Nelson Mathematics 8

Series Authors and Senior Consultants
Marian Small • Mary Lou Kestell

Senior Author
David Zimmer

Assessment Consultant
Damian Cooper

Authors
Bernard A. Beales • Maria Bodiam • Doug Duff
Robin Foster • Cathy Hall • Jack Hope • Chris Kirkpatrick
Beata Kroll Myhill • Geoff Suderman-Gladwell • Joyce Tonner

THOMSON
NELSON

Australia Canada Mexico Singapore Spain United Kingdom United States

Nelson Mathematics 8

Series Authors and Senior Consultants
Marian Small, Mary Lou Kestell

Senior Author
David Zimmer

Authors
Bernard A. Beales, Maria Bodiam, Doug Duff, Robin Foster, Cathy Hall, Jack Hope, Chris Kirkpatrick, Beata Kroll Myhill, Geoff Suderman-Gladwell, Joyce Tonner

Assessment Consultant
Damian Cooper

Director of Publishing
Beverley Buxton

General Manager, Mathematics, Science & Technology
Lenore Brooks

Publisher, Mathematics
Colin Garnham

Executive Managing Editor, Special Projects
Cheryl Turner

Managing Editor, Development
David Spiegel

Program Managers
Shirley Barrett, Mary Reeve, Tony Rodrigues

Developmental Editors
Lynda Cowan, Santo D'Agostino, Wendi Morrison, Bob Templeton

Editorial Assistant
Amanda Davis

Executive Managing Editor, Production
Nicola Balfour

Senior Production Editor
Debbie Davies-Wright

Copyeditor/Proofreader
Paula Pettitt-Townsend

Indexer
Jin Tan

Senior Production Coordinator
Sharon Latta Paterson

Design Director
Ken Phipps

Interior Design
Ken Phipps, Peggy Rhodes

Cover Design
Ken Phipps

Cover Image
Ko Fujiwara/Photonica

Composition Team
Kyle Gell, Kathy Karakasidis, Allan Moon

Illustrators
Steve Corrigan, Deborah Crowle, Kyle Gell, Kathy Karakasidis, Steve MacEachern, Allan Moon, Valentino Sanna

Photo Research and Permissions
Kristiina Bowering

Set-up Photos
Dave Starrett

Printer
Transcontinental Printing Inc.

COPYRIGHT © 2006 by Nelson, a division of Thomson Canada Limited.

Printed and bound in Canada
2 3 4 08 07 06 05

For more information contact Nelson, 1120 Birchmount Road, Toronto, Ontario, M1K 5G4, or you can visit our Internet site at http://www.nelson.com.

ALL RIGHTS RESERVED. No part of this work covered by the copyright herein may be reproduced, transcribed, or used in any form or by any means—graphic, electronic, or mechanical, including photocopying, recording, taping, Web distribution, or information storage and retrieval systems—without the written permission of the publisher.

For permission to use material from this text or product, submit a request online at www.thomsonrights.com.

Every effort has been made to trace ownership of all copyrighted material and to secure permission from copyright holders. In the event of any question arising as to the use of any material, we will be pleased to make the necessary corrections in future printings.

National Library of Canada Cataloguing in Publication Data

Nelson mathematics 8 / Marian Small ... [et al.].

Includes index.
ISBN 0-17-626920-7

1. Mathematics—Textbooks.
I. Small, Marian

QA107.3.N448 2005
510 C2004-905058-3

Advisory Panel

Michael Babcock
Teacher
Enterprise Public School
Limestone District School Board
Enterprise, Ontario

Beth Bond
Grade 8 Teacher
Toniata School
Brockville, Ontario

Mark Cassar
Vice Principal
Holy Cross Catholic School
Malton, Ontario

Donna Commerford
Retired Principal
Burlington, Ontario

Ron Curridor
Vice Principal
York Catholic District School Board
Maple, Ontario

Lee Jones-Imhotep
Teacher, Literacy Coordinator
Lawrence Heights Middle School
Toronto District School Board
Toronto, Ontario

Peter Martindale
Teacher
Hamilton-Wentworth District School Board
Hamilton, Ontario

Lee McMenemy
Elementary Coordinator
Algoma District School Board
Sault Ste. Marie, Ontario

Kevina Morrison
Intermediate Math Teacher
Highbush Public School
Durham District School Board
Pickering, Ontario

Wayne Murphy
Department Head of Mathematics
Ajax High School
Durham District School Board
Ajax, Ontario

Barbara Nott
Teacher
Rainbow District School Board
Sudbury, Ontario

Silvana F. Simone
Mathematics Instructor
Ontario Institute for Studies in Education of the University of Toronto
Toronto, Ontario

Susan Stuart
Assistant Professor
Nipissing University
North Bay, Ontario

James Williamson
Teacher
Nipissing-Parry Sound Catholic District School Board
North Bay, Ontario

Rod Yeager
Independent Mathematics Education Consultant
Department Head of Mathematics (retired)
Orangeville District Secondary School
Upper Grand District School Board
Orangeville, Ontario

Reviewers

Equity Reviewer

Mary Schoones
Educational Consultant/Retired Teacher
Ottawa-Carleton District School Board
Ottawa, Ontario

Literacy Reviewer

Kathleen Corrigan
Consultant
Simcoe County District School Board
Midhurst, Ontario

Contents

● Guided Activity ● Direct Instruction ● Exploration

Chapter 3: Collecting, Organizing, and Displaying Data 89

Chapter 4: Patterns and Relationships 121

● Guided Activity ● Direct Instruction ● Exploration

Chapter 5: Measurement of Circles 149

Chapter 6: Integer Operations 179

Guided Activity · Direct Instruction · Exploration

● Guided Activity ● Direct Instruction ● Exploration

● Guided Activity ● Direct Instruction ● Exploration

Chapter 11: Geometry and Measurement Relationships 369

Chapter 12: Probability 399

● Guided Activity ● Direct Instruction ● Exploration

CHAPTER 1

Number Relationships

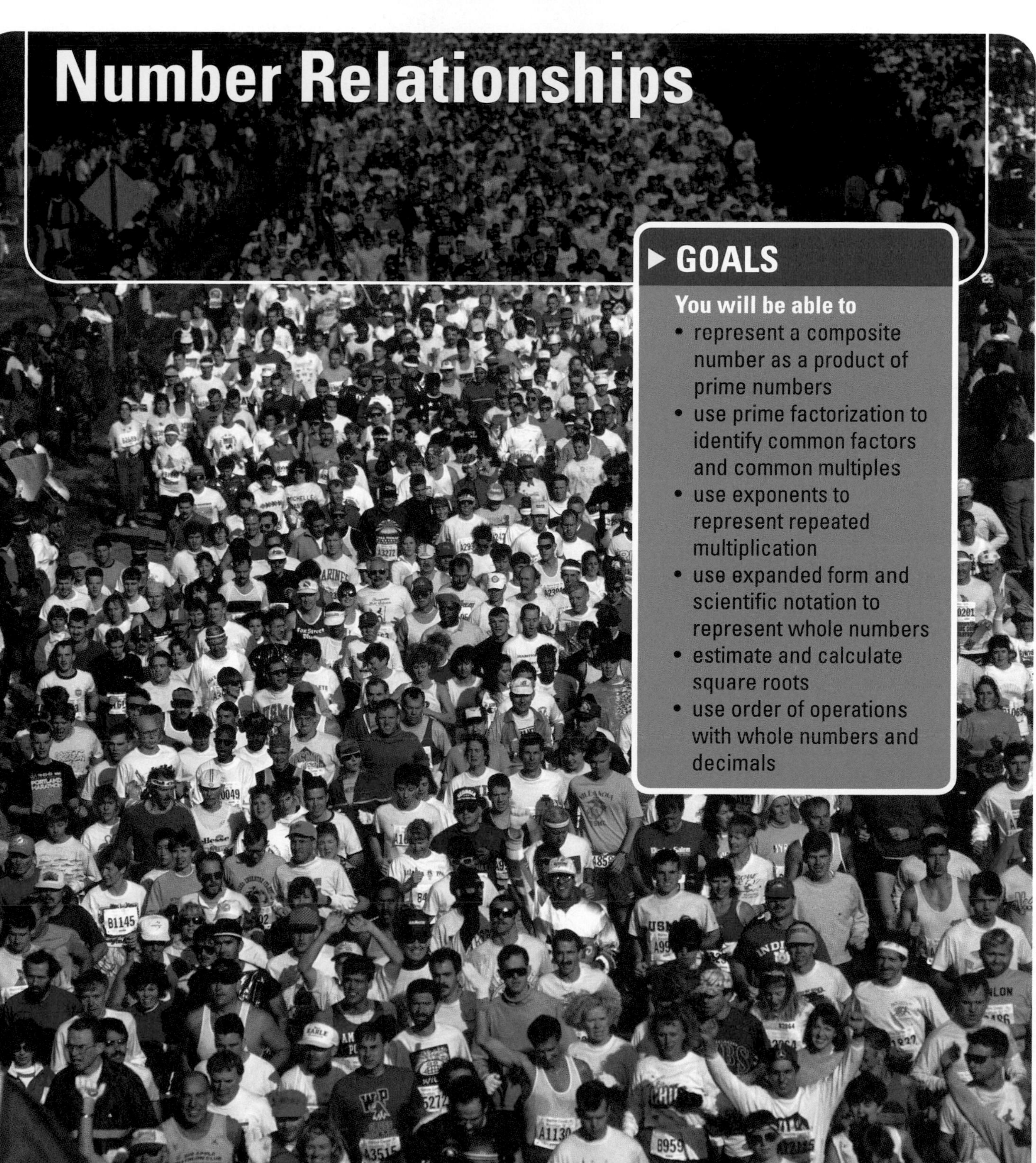

GOALS

You will be able to

- represent a composite number as a product of prime numbers
- use prime factorization to identify common factors and common multiples
- use exponents to represent repeated multiplication
- use expanded form and scientific notation to represent whole numbers
- estimate and calculate square roots
- use order of operations with whole numbers and decimals

Getting Started

Filling Boxes

Reilly has a collection of model cars, which he stores in small cardboard boxes. He can pack several of these small boxes into larger boxes, with no space left over.

? Which boxes can be used to fill other boxes, with no space left over?

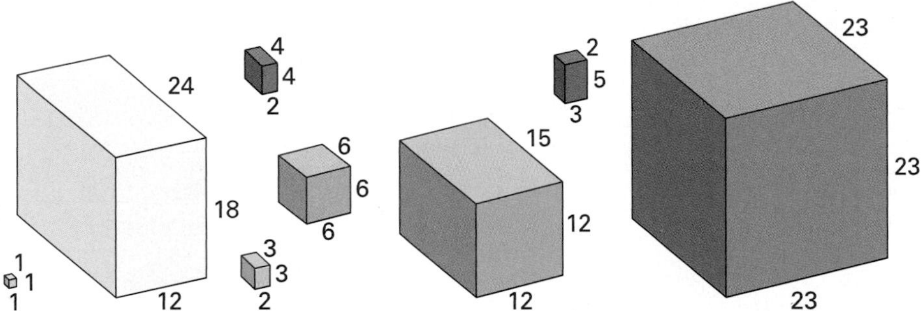

A. Boxes that measure 1 unit by 1 unit by 1 unit can be used to fill any of the larger boxes, with no space left over. Explain why.

B. How do you know that 3-by-5-by-2 boxes cannot be used to fill the 6-by-6-by-6 box?

C. List the small boxes that can be used to fill the 6-by-6-by-6 box. Repeat for the yellow, blue, and purple larger boxes.

D. How can you use the factors of the dimensions of a large box to determine if a smaller box can be used to fill it?

Do You Remember?

1. a) A **common factor** of 6 and 8 is 2. List all the common factors of 12 and 18.
   b) A **common multiple** of 6 and 8 is 24. List three common multiples of 12 and 18.

2. A century year (such as 1900, 2000, or 2100) is a leap year only if it is a multiple of 400.
   a) Was the year 1900 a leap year? How do you know?
   b) What was the last century year that was a leap year?
   c) What is the next century year that will be a leap year?

3. Identify each number as a **prime number** or a **composite number**. If the number is composite, list all of its factors.
   a) 48 b) 29 c) 36 d) 120

4. A **divisibility rule** is a way to determine if one number is a factor of another number, without dividing that number.
   a) 4230 can be divided evenly by 2, 5, and 10. How do you know?
   b) Here is the divisibility rule for 3 and 9: "If the sum of the digits can be divided by 3 and 9, the number can be divided by 3 and 9." Can 4230 be divided by 3 and 9?
   c) Can 98 022 be divided by 2, 3, 5, 9, or 10? Use divisibility rules.

5. A room contains eight crates. Each crate contains eight boxes. Each box contains eight bags. Each bag contains eight balloons.
   a) How many balloons are in the room?
   b) Express the number of balloons as a **power**. Identify the **base** and the **exponent**.

6. Use powers to represent each multiplication. Then calculate the product.
   a) $2 \times 2 \times 2 \times 2 \times 2$
   b) $10 \times 10 \times 10$

7. Express 64 as a power in two ways.

8. A square room has an area of 144 m^2. Draw a picture to show the **square root** of 144. Label the length of each side of the room.

9. Calculate each square root. Use mental math.
   a) $\sqrt{1}$ d) $\sqrt{64}$
   b) $\sqrt{25}$ e) $\sqrt{100}$
   c) $\sqrt{81}$ f) $\sqrt{36}$

10. Suppose that you have $200 worth of $2 coins.
    a) If you stack the coins, how high will the stack be?
    b) If you place the coins side by side in a row, how long will the row be?
    c) What is the total mass of the coins?

diameter 2.8 cm
thickness 0.18 cm
mass 7.3 g

11. Use = or ≠ to make each statement true. Use the **rules for order of operations.**
    a) $12 + 3 \times 9$ ▒ 135
    b) $(1 + 3 \times 3)^2 + 8$ ▒ 108

1.1 Identifying Prime and Composite Numbers

You will need
- a calculator
- grid paper

▶ **GOAL**

Determine whether a number is prime or composite.

Learn about the Math

Jordan and her friends have discovered a new Web site that sells legal music downloads. Each of the first 100 customers will be randomly assigned a number from 1 to 100 for a chance to win a prize. Customers who receive a **prime number** will win a free music download. Customers who receive a **composite number** will win nothing.

prime number

a number that has only two factors, 1 and itself; for example, 17 is a prime number because its only factors are 1 and 17

composite number

a number that has more than two factors; for example, 12 is a composite number because its factors are 1, 2, 3, 4, 6, and 12

? Which students will win a free music download?

A. Identify all the factors of 24, 27, 36, and 45.

B. How do your results in step A show that none of the students who received these numbers will win a free music download?

C. Will any student who receives an even number other than 2 win a free music download? Explain your reasoning.

D. Will any student who receives a multiple of 3 other than 3, or a multiple of 5 other than 5, win a free music download? Explain your reasoning.

E. Tamara received the number 61. To determine if 61 is a composite number, why would you divide 61 by prime numbers only?

F. Which students will win a free music download?

Reflecting

1. Which digits cannot be the last digit of a prime number greater than 10?

2. What steps would you follow to determine whether a number is prime?

Work with the Math

Example: Using divisibility rules to determine factors

Is 187 a prime number or a composite number?

Jordan's Solution

2 is not a factor of 187 because 187 is an odd number.

I used divisibility rules to see if prime numbers from 2 onward are factors of 187.

3 is not a factor of 187 because the sum of the digits is $1 + 8 + 7 = 16$, and 3 is not a factor of 16.

5 is not a factor of 187 because the last digit is not 0 or 5.

$$7\overline{)187} = 26.71$$

7 is not a factor of 187 because the quotient is not a whole number.

$$11\overline{)187} = 17$$

11 is a factor of 187 because the quotient is a whole number.
187 is a composite number.

I stopped testing for prime factors after I divided by 11 because I knew that 187 has more than two different factors. It has 1, 11, 17, and 187 as factors.

A Checking

3. Some students received numbers from 70 to 80 in the music download contest. Which students will win a free download? Explain your reasoning.

4. a) Examine the numbers listed below. Identify the only number that might be prime. Explain how you know that the other numbers are composite.

163
23 452
1 000 000
123 123 123
2175

b) Explain how you can prove that the number you identified is prime.

B Practising

5. Identify each number as prime or composite. If the number is composite, list all of its factors.

a) 17 **e)** 67
b) 25 **f)** 99
c) 47 **g)** 161
d) 48 **h)** 171

6. Which numbers between 30 and 40 are prime?

31 32 33 34 35 36 37 38 39

7. Show that there are no prime numbers from 200 to 210.

200 201 202 203 204 205
206 207 208 209 210

8. How do you know that the product of any two numbers greater than 1 must be a composite number?

9. If you add a prime number to itself, is the sum composite or prime? Explain your reasoning.

10. a) Write the numbers 1 to 60 on grid paper, in rows of six. Circle the prime numbers.

1	(2)	(3)	4	(5)	6
(7)	8	9	10	11	12
13	14	15	16	17	18

b) What do you notice about the locations of the prime numbers greater than 3?

11. The consecutive numbers 2 and 3 are both prime. How do you know that there are no other consecutive prime numbers?

12. Twin primes are pairs of primes that differ by 2. The first twin primes are 3 and 5. List all the twin primes less than 100.

13. The area of a rectangle is 991 cm^2. If 991 is a prime number, what are the whole number dimensions of the rectangle? Explain your reasoning.

14. A classroom of students can be divided into two, three, and five groups, with no students left over. How many students are likely in the class?

15. Explain why there are no square prime numbers.

16. What prime numbers do you get when you enter each number from 0 to 10 in this expression?

$\blacksquare^2 + \blacksquare - 1$

17. The number 123 123 123 123 123 12■ is divisible by 3 and 9. What is the missing digit? Explain your reasoning.

C Extending

18. You get prime numbers when you enter the numbers from 1 to 40 in the expression $\blacksquare^2 - \blacksquare + 41$.

For example, $8^2 - 8 + 41 = 97$.

Explain why this expression does not give a prime number when you enter 41.

19. When the marbles in a bag are divided evenly between two friends, there is one marble left over. When the same marbles are divided evenly among three friends, there is one marble left over. When the marbles are divided evenly among five friends, there is one marble left over.

a) What is the least possible number of marbles in the bag?

b) What is another possible number of marbles in the bag?

20. What is the least number that is divisible by 2, 3, 4, 5, and 7? Explain your reasoning.

21. A number is **perfect** if all of its factors, other than the number itself, add up to the number. For example, the factors of 6 are 1, 2, 3, and 6. Since $6 = 1 + 2 + 3$, 6 is a perfect number.

a) Why is no prime number a perfect number?

b) Show that 496 is a perfect number.

c) There is one perfect number greater than 6 and less than 50. Determine the number.

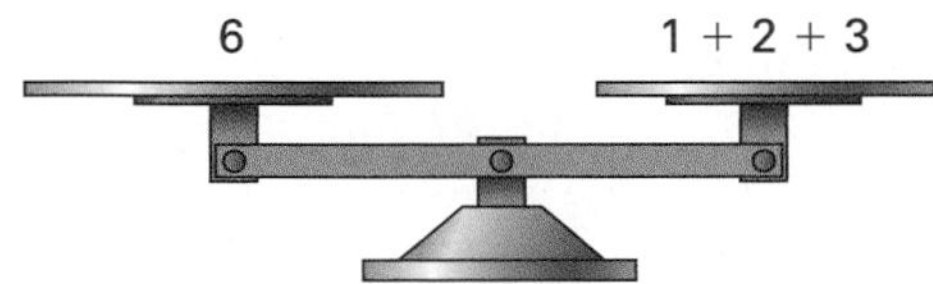

22. Suppose that you and a partner are playing a game with two dice. You roll the dice and add the numbers. You get 1 point if the sum is a prime number. Your partner gets 1 point if the sum is a composite number. Who is more likely to win? Explain your reasoning.

23. In a different game, you roll two dice and multiply the numbers. You get 1 point if the product is a prime number. Your partner gets 1 point if the product is a composite number. Who is more likely to win? Explain your reasoning.

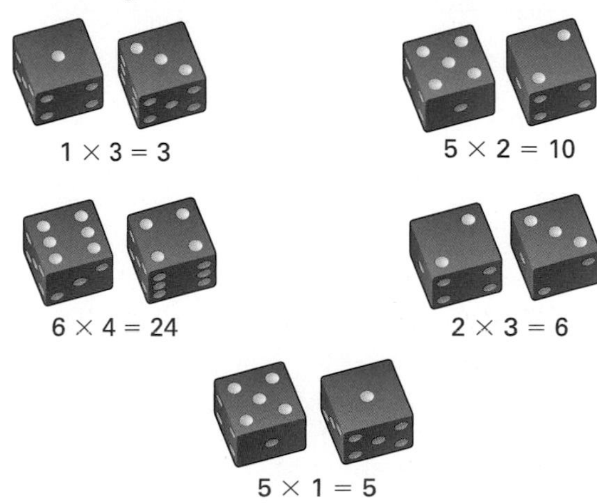

1.2 Prime Factorization

▶ **GOAL**

Express a composite number as the product of prime factors.

Learn about the Math

Teo and Sheree need passwords for their e-mail accounts. They want to use numbers that they can remember, but will be difficult for others to figure out. Sheree uses the **prime factorization** of her address, 1050, to form part of her password. Teo uses the prime factorization of his date of birth, 330 (March 30).

prime factorization

the representation of a composite number as the product of its prime factors; for example, the prime factorization of 24 is $24 = 2 \times 2 \times 2 \times 3$, or $2^3 \times 3$; usually, the prime numbers are written in order from least to greatest

? What are Teo's and Sheree's passwords?

Example 1: Using a factor tree to determine prime factors

If Sheree's address is 1050, what will her password be?

Sheree's Solution

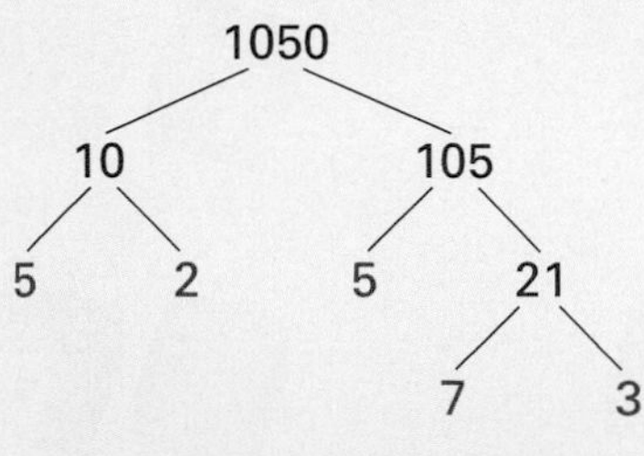

I know that 10 is a factor of 1050. I divided by 10 to determine another factor, 105. I used a factor tree to show these two factors.

5 is a factor of both 10 and 105. I divided each number by 5 to determine two more factors, 2 and 21.

I continued to calculate factors until only prime factors were left at the ends of the branches.

$$1050 = 2 \times 3 \times 5 \times 5 \times 7$$
$$= 2 \times 3 \times 5^2 \times 7$$

I wrote the prime numbers in order, from least to greatest, to create the prime factorization of 1050.

Then I used **exponents** to write the prime factorization a different way.

My e-mail password will be my address followed by its prime factors: 105023557.

NEL

Example 2: Using repeated division to determine prime factors

If Teo's date of birth is 330, what will his password be?

Teo's Solution

I divided by prime factors.

$$2\overline{)330} = 165$$

The prime number 2 is a factor of 330. So, I divided by 2 to determine another factor, 165.

$$5\overline{)165} = 33$$

The prime number 5 is a factor of 165. I divided by 5 to determine another factor, 33.

$$3\overline{)33} = 11$$

I divided by 3 to get the last prime factor.

$330 = 2 \times 3 \times 5 \times 11$

I wrote the prime factors as a multiplication sentence to show the prime factorization of 330.

My e-mail password will be my date of birth followed by its prime factors: 33023511.

Reflecting

1. What might Sheree's factor tree have looked like if she had started dividing by 50 instead of 10?
2. Does the order in which you divide by factors change the prime factorization? Provide an example to support your answer.
3. a) What divisibility rules might Sheree have used to determine some factors of 1050, without dividing the number?
   b) What divisibility rules might Teo have used to determine some factors of 330, without dividing the number?
4. If you used Sheree's strategy and Teo's strategy for the same number, would you get the same prime factorization? Explain. Use an example to support your explanation.

Work with the Math

Example 3: Writing the prime factorization of a composite number

What is the prime factorization of 1470?

Solution A: Creating a factor tree

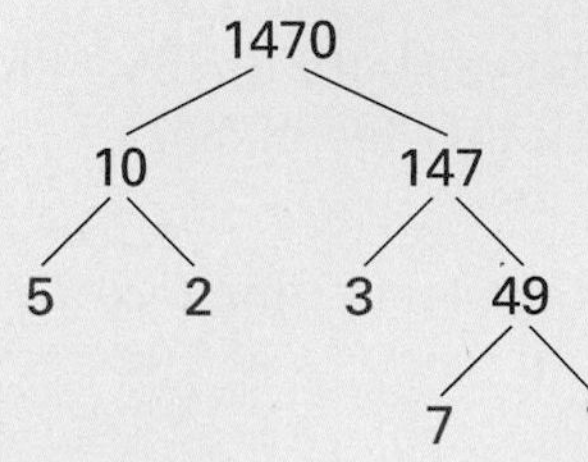

Write the prime numbers at the ends of the branches in order, from least to greatest, to show the prime factorization.

$1470 = 2 \times 3 \times 5 \times 7 \times 7$
$ = 2 \times 3 \times 5 \times 7^2$

Solution B: Using repeated division

```
      3
   7)21
  7)147
  5)735
2)1470
```

Write the prime numbers in the divisors and quotient in order, from least to greatest, to show the prime factorization.

$1470 = 2 \times 3 \times 5 \times 7 \times 7$
$ = 2 \times 3 \times 5 \times 7^2$

A Checking

5. Determine the prime factorization of each number.

a) 117
b) 147
c) 220
d) 270

6. a) Rivka used the last four digits of her telephone number, 1048, followed by its prime factorization to create her e-mail password. Determine her password.

b) Identify any divisibility rules you used.

B Practising

7. Determine the prime factorization of each number.

a) 100
b) 102
c) 320
d) 375
e) 412
f) 2055
g) 512
h) 3675

8. Factor trees are being used to determine the prime factorizations of 1755 and 2180.

a) Explain how you know that each factor tree is not complete.

b) Copy and complete each factor tree to determine the prime factorization.

9. Determine the missing number in each prime factorization.

a) $200 = 2 \times 2 \times \blacksquare \times 5 \times 5$

b) $216 = 2^3 \times 3^{\blacksquare}$

c) $8281 = 7 \times 7 \times 13 \times \blacksquare$

d) $1568 = \blacksquare^5 \times 7^2$

10. a) Determine the prime factorization of each number.

64 256 1024

b) What does the prime factorization tell you about each number?

11. a) Determine the prime factorization of a three digit or four-digit composite number of your choice.

b) Create an e-mail password using the composite number you chose, followed by its prime factorization.

12. Why would you determine the prime factorization of only composite numbers? Use an example to support your explanation.

13. How can you use the prime factorization of a number to determine whether the number is even or odd? Use an example to support your explanation.

C Extending

14. The prime factorization of a number is $2^3 \times 5 \times 7$.

a) Explain how you can use the prime factorization to determine whether 35 is a factor of the number.

b) Explain how you can use the prime factorization to determine whether 8 is a factor of the number.

c) How do you know, without multiplying the prime factors, that the last digit of the number is 0?

15. The prime factorizations of two numbers are shown.

$2^5 \times 3 \times 5^2 \times 7^{10}$

$3^8 \times 5 \times 7 \times 41^{12}$

a) How do you know that 2 is not a common factor of the numbers?

b) How do you know that 35 is a common factor?

c) List another common factor of the numbers. Explain your reasoning.

16. a) Multiply any three-digit number by 1001 to get a six-digit number.

1001

× 

b) Divide your six-digit number by 7, 11, and then 13. What is the quotient?

c) Show the prime factorization of 1001.

d) Explain how you could use the prime factorization of 1001 to predict the quotient you calculated in part (b).

17. a) Multiply two different prime numbers. List all the possible factors of the product.

b) Repeat part (a) with two other prime numbers.

c) What do you notice about the number of factors each product has?

18. a) Multiply three different prime numbers. List all the possible factors of the product.

b) Repeat part (a) with three other prime numbers.

c) What do you notice about the number of factors each product has?

19. Use your results in questions 17 and 18 to predict the number of factors the product of four different prime numbers will have. Use an example to check your prediction.

20. The prime factorization of a number is $2^5 \times 3^8 \times 5^7 \times 7^4 \times 11 \times 13$. Which statements are true about the number? Explain your reasoning.

a) The number is even.

b) The number is a multiple of 10.

c) 15 is a factor of the number.

d) 17 is not a factor of the number.

e) 77 is a factor of the number.

1.3 Common Factors and Common Multiples

You will need
- a calculator

▶ **GOAL**
Use prime factorization to identify common factors and common multiples.

Learn about the Math

Jordan and Reilly are creating a large square mural. The mural will be made of 36 cm by 48 cm rectangles covered with coloured squares. They want these squares to be as large as possible, measured in whole numbers of centimetres.

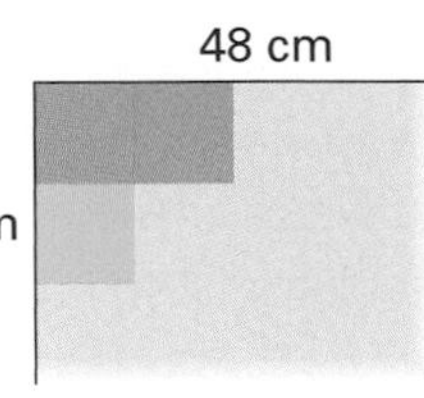

Then Jordan and Reilly plan to arrange copies of the 36 cm by 48 cm rectangle to form a large square mural that measures the least possible whole number of centimetres.

They decide to use the **greatest common factor (GCF)** and **least common multiple (LCM)** of 36 and 48 to determine the dimensions of both sizes of squares.

greatest common factor (GCF)
the greatest whole number that divides into two or more other whole numbers with no remainder; for example, 4 is the greatest common factor of 8 and 12

least common multiple (LCM)
the least whole number that has two or more given numbers as factors; for example, 12 is the least common multiple of 4 and 6

? What are the dimensions of the small squares and the large square mural?

Example 1: Using a Venn diagram to identify the GCF

What are the dimensions of the small squares? Use the greatest common factor (GCF) of 36 and 48.

Jordan's Solution

$36 = 2 \times 2 \times 3 \times 3$
$48 = 2 \times 2 \times 2 \times 2 \times 3$

First I wrote the prime factorization of 36 and 48.

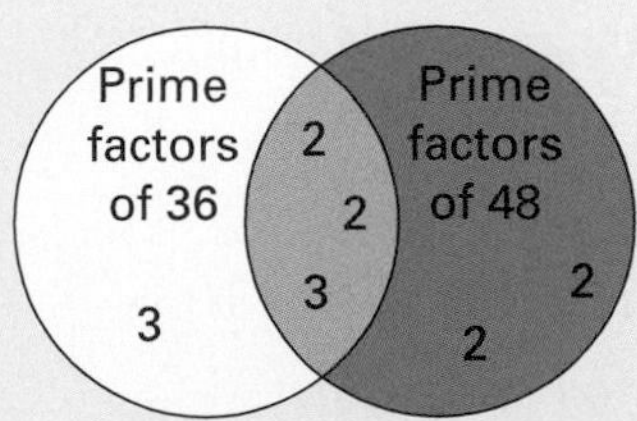

Then I arranged the prime factors in a Venn diagram. The common prime factors are in the overlap.

I multiplied the common prime factors to determine the other common factors of 36 and 48. So, 2, 3, 4 (2×2), 6 (2×3), and 12 $(2 \times 2 \times 3)$ are the common factors of 36 and 48.

The GCF is $2 \times 2 \times 3 = 12$.
A 12 cm by 12 cm square is the largest possible square that divides a 36 cm by 48 cm rectangle.

Example 2: Using a Venn diagram to identify the LCM

What are the dimensions of the final square mural? Use the least common multiple (LCM) of 36 and 48.

Reilly's Solution

$36 = 2 \times 2 \times 3 \times 3$
$48 = 2 \times 2 \times 2 \times 2 \times 3$

First I wrote the prime factorization of 36 and 48.

Then I arranged the prime factors in a Venn diagram.

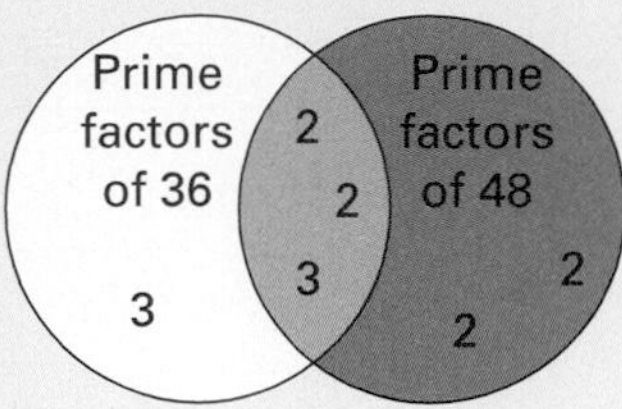

I multiplied all the prime numbers in both circles to determine the LCM of 36 and 48.

The LCM is $3 \times 2 \times 2 \times 3 \times 2 \times 2 = 144$.

The final mural will be a 144 cm by 144 cm square.

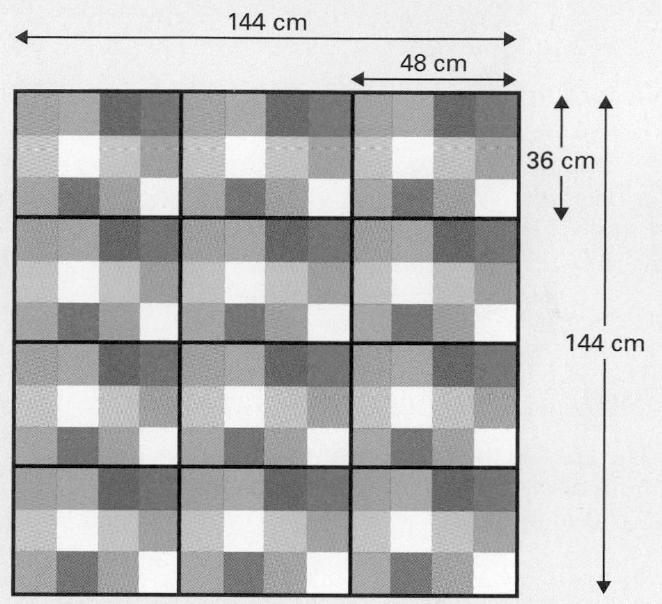

Reflecting

1. How did identifying the GCF and LCM help Jordan and Reilly decide on the dimensions of the small squares and the large square mural?

2. Why do you think Jordan multiplied the factors in the overlap of the Venn diagram to determine other common factors of 36 and 48?

3. Why do you think Reilly multiplied the numbers in the three sections of the Venn diagram to determine the LCM of 36 and 48?

Work with the Math

Example 3: Using Venn diagrams to identify the GCF and LCM

Show how to use prime factorization to identify the GCF and LCM of each pair of numbers.

a) 27 and 42

b) 18 and 35

Solution A

Write the prime factorization of 27 and 42.

$27 = 3 \times 3 \times 3$

$42 = 2 \times 3 \times 7$

Record the prime factors in a Venn diagram.

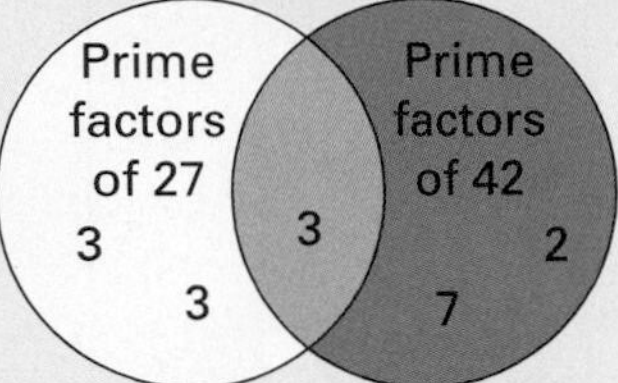

The GCF is the product of the numbers in the overlap. The GCF of 27 and 42 is 3.

The LCM is the product of the numbers in both circles. The LCM of 27 and 36 is $3 \times 3 \times 3 \times 2 \times 7 = 378$.

Solution B

Write the prime factorization of 18 and 35.

$18 = 2 \times 3 \times 3$

$35 = 5 \times 7$

Record the prime factors in a Venn diagram.

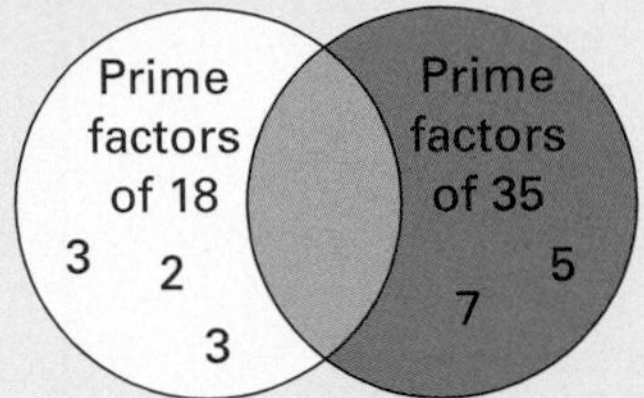

The GCF is the product of the numbers in the overlap. There are no prime factors in the overlap, but 1 is a common factor of both 18 and 35. So, the GCF of 18 and 35 is 1.

The LCM is the product of the numbers in both circles. The LCM of 18 and 35 is $2 \times 3 \times 3 \times 5 \times 7 = 630$.

A Checking

4. Identify the GCF and LCM of each pair of numbers.

a) $120 = 2 \times 2 \times 2 \times 3 \times 5$
$210 = 2 \times 3 \times 5 \times 7$

b) $252 = 2 \times 2 \times 3 \times 3 \times 7$
$60 = 2 \times 2 \times 3 \times 5$

5. a) Identify another common factor of each pair of numbers in question 4.

b) Identify another common multiple of each pair of numbers in question 4.

B Practising

6. Use prime factorization to identify at least three common factors and at least three common multiples of each pair of numbers.

a) 48 and 60

b) 32 and 64

c) 24 and 32

d) 512 and 648

7. Identify the GCF and LCM of each pair of numbers.

a) $78 = 2 \times 3 \times 13$
$442 = 2 \times 13 \times 17$

b) $32 = 2 \times 2 \times 2 \times 2 \times 2$
$24 = 2 \times 2 \times 2 \times 3$

NEL

8. Use prime factorization to identify four common factors and four common multiples of each pair of numbers.

a) $468 = 2^2 \times 3^2 \times 13$
$396 = 2^2 \times 3^2 \times 11$

b) $840 = 2^3 \times 3 \times 5 \times 7$
$2000 = 2^4 \times 5^3$

c) $1818 = 2 \times 3^2 \times 101$
$606 = 2 \times 3 \times 101$

9. Identify the GCF and LCM of each pair of numbers.

a) 64 and 240
b) 55 and 275
c) 48 and 72
d) 120 and 200

10. a) Identify the GCF and LCM of 360 and 480.

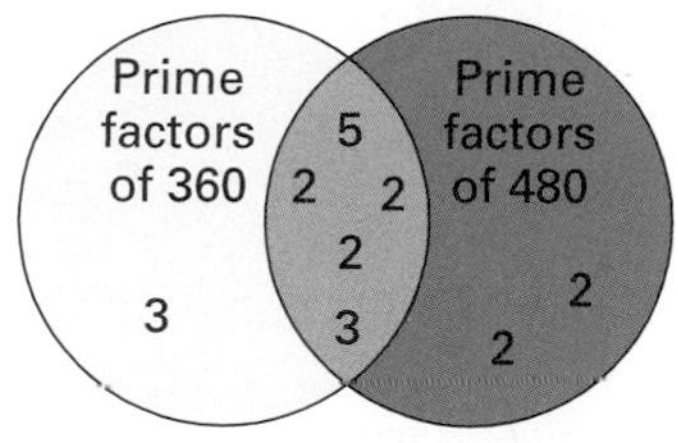

b) Identify four other common factors.

c) Identify four other common multiples.

11. A rectangle measures 72 cm by 108 cm.

a) A 2 cm by 2 cm square can be used to cover the rectangle without any spaces or overlapping. Explain why.

b) How can you use the common factors of 72 and 108 to identify all the squares that can be used to cover the rectangle?

c) List all other squares with whole-number dimensions that can be used to cover the rectangle.

12. Identify the GCF and LCM of each pair of numbers.

a) 40 and 48
b) 120 and 400
c) 101 and 200
d) 1024 and 1536

13. Given the GCF or LCM, what else do you know about each pair of numbers?

a) Two numbers have a GCF of 2.

b) Two numbers have an LCM of 2.

c) Two numbers have a GCF of 3.

d) Two numbers have an LCM of 10.

14. Explain how you can use these centimetre bars to identify the common factors and GCF of 6 and 8.

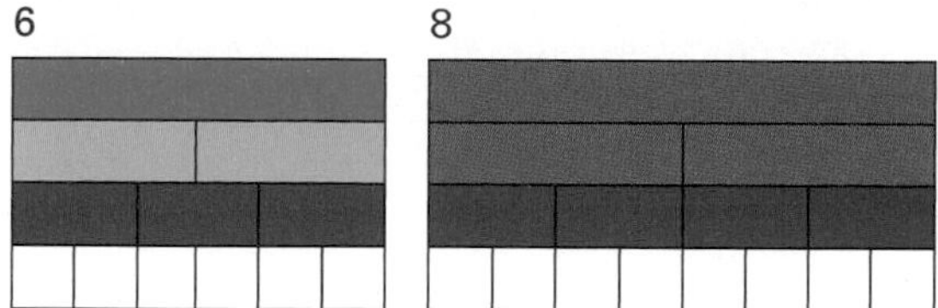

15. Explain how to identify the GCF and LCM of a pair of numbers, if one number is a factor of the other number.

16. What pairs of numbers fit this description? List as many pairs as you can.

"A pair of numbers has a sum of 100. One number is a multiple of 3. The other number is a multiple of 11."

C Extending

17. The prime factorizations of two numbers, a and b, have some missing prime factors.

$a = 2 \times 3 \times$ ▢

$b =$ ▢ $\times$ ▢

a) The GCF of a and b is 5. What is the value of a?

b) The LCM of a and b is 210. What is the value of b?

18. Show how you can use prime factorization and a Venn diagram to identify the GCF and LCM of 12, 48, and 64.

1.4 Calculating Powers

You will need
- a calculator

▶ **GOAL**
Represent and calculate numbers expressed as powers.

Learn about the Math

Tamara cuts a piece of paper, 0.1 mm thick, in two. She stacks one piece on top of the other. She cuts the stack of two pieces to form four pieces. Then she cuts the stack of four pieces to form eight pieces. She keeps cutting and stacking.

? How high, in metres, will the stack of paper be after 20 cuts?

A. Complete a table like this one to show the number of pieces of paper after each cut.

Number of cuts	1	2	3						
Number of pieces	2	4	8						

B. How many pieces of paper are stacked after 10 cuts?

C. Explain why you can write the number of pieces after 10 cuts as $2 \times 2 \times 2 \times 2 \times 2 \times 2 \times 2 \times 2 \times 2 \times 2$.

D. Explain why you can write the total number of pieces after 10 cuts as the **power** 2^{10}.

E. Use the table to predict the total number of pieces stacked after 11 cuts.

F. Use your calculator to determine the number of pieces stacked after 20 cuts.

G. What is the height, in metres, of the stack of paper after 20 cuts? Show your work.

power
a numerical expression that shows repeated multiplication; for example, the power 5^3 is a shorter way of writing $5 \times 5 \times 5$; a power has a **base** and an **exponent**: the exponent tells the number of equal factors there are in a power

3 is the exponent of the power.

$5^3 = 125$

5 is the base of the power.

Reflecting

1. When you calculate 2^{20} on your calculator, you get 1 048 576. If you wanted to calculate 2^{21}, what number would you multiply 1 048 576 by?

2. Why do you write 2^{20}, not 20^2, to represent the number of pieces of paper stacked after 20 cuts?

Work with the Math

Example: Using a calculator to determine powers of a number

A baseball bounces to about 0.32 times its previous height. If it is dropped from an initial height of 1.00 m, about how high will it be after three bounces?

Teo's Solution: Using repeated multiplication

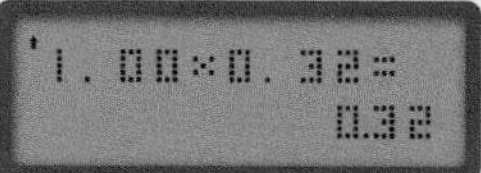

0.32×0.32=
0.1024

0.1024×0.32
= 0.032768

The height after each bounce is 0.32 times the previous height. I multiplied by 0.32 each time. Since 0.32 is less than 1, the product becomes less and less.

The height after the first bounce will be 1.00 m × 0.32 = 0.32 m, or about 32 cm.
The height after the second bounce will be 0.32 m × 0.32 = 0.1024 m, or about 10 cm.
The height after the third bounce will be 0.1024 m × 0.32 = 0.032 768 m, or about 3 cm.

The height after the third bounce will be 0.032 768 m, which is about 0.03 m, or about 3 cm.

I rounded to two decimal places, or to the nearest centimetre, because this is the number of decimal places given for the height in the problem.

Tamara's Solution: Using a power key

Number of bounces	Height (m)
1	0.32
2	$0.32 \times 0.32 = 0.32^2$
3	$0.32 \times 0.32 \times 0.32 = 0.32^3$

I used exponents to show the height after each bounce.

0.32 [^] 3 [Enter]

0.32^3=
0.032768

To calculate 0.32^3, I used the power key [^] on my TI-15 calculator. The result should be less than 0.32 because I multiplied 0.32 (which is less than 1) three times.

The height of the baseball after three bounces is about 0.03 m, or about 3 cm.

Calculator Tip

- Some calculators have a [y^x] key to enter powers. For example, to calculate 0.32^3, press 0.32 [y^x] 3 [=].
- When multiplying decimals, your calculator will often display many decimal places. Usually, you can round to three decimal places. If the decimals represent measurements, round to the same number of decimal places given in the problem.

A Checking

3. Calculate each power.

   a) 2^{14} b) 1.4^5 c) 0.69^3

4. A long board, 4.7 cm thick, is cut into three pieces of equal length. These three pieces are then stacked. The stack is cut in three equal pieces to form nine pieces.

   a) Use a power to express the number of pieces in a stack after three sets of cuts.

   b) If the cutting and stacking is continued, what is the height of the stack after 10 sets of cuts? Show your work.

B Practising

5. Write each power as repeated multiplication. Calculate.

   a) 2^5 c) 10^6 e) 1.2^2

   b) 25^3 d) 3^4 f) 0.4^2

6. Write each repeated multiplication as a power. Calculate.

   a) $2 \times 2 \times 2$

   b) 2.5×2.5

   c) $10 \times 10 \times 10 \times 10 \times 10$

   d) $0.3 \times 0.3 \times 0.3 \times 0.3$

7. A crate contains 12 boxes. Each box contains 12 packages. Each package contains 12 pencils. Express the number of pencils in a crate as a power. How many pencils are in a crate?

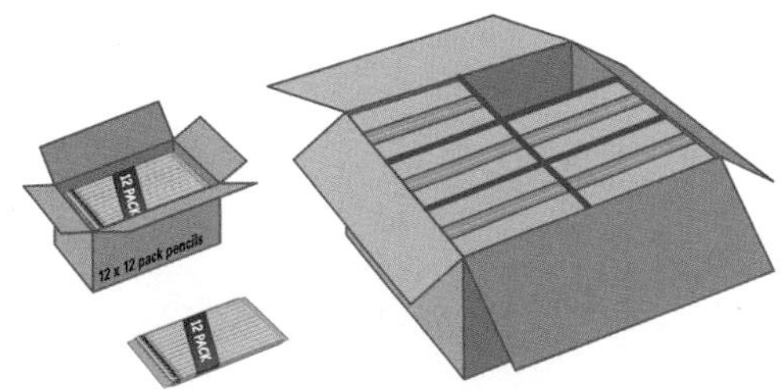

8. Explain how you can use mental math to calculate 2^8.

9. This line represents the distance from Earth to the star Polaris, which is about 2^{52} km.

   0 A B C D 2^{52}

   a) Which letter best represents a distance of 2^{51} km? Explain your reasoning.

   b) Copy the line. Then draw a line that represents a distance of 2^{53} km. Explain your reasoning.

10. a) Choose a number greater than 1. Copy these powers, with your number in both boxes. Which power is greater?

    $\square^{8}$ $\square^{10}$

    b) Choose a number between 0 and 1. Copy these powers, with your number in both boxes. Which power is greater?

    $\square^{8}$ $\square^{10}$

11. Lang withdrew half of his money from his bank account on the last day of January. Then he withdrew half of the remaining amount on the last day of February. He continued withdrawing half of his money on the last day of March, April, May, and June. His final balance was $1.50. How much money did Lang have in his bank account before his first withdrawal?

12. a) Calculate each power of 10.

    10^4 10^3 10^2 10^1

    b) What pattern do you see in part (a)?

    c) Explain how your pattern can show that $10^0 = 1$.

C Extending

13. a) Calculate each power of 0.1.

    0.1^2 0.1^3 0.1^4 0.1^5

    b) Compare the value of each power of 0.1 with its exponent. What pattern do you see?

    c) Predict the value of 0.1^6.

NEL

Mental Math

MULTIPLYING AND DIVIDING BY POWERS OF 10

You can use patterns to multiply and divide by powers of 10.

Example 1: Calculate 15.6×10^3.

$15.6 \times 10 = 156$
$156 \times 10 = 1560$
$1560 \times 10 = 15\,600$

$15.6 \times 10^3 = 15\,600$

100 000	10 000	1000	100	10	1
	1	5	6	0	0

Multiplying 15.6 by 10^3 means multiplying 15.6 by 10 three times.

Each time you multiply by 10, the place value of every digit increases by a factor of 10.

Every digit in 15.6 increases by a factor of 10^3, or 1000.

Example 2: Calculate $15.6 \div 10^3$.

$15.6 \div 10 = 1.56$
$1.56 \div 10 = 0.156$ (156 thousandths)
$0.156 \div 10 = 0.0156$ (156 ten thousandths)

$15.6 \div 10^3 = 0.0156$

1	0.1	0.01	0.001	0.0001
0	0	1	5	6

Dividing 15.6 by 10^3 means dividing 15.6 by 10 three times.

Each time you divide by 10, the place value of every digit decreases by a factor of 10.

Every digit in 15.6 decreases by a factor of 10^3, or 1000. This is the same as multiplying by $\frac{1}{1000}$, or 0.001.

1. Calculate each product.

a) $10^2 \times 45$
b) $10^3 \times 0.31$
c) 2.01×10^4
d) $10^6 \times 3.1$
e) 0.004×10^3
f) $10^8 \times 1.003$

2. Calculate each quotient.

a) $1.3 \div 10^2$
b) $4 \div 10^3$
c) $1000 \div 10^4$
d) $14\,567 \div 10^6$
e) $300.5 \div 10^3$
f) $15.0 \div 10^3$

3. Determine each missing exponent.

a) $10^{\blacksquare} \times 1.4 = 140$
b) $6.25 \div 10^{\blacksquare} = 0.006\,25$
c) $0.15 \times 10^{\blacksquare} = 150$
d) $25\,000 \div 10^{\blacksquare} = 0.25$
e) $35.2 \times 10^{\blacksquare} = 35\,200\,000$
f) $0.01 \div 10^{\blacksquare} = 0.0001$

1.5 Expanded Form and Scientific Notation

You will need
- a calculator

▶ **GOAL**

Express and compare numbers using expanded form and scientific notation.

Learn about the Math

Manuel's grandfather is 75 years old and has a heart rate of about 70 beats per minute. Manuel uses his calculator to estimate the total number of times his grandfather's heart has beat over the 75 years.

75×365×24
×60×70

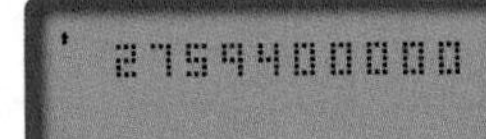

Manuel's grandfather has an African grey parrot. The parrot is 45 years old and has a heart rate of about 550 beats per minute. Manuel uses his calculator to estimate the total number of times the parrot's heart has beat during its lifetime. Manuel's calculator displays a number in **scientific notation**.

45×365×24
×60×550

You can compare large numbers using scientific notation or **expanded form**.

scientific notation

a way of writing a number as a decimal between 1 and 10, multiplied by a power of 10; for example, 70 120 is written as 7.012×10^4

number between 1 and 10

7.012×10^4

power of 10

expanded form

a way of writing a number that shows the value of each digit as a power of 10; for example, 1209 in expanded form is $1 \times 10^3 + 2 \times 10^2 + 9 \times 1$

? Which heart has beat more times?

Communication Tip

The TI-15 calculator uses the carat symbol, ^, for scientific notation. For example, 1.81×10^{11} can be entered like this: 1.81 [×] 10 [^] 11 [Enter]

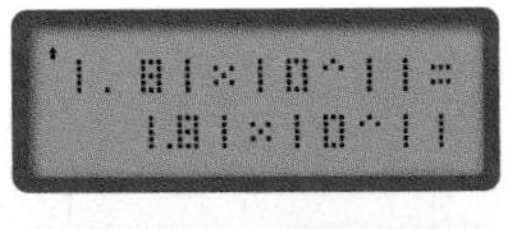

Some calculators use the letter **E** in the display to express numbers in scientific notation.

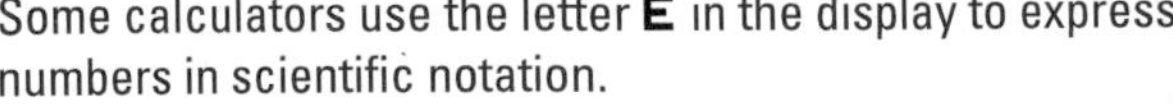

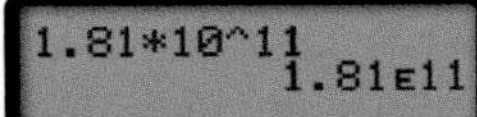

Other calculators use a shorter form to express the same scientific notation.

Example 1: Comparing large numbers

Compare the number of heartbeats for Manuel's grandfather and the parrot. Use scientific notation and expanded form.

Manuel's Solution

I had to determine which calculator answer, 2759400000 or 1.301 × 10^10, is greater.

1.301×10^{10}

10^{10}	10^9	10^8	10^7	10^6	10^5	10^4	10^3	10^2	10^1	1
1.301	0	0	0	0	0	0	0	0	0	0

I decided to write both numbers in expanded form. I represented 1.301×10^{10} in a place value chart.

10^{10}	10^9	10^8	10^7	10^6	10^5	10^4	10^3	10^2	10^1	1
1	3	0	1	0	0	0	0	0	0	0

I regrouped to determine the place value of each digit.

$1.301 \times 10^{10} = 1 \times 10^{10} + 3 \times 10^9 + 1 \times 10^7$

I showed each digit multiplied by its place value. Then I showed the sum of the products.

2 759 400 000

The number 2 759 400 000 is in standard form. The front digit has the greatest place value—billions or 10^9.

10^{10}	10^9	10^8	10^7	10^6	10^5	10^4	10^3	10^2	10^1	1
	2	7	5	9	4	0	0	0	0	0

2 759 400 000
$= 2 \times 10^9 + 7 \times 10^8 + 5 \times 10^7 + 9 \times 10^6 + 4 \times 10^5$

I showed each digit multiplied by its place value. Then I showed the sum of the products.

$1 \times 10^{10} + 3 \times 10^9 + 1 \times 10^7$
$> 2 \times 10^9 + 7 \times 10^8 + 5 \times 10^7 + 9 \times 10^6 + 4 \times 10^5$

I compared the expanded forms of the two numbers. One number has billions and the other has 10 billions.
$1 \times 10^{10} > 2 \times 10^9$

The parrot's heart has beat more times than my grandfather's heart.

I could have used scientific notation to compare the two numbers.

$2\,759\,400\,000 = 2.7594 \times 10^9$
$1.301 \times 10^{10} > 2.7594 \times 10^9$

Reflecting

1. Why is ☐.☐ $\times 10^9$ always less than ☐.☐ $\times 10^{10}$?

2. How do you know what power of 10 to use when you want to write a number in scientific notation? Use an example to support your explanation.

3. How do you know what powers of 10 to use when you want to write the expanded form of a number? Use an example to support your explanation.

Work with the Math

Example 2: Comparing numbers using scientific notation

Which travelled farther?

- a ray of light travelling at a speed of about 300 000 km per second for one week
- the spacecraft *Voyager 1* travelling at a speed of about 63 000 km per hour for 100 years

Solution

The ray of light travelled about 1.814×10^{11} km.

Voyager 1 travelled about 5.519×10^{10} km.

$1.814 \times 10^{11} > 5.519 \times 10^{10}$

$10^{11} > 10^{10}$

The ray of light travelled farther.

A Checking

4. State whether each number is in scientific notation, standard form, or expanded form.

a) 1 300 000

b) 1.235×10

c) $1 \times 10^3 + 2 \times 10^2 + 3 \times 10 + 5 \times 1$

5. Copy and complete the chart.

Standard form	Expanded form	Scientific notation
360	$3 \times 10^2 + 6 \times 10$	3.6×10^2
	$3 \times 10^3 + 6 \times 10^2$	
		3.6×10^4
360 000		

6. Which number is greatest?

4376

$5 \times 10^3 + 4 \times 10^2$

6.13×10^3

B Practising

7. Express each number in expanded form.

a) 2345

b) 11 289

c) 105 284

d) 1 045 605

8. Express each number in standard form.

a) $1 \times 10^3 + 0 \times 10^2 + 4 \times 10 + 9 \times 1$

b) $4 \times 10^4 + 3 \times 10^3 + 8 \times 10^2 + 7 \times 10 + 0 \times 1$

c) $8 \times 10^6 + 1 \times 10^5 + 5 \times 1$

9. Decide whether or not each number is in scientific notation. Explain your reasoning.

a) 12.5×10^7

b) 5.688×10^{12}

c) 0.43×10^6

d) 4.5×5^6

10. Express each number in scientific notation.

a) 1 300 000

b) 12 500

c) 882 500 000

d) 51 670 000

11. a) Calculate each power of 10.

10^3 10^6 10^9 10^{12}

b) Compare the value of each power of 10 in part (a) with its exponent. What pattern do you see?

c) Predict the value of 10^{15}.

12. Express each number in standard form.

a) 1.235×10
b) 8.01×10^6
c) 5.688×10^{12}
d) 3.5×10^{10}

13. Which number is greatest? Explain your reasoning.

987 098

$6 \times 10^5 + 3 \times 10 + 1 \times 1$

1.0×10^6

14. Why does a calculator express some numbers in scientific notation rather than in standard form?

15. The media often use decimals to report large numbers. Express each number using scientific notation.

a) 1.4 million, the approximate number of bytes of storage in a floppy diskette (one million bytes = one megabyte)

b) 1.4 billion, the approximate number of bytes of computer storage needed to store all the information in an encyclopedia (one billion bytes = one gigabyte)

c) 2.5 trillion, the approximate number of bytes of storage capacity in the computers at Statistics Canada (one trillion bytes = one terabyte)

16. a) Explain how you can change a number in standard form to expanded form. Use an example to clarify your explanation.

b) Explain how you can change a number in scientific notation to standard form. Use an example to clarify your explanation.

17. Answer each question. Show your work, and write your answer in expanded form or scientific notation.

a) About how many times has your heart beat in your lifetime?

b) Most people blink about every 2 to 10 s. About how many times have you blinked in your lifetime?

c) The human eye can process about 36 000 bits of information every hour. About how many bits of information have you processed in your lifetime?

18. Which prize is worth more? Explain your reasoning.

- a prize on March 31, if the amount is tripled each day, beginning with $3 on March 1
- a prize after 50 years, if $1 million is added each day

C Extending

19. In 2004, William Gates III of Microsoft had assets worth about $46.6 billion U.S.

a) What is this amount worth in Canadian dollars? Each U.S. dollar was worth about $1.29 Canadian.

b) Express the amount in Canadian dollars using scientific notation.

Mid-Chapter Review

Frequently Asked Questions

Q: How can you determine whether or not a number is a prime number?

A: Use divisibility rules or division to see if prime numbers less than the number are divisors.

For example, you can tell that 141 can be divided by 3 because the sum of the digits is $1 + 4 + 1 = 6$, which is divisible by 3. So, 141 is not a prime number because it has more than two factors.

Q: How can you use prime factorization to determine the LCM and GCF of two numbers?

A: Use a factor tree or repeated division to determine all the prime factors of each number. Divide by prime numbers until all the factors are prime numbers.

The prime factorization of 42 is $2 \times 3 \times 7$.

The prime factorization of 36 is $2 \times 2 \times 3 \times 3 = 2^2 \times 3^2$.

Use a Venn diagram to display the factors of the two numbers. The common factors are 2 and 3. The greatest common factor (GCF) is $2 \times 3 = 6$.

The least common multiple (LCM) is the product of the GCF and the extra prime factors.

$6 \times 2 \times 3 \times 7 = 252$

Q: How can you express a number in expanded form and in scientific notation?

A: The number 150 000 is in standard form. Before you express it in scientific notation, describe the place value of its digits.

In scientific notation, one factor must be a decimal number between 1 and 10, and the other factor must be a power of 10. The first digit tells you that the power of 10 is 10^5.

The decimal number is 1.5.

$150\,000 = 1.5 \times 10^5$

10^5	10^4	10^3	10^2	10^1	1
1	5	0	0	0	0

For expanded form, show each digit multiplied by its place value. Write the sum of these products.

$$150\,000 = 1 \times 10^5 + 5 \times 10^4 + 0 \times 10^3 + 0 \times 10^2 + 0 \times 10 + 0 \times 1$$
$$= 1 \times 10^5 + 5 \times 10^4$$

Practice Questions

(1.1) **1.** How do you know that each number is a composite number?

a) 111 704 **c)** 111 111

b) 1 250 005 **d)** 2^{10}

(1.1) **2.** The first two digits of Oliver's three-digit apartment number are 1 and 2. His apartment number is a prime number. What is Oliver's apartment number?

(1.1) **3.** Jocelyn is trying to determine whether or not 247 is a prime number.

a) How can she tell, without dividing, that 2, 3, and 5 are not factors?

b) What other numbers should she divide by to determine whether or not 247 is a prime number? Explain your reasoning.

c) Is 247 a prime or composite number? Explain.

(1.2) **4.** Determine the prime factorization of each number.

a) 30 **b)** 75 **c)** 165 **d)** 1122

(1.2) **5.** Complete each prime factorization.

a) $210 = 2 \times 3 \times \blacksquare \times \blacksquare$

b) $196 = 2^2 \times \blacksquare^2$

c) $216 = 2^3 \times 3^{\blacksquare}$

d) $910 = 2 \times \blacksquare \times \blacksquare \times 13$

(1.3) **6.** Identify three common factors and three common multiples of 70 and 56.

$70 = 2 \times 5 \times 7$

$56 = 2^3 \times 7$

7. a) Determine the GCF of 24 and 30.

b) Determine the LCM of 24 and 30. (1.3)

8. Calculate. (1.4)

a) 3^5 **b)** 2^6 **c)** 0.2^4 **d)** 1.5^3

9. Five DVDs are packaged in plastic wrap. Five packages are packed in a box. Five boxes are packed in a crate. (1.4)

a) How many DVDs are packed in a crate?

b) Represent the number of DVDs in a crate as a power.

10. Copy and complete the chart. (1.5)

Standard form	Expanded form	Scientific notation
456	$4 \times 10^2 + \blacksquare \times 10 + \blacksquare \times 1$	4.56×10^2
	$1 \times 10^4 + 3 \times 10^2 + 9 \times 1$	
		4.5×10^4
123 123		

11. Express each number in expanded form and in scientific notation. (1.5)

a) 12 500, the number of seats in the Rexall Centre for tennis in Toronto

b) 32 000 000, the approximate population of Canada in 2004

c) 230 000 000, the approximate number of years for our galaxy to complete one rotation

d) 13 800 000 000, the approximate number of kilometres from the *Voyager 1* spacecraft to the Sun in May 2004

Math Game

DETERMINING PRIME FACTORS

You will need
- a die

The goal of this game is to determine the prime factorization of three-digit numbers and score the most points for the number of prime factors.

Number of players: 2 to 4

Rules

1. The first player rolls a die three times to make a three-digit number.
2. If the number is a prime number, the player scores no points.
3. If the number is a composite number, the player determines its prime factorization. The player's score is the number of prime factors in the prime factorization, including repeats of the same factor.
4. Players take turns rolling the die and determining the prime factorization of the numbers formed. The first player to score 10 points wins.

Prime Numbers							
2	3	5	7	11	13	17	19
23	29	31	37	41	43	47	53
59	61	67	71	73	79	83	89
97	101	103	107	109	113	127	131
137	139	149	151	157	163	167	173
179	181	191	193	197	199	211	223
227	229	233	239	241	251	257	263
269	271	277	281	283	293	307	311
313	317	331	337	347	349	353	359
367	373	379	383	389	397	401	409
419	421	431	433	439	443	449	457
461	463	467	479	487	491	499	503
509	521	523	541	547	557	563	569
571	577	587	593	599	601	607	613
617	619	631	641	643	647	653	659
661	673	677	683	691	701	709	719

Jordan's turn:

I rolled 441.

I drew a factor tree to determine the prime factors.

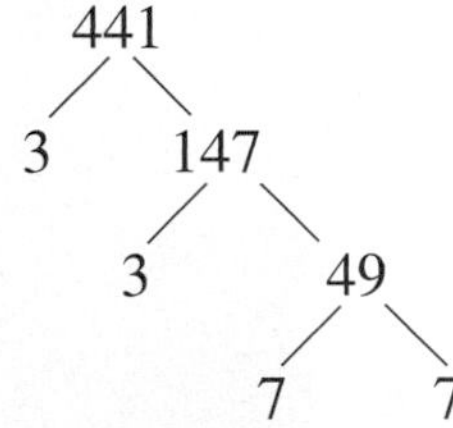

The prime factorization of 441 is $3 \times 3 \times 7 \times 7$.
I scored 4 points for the four prime factors.

Curious Math

SUBTRACTING TO CALCULATE SQUARE ROOTS

You can calculate the **square root** of a perfect square by determining the length and width of a square with a given area.

Area = length × width

4

4

area = 16 square units

For example, to calculate the square root of 16, you can solve the equation $16 = \square \times \square$.

Since the length and width of a square are equal, $\square = \sqrt{16}$, which is 4.

You can also calculate the square root by subtracting consecutive odd numbers.

$$\begin{array}{r}16\\-\ 1\\\hline 15\end{array}$$ one subtraction

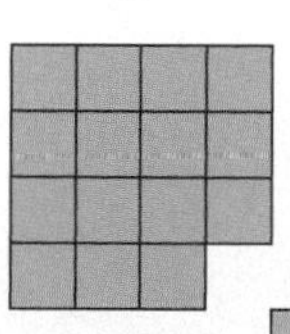

$$\begin{array}{r}15\\-\ 3\\\hline 12\end{array}$$ two subtractions

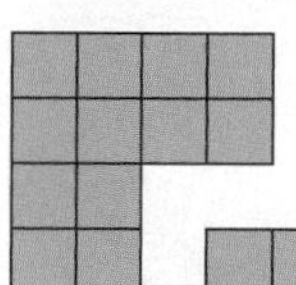

$$\begin{array}{r}12\\-\ 5\\\hline 7\end{array}$$ three subtractions

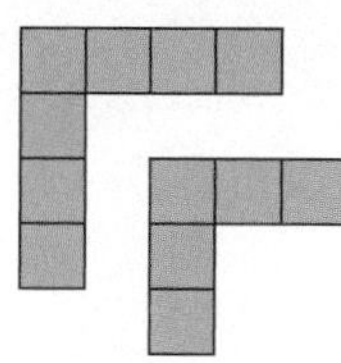

$$\begin{array}{r}7\\-\ 7\\\hline 0\end{array}$$ four subtractions

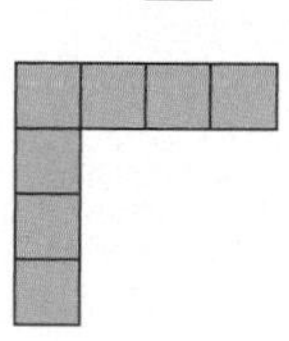

The square root is equal to the number of consecutive odd numbers subtracted to equal 0. Four odd numbers were subtracted from 16, so $\sqrt{16} = 4$.

1. Calculate each square root by subtracting consecutive odd numbers.

a) $\sqrt{9}$ **b)** $\sqrt{25}$ **c)** $\sqrt{64}$ **d)** $\sqrt{100}$

1.6 Square Roots

You will need
- grid paper
- a calculator

▶ **GOAL**
Estimate and calculate the square root of a whole number.

Learn about the Math

Sandra and her father cut a hole in the ice on a lake to measure the thickness of the ice. Then they used a formula with a **square root** ($\sqrt{\ }$) to determine if 30 cm of ice could safely support their total mass of 125 kg.

square root ($\sqrt{\ }$)
one of two equal factors of a number; for example, the square root of 100 is represented as $\sqrt{100}$ and is equal to 10 because 10×10 or $10^2 = 100$

Required thickness $= 0.38\sqrt{\blacksquare}$ ← load in kilograms

Communication Tip

- In many formulas, the multiplication symbol is not included. For example, $0.38\sqrt{\blacksquare}$ represents $0.38 \times \sqrt{\blacksquare}$.
- You can use the symbol $\doteq$ to show that a number is approximately equal to another number. For example, $\sqrt{2} \doteq 1.414$.

? Is the ice thick enough to support the total mass of Sandra and her father?

A. Draw a 10-by-10 square, an 11-by-11 square, and a 12-by-12 square on grid paper. Calculate the area of each square.

B. How can you calculate the length of each side of a square if you know only the area of the square?

C. Does a square with an area of 125 square units have whole-number dimensions? Explain your reasoning.

D. How can you use the side lengths of the squares you drew in step A to estimate $\sqrt{125}$?

E. Use a calculator to determine $\sqrt{125}$. Round your answer to two decimal places.

Calculator Tip

Different calculators require different key sequences to calculate square roots.

TI-15:
[√] 125 [)] [Enter]

Other calculators:
125 [√]

F. Is the ice thick enough to support the total mass of Sandra and her father? Show your work.

Reflecting

1. Explain how to use the square key x^2 or the power key ^ on your calculator to check your answer in step E.

2. When you square your answer in step E, why do you not get exactly 125?

Work with the Math

Example 1: Estimating a square root by squaring numbers

The area of a square floor is 82.0 m². Estimate the length of each side of the floor.

Reilly's Solution

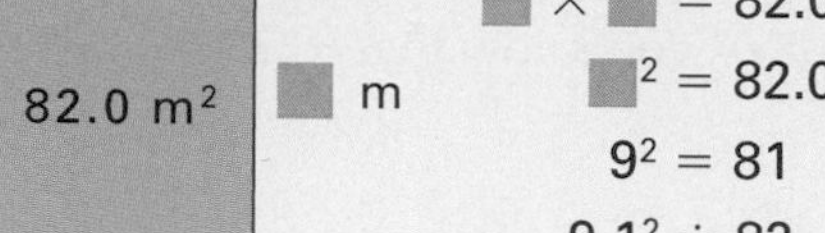

$$■ \times ■ = 82.0$$
$$■^2 = 82.0$$
$$9^2 = 81$$
$$9.1^2 \doteq 82$$
$$9.1 \doteq \sqrt{82}$$

I can find the side length of a square with an area of 82.0 square units by calculating $\sqrt{82}$.

The square root of 81 is 9. So, the square root of 82 must be a bit more than 9. I picked 9.1.

The side length of the square is between 9.0 and 9.1 m².

Example 2: Using the square root key on a calculator

The mass of a truck is 5000 kg. What thickness of ice is needed to support the truck?

Tamara's Solution

First I estimated the thickness: $0.38\sqrt{5000}$.

$\sqrt{5000}$ must be close to 70 because $70^2 = 4900$.

Multiplying 70 by 0.38 is less than half of 70, or about 30 cm.

Then I used a calculator to calculate the thickness.

Using the TI-15:

.38 ⊠ √ 5000) Enter

Using another calculator:

5000 √ → 70.71067812

× .38 = → 26.87005769

The ice needs to be about 27 cm thick to support the truck.

A Checking

3. Estimate each square root to one decimal place.

   a) $\sqrt{15}$ c) $\sqrt{50}$
   b) $\sqrt{300}$ d) $\sqrt{122}$

4. State whether the square root is a whole number. Then calculate the square root. Round to three decimal places, if necessary.

   a) $\sqrt{42}$ c) $\sqrt{961}$
   b) $\sqrt{144}$ d) $\sqrt{2052}$

5. Use the following formula to estimate the thickness of ice, in centimetres, needed to support each vehicle.

   Thickness (cm) $= 0.38\sqrt{\text{load (kg)}}$

   a) a car with a mass of 800 kg
   b) a truck with a mass of 1800 kg

B Practising

6. Use estimation to determine whether or not each answer is reasonable. Use the square root key on your calculator to correct any unreasonable answers.

   a) $\sqrt{8} \doteq 2.8$ d) $\sqrt{342} \doteq 28.5$
   b) $\sqrt{10} \doteq 3.2$ e) $\sqrt{1482} \doteq 38.5$
   c) $\sqrt{289} = 27$ f) $\sqrt{3052} \doteq 55.2$

7. Calculate.

   a) $\sqrt{18}$ c) $\sqrt{150}$ e) $\sqrt{800}$
   b) $\sqrt{75}$ d) $\sqrt{38}$ f) $\sqrt{3900}$

8. A square field has an area of 3000 m^2.

   3000 m^2

   a) Is the side length of the field a whole number of metres? Explain how you know.
   b) Estimate the side length of the square.
   c) How do you know that the side length is between 50 m and 60 m?
   d) Calculate the side length of the square field.

9. Explain how you know that $\sqrt{71}$ is between 8 and 9.

10. Explain how you can use squaring to estimate $\sqrt{7}$.

11. Use mental math to calculate each square root. Then use squaring to check your answer.

    a) $\sqrt{100}$ c) $\sqrt{400}$ e) $\sqrt{1600}$
    b) $\sqrt{144}$ d) $\sqrt{900}$ f) $\sqrt{3600}$

12. Use the following formula to estimate the time an object takes to fall from each height below.

    Time (s) $= 0.45\sqrt{\text{height (m)}}$

    a) 100 m d) 900 m
    b) 200 m e) 2000 m
    c) 400 m f) 10 000 m

13. Nico squared some numbers and got these answers. Use mental math to determine each number she squared. Explain your reasoning.

    a) 49 c) 30 e) 169
    b) 1225 d) 72 f) 625

NEL

14. a) Choose a number.

b) Name a number that has a square root less than your chosen number.

c) Name the number whose square root is your chosen number.

d) Name a number that has a square root greater than your chosen number.

15. a) Try Tamara's number trick:

- Choose any whole number greater than 0.
- Square it.
- Add twice your original number.
- Add 1.
- Calculate the square root of the sum.
- Subtract your original number.
- Record your answer.

b) Try Tamara's number trick with four other numbers.

c) What do you notice about your answers in parts (a) and (b)?

16. The year 1936 is the last year whose square root was a whole number. What is the next year whose square root will be a whole number? Explain your reasoning.

17. Examine each number. What number can you add to this number to make a number that has a whole-number square root?

a) 42 **c)** 470

b) 101 **d)** 1000

18. A palindrome is a number that is the same when it is read from left to right and from right to left. Both 14 641 and its square root, 121, are palindromes. Find at least three other numbers that are palindromes and have square roots that are palindromes.

19. a) Calculate these square roots.

$\sqrt{5}$ $\sqrt{50\ 000}$

$\sqrt{500}$ $\sqrt{5\ 000\ 000}$

b) Describe any patterns you see in part (a).

c) Identify the next calculation in the pattern.

C Extending

20. Ken calculated the square root of a number. Then he calculated the square root of the square root. His answer was 25. What was his original number? Explain your reasoning.

21. a) Choose three different two-digit numbers. Determine the prime factorization of each number.

b) Calculate the square of each number in part (a). Determine the prime factorization of each square.

c) Compare the prime factorization of each square with the prime factorization of its square root. How can you use the prime factorization of a square to calculate its square root?

d) Use the prime factorization of 23 409 to calculate its square root.

$23\ 409 = 3^4 \times 17^2$

22. a) Try Sheree's number trick:

- Choose any two-digit number.
- Subtract 2 from this number.
- Calculate the product of the two numbers.
- Add 1 to the product.
- Calculate the square root of the sum.

b) Repeat Sheree's number trick with another two-digit number.

c) What do you notice about your answers in parts (a) and (b)?

1.7 Exploring Square Roots and Squares

You will need
- centimetre dot paper
- a calculator

▶ **GOAL**

Determine the diagonal lengths, side lengths, and areas of squares.

Explore the Math

Manuel drew the following squares on centimetre dot paper. Then he compared the side lengths and areas of the upright squares with the diagonal lengths, side lengths, and areas of the slanted squares.

Upright Squares

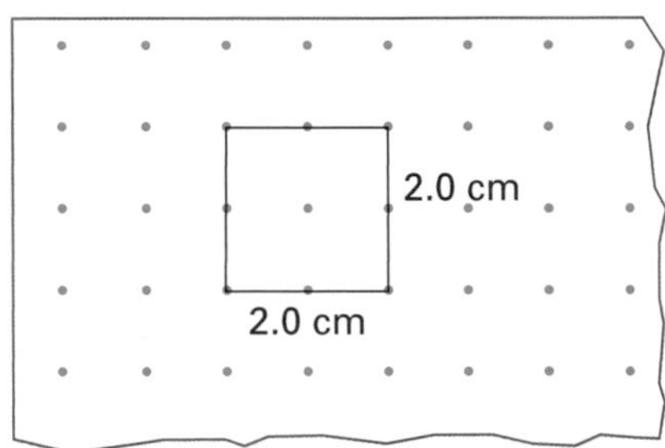

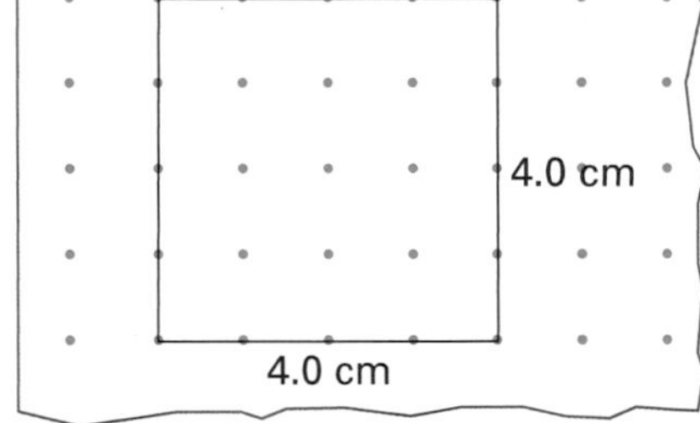

Slanted Squares

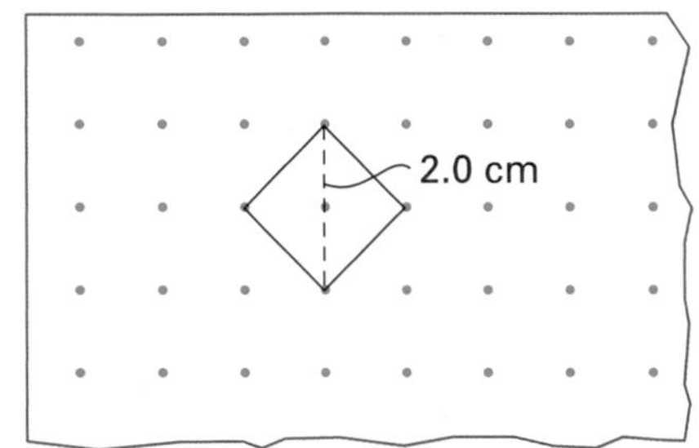

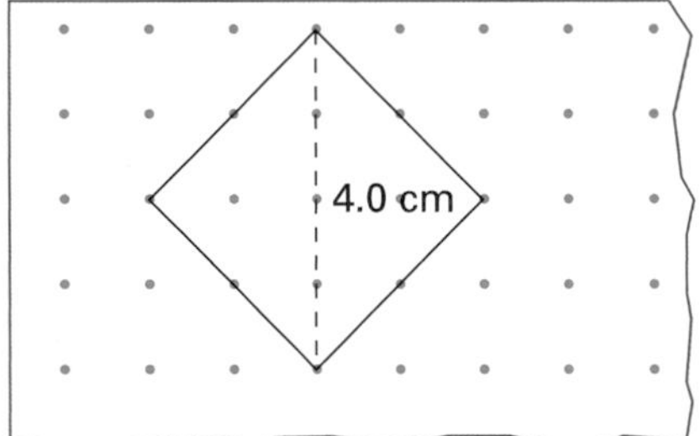

? How can you determine the area of a square on dot paper?

A. Copy each upright and slanted square onto centimetre dot paper. Determine the area of each square.

B. Draw an upright square with a side length of 6 cm on centimetre dot paper. Then draw a slanted square with a diagonal length of 6 cm. Determine the area of each square.

C. Draw another upright square and its corresponding slanted square. Make sure that the diagonal length of the slanted square is equal to the side length of the upright square. Compare the areas of the two squares.

D. How can you predict the area of a slanted square if you know its diagonal length? Draw another slanted square and calculate its area to check your prediction.

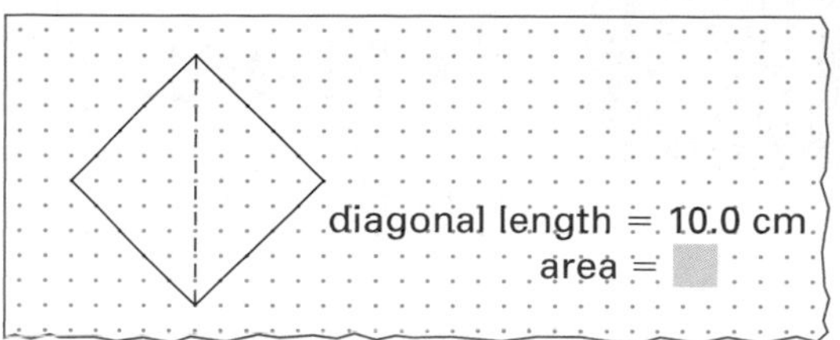

E. How can you determine the side length of a square if you know its area?

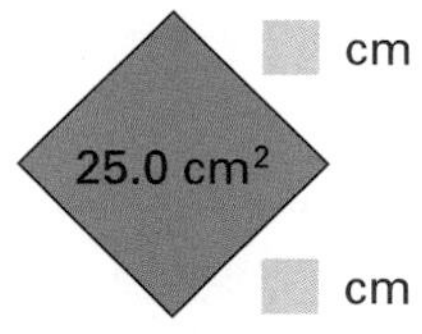

F. How can you use your answers in steps A to E to determine the side length of each slanted square you drew on dot paper? Record the diagonal length, area, and side length of each slanted square in a chart like this:

Diagonal length (cm)	Area (cm^2)	Side length (cm)
2.0		
4.0		
6.0		
		10.0
	25.0	

G. What is the area and diagonal length of the largest slanted square you can draw on centimetre dot paper? Show your work.

Reflecting

1. The diagonal length of a slanted square is 2 cm. How do you know that the side length of this square is greater than 1 cm?

2. The area of a square with a diagonal length of 10 cm has to be less than the area of a square with a side length of 10 cm. Explain why.

3. a) What is the area of a square with a diagonal length of 100 cm? Explain your reasoning.
   b) What is the side length of this square? Explain your reasoning.

4. a) How can you determine the area of a square if you know its side length?
   b) How can you determine the area of a square if you know its diagonal length?
   c) How can you determine the side length of a square if you know its diagonal length?

1.8 Order of Operations

You will need
- a calculator
- a watch with a second hand

▶ **GOAL**

Apply the rules for order of operations to whole numbers and decimals.

Learn about the Math

Reilly is beginning a fitness program. He read that his heart rate has to increase in order to receive any benefits from the program. He used the following formula to determine the minimum training heart rate for a beginner:

Minimum training heart rate = 0.5 × (220 − age + resting heart rate)

Reilly is 13 years old. His resting heart rate is 73 beats per minute.

? What is Reilly's training heart rate?

Example 1: Using the rules for order of operations

What is Reilly's training heart rate?

Reilly's Solution

Minimum training heart rate = 0.5 × (220 − age + resting heart rate)	
= 0.5 × (220 − 13 + 73)	I substituted my age and resting heart rate into the formula.
= 0.5 × (207 + 73)	
= 0.5 × (280)	I did the operations in the brackets first.
= 140	Then I multiplied by 0.5 by taking half the number.
My training heart rate should be 140 beats per minute.	28 ÷ 2 = 14, so 280 ÷ 2 = 140

Reflecting

1. Use estimation to show that Reilly's calculation of his training heart rate is reasonable.
2. How would Reilly's answer change if he ignored the brackets in the formula?
3. Does it matter which operation within brackets you do first? Explain.

Communication Tip

- You can use the memory aid **BEDMAS** to remember the rules for order of operations.
  Perform the operations in **B**rackets first.
  Calculate **E**xponents and square roots next.
  Divide and **M**ultiply from left to right.
  Add and **S**ubtract from left to right.
- Brackets can be many different shapes, such as [ ], { }, and ( ). Curved brackets ( ) are sometimes called parentheses. Some calculators have brackets you can enter when performing a calculation.
- When a square root sign covers an expression, it behaves like brackets.
- When there are multiple brackets, complete the operations in the inner brackets first. For example:
  $[(2 + 3) \times 3]^2$
  $= [5 \times 3]^2$
  $= 15^2$
  $= 225$

Work with the Math

Example 2: Using the rules for order of operations in a formula

Sometimes, doctors need to estimate the surface area of a patient's skin to determine the dosage of a medicine. They use the patient's height (in centimetres) and mass (in kilograms) in the following formula:

Body surface area $= \sqrt{\text{height} \times \text{mass} \div 3600}$

A patient is 2.10 m tall and has a mass of 150 kg. Use the formula to estimate the surface area of the patient's skin.

Sheree's Solution

$$\begin{aligned}\text{Body surface area} &= \sqrt{\text{height} \times \text{mass} \div 3600}\\ &= \sqrt{210 \times 150 \div 3600}\\ &= \sqrt{31\ 500 \div 3600}\\ &= \sqrt{8.75}\\ &\doteq 2.958\end{aligned}$$

The patient's body surface area is about 3 m^2. That surface area is almost equal to the area of a 1 m by 3 m rectangle.

I estimated to check my calculation. Height $\times$ mass is about $200 \times 150 = 30\ 000$. $30\ 000 \div 3600$ is less than $30\ 000 \div 3000$, which is about 10. The answer is less than $\sqrt{10}$, which is close to 3. So, my calculation looks reasonable.

Example 3: Using multiple brackets

Evaluate $[2 + (6 + 2^2)]^2$. Show each step.

Solution A: Using mental math

$[2 + (6 + 2^2)]^2$
$= [2 + (6 + 4)]^2$
$= [2 + (10)]^2$
$= [12]^2$
$= 144$

Solution B: Using a calculator with parentheses keys

$[2 + (6 + 2^2)]^2$

(2 + (6 + 2 ^ 2)) ^ 2 Enter

(2+(6+2^2))^2= 144

A Checking

4. Evaluate each expression. Express your answer to no more than three decimal places.
   a) $3.5 + 16 - 2.5^2$
   b) $4.2 \times \sqrt{3 \times 5 + 1} \times 9.8$
   c) $6 \times 9.5 - 10.6 \div 2 + 1.5 \times 3.6$
   d) $(7.3^3 - \sqrt{3 \times 5 + 7^2})^2$

5. Use estimation to check that one calculation in question 4 is reasonable.

B Practising

6. Evaluate each expression. Express your answer to no more than three decimal places.
   a) $12 \times 5.5 - 3 \times 1.5^3$
   b) $(8.75 + 3 \times 16)^2 - 3.5^2$
   c) $(4.5 + 2.5 \times 8.2^2 + 4)^2$
   d) $[(6.5^2 - 4)^2 + \sqrt{40 + 9 \times 9}\,]^2$

7. Explain the errors that were made in this calculation. Show the corrections.

   $72.55 - 4 \times 3.75^2$
   $= 68.55 \times 3.75^2$
   $= 68.55 \times 14.0625$
   $= 963.984\ 375$
   $\doteq 963.984$

8. Measure your heart rate. Calculate your minimum training heart rate.

9. The following formulas can be used to determine the training heart rate for average and high fitness levels:

   Average fitness training heart rate
   $= 0.60 \times (220 - \text{age} + \text{resting heart rate})$

   High fitness training heart rate
   $= 0.75 \times (220 - \text{age} + \text{resting heart rate})$

   a) What are the average and high fitness training heart rates of a 30-year-old with a resting heart rate of 75?
   b) What are your average and high fitness training heart rates?
   c) Show how to use estimation to check that your answers in part (b) are reasonable.

10. Determine whether each calculation is correct. Show your work.
    a) $(8.4 - 3.8)^2 + 18.1 = 39.26$
    b) $4.5 + \sqrt{1681} \times 9.5 - 18.35 \div 2 = 206.95$
    c) $8.3^3 + 3.4 + 4 \times 8.8 = 5096.845$
    d) $21.1 \div (4.3 + 2.5^2) = 2$
    e) $4.55 + 8^2 \times 0.25 - 3.45 = 13.687$
    f) $45 \times \sqrt{5^2 + 12^2} \div (100 + 32^2 - 539) = 1$

11. Evaluate each expression. Show your work.

a) $(\sqrt{19} - 6)^2 \div 6.5$

b) $14.1 - 45.6 \div 2.5^2$

c) $6 + \sqrt{1225} + (3 + 2 \times 3)^3$

d) $[2.5 + (4.3 - 1.1^2)]^2$

12. Use one or more sets of brackets to calculate at least three different answers for this expression:

$4.5 + 2 \times 2.5^2 - 6$

13. a) Explain why the instructions below do not match the numerical expression $4.5^2 + 4.75 \div 5^2$.

> Square 4.5, add 4.75 to this number, divide the sum by 5, and square the quotient.

b) Use brackets so that the numerical expression matches the words.

c) Calculate your numerical expression in part (b). Show each step.

d) Evaluate the numerical expression in part (a). Show each step.

14. Explain the errors that were made in this calculation. Show the corrections.

$$\begin{aligned} & 4.5 \times \sqrt{6.5^2 + 3 \times 2.25} \\ &= 4.5 + 6.5 + 3 \times 2.25 \\ &= 11 + 3 \times 2.25 \\ &= 14 \times 2.25 \\ &= 31.5 \end{aligned}$$

15. Which expressions would have the same answer with and without the brackets? Explain your reasoning. Calculate each answer.

a) $4.5 \times (3.8 \times 3.2)$

b) $4.8 + (3.5^2 + 5.75) \times 3$

c) $[(4 \times 5)]^2$

16. Tiffany took a boat safety course. She learned how to use this formula to estimate the distance to an object on the horizon:

Distance (km) $= 3.57 \sqrt{\text{eye height (m)}}$

a) About how far can you see from a ferry if your eye height is 8 m?

b) About how far can you see from the outdoor observation deck of the CN Tower, at a height of 342 m?

c) About how far can you see if you are standing on a beach, at the edge of the water?

C Extending

17. a) Calculate $[(4^2)^2]^2$.

b) Calculate 4^8.

c) Compare your answers. What do you notice?

d) Show how you can use only one exponent to calculate $[(5^2)^2]^2$.

18. Write an expression that matches each set of instructions. Add brackets if required.

a) Subtract 1.5 from 3.75, square this number, and divide by 2.

b) Divide 12.25 by 0.25, take the square root of this number, and multiply by 7.

1.9 Communicating about Number Problems

You will need
- a calculator

▶ **GOAL**
Explain how to create and solve problems that involve numbers.

Communicate about the Math

A school Web site presented a challenge for students. They were asked to create and solve a problem that involved whole numbers and decimal numbers. The numbers had to come from an article on the Internet, in a newspaper or magazine, or in another type of publication. The students' problems and solutions would be posted on the Web site.

? How can you create a number problem and explain your solution?

Sheree used some numbers in an *Envirozine* article to create a problem. Then she explained how she solved her problem, and she asked Jordan to review her work.

Envirozine Fast Facts

More than 140 thousand tonnes of computer equipment, phones, televisions, stereos, and small home appliances accumulate in Canadian landfills each year. That's equivalent to the weight of about 28 thousand adult African elephants, or enough uncrushed electronic waste to fill up the Toronto Rogers Centre every 15 years.

Sheree's Problem
Each year, Canadians send 140 thousand tonnes of electronic waste to landfill sites. About how many kilograms of electronic waste are sent to landfills each month? Write your answer in scientific notation.

Sheree's Solution and Explanation	Jordan's Questions
The mass of electronic waste each year is 140 000 t. This mass is equal to 140 000 000 kg. ←	How did you calculate 140 000 000 kg?
I divided 140 000 000 kg by 12. ←	Why did you divide by 12?
140 000 000 kg $\div$ 12 $\doteq$ 11 666 667 kg ←	How did you make this estimate?
This mass is about 11.7 million kg, or 1.17×10^7 kg, each month. ←	How did you change 11.7 million to scientific notation?

A. How should Sheree answer each of Jordan's questions?

B. What other questions might Jordan ask to improve Sheree's solution?

C. Improve Sheree's solution. Use the Communication Checklist to help you.

Reflecting

1. Which questions in the Communication Checklist were covered well in Sheree's solution?

2. Why should you explain your thinking when you are solving a problem?

Communication Checklist

- ☑ Did you identify the given information?
- ☑ Did you show how to solve your problem step by step?
- ☑ Did you explain each calculation?
- ☑ Did you explain why each calculation is reasonable?

Work with the Math

Example: Creating a problem and explaining your solution

Use this information to create and solve a problem.

The official size of a tennis court for singles is 23.88 m by 8.23 m. The official size for doubles is 23.88 m by 10.97 m.

Teo's Solution

My Problem:

A tennis court for doubles is a 23.88 m by 10.97 m rectangle. What is the side length of a square with the same area as the doubles tennis court?

My Solution:

I calculated the area of the rectangle by multiplying its dimensions. I used my calculator to multiply 23.88 by 10.97.

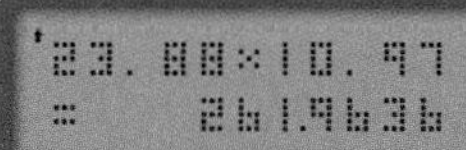

The area of the tennis court is about 261.96 m^2. I rounded to two decimal places because this is the number of decimal places in the measurements given. I know my calculation is reasonable because 10.97 is about 10, 23.88 is about 24, and $10 \times 24 = 240$.

To calculate the area of a square, I square the side length. If I know the area of a square and want to determine the side length, I calculate the square root of the area. I used my calculator to calculate the square root of 261.96.

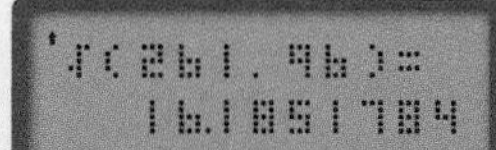

The square has a side length of about 16.19 m. This is close to 16 m. I checked my answer by squaring 16 on my calculator.

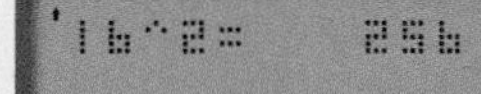

My answer is reasonable because 256 is close to 261.96.

A Checking

3. Manuel used information about the heart to create a problem. Then he solved his problem and explained his solution. How can you improve Manuel's explanation? Use the Communication Checklist to help you.

> The heart is a powerful muscle. It beats without stopping throughout a lifetime. An adult heart pumps 55 to 80 mL of blood per beat. A child's heart pumps 25 to 85 mL of blood per beat.

> My Problem:
> My heart pumps about 80 mL of blood per beat. My heart rate is about 85 beats per minute. About how many kilolitres of blood have been pumped through my body in my lifetime of 14 years?
>
> My Solution:
> 85 × 80 mL = 6800 mL
> = 6.8 L
>
> I multiplied 85 by 80 mL to get the amount of blood each minute.
>
> 6.8 L × 60 = 408 L
> ≐ 0.4 kL
>
> I calculated the number of litres pumped per hour and per day and per year.
>
> 0.4 × 24 = 9.6 kL
> 9.6 × 365 = 3504 kL
>
> 3504 kL × 14 = 49 056 kL

B Practising

For questions 4 to 7, use numbers from each newspaper clipping, as well as any other numbers you need, to create and solve a problem. Use the Communication Checklist to help you explain your solution.

4. In one day, the movie *Star Wars: Episode III — Revenge of the Sith* earned $50 013 859 U.S. at the box office.

5. A space vehicle must move at a rate of 11.3 km per second to escape Earth's gravitational pull.

6. An IMAX film is fed through a projector at a rate of 24 frames per second. The width of each frame is about 70 mm.

7. The mass of an adult caterpillar is about 27 000 times its mass at birth.

8. Collect whole numbers and decimal numbers from magazines and newspapers, or from the Internet. Use these numbers, as well as other numbers, to create and solve a problem. Explain your solution, using the Communication Checklist to help you.

Chapter Self-Test

1. Explain why 143 is not a prime number.

2. How do you know that 3^6 is not a prime number?

3. Determine the prime factorization of each number.

   a) 360 c) 560
   b) 245 d) 1620

4. a) Identify the common factors of 54 and 36.
   b) Identify three common multiples of 54 and 36.
   c) Identify the GCF and LCM of 54 and 36.

5. a) Identify 10 different rectangular prisms with whole-number dimensions that have a volume of 144 cm^3. Show your work.
   b) The volume of a rectangular prism with whole-number dimensions has a volume that is a prime number. What are its dimensions? Use an example to support your explanation.

6. a) Calculate each power.

   2^3 20^3 200^3 2000^3

   b) Describe any patterns you see.
   c) Use your pattern to calculate $20\,000^3$.

7. Determine the missing numbers to make each statement true.

   a) $0.5^{■} = 0.5 \times 0.5 \times 0.5 \times 0.5$
   b) $1.3^3 = ■ \times ■ \times ■$

8. Which prize is worth more? Explain your reasoning.
   - a prize on March 21, if \$5 is given on March 1, five times as much on March 2 (\$25), five times as much on March 3 (\$125), and so on, to March 21
   - a prize of \$9.5 billion

9. A total of 8 058 044 651 Web pages were searched by Google by the end of 2004. Express this number in scientific notation and in expanded form.

10. Write each number in standard form.

    a) 1.45×10^5
    b) 9.6×10^7
    c) 4.888×10^4
    d) 5.67×10^{12}

11. The total area of Canada is 9 984 670 km^2. Calculate the side length of a square with the same area. Show your work.

12. Calculate. Explain how you know that each answer is reasonable.

    a) $\sqrt{20}$ c) $\sqrt{775}$
    b) $\sqrt{345}$ d) $\sqrt{2025}$

13. Evaluate each expression.

    a) $8.8 \div 2.2 \times 4 + (5.4 - 4.2)^2$
    b) $4 \times 2.8 - 1^5 + 4.8 \times 5$
    c) $\sqrt{31 + 10 \div 2} + 3 \times 2.5$
    d) $[12.5^2 - (3 + 2.6)^2]^2$
    e) $[(10 - 2 \times 3)^2]^3$
    f) $5^2 - (11 - 7)^2 \div (1 + 2^2)$

Chapter Review

Frequently Asked Questions

Q: What is a square root, and how do you calculate one?

A: The square root of a number n is a number you can multiply by itself to get the number n. For example, $\sqrt{64} = 8$ because $8^2 = 64$.

You can estimate the square root of a number by calculating the square roots of square numbers close to this number. For example, to estimate the square root of 5000, think of $70^2 = 4900$ and $80^2 = 6400$. The number 5000 is between 4900 and 6400, but closer to 4900. So, $\sqrt{5000}$ is close to 71.

You can calculate the square root of a number by using the $\sqrt{\ }$ key on your calculator.

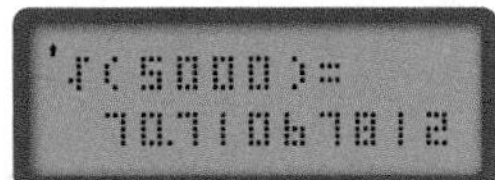

$\sqrt{5000} \doteq 70.711$

Check: $70.711^2 \doteq 5000.046$, which is close to 5000

Q: What are the rules for the order of operations?

A: These are the rules for evaluating an expression with mixed operations, so that everyone gets the same result:

Perform the operations in **B**rackets first.
Calculate **E**xponents and square roots next.
Divide and **M**ultiply from left to right.
Add and **S**ubtract from left to right.

You can use the term **BEDMAS** to remember the rules.

For example,

		Check by estimating:
$[4.35 \times (100 - \sqrt{3^2 \times 4})]^2$	Perform the operations in the inner brackets first. Do square root operations by squaring first and then multiplying.	$[4.35 \times (100 - \sqrt{3^2 \times 4})]^2$ is about $[4 \times (100 - \sqrt{36})]^2$.
$= [4.35 \times (100 - \sqrt{9 \times 4})]^2$		
$= [4.35 \times (100 - \sqrt{36})]^2$	Calculate the square root.	4×94 is about 400.
$= [4.35 \times (100 - 6)]^2$	Subtract in the brackets.	400^2 is 160 000.
$= [4.35 \times 94]^2$	Multiply and square.	
$= 408.90^2$		
$= 167\ 199.21$		

Practice Questions

(1.1) **1.** Identify the only prime number below. How do you know that the other numbers are composite numbers?

128 405 999 1579

(1.2) **2.** Determine the prime factorization of each number.

a) 235 **c)** 1218

b) 468 **d)** 44 100

(1.3) **3.** A square measures 72 cm by 72 cm.

a) Which of these rectangles can be used repeatedly to cover the square without any spaces or overlapping?

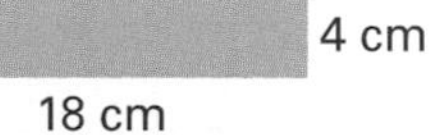

b) Determine two other rectangles with whole-number dimensions that can be used to cover the square.

c) How can you tell from the dimensions of a rectangle whether or not it will cover the square?

(1.4) **4.** Kim keeps 0.9 of a 1.00 m rope. Shaun keeps 0.9 of Kim's piece. Kent keeps 0.9 of Shaun's piece. Charlene keeps 0.9 of Kent's piece.

a) How long is Charlene's piece of rope?

b) Explain how you can use powers of 0.9 to solve the problem.

c) How many more people need to be involved for the last person to have a piece of rope that is just under 0.5 m? Explain your reasoning.

5. The average human body contains about 40 L of water. What is the total amount of water contained in the 6.4 billion people in the world? Show each step in your solution. Express your answer in scientific notation. (1.5)

6. Write each number in expanded form and in scientific notation. (1.5)

a) 160 000 **c)** 145 000 000

b) 2 240 000 **d)** 23 000 000 000

7. Explain how to estimate $\sqrt{1659}$. (1.6)

8. Calculate.

a) $\sqrt{35}$ **c)** $\sqrt{169}$

b) $\sqrt{500}$ **d)** $\sqrt{70}$

9. The square root of a whole number is about 5.2. What is the number? Explain your reasoning. (1.6)

10. Evaluate each expression. Use the rules for order of operations. (1.8)

a) $5.5 + 3.5 \times 4.5$

b) $(1 + 2.46^2) \div 2 + 3.5^2$

c) $[(2.5 + 6.5 \times 2.3^2) - 1.5]^2$

d) $\sqrt{39} - 3 \times 4.5 + 3.5^2$

11. Derek wants to buy a cell phone. He wants to know which monthly plan is best if he uses the phone 8 h each month. (1.8)

- Plan 150:
  Cost = \$20 + (time in minutes − 150) × \$0.30
- Plan 400:
  Cost = \$40 + (time in minutes − 400) × \$0.25

Calculate the cost of each plan for 8 h per month. Which plan is better for Derek?

Chapter Task

Describing Numbers

The United Nations declared October 12, 1999, as *The Day of 6 Billion*. According to experts, the population of the world reached 6 billion on this day.

12 October 1999
the Day of 6 Billion
Reaching 6 billion is not about numbers...
...It is about people.
Estimated World Population Today

? In how many different ways can you describe the number 6 billion?

A. Show how to write 6 billion using
- prime factorization
- expanded form
- scientific notation

B. Explain how you know that 6 billion is the same as 6000 million.

C. Heidi said that 6 billion can represent the area of a square. About how many units is the length of the square? How do you know?

D. Nicolai said that 6 billion can represent the volume of a cube. How many units long is the cube? How do you know?

E. Jay said that 6 billion people could stretch around Earth at the equator more than 200 times. Show why his claim makes sense. (The distance around the equator is about 40 000 km.)

F. Think of two other ways to describe the number 6 billion. Which way do you think is most interesting? Why?

Task Checklist

- ☑ Did you show all the steps you used?
- ☑ Did you use correct mathematical language?
- ☑ Did you explain your thinking?

CHAPTER 2

Proportional Relationships

▶ GOALS

You will be able to

- represent and compare fractions as decimals and percents
- multiply and divide decimals
- solve problems that involve ratios and rates
- solve a variety of problems that involve percents

Getting Started

You will need
- a calculator

Buying Fish

Annika is buying a new fish tank and tropical fish. She wants 20 different kinds and sizes of fish. Based on the size of the tank she wants, the salesperson recommends that no more than 35% of the fish should be longer than 8 cm.

Type of fish	Number of fish Annika would like in her tank	Average length (cm)
neon tetra	8	4
orange swordtail	3	10
black molly	6	7
angel fish	2	11
algae eater	1	15

? Does Annika's list meet the salesperson's recommendations?

A. Write the ratio of the number of neon tetra to the total number of fish in Annika's list. Write a similar ratio for each type of fish.

B. **a)** Calculate the percent of each type of fish in Annika's list.

b) What strategy did you use for your calculations?

C. **a)** Determine the decimal equivalent for each percent.

b) What strategy did you use to calculate the decimals?

D. How many fish in Annika's list are longer than 8 cm?

E. What percent of the fish in Annika's list are longer than 8 cm? What percent of the fish are shorter than or equal to 8 cm?

F. Does Annika's list follow the salesperson's recommendations? Explain how you know.

Do You Remember?

1. a) Write the ratio of white squares to green squares.
   b) What fraction of the squares are white?
   c) What percent of the squares are green?

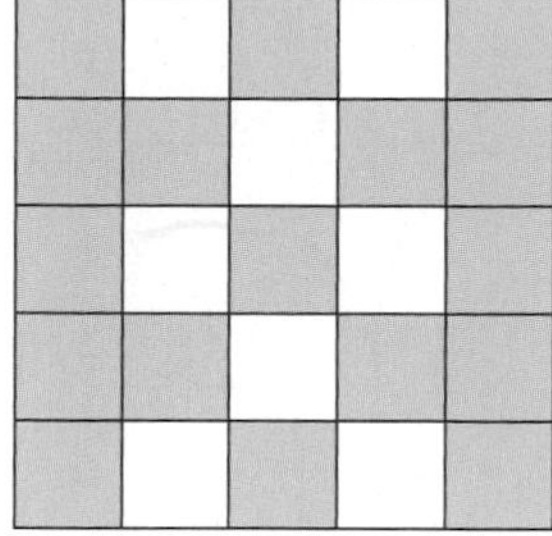

2. Write three ratios that are equivalent to 3 : 8.

3. Write the scale factor in each proportion. Then solve for the missing term.

   a) $\frac{4}{9} = \frac{■}{18}$ c) $\frac{3}{■} = \frac{15}{45}$

   b) $\frac{55}{■} = \frac{11}{7}$ d) $\frac{14}{18} = \frac{■}{9}$

4. Write the decimal equivalent for each fraction.

   a) $\frac{1}{4}$ b) $\frac{1}{2}$ c) $\frac{1}{10}$ d) $\frac{1}{5}$

5. Copy the chart, and determine the equivalent forms of each given number.

Ratio	Decimal	Percent
$\frac{3}{5}$		
	0.76	
		41%

6. The ratio of cars to other vehicles in the school parking lot is 3 : 2.
   a) What percent of the vehicles are cars?
   b) What percent of the vehicles are not cars?

7. Copy each statement. Write and solve the proportion to fill in the blank.
   a) 40% of 35 is ■.
   b) 21 out of 25 is ■%.
   c) 10% of ■ is 9.

8. Calculate.

   a) $3.0 \div 5$ d) $1.44 - 0.92$
   b) 4.6×7 e) 0.8×2.2
   c) $52.6 + 3.7$ f) $12.25 \div 5$

9. At a grocery store, two 1 L bottles of pop cost $1.98. Kamilah wants to buy 12 bottles of pop. How much do 12 bottles cost?

10. Daniel received a mark of 80% on his science test. If the test was out of 75, what was his score on the test?

11. A store advertises chicken for sale at $2.45/kg. How much does 4.2 kg of chicken cost?

12. Copy and complete the factor tree to determine the prime factors of 18.

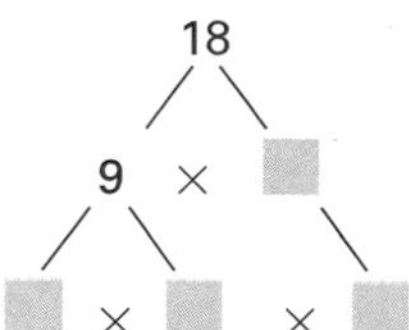

13. Determine the prime factorization of each number.

    a) 20 b) 36 c) 120

14. The scale of a floor plan is 1 : 200.
    a) In the scale diagram, the width of the building is 14 cm. Calculate the width of the building in metres.
    b) The length of the building is 32 m. Calculate the length of the building in the scale diagram in centimetres.

You will need

- a calculator

2.1 Expressing Fractions as Decimals

▶ **GOAL**

Use division to express fractions as decimals.

Learn about the Math

Eva and her friends are going on a hike. Eva buys 2 kg of trail mix to share with her friends.

? How much trail mix will each hiker receive?

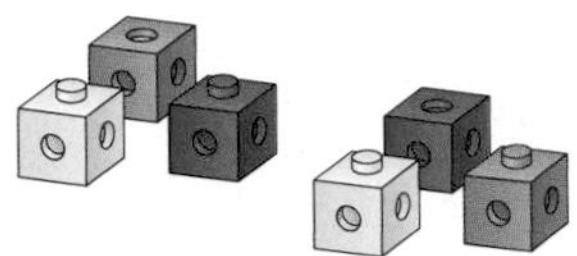

A. Suppose that there are three hikers. How can this picture be used to show that each hiker will get $\frac{2}{3}$ of a kilogram of trail mix?

B. Write a division statement to represent 2 kg of trail mix shared equally by three hikers.

C. Divide 2 by 3 on your calculator.

a) What is the result?

b) Why might this number be called a **repeating decimal** ?

c) Complete the division $2 \div 3$ using pencil and paper. What do you notice about the remainder after each step?

repeating decimal

a decimal in which a block of one or more digits eventually repeats in a pattern; for example,

$\frac{25}{99} = 0.252\ 525...$

$\frac{1}{7} = 0.142\ 857\ 142\ 857...$

$\frac{31}{36} = 0.861\ 111\ 1...$

D. Suppose that there is a different number of hikers, and each will get an equal share of the 2 kg of trail mix. Copy and complete the table to show how much trail mix each hiker will get.

Number of hikers		2	3	4	5	6	7	8	9	10
Mass of trail mix each hiker gets (kg)	As a fraction		$\frac{2}{3}$							
	As a decimal									

E. Write the prime factors of each denominator.

F. Which fractions in your table have repeating decimal equivalents?

G. Which fractions have **terminating decimal** equivalents?

H. Predict which decimals will terminate and which will repeat if you extend your table to include 11, 12, 13, and so on, up to 20 hikers. Test your predictions.

terminating decimal

a decimal that is complete after a certain number of digits, with no repetition; for example,

$\frac{29}{40} = 0.725$

NEL

Reflecting

1. Why are "terminating" and "repeating" appropriate names for the two types of decimals?

2. How can you predict whether the decimal equivalent of a given fraction will terminate?

3. How can you predict whether the decimal equivalent of a given fraction will repeat?

Communication Tip

In repeating decimals, instead of writing the repeating digits over and over, a horizontal bar is used to mark them. For example, 0.143 514 351 435... is written as $0.1\overline{435}$.

Work with the Math

Example 1: Comparing using equivalent decimals

Susan has three bags of popcorn to share with seven other people. Nathan has four bags of popcorn to share with eight other people. If all the bags of popcorn are the same size, which group will receive larger portions of popcorn?

Eva's Solution

3 bags shared among 8 people is
$3 \div 8 = 0.375$ bags.

4 bags shared among 9 people is
$4 \div 9 = 0.\overline{4}$ bags.

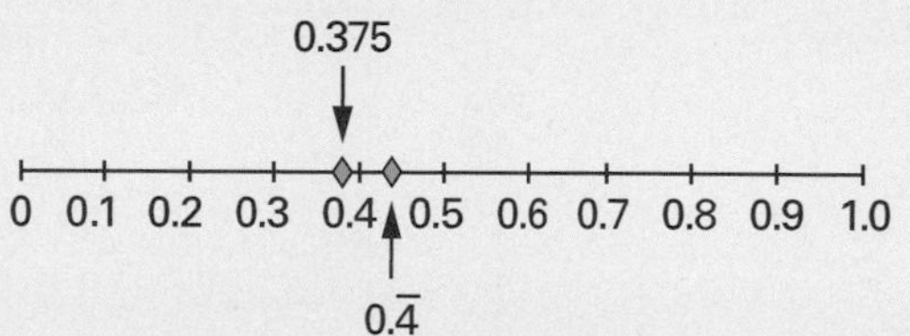

I know that $0.\overline{4} > 0.375$. So, the people in Nathan's group will receive larger portions.

Example 2: Predicting whether a decimal will terminate or repeat

Predict whether the decimal equivalent of each fraction will terminate or repeat.

a) $\frac{7}{9}$ **b)** $\frac{53}{80}$

Ken's Solution

a) $9 = 3 \times 3$

b) $80 = 2 \times 2 \times 2 \times 2 \times 5$

I can predict whether a decimal will terminate or repeat by looking at the prime factorization of the denominator of the fraction. If the prime factors are any combination of 2s and/or 5s, the decimal will terminate. Any other prime factors mixed with the 2s and/or 5s will result in a repeating decimal.

Based on the prime factors I found, I predict that $\frac{7}{9}$ will repeat and $\frac{53}{80}$ will terminate.

$\frac{7}{9} = 0.\overline{7}$ and $\frac{53}{80} = 0.6625$

I used a calculator to check my predictions.

A Checking

4. Write each repeating decimal using bar notation.

a) 0.555 555 55…

b) 0.134 561 345 613 456…

5. Which is greater?

a) $\frac{5}{16}$ or $\frac{2}{9}$ b) $\frac{7}{11}$ or $\frac{5}{8}$

6. Use prime factorization to determine which fractions have decimal equivalents that repeat.

a) $\frac{3}{4}$ b) $\frac{5}{9}$ c) $\frac{9}{14}$ d) $\frac{19}{20}$

B Practising

7. Write each fraction as a terminating decimal.

a) $\frac{14}{25}$ c) $\frac{1}{16}$ e) $\frac{19}{20}$

b) $\frac{5}{8}$ d) $\frac{4}{5}$ f) $\frac{22}{32}$

8. Write each fraction as a repeating decimal.

a) $\frac{1}{6}$ c) $\frac{7}{11}$ e) $\frac{48}{99}$

b) $\frac{8}{9}$ d) $\frac{7}{15}$ f) $\frac{57}{111}$

9. a) Predict whether the decimal equivalent of each fraction will be a terminating or repeating decimal. Use a calculator to check your predictions.

i) $\frac{4}{9}$ iii) $\frac{5}{6}$ v) $\frac{5}{18}$

ii) $\frac{3}{5}$ iv) $\frac{15}{16}$ vi) $\frac{19}{32}$

b) Order the decimals from least to greatest.

10. a) Express each fraction in the first three terms of this pattern as a repeating decimal.

$\frac{1}{11}, \frac{2}{11}, \frac{3}{11}, \ldots$

b) Describe the pattern.

c) Use the pattern to predict the decimal equivalents for $\frac{6}{11}$ and $\frac{9}{11}$.

11. Use >, <, or = to make each statement true.

a) 0.2 ■ $0.\overline{2}$

b) $\frac{45}{99}$ ■ $0.\overline{45}$

c) $0.\overline{82}$ ■ $\frac{4}{5}$

d) $\frac{6}{11}$ ■ $\frac{7}{13}$

e) 0.357 357 357… ■ $0.\overline{375}$

12. Order the numbers from least to greatest.

a) $\frac{1}{8}, \frac{5}{7}, 0.35, 0.\overline{39}, \frac{9}{10}$

b) $0.56, 0.5\overline{6}, 0.\overline{56}, \frac{5}{9}, \frac{27}{50}$

C Extending

13. Write each decimal as a fraction.

a) 0.1625 c) 0.272 727…

b) 0.0777… d) 0.065 656 5…

14. Use the fact that $\frac{1}{3} = 0.3333\ldots$ to predict the decimal equivalent for each fraction.

a) $\frac{2}{3}$ c) $\frac{1}{30}$

b) $\frac{1}{9}$ d) $\frac{1}{2} + \frac{1}{3} = \frac{5}{6}$

15. Determine fractions of the form $\frac{1}{■}$, in which the digits after the first two digits after the decimal place repeat. What do the denominators have in common?

Curious Math

REPEATING DECIMAL PATTERNS

Denis found that the decimal equivalent of $\frac{1}{13}$ is $0.\overline{076\ 923}$. He put pairs of successive digits from the repeating portion of this decimal into a table of values and plotted the points. Then he connected the points in the order they were plotted and joined the last point with the first.

x	y
0	7
7	6
6	9
9	2
2	3
3	0

Denis did this for all the other fractions in the family, from $\frac{2}{13}$ to $\frac{12}{13}$. He found that all the graphs were one of two shapes. Here are his graphs.

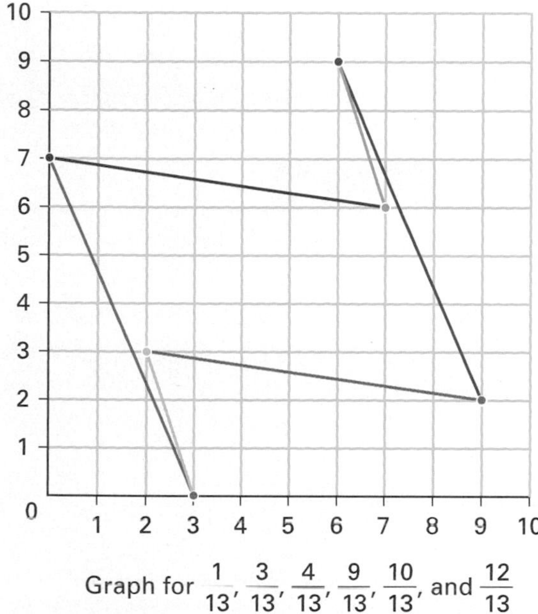

Graph for $\frac{1}{13}, \frac{3}{13}, \frac{4}{13}, \frac{9}{13}, \frac{10}{13}$, and $\frac{12}{13}$

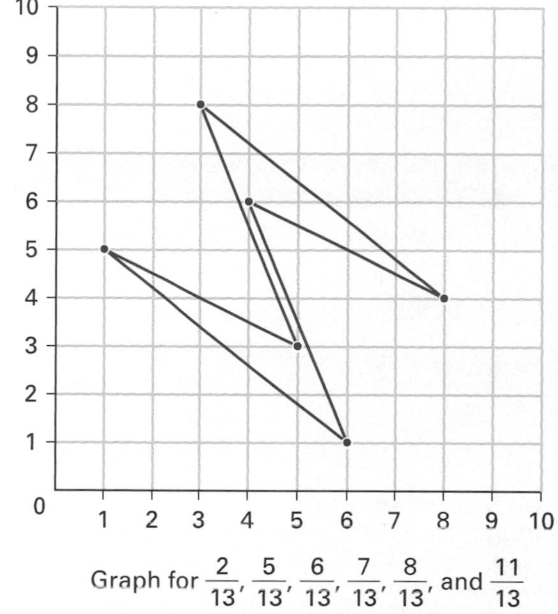

Graph for $\frac{2}{13}, \frac{5}{13}, \frac{6}{13}, \frac{7}{13}, \frac{8}{13}$, and $\frac{11}{13}$

1. Choose one of the following fraction families.

$\frac{1}{7}, \frac{2}{7}, \ldots \frac{6}{7}$ or $\frac{1}{14}, \frac{2}{14}, \ldots \frac{13}{14}$

2. Write each fraction in the family as a repeating decimal. Then graph the pairs of digits as Denis did, and join the points in the order you plotted them.

3. How many different graphs did your fraction family have?

4. What shape of graph do you think you would get from a terminating decimal? (*Hint:* Recall, for example, that 0.375 = 0.375 000….)

You will need
- a calculator

2.2 Multiplying and Dividing Decimals

▶ **GOAL**
Understand and apply multiplication and division of decimals.

Learn about the Math

Costas works part time as an usher at a movie theatre. Until this week, he earned \$8.25 per hour and worked 29.5 h a week. This week, he received a raise of \$0.35 per hour.

? How many hours would Costas need to work now to earn the same amount he earned before he got the raise?

Example 1: Multiplying decimals

How much did Costas earn each week before he got the raise?

Annika's Solution

My estimate is \$8/h × 30 h = \$240

I estimated what Costas earned by multiplying \$8 per hour by 30 h of work.

$$\begin{array}{r} 29.5 \\ \times\ 825 \\ \hline 1475 \\ 5900 \\ 236000 \\ \hline 24337.5 \end{array}$$

To calculate what he earned, I had to multiply 29.5 × \$8.25. I multiplied \$8.25 by 100 to get a whole number. Then I multiplied 29.5 h by 825 pennies.

24 337.5 ÷ 100 = 243.375

Then I divided by 100 to change my answer back to dollars.

Costas earned \$243.38 each week before he got the raise.

I rounded my answer to the nearest cent. Based on my estimate, my answer of \$243.38 is reasonable.

Communication Tip

When a calculation involves money, the answer is usually rounded to the nearest hundredth, or cent. For example, \$28.875 is rounded to \$28.88.

Example 2: Dividing decimals

How many hours would Costas need to work now to earn the same amount that he used to earn each week?

Nathan's Solution

My estimate is 28 h.

If Costas is earning more, he should be able to work fewer than 29.5 h to earn the same amount.

Number of hours = 243.38 ÷ 8.60
= (243.38 × 100) ÷ (8.60 × 100)
= 24 338 ÷ 860

Costas received a raise of $0.35 per hour, so he now earns $8.60 per hour. To calculate the number of hours he needs to work, I have to divide his earnings by his hourly wage.

```
      28.3
860 )24338.0
     1720
      7138
      6880
       2580
       2580
          0
```

Keep adding zeros after the decimal until the quotient has the desired number of decimal places.

I multiplied both the divisor and dividend by 100 to express both amounts in cents. This allowed me to divide by a whole number.

Costas must work 28.3 h at $8.60 per hour to earn the same amount he earned working 29.5 h at $8.25 per hour.

Based on my estimate, my answer of 28.3 h is reasonable.

Reflecting

1. How do you know that the answer to 243 ÷ 8.60 is the same as the answer to 24 300 ÷ 860?

2. How are multiplication and division calculations with decimals the same as multiplication and division calculations with whole numbers that have the same digits? How are these calculations different?

Work with the Math

Example 3: Solving a division problem

Linda's dial-up Internet service provider (ISP) claims to have a speed of 56.9 kilobytes per second. Bharat's cable ISP has a speed of 1556.44 kilobytes per second. How much faster is Bharat's ISP?

Solution

Divide the faster speed by the slower speed.

Estimate first: $1500 \div 50 = 30$. Bharat's ISP should be about 30 times as fast.

$1556.44 \div 56.9 = 27.353\,954\,31$

This answer seems reasonable. Bharat's cable ISP is about 27 times as fast as Linda's dial-up ISP.

Example 4: Solving a problem using several operations

Marina needs 0.75 kg of chocolate chips and 0.5 kg of pecans for a cookie recipe. The bulk food store sells chocolate chips for $7.99 per kilogram and pecans for $19.45 per kilogram. How much will Marina pay for these ingredients?

Solution

Multiply the quantity by the cost to calculate the total cost for each ingredient.

Cost of chocolate chips = 0.75 kg × \$7.99/kg
= \$5.9925

Cost of pecans = 0.5 kg × \$19.45/kg
= \$9.725

The cost of 0.75 kg of chocolate chips is $5.99. The cost of 0.5 kg of pecans is $9.73.

Total cost = \$5.99 + \$9.73
= \$15.72

Marina will pay $15.72 for these ingredients.

A Checking

3. Complete each solution by placing the decimal point correctly.

a) $3.1 \times 1.2 = 372$

b) $5.4 \div 1.2 = 45$

c) $26.45 \times 2.162 = 571849$

d) $12.18 \div 0.005 = 2436$

4. Calculate.

a) 4.5×3.6

b) 12.23×3.6

c) $56.58 \div 6.9$

d) $10.71 \div 0.75$

5. The price of gas is 85.9¢ per litre. If Brenda needs 48.3 L of gas to fill her gas tank, how much will she pay?

B Practising

6. Calculate.

a) 32.25 × 1.8
b) 0.45 × 2.6
c) 12.347 × 0.64
d) 48.87 ÷ 1.35
e) 1.862 ÷ 0.38
f) 0.2419 ÷ 0.59

7. Sheila has $4.75 to buy pencils for art class. Each pencil costs 89¢.

a) Estimate the number of pencils she can buy.

b) Calculate the number of pencils she can buy.

8. Suppose that you have 5.25 kg of jellybeans. How many 0.25 kg bags can you fill?

9. If one postage stamp costs $0.85, how much does a book of 25 stamps cost?

10. To rent a carpet cleaner, Tools To Go charges $15.00 for the first hour or part of an hour plus $3.50 for each additional half hour or part of a half hour.

a) Tim picked up a carpet cleaner at 8:10 a.m. and returned it at 4:10 p.m. Determine his rental charge.

b) Calculate the average cost per hour for Tim's rental.

c) Charmaine rented a carpet cleaner from Carpet Emporium. Her bill was $59.40 for 5.5 h. Compare the average cost per hour for Charmaine's rental with the average cost per hour for Tim's rental. How many times as much was Charmaine's rental?

11. Mary and Aperna worked together to mow a neighbour's lawn. They were paid $25.50. To split the money equally, Mary wants to divide by 2. Aperna disagrees and says that they need to multiply. By how much do they need to multiply? Explain.

12. How many 0.4 L glasses can be filled from a 4.75 L jug of juice?

13. A single subway token costs $2.25. A machine dispenses eight tokens for $15.00. If you need eight tokens, how much would you save by buying the tokens from the machine?

14. A carpenter charged $1455.98 for materials plus $35.75 per hour for 22.5 h of labour. What was the total bill?

C Extending

15. Marcus wants to carpet the floor of his bedroom. If the carpet costs $23.99 per square metre, how much will he pay?

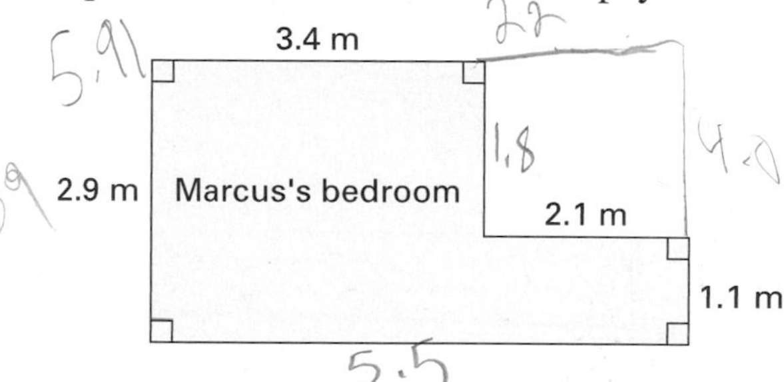

16. Calculate the area of the shaded part of this diagram.

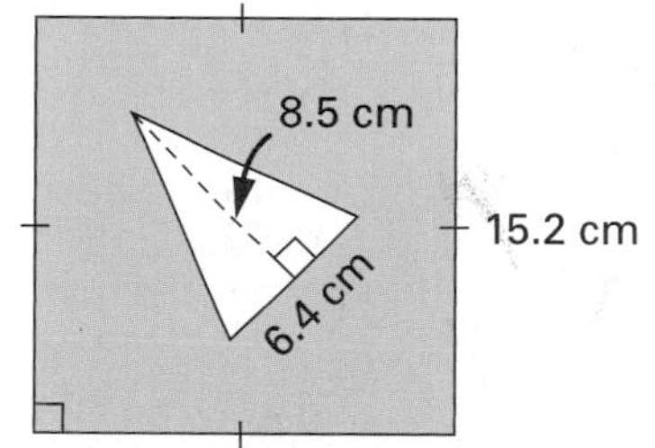

2.3 Exploring Ratios

You will need
- pattern blocks
- large triangle dot paper

▶ **GOAL**

Investigate the ratios of areas created by pattern block designs.

Explore the Math

Susan made pattern block designs by placing two colours of pattern blocks on large triangle dot paper. For each design, she wrote a **ratio** to compare the areas of the two colours.

Susan used a chart to show her results.

Pattern block design	Ratio of areas
	green : red = 1 : 3
	blue : yellow = 4 : 6

? What designs can you make using ratios with numbers that are less than 10?

ratio

a comparison of two or more quantities with the same units; for example, if the heights of three students are 164 cm, 175 cm, and 180 cm, the ratio of their heights can be written as 164 : 175 : 180

A. Make a design using any two colours of blocks to represent an area ratio of 1 : 2. Complete a chart like Susan's.

B. How can you make more than one design for an area ratio of 1 : 2?

C. Now consider other area ratios in the form 1 : ■, where ■ is less than 10. Make designs using two colours of blocks to represent as many of these area ratios as possible. Record your results in your chart. How many of these area ratios can you represent?

D. What other area ratios with numbers less than 10 can you show using two colours of blocks? Record your results in your chart.

Reflecting

1. Which ratios were you able to use to make designs?
2. Which ratios were you not able to use? Why did these ratios not work?
3. What strategy did you use to make a design for the area ratio 3 : 4? Did you use the same strategy to make a design for the area ratio 5 : 6?

Math Game

EQUIVALENT CONCENTRATION

Make playing cards like these for equivalent concentration:

You will need
- 18 index cards
- a calculator

0.875	$\frac{5}{9}$	0.9	$\frac{5}{11}$	$\frac{39}{50}$	35%	$0.\overline{45}$	$\frac{24}{100}$	75%
65%	24%	0.35	$\frac{7}{8}$	$\frac{13}{20}$	0.78	$0.\overline{5}$	90%	$\frac{18}{24}$

Number of players: 2

Rules

1. Shuffle the cards. Then place them face down on a desk in a 3-by-6 array.
2. Player 1 turns over a pair of cards. If the cards have equivalent numbers, player 1 takes the cards and plays again. If the cards do not match, player 1 turns over both cards again. Player 2 then takes a turn.
3. Take turns until all the matches have been made. The player with the most cards wins.

Variations

1. Create your own set of cards using fractions, decimals, and percents. Play the game again with your new game cards.
2. Join with another pair of students in your class, and combine your cards. Play the game with four players as two-person teams.

2.4 Ratios

You will need
- a calculator

▶ **GOAL**

Solve problems that involve ratios.

Learn about the Math

Michael has a summer job as a bricklayer's assistant. He is responsible for mixing the concrete. Concrete is made of cement, sand, and gravel in a **ratio** of 1 : 3 : 4 by mass. Michael needs to make 80 kg of concrete.

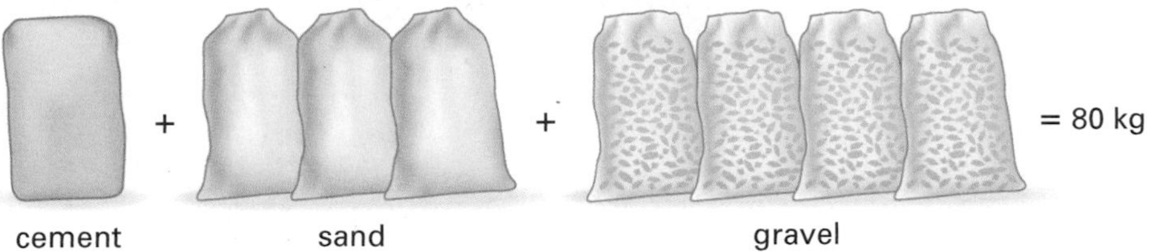

? How much cement, sand, and gravel does Michael need to mix together to make 80 kg of concrete?

A. How many parts, in total, are in a mixture of concrete?

B. Write each ratio.

a) the ratio of cement to sand

b) the ratio of sand to gravel

c) the ratio of cement to gravel

C. All the parts must total 80 kg. Write a **proportion** that compares 80 kg of concrete to the mass of the sand.

D. What is the **scale factor** in the proportion you wrote? Solve the proportion to determine the mass of sand that Michael needs.

E. Calculate the mass of gravel and the mass of cement that Michael needs to make 80 kg of cement.

proportion

a number sentence that shows two equivalent ratios; for example,
1 : 2 : 3 = 3 : 6 : 9

scale factor

a number that you can multiply or divide each term in a ratio by to get the equivalent terms in another ratio; it can be a whole number or a decimal; for example,

$$\frac{2}{3} = \frac{10}{15} \text{ (} \times 5 \text{ on numerator and denominator) or } \frac{2 \times 5}{3 \times 5} = \frac{10}{15}$$

Communication Tip

The ratio 1 : 3 : 4 is a three-term ratio, or a comparison between three quantities. It compares the number of equal parts in a mixture that consists of three different items. It is read as 1 part to 3 parts to 4 parts.

Reflecting

1. How can you calculate the total number of parts when you know the ratio of the parts?

2. How can you use the total number of parts and the total mass to determine the mass of each part?

3. How can your solution to the cement problem be expressed as a ratio that is equivalent to 1 : 3 : 4?

Work with the Math

Example: Using proportions with three-term ratios

The chart below is printed on a box of pancake mix.

Number of pancakes	Amount of mix	Amount of water
6	1 cup	$\frac{3}{4}$ cup

Daniel is making 120 pancakes for an athletic awards breakfast. How much mix and water does he need?

Denis's Solution

number of pancakes : mix : water = 6 : 1 : 0.75

I wrote a three-term ratio that relates the number of pancakes to the required ingredients.

I changed $\frac{3}{4}$ to its decimal equivalent, 0.75.

I used a proportion to solve the problem.

I used [measuring cup] to represent the amount of mix needed and [glass] to represent the amount of water needed.

$120 \div 6 = 20$

I knew the first term in each ratio in the proportion. To calculate the scale factor, I divided 120 by 6 on my calculator.

$6 \times 20 : 1 \times 20 : 0.75 \times 20 = 120$: [measuring cup] : [glass]

$= 120 : 20 : 15$

I multiplied by the scale factor, 20, to determine the missing terms in the proportion.

$6 : 1 : 0.75 = 120 : 20 : 15$

Daniel needs 20 cups of mix and 15 cups of water.

I expressed the amounts in cups.

Ⓐ Checking

4. The ratio for concrete on page 58 is $1:3:4$. Michael now needs to make 64 kg of concrete. Determine the mass of cement, sand, and gravel he needs to mix together.

5. What are the missing terms in each proportion?
   a) $2:3 = \blacksquare:15$
   b) $2:5:8 = \blacksquare:15:\blacksquare$
   c) $\blacksquare:\blacksquare:5 = 56:24:40$
   d) $\blacksquare:5:9 = 6:\blacksquare:27$

6. There are 30 students in Cassandra's art class. The ratio of boys to girls is $2:3$.
   a) How many boys and girls are in the class?
   b) What percent of the class are boys? What percent are girls?

Ⓑ Practising

7. Calculate the missing terms.
   a) $3:7 = 12:\blacksquare$
   b) $\blacksquare:45 = 3.2:15$
   c) $\blacksquare:2:7 = 7:14:\blacksquare$
   d) $\blacksquare:3.2:11.6 = 10:12.8:\blacksquare$

8. The following chart is printed on a package of cookie mix. Marina wants to make six dozen cookies for the school bake sale. How much mix and milk does she need?

Number of cookies	Amount of mix	Amount of milk
24	$2\frac{1}{2}$ cups	$1\frac{1}{4}$ cups

9. In a 500 g bag of trail mix, the ratio of raisins to peanuts to cashews is $9:6:1$ by mass. Determine the masses of raisins, peanuts, and cashews in a 2 kg bag.

10. The aspect ratio of a television or movie screen is the ratio of the width of the screen to its height. A high-definition television has an aspect ratio of $16:9$. The movie *Star Wars* was filmed in cinemascope, which has an aspect ratio of $2.35:1$. Are these aspect ratios equivalent? Explain.

11. Costas and Sheila bought a raffle ticket for a charity. The grand prize is $1000.00. Costas contributed $3.50 and Sheila contributed $1.50 to the price of the ticket. If they win the grand prize, they will share the money in the same proportion that they paid for the ticket. How much of the money should each person receive?

12. One brand of horse feed is made of oats and barley. The ratio of oats to barley is $4:11$ by mass. How many kilograms of each grain are needed to make 150 kg of feed?

13. In a 2 kg bag of building blocks, the ratio of red blocks to green blocks to yellow blocks is $5:3:2$ by mass. Determine the masses of the red, green, and yellow blocks in the bag.

14. In Heavenly Hash ice cream, the ratio of cashews to marshmallows to chocolate ice cream is $1:3:36$ by volume.
   a) What is the ratio of marshmallows to ice cream?
   b) What percent of Heavenly Hash ice cream is chocolate ice cream?
   c) How much of each ingredient is needed to make a 20 L tub of Heavenly Hash ice cream?

15. To make a batch of four dozen cookies, Denis needs $1\frac{3}{4}$ cups of flour, 1 cup of sugar, and $\frac{1}{3}$ cup of milk. Calculate the amount of each ingredient that Denis needs to make 12 dozen cookies.

16. A snack mix contains toasted oat cereal, pretzels, and nuts in a ratio of 2 : 2 : 1 by mass. What mass of each ingredient is needed to make the following amounts of snack mix?

a) 330 g
b) 210 g
c) 500 g
d) 750 g

17. Katie collects stamps. She has stamps from Canada, the United States, and the rest of the world in a ratio of 1 : 1.2 : 1.5. She has 135 stamps from the rest of the world.

a) How many stamps are from Canada?

b) How many stamps are from the United States?

c) What is the total number of stamps in Katie's collection?

18. The longest glacier in the world is Lambert Glacier in Antarctica. It is 403 km long.

The longest glacier in the Himalayas is the Siachen. It is 76 km long.

a) Write a ratio to compare the lengths of the glaciers.

b) Round off the terms of the ratio to make a ratio that is approximately equivalent.

c) About how many times as long as the Siachen Glacier is the Lambert Glacier?

d) Write a ratio to compare your height with the length of the Lambert Glacier. About how many times as long as you is the glacier?

19. Park rangers captured, tagged, and released 82 grizzly bears in Banff National Park. A month later, when the rangers captured 20 bears, 2 had tags. Estimate the park's grizzly bear population.

20. Two numbers are in the ratio of 4 to 7. Their sum is 55. What are the numbers?

C Extending

21. **a)** Follow these steps.
- Draw a square.
- Measure one side and one diagonal to the nearest millimetre.
- Determine the ratio of side length to diagonal length.

b) Repeat part (a) for three different-sized squares. What do you notice?

22. A rectangular prism has a volume of 960 cm^3. Its width, length, and height are in the ratio 3 : 5 : 8.

a) Determine the dimensions of the prism.

b) What is the ratio of the left side to the front to the top of the prism by surface area?

c) Calculate the surface area of the prism.

23. The measures of the angles in $\triangle ABC$ are in the ratio 3 : 7 : 8. Determine the measure of each angle.

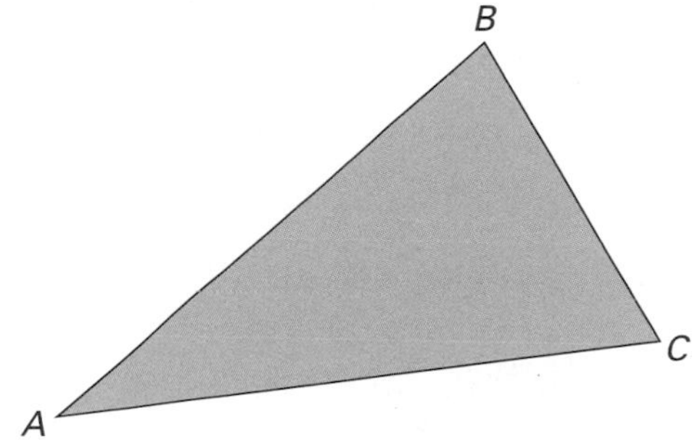

Mid-Chapter Review

Frequently Asked Questions

Q: How do you know whether the decimal equivalent of a fraction will be a repeating decimal?

A: If the denominator of the fraction has only 2s and/or 5s in its prime factorization, its decimal equivalent will terminate. A terminating decimal is a decimal that is complete after a certain number of digits, with no repetition.

For example, $40 = 2 \times 2 \times 2 \times 5$ and $\frac{3}{40} = 0.075$.

If the denominator of the fraction has any other numbers (perhaps in addition to 2s and 5s) in its prime factorization, its decimal equivalent will be a repeating decimal. A repeating decimal is a decimal that has a number or block of numbers that repeats over and over.

For example, $\frac{2}{11} = 0.181\ 818\ldots$, or $0.\overline{18}$.

Q: What strategies can you use to multiply and divide two decimals?

A: **Multiplying decimals**

Multiply both decimals by powers of 10 to eliminate the decimal points. Then divide your result by the same powers of 10.

For example, 8.2×1.4

$(8.2 \times 10) \times (1.4 \times 10) = 82 \times 14$

$$\begin{array}{r} 82 \\ \times\ 14 \\ \hline 328 \\ 820 \\ \hline 1148 \end{array}$$

$1148 \div 100 = 11.48$

$8.2 \times 1.4 = 11.48$

Dividing decimals

Multiply both the dividend and divisor by the same power of 10 to eliminate the decimal points.

For example,

$$\begin{aligned} 12.75 \div 1.25 &= (12.75 \times 100) \div (1.25 \times 100) \\ &= 1275 \div 125 \end{aligned}$$

$$\begin{array}{r} 10.2 \\ 125\,\overline{)1275.0} \\ \underline{125} \\ 250 \\ \underline{250} \\ 0 \end{array}$$

$12.75 \div 1.25 = 10.2$

Q: How do you solve a ratio problem?

A: Write a proportion to represent the problem. Calculate the scale factor. Then multiply or divide to determine the missing term.

For example,

$$3:8 = \blacksquare:24$$

(× 3 from 8 to 24; × 3 from 3 to the missing term)

The missing term is 9.

Practice Questions

(2.1) **1.** Write each repeating decimal using bar notation.

a) 0.777 77…

b) 0.127 512 751 275 1…

c) 0.485 621 621 621 6 …

(2.1) **2.** Write each fraction as a decimal.

a) $\frac{17}{20}$ **b)** $\frac{4}{9}$ **c)** $\frac{3}{16}$ **d)** $\frac{10}{11}$

(2.1) **3.** How can you tell, without dividing, whether the decimal equivalent of a fraction will be a terminating or repeating decimal?

(2.1) **4.** Order the numbers from least to greatest.

$\frac{8}{11}$, 0.72, $\frac{17}{25}$, $0.\overline{75}$, 0.7

(2.2) **5.** Calculate.

a) 28.54×1.2

b) 52.256×0.05

c) 3.142×0.007

(2.2) **6.** Calculate.

a) $66.304 \div 2.59$

b) $280.6542 \div 22$

c) $17.638 \div 1.38$

(2.2) **7.** At one gas station, unleaded gasoline costs 84.9¢ per litre. Corey needs 48.7 L to fill the gas tank of his car. Wendy needs 74.3 L to fill the gas tank of her SUV. Determine the difference in the cost to fill their gas tanks.

(2.2) **8.** Kendra is making hamburgers for her family barbecue. She has bought three packages of ground beef with masses of 0.652 kg, 0.545 kg, and 0.824 kg. If each hamburger she makes has a mass of about 0.125 kg, how many whole hamburgers can she make?

9. Mr. Schneider paid $2276.35 to have a landscaper build a patio with the dimensions below. How much did the landscaper charge for each square metre of patio? (2.2)

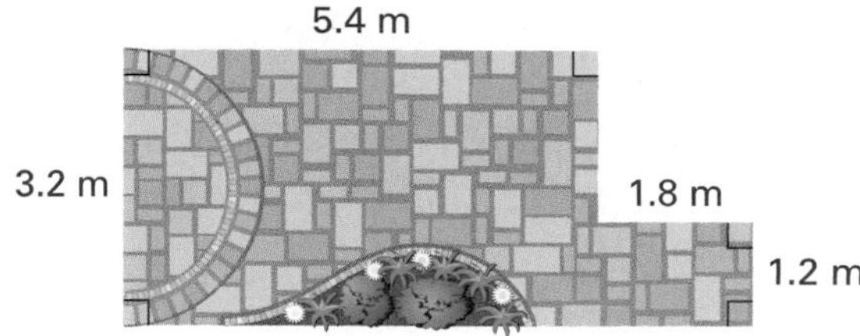

10. Calculate the missing terms in each proportion. (2.4)

a) ■ : 11 = 11 : 121

b) 5 : 2 : 1 = ■ : 14 : ■

c) 1.5 : ■ : 2.4 = 6 : 5 : ■

11. One brand of lawn fertilizer consists of nitrogen, phosphorus, and potassium in the ratio 3 : 1 : 2 by mass. Determine the amount of each nutrient in an 18 kg bag of this fertilizer. (2.4)

12. Eva makes bracelets from beads. Each bracelet consists of solid, opaque, and transparent beads in the ratio 5 : 3 : 1. One style of bracelet has 36 beads. How many of each type of bead did Eva use to make this bracelet? (2.4)

2.5 Rates

You will need
- grid paper
- a ruler
- coloured pencils
- a calculator

▶ **GOAL**

Determine and apply rates to solve problems.

Learn about the Math

During his Marathon of Hope, Terry Fox ran from Pickering to Scarborough Town Centre in Toronto. He covered the distance of 30 km in about 8 h. Terry also ran from Sudbury to Sault Ste. Marie. He took about 56 h (over an eight-day period) to travel the 245 km distance.

? During which of these two parts of his marathon was Terry Fox faster?

A. **Speed** is an example of a **rate**. It compares the distance travelled to the time taken to travel this distance. Estimate the average speed at which Terry ran from Pickering to Toronto. Then estimate his average speed from Sudbury to Sault Ste. Marie.

B. Write the rates that represent the average speeds you estimated in step A.

C. Express each rate in step B as a **unit rate** by writing a proportion and dividing by the appropriate scale factor.

D. Make two tables of values. Use your unit rates from step C to complete your tables of values.

Pickering to Toronto

Time (h)	Distance (km)
0	
1	
2	
3	
4	
5	
8	

Sudbury to Sault Ste. Marie

Time (h)	Distance (km)
0	
1	
2	
3	
4	
5	
8	

E. Use your table of values to plot the points for Terry's run from Pickering to Toronto. Put time on the horizontal axis and distance on the vertical axis. Join the points with a line to show Terry's average speed.

speed

the rate at which a moving object changes position with time; for example, a sprinter who runs 100 m in 10 s has an average speed of 100 m/10 s = 10 m/s

rate

a comparison of two quantities measured in different units; unlike ratios, rates include units

unit rate

a rate in which the second term is 1; for example, 60 km/h is a unit rate because it compares the distance travelled (60 km) to 1 h of time

F. On the same pair of axes, plot the points for Terry's run from Sudbury to Sault Ste. Marie. Use a different colour to join the points with a line.

G. a) During which part of the marathon did Terry run faster, on average?

b) Explain how you could answer the question in part (a) using unit rates.

c) Explain how you could answer this question using the graph you created.

Communication Tip

A unit rate may look like a decimal number, but it isn't a decimal number. For example, a speed of 56.58 km/h means that a distance of 56.58 km was travelled (on average) in 1 h. So, this rate should be written as 56.58 km/1 h. For convenience, however, we write it as 56.58 km/h because the second term is known to be 1.

Reflecting

1. Suppose that Terry Fox ran from Pickering to Toronto at a speed of 4 km/h. Can you be sure that he travelled a distance of 4 km each hour? Explain.
2. Why was it difficult to compare the rates at which Terry ran before you calculated the unit rates?

Work with the Math

Example 1: Working with unit rates

At last year's family picnic, the organizers served about 160 L of lemonade to 250 people. Determine the average amount of lemonade served to each person.

Susan's Solution

The rate is $\frac{160\text{ L}}{250\text{ people}}$.

$$\frac{160\text{ L}}{250\text{ people}} = \frac{■\text{ L}}{1\text{ person}}$$

I needed to determine the average number of litres served to each person. This is the same as finding the unit rate measured in litres per person. I divided both terms in my rate by the scale factor 250 to get a rate out of 1.

$$\frac{160\text{ L} \div 250}{250\text{ people} \div 250} = \frac{0.64\text{ L}}{1\text{ person}}$$

I used my calculator to divide.

Each person drank an average of 0.64 L, or 640 mL.

I wrote my answer in millilitres per person since there are 1000 mL in 1 L.

Example 2: Using unit costs to determine the best buy

Tim's favourite cereal comes in two sizes. The small box contains 650 g of cereal and is on sale for \$3.29. The large box contains 1.45 kg of cereal and costs \$6.99. Which size should Tim buy to get the best buy?

Ken's Solution

I can compare the costs by calculating the unit cost for each box. This will give me the price of 1 kg for each box. The lowest cost per kilogram is the best buy.

$$\text{Unit cost (large box)} = \frac{\$6.99}{1.45\text{ kg}} = \frac{\$6.99 \div 1.45}{1.45\text{ kg} \div 1.45} \doteq \frac{\$4.820\,689\,655}{1\text{ kg}} \doteq \$4.82/\text{kg}$$

$$\text{Unit cost (small box)} = \frac{\$3.29}{0.65\text{ kg}} = \frac{\$3.29 \div 0.65}{0.65\text{ kg} \div 0.65} = \frac{\$5.061\,538\,462}{1\text{ kg}} \doteq \$5.06/\text{kg}$$

Tim should buy the large box. It is the best buy.

Communication Tip

Unit cost is the name given to any unit rate that represents the cost per one unit of quantity. The most common units for measuring quantity are litres, millilitres, grams, kilograms, metres, and square metres. For example, if the unit cost of carpet is \$19.59/m^2, this means that 1 m^2 of carpet costs \$19.59.

A Checking

3. What two quantities are being compared in each rate? Calculate the equivalent unit rate.

   a) 135 words typed in 2.5 min

   b) 400 m run in 55.0 s

4. Calculate the unit cost.

   a) \$2.43 for 5.4 m of ribbon

   b) \$3.00 for 24 bottles of water

B Practising

5. Bharat types 20 words/min. How many words can he type in each length of time?

   a) 5 min **b)** 30 min **c)** 23 min

6. Calculate the hourly rate.

   a) Serena worked 11 h and earned \$83.05.

   b) Abdul earned \$141.95 for 17 h of work.

7. Calculate the unit cost.

   a) \$1.85 for 4 kg of peaches

   b) \$16.99 for a 454 g package of cooked shrimp

   c) \$2.99 for a 1.89 L bottle of juice

   d) \$283.28 for 22.5 m^2 of flooring tiles

8. Hannah drove her car 318.4 km in 4 h.

   a) Calculate her average speed.

   b) At this speed, how far can she expect to travel in 5.5 h?

9. Wayne Gretzky holds the NHL record for the most points scored in a career. He scored 2857 points in 1487 games.

   a) Calculate his average points per game.

   b) At this rate, how many more points might he have scored if he had played 79 more games?

10. Order the following employees from least to greatest earnings per hour.

Employee	Hours (h)	Earnings ($)
Carla	32	286.40
Gemsy	29	265.35
Avril	25	235.50
Chantelle	34	290.70

11. Determine the best buy in each situation.

   a) Station A: 45 L of gas for $37.15
   Station B: 50 L of gas for $39.50

   b) Store A: $4.99 for 1.2 kg of peanut butter
   Store B: $9.88 for 2.5 kg of peanut butter

   c) Store A: 55 m^2 of carpet for $1676.95
   Store B: 40 m^2 of carpet for $1119.60

12. In the 2004 Summer Olympics, Adam van Koeverden of Oakville, Ontario, won two medals. He won the gold medal in the men's 500 m kayak race, with a time of 1 min 37.9 s. He also won the bronze medal in the 1000 m race, with a time of 3 min 28.2 s. In which race did he row with greater speed?

13. Kamilah noticed that three different-sized boxes of the same cookies were on sale at a grocery store. The 425 g box was on sale for $3.59, the 740 g box was on sale for $4.88, and the 950 g box was on sale for $7.29. Which box of cookies was the best buy?

C Extending

14. Use the exchange rates in the chart below to convert $500 Canadian to each currency given.

Country	Monetary unit	Value in Canadian dollars ($)
Argentina	peso	0.474 697
Germany	euro	1.582 54
India	rupee	0.027 881 9
Japan	yen	0.011 756 4
Russia	ruble	0.043 995 9
South Africa	rand	0.193 159
Sweden	kronor	0.182 995
United Kingdom	pound	2.301 90
United States	dollar	1.222 9

15. In the 2004 Summer Olympics, Marie-Hélène Premont of Chateau-Richer, Quebec, won the silver medal in the women's mountain bike race. She completed the 31.3 km course in 1 h 57 min 50 s.

   a) Determine Premont's average speed in kilometres per hour.

   b) At this rate, how long would she take to complete a course of 45 km? Express your answer in hours, minutes, and seconds.

16. In 2004, the world's fastest knitter was able to knit 225 stitches in 3 min. How long would she take to knit a scarf that was 20 cm wide and 1.2 m long, if she used yarn that resulted in 1.6 stitches per centimetre?

2.6 Representing Percent

You will need
- 10-by-10 grids
- coloured pencils
- a calculator

GOAL

Represent and calculate percents that involve whole numbers or decimals, and whole number percents that are greater than 100%.

Learn about the Math

Exactly 800 students were enrolled at Susan's school last year. This year, the enrolment went up 3.5%.The new enrolment is 150% of what the enrolment was 10 years ago.

? How many students are enrolled this year, and how many were enrolled last year?

To model a percent, you can shade squares in a grid of 100 squares. If the percent is less than 100, you use only part of the grid. If the percent is greater than 100, you need to use more than one grid.

Example 1: Representing and calculating a fractional or decimal percent

How many students are enrolled this year, if there is a 3.5% enrolment increase from last year?

Susan's Solution

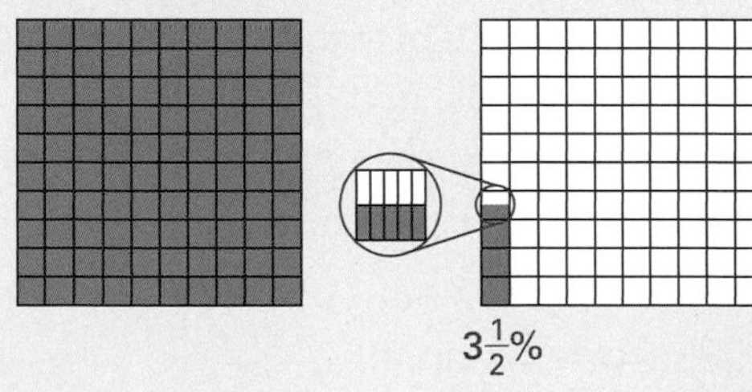

I modelled the enrolment of 800 from last year as a hundredths grid. The grid represents 100% of the enrolment last year.

To show the 3.5% increase, I coloured 3 squares out of 100 and I coloured 5 tenths of a fourth square, which are 5 thousandths of the whole grid.

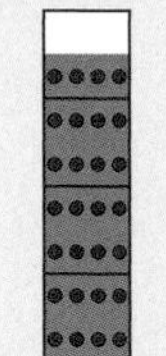

Since an increase means more, there must be more than 800 students enrolled this year.

Since the whole grid of 100 squares represents the 800 students from last year, each square represents $\frac{800}{100}$, or 8 students. So, 3.5% more students this year is 8 + 8 + 8 + 4 = 28 more students.

The number of students enrolled this year is 800 + 28 = 828.

Example 2: Representing and calculating a percent greater than 100%

How many students were enrolled 10 years ago?

Nathan's Solution

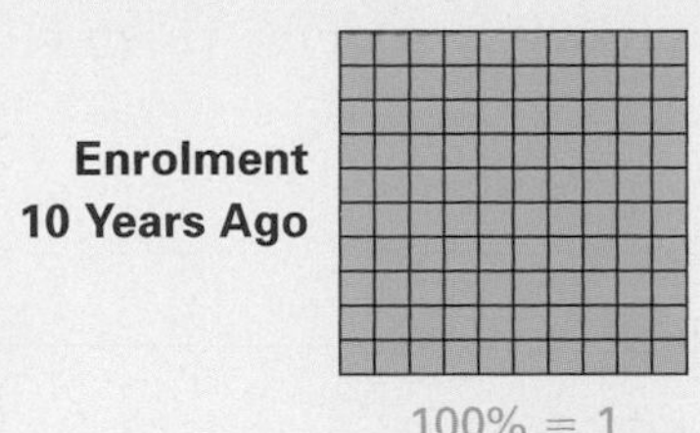

$100\% = 1$

I used a hundredths grid to model the enrolment 10 years ago.

The new enrolment is 150% of what the enrolment was 10 years ago.

150% means 100% and another 50%.

100% is the whole grid I already coloured.

50% is another half of a grid.

Another way to write 150% is $1\frac{1}{2}$, or 1.5.

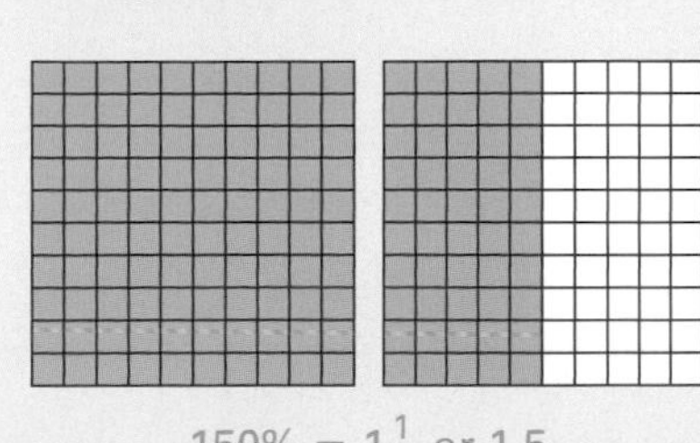

$150\% = 1\frac{1}{2}$ or 1.5

Enrolment Now

Enrolment 10 Years Ago

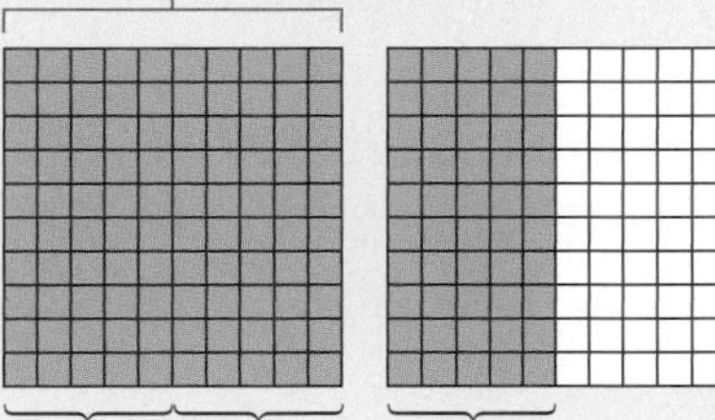

828 students ÷ 3 groups = 276 students in each group

I shaded three half-grids to represent the 828 students enrolled now.

Each half-grid shows $\frac{1}{3}$ of 828, or 276 students.

Two groups of 276 students are 552 students, which is the number in one whole grid.

Therefore, $2 \times 276 = 552$ students were enrolled 10 years ago.

Reflecting

1. How did the hundredths grid model help you determine that 3.5% represented 28 students?

2. How did knowing that a percent can be written as a number out of 100 help you express a percent as a decimal or a fraction? (For example, $3.5\% = \frac{3.5}{100}$ and $150\% = \frac{150}{100}$.)

3. How did the hundredths grid model help you calculate percents greater than 100% and percents expressed using decimals and fractions?

Work with the Math

Example 3: Representing a percent less than 1%

About 0.9% of the volume of air is argon gas. In 50 m^3 of air, about how much of the volume (in cubic metres) is argon gas?

Solution

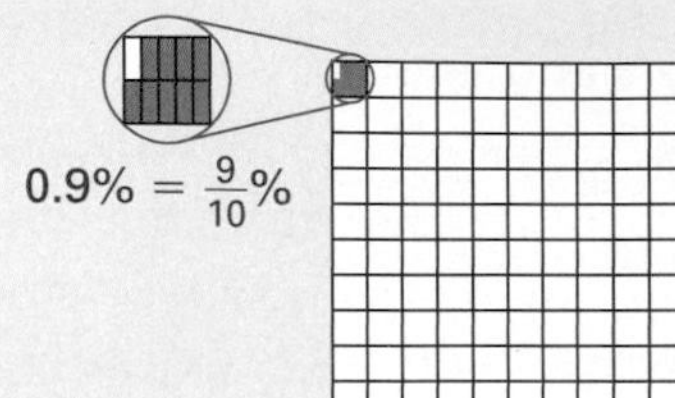

The whole grid is 100%, which represents 50 m^3.

One square on the grid is 1%. This represents $50 \text{ m}^3 \div 100 = 0.5 \text{ m}^3$.

The argon gas can be represented by 0.9 of one square on the grid.

The amount of argon gas is $0.9 \times 0.5 \text{ m}^3 = 0.45 \text{ m}^3$.

A Checking

4. What percent does each diagram show? One full grid represents 100%.

a) 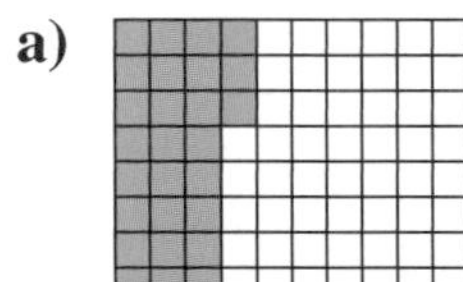

b) 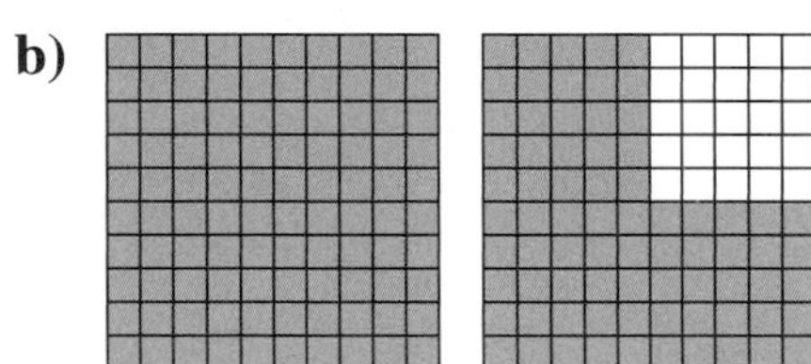

c) 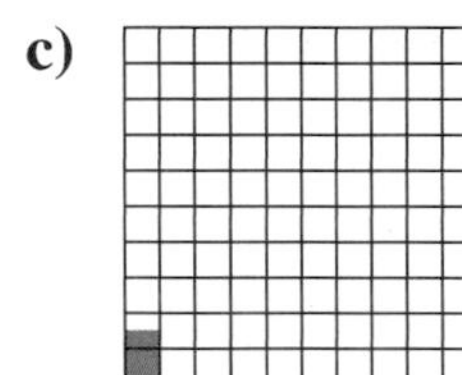

5. Yanir has \$50 in pennies. Use grids to model and calculate each amount.

a) 9% of \$50
b) 310% of \$50
c) 0.5% of \$50
d) 165% of \$50

6. At the beginning of this year, there were 360 students in Samantha's school. Last year, there were 125% as many students.

a) How many students were in Samantha's school last year?
b) By the end of this year, 2.5% of the students moved and left the school. How many students left the school?

B Practising

7. What percent does each diagram show? One full grid represents 100%.

a) 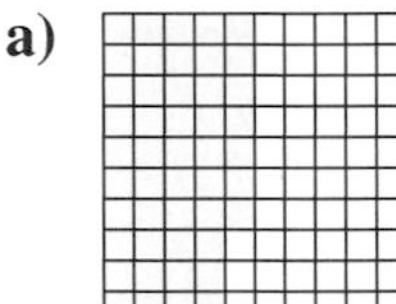

b) 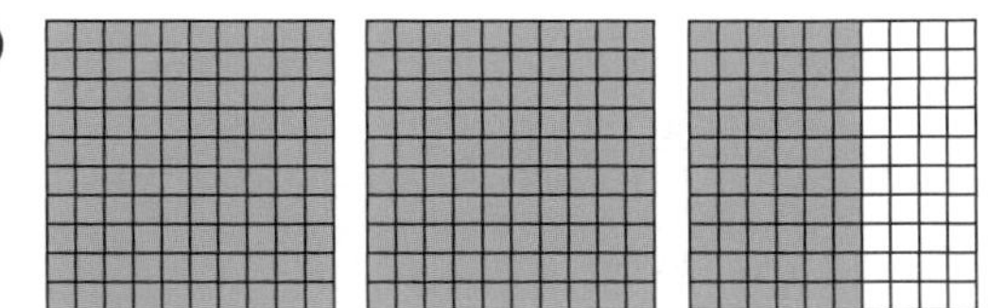

c) 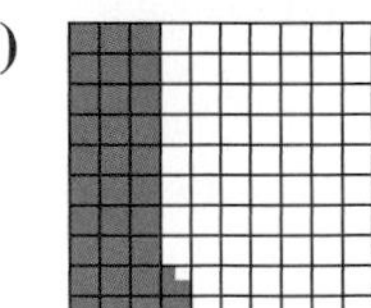

NEL

8. The population of a town is 600. Use grids to model and calculate each number.

a) 12% of 600
b) 240% of 600
c) 185% of 600
d) 11.5% of 600
e) 0.5% of 600
f) 33.5% of 600

9. a) Colour a hundredths grid to show 25%. What fraction of the whole grid is this?

b) Colour 12.5% of the grid. What fraction of the whole grid is this?

c) How can you use mental math to calculate 12.5% of 800?

10. Use the hundredths grid model to help you order these numbers from least to greatest.

212%, 1.56, 0.72, 77.6%, 0.3%, $4\frac{1}{2}$

11. A 250 mL glass of cranberry juice provides 100% of the recommended daily intake of vitamin C. Use a hundredths grid to model each solution.

a) Suppose that you drank two 250 mL glasses of cranberry juice with your breakfast. What percent of the recommended daily intake would you get?

b) A 250 mL glass of grape juice provides 50% of the recommended daily intake of vitamin C. How many glasses of grape juice would you have to drink in a day to get 100% of the recommended daily intake of vitamin C?

12. Every secondary-school student has to complete 40 h of community service. Four students completed the following percents of their community service hours. Use a hundredths grid to model and then calculate the number of hours each student completed.

a) 50%
b) 7.5%
c) 88%
d) 104%

13. Decide whether each method for calculating 225% of a number is correct. Use a model to justify your decision.

a) Double the number, and add one fourth of the number.

b) Multiply the number by 2.25.

c) Multiply the number by 225.

d) Calculate 1% of the number, and then multiply by 225.

14. In a survey, 40 students were asked this question: What type of video game do you prefer? The circle graph shows their responses. Use a hundredths grid to model the number of students who preferred each type of game.

Favourite Video Games

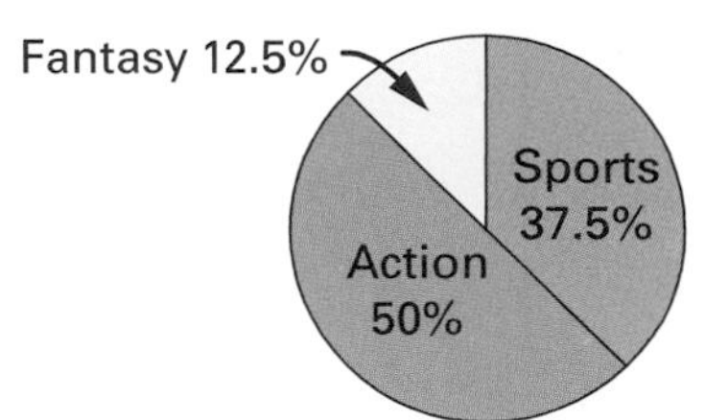

C Extending

15. Copy and complete the chart.

Percent	Fraction	Decimal
$187\frac{1}{2}\%$		
	$2\frac{1}{8}$	
		0.0075

16. What percent of the probability number line would you colour to show each probability?

0, $\frac{1}{6}$, $\frac{1}{3}$, $\frac{3}{6}$, $\frac{2}{3}$, $\frac{5}{6}$, 1

a) the probability of rolling a number less than 5 with one die

b) the probability of rolling a sum of 7 with two dice

2.7 Solving Percent Problems

You will need
- a calculator

▶ **GOAL**

Use proportions to solve percent problems.

Learn about the Math

A music station reported that 4015 people under the age of 16 attended a concert. This was 22% of the total attendance.

? How many people attended the concert?

A. Estimate the total number of people at the concert.

B. Use the given information to write a proportion that shows $\frac{\blacksquare}{100} = \frac{\text{part}}{\text{whole}}$. (Use a box for the missing term.)

C. What scale factor can you multiply or divide each number on the left side by to make the ratios equivalent?

D. Use your scale factor to solve your proportion.

E. How many people attended the concert? Check that your solution is reasonable by comparing it with your estimate in step A.

Reflecting

1. How did you know that the total number of people at the concert was between four and five times the number of people under the age of 16?
2. What sequence of calculations did you use to solve the proportion?
3. How could you use a calculator to check that your solution is correct?

Work with the Math

Example 1: Determining a percent of a whole

On a multiple-choice science test, Marcus answered 65% of the questions correctly. If there were 40 questions on the test, how many did he answer correctly?

Denis's Solution

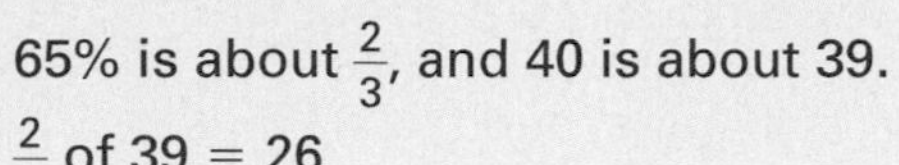

65% is about $\frac{2}{3}$, and 40 is about 39.

$\frac{2}{3}$ of 39 = 26

I estimated. Since 65% is about $\frac{2}{3}$, I used a convenient number that works with thirds.

$\frac{1}{3}$ of 39 = 13

So, $\frac{2}{3}$ of 39 = 26

$$\frac{65}{100} = \frac{■}{40} \quad (\div 2.5)$$

In the proportion $\frac{■}{100} = \frac{\text{part}}{\text{whole}}$, I didn't know the number for "part."

$$\frac{65}{100} = \frac{26}{40} \quad (\div 2.5)$$

I divided both terms in the first ratio by 2.5 to get the equivalent terms in the second ratio.

Marcus answered 26 questions correctly.

I looked back at my estimate to see that my answer is reasonable.

Example 2: Determining a percent

In last year's softball games, Aimee had 34 hits in 80 times at bat. What percent of Aimee's times at bat did she get a hit?

Ken's Solution

$\frac{40}{80}$ is 50%.

I had to express $\frac{34}{80}$ as a percent.

$\frac{34}{80}$ will be less than 50%.

I estimated that 34 is close to 40, which is half of 80.

$$\frac{■}{100} = \frac{34}{80}$$

In the proportion $\frac{■}{100} = \frac{\text{part}}{\text{whole}}$, I didn't know the percent.

$$= \frac{34 \times 1.25}{80 \times 1.25}$$

I calculated the scale factor.
100 ÷ 80 = 1.25

$$\frac{■}{100} = \frac{42.5}{100}$$

Aimee got a hit 42.5% of her times at bat.

My answer looks reasonable because it's a bit less than 50%.

Example 3: Determining the whole from a percent

Daniel's school choir has 15 girls in it. If 37.5% of the students in the choir are girls, how many students are in the choir?

Annika's Solution

37.5% is about $\frac{1}{3}$.

First I estimated. I knew that $33\frac{1}{3}\% = \frac{1}{3}$.

I estimate that about $\frac{1}{3}$ are girls, so the choir has about $3 \times 15 = 45$ students.

If $\frac{1}{3}$ is 15 girls, then $\frac{2}{3}$ is 30 girls, and $\frac{3}{3}$ is 45 girls.

In the proportion $\frac{■}{100} = \frac{\text{part}}{\text{whole}}$, I didn't know the number for "whole."

$$\frac{37.5}{100} = \frac{15}{■}$$

I had to ask myself, "37.5% of what number is 15?"

$$\frac{37.5 \times 0.4}{100 \times 0.4} = \frac{15}{■}$$

The scale factor is $15 \div 37.5 = 0.4$.

$100 \times 0.4 = 40$

$$= \frac{15}{40}$$

Daniel's school choir has 40 students.

My answer is close to my estimate of 45.

A Checking

4. Estimate, and then calculate.

a) 16% of 90 = ■

b) $\frac{18}{40} = ■\%$

c) 15.5% of ■ = 9.3

5. In a class of 30 students, 60% said they walk to school.

a) Estimate how many students in the class walk to school.

b) Write a proportion that you could use to determine the number of students in the class who walk to school.

c) Solve your proportion. Check that your answer is reasonable.

6. A dog has a litter of three male pups and five female pups. What percent of the pups in the litter are male?

7. On a multiple-choice history test, Rita received a mark of 80%. She answered 32 questions correctly.

a) Write a proportion that you could use to determine the number of questions on the test.

b) Solve your proportion. Check that your answer is reasonable.

B Practising

8. On a school basketball team, 13 out of 16 students are in Grade 8.

a) Write a proportion that you could use to calculate the percent of the students who are in Grade 8.

b) Solve your proportion. Check that your answer is reasonable.

9. In a survey of 80 students at Jim's school, 45% like rap music. Estimate and then calculate how many students like rap music.

10. 24 students in Sharon's art class say that blue is their favourite colour. This is 75% of the entire class.

a) Determine the number of students in the whole class.

b) Check that your answer is reasonable.

11. Calculate each number.

a) 15% of 80 c) 4.2% of 550

b) 28% of 150 d) 108% of 240

12. Calculate each percent. Round to one decimal place if necessary.

a) $\frac{18}{25} = \blacksquare\%$ c) $\frac{54}{72} = \blacksquare\%$

b) $\frac{15}{75} = \blacksquare\%$ d) $\frac{7}{8} = \blacksquare\%$

13. Calculate each whole.

a) 40% of ■ = 30

b) 15% of ■ = 3

c) 25% of ■ = 60

d) 5.2% of ■ = 1.3

14. Estimate the equivalent percent of each fraction. Explain your reasoning.

a) $\frac{45}{95}$ b) $\frac{29}{26}$ c) $\frac{57}{64}$

15. The chart shows the four different blood types and the percent of the human population that has each blood type. In a town of 4600 people, how many people would you expect to have each blood type?

Blood type	Percent of human population (%)
O	45
A	41
B	10
AB	4

16. Manuel is saving for a new mountain bike. Every week he deposits 25% of his paycheque in a savings account. This week his paycheque is $80.52.

a) Estimate how much Manuel will put in his bank account this week.

b) Why would you multiply 0.25×80.52 to calculate how much Manuel will put in his bank account this week?

17. When water freezes, its volume increases by 10.1%.

a) If 150 L of water freezes, what is the increase in volume?

b) Estimate the original volume of water frozen if the increase in volume is 22 L.

C Extending

18. In a survey, 5700 Canadian students across Canada in Grades 3 to 10 were asked the following question: What are your favourite weekend activities? The table below shows the percent of responses for 365 girls and 345 boys in Grade 8.

Activity	Girls (%)	Boys (%)
spending time with friends	32.6	30.7
shopping	17.8	2.6
playing sports	11.2	21.4
watching TV and videos	7.4	10.1
reading	4.1	1.2
playing video games	3.8	18.3

a) How many more Grade 8 boys than Grade 8 girls chose watching TV and videos? Express your answer as a percent.

b) Create and solve another problem using some of the data in the table.

2.8 Solving Percent Problems Using Decimals

You will need
- a calculator

▶ **GOAL**
Use percents to solve problems that involve everyday situations.

Learn about the Math

Miranda wants to buy an MP3 player. In a newspaper, she sees an MP3 player that regularly sells for $119.95 advertised at 20% off. She would also have to pay 15% in taxes. She has saved $115.00 from babysitting.

? Does Miranda have enough money to buy the MP3 player?

Example 1: Working with discounts and sales tax

How much does Miranda need to buy the MP3 player? Does she have enough?

Eva's Solution

discount = 20% of $119.95
= 0.2 × $119.95
= $23.99

The discount is 20% of $119.95. I converted the percent discount to a decimal.

I calculated the discount by multiplying the regular price by the discount expressed as a decimal.

sale price = regular price − discount
= $119.95 − $23.99
= $95.96

I calculated the sale price by subtracting the discount from the regular price.

taxes = 15% of sale price
= 0.15 × $95.96
= $14.39

I calculated the taxes by multiplying the sale price by the tax rate. I changed 15% to 0.15 and rounded my answer to the nearest cent.

purchase price = sale price + taxes
= $95.96 + $14.39
= $110.35

I determined the purchase price by adding the taxes to the sale price.

Miranda will spend $110.35.

The purchase price is less than Miranda's savings, so she has enough money to buy the MP3 player.

Reflecting

1. How do you know that calculating 80% of the regular price gives you the same result as subtracting 20% from the regular price?

2. How do you know that multiplying the sale price by 1.15 gives the purchase price?

3. How do you know that calculating $119.95 × 0.8 × 1.15 gives the correct purchase price?

Work with the Math

Example 2: Calculating interest

Raul took out a loan to buy a computer. The computer cost $1299.00. The interest rate on the loan is 8.25% each year. Calculate the amount of interest Raul will pay back over the two years.

Solution

yearly interest = amount of loan × annual interest rate
= $1299.00 × 8.25%
= $1299.00 × 0.0825
= $107.1675

total interest = yearly interest × length of loan in years
= $107.1675 × 2
= $214.335

Raul will pay $214.34 in interest.

A Checking

4. A television is on sale for 25% off the regular price of $339.95. Calculate the discount and the purchase price if the taxes are 15%.

B Practising

5. Mikael's father bought a new car for $35 500. The car decreased in value by 20% after one year. What was the value of the car after one year?

6. a) Calculate the 8% Ontario provincial sales tax (PST) and the 7% goods and services tax (GST) for each item.

b) Calculate the purchase price for each item in part (a).

7. a) Calculate the discount and the sale price for each item.

b) Calculate the purchase price for each item in part (a). All the items were purchased in Alberta (0% PST and 7% GST).

8. Lawrence added the taxes to the price of an item before taking off the discount. Tina took off the discount and then added the taxes. Will they get the same purchase price? Explain why or why not.

9. Calculate the simple interest on each amount and the total amount at the end.

a) a loan of $250 at 5% per year over three years

b) a deposit of $500 that pays 3.5% per year over five years

c) a loan of $1200 at 6.9% per year over four years

d) a deposit of $2550 that earns 3% interest over 30 months

e) a loan of $5000 at 8% per year over 39 weeks

10. Miriam wants to buy a pair of inline skates. One store is selling the skates Miriam wants at 15% off the regular price of $149.95. Another store is selling the skates for $139.95, with 10% off. Which store has the better price?

11. An electronics store offers its customers the choice of two payment plans to finance their stereo purchases. A customer makes a down payment and pays the remaining amount over time.

- Plan A: financing the remaining amount at 8% per year, simple interest, for 2 years
- Plan B: financing the remaining amount at 4% per year, simple interest, for 5 years

Stefan wants to buy a stereo system that sells for $459.95 including taxes. Which plan should he choose to pay the least amount of money if he makes a down payment of $100 today?

C Extending

12. Jude bought a T-shirt during a store's annual super sale. The regular price of the T-shirt was $25.99, but it was on sale at 20% off. Because of the super sale, Jude received an additional 10% off the sale price. Calculate the purchase price of the T-shirt, including 15% tax.

13. Terry has a savings account that pays 1.9% interest per year. Terry's grandmother opened the account for him on his 10th birthday and deposited $500. How much will Terry have in the account on his 14th birthday if no other deposits or withdrawals are made? Interest earned each year is added to the account at the end of the year.

14. Charlene's bank account pays 1.5% interest each year. Charlene currently has $450 in the account. She is planning to deposit $50 three months from now and $200 six months from now. What will her account balance be one year from now?

15. Nalini is a real estate agent. She is paid 2.9% commission on the sale of a home. If she sells a home for $259 000, what will her commission be?

Mental Math

SIMPLIFYING PERCENTS AND FRACTIONS

You can express a percent as a fraction by dividing the numerator and the denominator by the same whole number.

Example 1: $60\% = \frac{60}{100}$

$= \frac{60 \div 20}{100 \div 20}$

$= \frac{3}{5}$

Divide both the numerator and the denominator by 20 to determine an equivalent fraction. The fraction $\frac{3}{5}$ is in lowest terms.

You can express a fraction as a percent by multiplying the numerator and the denominator by the same whole number.

Example 2: $\frac{18}{50} = \frac{18 \times 2}{50 \times 2}$

$= \frac{36}{100}$

$= 36\%$

Multiply both the numerator and the denominator by 2 to determine an equivalent fraction.

1. In Example 1, why were the numerator and the denominator divided by 20?

2. In Example 2, why were the numerator and the denominator multiplied by 2?

3. Express each percent as a fraction in lowest terms.

a) 20% **c)** 40% **e)** 80% **g)** 90%

b) 5% **d)** 50% **f)** 25% **h)** 75%

4. Express each fraction as a percent.

a) $\frac{1}{4}$ **c)** $\frac{11}{20}$ **e)** $\frac{22}{25}$ **g)** $\frac{9}{20}$

b) $\frac{3}{4}$ **d)** $\frac{4}{5}$ **f)** $\frac{29}{50}$ **h)** $\frac{15}{25}$

2.9 Solve Problems by Changing Your Point of View

You will need
- a calculator

▶ **GOAL**
Solve problems by looking at situations in different ways.

Learn about the Math

Courtney wants to buy a new guitar. She finds the guitar she wants on sale for 25% off the regular price of $329.98.

? How can Nathan and Annika calculate the purchase price of the guitar, including taxes?

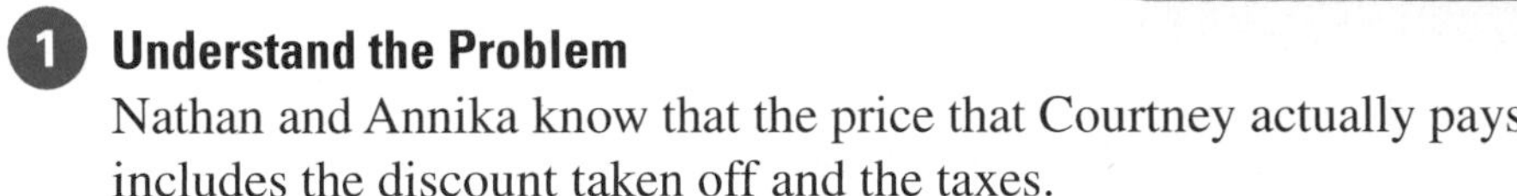

1 Understand the Problem

Nathan and Annika know that the price that Courtney actually pays includes the discount taken off and the taxes.

2 Make a Plan

Nathan's Plan

The discount is 25% of the regular price. This is the same as saying the sale price is 75% of the regular price.

The taxes are 15% of the sale price. This is the same as saying the purchase price is 115% of the sale price.

Annika's Plan

Instead of using two steps to calculate the purchase price, I can use a single calculation. The purchase price is 115% of the sale price, and the sale price is 75% of the regular price.

3 Carry Out the Plan

Nathan's Solution

$$\begin{aligned}\text{sale price} &= 75\% \text{ of } \$329.98\\ &= 0.75 \times \$329.98\\ &= \$247.485\\ &= \$247.49\end{aligned}$$

$$\begin{aligned}\text{purchase price} &= 115\% \text{ of } \$247.49\\ &= 1.15 \times \$247.49\\ &= \$284.6135\end{aligned}$$

The purchase price is $284.61.

Annika's Solution

$$\begin{aligned}\text{purchase price} &= 115\% \text{ of sale price}\\ &= 115\% \text{ of } (75\% \text{ of the regular price})\\ &= 115\% \text{ of } 75\% \text{ of the regular price}\end{aligned}$$

$$\begin{aligned}\text{purchase price} &= 1.15 \times 0.75 \times \$329.98\\ &= \$284.607\,75\end{aligned}$$

The purchase price is $284.61.

4 Look Back

My answer seems reasonable. I know the sale price has to be less than the regular price by about $\frac{1}{4}$, or \$80. When the taxes are added, the purchase price will still be less than the regular price because it was discounted by 25% and increased by only 15%.

Reflecting

1. How was Nathan's reasoning different from Annika's?
2. How did Nathan's approach demonstrate that changing your point of view can simplify the solution to a problem?

Work with the Math

Example: Changing your point of view to calculate area

Kris's father wants to replace the carpet in the family room. Determine the amount of carpet he needs.

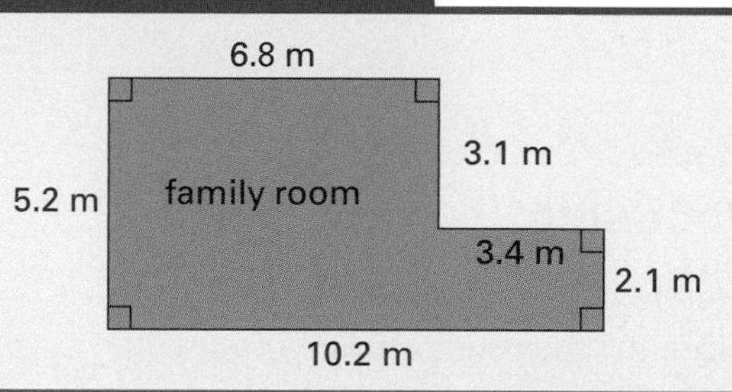

Denis's Solution

1 Understand the Problem

I need to calculate the area of the family room.

2 Make a Plan

I can subtract the area of the small rectangle from the area of the large rectangle.

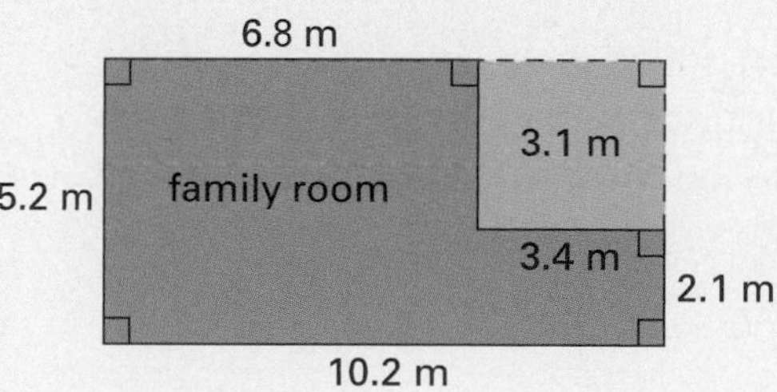

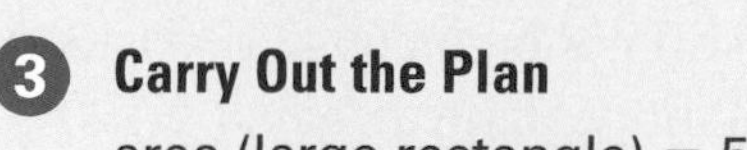

3 Carry Out the Plan

area (large rectangle) = 5.2 m × 10.2 m
= 53.04 m^2

area (small rectangle) = 3.1 m × 3.4 m
= 10.54 m^2

area (family room) = 53.04 m^2 − 10.54 m^2
= 42.5 m^2

Kris's father needs 42.5 m^2 of carpet.

4 Look Back

I can estimate to check my answer: (5 × 10) − (3 × 3) is about 40.

A Checking

3. Describe how you could change your point of view to solve each problem. You do not need to solve the problem.
   a) Joel buys a new goalie stick, which is on sale for 30% off the regular price of $59.95. What is the sale price?
   b) Marilyn buys a calculator for $15.95. What is the purchase price if her bill includes 15% tax?
   c) What is the area of the shape?

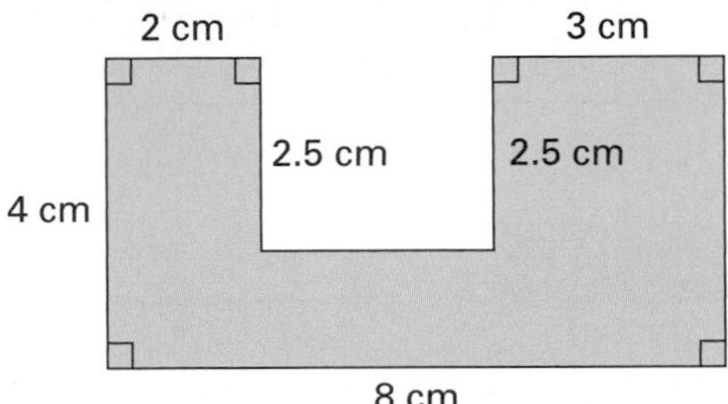

B Practising

4. Daniel buys a video game, which is on sale for 30% off the regular price of $69.98. The combined taxes are 15%. How much does Daniel pay?

5. Kamilah's parents buy her a motorized scooter, which is on sale for 15% off the regular price of $89.95. Today, they only have to pay the GST. What is the purchase price?

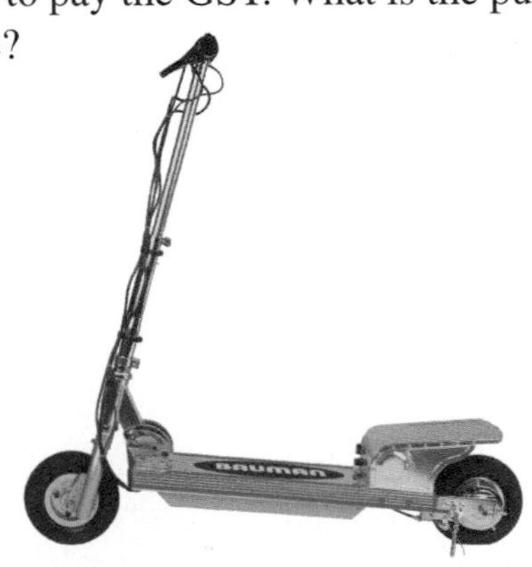

6. A used kayak sells for $450 and 13% tax. What is the purchase price?

7. Determine the area of each figure.
   a)

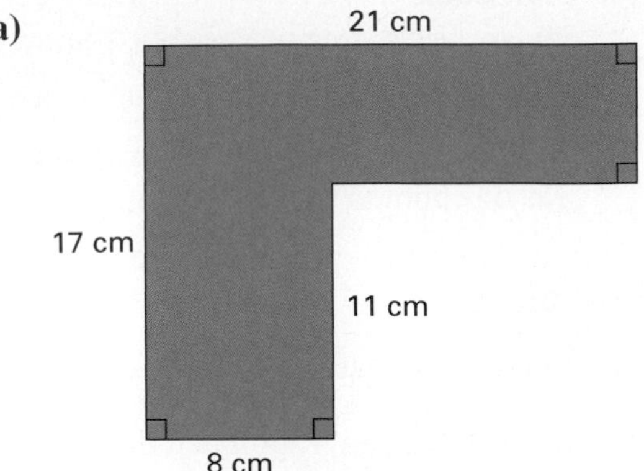

   b)

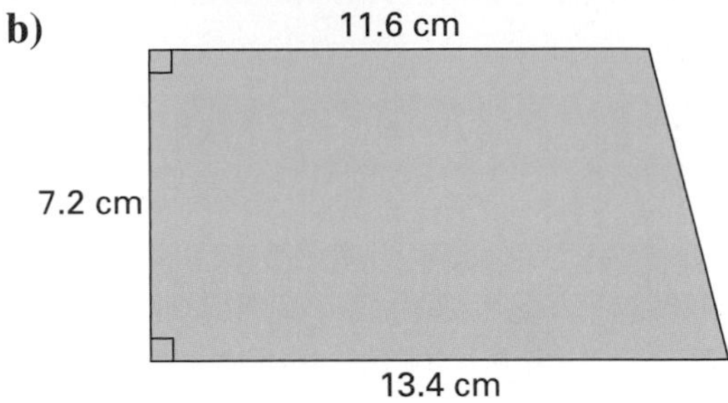

8. A picture for the school yearbook has an area of 80 cm^2. The picture was reduced by 20% to fit in the space available, but it didn't fit. It was reduced by a further 15%. What is the final area of the reduced picture?

9. Mark made a poster for his room by enlarging a picture of his favourite hockey player, which he had taken himself. The original picture had dimensions of 6 cm by 9 cm. Mark enlarged it by 180% but found that it was still not big enough. He had the enlarged picture enlarged again by 190%. What are the dimensions of his poster?

Chapter Self-Test

1. Express each fraction as a decimal. Explain how you can tell whether the decimal will terminate or repeat without dividing.

a) $\frac{17}{20}$ **b)** $\frac{11}{16}$ **c)** $\frac{67}{99}$ **d)** $\frac{2}{7}$

2. Calculate.

a) 1.38×2.7

b) 0.43×9.15

c) 18.4×6.55

3. Calculate.

a) $6.4 \div 1.6$

b) $32.83 \div 0.14$

c) $156.48 \div 6.4$

4. Use $>$, $<$, or $=$ to make each statement true.

a) 0.6 ■ $0.\overline{6}$ **b)** $\frac{7}{9}$ ■ $0.\overline{7}$

5. Calculate the missing terms.

a) $2:7 = 8:$ ■

b) ■ $:39 = 2.7:13$

c) ■ $:4.2:6.3 = 8.5:$ ■ $:31.5$

6. What percent does each diagram show? One full grid represents 100%.

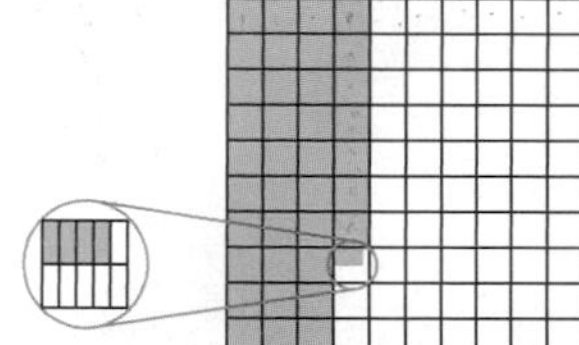

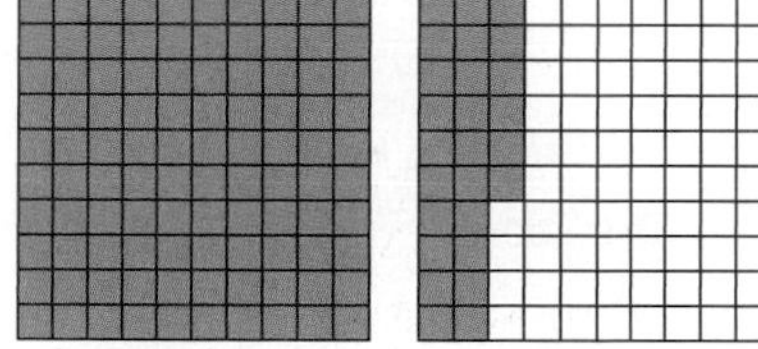

7. Use grids to model and calculate.

a) 78% of 300 **b)** 12.5% of 180

8. Sylvia is training for a triathlon. She cycles 6.25 km in 25 min.

a) What is her average speed, in kilometres per hour?

b) Solve a proportion to determine how long she would take to cycle 40 km. Use the speed in part (a).

9. Ethan bought 0.7 kg of tomatoes. If the tomatoes sell for \$1.96/kg, how much did he pay?

10. Hannah filled her car at the gas station. She bought 48.3 L, and her bill was \$37.43. What was the price of the gasoline, in cents per litre?

11. An addition to a house increases the floor area from 275 m^2 to 300 m^2. By what percent was the original floor area increased?

12. The ratio of cats to dogs at a Humane Society is 5 : 2. There are 63 cats and dogs currently available for adoption. How many are cats?

13. The table below is printed on a box of biscuit mix. How much mix and water are needed to make six dozen biscuits?

Number of biscuits	Amount of mix	Amount of water
24	$1\frac{3}{4}$ cups	$\frac{3}{4}$ cups

14. Esme bought a laptop computer. The regular price of the computer was \$998.95, but it was on sale for 25% off. The taxes were 15%. Determine the purchase price.

Chapter Review

Frequently Asked Questions

Q: How do you use rates to solve problems?

A: A unit rate is a rate that has 1 as its second term. For example, 10 m travelled in 2 s is equivalent to the unit rate 5 m/1 s (the distance travelled in 1 s). This is written as 5 m/s. Unit rates are used to make comparisons between rates. For example, suppose that a car travelled 285 km in 3 h and a motorcycle travelled 225 km in 2.5 h. To determine which travelled at a faster average speed, you can calculate the unit rate.

Car: $\frac{285 \text{ km}}{3 \text{ h}} = 95 \text{ km/h}$

Motorcycle: $\frac{225 \text{ km}}{2.5 \text{ h}} = 90 \text{ km/h}$

The car travelled at a faster average speed.

Q: How can you solve a problem that involves percents?

A: You can use the proportion $\frac{\blacksquare}{100} = \frac{\text{part}}{\text{whole}}$ to solve the problem.

The calculation may involve multiplication or division, depending on the problem. For example, to calculate 35% of 80 you can solve the proportion $\frac{35}{100} = \frac{\blacksquare}{80}$.

To calculate the whole if 45% is 95, you can solve the proportion $\frac{45}{100} = \frac{95}{\blacksquare}$.

To calculate what percent 3 is of 4, you can solve the proportion $\frac{\blacksquare}{100} = \frac{3}{4}$.

Q: What are some applications of percents?

A: Some applications are discounts, taxes, and interest.

Example 1: A pair of sunglasses sells for $25. Calculate a 20% discount off the sunglasses.

$$\begin{aligned} 20\% \text{ of } \$25 &= 0.2 \times \$25 \\ &= \$5 \end{aligned}$$

The discount is $5.

Example 2: Reece took out a loan of $15 000 to buy a car. The interest rate on the loan is 9.5% each year. How much interest will he pay back after one year?

$$\begin{aligned} 9.5\% \text{ of } \$15\,000 &= 0.095 \times \$15\,000 \\ &= \$1425 \end{aligned}$$

Reece will pay $1425 in interest.

NEL

Practice Questions

(2.1) **1.** Express each fraction as a decimal.

a) $\frac{11}{25}$ **b)** $\frac{5}{6}$ **c)** $\frac{13}{15}$

(2.1) **2.** Order the numbers from least to greatest.

$0.25, 0.2\overline{5}, 0.\overline{25}, \frac{2}{9}, \frac{13}{25}$

(2.2) **3.** Calculate.

a) 41.25×4.3 **b)** $24.351 \div 1.5$

(2.2) **4.** A single bus fare costs \$2.35. A monthly pass costs \$45.75. Celine estimates that she will ride the bus 25 times this month. Kamal estimates that he will ride the bus 18 times. Should they both buy monthly passes? Explain.

(2.4) **5.** Determine the missing terms.

a) $4:7:3 = \square:28:\square$

b) $\square:\square:6 = 5:9:2$

(2.4) **6.** In a 750 g bag of mixed nuts, the ratio of peanuts to cashews to almonds is 8 : 4 : 3 by mass. Determine the masses of the peanuts, cashews, and almonds in the bag.

(2.5) **7.** Calculate the unit rate.

a) 15 km travelled in 10 min

b) \$13.95 for 0.45 kg of tuna fish

(2.5) **8.** Marian bought a 2 L bottle of fruit juice for \$5.99. Ivan bought a 0.75 L bottle of the same juice for \$2.95. Which was the better buy? Explain.

(2.5) **9.** State the two quantities that are being compared in each rate. Then calculate the equivalent unit rate.

a) \$101.25 earned in 9 h

b) 400 m travelled in 50 s

10. Use grids to model each percent. Then express the percent as a decimal. (2.6)

a) 23% **b)** 245% **c)** 0.7% **d)** 120%

11. Use grids to determine which is the greater amount, 30% of \$500 or 500% of \$30. (2.6)

12. Determine the missing value. (2.7)

a) $\frac{64}{80} = \square\%$

b) $15\% \text{ of } \square = 6$

c) $32\% \text{ of } 65 = \square$

d) $\frac{45}{18} = \square\%$

e) $0.8\% \text{ of } 2\,500\,000 = \square$

13. Exactly 799 students voted in the student council election. This represented 85% of eligible voters. How many students were eligible to vote? (2.7)

14. Samuel earns 0.2% interest each year on his savings account. If he has \$3500 in his account for a year, how much interest will he have at the end of the year? (2.7)

15. Luke bought a hockey sweater with a regular price of \$68.95. The sweater was on sale for 35% off, and the taxes were 15%. Determine each amount. (2.8)

a) the discount **c)** the taxes

b) the sale price **d)** the purchase price

16. Calculate the interest and the total amount. (2.8)

a) a loan of \$1750 at 4.8% per year over five years

b) an investment of \$1500 at 3% per year over three years

Chapter Task

An Unexpected Inheritance!

Suppose that you have inherited $2500.00 from your uncle. His will states that you must put 65% of your inheritance into a savings account for your post-secondary education. You may spend the remaining amount of money on exactly 10 items of your choice, with the following conditions:

- You must research and find the best interest rate available for the money you are investing.
- You cannot spend more than $100 on any single item.
- You must find the best buy for each item.

? How will you meet the conditions of your uncle's will?

A. How much money will you invest? How much money do you have to spend?

B. How will you invest your money for your education?

C. How much money will you have in your savings account in five years? How much of this money will be interest?

D. Make a list of 10 items that you would like to buy with the remaining money.

E. Use a newspaper or the Internet, or go shopping, to find the best buy for each item on your list.

F. For each item, record the regular price, the sale price, and the name of the store where you found the best buy.

G. Verify, through calculations, that you can purchase all the items on your list with your money. Remember to include 15% tax.

H. Compare the total cost of the 10 items purchased on sale with the total cost at the regular price. How much did you save? Determine your savings as a percent.

Task Checklist

- ☑ Did you find the best interest rate available?
- ☑ Did you find the best buy for each item?
- ☑ Did you show all your calculations?
- ☑ Did you check your answers?

Math in Action

Coach

Al Morrow is a rowing coach for the National Rowing Association, Rowing Canada. He prepares athletes for competitions such as the Olympic Games and World Rowing Championships. In 1992, he coached three gold medalist crews for the Barcelona Olympic Games. His teams won medals at World and Olympic Championships every year from 1991 to 2003.

Al says, "I enjoy the opportunity of working with young people and helping them become better people. I want the athletes I work with to obtain more pleasure from their sport, become fitter, and learn skills that will benefit them through their lifetime. Often, winning is a byproduct of this process. And when that happens, it's really exciting."

Problems, Applications, and Decision Making

"Often a coach makes team selections. I have to … compare team candidates' performances," explains Al.

1. A coach noted these stroke rates for rowing crews of eight. Calculate each stroke rate per minute, to the nearest tenth. Then order the stroke rates per minute, from least to greatest.

   a) 195 strokes in 6 min

   b) 181 strokes in 5 min

   c) 214 strokes in 7 min

2. Coaches compare rowing speeds by calculating the distance per second. Calculate the speed in each situation, to the nearest tenth of a metre per second.

   a) A crew of eight in a men's race rowed 2000 m in 5:35.98. (The time 5:35.98 means 5 min 35.98 s.)

   b) A crew of four in a women's race rowed 2000 m in 6:31.40.

   c) A single rower in a men's single scull rowed 2000 m in 7:06.76.

3. Why would the unit rates in questions 1 and 2 be useful for a coach?

The gold medal standard times for quadruple sculls are 5:33 for men and 6:08 for women. A gold medal standard time is based on fastest times that have been recorded. Expressing a gold medal standard time as a percent of a crew's time provides a method of comparison.

4. a) In a quadruple sculls competition, the time for a men's crew was 6:14.25. Express the men's gold medal standard time as a percent of this crew's time, to the nearest percent.
   b) The time for a women's quadruple sculls crew was 6:57.73. Express the women's gold medal standard time as a percent of this time, to the nearest percent.
   c) Which crew is closer to the gold medal standard time for quadruple sculls? Explain how percents show this.

5. A women's double scull rowed 1525 m in 5 min at practice. At this pace, how far would the crew row in 8 min? Why is it necessary to include "at this pace" in the question?

6. A men's crew of two rowed 900 m in 3:15.37. At this pace, what would be their time, to the nearest second, for 2000 m?

Advanced Applications

"There's the actual coaching side to it," Al commented. "Then there's the whole motivational side."

7. The stroke rate goal for a crew of eight is 34.8 strokes/min. Choose two lengths of time, from 5 min to 10 min. How many strokes in each length of time would achieve this goal? Explain your strategy.

8. A coach set the goal of 92% of the men's gold medal standard time for quadruple sculls. What is the slowest time, in hundredths of a second, that would achieve this goal? Explain your strategy.

9. What is the slowest time, in hundredths of a second, that would achieve the goal of 90% of the women's gold medal standard time for quadruple sculls?

CHAPTER 3

Collecting, Organizing, and Displaying Data

▶ GOALS

You will be able to

- collect, organize, and display data
- construct histograms to represent appropriate data
- evaluate representations of data
- analyze and evaluate arguments based on mean, median, and mode

Getting Started

You will need
- a container
- centimetre cubes
- grid paper
- a ruler

The Biggest Handful—Up or Down?

Kayley won the school raffle. Her prize is a handful of toonies from the bowl. Kito thinks that Kayley will get more coins if she holds her hand with the palm up. They decide to try this with cubes first.

? Can you gather more cubes using Kito's method or Kayley's method?

A. Remove a handful of cubes from the container using Kayley's method. Record the number of cubes you removed. Then put the cubes back in the container. Repeat until you have drawn five handfuls.

B. Repeat step A using Kito's method.

C. Calculate the **mean** number of cubes you removed using each method. Calculate the ratio of the two means to one decimal place. Record your data in a class chart like this one:

Student	Mean number of cubes using Kayley's method	Mean number of cubes using Kito's method	Ratio of mean using Kayley's method to mean using Kito's method
1			
2			
3			

D. Use the class data to create a graph that compares the number of cubes removed using both methods.

E. How does your graph show which method allows you to remove more cubes?

Do You Remember?

1. State whether you would take a **census** or collect data from a **sample** to answer each question. Explain your choice.
   a) What is the favourite colour of the students in your class?
   b) What is the preferred vacation destination of families living in Ontario?
   c) Does your community need a new arena?
   d) Do the Grade 8 students in your school want to have e-mail pals?

2. This database shows the amount of time that Canadians listen to different types of radio programs, by percent.

Type of radio program	Listening time for ages 12 to 17 (%)	Listening time for all ages (%)
talk	2.3	11.4
sports	0.6	2.5
music	86.3	66.1
other	10.8	20.2

Source: Statistics Canada

Which set of data does each circle graph match?

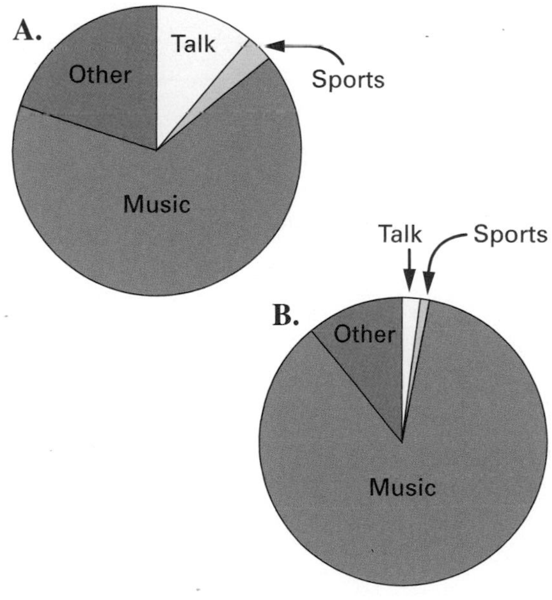

3. The scatter plot shows the population growth of a town over a 10-year period.

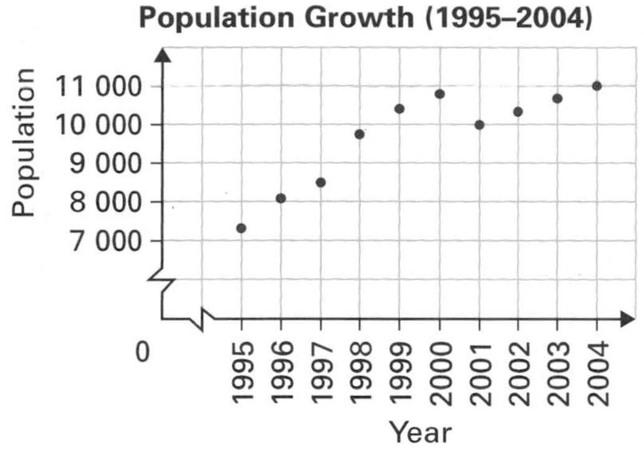

   a) Estimate the town's population in each year.
      i) 1997 ii) 2000 iii) 2003
   b) Between which years was the growth the greatest? By how much did it increase?

4. The class marks for an English assignment are given below.

   88 90 71 93 55 46 82 87 86 75

   55 81 83 91 84 85 89 63 79 88

   a) Organize these marks into a **stem-and-leaf plot**.
   b) Use your stem-and-leaf plot to describe the data.

5. Display these data as a bar graph.

City	Average monthly sunshine in September (h)
Kamloops, BC	194
Schefferville, QU	101
St. John's, NF	145
Sydney, NS	168
Prince Rupert, BC	95
Coppermine, NWT	69

6. Determine the mean, **median**, and **mode** of these data.

   9, 17, 53, 15, 18, 33, 17, 22

3.1 Organizing and Presenting Data

You will need
- grid paper
- a ruler

▶ **GOAL**

Organize and present data to solve problems and make decisions.

Learn about the Math

On July 15, 2004, the city of Peterborough, Ontario, declared a state of emergency due to flooding. Approximately 191 mm of rain had fallen in 24 h, causing an estimated $110 million in damages.

Jude and Samantha are writing an article for the school newspaper about fundraising efforts to help flood victims. They want to compare the amounts earned by different fundraising events, so they researched past fundraising events held at their school.

Fundraising event	Amount raised ($)
bake sale	75
book sale	128
raffle	320
car wash	65
silent auction	156
garage sale	284
sponsored 10 km run	680
bike-a-thon	300
concert	2500
talent show	1250
donations	473
CD sale	145
winter carnival	411

Fundraising event	Amount raised ($)
jellybean count	188
walk-a-thon	390
battle of the bands	670
pledges	433
sponsored community service	225
swim-a-thon	240
bingo	175
international dinner	135
scavenger hunt	105
charity ball	1650
karaoke	180
recipe book	114
toy sale	57

? Which type of fundraising event is most successful?

A. Organize the data into three or four categories. Choose a type of graph (a bar graph, a pictograph, a line graph, a scatter plot, a stem-and-leaf plot, or a circle graph) that would be appropriate to compare the categories. Construct the graph.

B. What conclusions can you make from your graph?

Reflecting

1. Why did you choose the type of graph you used?
2. What other way could you organize the data to determine which type of fundraising event is most successful?

Work with the Math

Example: Organizing and analyzing data to look for a relationship

Is there a relationship between the amount of damage that is caused by a flood and the amount of rain that fell?

Carina's Solution

Location	Amount of rain (mm)	Amount of damage ($ millions)
ON	450	40
AB	160	48
QC	155	93

I used the Canadian Disaster Database Web site for my information. I sorted the data by year to find recent floods in Canada. Then I looked for floods caused by heavy rainfall in a short period of time. I organized the information in a table.

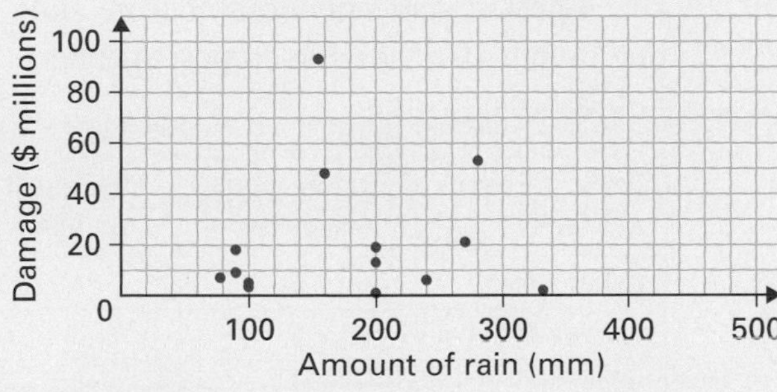

Since I was looking for a relationship between two variables, I decided to construct a scatter plot. I plotted flooding damage versus amount of rain.

I didn't see any pattern in the data points. They were all over the grid.

I cannot see a relationship between the amount of damage that is caused by a flood and the amount of rain that fell.

A Checking

3. Which type of graph (a bar graph, a pictograph, a line graph, a scatter plot, a stem-and-leaf plot, or a circle graph) would you use to display the data for each purpose below?
   a) to predict the world's population growth in the future
   b) to compare the percent of Canada's population with each blood type
   c) to look for a relationship between the number of hours your classmates watch television and the number of hours they play sports each month
   d) to order NBA basketball players by height

B Practising

4. State the types of graphs that you could use to present each set of data below. Which type of graph do you think is most appropriate?

	Data	Purpose of graph
a)	temperature readings taken over five years	to look for a trend
b)	number of baskets scored in one year for five NBA players	to compare player performance
c)	percent of students with asthma each year over a 20-year period	to predict the percent of students with asthma in the future
d)	types of garbage collected in one community	to distribute resources for recycling and waste collection
e)	number of games won by the Toronto Blue Jays in each of their first 25 years	to determine if the team's performance is improving

5. This chart shows the estimated dog and cat populations in several countries in 2002.

Country	Millions of dogs	Millions of cats
USA	61.1	76.4
Brazil	30.1	12.5
China	22.9	53.1
Japan	9.7	7.3
Russia	9.6	12.7
France	8.2	9.6
Italy	7.6	9.4
Canada	3.9	6.8

a) Construct the most appropriate type of graph to compare the two types of pet populations. Why did you choose this type of graph?

b) How does your graph quickly show if there are more dogs or more cats in a country?

6. The speed that a car is driven affects the amount of gasoline that the car consumes. One car manufacturer recorded the following gasoline consumption for a new model of car.

Speed (km/h)	25	40	55	70	85	100	115
Gasoline consumed (L/100 km)	10.2	8.4	8.1	7.8	7.5	9.0	10.7

a) Construct a graph to show the relationship between speed and gasoline consumed.

b) Use your graph to estimate the driving speed that consumes the least amount of gas.

c) At 100 km/h, 9.0 L of gas is needed to travel 100 km. Use your graph to estimate another speed at which 9.0 L of gas is needed to travel 100 km.

d) Predict the amount of gas that is needed to travel 100 km at 95 km/h.

7. Gerald's Grade 8 class was surveyed about snack preferences one month before and one month after hearing a guest speaker talk about nutrition.

Preferred type of snack	Before guest speaker	After guest speaker
potato chips	7	4
chocolate bar	9	3
apple	1	5
plain cereal bar	3	7
candy	5	3
carrot sticks	5	8

a) Based on the data in the chart, did the guest speaker convince students to eat healthier snacks? Construct a graph to support your answer.

b) Justify the type of graph you chose to draw in part (a).

C Extending

8. a) Survey the students in your class about their snack preferences, using the types of snacks in question 7.
   b) Organize your data in a chart. Then display your data in a graph.
   c) How do your results compare with the results in question 7?

9. The September 7, 1992, issue of *Fortune* magazine listed 233 billionaires and their ages. The table shows the ages and wealth (in billions of U.S. dollars) of the 60 wealthiest people in this list. Does the data show a relationship between age and wealth?

Age	Wealth	Age	Wealth	Age	Wealth	Age	Wealth
50	37	69	7.0	23	4.7	68	4.0
88	24	36	6.2	70	4.6	40	4.0
64	14	49	5.9	59	4.6	62	4.0
63	13	73	5.3	96	4.5	69	4.0
66	13	52	5.2	84	4.5	49	4.0
72	11.7	77	5.0	40	4.5	64	3.9
71	10.0	73	5.0	60	4.3	83	3.9
77	8.2	62	4.9	77	4.0	41	3.8
68	8.1	54	4.8	68	4.0	78	3.8
66	7.2	63	4.7	83	4.0	80	3.6
68	3.5	65	3.0	69	3.3	71	3.0
67	3.4	50	3.0	58	3.3	68	3.0
71	3.4	64	3.0	71	3.2	68	3.0
54	3.4	57	3.0	55	3.2	54	3.0
62	3.3	86	3.0	66	3.0	68	2.8

Mental Math

CALCULATING A FRACTION OF A WHOLE NUMBER

Suppose that you want to determine the number of slices in $\frac{3}{4}$ of a 24-slice pizza. Because the denominator of the fraction $\frac{3}{4}$ is a factor of the whole number 24, you can use a shortcut. First divide the whole number by the denominator, and then multiply by the numerator.

Example: Calculate $\frac{3}{4}$ of 24.

Step 1: Calculate $\frac{1}{4}$ of 24 by dividing 24 by the denominator, 4.

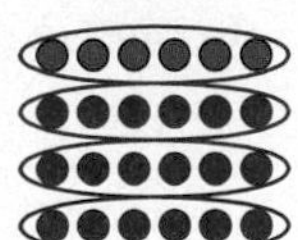

$\frac{1}{4}$ of 24 = 24 ÷ 4
= 6

Step 2: Multiply by the numerator, 3.

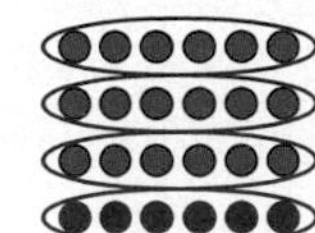

$\frac{3}{4}$ of 24 = 3 × 6
= 18

1. Use $\frac{1}{6}$ of 42 = 7 to calculate $\frac{5}{6}$ of 42.

2. Calculate.
   a) $\frac{3}{5}$ of 15 b) $\frac{3}{4}$ of 12 c) $\frac{3}{8}$ of 48 d) $\frac{4}{11}$ of 55

3.2 Exploring Sample Size

You will need
- slips of paper
- a paper bag

▶ **GOAL**

Explore how sample size represents a population.

Explore the Math

Rishi volunteered to run the milkshake stand at his school's Fun Fair. Before buying the ingredients, he wanted to know flavour preferences. Instead of taking a **census**, he decided to use a **sample** from his class to represent the people who will attend the Fun Fair. He wondered what sample size he should use.

? How does the size of the sample affect Rishi's conclusions?

A. Have each student in your class secretly record his or her preference for milkshake flavour (chocolate, vanilla, or strawberry) on a slip of paper. Place all the slips of paper in a bag.

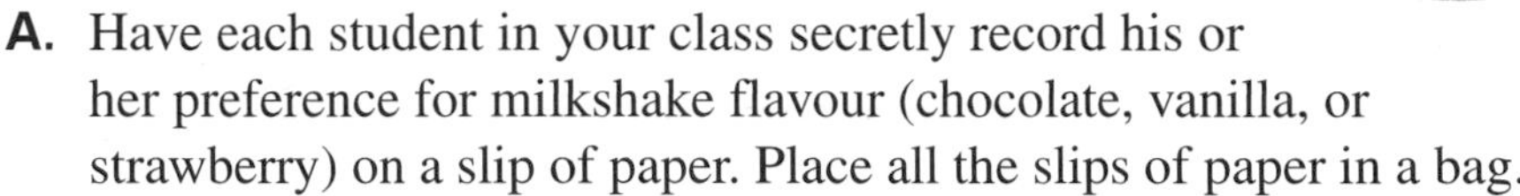

B. Take a sample of one slip of paper from the bag. Record the flavour in a chart like the one below. Return the slip to the bag.

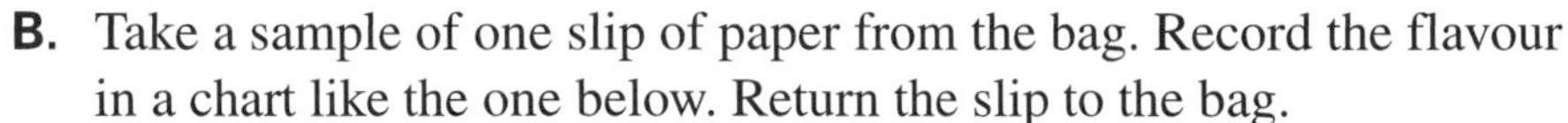

	Preferred flavour		
Sample number	**Chocolate**	**Strawberry**	**Vanilla**
1			
2			

C. Repeat step B until you have taken five samples from the bag.

D. Based on your results, predict the preferences for the **population**. How confident are you in your prediction? Why?

E. Repeat steps B to D for samples of 5 slips and samples of 10 slips.

F. Which sample size has the most variation in the results? Which sample size has the least variation?

G. Look at all the slips of paper to determine the preferences for the whole class. Based on the class preferences, which sample size gave you the best prediction? Did you expect this?

H. Is your class a **representative sample** of your school? Explain.

census

a survey of all the people in a population; for example, a census would involve asking everyone who is going to the Fun Fair what flavour they prefer

sample

a part of a population that is used to make predictions about the whole population

representative sample

a sample from a population such that the properties of the sample reasonably reflect the properties of the population

Reflecting

1. Why do you think a sample is often used instead of a census?

2. Why is a large sample likely to be a better predictor of a population's preferences than a small sample?

3. Suppose that you want to know the cartoon-watching habits of students. You decide to use a sample from a class at a high school. Is this a representative sample of your school? Explain.

Curious Math

WHEN IS A LOW SCORE NOT A BAD SCORE?

Percentiles are a way to compare numerical data that have been put in order from least to greatest. A percentile tells the percent of the data that is less than or equal to a value.

This diagram represents 10 student test scores. The percent of scores at or below each score is shown.

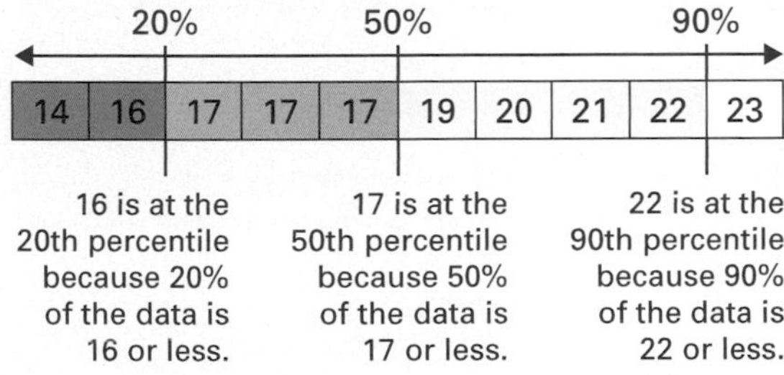

1. Use the diagram above to answer these questions.
   a) At what percentile is the data value 20? At what percentile is the data value 23?
   b) What data value is at the 80th percentile? What data value is at the 10th percentile?
   c) Why is there no value at the 40th percentile for these data?

2. In 2003, 3615 North American university students competed for a grand prize of $25 000 U.S. in the annual William Lowell Putnam Mathematical Competition.
   a) The students who scored 10 out of 120 were at the 78th percentile. How many students scored 10 marks or less?
   b) 1005 of the 3615 students received 0 out of 120 on the Putnam exam. What percentile corresponds to a mark of 0?
   c) The students who scored 1 mark out of 120 were at the 52nd percentile. How many students scored 1 mark or less? How many scored 1 mark exactly?
   d) If you scored $\frac{15}{120}$ on a test at school, would you be satisfied with your score? If you scored $\frac{15}{120}$ on the Putnam exam, how would you feel? Explain the difference.

3.3 Using Electronic Databases

You will need
- Internet access
- *Fathom*™ software
- spreadsheet software

▶ **GOAL**

Use statistics software to display data from electronic databases, and use the data to solve problems.

Learn about the Math

Rowyn and Stefan read that Canada's population in 1930 was about 10 million people. They wondered what the population would be 100 years later, in 2030.

? How can you use data to predict the population of Canada in 2030?

Example 1: Finding population data on the Internet

Locate information about Canada's population since 1930.

Stefan's Solution

I used my Web browser to go to the Statistics Canada Web site, www.statscan.ca.
I found a Web page with Canadian population growth data by following the steps below.
Enter "population growth" in the search window.

A.

B. Canadian Statistics

C. Search Canadian Statistics | population growth | Search | Tips

D.
1. Components of population growth, by province and territory (3 tables) *2005-05-10.*

2. Population and growth components (1851-2001 Censuses) *2005-01-28.*

E.

Population and growth components (1851-2001 Censuses)

Definitions and notes	Census population at the end of period	Total population growth[1]	Births	Deaths	Immigration	Emigration
Period	thousands					
1851-1861	3,230	793	1,281	670	352	170
1861-1871	3,689	459	1,370	760	260	410
1871-1881	4,325	636	1,480	790	350	404
1881-1891	4,833	508	1,524	870	680	826
1891-1901	5,371	538	1,548	880	250	380
1901-1911	7,207	1,836	1,925	900	1,550	740
1911-1921	8,788	1,581	2,340	1,070	1,400	1,089
1921-1931	10,377	1,589	2,415	1,055	1,200	970
1931-1941	11,507	1,130	2,294	1,072	149	241
1941-1951[2]	13,648	2,141	3,186	1,214	548	379
1951-1956	16,081	2,433	2,106	633	783	185
1956-1961	18,238	2,157	2,362	687	760	278
1961-1966	20,015	1,777	2,249	731	539	280
1966-1971[3]	21,568	1,553	1,856	766	890	427
1971-1976	23,450	1,488	1,760	824	1,053	358
1976-1981	24,820	1,371	1,820	843	771	278
1981-1986	26,101	1,281	1,872	885	678	278
1986-1991	28,031	1,930	1,933	946	1,164	213
1991-1996	29,611	1,580	1,936	1,024	1,118	338
1996-2001	31,021	1,410	1,705	1,089	1,217	376

Source: Statistics Canada, Census of Population.
Last modified: 2005-01-28.

I found the data I needed. I can see a trend. I will be able to use the data to predict the population in 2030.

Example 2: Displaying data using statistics software

Use a graph to predict the population of Canada in 2030.

Rowyn's Solution

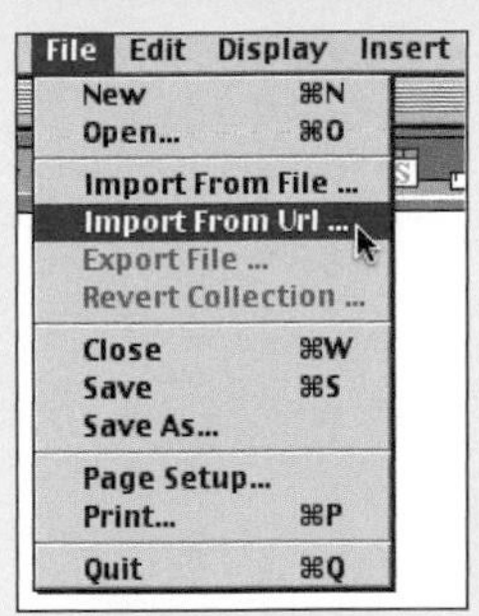

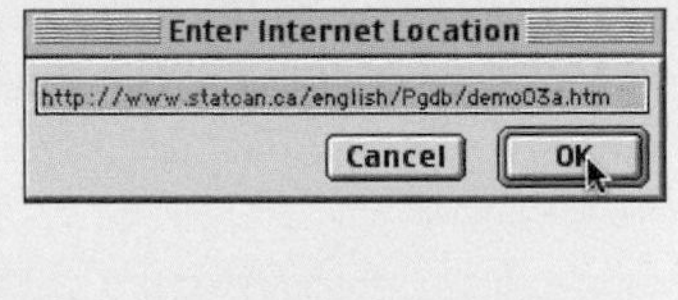

I used *Fathom*™ software to import the data from the Statistics Canada Web site. I selected the **Import From Url** command to do this.

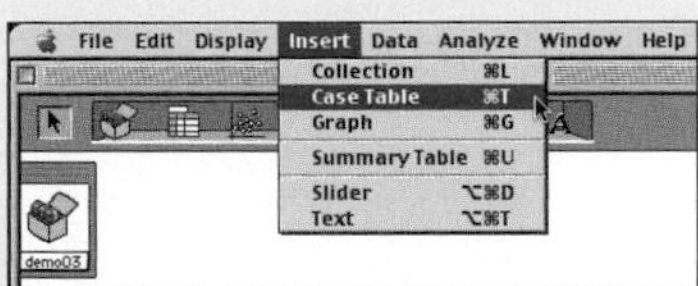

I selected the collection and used **Insert: Case Table** to show all the data in the collection.

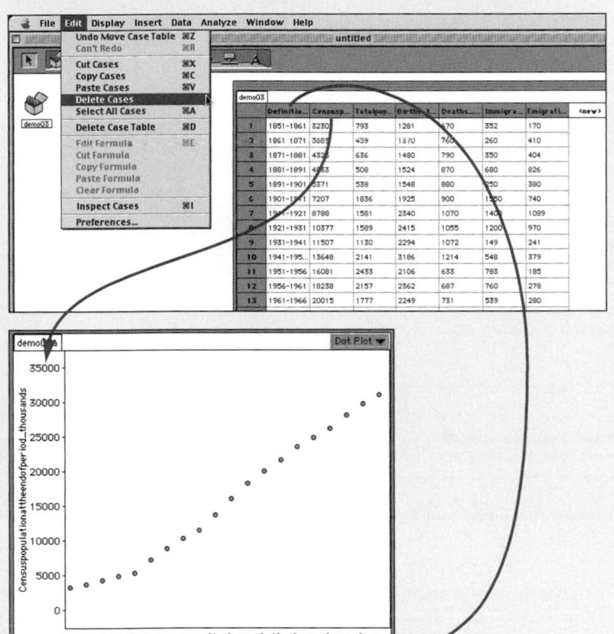

The table contained one case for each row of the original data table. I used **Edit: Delete Cases** to delete the last two cases because they contained non-numeric data.

I used the graph icon to create a graph on the *Fathom*™ workspace.

I dragged the "Definitions and notes_Period" attribute to the *x*-axis of the graph. Then I dragged the "Census population at the end of period_thousands" attribute to the *y*-axis. *Fathom*™ made a dot plot from the data.

I noticed that the census periods changed in 1951 from every 10 years to every 5 years.

The graph shows a trend in the last few census periods. I looked at the data in the table and saw an annual increase of about 1 000 000 per census period.

I estimate that the population in 2030 will be about 6 000 000 more than it was in the 2001 census. This means that it should be about 30 000 000 + 6 000 000 = 36 000 000 in 2030.

Reflecting

1. How did Rowyn use the graph she made with *Fathom*™ to predict the population of Canada in 2030?

2. How did Rowyn use the information from the database to predict the population?

Work with the Math

Example 3: Using a spreadsheet to compare data

Use a spreadsheet to make a graph that compares growth in personal computer availability in Canada with growth in personal computer availability in the United States.

Rishi's Solution

I found data about personal computers on the United Nations Statistics Division Web site.

I downloaded the data into a spreadsheet program. I copied the data for Canada and the United States to a new spreadsheet.

◇	A	B	C	D	E	F	G	H	I	J	K	L	M	N	O
1	Country	1990	1991	1992	1993	1994	1995	1996	1997	1998	1999	2000	2001	2002	
2	Canada	0.37	0.59	0.94	1.22	2.45	4.28	6.93	15.48	25.59	37.24	42.13	45	51.28	
3	United States	0.8	1.19	1.77	2.32	4.97	9.45	16.8	22.13	30.81	36.7	44.06	50.15	55.14	
4															

I used the spreadsheet program to make a comparative bar graph that shows how the number of personal computers per 100 people in Canada and the United States changed each year from 1990 to 2002.

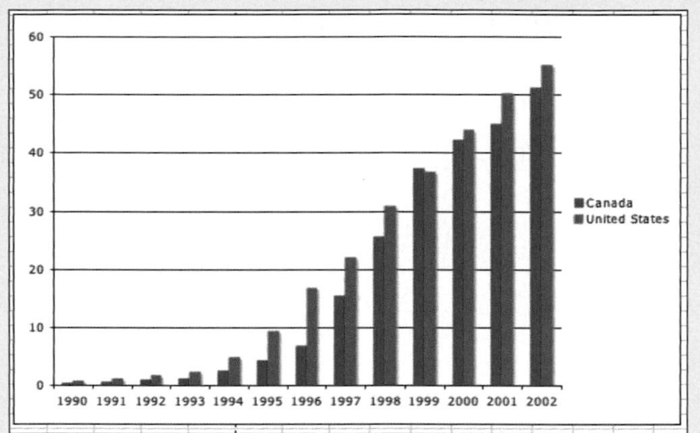

A Checking

Use the database at the right to answer questions 3 to 5.

Average Number of Hours of Television Viewing per Week

	All ages	Ages 2–11	Ages 12–17	Ages 18 and over	
				Male	Female
Canada	21.6 h	14.6 h	13.7 h	21.0 h	25.8 h
NL	22.7	17.0	13.7	22.1	26.6
PE	21.5	15.7	15.7	21.0	25.1
NS	23.7	16.1	15.9	23.0	27.8
NB	23.3	16.3	13.4	21.8	28.4
QC	23.8	14.7	14.4	23.0	28.9
ON	20.6	14.5	13.8	20.0	24.5
MB	21.6	15.0	13.9	20.9	26.3
SK	21.2	16.0	12.3	20.8	25.4
AB	20.0	14.2	12.4	19.4	24.3
BC	20.8	13.1	12.5	20.9	24.3

Source: Statistics Canada

3. Construct a bar graph that compares the number of hours of television viewing for each age group in Ontario with the number of hours of television viewing for each age group in Canada.

B Practising

4. Construct a bar graph that compares the number of hours of television viewing for all ages in Ontario and Canada.

NEL

5. Use *Fathom*™ or a spreadsheet program to make a bar graph that displays the number of hours of television viewing per week by age group in Canada.

6. Use the Statistics Canada Web site, www.statscan.ca, to answer the following questions.
   a) What type of reading material is read the most by Canadians? Explain why this might be so.
   b) What types of reading material do female Canadians read more than male Canadians?
   c) What graphs could you construct to represent the data in this database? For each graph, state the type of graph, the data you would use, and a possible purpose.

7. Use an Internet database to create a graph that compares the rate of growth for the population of Canada with the rate of growth for the population of your community.

8. Use a database to find information about the average total income of families in Canada over the last 20 years. Create a graph to predict the average income in the year 2025.

9. a) Create a database with these fields: country name, land area, gross domestic product (GDP), population, literacy rate, and life expectancy.
   b) Find databases that will give you data for your database, for 10 countries of your choice.
   c) Use the data in your database to rank the countries according to your desire to live there.
   d) Construct a graph that supports your rankings in part (c).

C Extending

10. a) How would you reorganize the following two databases to create one database?

Database A

Country	Area (km^2)	Imports to Canada ($ millions)	Continent
China	9 596 960	15 982	Asia
Norway	324 220	3 933	Europe
Spain	504 782	1 025	Europe
Taiwan	35 980	4 240	Asia
USA	9 629 091	218 272	North America

Database B

Country	Population	Exports from Canada ($ millions)
China	1 284 303 705	4 126
USA	280 562 489	345 317
Spain	40 077 100	948
Taiwan	22 548 009	1 119
Norway	4 525 116	928

   b) How would you sort your database to find the European country with the greatest population that trades with Canada?
   c) How would you find the country in Asia whose exports to Canada and imports from Canada have the greatest total?
   d) Which country comes closest to breaking even in trade with Canada (that is, whose imports to Canada are almost equal to Canada's exports)?
   e) To which country does Canada export the most? To which country does Canada export the least?

Mid-Chapter Review

Frequently Asked Questions

Q: How do you decide which type of graph you should use to represent data?

A: The type of graph depends on what you want the graph to show.

Type of graph	What graph shows
line graph	trends
circle graph	how a whole is divided
scatter plot	relationships
bar graph/pictograph	frequency in different categories

Q: What is the relationship between the size of a sample and how confident you can be in the results?

A: As you increase the size of a sample, the size of the sample gets closer to the size of the population. Therefore, the results you get should be more representative of the entire population.

For example, a sample consisting of students from four classes is more representative of the entire school than a sample consisting of students from only one class.

Q: How can you use technology to compare data?

A: You can use the Internet to find a database with data that will help you answer the question. Then you can transfer the data to a spreadsheet program or a statistics program. Use this software to graph the data, to see if there are any trends that will help you answer the question.

For example, this database shows information about the new housing price index for major cities across Canada.

Definitions and notes	2000	2001	2002	2003	2004
	1997=100				
Canada	**104.1**	**107.0**	**111.3**	**116.7**	**123.2**
St. John's (NL)	101.2	103.2	107.7	112.5	118.6
Halifax (NS)	107.4	110.5	114.4	119.1	121.6
Vancouver (BC)	90.2	90.9	93.2	96.2	101.0

Source: Statistics Canada

To compare the changes in the housing price index in 2004 for major Canadian cities, download the data into a spreadsheet program. Copy the data for 2003 and 2004 to a new spreadsheet. Then use the spreadsheet to make a comparative bar graph that shows how the housing price index in 2003 and 2004 changed for each city.

Practice Questions

(3.1) **1.** The data below show the percent of Canada's adult population with various levels of schooling.

Location	No higher than secondary	Post-secondary non-university	University without a degree	University with a degree
Canada	41.8	34.3	11.3	19.5
NL	48.7	34.4	10.9	12.4
PE	45.2	34.8	12.3	15.1
NS	41.5	35.3	13.3	18
NB	49.1	31.7	11.7	14.4
QC	46.9	32.8	6.8	18.6
ON	39.9	33.9	12	21.4
MB	45.8	31.7	14	16.7
SK	46	32.5	15.2	15.4
AB	37.7	38.3	12.5	18.8
BC	36.6	36.7	15	20.9
YT	29	45.7	2.4	26.7
NT	38.3	40.6	10.1	17
NU	48.5	39.7	4.8	10

Source: Statistics Canada

a) Construct a graph to compare the data for Ontario with the data for New Brunswick.

b) Construct a graph to compare the percent of the population with no higher than secondary education in all the provinces and territories.

c) Which province or territory is most representative of Canada, in terms of level of schooling?

d) Which provinces or territories are above the Canadian percentage for population with a university degree?

e) Suppose that you were promoting post-secondary education to students in Canada. What two provinces or territories would you target? Give reasons for your choices.

f) What type of graph would be effective for promoting post-secondary education to students in Canada?

2. Describe three situations in which you might use each type of graph. (3.1)

a) a bar graph **b)** a scatter plot

3. Magda and Trevor want to know what is the most popular spectator sport at their school. Instead of asking every student, Magda asks 25 students in her school and Trevor asks 15 students in his class. Whose results would you have more confidence in? Explain why. (3.2)

4. This database gives the gross income, in thousands of U.S. dollars, for five of the highest-grossing films. (3.3)

Film	North America	Overseas
Titanic	600 800	1 234 200
The Lord of the Rings: The Return of the King	377 000	752 200
Harry Potter and the Philosopher's Stone	317 600	651 100
Stars Wars: Episode I—The Phantom Menace	431 100	494 400
The Lord of the Rings: The Two Towers	340 500	580 000

a) Create a spreadsheet for the data.

b) Construct a bar graph that compares the gross income for each movie in North America and overseas.

c) Use your graph to determine which movie had the least gross income in North America and overseas.

3.4 Histograms

You will need
- grid paper
- a ruler

▶ **GOAL**

Use histograms to describe appropriate data.

Learn about the Math

Rishi's Grade 8 class is planning a trip to Canada's Wonderland. Many of the attractions have minimum or maximum height requirements. The heights (in centimetres) of the students in Rishi's class are given below.

168	173	157	160	165
160	148	160	150	155
155	150	160	163	152
152	163	157	155	157
160	157	152	147	165
155	157	168	160	163

Some students want to use a bar graph to display the heights. Other students want to group the heights to create a **histogram**.

histogram
a graph with bars that show frequencies of data organized into intervals; the intervals line up side by side, without gaps, on the number line

? **How can you use each type of graph to display the heights of the students in Rishi's class?**

Example 1: Displaying data using a bar graph

Create a bar graph to display the heights of the students in Rishi's class.

Kayley's Solution

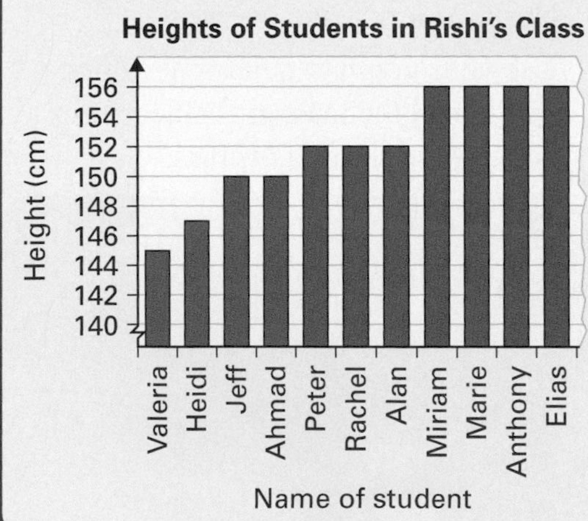

I used a student name for each category.

My bar graph is very large, but it clearly shows who can go on rides with height restrictions.

Example 2: Displaying data using a histogram

Create a histogram to display the heights of the students in Rishi's class.

Kito's Solution

Height (cm)	Frequency
145–150	2
150–155	5
155–160	9
160–165	9
165–170	4
170–175	1

First, I organized the heights in a frequency table. I needed intervals to represent heights from 147 cm to 173 cm. This is a range of 26 cm.

If I used multiples of 2 for my intervals, I would have 13 intervals. That's too many.

If I used multiples of 10, I would have three intervals. That's too few.

I chose multiples of 5. This gave me six intervals. I decided to start the first interval at 145 because 145 is a multiple of 5.

Heights of Students in Rishi's Class

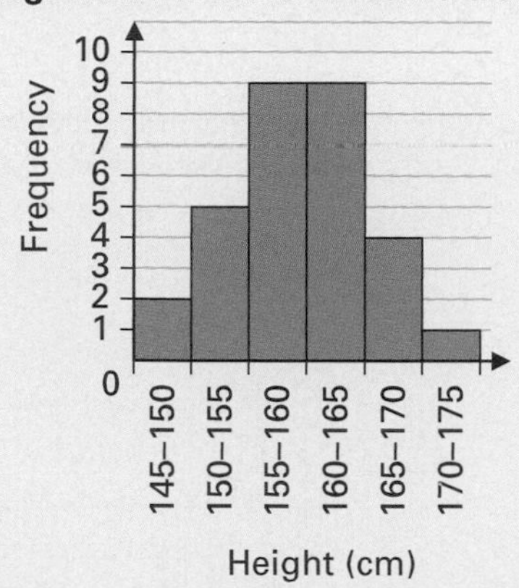

My histogram looks a lot like a bar graph. But the bars have no spaces between them since the intervals have no gaps between them.

I can tell how many heights are in each interval, but I don't know what the exact heights are or which students have these heights.

Reflecting

1. How are bar graphs and histograms similar?

2. In what situations would you use a histogram instead of a bar graph? Why?

Communication Tip

Data values that fall at a value where two intervals intersect are usually placed in the higher interval. For example, 155 would usually be placed in the interval 155–160, not in the interval 150–155.

Work with the Math

Example 3: Displaying data in a histogram

The students in Brenda's class think that a crossing guard is needed at a nearby intersection before and after school. They decide to research the traffic at the intersection. Their results are shown in the table below.

Number of Vehicles Passing Through Intersection Each Hour							
7:00–8:00 a.m.	253	10:00–11:00 a.m.	199	1:00–2:00 p.m.	143	4:00–5:00 p.m.	370
8:00–9:00 a.m.	364	11:00–12:00 p.m.	175	2:00–3:00 p.m.	137	5:00–6:00 p.m.	441
9:00–10:00 a.m.	217	12:00–1:00 p.m.	220	3:00–4:00 p.m.	150	6:00–7:00 p.m.	289

Create a histogram to display the data. Does your histogram support the need for a crossing guard?

Solution

There are 12 intervals in the table, but 12 intervals would make the graph hard to read. Group the frequencies into 2 h intervals.

The traffic is greater between 7:00 and 9:00 a.m., and between 3:00 and 5:00 p.m., than it is at most other times during the day. Therefore, the histogram supports the need for a crossing guard because these are the same times that students are travelling to and from school.

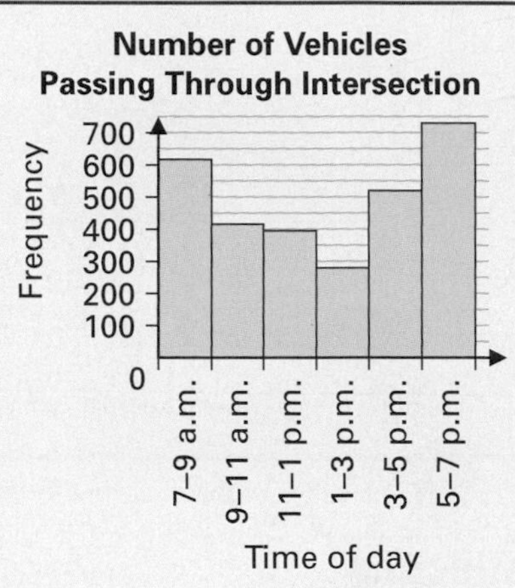

A Checking

3. a) How many intervals are in this histogram? What is the size of each interval?

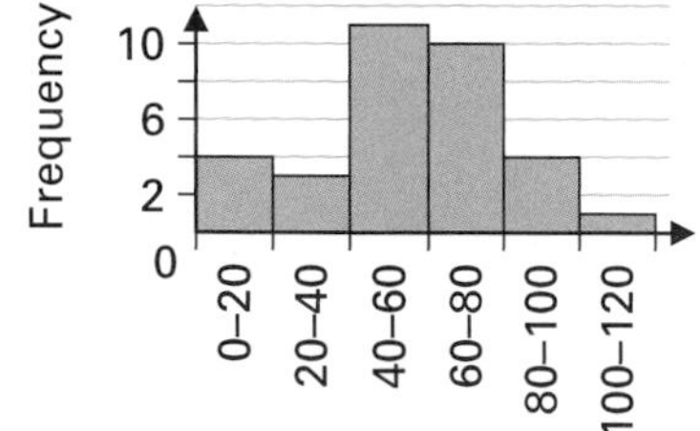

b) Todd spends 35 min on homework per day, on average. In which interval does his daily time belong?

c) About how much time do you spend doing homework each day, on average? In which interval does it belong?

4. Organize these temperatures (°C) into a frequency table. Then use your table to construct a histogram.

1.1	8.7	30	23.5	33.9	40.1
27.2	31.4	19.6	6.7	14.8	33.3
7.1	39.4	22.9	29.1	16.6	9.7
43.5	48.4	46.8	11.2	33.1	45

B Practising

5. Display the following information in a histogram.

Time Spent on Computer by Students

Time spent on a computer daily (min)	Number of students
0–30	24
30–60	40
60–90	57
90–120	23
over 120	8

6. These are Ravi's mean bowling scores for the past 24 weeks.

110.7	120.4	115.2	106.2	107.1	122.6
130.0	129.5	119.2	113.4	100.2	95.4
103.0	129.9	105.7	125.0	122.6	111.5
112.4	114.7	101.8	129.0	103.1	140.9

a) Organize the scores in a frequency table. Explain your choice of intervals.

b) Display the scores in a histogram.

c) Display the scores in a stem-and-leaf plot.

7. a) How many intervals are in this histogram? What is the size of the intervals?

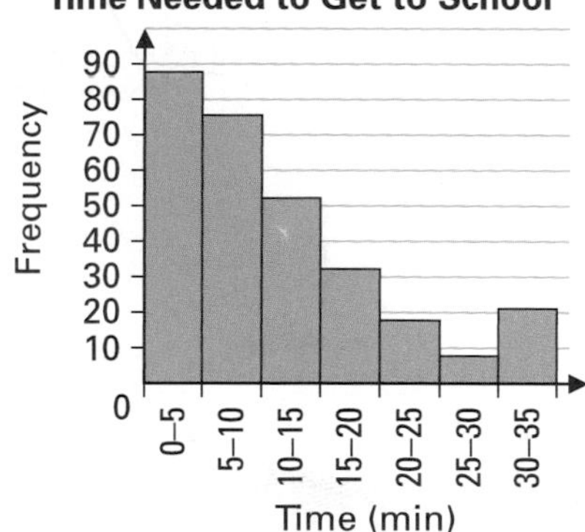

b) James takes 25 min to walk to school. Which interval does his time belong in?

c) What percent of the students needs 30 min or more to get to school?

8. Manon and Juan recorded the running time for 100 movies. Manon displayed the data in a bar graph that listed each movie individually. Juan combined the data to create seven intervals and displayed the intervals in a histogram.

a) Could Juan have used Manon's bar graph to create his histogram? How?

b) Could Manon have used Juan's histogram to create her bar graph? How?

c) What was the benefit of using a histogram?

9. The following times, in seconds, were recorded for a 100 m race.

13.9	14.3	14.4	13.7	15.2	15.4	13.9
13.9	14.5	14.7	14.4	13.8	13.1	13.8
12.4	13.8	12.7	13.4	13.9	14.0	14.4
14.3	14.5	11.8	12.9	12.3	12.8	13.7
13.1	15.0	14.8	14.2	14.4	14.8	

a) Explain how you would sort the data into **i)** three intervals **ii)** five intervals

b) Which number of intervals in part (a) would be the most appropriate? Explain.

c) Use this number of intervals to construct a histogram.

C Extending

10. Two students drew histograms that showed the ages of 40 people. The students used different numbers of intervals. Figure out a possible distribution of the 40 ages that makes both histograms accurate.

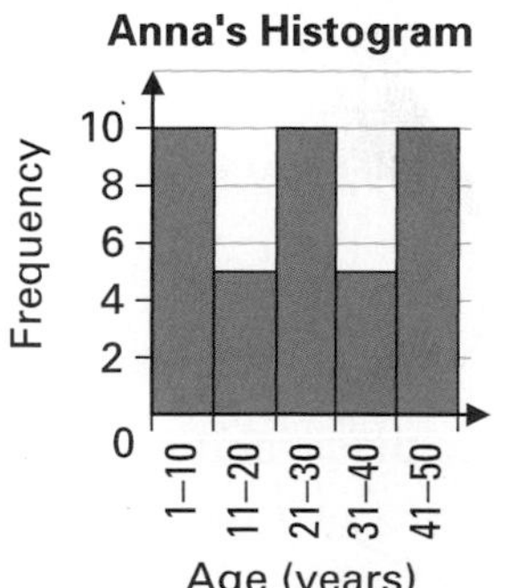

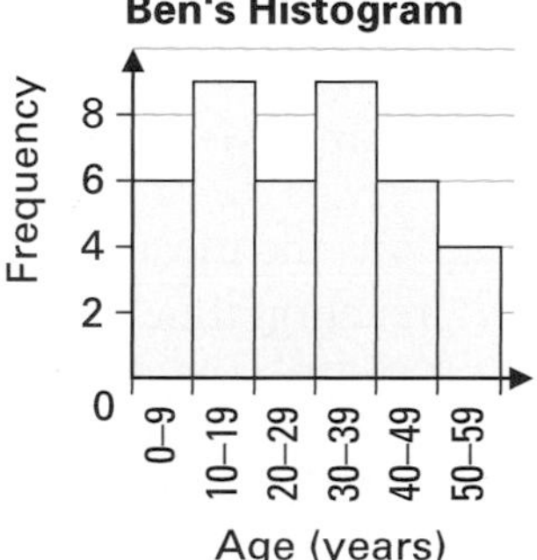

3.5 Mean, Median, and Mode

You will need
- a metre stick
- a calculator or spreadsheet software

▶ **GOAL**

Use means, medians, and modes to compare groups of data.

Learn about the Math

Carina and Stefan have designed an experiment to measure their reaction times using a metre stick.

? How quick is your reaction time?

A. Hold a metre stick at the end marked 100 cm. Have your partner place his or her thumb and forefinger near the end marked 0 cm, without touching the stick.

B. Without warning your partner, let go of the metre stick. Record the centimetre mark at which your partner catches it.

C. Repeat step B nine more times.

D. Switch roles with your partner, and repeat steps A to C.

E. Determine the mean, the median, and the mode (if it exists) of each set of reaction times.

F. Repeat step E, leaving out the least measurement for each set of reaction times.

G. Repeat step E, leaving out the greatest measurement.

H. Repeat step E, leaving out both the least and the greatest measurements.

I. Compare your reaction time with the reaction times of the other students in your class. Use the means, medians, and any modes you calculated in steps E to H for your comparison.

Reflecting

1. In steps E to H, was the mean, the median, or the mode affected more by leaving out the least and greatest measurements? Why?

2. Was the mean, the median, or the mode a better indicator of your reaction time? Justify your answer.

3. How did your means, medians, and modes help you compare your reaction time with the reaction times of the other students in your class?

Work with the Math

Example 1: Using a spreadsheet to calculate mean and median

Lesley recorded her distances for a 10 min run over 10 consecutive days.

◇	A	B	C	D	E	F	G	H	I	J	K
1	**Day**	**1**	**2**	**3**	**4**	**5**	**6**	**7**	**8**	**9**	**10**
2	**Distance (km)**	**1.4**	**1.4**	**1.3**	**1.5**	**1.5**	**1.6**	**0.9**	**1.6**	**1.5**	**1.5**

She wants to run at least 1.5 km on fitness-testing day. Do you think she will meet her goal? Does the mean, the median, or the mode provide a better prediction of whether she will meet her goal?

Rowyn's Solution

L	M
mean =	1.42
median =	1.5
mode =	1.5

I typed the data into a spreadsheet.

Then I entered formulas into column M to calculate the mean, the median, and the mode.

I used =AVERAGE(B2:K2) for the mean, =MEDIAN(B2:K2) for the median, and =MODE(B2:K2) for the mode.

One very low distance—0.9 km on day 7—lowered the mean. Most of Lesley's other distances were at or over her goal of 1.5 km. Even the distances that were lower were close to 1.5 km. The median and the mode show this better.

I think the median and mode provide a better prediction. Based on the median and the mode, I think she will likely meet her goal of running 1.5 km on fitness-testing day.

Example 2: Analyzing effect of removing data on measures of average

The marks that Dale received on his math assignments are given below.

55, 99, 75, 75, 75, 82, 90, 84, 88, 80

Dale's teacher is giving all the students the option of dropping their greatest and least marks to determine their average mark. Would this give Dale a better average than if all of his marks were used?

Rishi's Solution

Stem	Leaf
4	
5	5
6	
7	5 5 5
8	0 2 4 8
9	0 9

I used a stem-and-leaf plot to organize Dale's marks.

The median is $(80 + 82) \div 2 = 81$.
The mean is $80.\dot{3}$.
The mode is 75.

When I removed 55 and 99, the median and the mode didn't change. The mean went up to 81.1, however.

If Dale's teacher uses the mean, Dale should drop his greatest and least marks.

A Checking

4. a) Determine the mean, the median, and the mode of these data.
18, 19, 19, 12, 17, 19, 18, 18, 18, 25
   b) Remove the greatest and least values. Determine the mean, the median, and the mode.
   c) Which changed the most—the mean, the median, or the mode?

B Practising

5. a) Determine the mean, the median, and the mode of these data.
4.5, 4.7, 4.9, 5.5, 1.3, 1.5, 2.7, 3.9, 4.9, 2.7, 5.6
   b) Remove the greatest and least values. Determine each measure. Which changed the most—the mean, the median, or the mode?

6. According to Statistics Canada, the number of cable television subscribers increased from about 1 151 000 in 2002 to about 1 393 000 in 2003. What was the mean number of new subscribers per month during that year?

7. a) The mode of 59, 85, 72, 42, 62, 72, 53, 59, 63, and ■ is 72. Determine the missing value.
   b) The median of 15, 17, 13, 19, 20, 33, 22, 12, 18, and ■ is 18.5. Is it possible to determine the missing value? Explain.
   c) The mean of 79, 76, 55, 20, 14, 68, 30, 29, and ■ is 52. Calculate the missing value.

8. The class with the greatest mean sales in a spring fundraiser will win a prize. The mean for Eric's class is $148. The mean for Natalia's class is $152. Natalia's sales total $150. If Natalia moves to Eric's class, the mean for each class increases. Explain why.

9. In a skating competition, the marks of judges are randomly selected to count. Then the highest and lowest marks are dropped, and the skater receives the mean of the remaining marks.

These are some of the marks that 11 judges gave a skater for a free-skating program.

6.75	6.25	6.50
6.00	5.75	6.50
7.25	7.00	6.75
6.50	6.25	

Suppose that four marks were dropped.

   a) Remove four marks that would lower the mean score the most. Calculate the new mean and median.
   b) Remove four marks that would raise the mean score the most. Calculate the new mean and median.

10. Remove one value from the following data to make each statement true.
32, 45, 82, 99, 15, 102, 75, 15, 15, 75, 2, 75
   a) The median is 45.
   b) The mean is 56.09.

C Extending

11. a) Choose a novel and a textbook. Record the number of letters in the first 100 words in each book.
   b) How could you use the mean, the median, and the mode as average word length to measure readability?
   c) Remove the two longest words in each set of data. How does this affect each measure?

Math Game

WHAT'S THE AVERAGE?

The goal of this game is to determine the mean, median, and mode of the numbers you roll with four dice and to find one of these values on your game card.

Number of players: 2 to 4

You will need
- game cards
- four dice

Rules

1. Players have their own game cards and take turns rolling four dice.
2. On your turn, determine the mean, mode, and median of the numbers you roll. (Do not round.)
3. If possible, put a check mark in an empty box beside the correct mean, mode, or median on your game card.
4. If you cannot find an empty box that matches one of these values, put an X in any empty box.
5. When all the cards are filled, the player with the most check marks is the winner.

Example	Mean	Mode	Median	Action
Rowyn's roll	4	6	4.5	Rowyn could put a check mark beside a mean of 4 or a mode of 6. Both boxes were empty, so she chose the mean of 4.
Stefan's roll	4	4	4	Stefan could put a check mark beside a mean of 4, a mode of 4, or a median of 4. He chose the mode of 4 because it was the only empty box.
Kito's roll	3.5	none	3.5	Because Kito's mean and median were not whole numbers, and he did not have a mode, he could not put a check mark on his game card. So, he put an X beside the median of 3.

Rowyn's Card	
Mean Value	**✔/✘**
1	
2	
3	
4	✓
5	
6	
Mode Value	**✔/✘**
1	
2	
3	
4	
5	
6	
Median Value	**✔/✘**
1	
2	
3	
4	
5	
6	

3.6 Communicating about Graphs

You will need
- grid paper
- a ruler

▶ **GOAL**

Use data and graphs to support conclusions.

Communicate about the Math

Kayley researched the spending and saving habits of 13-year-olds to convince her mother that she needs an increase in her allowance. She surveyed 10 of her classmates and reported the average amounts. Then she used a spreadsheet and a graph to present her findings in a report. She asked Carina to comment on her report.

? How can Kayley improve her report?

Kayley's Report

Allowance	Amount earned	Amount spent on entertainment	Amount spent on food	Amount spent on clothes	Amount spent on CDs	Amount saved
$960	$500	$425	$450	$200	$175	$210

Spending Habits of 13-Year-Olds

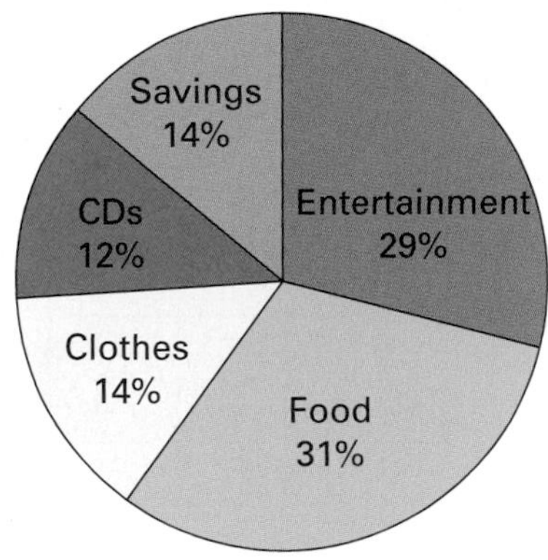

I organized the data I collected from my classmates in a spreadsheet. Then I used the graphing program on my computer to construct a circle graph.

I chose a circle graph to show the spending and saving habits of 13-year-olds because a circle graph shows how something is divided up. I knew that a line graph would not be appropriate because I am not showing any change over a time period.

I gave my graph a title and labelled the sections of the graph with percents. From my graph, I can conclude that 13-year-olds spend more than they save.

Carina's Questions

What was the sample size?

Was your sample representative of all 13-year-olds?

How did you use the spreadsheet program?

Why didn't you use a bar graph, a histogram, or a pictograph?

What other conclusions can you make from your graph?

A. Which of Carina's questions do you think is most important for improving Kayley's report? Why?

B. Kayley did not comment on the amount of money that her friends earn or get for allowance. How could she use this information in her report?

C. Why was Kayley's decision to use a graph to communicate her findings appropriate?

Communication Checklist

- ☑ Did you include all the important details?
- ☑ Did you make reasonable conclusions?
- ☑ Did you justify your conclusions?
- ☑ Were you convincing?

Reflecting

1. Which parts of the Communication Checklist did Kayley cover well? Explain.
2. What additional suggestions can you make to help Kayley improve her report?

Work with the Math

Example: Using a histogram

Rohan wanted to find out how important music is to 13-year-olds. He conducted a survey and presented his findings in a histogram. Based on his histogram, he concluded that music is very important to 13-year-olds.

a) How does Rohan's histogram support his conclusion?

b) Why is a histogram an appropriate graph to use?

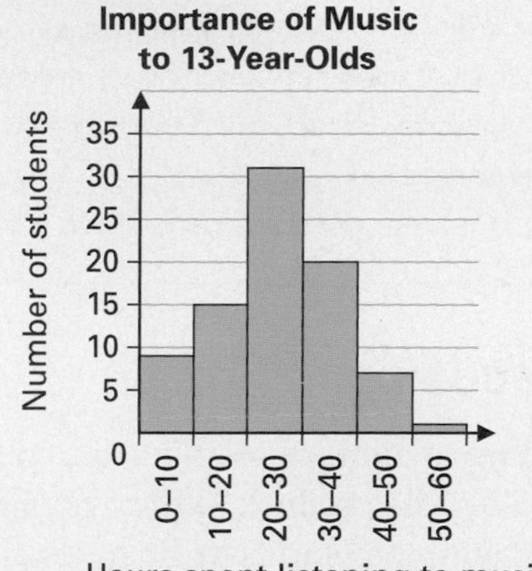

Carina's Solution

a) Rohan's histogram shows the distribution of hours that 13-year-olds listen to music over a week. Based on the histogram, I can conclude that most 13-year-olds listen to music for 20 to 40 h a week, with the majority listening to music for 20 to 30 h.

b) A histogram shows a frequency distribution, using intervals on a number line. A circle graph would not be appropriate because Rohan is not showing how a whole is divided. A line graph would not be appropriate either because he is not showing how something changes over time.

A Checking

3. Kevin produced a report to show the food he ate over a week. He used a circle graph. What questions would you ask Kevin to help him improve his report?

Kevin's Report

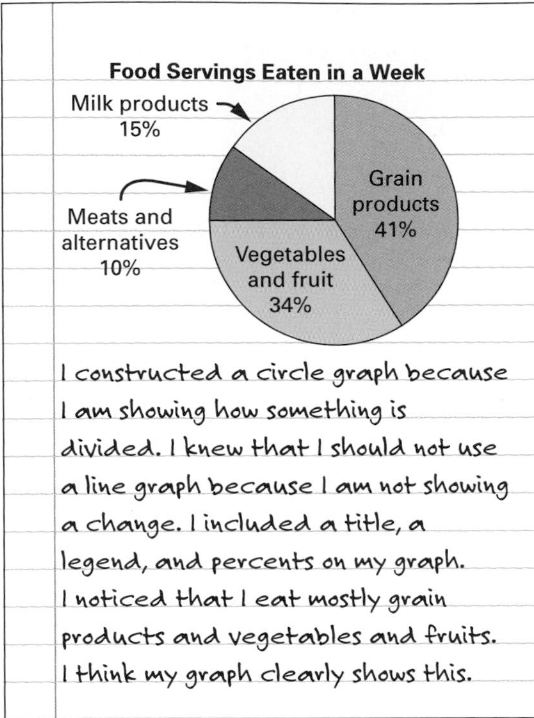

B Practising

4. A battery manufacturer is interested in the lifetime of its products. Thirty batteries are tested until they fail. The times to failure (in hours) are given below.

41.3	21.1	35.6	13.5	4.2	15.8
5.5	5.8	33.6	18.6	24.3	18.1
3.5	8.4	42.1	9.4	10.6	8.9
13.7	19.6	9.2	5.9	19.4	24.2
27.3	30.6	29.4	18.0	32.8	15.6

a) Construct a graph to display the data.

b) The manufacturer claims that 50% of its batteries last longer than 20 h. Describe how your graph shows whether or not this is true.

5. The countries that won medals in the winter Olympics from 1924 to 2002 are listed in this table.

Country	Gold	Silver	Bronze
Germany/East Germany/ West Germany	108	105	87
USSR/Unified Team/ Russia	114	83	78
Norway	94	94	75
United States	69	72	52
Austria	41	57	64
Finland	42	51	49
Sweden	39	30	39
Switzerland	32	33	38
Canada	31	28	37

a) Organize the data to compare the overall medal standings for four regions: Scandinavia (Sweden, Norway, and Finland), North America (Canada and the USA), the Alps (Switzerland, Austria, Germany, and East and West Germany), and USSR/Unified Team/Russia.

b) Create a graph to display your organized data.

c) Use your graph to predict how the different regions will perform at the next winter Olympics. Explain your prediction.

6. This table shows the population of Earth at various times in the last 250 years.

Year	Population (billions)
1750	0.80
1800	0.95
1850	1.20
1900	1.70
1950	2.55
2000	6.00

a) Construct a graph to display the data.

b) Estimate the population of Earth in 2050. What assumptions did you make?

NEL

Chapter Self-Test

1. The following database shows precipitation totals (in millimetres) for various cities in Canada.

City	Prov.	Jan.	April	July	Oct.
Calgary	AB	11.6	23.9	67.9	13.9
Charlottetown	PE	106.4	87.8	85.8	108.6
Churchill	MB	16.9	19.0	56.0	46.9
Dawson	YT	19.2	8.0	48.4	31.6
Edmonton	AB	22.5	26.0	91.7	17.9
Fredericton	NB	109.6	87.4	87.1	97.7
Halifax	NS	134.7	114.3	107.4	126.6
Hamilton	ON	65.8	78.0	86.5	72.5
Iqualuit	NU	21.1	28.2	59.4	36.7
Kitchener	ON	64.4	76.9	91.8	65.6
Moncton	NB	119.2	99.3	103.3	103.8
Montreal	QC	70.4	76.1	90.1	77.6

   a) Construct a scatter plot to see if there is a relationship between the precipitation in January and the precipitation in April.

   b) Why was a scatter plot an appropriate graph to use in part (a)?

2. The mayor of a town has money in the budget to build a library, an arena, or a swimming pool. The population of the town is 30 000. The mayor wonders how many people she should survey to help her decide what to build: 25, 100, 2000, 4000, 5000, 10 000, 15 000, or 20 000 people.

   a) Which sample size would give the mayor the most confidence that she made the correct decision? Explain.

   b) Why might the mayor not use this sample size?

3. Use the database in question 1.

   a) Compare the precipitation in eastern cities and western cities during the fall and winter months. Explain how you used the database to do this.

   b) Is it reasonable to conclude that your results in part (a) can represent all cities in eastern and western Canada? Explain

4. People entering a mall were asked "What is your height?" Below are the heights of the first 30 people. The heights are rounded to the nearest centimetre.

162	171	181	166	182	176
183	187	166	188	188	190
177	168	184	174	183	171
180	169	175	179	164	178
174	170	184	172	177	177

   a) Organize the heights in a frequency table. How did you decide on your intervals?

   b) Use your frequency table to construct a histogram.

5. Below are daily temperature readings (in degrees Celsius) for the month of April last year.

10	30	22	10	13	14	5	13
10	14	15	13	23	17	16	12
5	15	12	17	11	16	14	12
15	5	25	12	12	10		

   a) Determine the mean, median, and mode temperatures for April.

   b) Repeat part (a) after removing the three greatest and three least temperatures. Which measure was affected the most? Explain.

Chapter Review

Frequently Asked Questions

Q: How are bar graphs and histograms similar and different?

A: Similarities

- The bars are the same width.
- Data categories are shown on the horizontal axis.

Differences

Bar graphs:

- Categories do not have to be numeric intervals.
- Categories can appear in any order.
- Spaces between bars indicate that the categories are separate from one another.
- Not all bar graphs show frequency.

Histograms:

- Categories must be numeric intervals.
- Categories must be in ascending order.
- The right boundary of an interval is the left boundary of the next interval.
- All histograms show frequency.

Comparing Number of Children with Number of Pets

Number of families: 0, 4, 8, 12

more children | more pets | same

Family make-up

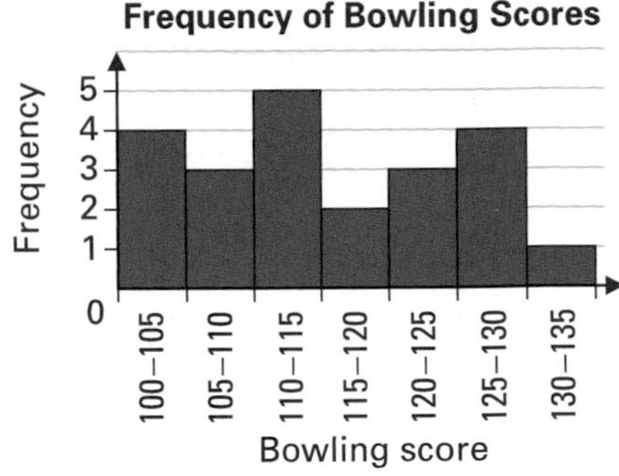

Q: How do you know when to use the mean, median, or mode to compare sets of data?

A: The mode is the only value that can be used for non-numeric data. A set of data could have no mode or several modes. Use the mode when you have non-numeric data or are only interested in the most frequently occurring data item.

The mean is calculated using every item of data, so it can be affected by extremely low or extremely high values. The median is not affected as much by extreme values. If you think extreme values should be taken into account, use the mean. If you think extreme values should not be taken into account, use the median.

NEL

Practice Questions

(3.1) **1.** The following database shows population characteristics for selected countries.

Country	Life expectancy (years)	Per capita income (U.S. $)	Number of people per motor vehicle
Bangladesh	57	230	1200
Brazil	66	3 370	9
Canada	78	19 570	1.6
China	70	530	225
Ethiopia	50	130	800
Iceland	79	24 590	1.8
India	59	310	225
Japan	80	34 630	2.1
Mexico	73	4 010	9
Norway	78	26 480	2.2

a) Compare the data to determine a relationship between life expectancy and income.

b) Construct a scatter plot to compare the number of people per motor vehicle and income. Is there a relationship between these two factors?

(3.2) **2.** When analyzing a survey, would you be more confident in the results from a census or a sample? Explain why.

(3.4) **3.** The distances, in kilometres, that employees of one company drive to work each day are listed below.

7.1	9.3	40.4	36.7	27.6	14.1
19.5	55.9	46.2	41.1	50	28.6
27.5	33.0	39.8	21.6	8.5	65
61.3	59.9	39.2	37.5	44.1	49.5
45.9	49.8	31.5	29.7	22.6	19.4

a) Organize the distances in a frequency table. Explain your choice of intervals.

b) Display the data in a histogram.

4. a) Organize the following data in a stem-and-leaf plot.

219 151 199 186 170 186 194
184 196 185 174 186 197 170
178 179 182 193 195 171

b) Use your stem-and-leaf plot to determine the median and the mode.

c) Calculate the mean of the data.

d) Remove the greatest and least values, and determine the mean, median, and mode. Which measure is affected the most? Explain why. (3.5)

5. Consider the following data:

525, 575, 495, 63, 450, 560, 500

Explain how the mean and the median are affected by including each value below with these data. (3.5)

a) 1500 **b)** 499 **c)** 1

6. This database shows the lunchtime beverage choices of the Grade 7 and 8 students in one school. (3.6)

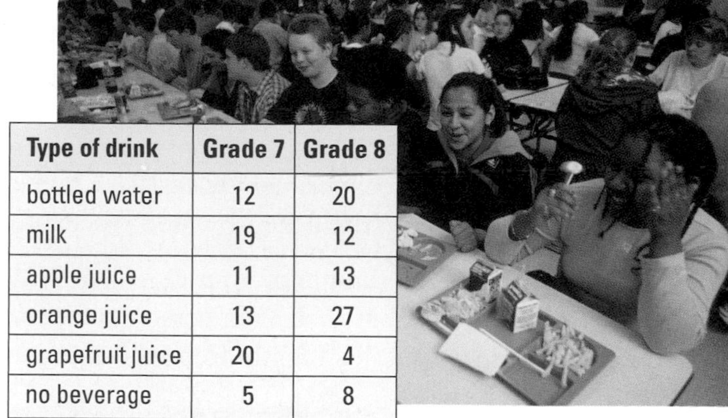

Type of drink	Grade 7	Grade 8
bottled water	12	20
milk	19	12
apple juice	11	13
orange juice	13	27
grapefruit juice	20	4
no beverage	5	8

a) Which grade has a greater percent of students who prefer juice?

b) Which three beverages should be offered at lunch? Present your opinion in a letter to the principal. Include a graph to make your argument convincing.

Chapter Task

Jumping Ability

Many sports involve vertical jumping.

What factors affect how high a person can jump? Is there a relationship between height and vertical jumping ability? Is there a relationship between arm or leg length and vertical jumping ability?

? Which measure is the best predictor of vertical jumping ability for students in your class—height, arm length, or leg length?

A. Design an experiment to test how high a person can jump, on average. Write a step-by-step procedure for your experiment.

B. Choose a sample of your classmates. Measure the height of each student. Ask each person to measure his or her arm length and leg length. Record these measurements.

C. Use your experiment to test the average vertical jumping ability of each student in your sample. Organize and present your findings.

D. Use graphs and your data in steps B and C to look for relationships between average vertical jumping ability and height, arm length, or leg length. Based on your sample, which measure is the best predictor of vertical jumping ability?

Task Checklist

- ☑ Did you use a large enough sample to have confidence in your results?
- ☑ Did you use an appropriate method to organize your data?
- ☑ Are your graphs appropriate for your data?
- ☑ Did your graphs answer the question and justify your conclusion?

Cumulative Review
Chapters 1–3

Cross-Strand Multiple Choice

(1.2) **1.** What is the prime factorization of 7056?

A. $2^2 \times 3^2 \times 5^2$ **C.** $2^4 \times 3^3 \times 7$

B. $2^4 \times 3^2 \times 7^2$ **D.** $2^3 \times 3^2 \times 7^2$

(1.6) **2.** Which value is closest to $\sqrt{640}$?

A. 25 **C.** 27

B. 80 **D.** 8

(1.7) **3.** What is the result of $(3.5 + 4.2 \times 1.6^2 + 3)^2$, to three decimal places?

A. 234.702 **C.** 11 545.158

B. 17.252 **D.** 297.632

(2.1) **4.** Which set of numbers is ordered from least to greatest?

A. $0.6, 0.6\overline{1}, \frac{5}{8}, \frac{7}{11}, 0.\overline{6}$

B. $0.6\overline{1}, 0.6, \frac{5}{8}, \frac{7}{11}, 0.\overline{6}$

C. $0.\overline{6}, 0.6, \frac{7}{11}, \frac{5}{8}, 0.6\overline{1}$

D. $0.6, 0.6\overline{1}, \frac{7}{11}, \frac{5}{8}, 0.\overline{6}$

(2.4) **5.** Reilly, Maria, and Tamara figured out that the ratio of the times they spent painting a deck is 3:5:1. They are going to use this ratio to share the $36.90 they earned. How much will Maria get?

A. $4.10 **C.** $12.30

B. $16.40 **D.** $20.50

(2.5) **6.** Jacob travelled 708 km on a bus in 8 h. Alissa travelled 496 km on a train in 5 h. What was the speed of the faster vehicle?

A. 99.2 km/h **C.** 141.6 km/h

B. 62.0 km/h **D.** 88.5 km/h

7. Peter bought a snowboard for $326. Marcy bought a snowboard for 135% of this price. How much did Marcy pay? (2.6)

A. $211.90 **C.** $4401

B. $114.10 **D.** $440.10

8. This cordless mouse is on sale. What is the discount? (2.8)

A. $71.92 **C.** $107.88

B. $17.98 **D.** $71.20

9. Which statement about a histogram is not true? (3.4)

A. A histogram shows the number of values in each category.

B. Any data that can be displayed using a bar graph can also be displayed using a histogram.

C. All the bars of a histogram are the same width.

D. There are no spaces between the bars.

10. An athlete received these scores at a competition. What is the mean (to the nearest tenth) after removing the greatest and least scores? (3.5)

9.8
8.8
7.6
10.0
9.0
8.6
8.8

A. 8.9 **C.** 9.1

B. 6.4 **D.** 9.0

Cross-Strand Investigation

Eastside Arena held a student job fair. Chang and Martina visited several booths at the fair and collected the following data about hourly rates of pay.

Type of job	Hourly rates of pay ($)								
restaurants	7.55	8.00	9.90	10.75	8.45	8.45	7.75	8.75	7.95
stores	12.30	7.80	8.10	7.75	10.00	9.25	7.85	9.15	7.85
recreation	10.20	9.50	11.80	8.70	12.20	12.95	8.90	7.90	10.50
advertising	9.20	10.50	10.00	11.15	8.45	8.00	9.25	9.20	11.10

Note: If possible, use a spreadsheet program for this investigation. If you do not have access to a computer with a spreadsheet program, use a calculator.

11. a) Calculate the mean hourly rate of pay for restaurants. Then remove the greatest and least hourly rates of pay, and determine the mean. Which mean do you think better represents the hourly rates of pay? Why?

b) Organize the hourly rates of pay for all employees in a frequency table. Explain your choice of intervals.

c) Use your frequency table to construct a histogram. Explain what your histogram shows about the hourly rates of pay.

d) The job fair committee decided to give a button and a bookmark to each student who visited the fair. The buttons came in packages of 30. The bookmarks came in packages of 50. The committee needed the same number of each left over for another fair. The committee estimated that 400 students would visit the fair. How many packages of buttons and packages of bookmarks did they need? Explain your reasoning.

Job Fair

I went to the job fair.

CHAPTER 4

Patterns and Relationships

▶ GOALS

You will be able to

- identify and extend patterns
- use algebra to describe pattern rules
- represent relationships using tables of values and scatter plots
- solve problems that involve patterns

Getting Started

You will need
- grid paper
- a ruler

Calendar Patterns

Hoshi coloured seven spaces on a calendar page to create an H-pattern.

? Which sums between 80 and 90 are possible in an H-pattern on a calendar?

A. Calculate the sum of the numbers in the H-pattern on the calendar page shown.

B. Repeat step A for three more H-patterns in other locations on the calendar page.

C. Describe, in words, how the sum of each H-pattern is related to its middle number.

D. Consider the H-pattern shown above. Add two numbers shaded with the same colour. How does the sum compare with the middle number in the H-pattern? Repeat for the two other pairs of shaded numbers.

E. Repeat step D for each of your three H-patterns.

F. Copy and complete this H-pattern diagram, replacing each ? with an algebraic expression.

?		?
$n - 1$	n	?
?		$n + 8$

G. Use step D, E, or F to explain why your rule in step C is correct.

H. Hoshi coloured another H-pattern on a different calendar page. The sum of the numbers in this H-pattern is 77. What are the numbers?

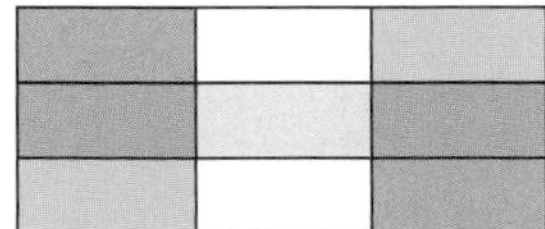

I. How do you know that a sum of 78 is not possible for an H-pattern on a calendar page?

J. Which sums between 80 and 90 are possible for an H-pattern on a calendar page?

Do You Remember?

1. Determine the greatest common factor of each set of numbers.
   - a) 12 and 28
   - b) 16 and 60
   - c) 44, 22, and 88
   - d) 95, 25, and 55

2. a) Copy and complete the table of values.

Figure number	Figure	Number of counters
1	● ● ● (vertical column of 3 counters)	
2	cross of 5 counters	
3	cross of 7 counters	
4		
5		

   b) Describe the patterns you see in the table of values.

   c) What is the relationship between the figure number and the number of counters in each figure?

   d) How many counters would you need to make the 10th figure in the sequence?

3. Write the next three terms in each sequence. Describe the pattern rule.
   - a) 3, 6, 9, 12, …
   - b) 2, 6, 10, 14, …
   - c) 1, 3, 6, 10, …
   - d) 1, 4, 9, 16, …

4. Write an algebraic expression for each phrase, using the variable n.
   - a) a number increased by four
   - b) five times a number, plus two
   - c) a number tripled
   - d) four times a number, minus one

5. Substitute for the variable in each expression and evaluate, if $a = 4.8$ and $b = 14$.
   - a) $15 - a$
   - b) $3b + 2$
   - c) $6b - 5$
   - d) $0.8 + 4a$

6. a) What stays the same and what changes in this pattern?

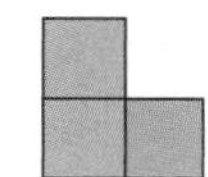

Figure 1

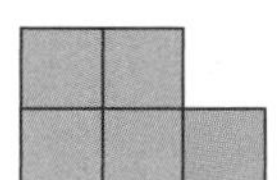

Figure 2

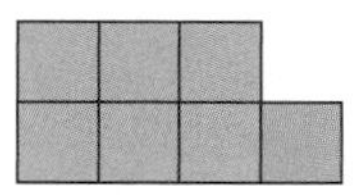

Figure 3

   b) Describe the pattern rule in words.

   c) Write a pattern rule using a variable.

   d) How many square tiles will there be in figure 5?

7. Rosa uses a table of values to record her savings from her weekly paycheque.

Number of weeks	Savings ($)
1	15
2	30
3	45
4	60

   a) Use Rosa's data to make a scatter plot.

   b) Use your scatter plot to determine how much Rosa will have saved by the end of nine weeks.

   c) By the end of which week will she have saved $90?

4.1 Exploring Relationships in the Fibonacci Sequence

You will need
- a calculator
- a highlighter pen

▶ **GOAL**

Identify and discuss relationships within a number pattern.

Explore the Math

The following problem was proposed by an Italian mathematician named Leonardo of Pisa, also known as Fibonacci, who lived about 800 years ago.

Suppose that a pair of rabbits (male and female) cannot reproduce until they are mature at two months old. Also suppose that every month from then on, a new pair of rabbits (also male and female) is born. If the pattern continues, how many pairs of rabbits are there at the beginning of each month?

Month	Mature pairs	Immature pairs	Total pairs
1		1	1
2	1		1
3	1	1	2
4	2	1	3
5	3	2	5
6	5	3	8
7	8	5	13

The solution to this problem is a number pattern called the Fibonacci sequence:
1, 1, 2, 3, 5, 8, 13, 21, 34, …

Starting from the 3rd number, each **term** in the Fibonacci sequence is the sum of the two preceding terms.

term
each number in a sequence; for example, in the sequence 1, 3, 5, 7, …, the 3rd term is 5

? What number relationships can you identify in the Fibonacci sequence?

A. Copy the Fibonacci sequence. Highlight every 3rd term in the sequence. What is the greatest common factor of these terms?

1, 1, 2, 3, 5, 8, 13, 21, 34, …

B. Copy the Fibonacci sequence. Highlight every 4th term in the sequence. What is the greatest common factor of these terms?

1, 1, 2, 3, 5, 8, 13, 21, 34, 55, 89, 144, …

C. Repeat step B for every 5th term and for every 6th term in the Fibonacci sequence.

D. Summarize your results in steps A, B, and C. What can you conclude?

E. Copy the Fibonacci sequence. Highlight the 1st, 2nd, and 3rd terms in the sequence. Determine the sum.

F. Copy the Fibonacci sequence. Highlight the 2nd, 3rd, and 4th terms in the sequence. Determine the sum.

G. Continue the pattern in steps E and F to determine six more sums. Record these sums as a new sequence. (The first three sums are listed for you below.) Does the new sequence have properties that are similar to properties of the Fibonacci sequence? If so, describe these properties.

1, 1, 2, 3, 5, 8, 13, 21, 34, … Sum: $1 + 1 + 2 = 4$
1, 1, 2, 3, 5, 8, 13, 21, 34, … Sum: $1 + 2 + 3 = 6$
1, 1, 2, 3, 5, 8, 13, 21, 34, … Sum: $2 + 3 + 5 = 10$
The new sequence is 4, 6, 10, ….

H. Repeat step G, but add four terms each time. What can you conclude?

I. Choose three consecutive terms in the Fibonacci sequence. Square the middle term. Calculate the product of the other two terms. What is the relationship between these two values?

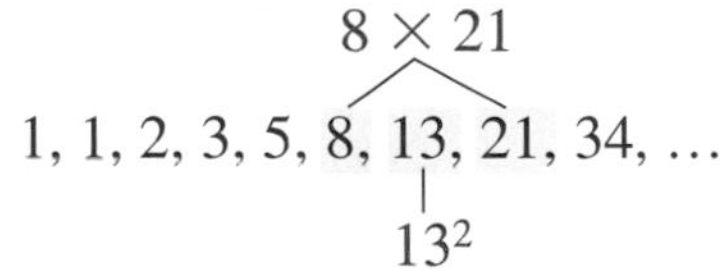

J. Check to see if the relationship you discovered in step I is true for other sets of three consecutive terms in the Fibonacci sequence.

K. Identify other relationships using the Fibonacci sequence.

Reflecting

1. Describe the relationships you discovered in the Fibonacci sequence.

2. What strategies did you use to search for relationships?

3. How many examples of a relationship do you need to check before you start to believe that the relationship might be true for the entire Fibonacci sequence?

4.2 Creating Pattern Rules from Models

You will need
- coloured square tiles
- toothpicks
- coloured pencils

▶ **GOAL**

Use algebraic expressions to describe patterns.

Learn about the Math

Chad, Benjamin, and Toma used coloured tiles to create three different models that represent the same pattern. Each student then used the **variable** t to write a different **algebraic expression** to describe the number of tiles in each figure in the pattern.

variable

a letter or symbol, such as *a*, *b*, or *n*, that represents a number

algebraic expression

a combination of one or more variables; it may include numbers and operation signs

Chad's model shows $3t + 3$.

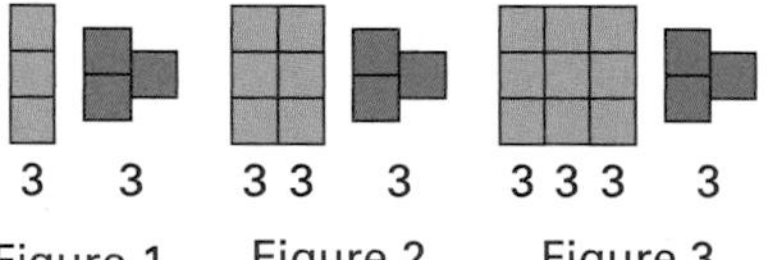

Benjamin's model shows $t + t + t + 3$.

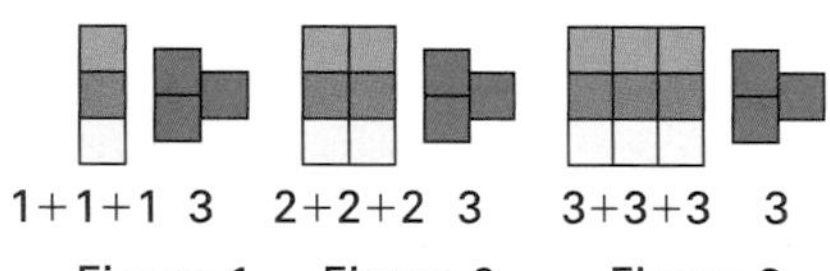

Toma's model shows $3(t + 1)$.

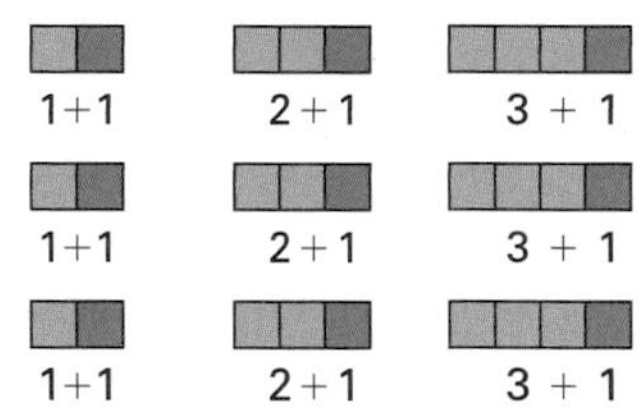

? How do the students' models relate to their algebraic pattern rules?

A. How did Chad use colour to show which part of his pattern stays the same and which part changes?

B. How does Chad's model relate to his algebraic pattern rule?

C. Repeat steps A and B for Benjamin's and Toma's models and algebraic expressions.

D. The total number of tiles in each figure of the pattern is a multiple of 3. Which pattern rule shows this most clearly?

Reflecting

1. How could you use coloured tiles to show that the pattern rule $6 + 3 \times (n - 1)$ also represents the same pattern?

2. How do you know that all these pattern rules must be equivalent?

Work with the Math

Example: Identifying and describing a pattern rule

Write a pattern rule to describe the number of toothpicks in each figure of this toothpick fence.

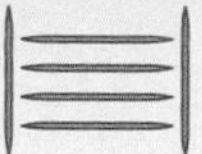
Figure 1

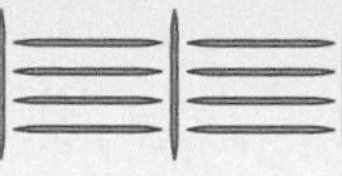
Figure 2

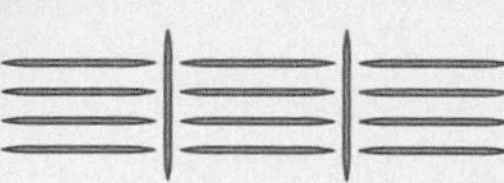
Figure 3

Hoshi's Solution

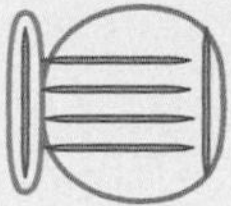
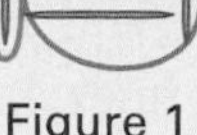
Figure 1

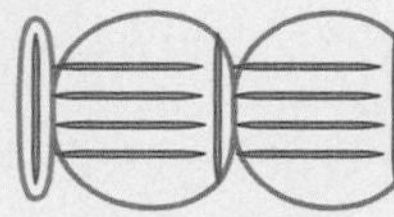
Figure 2

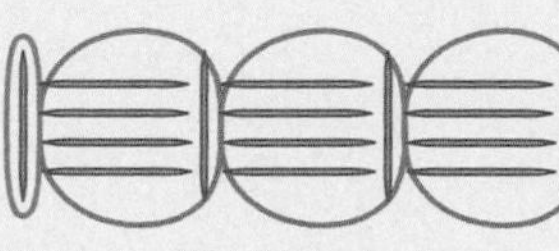
Figure 3

I used a purple pencil to circle the part of the pattern that changes. I see that each new section of fence has 5 more toothpicks.

I used a red pencil to circle the part of the pattern that stays constant. There is always 1 post at the beginning of each figure.

I wanted the number of sections in each figure to be the same as the figure number.

I checked to make sure that my pattern rule works.

My variable is n. It represents the number of sections of fence. My pattern rule is $5n + 1$.

Check:
In figure 1, the total is $5(1) + 1 = 6$. ✓
In figure 2, the total is $5(2) + 1 = 11$. ✓
In figure 3, the total is $5(3) + 1 = 16$. ✓

Tran's Solution

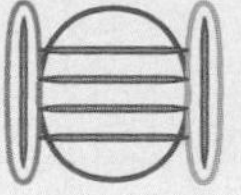
Figure 1

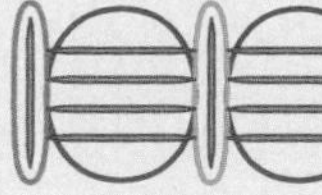
Figure 2

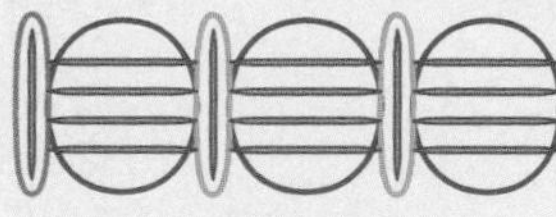
Figure 3

I circled the first post in red because that's what each figure begins with. It doesn't change.

The rest of each figure is the part that changes. Each section of fence that is added has 4 rails and 1 post.

My pattern rule describes the relationship between the figure number and the total number of toothpicks.

I checked to make sure that my pattern rule works.

I used the variable s to represent the number of sections of fence after the first post.

My pattern rule is $s(4 + 1) + 1$.

Check:
In figure 1, I get $1(4 + 1) + 1 = 6$. ✓
In figure 2, I get $2(4 + 1) + 1 = 11$. ✓
In figure 3, I get $3(4 + 1) + 1 = 16$. ✓

A Checking

3. a) Which part of this pattern changes? Which part stays the same?

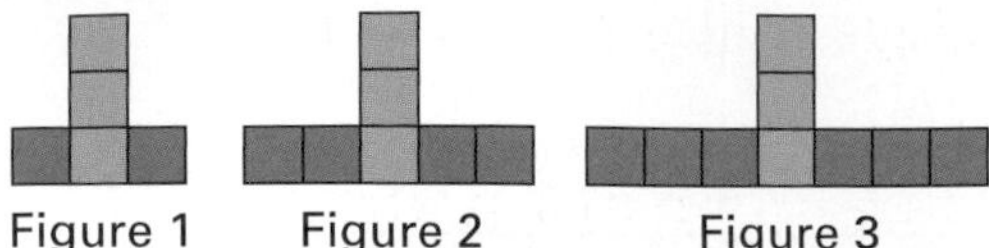

b) Use an algebraic expression to describe the number of tiles in terms of the figure number.

4. Describe this pattern rule in words. Then write two different algebraic expressions to describe the pattern rule.

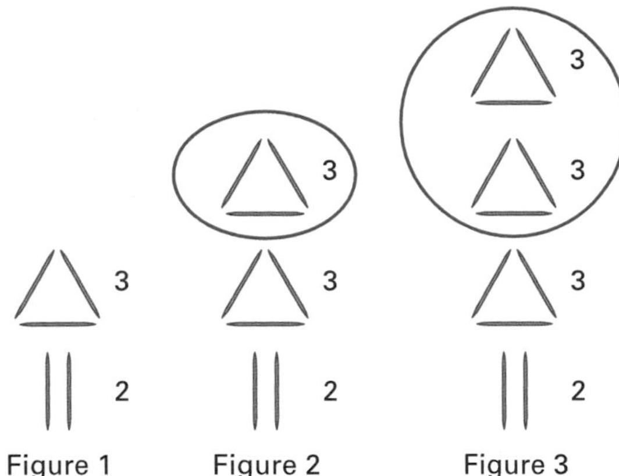

B Practising

5. These two models show the same pattern in two different ways.

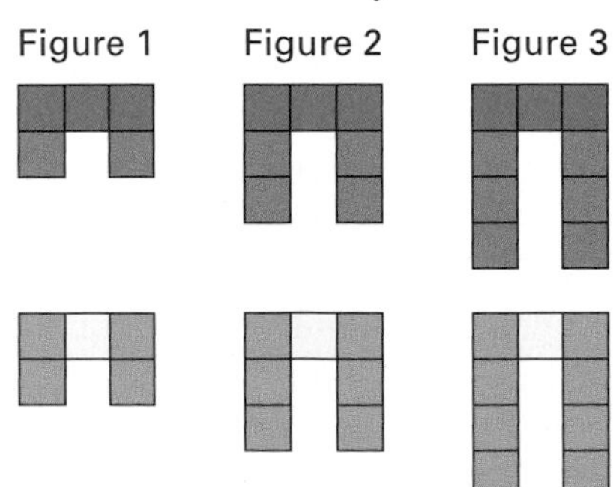

a) Describe what changes and what stays the same in each model.

b) Write an algebraic pattern rule for each model.

6. The variable n represents the figure number in the following algebraic pattern rules:

A. $4n$ **B.** $2n + 2$ **C.** $3n + 1$ **D.** $4n - 1$

Which of these pattern rules describes the toothpick pattern shown below? Explain how you know.

7. Write two algebraic pattern rules for this toothpick pattern.

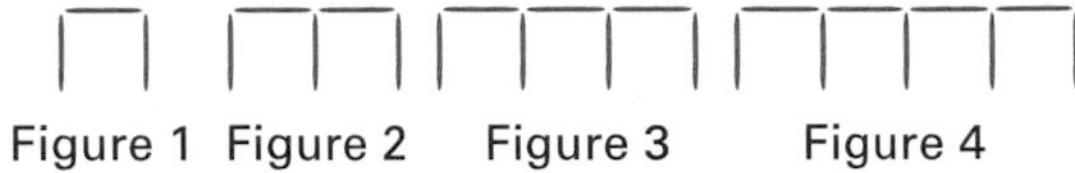

8. The following fence pattern starts with a gate and increases by one section in each consecutive figure. Write two algebraic pattern rules for this pattern.

9. a) Write an algebraic expression that describes the pattern rule for the number of red tiles.

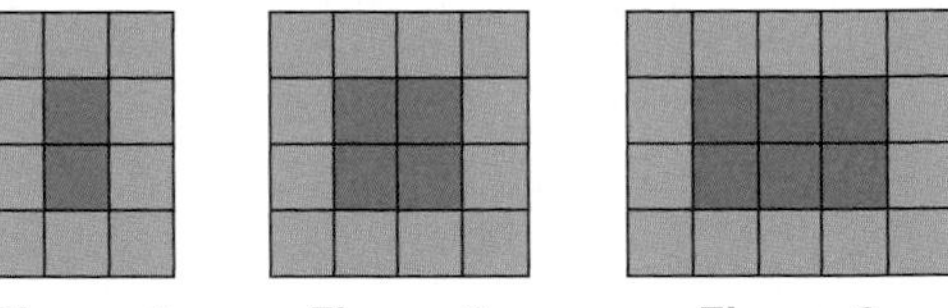

b) Repeat part (a) for the blue tiles. Explain your thinking.

10. Use the pattern in question 9.

a) Can you make a figure with an odd number of blue tiles? Explain.

b) How many blue tiles would you need to make a figure that has 10 red tiles?

NEL

11. Describe this pattern rule in words, and then with an algebraic expression.

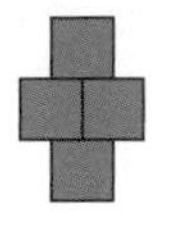

Figure 1

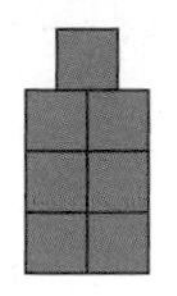

Figure 2

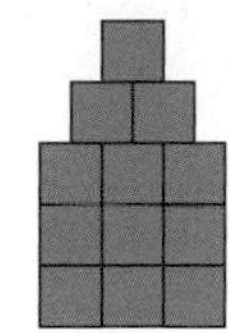

Figure 3

12. Use each description to draw a diagram and write an algebraic pattern rule.

a) In figure 1, there are four tiles in a row and two tiles on top. Another row of four tiles is added on the bottom of each consecutive figure.

b) In figure 1, there are four tiles in a row and two tiles on top. Another two tiles are added on the top of each consecutive figure.

c) The total number of tiles is the figure number squared, plus the figure number.

C Extending

13. a) Write an algebraic expression that describes the pattern rule for the number of red tiles.

Figure 1

Figure 2

Figure 3

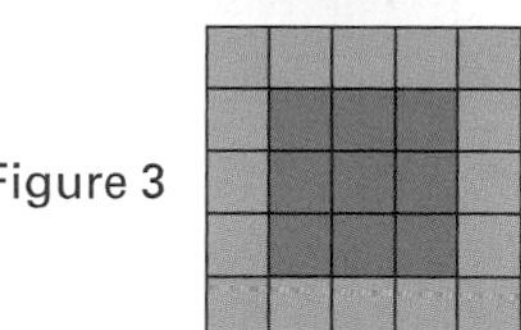

b) Repeat part (a) for the blue tiles.

c) Write two different algebraic expressions that describe the total number of tiles in the pattern.

Mental Imagery

MOVING TOOTHPICKS

You will need
- toothpicks

Maria's little brother made the following pens for his tiny toy animals, using toothpicks.

1. How can you move only two toothpicks to leave four square pens?

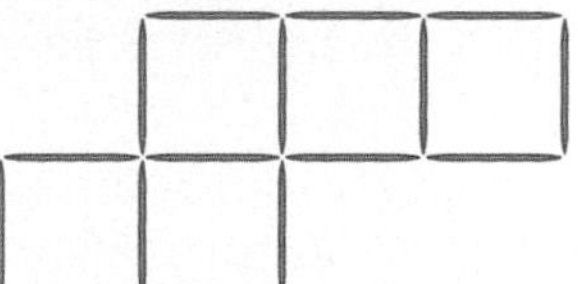

2. How can you move only two toothpicks to turn the L shape upside down?

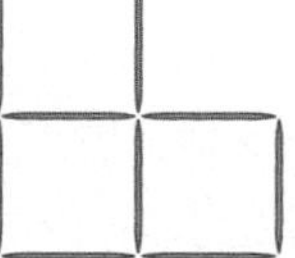

3. How can you remove only two toothpicks to leave two square pens?

4. How can you remove only three toothpicks to leave three triangular pens?

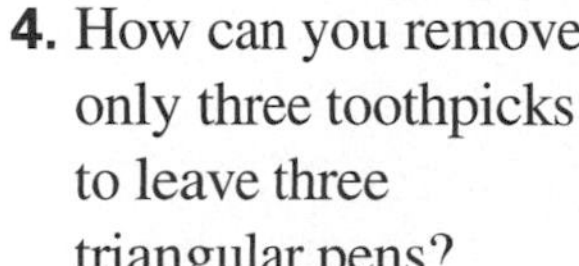

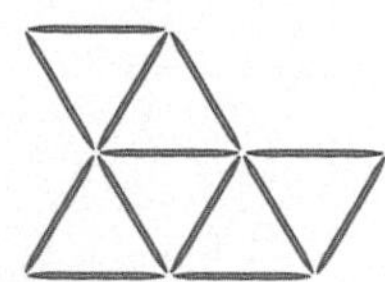

4.3 The General Term of a Sequence

You will need
- counters

▶ **GOAL**
Write an algebraic expression for the general term of a sequence.

Learn about the Math

Maria is using counters to make a sequence of rectangular figures. The first three figures have 6, 9, and 12 counters.

? How many counters would Maria need to make the 100th figure?

Example 1: Using systematic trial

Determine a pattern rule for the sequence 6, 9, 12, 15, ...

Maria's Solution

Term number	Term value
1	6
2	9
3	12
4	15

I made a table of values using the first few terms in the sequence.

Then I used guess and test to find the pattern rule with variable t.

First I tried $6t$ because when $t = 1$, $6t$ is $6(1) = 6$. However, $6t$ doesn't work when $t = 2$ because $6(2) \neq 9$.

Next I tried $5t + 1$ because when $t = 1$, you get $5(1) + 1 = 6$. But $5t + 1$ doesn't work when $t = 2$ because $5(2) + 1 \neq 9$.

Next I tried $4t + 2$. It works when $t = 1$, but not when $t = 2$ because $4(2) + 2 \neq 9$.

Then I tried $3t + 3$. It works when $t = 1$. It also works when $t = 2$ because $3(2) + 3 = 9$, when $t = 3$ because $3(3) + 3 = 12$, and when $t = 4$ because $3(4) + 3 = 15$.

The pattern rule is $3t + 3$, where t is the term number.

NEL

Example 2: Using logical reasoning

Determine a pattern rule for the sequence 6, 9, 12, 15, ...

Toma's Solution

Term number	Term value
1	6
2	9
3	12
4	15

+ 3
+ 3
+ 3

If t represents the term number, the rule is $3t + 3$.

I used a table of values. I noticed that when you go down the second column, you add 3 more counters for each new row.

I know that repeated addition is the same as multiplication. So, I know that the pattern rule has to include $3t$.

If I try $3t$ by itself as the pattern rule, I get 3, 6, 9, 12, ... This is not corrrect because each term is too low by 3.

If I add 3, I'll have the right pattern rule: $3t + 3$.

I checked my pattern rule on all the term numbers, and it works.

Using the pattern rule $3t + 3$, the value of the 100th term is

$$\begin{aligned} 3(100) + 3 &= 300 + 3 \\ &= 303 \end{aligned}$$

Maria would need 303 counters to make the 100th figure.

Communication Tip

A pattern rule that uses a variable, such as n, to describe term values in a sequence is usually called the nth term of the sequence. It is also called the general term.

Reflecting

1. Why is it useful to create an algebraic expression for the general term of a sequence?
2. What strategies can you use to create an algebraic expression for the general term of a sequence?

Work with the Math

Example 3: Representing the nth term of a sequence

Determine an algebraic expression for the nth term of the sequence 2, 6, 10, 14, ...

Solution

Term number	Term value
1	2
2	6
3	10
4	14

+ 4
+ 4
+ 4

The term value increases by 4 each time.
If you use the expression $4n$, you get the sequence 4, 8, 12, 16, ... Each term is too high by 2.
So, the correct expression for the nth term is $4n - 2$.

When you check this expression using each term number, you get the original sequence: 2, 6, 10, 14, ...

A Checking

3. a) Copy and complete the table of values for the sequence shown.

Term number (figure number)	Picture	Term value (number of squares)
1		2
2		
3		
4		
5		

b) Create an algebraic expression for the nth term of the sequence.

c) Use your algebraic expression to calculate the 30th term in the sequence.

B Practising

4. a) Make a table of values for the sequence 6, 11, 16, 21, 26, ...

b) Write an algebraic expression for the general term of the sequence.

c) Use your expression for the general term to calculate the 25th term in the sequence.

5. Hendryk and Nilay are looking at this table of values. Hendryk says that the pattern rule is $2n + 3$. Nilay says that the pattern rule is $3n + 2$. Which student is right? Explain your thinking.

Term number	Term value
1	5
2	7
3	9
4	11
5	13

6. a) Write an algebraic expression for the nth term of this sequence.

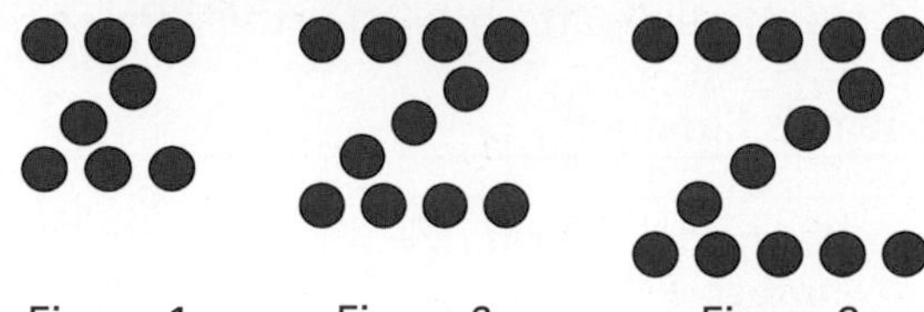

Figure 1 Figure 2 Figure 3

b) Calculate the number of counters you would need to make the 80th figure in this sequence.

c) Determine the figure number of the Z you could make using 41 counters.

7. Vanya says that the 15th figure in this sequence contains 225 small triangles. Is she correct? Explain your thinking.

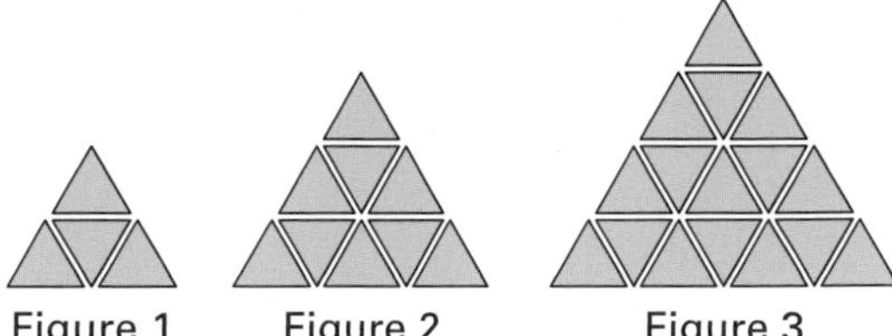

Figure 1 Figure 2 Figure 3

8. Benjamin made a rectangular sequence using coloured counters.

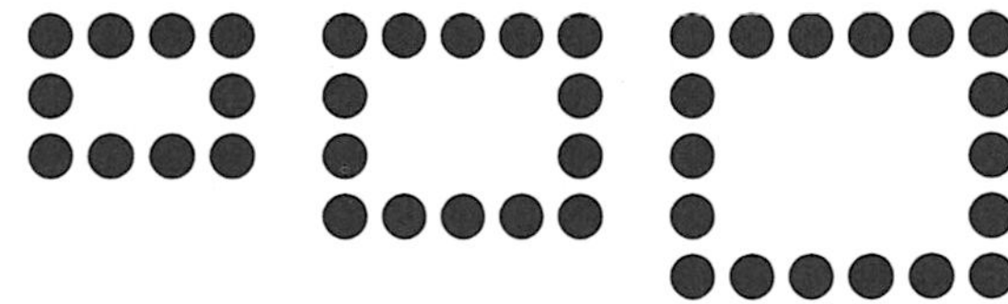

Figure 1 Figure 2 Figure 3

a) Describe the pattern rule in words.

b) Write an algebraic expression for the general term of the sequence.

c) Determine the figure number of the rectangle you could make using 50 counters.

d) Calculate the number of blue counters you would need to make the 75th rectangle in the sequence.

9. Write an algebraic expression for the nth term of each sequence. Then use your expression to calculate the 50th term in the sequence.
   a) 5, 9, 13, 17, 21, …
   b) 11, 13, 15, 17, 19, …
   c) 26, 31, 36, 41, 46, …
   d) 10, 40, 70, 100, 130, …
   e) 101, 201, 301, 401, 501, …

10. a) Start with the 5th row of a multiplication table (the multiplication-by-5 row). Add 3 to each number in the row.
   b) Determine an algebraic pattern rule for the sequence in part (a).
   c) Choose a different row of the multiplication table. Add (or subtract) a number of your choice to each number in the row. Then determine an algebraic pattern rule for the resulting sequence.
   d) Discuss how the sequences in parts (b) and (c) are similar to those in question 9.

11. a) The terms of a sequence increase by the same amount. The 1st term is 7, and the 3rd term is 15. Calculate the 7th term. Then write an algebraic expression for the general term.
   b) The terms of a different sequence also increase by the same amount. The 3rd term is 7, and the 7th term is 15. Calculate the 17th term. Then write an algebraic expression for the general term.

C Extending

12. Write an algebraic expression for the nth term of each sequence. Then use your expression to calculate the 50th term in the sequence.
   a) 29, 27, 25, 23, 21, …
   b) 118, 117, 116, 115, 114, …

13. a) Write an algebraic expression for the nth term of this sequence.

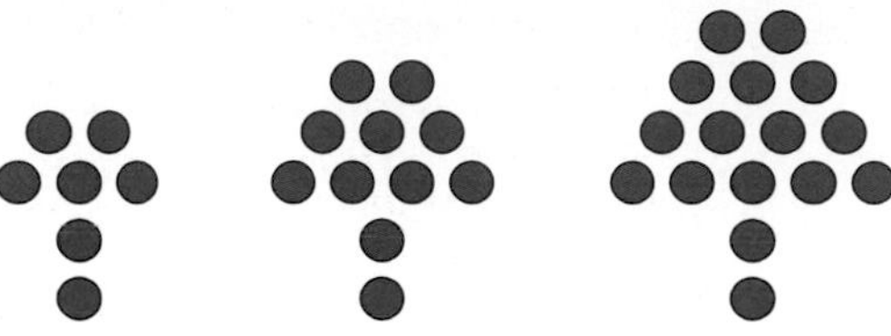

   b) Use your expression to predict the number of blue counters in the 100th figure.
   c) Describe another strategy you could use to predict the number of blue counters in the 100th figure.

14. a) Make a table of values that shows the total number of cubes in the first five figures of this staircase pattern.

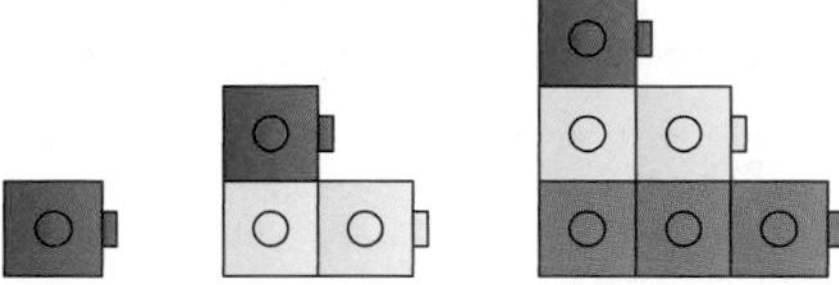

   b) Write an algebraic pattern rule.
   c) Calculate the number of cubes you would need to build the 10th figure in this staircase pattern.

15. Consider the staircase pattern in question 14.
   a) Imagine a staircase with many rows in this pattern. Use your imaginary staircase to make a new pattern, in which the 1st term is the number of cubes in the 1st row, the 2nd term is the number of cubes in the 2nd row, and so on. Write the first six terms in your new pattern.
   b) Suppose that you made the original staircase pattern out of cubes. Could you split this pattern to show an adding strategy to calculate the total number of cubes? If so, explain how.

Mid-Chapter Review

Frequently Asked Questions

Q: How can you use a model of a sequence to determine a pattern rule?

A: You can colour code the model to help you see the parts that change and the parts that stay the same.

For example, the rule for the pattern at the right can be described as follows: "Start with a row of two red squares and a column of four blue squares. Add another row of two red squares in each consecutive figure." For figure n, there are $2n$ red squares and four blue squares. An algebraic expression for the pattern rule is $2n + 4$, where n represents the figure number.

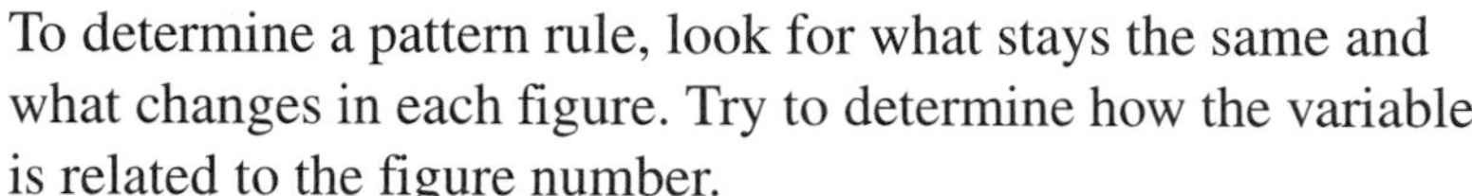

Figure 1 Figure 2 Figure 3

To determine a pattern rule, look for what stays the same and what changes in each figure. Try to determine how the variable is related to the figure number.

You can check that your algebraic expression is correct by substituting the figure number into your expression and calculating the total number of squares.

Q: How can you use a table of values to create an algebraic expression for the *n*th term, or general term, of a sequence?

A: The term numbers are listed in the first column of the table. The term values are listed in the second column. An example for the sequence 7, 9, 11, 13, … is shown.

Term number	Term value
1	7
2	9
3	11
4	13

One way to determine the *n*th term of the sequence is to use reasoning. Since the term value increases by 2 every time, you can be sure that $2n$ appears in the expression for the *n*th term. Substituting the term numbers into the expression $2n$, you get 2, 4, 6, 8, …. You can see that the terms are all too low by 5. So, the correct expression for the *n*th term is $2n + 5$.

Another way to determine the *n*th term is to use systematic trial. For example, you could try $7t$, then $6t + 1$, then $5t + 2$, then $4t + 3$, then $3t + 4$, and finally $2t + 5$. The expression $2t + 5$ works when $t = 1$ $(2 \times 1 + 5 = 7)$, $t = 2$ $(2 \times 2 + 5 = 9)$, and so on.

Practice Questions

(4.1) **1. a)** Describe the following sequence in words:

2, 2, 4, 6, 10, 16, 26, …

b) Could 947 be a term in the sequence? Explain.

c) Compare the square of the 4th term with the product of the previous term (3rd term) and the following term (5th term). Describe the relationship. Is this relationship valid for other terms in the sequence?

d) How does the relationship in part (c) compare with the relationship between the square of a term and the product of the previous and following terms of the Fibonacci sequence?

(4.1) **2. a)** Determine an algebraic expression for the *n*th term of the following sequence.

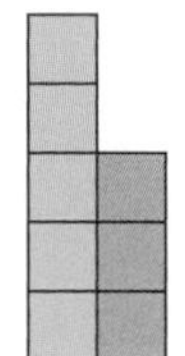
Figure 1

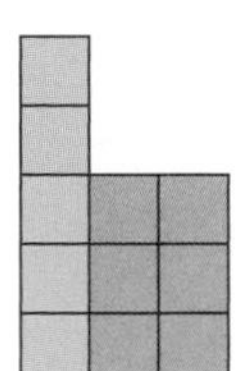
Figure 2

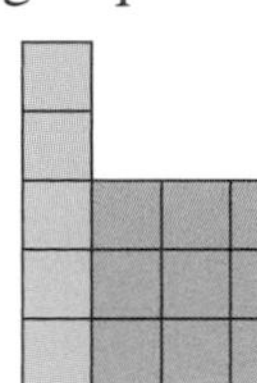
Figure 3

b) Explain how the colours of the tiles in the diagrams are related to the algebraic expression.

(4.2) **3. a)** Use colour to model this pattern in two ways.

Figure 1

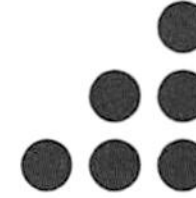
Figure 2

Figure 3

b) Write the algebraic pattern rule for each of your models.

4. a) Determine an algebraic expression for the *n*th term of the sequence 7, 10, 13, 16, ….

b) Determine an algebraic expression for the *n*th term of the sequence 8, 11, 14, 17, ….

c) Compare your algebraic expressions in parts (a) and (b). (4.2)

5. Simone wrote the sequence 5, 7, 9, 11, …. (4.3)

a) Write an algebraic expression for the *n*th term of the sequence.

b) Calculate the 50th term in the sequence.

c) Determine which term has a value of 25.

6. Write an algebraic expression for the *n*th term of each sequence. Then use your expression to calculate the 100th term in the sequence. (4.3)

a) 8, 14, 20, 26, 32, …

b) 15, 18, 21, 24, 27, …

c) 11, 22, 33, 44, 55, …

d) 9, 10, 11, 12, 13, …

e) 47, 63, 79, 95, 111, …

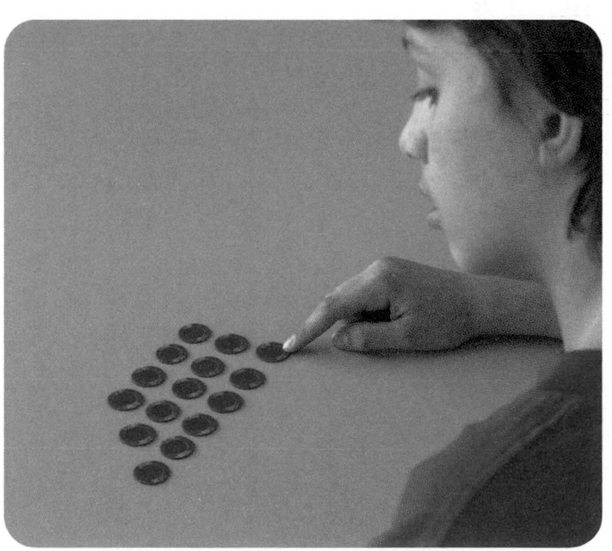

You will need
- a calculator

4.4 Solve Problems by Examining Simpler Problems

▶ **GOAL**
Solve problems by examining simpler problems first.

Learn about the Math

Tran works at a golf course, setting up practice balls on the driving range.

? How many golf balls are in Tran's pyramid?

1 Understand the Problem

Tran knows that the golf balls are arranged in layers to form a square-based pyramid. There are 8 layers in total.

2 Make a Plan

Tran realizes that solving a simpler problem first might help him solve the problem. He decides to figure out how many golf balls there would be in a smaller pyramid.

3 Carry Out the Plan

Tran makes a table of values to organize his information. Then he looks for a pattern.

Layer number	Number of golf balls in each layer	Pattern	Total number of golf balls
1	$1^2 = 1$	1	1
2	$2^2 = 4$	$1 + 4$	5
3	$3^2 = 9$	$1 + 4 + 9$	14

Tran notices that the number of golf balls in each layer is the layer number squared. This means that layer 4 contains $4^2 = 16$ golf balls. The pattern continues to layer 8, which contains $8^2 = 64$ golf balls.

Tran adds the number of golf balls in all the layers to determine the total number of golf balls.

NEL

Total number of golf balls
$= 1 + 4 + 9 + 16 + 25 + 36 + 49 + 64$

There are 204 golf balls in the pyramid.

4 Look Back

Tran estimates to check whether his solution makes sense.

In the photo, about half of the golf balls appear to be in the bottom two layers. Tran knows that the sum of the last two numbers, 64 and 49, is about 100. This means that the total number of golf balls should be about 200.

Reflecting

1. What other strategies could Tran have used to solve the problem?
2. What was the simpler problem that Tran examined? Why was the table of values helpful?
3. How did solving a simpler problem help Tran solve the problem?

Work with the Math

Example: Using a simpler problem to solve a problem involving coins

Suk-yin has 29 coins in her purse. The coins have a total value of $6.05. If the coins are quarters and nickels only, how many of each coin does Suk-yin have?

Chad's Solution

1 Understand the Problem

I know that there are 29 coins. I also know that the total value of the coins is $6.05. I need to determine how many of the coins are quarters and how many are nickels.

2 Make a Plan

I could check the value of each possible combination of quarters and nickels, but that might take a long time. Maybe I can solve a simpler problem like this: "Suppose I have just nickels, worth $6.05. How many nickels would I have?"

3 Carry Out the Plan

If I have all nickels and the value is $6.05, then I have 121 coins. But I'm only supposed to have 29 coins—that's 92 fewer coins.

If I trade 5 nickels for a quarter, I'll have 4 fewer coins each time I make a trade. I know that $92 \div 4 = 23$, so I have to make 23 trades. I must have 23 quarters and 6 nickels.

4 Look Back

The value of 23 quarters and 6 nickels is 23($0.25) + 6($0.05) = $6.05.

A Checking

4. At a historical site, cannonballs are stacked in a rectangular pyramid. The top layer of the pyramid has only 3 cannonballs arranged in one row. The 2nd layer has a 2-by-4 arrangement. If this pattern continues, how many cannonballs are in the 9th layer?

B Practising

5. A long strand of spaghetti is folded once. If this is cut 20 times, how many pieces of spaghetti will there be?

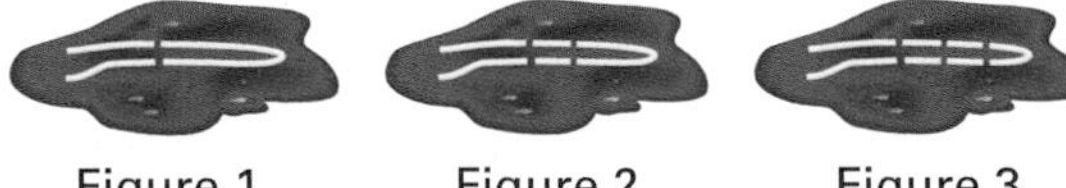

Figure 1 Figure 2 Figure 3

6. There are 14 teams in a basketball league. Each team plays every other team twice during the season.
   a) Suppose that you want to determine how many games, in total, are played. Suggest a simpler problem that you could solve first.
   b) How many games, in total, are played during the season?

7. Three different hoses, each with its own pump, can be used to fill a swimming pool. If hose A is used by itself, the pool takes 6 h to fill. If hose B is used by itself, the pool takes 3 h to fill. If hose C is used by itself, the pool takes 2 h to fill. If all three hoses are used at the same time, how long does the pool take to fill?

8. a) Four different-coloured pennants are going to be hung in a row to decorate a gymnasium wall. In how many different orders can the pennants be hung?
   b) Repeat part (a) for five different-coloured pennants.
   c) Repeat part (a) for 10 different-coloured pennants.

9. The side lengths and area of a rectangle increase according to a pattern of whole numbers.

Rectangle number	Side lengths of rectangle (units)	Area of rectangle (square units)
1	1×2	2
2	2×3	6
3	3×4	12
4	4×5	20

Use this pattern to determine the side lengths and area of the 100th rectangle.

10. A large window has 12 square panes on each side. The outside frame of the window will be painted green.

Figure 1 Figure 2 Figure 3

   a) How many panes will have two sides touching the green frame?
   b) How many panes will have one side touching the green frame?
   c) How many panes will have no sides touching the green frame?

11. A polygon has 20 sides. How many diagonals does it have?

12. Create a problem you can solve by solving a simpler problem first. Show how to solve your problem.

NEL

Curious Math

ADDING A SPECIAL SEQUENCE OF NUMBERS

Carl Gauss (1777–1855) was a German mathematician. When he was about 10 years old, his teacher asked his class to add all the whole numbers from 1 to 100. His teacher assumed that this would keep the students busy for a long time. A few moments later, Gauss showed the correct answer on his small slate to his surprised teacher!

To understand how Gauss solved this problem so quickly, think about solving a simpler related problem. Think about adding the numbers from 1 to 10.

1. a) Explain how using the adding pattern shown on the slate makes it easier to calculate the sum of the whole numbers from 1 to 10.

b) Calculate the sum. Use a calculator to check your result.

2. a) Use Gauss's adding strategy to add the whole numbers from 1 to 9.

b) One number was left over when you arranged the numbers in pairs. Explain how you adapted the adding strategy to include this number.

3. Use Gauss's adding strategy to calculate each sum. Show your work.

a) 1 + 2 + 3 + … + 99 +100

b) 21 + 22 + 23 + … + 79 + 80

c) 1 + 2 + 3 + … + 98 + 99

d) 0.1 + 0.2 + 0.3 + … + 0.8 + 0.9

e) 3 + 7 + 11 + 15 + … + 83 + 87

f) 2.3 + 2.5 + 2.7 + 2.9 + … + 4.9 + 5.1

4.5 Relating Number Sequences to Graphs

You will need
- grid paper
- a ruler
- coloured pencils

▶ **GOAL**

Relate a sequence to its scatter plot.

Learn about the Math

Ludek is offered eight days of work on his neighbour's farm. He has two options for payment:

- Option 1: $40 each day
- Option 2: $2 the first day, $4 the second day, $8 the third day, $16 the fourth day, and so on

? Which payment option results in greater total earnings?

A. Copy and complete a separate table of values, like the one below, for option 1 and for option 2.

Day number (term number)	Payment on this day	Total earnings (term value)
1		
2		
3		
4		
⋮		

B. Describe the pattern rules for options 1 and 2, using words or algebraic expressions.

C. For which option is predicting Ludek's total earnings for eight days more difficult? Explain.

D. Draw two scatter plots, using two different colours, to show the total earnings in both tables of values. Use the same pair of axes for both scatter plots.

E. Connect the points in each scatter plot. Extend each scatter plot to day 8.

F. Which payment option is better for Ludek? Explain.

Reflecting

1. Explain how you can use your scatter plots to determine the number of days that Ludek must work to make option 2 the better choice.
2. How is using a scatter plot like using a table of values to show a relationship?

Work with the Math

Example: Using a scatter plot to predict elapsed time

A backyard swimming pool contains 80 000 L of water. The pool needs to be emptied so that the bottom can be repaired. The water drains from the pool at a constant rate. It takes a total of 6 h 40 min to drain fully.

a) How much water is still in the pool after 2 h?

b) When 35 000 L of water remains in the pool, work can begin in the shallow end. When does this occur?

c) Create an algebraic expression for the volume of water remaining in the pool as it drains.

Benjamin's Solution

Time (min)	Volume of water (L)
0	80 000
400	0

I thought the problem would be easier to solve if I changed 6 h 40 min to 400 min. I organized the information in a table of values. Then I used my table to draw a scatter plot.

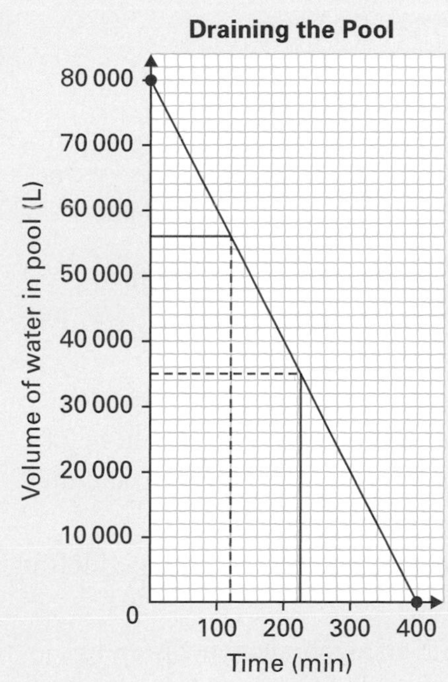

I drew a straight line between the two points on the scatter plot, since the water drains at a constant rate.

a) To determine how much water is still in the pool after 2 h, I drew a vertical broken red line on the scatter plot. Where the broken red line intersected the graph, I drew a horizontal solid red line. Then I read the volume from the vertical axis. About 56 000 L of water is still in the pool after 2 h.

b) I drew a horizontal broken blue line from 35 000. Where it intersected the graph, I drew a vertical solid blue line. Then I read the time from the horizontal axis. The time is about 225 min, which is 3 h 45 min.

c) I calculated the rate that the water drains:

$\frac{80\ 000\text{ L}}{400\text{ min}} = 200\text{ L/min}.$

The volume of water (in litres) remaining in the pool after t minutes is $80\ 000 - 200t$.

A Checking

3. Here are three different patterns. Pattern A is shown using a table of values. Pattern B is shown using a pattern rule. Pattern C is shown using models. Match each pattern with the correct scatter plot below. State the colour of the matching scatter plot.

Pattern A

Term number	Term value
1	6
2	11
3	16
4	21
5	26
6	31

Pattern B

$4n$

Pattern C

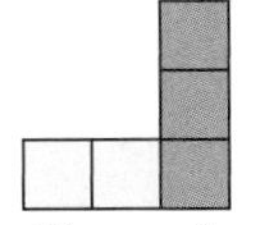
Figure 1

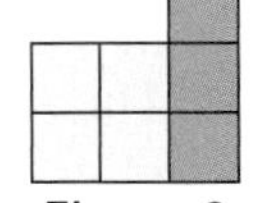
Figure 2

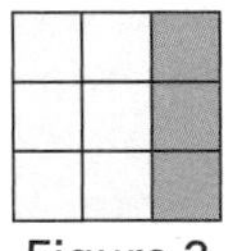
Figure 3

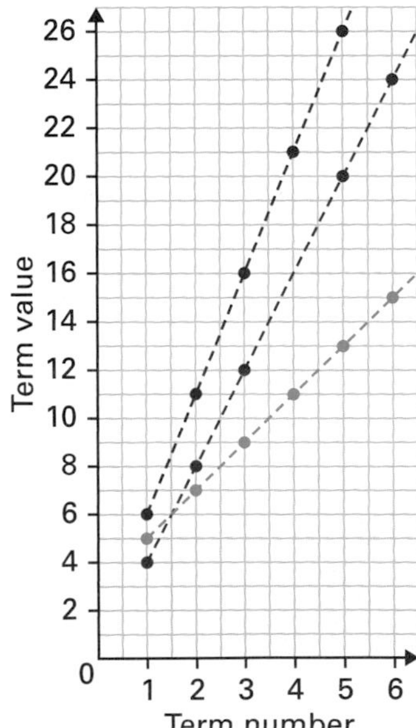

B Practising

4. Gilbert works picking strawberries. He earns $2.50 for each large basket he fills.
   a) Draw a scatter plot to represent the relationship between the number of baskets Gilbert fills and the money he earns.
   b) If Gilbert's goal is to earn $360, how many baskets must he fill?
   c) Write an algebraic expression to describe the relationship.

5. Match each algebraic expression with the colour of its scatter plot.
   a) $3x$
   b) $3x + 2$
   c) $3x - 2$

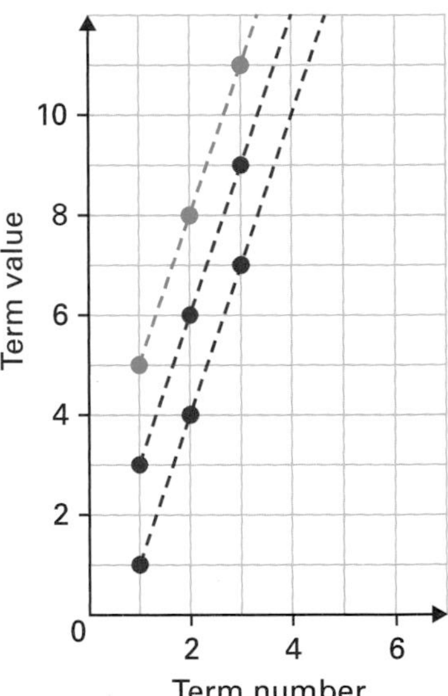

6. A 20 000 L tank in a chemical factory drains at a constant rate. It takes 100 min to empty the tank.
   a) Draw a scatter plot to represent the relationship between the volume of liquid remaining in the tank and the time in minutes.
   b) When is there 6000 L of liquid left in the tank?
   c) Write an algebraic expression to describe the relationship.

7. For a science investigation, Georgia puts 25 mL of water in a graduated cylinder in a sunny window. She records the rate of evaporation in the following table of values.

Elapsed time (in hours)	Volume of water (in millilitres)
0	25
1	22.5
2	20
6	10

a) Use the data in the table of values to draw a scatter plot.

b) How much time has passed when 17.5 mL of water remains in the cylinder?

c) Describe the relationship between the volume of water and the elapsed time.

8. a) Use the data in these tables of values to draw two scatter plots on the same pair of axes. Use a different colour for each scatter plot.

i)

Term number	Term value
1	1
2	4
3	9
4	16

ii)

Term number	Term value
1	4
2	8
3	12
4	16

b) Write each pattern rule as an algebraic expression.

c) Explain the similarities and differences between the two relationships.

9. The first six triangular numbers are 1, 3, 6, 10, 15, and 21. Plot these numbers on a scatter plot. Explain why the 11th term in the sequence is difficult to predict using a scatter plot.

C Extending

10. Write an algebraic expression for each set of points.

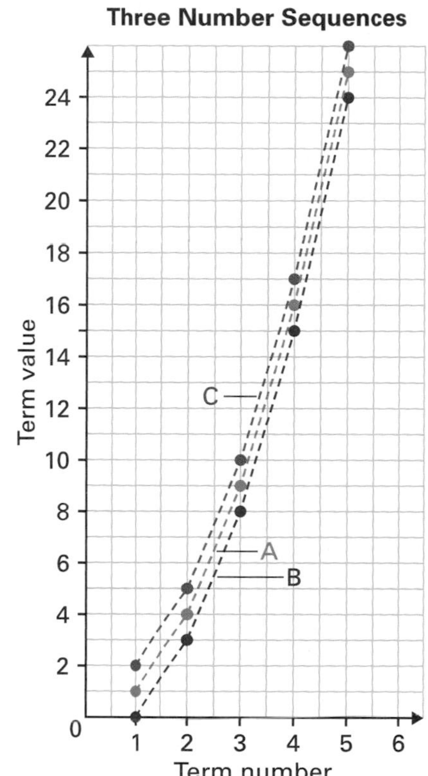

11. Use words or an algebraic expression to describe the pattern rule for the data in this table of values.

Term number	Term value
1	6
2	11
3	18
4	27

Math Game SPROUTS

The object of this game is to connect the dots. You might notice some interesting patterns as you play. Try to find a way to predict the winner of each game.

You will need
- 2 coloured pencils

Number of players: 2

Rules

1. Start by drawing one to five dots on a sheet of paper.
2. Take turns using a coloured pencil to
   a) draw a curve between two dots, or draw a loop starting and ending at the same dot, and
   b) make a new dot somewhere on the curve or loop you have just drawn
3. A curve cannot cross another curve.
4. No more than three curves can touch each dot.
5. The winner is the player who makes the last possible move.

Play this game a few times, starting with different numbers of dots. For each game, record the winner, the number of possible starting moves, and the number of moves needed to win in a chart like the one below. You should begin to see some interesting patterns.

Hints for Playing the Game

- Here are possible starting moves:
  - with 1 dot

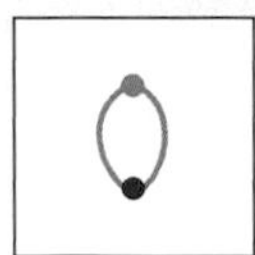

  - with 2 dots

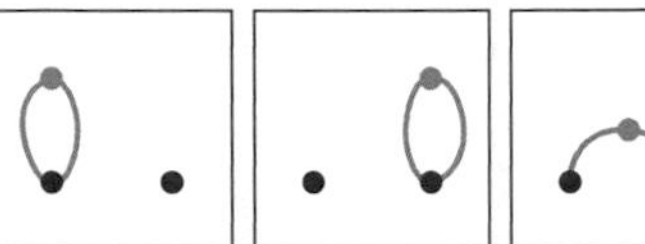

  - with 3 dots

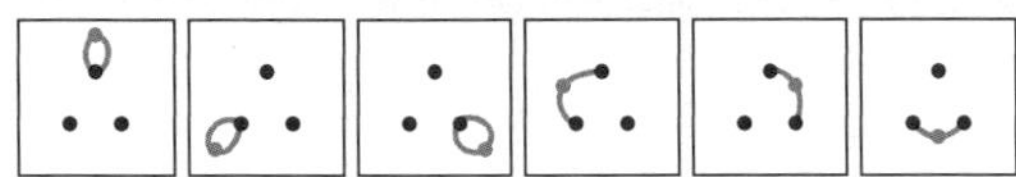

- Use a legend to show which colour belongs to which player.
- Circle used-up dots to make them easier to see.

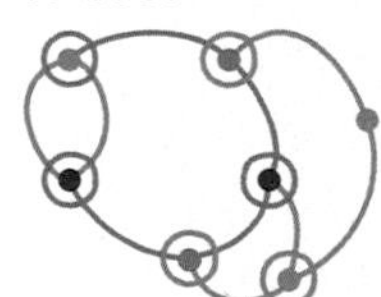

Player 1 is orange.
Player 2 is blue.
Player 1 wins.

Number of dots to start	Number of possible starting moves	Maximum number of moves to win	Winning player
1	1	2	
2	3	5	
3			
4			
5			

Chapter Self-Test

1. a) Use two colours to show which part of the pattern stays the same and which part changes.

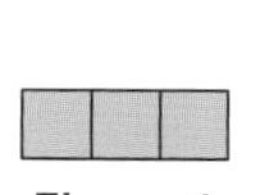
Figure 1

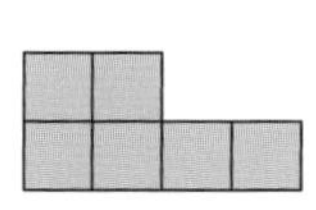
Figure 2

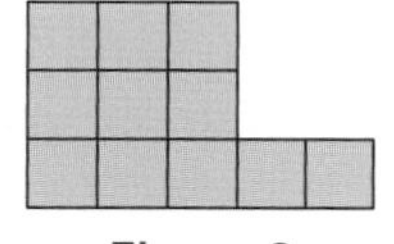
Figure 3

   b) Describe the pattern rule in words.
   c) Write an algebraic pattern rule.

2. Dylan wrote the sequence 7, 12, 17, 22, ….
   a) Use a table of values to determine a pattern rule for this sequence.
   b) Determine the 25th term.

3. Kirsten wrote the sequence 17, 24, 31, 38, ….
   a) Use words and an algebraic expression to describe the pattern rule.
   b) Determine the *n*th term.
   c) Determine the 77th term.

4. Mitchell made a triangular pyramid by gluing together small plastic balls.
   a) Use a table of values to determine the total number of balls needed to build a pyramid that is six levels high.
   b) How many more balls would he need to increase the number of levels to ten?
   c) How many levels would the pyramid have if Mitchell used 165 balls?

5. A long strand of spaghetti is folded twice to form a Z shape. If the spaghetti is cut vertically through the Z, how many pieces will there be after 75 cuts?

Figure 1

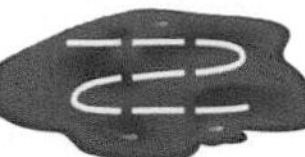
Figure 2

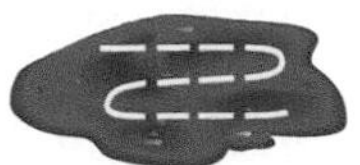
Figure 3

6. a) Use the data in these tables of values to draw two scatter plots on the same pair of axes. Use a different colour for each scatter plot.

   i)

Term number	Term value
2	6
5	12
7	16
10	22

   ii)

Term number	Term value
6	1
10	3
12	4
18	7

   b) For each scatter plot, determine the term number if the term value is 8.

7. John made a pattern with 9 toothpicks in the 1st figure, 14 in the 2nd figure, 19 in the 3rd figure, and 24 in the 4th figure.
   a) Write an algebraic expression for the *n*th term.
   b) Use a scatter plot to determine the figure number of the figure with 94 toothpicks.
   c) Check your result in part (b) by substituting for the variable and evaluating the algebraic expression.

Chapter Review

Frequently Asked Questions

Q: How can you use a scatter plot to represent a pattern?

A: A scatter plot shows the relationship between two quantities in a table of values. Use the x-axis to show the term number and the y-axis to show the term value.

For example, the table and graph show the number of trees planted in a park over several days. Each row of the table is represented as a point on the scatter plot. The points form a line, which can be extended to show other values in the pattern. The algebraic expression for this relationship is $2n + 1$.

Number of days	Number of trees planted
1	3
2	5
3	7
4	9
⋮	⋮
n	$2n + 1$

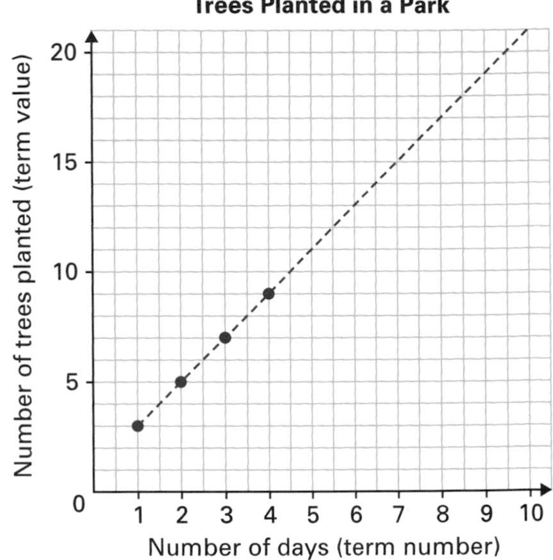

Q: What are the advantages and disadvantages of using a scatter plot to represent a pattern?

A: Advantages

A scatter plot is a visual representation of a pattern. You can use a scatter plot to predict trends without doing the calculations. You can also use a scatter plot to determine an unknown value when solving a problem.

For example, you can use the scatter plot on this page to determine the term value when the term number is 7, or the term number when the term value is 19. From the graph, you can tell that the coordinates of those points are (7, 15) and (9, 19).

Disadvantages

Sometimes the scale on an axis is too large or too small. Then a scatter plot may not be as accurate as a pattern rule for predicting term values.

For example, the scatter plot on this page is not very helpful for determining the term value when the term number is 195. Instead, you need to use the pattern rule:

$$\begin{aligned} 2n + 1 &= 2 \times 195 + 1 \\ &= 390 + 1 \\ &= 391 \end{aligned}$$

The 195th term is 391.

Practice Questions

(4.2) **1.** A student council is planning a penny drive for charity. To promote interest in the event, the students have designed a series of posters. Each poster uses pennies to form a figure in the following pattern:

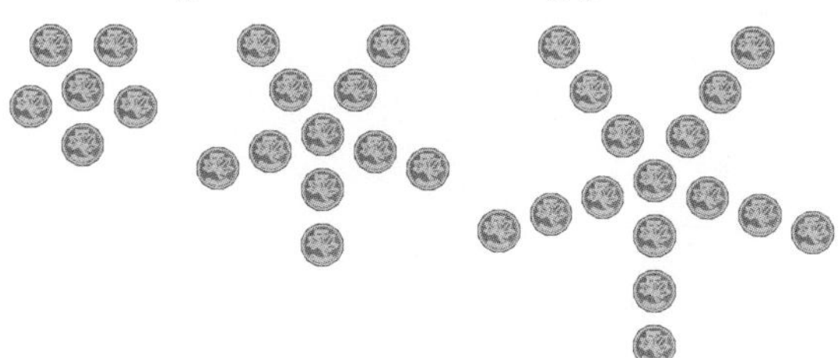

Figure 1 Figure 2 Figure 3

a) Which part of the pattern changes and which part stays the same in each figure?

b) Describe the relationship between the term number and the term value in the pattern.

c) Determine an algebraic pattern rule.

d) How many pennies are needed for the 12th poster in the pattern?

(4.3) **2. a)** Use a table of values to determine a pattern rule for the sequence 5, 7, 9, 11, ….

b) Write an algebraic expression for the *n*th term of the sequence.

c) Calculate the 70th term in the sequence.

(4.3) **3.** How many counters would you need to make the 50th term in this sequence?

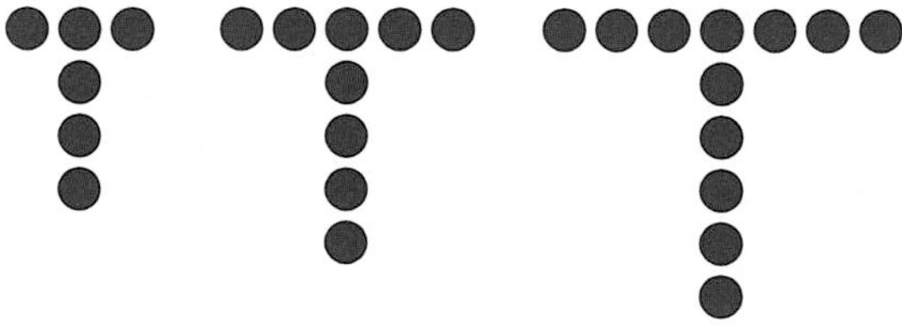

Figure 1 Figure 2 Figure 3

4. A right angle is formed by two rays extending from a common point. Seven more rays are then drawn inside the right angle. What is the total number of angles, of all sizes, that are formed by the rays? (4.4)

5. a) Use the data in the three tables of values to draw three scatter plots on the same pair of axes. Use a different colour for each scatter plot. (4.5)

i)

Term number	Term value
4	3
6	4
10	6
12	
1	

ii)

Term number	Term value
3	5
4	7
5	9
10	
11	

iii)

Term number	Term value
2	7
5	13
6	15
8	
9	

b) Determine the missing values in each table of values.

c) Write an algebraic expression for each pattern rule.

Chapter Task

Pyramid Patterns

Grade 8 students are collecting shoeboxes filled with school supplies for partner schools in developing countries. They collect 21 boxes by the end of day 1, 40 boxes by the end of day 2, and 59 boxes by the end of day 3. This pattern continues for the next four days.

Before the supplies are shipped, the students want to display the shoeboxes in a rectangular pyramid, with no shoeboxes left over. They have the following options for the top three rows of the pyramid:

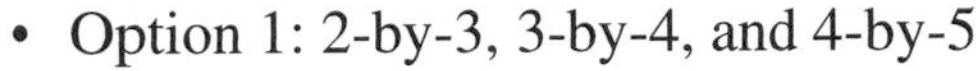

- Option 1: 2-by-3, 3-by-4, and 4-by-5
- Option 2: 2-by-2, 3-by-3, and 4-by-4
- Option 3: 3-by-5, 3-by-6, and 3-by-7

The lower rows extend the pattern from the top three rows.

? Which pyramid option should the students choose for their display?

A. Write an algebraic expression for the total number of shoeboxes collected by the end of any day.

B. How many shoeboxes have the students collected by the end of day 7?

C. For each pyramid option, calculate the total number of shoeboxes used after each row has been completed. That is, calculate the total number of shoeboxes in the top row, the total number of shoeboxes in the top two rows, the total number of shoeboxes in the top three rows, and so on.

D. Decide which pyramid option the students should choose, if they do not want any shoeboxes left over.

E. How many rows will be in the students' pyramid? Justify your answer.

Task Checklist

- ☑ Did you include diagrams, tables of values, an algebraic expression, and a scatter plot?
- ☑ Did you use the strategy of solving a simpler problem first?
- ☑ Did you use appropriate math vocabulary?
- ☑ Did you show all your work?

CHAPTER 5

Measurement of Circles

▶ GOALS

You will be able to

- describe the relationships among the radius, diameter, circumference, and area of a circle
- develop and apply formulas to determine the circumference of a circle and the area of a circle
- draw a circle with given measurements

Getting Started

You will need
- centimetre grid paper
- string
- tape
- a ruler
- a calculator

Designing a Label

Tamara and Teo are designing a label for the school yearbook CD. The label will be a polygon with a perimeter of 30 cm. Tamara and Teo want to know which polygon has the greatest area, so it will cover most of the CD.

? Which polygon will cover most of the CD?

A. On grid paper, draw a circle that is a life-sized model of the CD (12 cm wide and 12 cm high).

B. Draw a square around the circle to represent the package for the CD. The CD should just fit in the package.

C. Use a 30 cm length of string to create a triangle that would fit on the model of the CD.

D. Estimate the area of the triangle by counting the squares on the grid.

E. Calculate the area of the triangle using a formula.

F. Is there another triangle that would cover a greater area but still fit on the model of the CD?

G. Repeat steps C to F using a rectangle.

H. Which of your polygons covered the greatest area of the CD?

Do You Remember?

1. State whether each measurement is an area or a perimeter.
   a) the distance around a school track
   b) the amount of paper needed to wrap a gift
   c) the length of the boards needed to go around a skating rink

2. Use <, >, or = to make each statement true.
   a) 5 cm ■ 5 m
   b) 1 m ■ 100 cm
   c) 1.000 m ■ 1000 mm
   d) 13 km ■ 130 m

3. Determine the perimeter and the area of each shape.

   a)
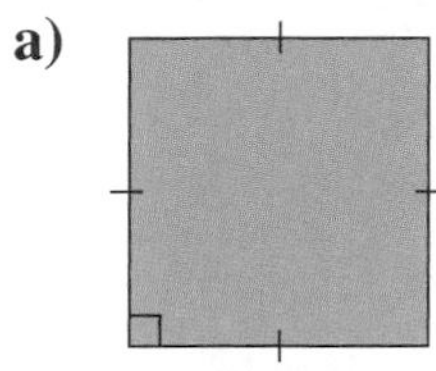

   b)
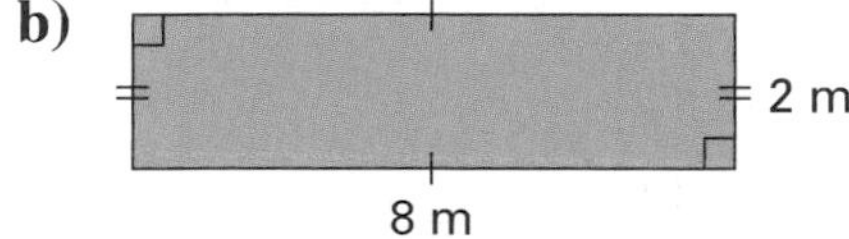

   c)
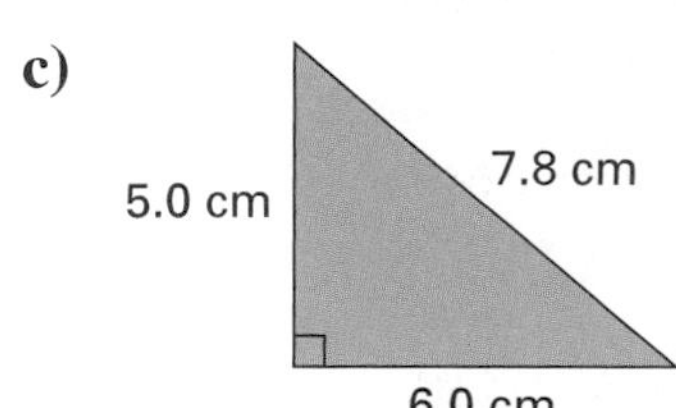

   d)
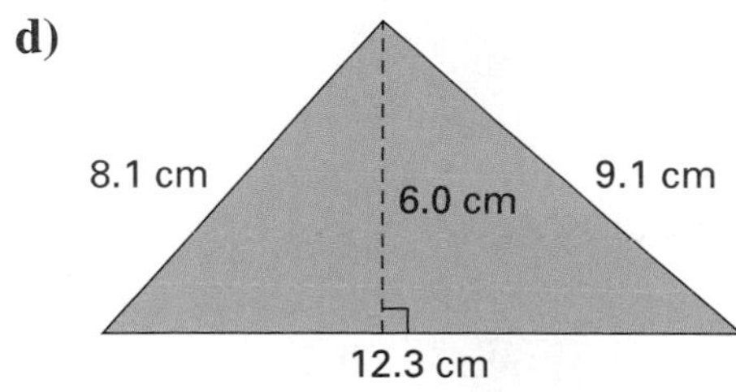

4. Determine the perimeter and the area of the parallelogram.

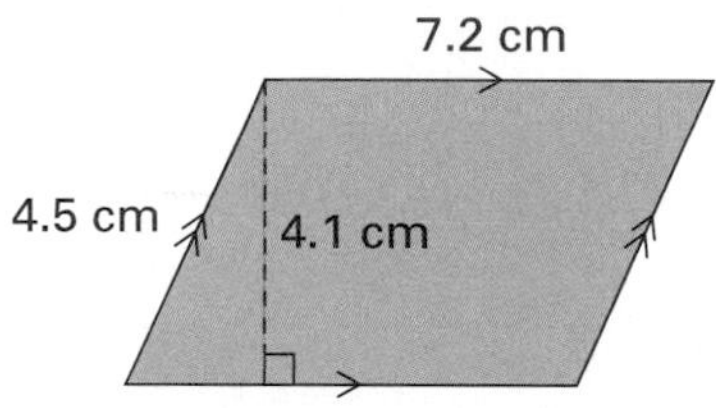

5. Sod is measured in square metres. What area of sod is needed to cover each lawn?

   a)
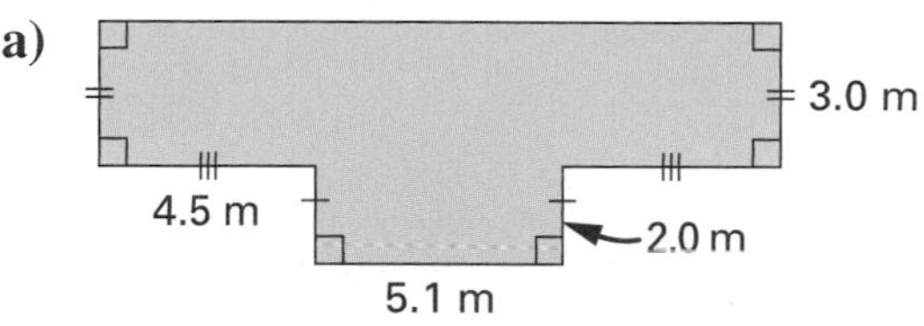

   b)
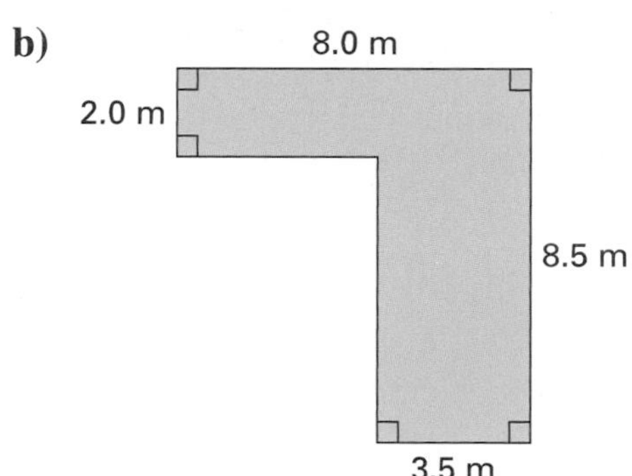

   c)
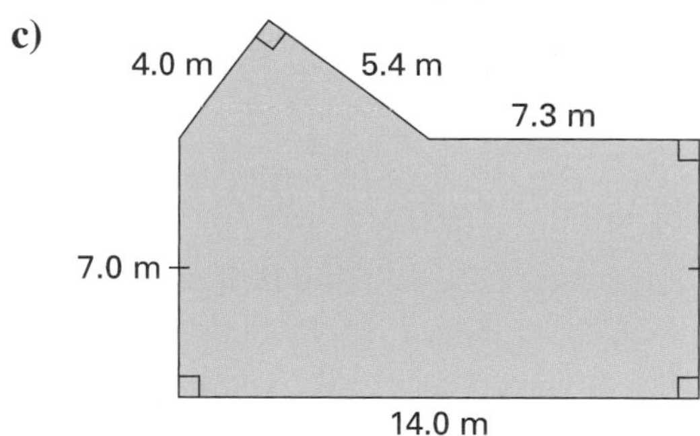

6. A right triangle has an area of 6 cm^2 and a base of 4 cm. What is its height?

5.1 Exploring Circles

You will need
- a compass
- scissors
- a ruler
- string
- a protractor

▶ **GOAL**

Draw circles and explore measurements.

Explore the Math

Jordan enjoys folding square origami paper to create figures. She wonders if she can fold circular paper to create polygons.

radius (pl. radii)

a line segment that goes from the centre of a circle to its circumference; the length of this line segment

? How can you use a circle to create a polygon?

A. Adjust a compass so that the pencil tip is 6 cm from the compass point. Draw three circles, and cut them out.

B. Measure the **radius** and the **diameter** of one circle with a ruler.

C. Measure the **circumference** of the circle with string and a ruler.

D. Fold the circle in half, along a diameter, to make a semicircle. Unfold the circle. Measure the **arc** of the semicircle with string and a ruler. Compare this measurement with your measurement in step C.

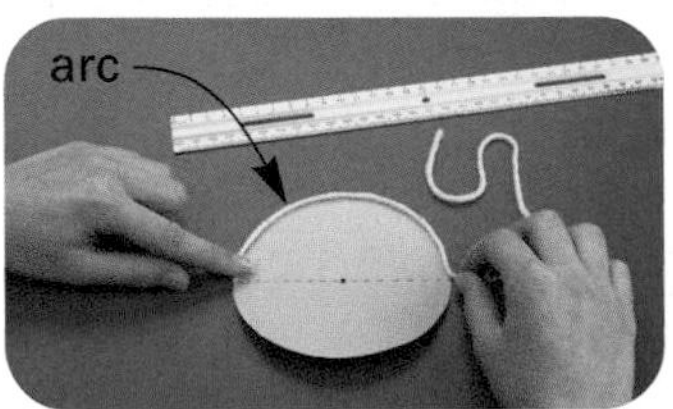

E. Mark the centre of the circle and a point on the circumference. Fold the point to the centre. The fold line is a **chord**. Make two more folds from points on the circumference to the centre to create two new chords that are the same length as the first. The ends of the chords should meet. Unfold the circle, and draw over the fold lines to create a triangle.

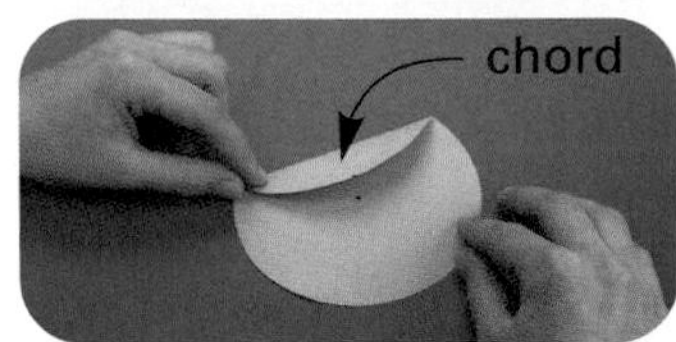

diameter

a line segment that runs from one side of a circle, through the centre, to the other side; the length of this line segment

circumference

the boundary of a circle; the length of this boundary

arc

a section of the circumference of a circle that lies between two ends of a chord (each chord creates two arcs); the length of this section

chord

a line segment that joins any two points on the circumference of a circle; the length of this line segment

Communication Tip

- The terms **arc, chord, circumference, diameter**, and **radius** refer to either a part of a circle or the length of the part. For example, you could say that the name of the radius of this circle is *OX and* that the radius measures 5 cm. The way in which the term is used will tell you which definition is intended.

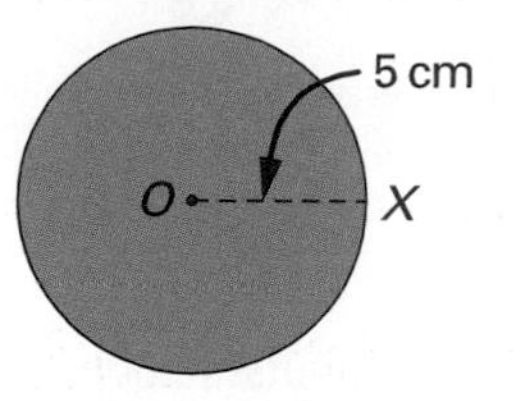

- The instrument that you use to draw circles can be called either a **pair of compasses** or a **compass**. In this book, the term **compass** is used.

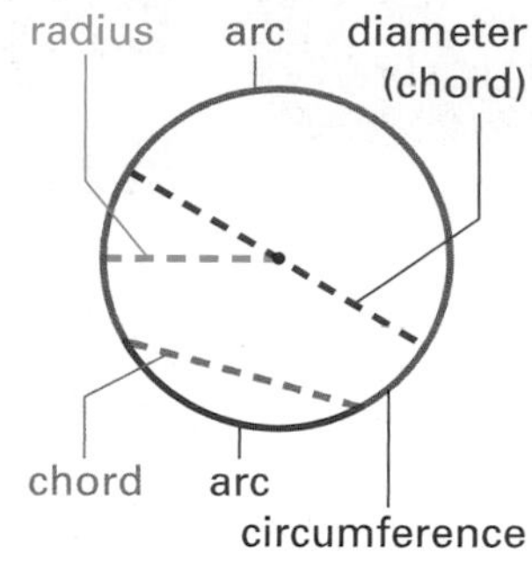

F. Measure the following parts of the shape you drew. Record your results in a chart like the one below.

- one interior angle of the shape
- one side (chord) of the shape
- one arc formed by the vertices of the shape
- the perimeter of the shape

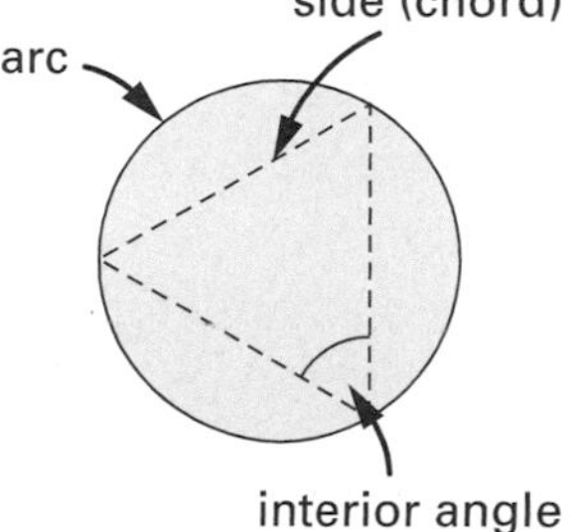

Polygon	Measure of one interior angle (°)	Length of one side (cm)	Length of one arc (cm)	Perimeter (cm)
triangle				

G. Fold your second circle in half, and then fold it in half again. Unfold it. Join the ends of the fold lines to make a square. Repeat step F.

H. Fold your third circle to create an octagon with all sides equal. Repeat step F.

Reflecting

1. How do you know that the diameter of a circle is the longest possible chord in the circle?

2. Examine the polygons you folded.

   a) As the number of sides increases, how do the side lengths change?

   b) As the number of sides increases, how do the measures of the interior angles change?

   c) As the measure of each interior angle increases, how do the lengths of the arcs change?

   d) As the number of sides increases, how do the perimeters change?

5.2 Exploring Circumference and Diameter

You will need
- centimetre cubes
- string
- a compass
- a ruler

▶ **GOAL**
Investigate the relationship between the diameter and circumference of a circle.

Explore the Math

Sheree and Reilly have been asked to mark their school logo on the floor of the gym using masking tape. The logo is a circle with a line through the centre. Sheree and Reilly need to know the diameter and circumference of the logo so they can estimate the number of rolls of tape to buy.

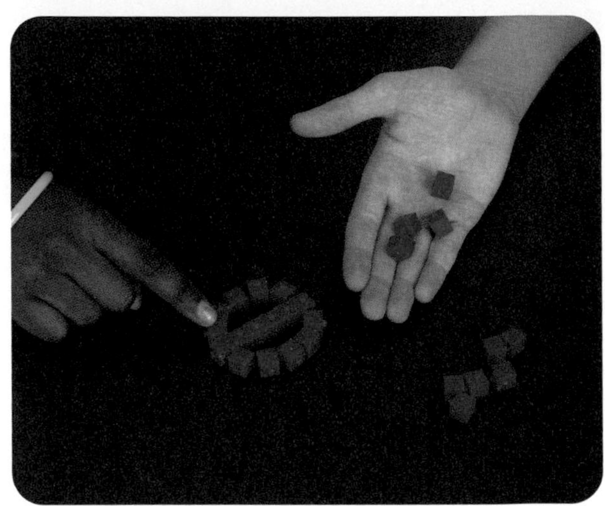

Sheree says, "It's easy to measure the diameter directly, using a measuring tape. But it's harder to measure the circumference directly."

They decide to make a model of the logo with centimetre cubes.

? How can you use the diameter of the logo to predict its circumference?

A. Use centimetre cubes to make a circle with a diameter of 4 cm. Count the cubes in the diameter and in the circumference. About how many times as long as the diameter is the circumference?

B. Draw a circle with a diameter of 4 cm.

C. Predict the circumference of the circle. Measure the circumference with string and a ruler. Record your data in a chart like the one below.

	Circumference	
Diameter (cm)	**Predicted (cm)**	**Measured (cm)**
4		

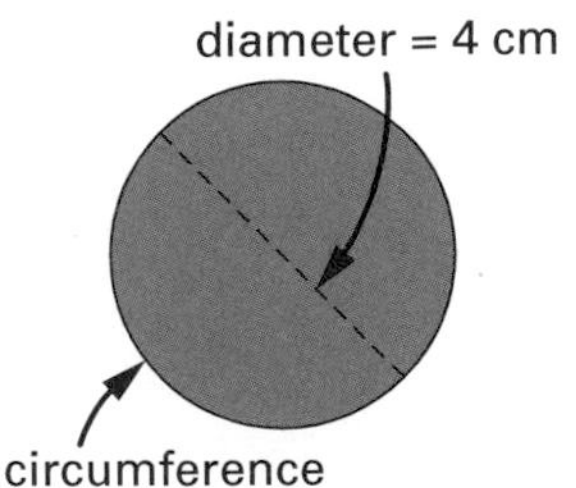

D. Repeat steps B and C using circles with diameters of 6 cm and 8 cm. Extend your chart to include the data.

E. Measure the diameter and circumference of two circular objects, such as a CD, a lid, or a coaster. Extend your chart to include the data.

F. What do you notice when you compare the diameter with the circumference?

G. The diameter of Sheree and Reilly's school logo is 12 m. About how long is its circumference?

Reflecting

1. Why is measuring the diameter of a circle easier than measuring its circumference?

2. a) If you know the diameter of a circle, how can you predict its circumference?
   b) Does your answer in part (a) depend on the size of the circle?

Mental Imagery

DETERMINING THE REGULAR PRICE

You can determine the regular price of an item if you know the amount of savings and the discount.

Example: Determine the regular price of an item if a 10% discount is a savings of \$16.50.

Use a circle to help you picture 10%. The whole circle represents the regular price, 100%. Each section, 10%, represents \$16.50.
$10 \times 10 = 100$, so the regular price is 10 times the savings of \$16.50.
The regular price is $10 \times \$16.50 = \$165.00$.

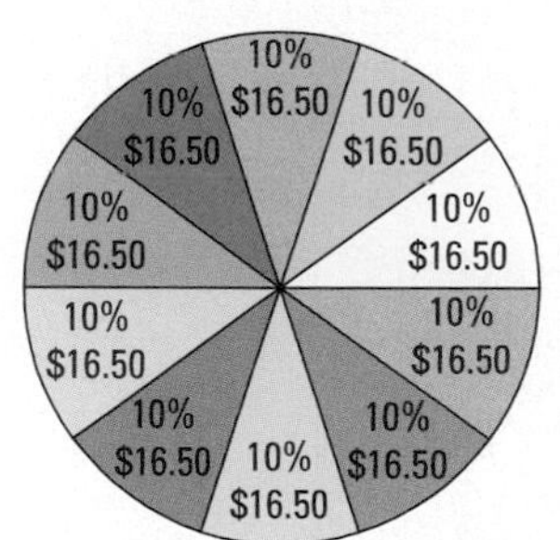

1. How can you show that 20% of \$165.00 is \$33.00?

2. The price of a sweater is discounted by 25%, or \$15.
   a) Draw a circle to represent the original price of the sweater.
   b) Determine the original price of the sweater.
   c) What is the sale price of the sweater?

5.3 Calculating Circumference

You will need
- a calculator
- a compass

▶ **GOAL**
Develop and apply the formula for the circumference of a circle.

Learn about the Math

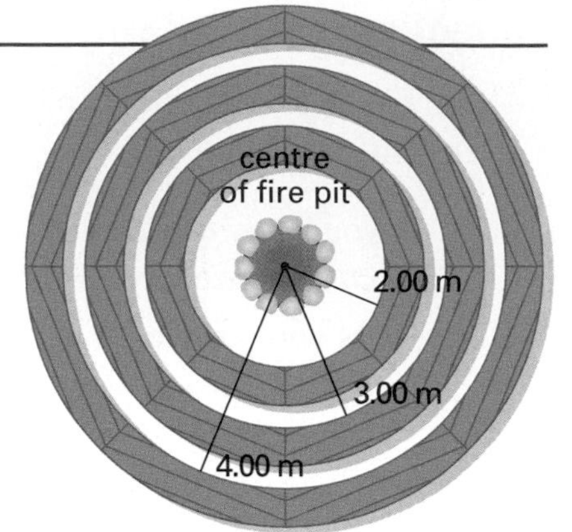

Tamara and Jordan are at summer camp. They want to build another log bench around the fire pit, 5.00 m from the centre.

? How can you determine the circumference of a bench that is 5.00 m from the centre of the fire pit?

Tamara says, "Let's measure the circumference of each bench."

Jordan says, "The circumference should be about three times the diameter. Let's check by dividing."

Diagram	Circumference (m)	Diameter (m)	Circumference ÷ diameter (m) (to two decimal places)	Radius (m)	Circumference ÷ radius (m)
centre, 2.00 m, log bench	12.56	4.00	3.14	2.00	6.28
centre, 3.00 m	18.84	6.00	3.14	3.00	6.28
centre, 4.00 m	25.12	8.00	3.14	4.00	6.28

Jordan observes, "The circumference of each bench is about 3.14 times the diameter. It's also the length of the radius multiplied by 6.28."

Tamara notices, "6.28 is twice 3.14."

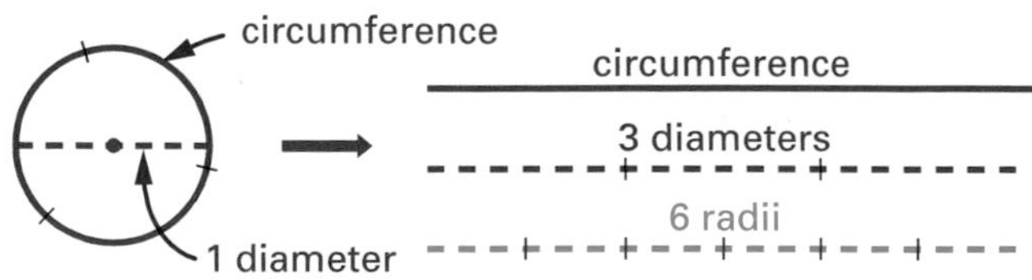

The ratio of the circumference to the diameter, or the number of times the diameter of a circle divides the circumference, is called **π (pi).**

π (pi)
the ratio of the circumference to the diameter of a circle; its value is 3.141 592 654 ..., or about 3.14, rounded to two decimal places

The formula for the circumference, C, of a circle with diameter d is $C = \pi d$. The formula for the circumference of a circle with radius r is $C = 2\pi r$.

Calculator Tip

Some calculators have a π key that automatically enters the value of π to the maximum number of decimal places for the calculator. On the TI-15, however, the following keys must be pressed to show the value of π:

Example 1: Determining the circumference of a circle from its diameter

Determine the circumference of a log bench that is 5.00 m from the centre of a fire pit.

Jordan's Solution

$C = \pi d$
$= \pi\ (10.00\ \text{m})$
$\doteq 3.14 \times 10.00\ \text{m}$
$\doteq 31.40\ \text{m}$

The circumference of the bench is about 31.40 m.

I drew this diagram. The radius is 5.00 m, so the diameter is 10.00 m.

First I estimated the circumference. The circumference is about 3 × 10 m, or 30 m.

Then I used the formula to calculate a closer estimate.

I rounded to the nearest hundredth of a metre because that's how the radius is measured.

Communication Tip

In the equation in Jordan's solution, the *C* and *d* are in italics because they are variables. The m is not in italics because it is a unit of measurement.

Reflecting

1. How would you calculate the circumference of a circle if you knew only its radius?

2. If you knew the circumference of a circle, how would you estimate its diameter?

3. Why would you use a formula to determine the circumference of a circle, rather than measuring the circumference?

Work with the Math

Example 2: Determining the circumference of a circle from its radius

Determine the circumference of a circle with a radius of 6.0 m.

Solution

Use the formula $C = 2\pi r$.

$C = 2\pi r$

$= 2 \times \pi \times 6.0$ m

$\doteq$

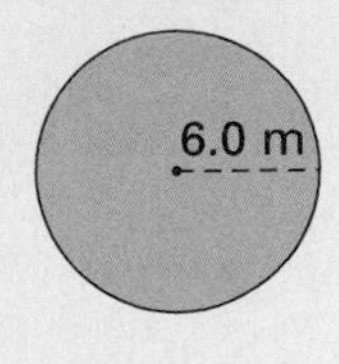

Use the [π] key on your calculator.

Round to the nearest tenth of a metre because this is how the radius is measured. The circumference is about 37.7 m.

Round your answers to the same number of decimal places as in the given measurements.

A Checking

4. Calculate the circumference of a circle with each diameter. Use the formula $C = \pi d$.

a) 5 cm b) 4.7 cm

5. Calculate the circumference of a circle with each radius.

a) 10 cm b) 8.2 m

B Practising

6. Calculate the circumference of a circle with each diameter.

a) 4.5 cm d) 36.0 m
b) 1.7 cm e) 7 mm
c) 6.4 cm f) 4.0 cm

7. Calculate the circumference of a circle with each radius.

a) 7 mm d) 9.0 cm
b) 19.5 cm e) 23.1 m
c) 6.3 cm f) 0.05 m

8. The diameter of the wheels on Xavier's bicycle is 80 cm. Calculate the circumference of the wheels.

9. a) Draw a circle with a diameter of 11 cm. Explain what you did.

b) What is the circumference of your circle?

10. At summer camp, Maria uses chalk to draw a meeting circle around a flagpole. The distance from one side of the circle, through the flagpole, to the other side is 11.0 m. How long is the chalk line around the circle?

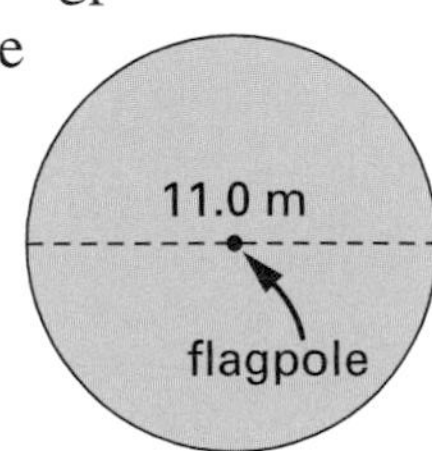

11. Copy and complete the chart.

Item	*r*	*d*	*C*
clock	9.0 cm		
watch		36 mm	
round tea bag	1.9 cm		
sewer cover		62 cm	
circle protractor	5.9 cm		
electric fan		201 mm	

NEL

12. At a zoo, the giraffes are fenced inside a circular field with a radius of 700 m. What length of fencing is needed?

13. The distance around a circular wading pool is 39.25 m. How far does a lifeguard have to walk from the edge of the pool to get to the centre of the pool?

14. This bicycle is called a penny-farthing. In one model, the diameter of the front wheel is 120.0 cm. In another model, the diameter is 150.0 cm. What is the difference in the circumferences of these front wheels?

15. For hockey practice, Rosa has to skate around a face-off circle five times. The face-off circle has a diameter of 9.0 m. About how far does Rosa have to skate?

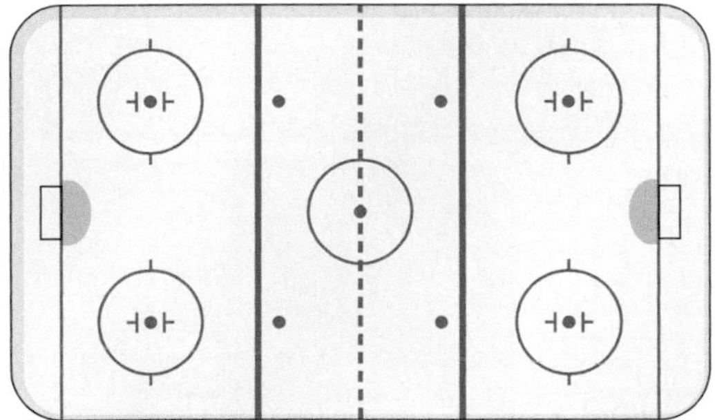

16. The circumference of this CD is about 37.7 cm. The diameter of the hole in the centre is 1.5 cm. What is the distance from the outside edge of the CD to the inside edge?

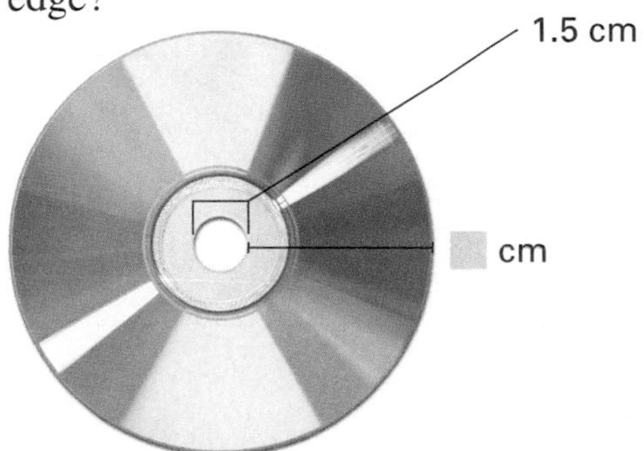

17. One of the largest trees in the world is a giant sequoia. It is over 90 m tall. The diameter of its base is about 9.2 m. What is the circumference of its trunk? (Assume that its trunk is a circle.)

18. Use each description to write a problem that involves circumference. Explain how to solve your problem.

    a) Earth orbits the Sun once each year. Assume that Earth's orbit is a circle with a radius of about 150 000 000 km.

    b) Doug is rolling a tire that is 50.0 cm in diameter. It makes 15 full turns.

C Extending

19. Sketch what the label looks like when it is removed from the can. Determine the length and width of the label. Show how you calculated the length of the label.

20. This racetrack consists of a rectangle and two semicircles. What is the length of one lap?

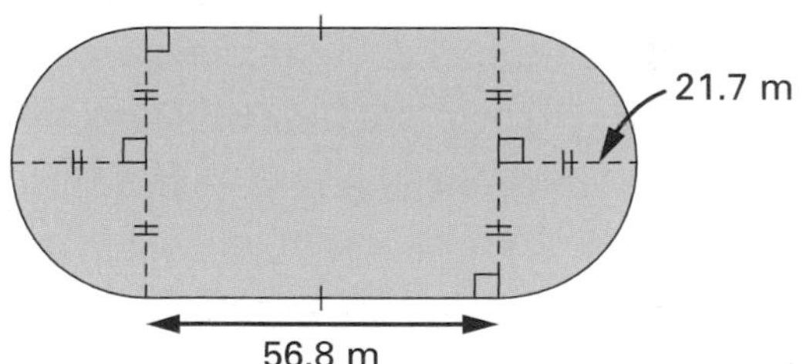

21. How does the length of the red arc compare with the circumference of the blue circle? Explain your reasoning.

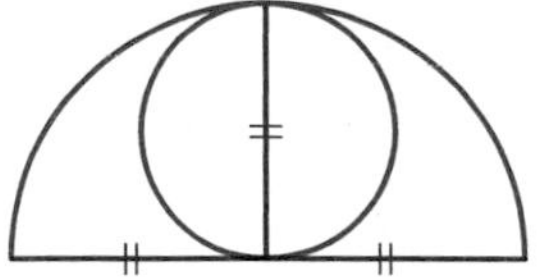

Mid-Chapter Review

Frequently Asked Questions

Q: What are the parts of a circle?

A: The **circumference** is the boundary of a circle. It is also the length of this boundary.

The **diameter** is a line segment that runs from one side of a circle, through the centre, to the other side. It is also the length of this line segment.

The **radius** is a line segment that goes from the centre of a circle to a point on its circumference. The radius is also the length of this line segment. The radius is half the diameter.

arc
radius
chord
diameter (chord)
arc
circumference

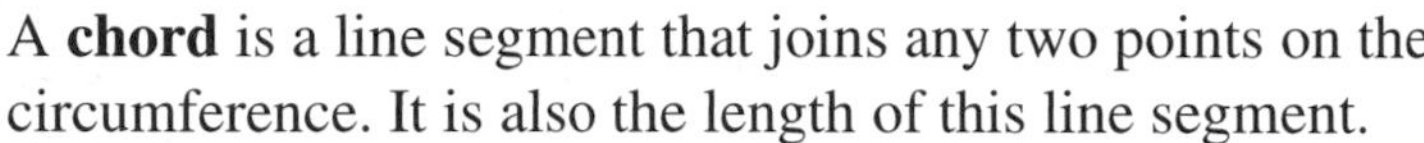

A **chord** is a line segment that joins any two points on the circumference. It is also the length of this line segment.

An **arc** is a section of the circumference that lies between the two ends of a chord. It is also the length of this section. A chord creates two arcs.

Q: How can you use a compass to draw a circle if you know its radius or diameter?

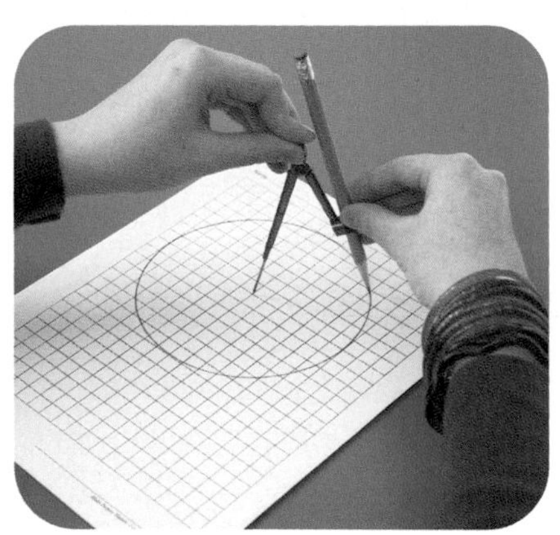

A: If you know the radius, go to step 2.

1. If you know the diameter, divide it by 2 to determine the radius. For example, a circle with a diameter of 14.0 cm has a radius of 7.0 cm.
2. Adjust the compass so that the distance between the compass point and the pencil tip is equal to the radius. Put the compass point where you want the centre of the circle to be. Then draw the circle.

Q: How can you determine the circumference of a circle if you know its diameter?

A1: You can estimate. Since the circumference of a circle is about three times its diameter, you can multiply its diameter by 3. For example, the circumference of a circle with a diameter of 6 cm is about 3×6 cm, or 18 cm.

A2: You can use a formula. The formula for the circumference, C, of a circle with diameter d is $C = \pi d$. Since the diameter is twice the radius, this formula can also be written as $C = 2\pi r$. You can use 3.14 as an approximate value for π. For example, the circumference of a circle with a diameter of 6.0 cm is calculated as follows:

$$\begin{aligned} C &= \pi d \\ &\doteq 3.14 \times 6.0 \text{ cm} \\ &\doteq 18.8 \text{ cm} \end{aligned}$$

Practice Questions

(5.1) **1.** Sketch a circle, and label the parts.

circumference

radius

diameter

chord

arc

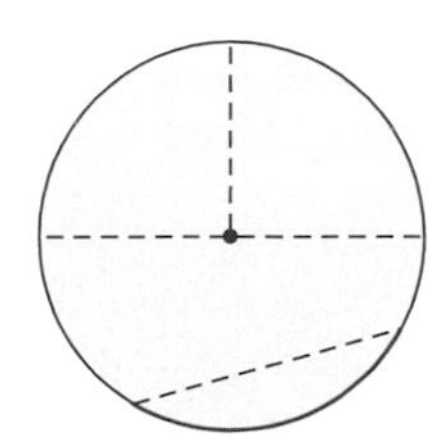

(5.1) **2.** Arrange the following measures of a circle in order, from shortest to longest: diameter, circumference, radius. Use drawings and words to explain your thinking.

(5.2) **3.** Diana is drawing a chalk circle on the gym floor for a game. The diameter of the circle is 3.0 m. Estimate the circumference of the circle.

(5.2) **4.** Estimate the circumference of a circle with each diameter.

a) 26 cm **c)** 17.2 cm

b) 10.8 m **d)** 3 km

(5.3) **5.** Copy and complete the chart.

Item	Diameter	Radius	Circumference
CD case		6.0 cm	
coaster	9.0 cm		
lock	26 mm		
coin		1.9 cm	

6. What is the circumference of the circle in each sign? (5.3)

a)

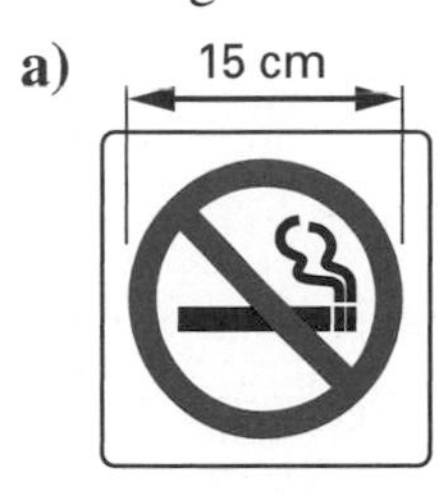

b)

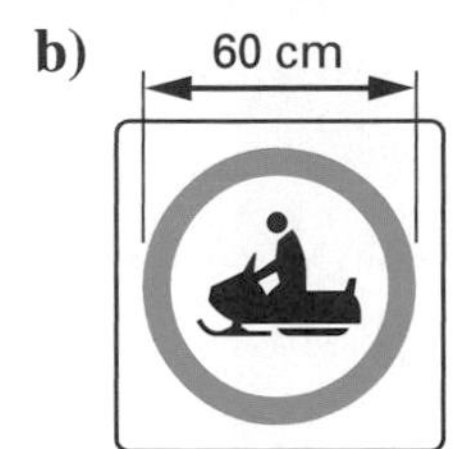

c)

d)

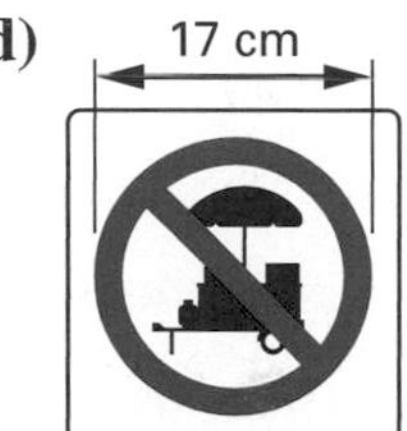

e)

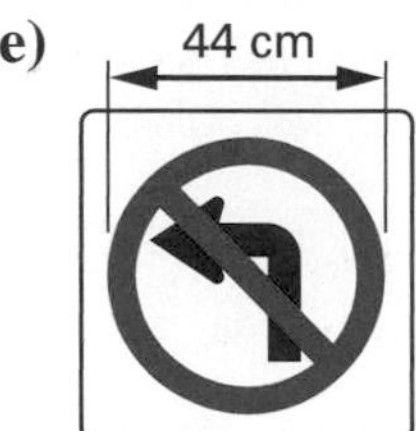

f)

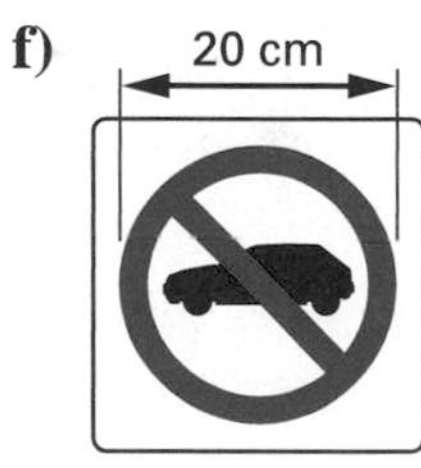

7. Suppose that you double the diameter of a circle. What happens to the circumference of the circle? Draw two circles to explain your answer. (5.3)

5.4 Estimating Area

You will need
- a compass
- scissors
- centimetre grid paper
- glue or tape

▶ **GOAL**

Estimate the area of a circle.

Explore the Math

Sheree's mother has made a CD of her songs. She plans to have 1000 copies produced. Sheree will make a circular label for each CD and paint the label. She needs to know the area of the label so that she can calculate the amount of paint she needs.

Sheree says, "I can estimate the area of the CD by drawing a model of it on grid paper. I can ignore the hole in the centre for my estimate. I'll draw a square outside the circle and a square inside the circle. The area of the CD should be between the areas of the two squares."

The area of the large square is 12 cm × 12 cm = 144 cm^2.

The area of the small square is 8 cm × 8 cm = 64 cm^2.

The area of the CD is about 104 cm^2.

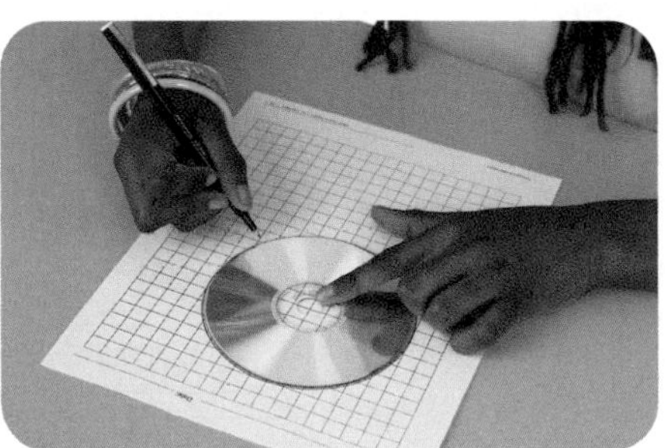

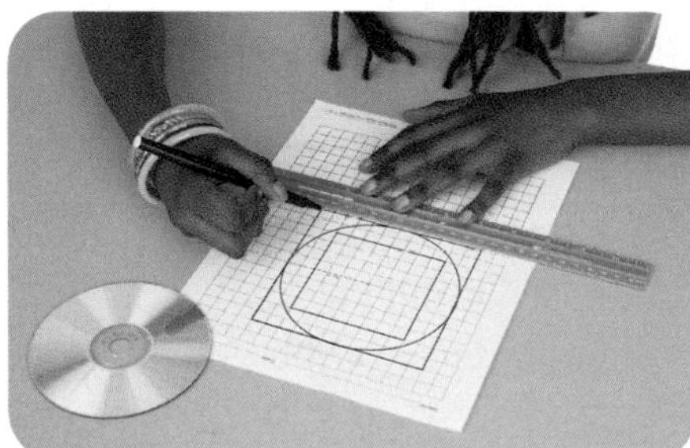

? How can you use the radius to improve Sheree's estimate of the area of the CD?

A. Draw three circles with a radius of 6 cm, and cut them out.

B. Fold one circle in half, and then fold it in half again. Unfold the circle, and cut out the four equal sections. Glue the sections onto grid paper to form a shape that almost fills a parallelogram. Sketch the parallelogram.

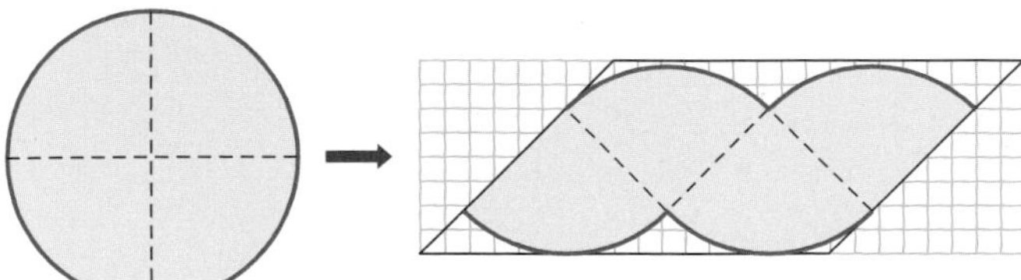

C. Measure the parallelogram, and record your data in a chart like the one below.

Number of sections	Length of base of parallelogram	Height of parallelogram	Area of parallelogram
4			

D. Repeat steps B and C, but this time fold and cut the circle into eight equal sections.

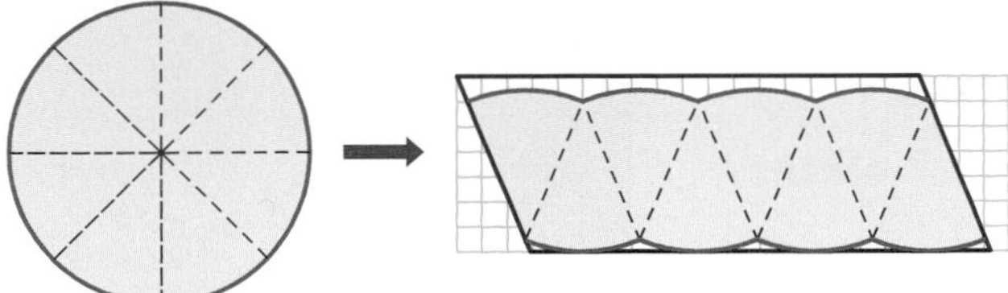

E. Repeat steps B and C again, but this time fold and cut the circle into 16 equal sections.

F. Use your results to estimate the area of the CD label.

Reflecting

1. How does the height of the parallelogram compare with the radius of the circle?
2. How does the length of the base of the parallelogram compare with the circumference of the circle?
3. How does the area of the parallelogram compare with the area of the circle?
4. How does the number of sections into which the circle is cut affect the area of the parallelogram?
5. How did you use the formula for the area of a parallelogram to estimate the area of the circle?

5.5 Calculating Area

You will need
- a calculator
- a compass
- scissors

▶ **GOAL**

Develop and apply the formula for the area of a circle.

Learn about the Math

Teo is arranging water sprinklers. Each sprinkler sprays water in a circle with a diameter of 8.0 m.

? What area of grass does each sprinkler water?

Teo uses the formula for the area of a parallelogram to develop a formula for the area of a circle. He draws a circle with a diameter of 8.0 cm to model the area that is watered.

He cuts the circle into 20 equal sections. Then he arranges the sections into a parallelogram.

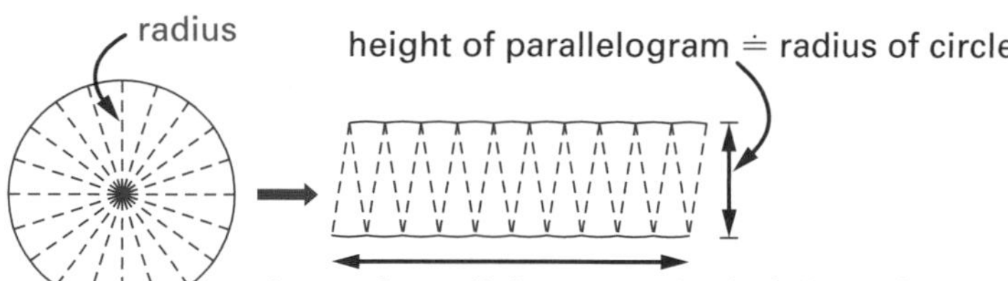

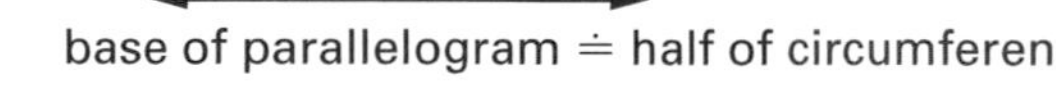

Area of parallelogram = base × height

Area of parallelogram $\doteq \frac{1}{2}$ of circumference × radius

Area of circle = $\frac{1}{2}$ of circumference × radius

The height of the parallelogram is close to the radius of the circle. The base of the parallelogram is about half the circumference of the circle. So, the area of the parallelogram can be used to calculate the area of the circle, using the radius and circumference of the circle.

The formula for the area, A, of a circle with circumference C and radius r is

$$A = \frac{1}{2} \times C \times r \qquad \text{Use } C = 2\pi r.$$

$$= \frac{1}{2} \times 2\pi r \times r$$

$$= 2 \times \frac{1}{2} \times \pi \times r \times r$$

$$= 1 \times \pi \times r^2$$

$$= \pi r^2$$

Example 1: Calculating the area of a circle

A sprinkler waters in a circle with a diameter of 8.0 m. Determine the area that is watered by the sprinkler.

Teo's Solution: Using a formula

$A = \pi r^2$
$\doteq 3.14 \times (4.0\text{ m})^2$
$\doteq 50.2\text{ m}^2$

I used the formula for the area of a circle. The diameter of the circular area is 8.0 m, so the radius is 4.0 m.

The area that is watered is about 50.2 m^2.

My answer uses the same number of decimal places as is given in the problem.

Manuel's Solution: Using the areas of squares

I drew a circle to model the watered area. I covered the circle with paper squares. The sides of the squares are the same length as the radius of the circle.

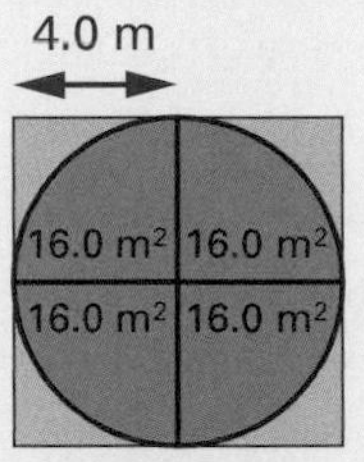

$4r^2 >$ area of the circle

Try four squares. The area of one square is r^2, so the area of four squares is $4r^2$, or 64.0 m^2. Four squares definitely cover more area than the circle does.

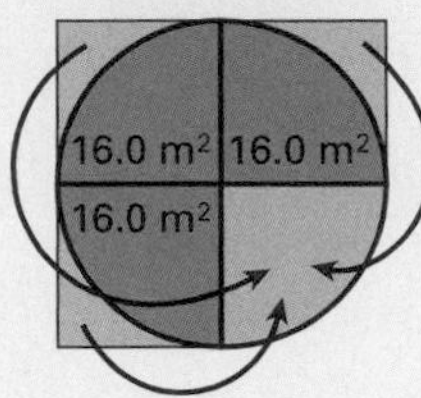

$3r^2$ is about equal to the area of the circle.

$A \doteq 3r^2$
$\doteq 3 \times (4.0\text{ m})^2$
$\doteq 48.0\text{ m}^2$

Try three squares. The area of three squares is $3r^2$, or 48.0 m^2. Three squares seem to cover almost the same area that the circle does. Altogether, the parts of the squares that are outside the circle seem to be about the same area as the uncovered part of the circle.

Since πr^2 is $3.14r^2$, it is reasonable that the area of the circle should be a little more than $3r^2$.

The area that is watered is a little more than 48.0 m^2.

Reflecting

1. How does knowing the formula for the circumference of a circle help you develop the formula for the area of a circle?

2. How can you calculate the area of a circle if you know its radius? What if you know its diameter?

3. Why would you use a formula to determine the area of a circle?

Work with the Math

Example 2: Calculating the area of a circle

A metal cover is needed for a circular fire pit with a radius of 250 cm. What is the area of the fire pit?

Solution

Substitute the radius in the formula for the area of a circle.

$A = \pi r^2$

$\doteq 3.14 \times (250 \text{ cm})^2$

$\doteq 196\ 250 \text{ cm}^2$

The answer is a lot of square centimetres, so I'd rather use square metres. The area of the fire pit is about 19.63 m^2.

Round your answers to the same number of decimal places as in the given measurements.

A Checking

4. Determine the area of each object. Use the formula $A = \pi r^2$.

a) radius 10.5 cm

b) diameter 14 cm

c) radius 13 cm

d) diameter 2.8 cm

B Practising

5. Calculate the area of a circle with each measurement.

a) diameter 7.3 cm

b) radius 2 cm

c) radius 2.7 cm

d) diameter 1.7 cm

6. Explain how to estimate and then calculate the area of the circle.

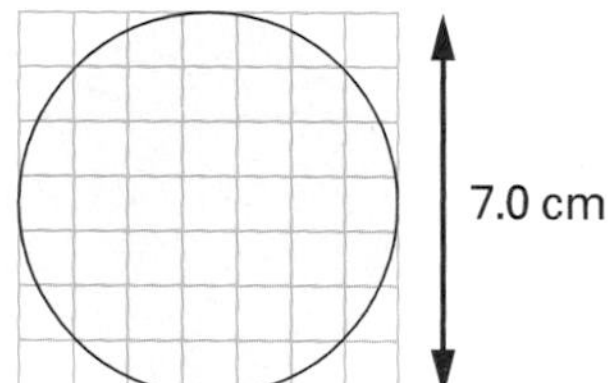

7. a) What area does this circle cover?

b) What is the area of each section?

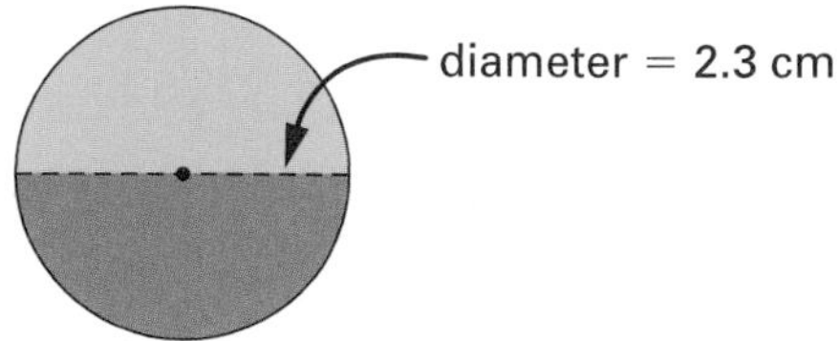

8. a) What area does this circle cover?
   b) The three sections are equal. What is the area of each section?

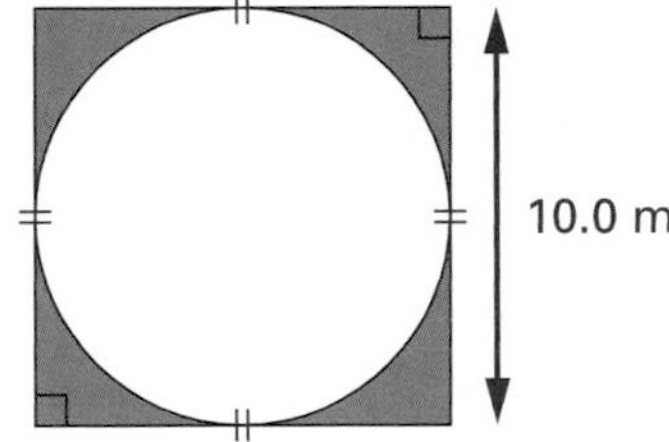

9. The radius of a circular pizza is 22.0 cm.
   a) What area does the pizza cover?
   b) If the pizza is cut into four equal pieces, what is the area of each piece?

10. a) What is the area of the square?
    b) What is the area of the white circle?
    c) What is the total area of the four red sections?

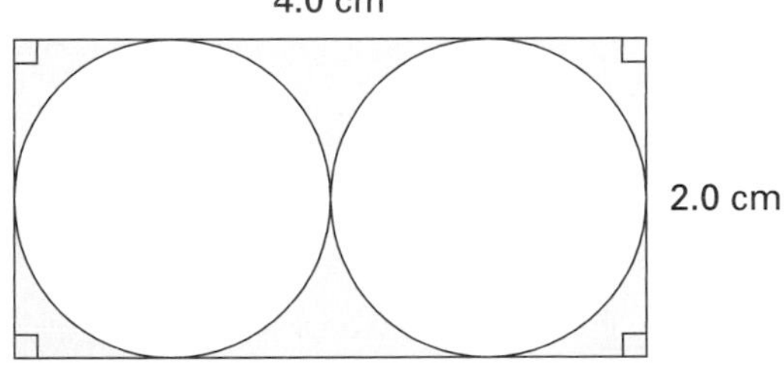

11. Explain the steps you would take to calculate the area of a circle with a circumference of 10.0 cm.

12. a) What is the area of the rectangle?
    b) What is the total area of the six yellow sections?

4.0 cm

2.0 cm

13. The diameter of a DVD is 12.0 cm. The diameter of the hole in the centre is 1.5 cm. Use this information to write a problem that involves area. Then solve your problem.

14. What is the total area of this figure?

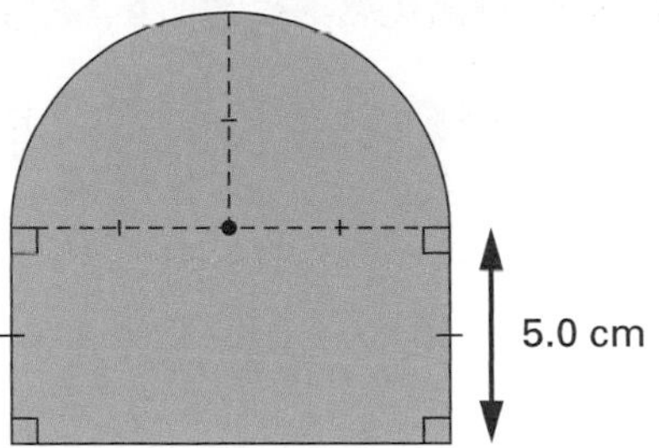

C Extending

15. Carla drew this target on the floor for a bean bag game. The radius of the target is 30.0 cm, and all bands are the same width. What area of the target is red?

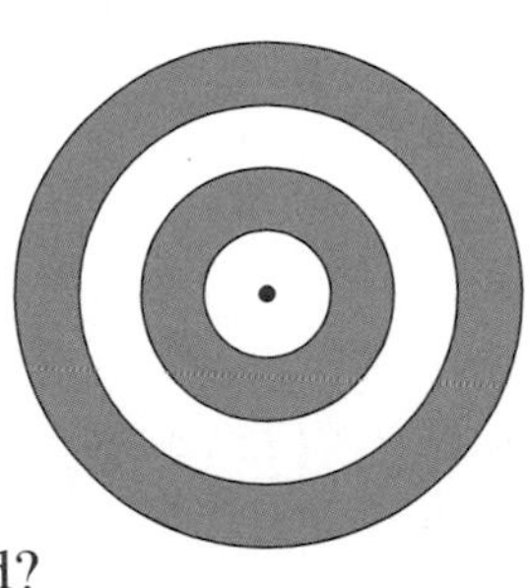

16. Roberto has designed this park for a new housing development. The park is a square with a semicircle at each end. It will be covered with sod and have a border made of paving stones.

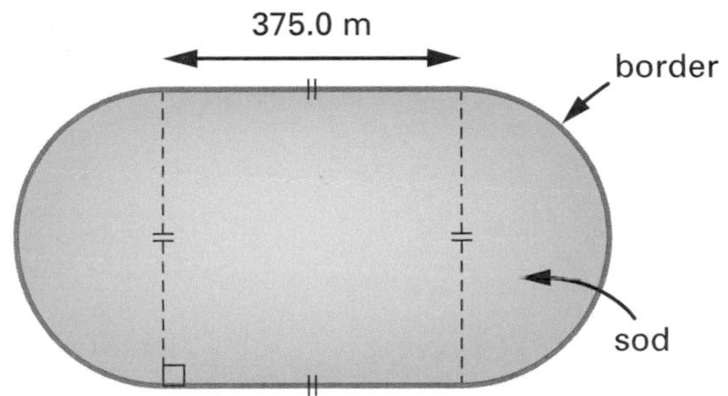

    a) What area of sod is needed to cover the park?
    b) Sod costs $1.25/m^2$. How much will the sod for the park cost?
    c) How long will the border be?
    d) The paving stones cost $2.75/m. How much will the border around the park cost?
    e) How much will the sod and paving stones cost, in total?

5.6 Solve Problems by Working Backward

You will need
- a compass

▶ **GOAL**
Work backward to solve problems.

Learn about the Math

John uses a trundle wheel to measure distance. Each time the wheel makes one complete turn of one metre, it clicks.

? How can you draw a full-sized diagram of a trundle wheel?

1 Understand the Problem

Manuel is going to use a compass to draw a diagram of the trundle wheel. The circumference of the trundle wheel is 1 m. Manuel needs to know the radius.

2 Make a Plan

Manuel knows the formula for circumference. He can work backward from the formula to determine the radius.

3 Carry Out the Plan

$C = \pi d$	Start with the formula for circumference.
$1.00 \text{ m} = \pi d$	Substitute the value of the circumference.
$1.00 \text{ m} \div \pi = d$	Calculate the diameter in metres.
$1.00 \text{ m} \div 3.14 \doteq d$	
$0.32 \text{ m} \doteq d$	The diameter is about 0.32 m, or 32 cm.

The radius is half the diameter, so the radius is about 16 cm.

4 Look Back

Manuel drew a circle with a radius of 16 cm. He measured the circumference with string to check that it was about 1 m.

Reflecting

1. What relationships about circle measurements were needed to solve the problem?

2. How did Manuel work backward to solve the problem?

Work with the Math

Example 1: Constructing a circle with a known area

A pizza parlour sells circular pizzas and square pizzas that require the same amount of dough. The box for a square pizza is 40 cm by 40 cm. What is the area of the smallest box that a circular pizza will fit into?

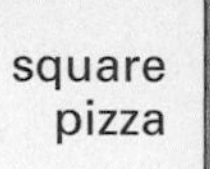

Reilly's Solution

1 Understand the Problem

The circular pizza requires the same amount of dough as the square pizza.

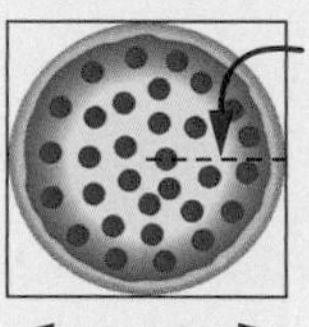

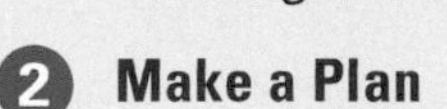

2 Make a Plan

I can calculate the area of the square pizza from the side length. I know that the formula for the area of a circle includes the radius. I can use this formula to work backward to determine the radius of the round pizza.

3 Carry Out the Plan

$A = \pi r^2$	I start with the area formula.
$1600 \text{ cm}^2 = \pi r^2$	The area of the square pizza is $40 \text{ cm} \times 40 \text{ cm} = 1600 \text{ cm}^2$.
$1600 \text{ cm}^2 \div \pi = r^2$	
$510 \text{ cm}^2 \doteq r^2$	The radius must be the square root of 510.
$23 \text{ cm} \doteq r$	

The radius is about 23 cm, so the diameter is about 46 cm (to the nearest centimetre). The box is 46 cm by 46 cm.

4 Look Back

I'll check by substituting the value of the radius into the area formula.

$A = \pi r^2$
$\doteq 3.14 \times (23 \text{ cm})^2$
$\doteq 1661 \text{ cm}^2$

There is a slight difference in the answers due to rounding.
I think my answer is correct.

Example 2: Calculating the original price

During a clothing sale, the price of an item goes down by half each day that it is not sold. If a jacket costs \$4.50 after six days, what was the original price?

Tamara's Solution

1 Understand the Problem

I know that the jacket costs \$4.50 now. I want to know what it cost six days ago.

2 Make a Plan

The price was halved each day. Doubling is the opposite of halving. I will start at the price on day 6 and double the price back to day 1. This will give me the original price.

3 Carry Out the Plan

Day	6	5	4	3	2	1
Price (\$)	4.50	9.00	18.00	36.00	72.00	144.00

$2 \times$ price

The original price of the jacket was \$144.00.

4 Look Back

To check my work, I start with \$144.00 and take half each day to day 6. I end up with \$4.50, so my answer is correct.

A Checking

3. Draw a circle with each measurement.

a) circumference 62.8 cm

b) area 314 cm^2

B Practising

4. Write the calculations in order, to determine the original number.

- Choose a number.
- Add -12.
- Subtract -10.
- Use its opposite.
- Add 12.
- The answer is -32.

5. The area of the circle in this figure is 78.5 m^2. What is the height of the triangle?

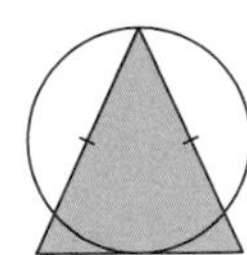

6. This figure covers an area of 706 cm^2.

a) What is the radius of each circle?

b) What is the circumference of each circle?

c) What area is covered by each colour?

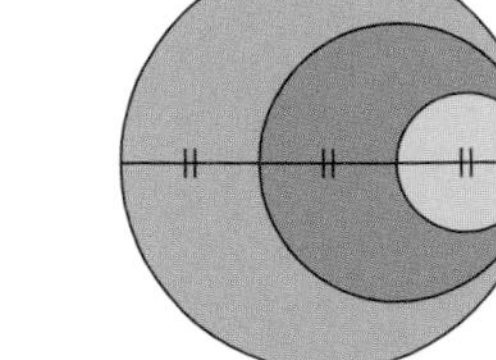

7. Fatouma is lifting weights over a 10-week training period. Every week, she lifts 2 kg more than she lifted the previous week. During the tenth week, she lifts 120 kg. What mass did she lift during the first week?

8. Henri cut away half of a shape five times. The following trapezoid is what remains. Draw what the original shape might have been.

9. Eastward High School needs a new logo for the gym floor. The logo must fit inside a square with an area of 25.0 m^2 and be bordered by a circle.

a) A line for basketball tip-offs will run through the middle of the circle. How long will this line be?

b) What will be the circumference of the circle around the logo?

10. The rim of a bicycle wheel has a circumference of 256.3 cm. Use this information to write three problems that can be solved by working backward. Solve your problems.

11. A lawn sprinkler rotates and sprays water in a circle. It sprays an area of 283 m^2. How far can it spray?

12. The Canadian $2 coin has a copper centre surrounded by a ring of nickel. The diameter of the coin is 2.8 cm. The area of the copper centre is 2.0 cm^2. What is the area of the nickel ring?

Curious Math

CUTTING PAPER STRIPS

Did you know that a piece of paper can have just one side?

You will need
- strips of paper
- tape
- scissors

1. Give a strip of paper half a twist. Tape the ends together.

2. Draw a line down the middle of the paper band. What do you think will happen if you cut along the line? Try it.

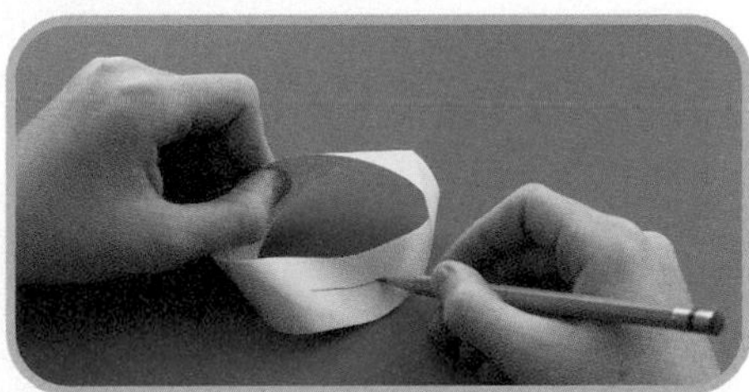

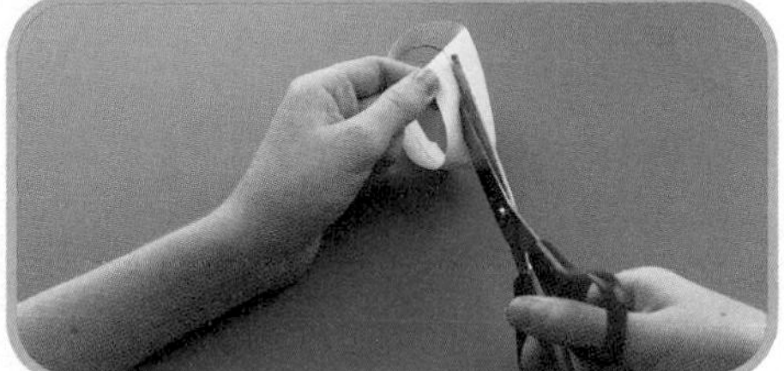

3. Tape two circular strips together as shown. Cut around the circumference of the two strips. Can you make a rectangle or a parallelogram?

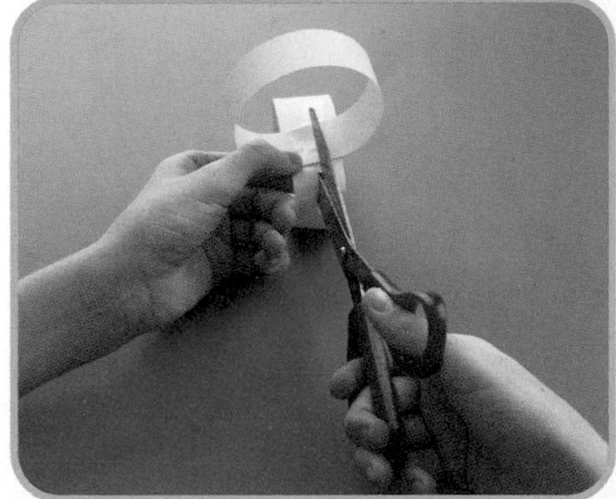

Math Game

ROLLING CIRCLES

You will need
- a 10-sided die numbered 0 to 9
- a pair of dice numbered 1 to 6
- a calculator

In this game, you will estimate the area of a circle, given its radius. Then you will try to form a two-digit number that is close to this area.

Number of players: 2 or more

Rules

1. Roll the 10-sided die. The number you roll represents the radius of a circle. Estimate the area of the circle.
2. Roll the pair of dice. Use the numbers you roll to form any two-digit number.
3. If the difference between the area of the circle and the two-digit number is 10 or less, score 4 points. If the difference is between 10 and 20, score 2 points.
4. Take turns.

The first player to score 10 points wins.

Example

I rolled a 2 with the 10-sided die.

Estimated area of circle $= \pi r^2$

$= \pi \times 2^2$

$\doteq 3 \times 4$

$\doteq 12$

Then I rolled a 3 and a 1 with the pair of dice. I can form 13 or 31 with these numbers. I'll use 13.

Difference $= 13 - 12$

$= 1$

$1 < 10$

My score is 4 points.

Chapter Self-Test

1. Draw a circle with a radius of 6.5 cm. Draw and label a chord, an arc, and a diameter.

2. State whether each measurement is an area or a circumference.
   a) the amount of sod needed to cover the circular green on a golf course
   b) the amount of material needed to make a pool cover
   c) the length of stone used for the border of a round garden
   d) the metal frame around a basketball hoop

3. Explain how to calculate the radius of a circle if you know its diameter.

4. Calculate the circumference of a circle with each measurement.
   a) radius 2.5 km
   b) radius 26 cm
   c) diameter 3.0 cm
   d) diameter 21 cm

5. Calculate the area of a circle with each measurement.
   a) radius 2 cm
   b) diameter 11 cm
   c) diameter 5.7 cm
   d) radius 6.2 cm

6. a) What is the area of the square?
   b) What is the area of the white circle?
   c) What is the area of the blue sections?

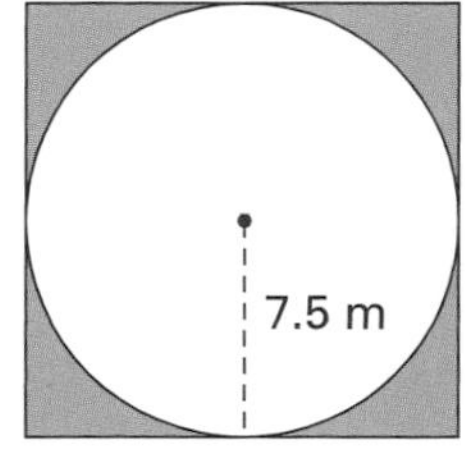

7. What is the area of the orange region?

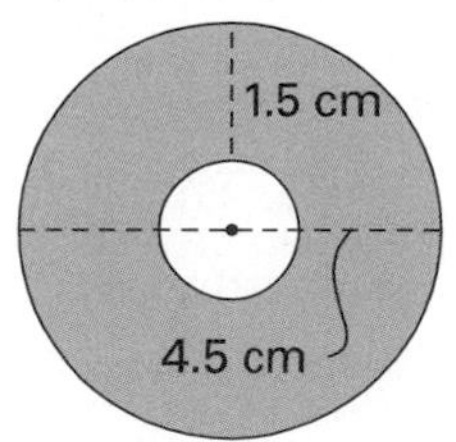

8. What is the area of the red region?

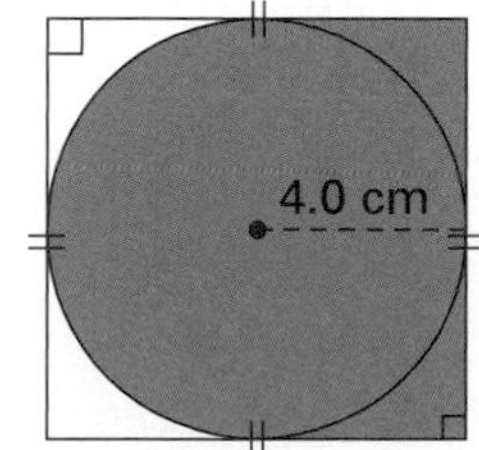

9. a) Determine the area of the park that is not covered by the wading pool.
   b) How much fencing is needed to surround the wading pool?

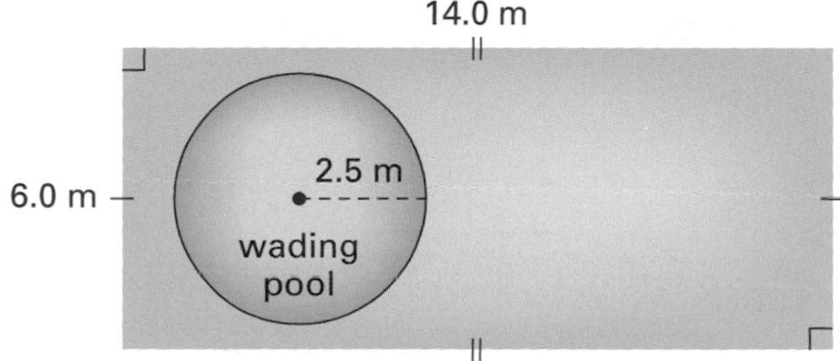

10. Draw a circle with each measurement.
    a) area 113 cm^2
    b) circumference 17.0 cm

11. The gravel bed for Taylor's pool is a circle with an area of 24.6 m^2. How many metres of fencing are needed to go around the bed?

Chapter Review

Frequently Asked Questions

Q: How can you determine the area of a circle?

A1: You can estimate the area using squares. The sides of the squares are the same length as the radius. The area of each square is r^2. About three of these squares cover the same area that the circle covers. For example, the area of a circle with a radius of 3.0 cm is about $3 \times (3 \text{ cm})^2$, or 27 cm^2.

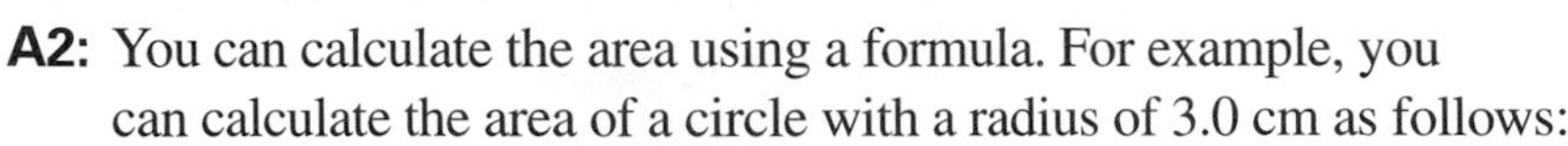

A2: You can calculate the area using a formula. For example, you can calculate the area of a circle with a radius of 3.0 cm as follows:

$$\begin{aligned} A &= \pi r^2 \\ &\doteq 3.14 \times (3.0 \text{ cm})^2 \\ &\doteq 28.3 \text{ cm}^2 \end{aligned}$$

Round to the nearest tenth because this is how the radius was measured.

Q: How can you draw a circle if you know its circumference or area?

A1: Use the formula for the circumference of a circle to determine the radius. For example, determine the radius of a circle with a circumference of 18.8 cm as follows:

$$C = 2\pi r$$

$18.8 \text{ cm} \div 2\pi = r$ Divide both sides by 2π.

$3.0 \text{ cm} \doteq r$ The radius is about 3.0 cm.

Adjust a compass so that the distance between the compass point and the pencil tip is equal to the radius. Put the compass point where you want the centre of the circle to be, and draw the circle.

A2: Use the formula for the area of a circle to determine the radius. For example, determine the radius of a circle with an area of 28.0 cm^2 as follows:

$$A = \pi r^2$$

$28.0 \text{ cm}^2 \div \pi = r^2$ Divide both sides by π.

$9.0 \text{ cm}^2 \doteq r^2$ Determine the square root of both sides.

$3.0 \text{ cm} \doteq r$ The radius is about 3.0 cm.

Use a compass to draw the circle, as described above.

Practice Questions

(5.1) **1.** Steve drew two circles, one with a radius of 10.0 cm and another with a diameter of 10.0 cm. Which circle is which?

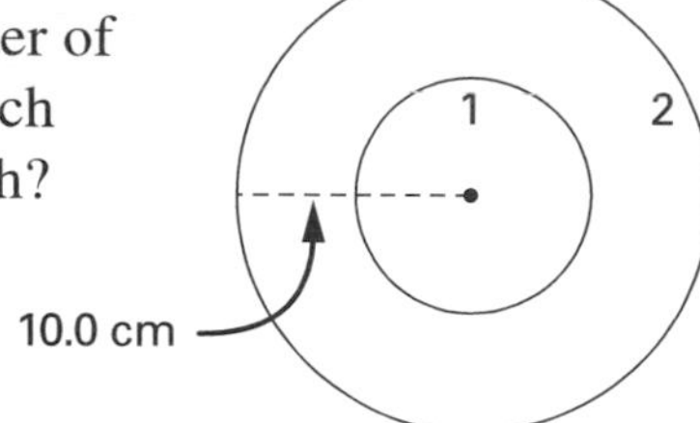

(5.2) **2.** Describe the relationship between the circumference and diameter of a circle.

(5.3) **3.** Calculate the circumference of each circle.

a) radius 2.6 cm

b) diameter 30 cm

c) diameter 1.2 km

d) diameter 8.3 cm

4. A straight boardwalk is being built over a circular wetlands area, so that it divides the area in half. A hiking path goes around the outside. The boardwalk is 50 m long. How long is the hiking path that goes around the wetlands? (5.3)

5. Suppose that you had to tile a circular wading pool. How would you estimate the area of the pool? (5.4)

6. Calculate the area of a circle with each measurement. (5.5)

a) diameter 50 km

b) radius 2 mm

c) radius 6.5 cm

d) diameter 11.0 m

7. Sarah's family has a circular swimming pool. The circumference of the pool is 25.12 m. What is its area? (5.5)

8. Each time a solid bicycle wheel turns, the bicycle travels 197 cm. What is the area of the wheel? (5.5)

9. a) What is the area of this square? (5.5)

b) What is the area of one white section? (*Hint:* It is one quarter of a circle.)

c) What is the area of the four white sections?

d) What is the area of the red section?

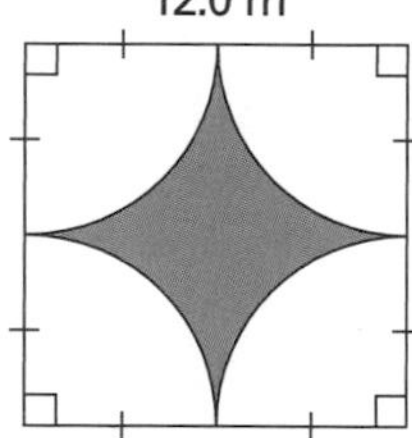

10. Draw a circle with each measurement. (5.6)

a) radius 5.7 cm

b) area 452 cm^2

c) circumference 34.5 cm

Chapter Task

Designing a Camp

The directors of a camp are planning to build a new cabin and a new climbing wall. They want your opinion on the best locations for these features. Keep in mind these requirements:

- The climbing wall must be within 100 m of all the cabins.
- For safety, a fence must be built around the area with the climbing wall. The enclosure must be circular.
- The new cabin must be within 50 m of a shower.
- The siren from the main lodge must be audible at the new cabin. It can be heard 75 m in any direction.

Task Checklist

- ☑ Did you measure accurately?
- ☑ Does your design meet the requirements?
- ☑ Did you include all the necessary information in your explanation?
- ☑ Did your explanation include terms such as "radius," "arc," and "circumference"?

? Where can you put the new cabin and climbing wall?

A. Sketch a map that shows the locations you recommend for the new cabin and climbing wall.

B. Determine the length of fencing that is needed to create the circular enclosure around the climbing wall.

C. Prepare a presentation for the director that shows your calculations and explains your thinking.

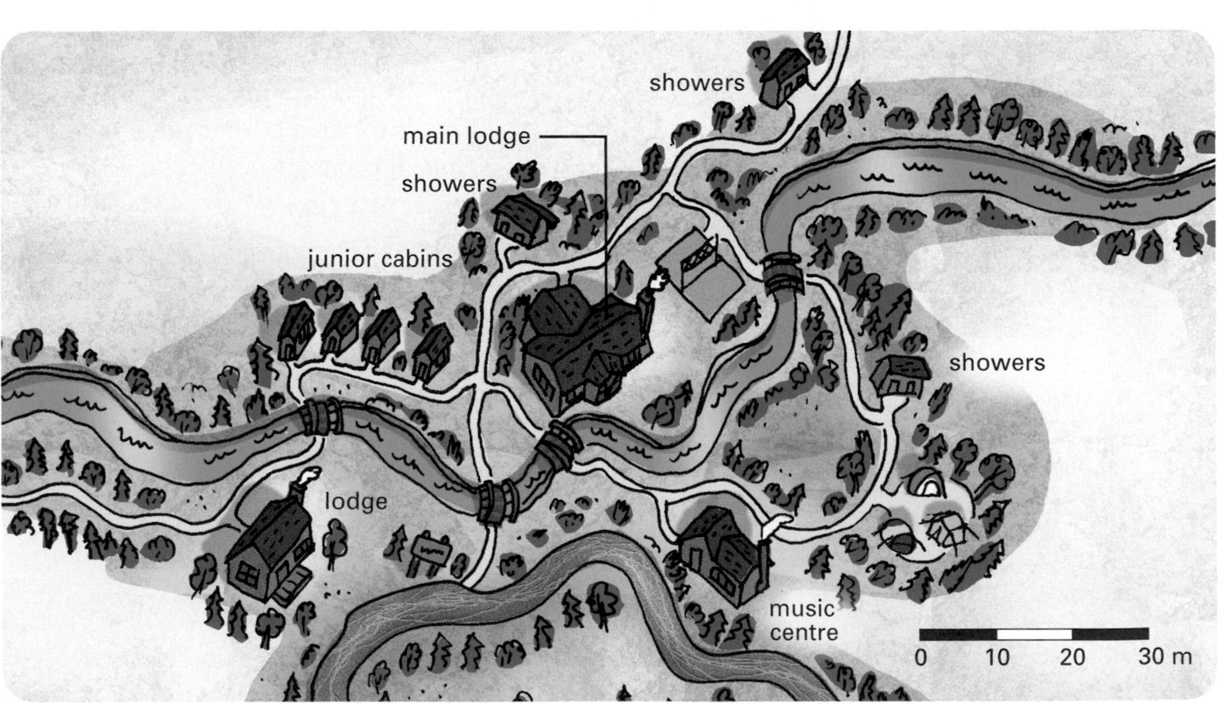

Math in Action

Architect

Douglas Joseph Cardinal is a world-famous Canadian architect. He was born in Calgary. The buildings he has designed include St. Mary's Church in Red Deer, the Telus World of Science in Edmonton, and the Museum of Civilization in Hull. These three buildings are unique because of their circular shape.

Problems, Applications, and Decision Making

When Cardinal designs a building, he begins with a sketch of his vision for the building. Then he uses Computer Assisted Design (CAD) software to draw building plans.

1. How does this view of the Canadian Museum of Civilization show the plan for the dome in the IMAX theatre?

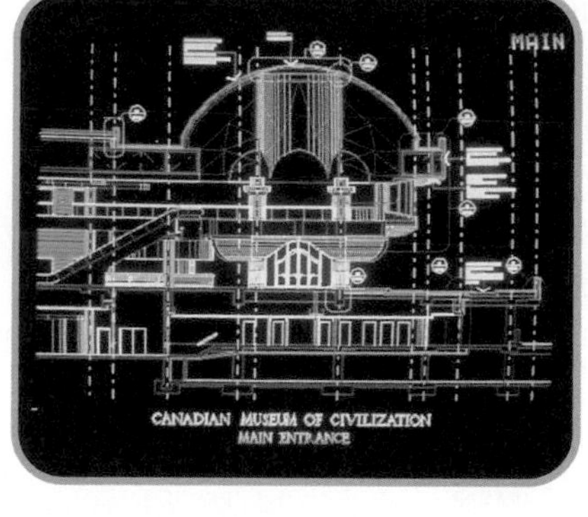

Canadian Museum of Civilization, Hull, Quebec, 1989

2. The diameter of the base of the dome in the IMAX theatre is 24 m.
   a) What is the circumference of the base of the dome, to the nearest metre?
   b) What floor area does the dome cover, to the nearest square metre?

Next Cardinal makes blueprints from the CAD screens.

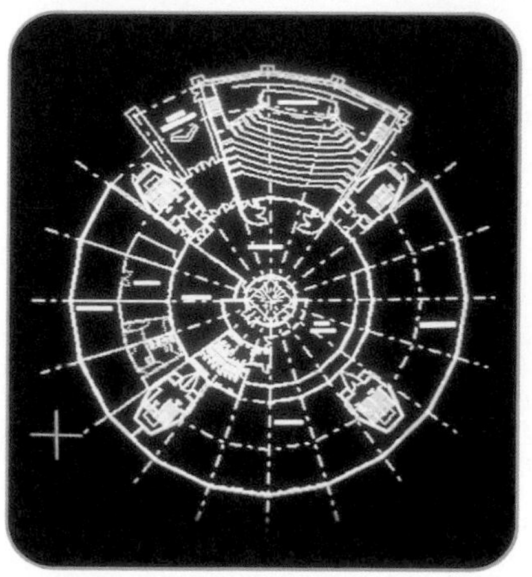

Telus World of Science, Edmonton, Alberta, 1984

3. The circumference of the dome of the planetarium in the Telus World of Science is 72 m.
   a) What is the diameter of the base of the dome, to the nearest metre?
   b) What is the area of the base of the dome, to the nearest square metre?

Cardinal explains, "CAD can provide automatic dimensions or determine exact building measurements. With my curving design for the roof of St. Mary's Church, it would have taken 10 people 100 years, working night and day, to do the calculations by hand."

4. a) What do you think were some of the challenges when designing St. Mary's Church?
   b) What do you think were some of the challenges when constructing St. Mary's Church?

St. Mary's Church, Red Deer, Alberta, 1967

Advanced Applications

Cardinal uses circular structures to enhance communication. "I watched how people work and noticed they don't sit in rows. They sit in circles to see each other. Curved spaces work better for communication."

5. a) Measure your classroom. Calculate its perimeter and area.
   b) Estimate the radius, diameter, and circumference of a circular classroom with the same area. Justify your estimation strategy.
   c) Draw a circular design for your classroom. Label the length of the diameter in your design.
   d) Which shape would you prefer for your classroom: the shape it is, a circular shape, or a different shape? Why?

CHAPTER 6

Integer Operations

▶ GOALS

You will be able to

- compare and order integers
- develop strategies to multiply and divide integers
- add, subtract, multiply, and divide integers
- solve problems that involve integers
- use order of operations with integers

Getting Started

You will need
- a red spinner and a blue spinner, each divided into eighths
- 2 paper clips
- red and blue counters
- number lines
- red and blue coloured pencils

Spinning Numbers

Eva has a red spinner that shows positive numbers and a blue spinner that shows negative numbers. Each spinner is divided into eight equal sections. She spins one spinner and records the number. She spins the other spinner and records the number.

? What are the greatest and least sums possible? What are the greatest and least differences possible?

A. Spin both spinners. Record the sum and the difference in a chart like the one to the right. (Use counters to help you calculate if you wish.) Repeat this nine more times.

Positive number (red)	Negative number (blue)	Sum	Difference

B. Does the order in which you spin the spinners affect the sum? Explain. Does the order in which you spin the spinners affect the difference? Explain.

C. Can you get a sum of 0? Can you get a difference of 0? Explain.

D. What is your greatest sum? What is the greatest sum you could get?

E. What is your least sum? What is the least sum you could get?

F. What is your greatest difference? What is the greatest difference you could get?

G. What is your least difference? What is the least difference you could get?

Do You Remember?

1. Is each statement true or false?

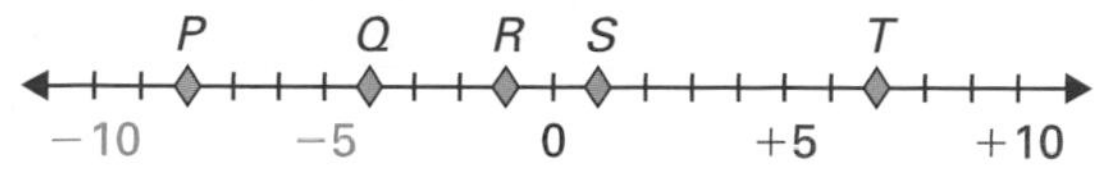

a) $P < S$ **c)** $R > S$

b) $T > Q$ **d)** $R < P$

2. Order the **integers** from least to greatest.

−7, +13, −26, −5, 0, +7

3. Write an integer for each situation.

a) Wanita earned $12.

b) Jeffrey lost $6.

c) The temperature is 11°C below freezing.

d) The highest point in Canada is Mount Logan. It is 5959 m above sea level.

4. Use red counters to model positive numbers, and blue counters to model negative numbers. Draw your models.

a) What is the **opposite integer** of +5?

b) What is the opposite integer of −4?

5. The **zero principle** says that the sum of two opposite integers is 0. Use the zero principle to show that (−3) + (+2) = (−1).

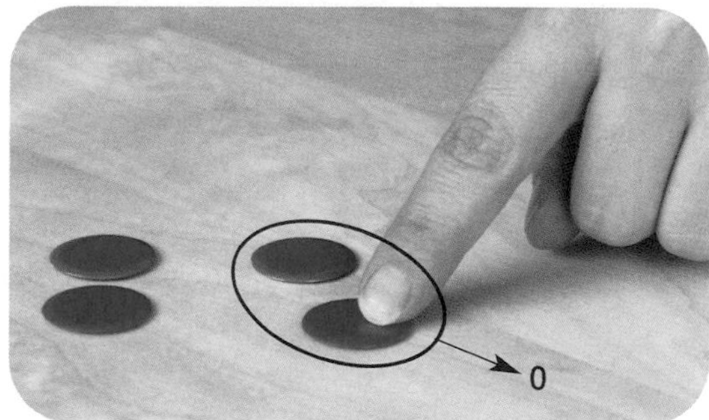

6. Calculate using red and blue counters or a number line as a model. Draw your model.

a) (+1) − (+3) **d)** (+8) − (−3)

b) 0 + (−6) **e)** (+11) + (−7)

c) (−4) + (−7) **f)** (−10) − 0

7. Copy and complete each chart. One is done for you as an example.

Counter model	●●●●●● + ●●●● = ●●
Number sentence	(−6) + (+4) = −2
Number line model	−6 −2 0

a)

Counter model	
Number sentence	(+5) + (−9) = ■
Number line model	−4 0 +5

b)

Counter model	
Number sentence	(+3) − (−2) = ■
Number line model	−2 0 +3

8. Determine the distance and direction on a number line from each starting integer to the ending integer given. Justify your answer using a number line.

Starting integer	Ending integer	Distance and direction
0	+5	
0	−3	
+4	+9	
+7	−4	
−3	−6	
−4	+6	

9. Calculate. Use counters if you wish.

a) (+6) + (+4) + (−5) + (−5)

b) (+5) + (−2) + 0 + (−2)

6.1 Exploring Integer Addition and Subtraction

▶ **GOAL**

Add and subtract integers.

Explore the Math

After being repaired, a zoo's Tropical Forest Exhibit and Antarctica Exhibit were at room temperature, 20°C.

To prepare for exhibiting plants and animals again, the temperature in the Tropical Forest Exhibit was warmed at a constant rate to 28°C. The temperature in the Antarctica Exhibit was cooled at a constant rate to –1°C.

The temperatures were checked after 4 h, 5 h, and 6 h, and recorded as follows:

Time (h)	Temperature in Tropical Forest Exhibit (°C)	Temperature in Antarctica Exhibit (°C)
0		
1		
2		
3		
4	24	8
5	25	5
6	26	2
7		
8		

Communication Tip

- The positive sign (+) is not usually included with positive integers.
- Brackets are only needed when the sign of a number follows an operation symbol and might be confused with the operation symbol. For example, $(+3) + (-6) - (+4)$ can be written as $3 + (-6) - 4$.

NEL

? How can you use integer operations to determine the missing temperatures in the table?

A. Copy and complete the table.

B. Look at the temperature pattern in the Tropical Forest Exhibit. How did the temperature change each hour? Express your answer as a rate, using °C/h.

C. Look at the temperature pattern in the Antarctica Exhibit. How did the temperature change each hour? Express your answer as a rate, using °C/h.

D. Explain why the equation $24 + 3 = \blacksquare$ can be used to calculate the temperature in the Tropical Forest Exhibit after 7 h.

E. Write an equation that can be used to calculate the temperature in the Antarctica Exhibit after 7 h.

F. Write an integer addition or subtraction equation that can be used to calculate the temperature in each exhibit

a) 3 h after the temperature started changing

b) 2 h after the temperature started changing

G. Suppose that the temperatures in both exhibits continued to change at the same rates. What would the temperature be in each exhibit 12 h after it started changing?

H. Suppose that the temperature in the Antarctica Exhibit continued to change at the same rate. If you knew that the temperature in the Antarctica Exhibit was −1°C, what equation could you use to determine the temperature 5 h later?

Reflecting

1. Why did you need to know the rate at which the temperature changed in each exhibit before you could calculate the temperatures that were not recorded?

2. How could you use a pattern, a number line, or integer calculations to help you complete the table?

3. How could you use integer calculations to calculate the temperatures in steps E and F?

6.2 Relating Integer Subtraction to Addition

You will need
- number lines
- coloured pencils
- red and blue counters
- a calculator

▶ **GOAL**

Subtract integers by measuring the distance between them.

Learn about the Math

The highest temperature ever recorded was 58°C in Libya in 1922.
The lowest temperature ever recorded was −89°C in Antarctica in 1983.

? What is the range of these temperatures?

Ken wrote 58 − (−89) but was not sure how to complete the calculation. Nathan suggested using a number line. Ken said that the numbers were too great to count the spaces.

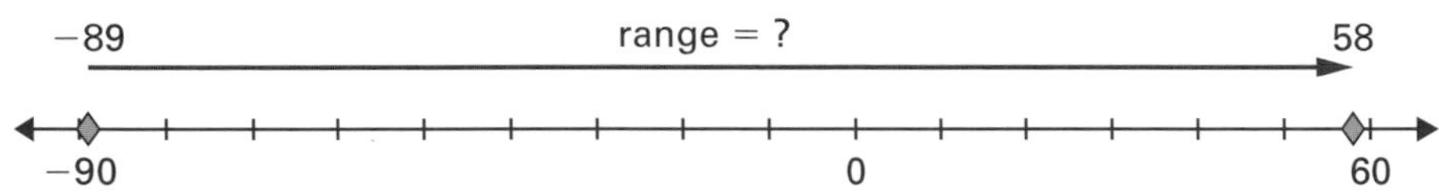

Example 1: Using a number line to solve a simpler problem first

What is the difference between 58°C and –89°C?

Nathan's Solution

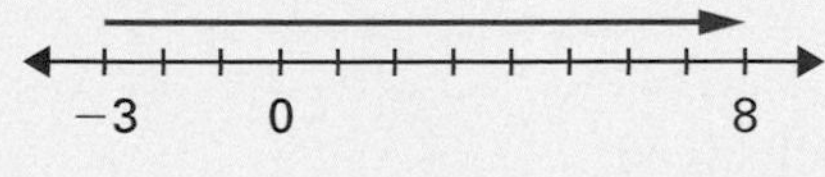

First I subtracted 8 − (−3) using a number line.

$8 - (-3) = 8 + 3$
$= 11$

To subtract −3 from 8, I drew an arrow to show what to add to −3 to get to 8. Since the arrow goes to the right, it represents a positive number. So I coloured it red. The arrow is 3 + 8 = 11 units long.

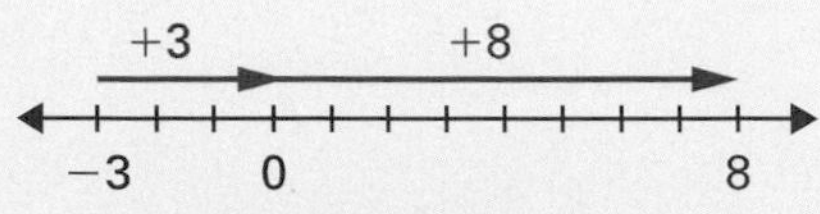

The part of the arrow from −3 to 0 is 3. The rest of the arrow, from 0 to 8, is 8.

Subtracting 8 − (−3) has the same result as adding 8 + 3.

$58 - (-89) = 58 + 89$
$= 147$

The range is 147°C.

It makes sense that subtracting an integer has the same result as adding its opposite. On a number line, the part of the arrow from −89 to 0 is 89. The rest of the arrow is 58.

58 − (−89) must equal 58 + 89.

NEL

Example 2: Using counters to solve a simpler problem first

What is the difference between 58°C and –89°C?

Ken's Solution

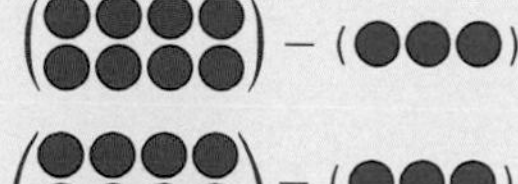

First I tried subtracting simpler numbers, using counters: 8 – (–3).

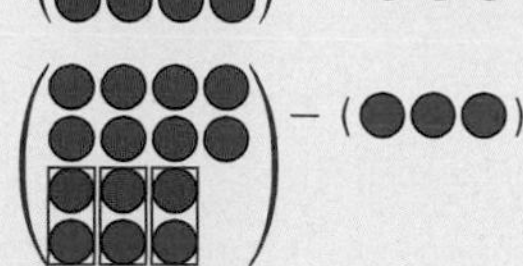

I used the zero principle to add enough blue and red counter pairs so that I could subtract.

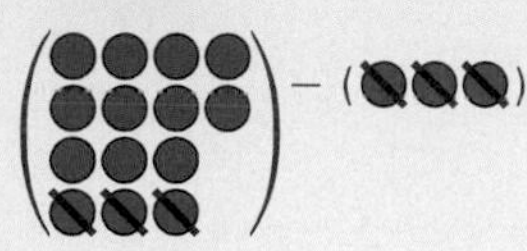

Then I subtracted –3 from both brackets. The answer is 11.

$8 - (-3) = 8 + 3$
$= 11$

Subtracting the three negative counters has the same result as adding three positive counters.

$58 - (-89) = 58 + 89$
$= 147$

The range is 147°C.

Subtracting –89 would have the same result as adding 89, since I'd add 89 blue and 89 red counters, but subtract the 89 blue counters. 58 + 89 is about 60 + 90, or 150. The exact answer 147 makes sense.

Reflecting

1. How does using counters and the zero principle show that subtracting 58 – (–89) has the same result as adding 58 and the opposite of –89?

2. Why does the order in which the numbers are written matter for subtraction but not for addition? Give examples to show your reasoning.

Work with the Math

Example 3: Subtracting using a calculator

Calculate 115 + (–218) – (–137).

Solution A: Using the negative sign key on a TI-15 calculator

115 [+] [(-)] 218 [–] [(-)] 137 [Enter]

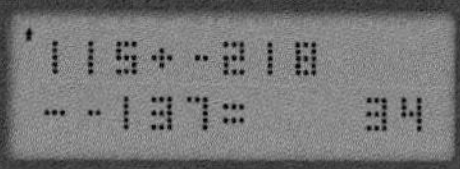

Solution B: Using the sign change key on other calculators

115 [+] 218 [+/–] [–] 137 [+/–] [=]

34.

Example 4: Comparing differences

Par is the standard score for the number of strokes a good player usually needs to complete a hole or an entire game of golf.

Golfer	Tuesday score	Wednesday score
Rae	6 above par = +6	3 below par = −3
Lorna	2 below par = −2	1 below par = −1
Megan	5 above par = +5	par = 0

a) By how many strokes did each golfer's score increase or decrease?

b) List the golfers in order, starting with the golfer whose score decreased the most.

Solution

a) $-3 - 6 = -3 + (-6)$
$= -9$ Rae's score decreased by 9 strokes.

$-1 - (-2) = -1 + 2$
$= 1$ Lorna's score increased by 1 stroke.

$0 - 5 = 0 + (-5)$
$= -5$ Megan's score decreased by 5 strokes.

b) The order, starting with the golfer whose score decreased the most, is Rae, Megan, and Lorna.

A Checking

3. a) Draw a number line to represent $5 - (-2)$.

b) Use counters and the zero principle to represent $5 - (-2)$. Draw your model.

c) Write the addition statement that is equivalent to $5 - (-2)$.

4. The temperature was −8°C on Tuesday night and 2°C on Wednesday afternoon. What was the temperature change?

B Practising

5. Calculate. Order the differences from greatest to least.

a) $7 - (-9)$ **c)** $-22 - (-10)$

b) $8 - 8$ **d)** $0 - 11$

6. Match the equivalent addition and subtraction expressions.

a) $-6 - 9$ **A.** $10 + (-12)$

b) $-10 - (-12)$ **B.** $-6 + (-9)$

c) $6 - 9$ **C.** $-12 + (-10)$

d) $10 - 12$ **D.** $6 + (-9)$

e) $-12 - 10$ **E.** $-10 + 12$

7. Write each subtraction as an addition. Then calculate without using a calculator.

a) $-10 - (-8)$ **d)** $0 - 10$

b) $3 - (-7)$ **e)** $-8 - 6$

c) $-6 - 0$ **f)** $-15 - (-5)$

8. Calculate. How could you estimate to see if each answer is reasonable?

a) $-32 - (-54)$ **c)** $19 - (-24)$

b) $36 - (-17)$ **d)** $-17 - 23$

9. For Example 3, Eva decided to estimate the answer for 115 + (−218) − (−137). She said, "About 100 minus about 200 is negative 100. Then add 137. My estimate is 37." Is her estimate reasonable? Explain.

10. Trevor recorded temperature changes for his science project. Copy and complete his chart.

Time	Temperature change (°C)	Temperature (°C)
Mon. a.m.	none	−7
Mon. p.m.	drop of 18	
Tues. a.m.	rise of 12	
Tues. p.m.		−23
Wed. p.m.		2

11. The highest point in North America is Mt. McKinley, and the lowest point is Death Valley. Mount McKinley is 6194 m above sea level. Death Valley is 87 m below sea level. Is 6100 m or 6300 m a better estimate of the difference between these heights? Explain.

12. Create a subtraction problem for each pair of integers.

a) −12 and 9 **b)** −1 and −14

13. Calculate.

a) 12 − (−5) + (−4)

b) −16 + 14 − 5

c) 22 − 30 + 0 − (−7)

d) −40 + (−50) + 90 − (−60)

14. Evaluate using a calculator.

a) −128 − (−306)

b) −119 + (−237) − (−155)

c) −7145 − 3658 + (−2159)

15. Erica had $45. She spent $18, earned $22, and then spent $6.

a) Write a number sentence, using only whole numbers, to show how much money Erica has.

b) Write another number sentence, using some negative integers, to show how much money Erica has.

16. a) What do you notice about subtracting 0 from an integer? Why does this make sense?

b) What do you notice about subtracting an integer from 0? Why does this make sense?

17. Dry ice is solid carbon dioxide. Its temperature is about −98°C. How much less is this temperature than room temperature, which is about 20°C?

18. Suppose that you randomly select two of the following integers and then subtract the integers in the order you selected them. Explain whether the difference is likely to be positive or negative.

−40, 3, −12, 83

19. Determine the tenth term in each number pattern.

a) 12, 3, −6, … **b)** −18, −7, 4, …

C Extending

20. When is the sum of two integers less than the difference?

21. When is the difference between two integers less than the sum?

6.3 Exploring Integer Multiplication

You will need
- red and blue counters
- number lines
- coloured pencils
- a calculator

▶ **GOAL**
Explore models of, and patterns for, integer multiplication.

Explore the Math

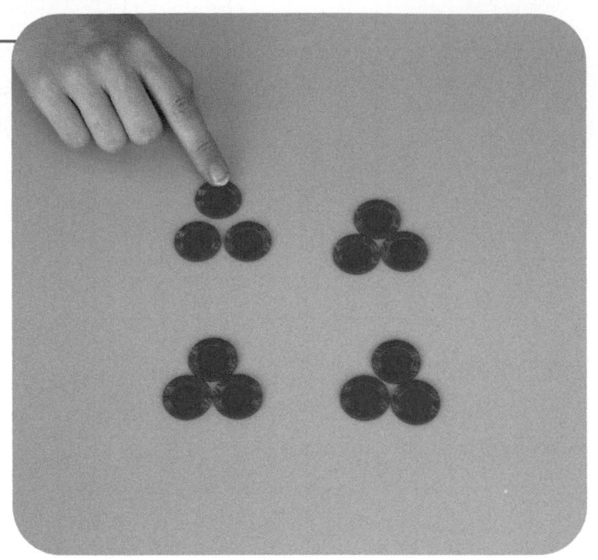

Susan's younger brother Sam is sending a package of three stickers to each of his four cousins. He wonders how many stickers are in the four packages. Susan shows Sam how to multiply 4×3.

"Multiplying 4×3 is the same as adding four groups of three."

Susan then shows Sam another way to multiply 4×3.

"Start at 0 on a number line, and skip count by 3 four times."

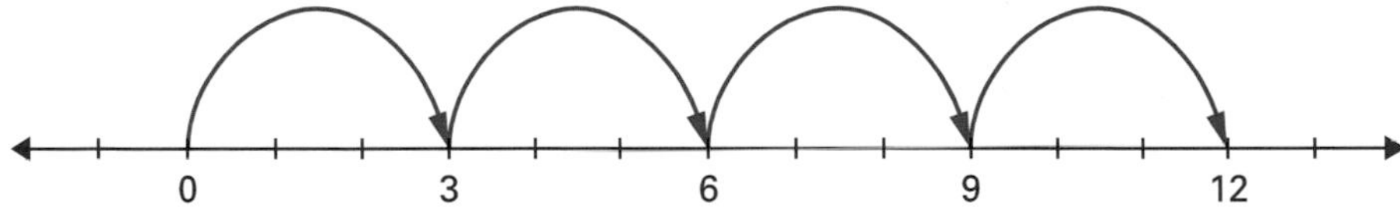

Susan knows that the product of two positive integers is positive. She wonders what will happen if she multiplies by a negative integer; for example, $4 \times (-3)$.

? What happens when you multiply a positive or negative integer by a negative integer?

A. Use blue counters to represent $4 \times (-3)$ as four groups of -3. What is the value of the product?

B. Start at 0 on a number line. Skip count by -3s, going to the left, four times. Where do you end up?

C. Use a calculator to verify your results in steps A and B.

D. Copy and complete the following chart.

Pattern 1	Pattern 2	Pattern 3	Pattern 4
$-2 \times 3 = ■$	$-5 \times 3 = ■$	$3 \times (-3) = ■$	$4 \times (-4) = ■$
$-2 \times 2 = ■$	$-5 \times 2 = ■$	$2 \times (-3) = ■$	$3 \times (-4) = ■$
$-2 \times 1 = ■$	$-5 \times 1 = ■$	$1 \times (-3) = ■$	$2 \times (-4) = ■$
$-2 \times 0 = ■$	$-5 \times 0 = ■$	$0 \times (-3) = ■$	$1 \times (-4) = ■$
$-2 \times (-1) = ■$	$-5 \times (-1) = ■$	$-1 \times (-3) = ■$	$0 \times (-4) = ■$
$-2 \times (-2) = ■$	$-5 \times (-2) = ■$	$-2 \times (-3) = ■$	$-1 \times (-4) = ■$
$-2 \times (-3) = ■$	$-5 \times (-3) = ■$	$-3 \times (-3) = ■$	$-2 \times (-4) = ■$

E. Use a calculator to verify the last product for each pattern in step D.

F. Each multiplication in Pattern 1 follows the pattern rule $-2 \times n$ or $-2n$, where n is any integer. Copy and complete this table of values.

Input integer (n)	Output integer ($-2n$)
3	$-2 \times 3 = -6$
2	$-2 \times 2 = ■$
1	$-2 \times 1 = ■$
0	$-2 \times 0 = ■$
-1	$-2 \times (-1) = ■$
-2	$-2 \times (-2) = ■$
-3	$-2 \times (-3) = ■$

G. Create a pattern rule for each of Pattern 2, Pattern 3, and Pattern 4.

H. Use your answers in steps D to G to complete this chart.

a	b	$a \times b$
positive	positive	
positive	negative	
negative	positive	
negative	negative	

Reflecting

1. Use a real-world meaning for -3 to explain why $4 \times (-3) = -12$ makes sense.
2. Why does it make sense that $4 \times (-3)$ and -3×4 have the same product?
3. Why is it easier to model $4 \times (-3)$ than $-4 \times (-3)$ using counters?
4. Explain your strategies for completing the chart in step H.

6.4 Multiplying Integers

You will need
- number lines
- coloured pencils
- red and blue counters
- a calculator

▶ **GOAL**
Develop and apply strategies to multiply integers.

Learn about the Math

Eva says, "I can hike about 3 km/h. Sometimes I walk east from my home. Other times I walk west."

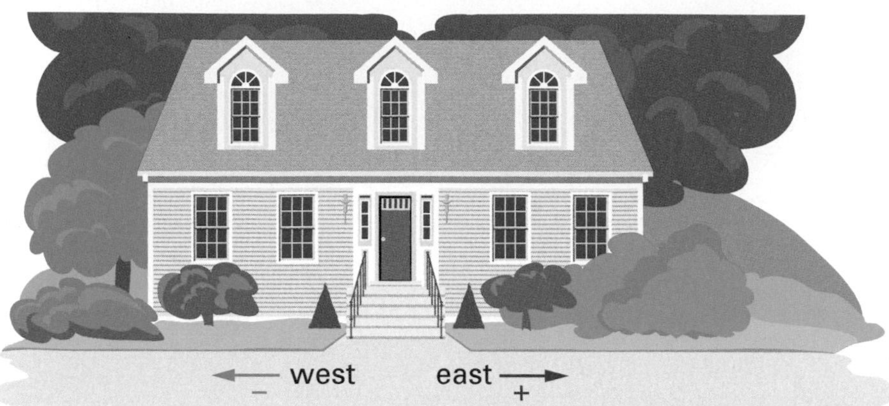

? If you know where Eva is now, how can you calculate where she was earlier?

Use a positive sign to mean hiking to the east. Use a negative sign to mean hiking to the west. Home is neither positive nor negative because it is located at 0.

A. How far from home is Eva if she hikes east for 10 h at 3 km/h? Draw this on a number line.

B. Describe your drawing in step A using a repeated addition sentence. Then describe your drawing using a multiplication sentence.

C. How far, and in which direction, has Eva hiked if her location can be determined using each of these calculations?

a) $4 \text{ h} \times 3 \text{ km/h}$ **b)** $2 \text{ h} \times (-3 \text{ km/h})$

D. Model each multiplication in step C on a number line.

E. Suppose that Eva has been hiking east for 6 h.

a) Why does $6 \text{ h} \times 3 \text{ km/h}$ represent her distance from home?

b) Why does $0 - 6 \text{ h} \times 3 \text{ km/h}$ represent how far, and in which direction, she would need to hike to get back home?

c) Why does $0 - 6 \text{ h} \times 3 \text{ km/h}$ have the same result as $-6 \text{ h} \times 3 \text{ km/h}$?

F. Model each multiplication in step E on a number line.

G. Suppose that Eva has been hiking west for 2 h.

a) Why does 2 h $\times$ (-3 km/h) represent her distance from home?

b) Why does $0 - 2$ h $\times$ (-3 km/h) represent how far she would need to hike to get back home?

Reflecting

1. Why does it make sense to describe east as positive (+) and west as negative (−)?

2. How does knowing $0 - 18 = -18$ show that $(-6) \times 3 = -18$ in step E?

3. How does knowing $0 - (-6) = 6$ show that $(-2) \times (-3) = 6$ in step G?

4. How can you predict the sign of the product of two integers?

Communication Tip

The multiplication of integers can be written without the multiplication symbol ($\times$). For example, $-10 \times (-20)$ can be written as $(-10)(-20)$.

Work with the Math

Example 1: Using integer products to solve distance problems

Eli walks to the west at 80 m/min.

a) Where will he be after 5 min?

b) Suppose that Eli walked west for 18 min. His position would be 18 min $\times$ (-80 m/min). How far must he walk to return to his starting position? What direction must he walk?

Denis's Solution

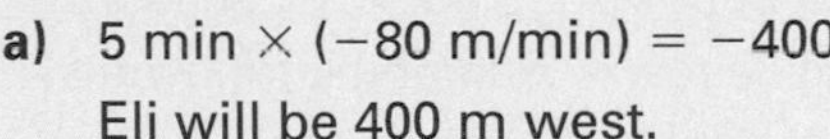

a) 5 min $\times$ (-80 m/min) $= -400$

Eli will be 400 m west.

I multiplied $5 \times 80 = 400$.

I know that a positive integer multiplied by a negative integer results in a negative integer. So the product must be -400.

b) 18 min $\times$ (-80 m/min) $= 18 \times (-80)$

$= -1440$

Eli must walk 1440 m east.

I multiplied $18 \times 80 = 1440$.

I know that a positive integer multiplied by a negative integer results in a negative integer. So the product must be -1440.

Eli walked 1440 m west. He must walk back the same distance, but in the opposite direction, to return to his starting position.

Example 2: Modelling integer multiplication

Multiply $-3 \times (-2)$ using a model.

Eva's Solution: Using counters

I can model $3 \times (-2)$ by adding three groups of two negative counters to 0.
So, I can model $-3 \times (-2)$ by subtracting three groups of two negative counters from 0.

I can't take away the six negative counters. So I used the zero principle to add six positive counters and six negative counters.

Then I subtracted.

(●● ●● ●● ●● ●● ●●) − (●● ●● ●●)
= (●●●●●●)

Six positive counters are left.
The answer is $-3 \times (-2) = 6$.

Nathan's Solution: Using a number line

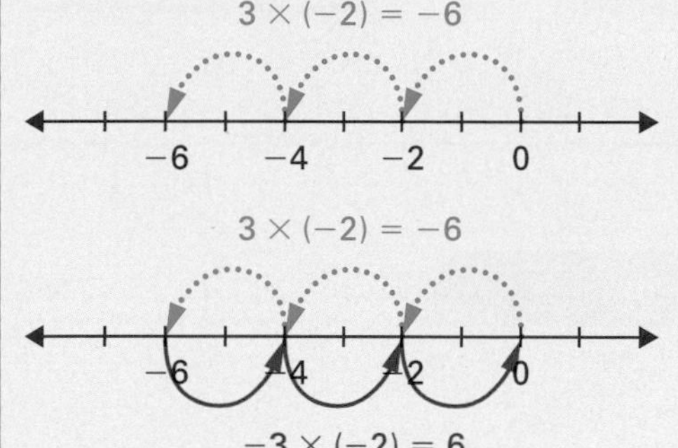

$-3 \times (-2)$ means the same as $0 - 3 \times (-2)$, which is the opposite of $3 \times (-2)$.

To show $3 \times (-2)$, I drew 3 dotted blue arrows going left from 0, with each arrow 2 units. The arrows stop at -6.

To show the opposite of $3 \times (-2)$, I drew 3 solid red arrows going right from -6 back to 0.

These red arrows go to the right 6 units. So the answer must be 6, which is the opposite of -6.

A Checking

5. Write the multiplication sentence that each model represents.

a) 

b) 0 − (●●●● ●●●● ●●●● ●●●● ●●●●)

c)

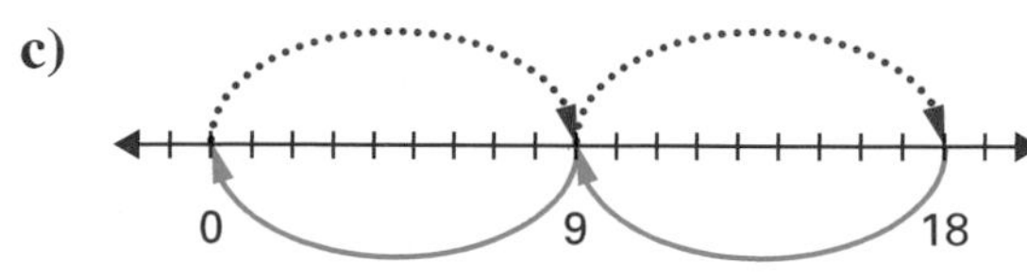

d)

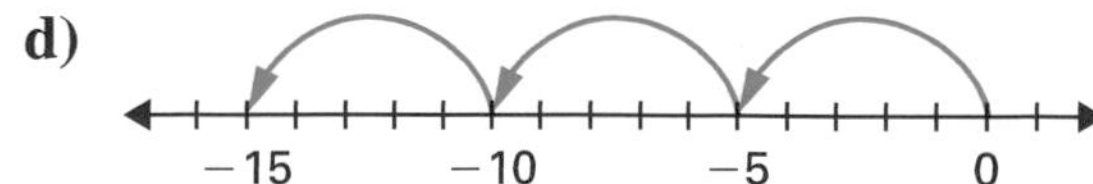

6. Dario is on a cycling trip. He started at 0 km. He is now at position 20 h × (−20 km/h). When did he reach each of the following positions? Explain your reasoning.

a) 10 h × (−20 km/h)

b) 8 h × (−20 km/h)

c) 0 km

B Practising

7. a) Model $-4 \times (-3)$ on a number line. Calculate the product. Explain what you did.

b) Model $-4 \times (-3)$ with counters. Calculate the product. Explain what you did.

8. How would you calculate $(-4)(-7)$? Justify your strategy.

9. Write each as a multiplication expression, and then solve.

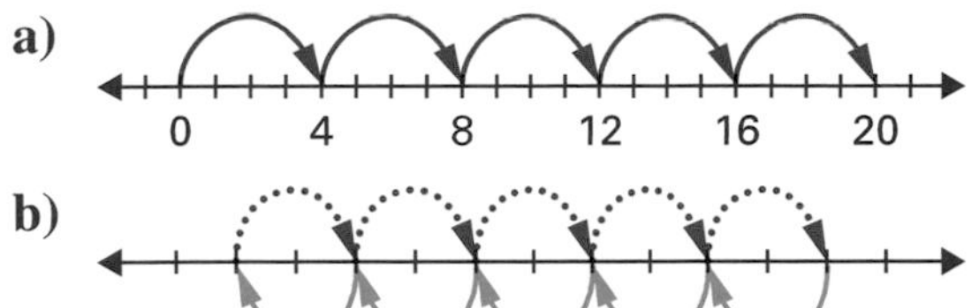

10. Write an integer multiplication sentence for each description.
    - **a)** Tyler rode a bus west for 4 h at 100 km/h.
    - **b)** Jenna babysat for 3 h, earning $5 an hour.
    - **c)** The temperature fell 2°C a day for 6 days.

11. Jasmine has 50 shares of a stock. The value of each share went down by $2 today. Express the total change in value of Jasmine's shares as an integer calculation.

12. Write a multiplication question for each repeated addition, and then solve.
    - **a)** $-5 + (-5) + (-5)$
    - **b)** $-8 + (-8) + (-8) + (-8) + (-8)$
    - **c)** $0 + 0 + 0 + 0 + 0 + 0 + 0$

13. Write a repeated addition question for each multiplication, and then solve.
    - **a)** $2 \times (-9)$
    - **b)** $(4)(8)$
    - **c)** $(3)(-6)$
    - **d)** $(7)(0)$

14. Multiply.
    - **a)** -2×4
    - **b)** $-8 \times (-9)$
    - **c)** $(7)(8)$
    - **d)** $(-9)(-9)$

15. Calculate each product. Order the products from greatest to least.
    - **a)** $(0)(-20)$
    - **b)** $(-6)(-30)$
    - **c)** $(7)(-80)$
    - **d)** $(-20)(50)$

16. What is the greatest possible product of any two numbers in this list? Explain your answer.

    $-3, -7, -15, 6$

17. The product of two integers is between -20 and -25. What are the integers? Give five answers.

18. Determine the missing integer for $-9 \times (■) = 63$. Explain what you did.

19. Continue each pattern for the next three terms. Explain the pattern rule.
    - **a)** $-2, 4, -8, 16,$ ■, ■, ■, ...
    - **b)** $-15, 30, 90, -360,$ ■, ■, ■, ...

20. Multiply.
    - **a)** $-5 \times 3 \times (-2)$
    - **b)** $-2 \times (-3) \times (-4) \times (-5)$
    - **c)** $4 \times (-3) \times (-2)$

21. The product of five different integers is -80.
    - **a)** What is the least possible sum of these five integers?
    - **b)** Is it possible for the product of four different integers to be -80? Explain.

22. Estimate each product.
    - **a)** $-35 \times (-25)$
    - **b)** $(-18)(38)$
    - **c)** $-21 \times 9 \times (-16)$

C Extending

23. Multiply any three integers that are not in the same row or column. Repeat with other sets of three integers. What do you notice?

−32	40	−24
28	−35	21
−8	10	−6

Mid-Chapter Review

Frequently Asked Questions

Q: How can you add integers?

A: You can use counters, a number line, or addition rules. Or you can use a calculator.

Addition question	Counter model	Number line model	Addition rule
5 + 2 = 7	(●●●●●) + (●●) = ●●●●●●●	0 5 7	5 + 2 = 7
−5 + (−2) = −7	(●●●●●) + (●●) = ●●●●●●●	−7 −5 0	(−5) + (−2) = −5 − 2 = −7
5 + (−2) = 3	(●●●●●) + (●●) = (●●● ●● ●●) = (●●●)	0 3 5	5 + (−2) = 5 − 2 = 3
−5 + 2 = −3	(●●●●●) + (●●) = (●●● ●● ●●) = (●●●)	−5 −3 0	−5 + 2 = −3

Q: How can you subtract integers?

A: You can use counters or a number line, or add the opposite. Or you can use a calculator.

Subtraction question	Counter model	Number line model	Addition of opposite
2 − 5 = −3	(●●) − (●●●●●) = (●● ●● ●● ●●) − (●●●●●) = ●●●	0 2 5	2 − 5 = 2 + (−5) = −3
−5 − (−2) = −3	(●●●●●) − (●●) = ●●●	−5 −2 0	−5 − (−2) = −5 + 2 = −3
5 − (−2) = 7	(●●●●●) − (●●) = (●●●●● ●● ●●) − (●●) = ●●●●●●●	−2 0 5	5 − (−2) = 5 + 2 = 7
−5 − 2 = −7	(●●●●●) − (●●) = (●●●●● ●● ●●) − (●●) = ●●●●●●●	−5 0 2	−5 − 2 = −5 + (−2) = −7

Q: How can you multiply integers?

A: You can use counters, a number line, or repeated addition. Or you can use a calculator. The following models show that

$(+) \times (+) = +$ $(-) \times (+) = -$ $(+) \times (-) = -$ $(-) \times (-) = +$

Multiplication question	Counter model	Number line model
$4 \times 3 = 12$	4 groups of 3 positive (red) counters give a total of 12 positive (red) counters.	0 3 6 9 12 4 arrows to the right, with each arrow 3 units long, give a result of 12 units to the right, or 12. $3 + 3 + 3 + 3 = 12$
$4 \times (-3) = -12$	4 groups of 3 negative (blue) counters give a total of 12 negative (blue) counters.	−12 −9 −6 −3 0 4 arrows to the left, with each arrow 3 units long, give a result of 12 units to the left, or −12. $-3 + (-3) + (-3) + (-3) = -12$
$-4 \times 3 = -12$	0−( ) = = $0 - 4 \times 3$ means subtract 4 groups of 3 red counters from 0. Use the zero principle, and add 4 groups of 3 red counters and 4 groups of 3 blue counters. Then subtract the 4 groups of 3 red counters. You're left with 4 groups of 3 blue counters, or 12 blue counters.	0 3 6 9 12 4 arrows to the left, with each arrow 3 units long, give a result of 12 units to the left, or −12. $0 - 4 \times 3$ means the opposite of 4×3, or the opposite of 12, which is −12.
$-4 \times (-3) = 12$	0−( ) = = $0 - 4 \times (-3)$ means subtract 4 groups of 3 negative (blue) counters from 0. The result is 4 groups of 3 positive (red) counters, or a total of 12 positive (red) counters.	−12 −9 −6 −3 0 4 arrows to the right, with each arrow 3 units long, give a result of 12 units to the right, or 12. $0 - 4 \times (-3)$ means the opposite of $4 \times (-3)$, or the opposite of −12, which is 12.

Practice Questions

(6.2) **1.** Calculate. Order the results from least to greatest.

a) $-30 - 8$ **c)** $2 + (-2)$

b) $4 - (-75)$ **d)** $39 - (-5)$

(6.2) **2.** Surface water temperatures on the Atlantic side of Newfoundland range from 13°C in the summer to −1°C in the winter. What is the range?

(6.2) **3.** Write integers to make this equation true. Give three possible answers.

$\blacksquare - \blacksquare + \blacksquare = -10$

(6.2) **4. a)** Explain why the sum of two negative integers is always less than each integer.

b) Use examples to show that the difference between two negative integers is not always less than either integer.

(6.2) **5.** Suppose that you randomly choose three of these four integers: −8, 8, −18, and 28. Is the sum likely to be positive, negative, or 0? Explain.

(6.3) **6.** Charlotte said, "If I multiply a negative integer and a positive integer, I know that the product is negative even without knowing the exact integers." Is Charlotte correct? Justify your answer.

(6.3) **7.** Write the multiplication equation that is modelled by each number line.

a) 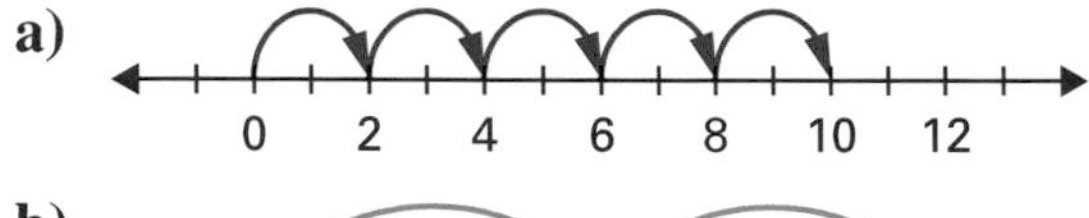

b)

(6.4) **8.** Use a model to explain why $-5 \times 8 = -40$.

9. Write a multiplication equation for each model. (6.4)

a) 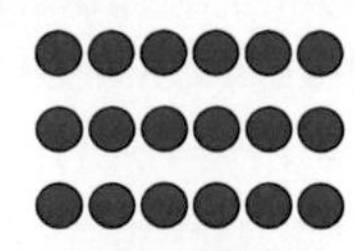

b) 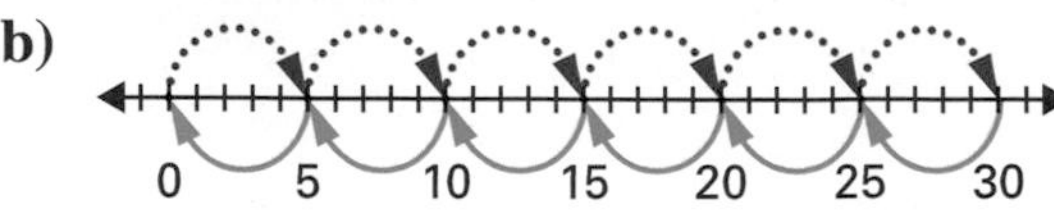

10. Multiply. (6.4)

a) $(+5)(+9)$ **c)** $(-8)(+11)$

b) $(-7)(-8)$ **d)** $0 \times (-12)$

11. Russell sold 40 shares of a stock. The value of each share has decreased by $1 since he bought the stock. Express the amount Russell gained or lost as an integer. (6.4)

12. When playing a game, Matt lost eight points in each of his last three turns. Show how to use integers to determine the change in his score after these three turns. (6.4)

13. Is it possible for the product of two consecutive integers to be negative? Explain. (6.4)

14. The product of three consecutive integers is −1716. What is the greatest of the three integers? (6.4)

15. a) List all the integer pairs of factors for −64.

b) Which pair has the greatest difference?

c) Which pair has the greatest sum?

d) Part (b) has two possible answers, but part (c) has only one answer. Explain why. (6.4)

16. Create and solve a problem for $8 \times (-10)$. (6.4)

Curious Math

SUBTRACTING WITH AN ADDING MACHINE

At the beginning of the 20th century, computing machines used gears and mechanical linkages to do additions. Since they could only add, they were called *adding machines*.

People used the *tens-complement* of numbers to subtract with these machines.

Example 1: Use the tens-complement to subtract $52 - 28$.

$100 - 28 = 72$	The tens-complement of 28 is what you get when you subtract 28 from the next highest positive power of 10. Use mental math to calculate the tens-complement of 28.
$52 + 72 = 124$	Add 52 to the tens-complement of 28 using an adding machine.
~~1~~24 → 24	Cross out the leading digit 1 to determine the difference.
$52 - 28 = 24$	This works because $52 - 28 = 52 + 100 - 28 - 100$ $= 52 + (100 - 28) - 100$

This method also works when you subtract negative integers.

Example 2: Use the tens-complement to subtract $16 - (-28)$.

$100 - (-28)$ $= 100 + 28$ $= 128$	The tens-complement of -28 is what you get when you subtract -28 from the next highest positive power of 10 compared to its opposite, 28. Use mental math to calculate it.
$16 + 128 = 144$	Add 16 and the tens-complement of the opposite of -28 using the adding machine.
~~1~~44 → 44 $16 - (-28) = 44$	Cross out the leading digit 1 to get the difference.

1. Use the tens-complement method to subtract each positive integer.

a) $23 - 16$ **b)** $94 - 87$ **c)** $67 - 20$

2. Use the tens-complement method to subtract each negative integer.

a) $15 - (-20)$ **b)** $30 - (-50)$ **c)** $-12 - (-10)$

3. Why did you subtract from 100 instead of 1000 in questions 1 and 2?

6.5 Exploring Integer Division

▶ **GOAL**
Explore models and patterns for integer division.

You will need
- red and blue counters
- integer number lines
- coloured pencils

Explore the Math

Annika and Susan are talking about division.

Annika says, "If we have eight counters, you and I can share them equally."

Susan says, "If two people share the eight counters equally, 8 ÷ 2 is what each person gets. If we divide 8 into 2 groups, we have 4 in each group."

Then she says, "8 ÷ 2 also tells how many groups of 2 are in 8. If we divide 8 into groups of 2, we have 4 in each group."

Annika says, "Finding the answer to 8 ÷ 2 is like finding what you need to multiply 2 by to get 8."

Susan wonders if she can use similar strategies to model what happens with negative integers.

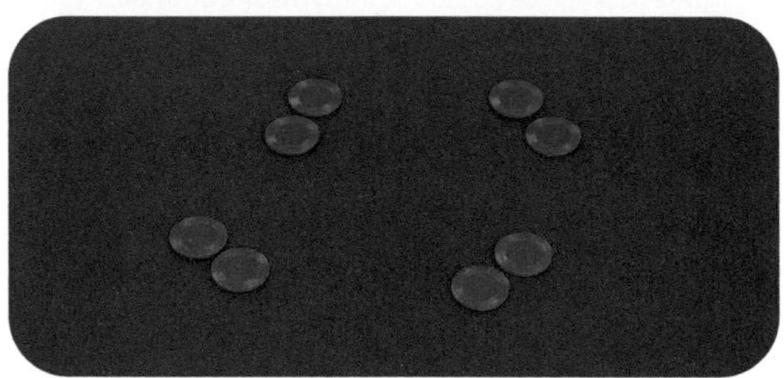

? How can you use models for division to calculate −8 ÷ (−2)?

A. Division can mean finding the size of each part when you share an amount equally. For example, −8 ÷ 2 means sharing 8 negative counters equally between 2 parts. Use this meaning to model −8 ÷ 2 using counters.

B. Draw a blue arrow from 0 to −8 on a number line. Use the "sharing" meaning of division to model −8 ÷ 2.

C. Draw your models for steps A and B in a chart like the one below.

Division sentence	Counter model	Number line model
−8 ÷ 2		

D. Repeat steps A and B to show other ways that -8 can be shared equally among parts. Draw all the counter and number line models in your chart.

E. Division can also mean finding how many small groups of a certain size can be created from a total amount. For example, $-8 \div (-2)$ means dividing 8 negative counters into groups of 2 negative counters. Use this meaning to model $-8 \div (-2)$ using counters. Draw your model.

F. Draw a blue arrow from 0 to -8 on a number line. Use the "counting groups" meaning of division to model $-8 \div (-2)$.

G. Draw your models for steps E and F in a chart.

Division sentence	Counter model	Number line model
$-8 \div (-2)$		

H. Repeat steps E and F to show other ways that -8 can be divided into groups of equal value. Draw all the counter and number line models in your chart.

I. Copy the following chart. Fill in the products you already know. What do you notice? Use your reasoning to continue the patterns.

Pattern 1	Pattern 2	Pattern 3	Pattern 4
$-6 \div 2 =$ ■	$-9 \div 3 =$ ■	$-9 \div (-3) =$ ■	$-6 \div (-2) =$ ■
$-4 \div 2 =$ ■	$-6 \div 3 =$ ■	$-6 \div (-3) =$ ■	$-4 \div (-2) =$ ■
$-2 \div 2 =$ ■	$-3 \div 3 =$ ■	$-3 \div (-3) =$ ■	$-2 \div (-2) =$ ■
$0 \div 2 =$ ■	$0 \div 3 =$ ■	$0 \div (-3) =$ ■	$0 \div (-2) =$ ■
$2 \div 2 =$ ■	$3 \div 3 =$ ■	$3 \div (-3) =$ ■	$2 \div (-2) =$ ■
$4 \div 2 =$ ■	$6 \div 3 =$ ■	$6 \div (-3) =$ ■	$4 \div (-2) =$ ■
$6 \div 2 =$ ■	$9 \div 3 =$ ■	$9 \div (-3) =$ ■	$6 \div (-2) =$ ■

Reflecting

1. Why can sharing negative blue counters be used as a model for $-8 \div 2$, but not for $-8 \div (-2)$?

2. Why can you not use negative blue counters, or divide an arrow on a number line, to model $8 \div (-2)$?

3. How does the relationship between multiplication and division help to confirm the patterns in step I?

6.6 Dividing Integers

You will need
- a calculator
- a ruler

▶ GOAL

Develop and apply strategies to divide integers.

Learn about the Math

Denis and Nathan keep track of changes in their weekly basketball scores. They record a positive change if a score goes up from the previous week, and a negative change if a score goes down. Their records for five weeks are given below.

Denis's Basketball Record

Week	2	3	4	5	6
Change in score	+5	−2	−2	−3	+7

Nathan's Basketball Record

Week	2	3	4	5	6
Change in score	−15	−8	−12	+20	+5

? What are Denis's and Nathan's mean weekly changes in score?

A. Determine the sum of each student's changes in score for the five-week period.

B. Why does it make sense that the mean change in score has the same sign as the total change in score?

C. Does the sign of the mean have to be the same as the sign that appears most often in the data? Explain how you know.

D. Calculate each student's mean change in score.

E. Multiply to check your division. Explain how this verifies your calculations in step D.

Communication Tip

Division can also be written in fraction form. The horizontal line means "divided by." For example, $48 \div (-12)$ can be written as $\frac{48}{-12}$, and $-48 \div 12$ can be written as $\frac{-48}{12}$.

Reflecting

1. How does thinking of $\frac{-10}{5}$ as the mean of five changes in score help to explain why a negative integer divided by a positive integer is negative?

2. How can you use the relationship between multiplication and division to verify your answer in question 1?

3. Why can you solve any integer division equation by solving a related multiplication equation?

Work with the Math

Example 1: Using multiplication rules to predict the sign of a quotient

Determine the answer to $-12 \div (-4)$.

Susan's Solution

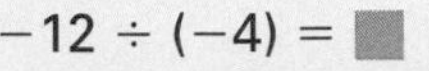

$-12 \div (-4) = ■$ $■ \times (-4) = -12$	I wrote the multiplication sentence that relates to the division equation.
$3 \times (-4) = -12$	I know that $3 \times 4 = 12$.
The answer is 3.	I also know that a positive integer multiplied by a negative integer results in a negative integer. So, the missing number must be 3.

Example 2: Using a calculator to divide integers

Thomas checks the value of his stock at the end of each day. Calculate the mean change in the value of his stock over a five-day period.

Day	1	2	3	4	5
Total change in value ($)	+20	−40	−11	−1	+12

Denis's Solution:

20 [+] [(-)] 40 [+] [(-)] 11 [+] [(-)] 1 [+] 12 [Enter] [÷] 5 [Enter]

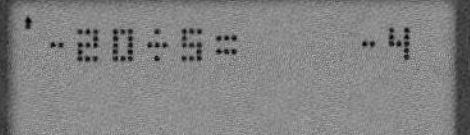

I calculated the mean by adding all the changes in value and then dividing the sum by 5.

A Checking

4. Divide. Multiply to check.

a) $-45 \div (-5)$

b) $\frac{0}{-8}$

c) $81 \div (-9)$

d) $\frac{-56}{7}$

5. Match each division equation with the related multiplication equation. Write the missing integers.

a) $-16 \div (-8) = ■$

b) $16 \div 8 = ■$

c) $-16 \div 8 = ■$

d) $16 \div (-8) = ■$

A. $■ \times (-8) = 16$

B. $■ \times (-8) = -16$

C. $■ \times 8 = 16$

D. $■ \times 8 = -16$

6. Andrea keeps track of changes in her weekly basketball scores. Her record for five weeks is given below.

Week	2	3	4	5	6
Change in score	+4	−11	−10	+15	−13

a) Use estimation to predict whether Andrea's mean weekly change will be positive or negative. Explain why.

b) Write a division equation to calculate Andrea's mean weekly change. What is Andrea's mean weekly change?

B Practising

7. Write the division equation represented by each model.

a) 

b)

8. Write a multiplication equation for each division. Then solve the division.

a) $-72 \div (-9)$

b) $84 \div 7$

c) $66 \div (-11)$

d) $-800 \div 20$

9. Divide.

a) $40 \div (-5)$

b) $-24 \div 6$

c) $\frac{-64}{-8}$

d) $-121 \div (-11)$

e) $0 \div (-10)$

f) $\frac{54}{9}$

10. Why can $\frac{-8}{-2}$ not represent calculating a mean change in score?

11. Copy and complete using + or −. Record two answers for each expression.

a) ▒ 300 ÷ ▒ 15 is negative.

b) ▒ 300 ÷ ▒ 15 is positive.

12. Estimate each quotient.

a) $844 \div (-4)$

b) $-319 \div (-11)$

c) $448 \div (-32)$

d) $-168 \div 8$

e) $136 \div (-17)$

f) $-575 \div (-23)$

13. Determine each quotient. Multiply to check.

a) $\frac{48}{-12}$

b) $\frac{-32}{8}$

c) $\frac{-27}{-9}$

d) $\frac{192}{-12}$

e) $\frac{-256}{32}$

f) $\frac{-243}{-9}$

14. a) Copy and complete the charts.

a	*b*	*a* × *b*	Example
+	+		
+	−		
−	+		
−	−		

a	*b*	*a* ÷ *b*	Example
+	+		
+	−		
−	+		
−	−		

b) How is determining the sign of a product the same as determining the sign of a quotient?

15. Determine the missing integer in each equation.

a) $40 \times$ ▒ $= -800$

b) ▒ $\times (-11) = -132$

c) $25 \times$ ▒ $= 2500$

d) ▒ $\times 24 = -192$

16. The quotient for $-35 \div 5$ is the opposite of the quotient for $-35 \div (-5)$. Why does this make sense?

17. Emma's scores for the first nine holes of a golf game are given below. Each positive integer represents a score above par. Each negative integer represents a score below par. What is Emma's mean score per hole?

Hole	1	2	3	4	5	6	7	8	9
Score	+1	−1	+3	+3	+2	0	0	−1	+2

18. Sanjay works in a recording studio. During a recent recording session, he noted the following decibel levels in a song:

−11 dB, −24 dB, +9 dB, +6 dB, +8 dB, −5 dB, +3 dB

a) What is the mean decibel level?

b) What is the difference between the mean decibel level and the lowest decibel level?

c) What is the difference between the mean decibel level and the highest decibel level?

19. What is the greatest integer quotient that can result from dividing one of these integers by another?

−120, −4, −15, −3

20. Write the next three terms.

a) 768, −384, 192, −96, ■, ■, ■, ...

b) −3645, 1215, −405, 135, ■, ■, ■, ...

21. How are multiplying integers and dividing integers similar? How are they different? Use examples to support your answers.

22. Calculate.

a) $-3 \times (-8) \div (-4)$

b) $\frac{(-6)(6)}{-4}$

c) $-63 \div (-7)(-9)$

d) $\frac{-144 \div 12}{-3}$

e) $(7)(-6) \div (3)(-7)$

f) $(-2)(-9) \div (2)(-3)$

23. Determine the missing integer.

a) $-49 \div$ ■ $= -7$

b) ■ $\div (-4) = 8$

24. Evaluate each expression when $x = -6$ and $y = 9$.

a) $-9x$

b) $-6y$

c) $5xy$

d) $6x + 7y$

e) $-8y - 5x$

f) $3xy \div y$

25. The Marianas Trench is the deepest spot in the oceans. It is located in the Pacific Ocean, just east of the Philippines. The maximum depth of the Marianas Trench is 10 962 m. The maximum depth of Lake Superior is 406 m. Create and solve an integer division question using this information.

C Extending

26. Suppose that you divided two integers. Then both integers are increased.

a) Can the quotient increase? Explain.

b) Can the quotient decrease? Explain.

c) Can the quotient be 0? Explain.

27. Suppose that you randomly choose an integer value between −80 and −90 for a and an integer value between −5 and −8 for b. What is the probability that $\frac{a}{b}$ is also an integer?

28. The product of three integers is negative. Suppose that you multiply this product by two other integers. If the final product is positive, what do you know about the other two integers?

29. Suppose that you divide integer a by integer b, and the result is negative. Then you divide integer a by an integer that is 2 greater than b. The result is positive. What did you divide by the first time?

6.7 Order of Operations with Integers

You will need
- a calculator

GOAL

Apply the rules for the order of operations with integers.

Learn about the Math

Suppose that you win a contest, but you have to answer the following skill-testing question before you can claim the prize:

$$\frac{6 \div (-3) + [(4 - (-5)) \times (-7)]}{4 - 5}$$

? What is the answer to the skill-testing question?

If there are brackets within brackets, or nested operations, perform the nested operations in the innermost brackets first.

When there is a dividing line separating the numerator of an expression from the denominator, calculate the value of the numerator, then the value of the denominator, and finally divide.

Communication Tip

- Different types of brackets can be used to make it easier to match beginning and end brackets.
- An expression that is written in fraction form can be evaluated by dividing the final value of the numerator by the final value of the denominator.

Example 1: Evaluating an expression in fraction form

Use the order of operations to evaluate the skill-testing question.

Annika's Solution

I started by determining the value of the numerator.

$$\frac{6 \div (-3) + [(4 - (-5)) \times (-7)]}{4 - 5}$$

I calculated what's in the innermost brackets.

$$= \frac{6 \div (-3) + [9 \times (-7)]}{4 - 5}$$

I calculated what's in the square brackets.

$$= \frac{6 \div (-3) + [-63]}{4 - 5}$$

I divided.

$$= \frac{-2 + [-63]}{4 - 5}$$

I added to calculate the numerator.

$$= \frac{-65}{4 - 5}$$

I subtracted to calculate the denominator.

$$= \frac{-65}{-1}$$

I divided the numerator by the denominator.

$$= 65$$

The answer is 65.

Example 2: Performing different calculations in the same step

How can you calculate the answer to the skill-testing question more efficiently?

Eva's Solution

$6 \div (-3) + [(4 - (-5)) \times (-7)]$

I calculated the numerator first. I did three steps at the same time, since they don't interfere with each other.

$6 \div (-3) = -2$, $4 - (-5) = 9$, and $9 \times (-7) = -63$

$-2 + (-63) = -65$

The numerator is -65.

$4 - 5 = -1$

Then I calculated the denominator. It's like an expression in brackets.

$-65 \div (-1) = 65$

I know that a fraction can represent division. I also know that a negative integer divided by a negative integer is positive.

Reflecting

1. What advantages does Eva's method of evaluating the expression have over Annika's method?

2. Nathan says, "If an expression has a numerator and a denominator, like $\frac{-6 + (-10)}{(-4)(2)}$, the last calculation is division." Is Nathan correct? Explain.

3. Why is it important to use the rules for the order of operations when you calculate the value of an integer expression?

Work with the Math

Example 3: Using a calculator to evaluate an expression

Calculate $\frac{106 + (-16) \div (-4)}{(-34 + 12) \div (-2)}$.

Solution

[(] 106 [+] [(-)] 16 [÷] [(-)] 4 [)] [÷]
[(] [(] [(-)] 34 [+] 12 [)] [÷] [(-)] 2 [)] [Enter]

Use the bracket keys, [(] and [)], to separate the numerator from the denominator and show the operation of division.

(106+-16÷-4
)÷((-34+12)

)÷((-34+12)
÷-2)◀

10

A Checking

4. Calculate.

a) $-9 - (-6) \div 6$

b) $4 \times (-8) - (-5)$

c) $-8 \times (-3) - (-8) \div (-4)$

d) $-16 \div [-2 - (-18)] \times (-1)$

B Practising

5. In each expression, which calculation(s) should you do first?

a) $-5 + (-6) \times (-8) \div 2$

b) $-8 \times 6 \div (-2) - [-9 \times (-3)]$

6. Calculate.

a) $-2 + (-3) \times (-8 + 4)$

b) $-9 - (-8) \times 7 + [6 \times (-2)]$

c) $7 \times [8 - (-2) \times (-6)]$

d) $-6 \div (-3) - [-8 \div (-2)]$

e) $0 + (-4) - 7 \times 5$

f) $[-14 + (-23)] - [(-17 - 2) \times 10]$

7. Calculate.

a) $7 \times [-3 - (-5)] \times 8$

b) $-3 - (-4) \times [2 \times (-6)]$

c) $-15 \div (-3) + 2 \times (-8)$

d) $[-2 - (-8)] \times (-5)$

e) $35 + (-4) \times (-8) - 7$

f) $18 \times (-3 - [8 \times (-5)])$

8. There is an error in this solution.

$$3 \times (-8) \div (-2 - 4) = -24 \div (-2 - 4)$$
$$= 12 - 4$$
$$= 8$$

a) Find the error.

b) Explain how to correct the error.

9. Calculate.

a) $\dfrac{-6 + (-10)}{(-4)(2)}$

b) $\dfrac{49 \div (-7)}{1 + (-2)(-3)}$

c) $\dfrac{28 \div (-4 - 3)}{(-2 + 4) \times 2}$

d) $\dfrac{27 + (-18) \div (-2)}{(-2 + 5)(-2)}$

e) $\dfrac{-9 + (-16) - 10}{(-7)(10) \div (-2)}$

f) $\dfrac{[6 + (-38)] \div 4\,(-2)}{(-2 + 4)(5 - 6)}$

10. Create an integer expression that shows why the rules for the order of operations are needed. Explain how your expression shows this.

11. Using brackets, group the terms in this expression to get the least possible result.

$40 \times 6 - 3 \times 4 - 5$

12. a) Evaluate with a calculator.

$-147 + 156 \div (-4) + 405 \div (-15)$

b) Does your calculator follow the order of operations? Explain how you know.

13. The formula for converting temperatures from Fahrenheit (F) to Celsius (C) is $C = (F - 32) \times 5 \div 9$. Use the formula to calculate each temperature in degrees Celsius.

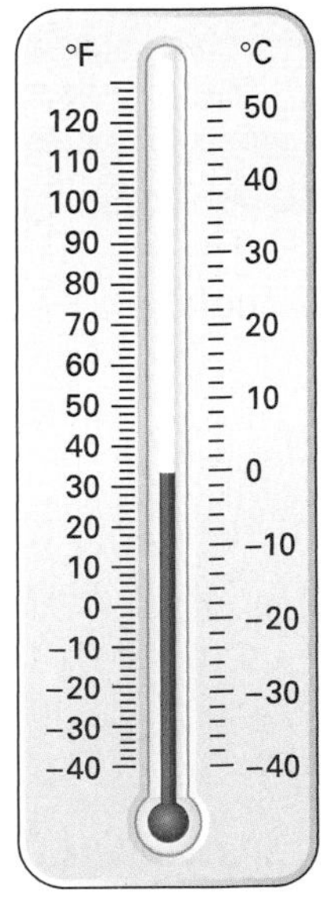

a) 32°F

b) 212°F

c) −4°F

d) −40°F

14. This chart shows the predicted high temperatures in Iqaluit for a week in November. Use an integer expression to determine the mean predicted high temperature for the week.

Day	Predicted high temperature (°C)
Mon.	−4
Tues.	−4
Wed.	0
Thurs.	1
Fri.	−1
Sat.	−2
Sun.	−4

15. Two sisters bought some shares in four stocks with money they earned cutting lawns. This chart shows how their stocks changed in value over one month. Write an integer expression that could be used to determine the change in the total value of their stocks. Evaluate your expression.

Stock	A	B	C	D
Number of shares	10	100	50	30
Value of each share Aug. 1 ($)	42	5	38	19
Value of each share Sept. 1 ($)	39	4	42	21

16. Copy each equation. Fill in the missing operation signs.

a) 36 ▒ (4 ▒ 1) ▒ 2 = 24

b) −12 ▒ 4 ▒ (−3) = −24

c) −15 ▒ (−12) ▒ 6 ▒ 16 = −47

17. The price of gold changes daily. One week, the price started at $350 per ounce on Monday and changed −$2 each day for 3 days, and then +$8 each day for the next 2 days.

a) Copy and complete the chart based on the data given.

Day	Starting price ($)	Final price ($)	Change in price ($)
Mon.	350		
Tues.			
Wed.			
Thurs.			
Fri.			

b) Calculate the mean final price of gold for the week.

c) Calculate the mean change in price for the week.

18. Evaluate each expression if $x = -2$, $y = 4$, and $z = -6$.

a) $\frac{2x + 7y}{z}$

b) $\frac{-4xz}{y^2}$

c) $\frac{y^2 - z^2}{x^2}$

C Extending

19. Calculate.

a) $(-3)^2 + (-8) \div (-2)$

b) $-3 \times [-4 + 2^3]$

c) $\frac{(-2 + 10)}{2^2}$

d) $\frac{-5 + (-3)(-6)}{(-2)^2 + (-3)^2}$

20. Copy and complete the equation using each digit from 1 to 5 once.

▒ × ▒▒ − (−▒) + (−▒) = 50

You will need
- a calculator

6.8 Communicating about Calculations

▶ **GOAL**
Explain your thinking when solving integer problems.

Communicate about the Math

The cards below were the last three cards that Ken got in a game. Ken followed the instructions correctly, but maybe not in the order shown. Now he is at −12. Where was he three turns ago?

Eva used a chart to keep track of the possibilities. Then she asked Susan to read her solution. Susan asked Eva the questions shown.

Divide by −2.
Multiply by −3.
Subtract 32.

If the last card was ...	Ken came from ...	If the card before was ...	Ken came from ...	If the other card was ...	Ken came from ...
Divide by −2.	24	Subtract 32.	56: impossible		
Divide by −2.	24	Multiply by −3.	−8	Subtract 32.	24
Subtract 32.	20	Multiply by −3.	impossible (not an integer)		
Subtract 32.	20	Divide by −2.	−40: impossible		
Multiply by −3.	4	Divide by −2.	−8	Subtract 32.	24
Multiply by −3.	4	Subtract 32.	36: impossible		

Susan's Questions

Why did you use a chart to solve the problem?

How did you choose the column headings?

How did you fill each "Ken came from ..." column?

How did you fill each "If the ... was ..." column?

Did you justify your conclusion that a position was not possible?

Did you state and justify your result for the problem?

? How can Eva improve her solution?

A. Which of Susan's questions do you think are good questions? Why?

B. How should Eva answer Susan's questions?

C. What other questions would be helpful to improve Eva's work?

D. Use the Communication Checklist to improve Eva's solution.

Communication Checklist

- ☑ Did you identify the information given?
- ☑ Did you show each step in your solution?
- ☑ Did you explain your thinking at each step?
- ☑ Did you check that your answer is reasonable?
- ☑ Did you state your conclusion clearly?

Reflecting

1. Which parts of the Communication Checklist did Eva cover well? Explain.

2. Why is it important to explain your thinking when solving a problem?

Work with the Math

Example: Using a chart to work backward

Carla climbed halfway down a cliff before resting the first time. Then she climbed halfway down the remaining distance and rested for a second time. After climbing halfway down the final distance, Carla was 6 m from the bottom of the cliff. Use an integer to describe Carla's distance, in metres, from the top of the cliff.

Ken's Solution

I drew a diagram to show the stages in Carla's climb down the cliff.

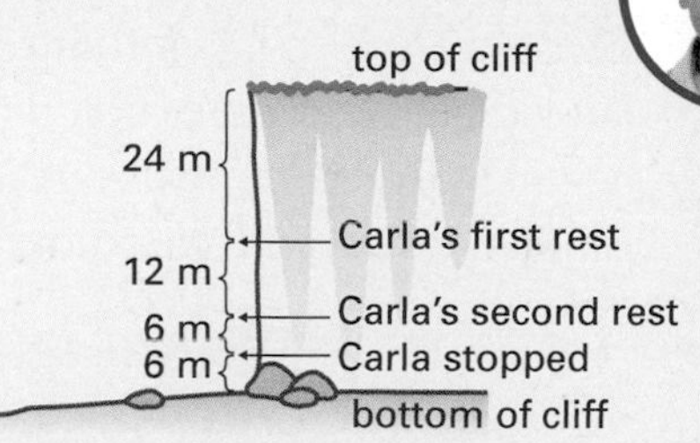

Carla finished 6 m from the bottom of the cliff, halfway between the bottom of the cliff and the location of her second rest. So, she climbed down 6 m after her second rest. At her second rest, Carla must have been 12 m from the bottom of the cliff.

Carla's second rest was halfway between the bottom of the cliff and the location of her first rest. At her first rest, Carla must have been 24 m from the bottom of the cliff. So, she climbed down 12 m after her first rest.

Carla's first rest was halfway between the bottom of the cliff and the top of the cliff. So, she climbed down 24 m before her first rest.

The bottom of the cliff is 48 m from the top.

Carla stopped 6 m from the bottom of the cliff. The top of the cliff is at 0 m, so climbing down is a negative value.

$48 \text{ m} - 6 \text{ m} = 42 \text{ m}$

The integer -42 describes Carla's distance in metres from the top of the cliff.

Refer to the game on page 208 to answer questions 3 to 5.

A Checking

3. a) Write the instructions for three cards to go from −10 to 10 on the game board. Then write two other solutions.

   b) Rewrite the instructions in part (a) to go from 10 to −10. Explain your thinking.

B Practising

Use the Communication Checklist to help you explain your answer to each question.

4. These were Ken's last three cards before he landed on −2. Where did he begin? Explain how you know.

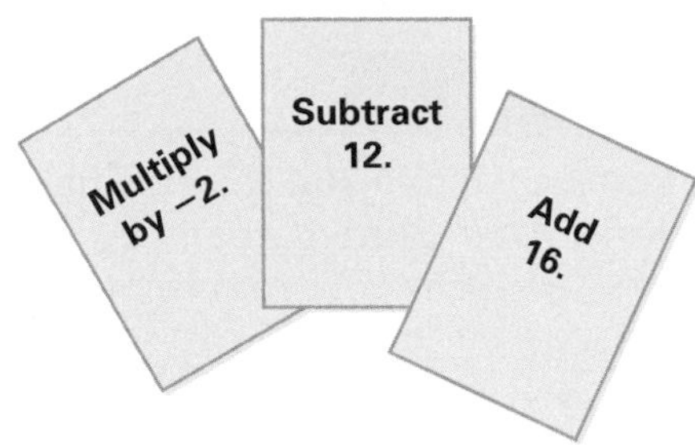

5. These were Ken's last four cards before he landed on −7. Where could he have begun? Give more than one answer. Explain how you figured out your answers.

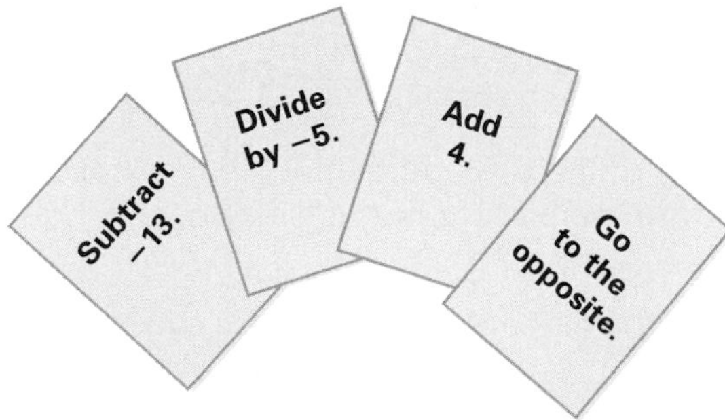

6. Susan said, "I have four negative (blue) counters. If I double the number of counters and then share them equally with Sam, I'll have as many as I started with." Use integers to show why this is correct.

7. Denis and four friends played a computer golf game in which the player with the fewest points wins the game. When they counted all their points, the mean number of points was −23. When Denis's points were not counted, the mean was −18.

   a) Explain how to estimate Denis's score.

   b) Test your explanation by asking someone to follow it. Make any changes to your explanation that you think would make it clearer.

8. Ethan has \$63 in his bank account at the end of June. During the month of June, he deposited \$285 and wrote cheques for \$85, \$41, and \$9. As well, he withdrew \$75 from a bank machine.

   a) Write an integer to represent the value of Ethan's bank account at the beginning of June.

   b) What does this integer show about the money that Ethan had in his bank account at the beginning of June? Explain how you know.

9. Abby walked 3 km west. Then she walked twice as far going east. She continued east for another kilometre, stopping 2 km east of Lauren's home. When Abby started walking, how far was she from Lauren's home? Explain how you know.

10. Gregory wrote four integers. Their sum is −22. The difference between the least integer and the greatest integer is 50. What could the integers be? How do you know?

11. a) Change a problem in this lesson to create a different problem, or make up a new integer problem.

    b) Explain how you know that your problem is an integer problem.

    c) Solve your problem.

Mental Math

USING FRACTIONS TO SOLVE PERCENT PROBLEMS

You can often change a percent to a fraction to solve percent problems.

Example 1: Calculate the amount of savings and the sale price.

25% means $\frac{25}{100} = \frac{1}{4}$.

$\frac{1}{4}$ of \$600 means \$600 ÷ 4 = \$150.

The sale price is \$600 − \$150 = \$450.

Example 2: Estimate the amount of savings and the sale price.

20% means $\frac{20}{100} = \frac{1}{5}$.

$\frac{1}{5}$ of \$30 means \$30 ÷ 5 = \$6.

The sale price is about \$30 − \$6 = \$24.

1. Calculate the amount of savings and the sale price.

a) 50% OFF \$25

b) 20% OFF \$160

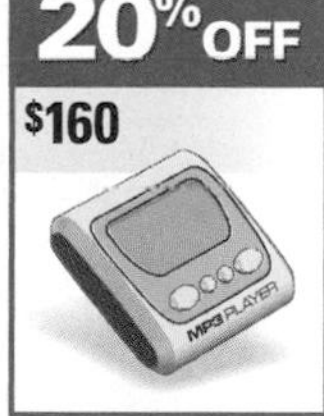

c) 10% OFF \$95

d) 25% OFF \$1200

2. Estimate the amount of savings and the sale price.

a) 20% OFF \$29.95

b) 15% OFF \$99.98

c) 25% OFF \$19.99

d) 50% OFF \$199.95

Math Game

TARGET ZERO

When using a standard deck of cards, aces count as 1, numbered cards count as their face values, and jokers count as 0. Red cards are positive, and black cards are negative.

Number of players: 2 to 4

You will need

- integer cards numbered −10 to 10 (two of each card) OR a standard deck of cards (including two jokers) with face cards removed

Rules

1. Shuffle the cards. Deal five cards to each player. Each card represents an integer.
2. Place the remaining cards in a pile with one card face up. This is the target card.
3. Players have one minute to write an integer expression that uses all of their five cards and has a value as close as possible to the value of the target card. The integers can be combined using operations and brackets.
4. Players evaluate their expressions. Each player receives a score equal to the positive difference between the value of her or his expression and the value of the target card. An exact match gives a score of 0.
5. Repeat steps 1 to 4 ten times. The winner is the player who has the lowest final score.

Chapter Self-Test

1. The mean depth of the Atlantic Ocean is 3332 m. Its greatest depth is 8605 m. The mean depth of the Indian Ocean is 3890 m. Its greatest depth is 7450 m.
   a) Which ocean has the greater depth? How much greater is its depth?
   b) Which ocean has the greater difference between its mean depth and its greatest depth?

2. Draw a counter model and a number line model for each expression.
   a) -2×4 b) $-12 \div 6$

3. Calculate without using a calculator.
   a) $5 + (-8)$
   b) $-10 + (-3)$
   c) $-7 - 2$
   d) $-8 - (-4)$
   e) $-4 + (-5) + 6$
   f) $10 + (-15) + (-5)$

4. Calculate without using a calculator.
   a) $-2 \times (-5)$
   b) $-15 \div 5$
   c) $3 \times (-10) + 1$
   d) $(-3 - 2) \times (-2)$
   e) $6 \times [3 - (-7)] \div 2$
   f) $\dfrac{-54 + 18 \div (-2)}{(-3 - 4)(-1)}$

5. Determine the missing value in each equation.
   a) $-34 \times \blacksquare = 306$
   b) $28 \times \blacksquare = -336$
   c) $\blacksquare \times (-17) = 255$
   d) $\blacksquare \times 37 = -555$

6. Determine the missing values.
   a) $-32 \div \blacksquare = -8$
   b) $-105 \div \blacksquare = 35$
   c) $\blacksquare \div 8 = -7$
   d) $\blacksquare \div (-18) = 23$

7. Evaluate using a calculator.
   a) $35 + (-4) \times (-8) - 7$
   b) $18 \times [-3 - (8 \times (-5))]$
   c) $5 + [6 \div (-2)] - 4$
   d) $-12 \div 4 \times (-7) - (-2) + 10$
   e) $9 \times 3 \times (-2) + (-36) \div 12 - 1$

8. Marcus recorded this information about his stocks. Estimate how much money, in total, he has gained or lost.

Stock	A	B	C	D
Number of shares	50	70	100	25
Change in stock price per share ($)	−2	+5	−3	−8

9. Which two integers have a product of -120 and a sum of -2?

10. How much greater or less is $5 + (-2)(-8)$ than $-8 + (-2)(5)$?

11. Clive's solution to a test question follows.

$$\begin{aligned} & 9 \div (-3) + 6 \times 2 - 7 \\ = & \ 9 \div (-3) + 6 \times (-5) \\ = & \ 9 \div (-3) + (-30) \\ = & \ (-3) + (-30) \\ = & \ -33 \end{aligned}$$

   a) What error did he make?
   b) Provide a correct solution.

Chapter Review

Frequently Asked Questions

Q: How can you divide integers?

A: You can use counters, a number line, or repeated subtraction. Or you can use a calculator. The models show that

$(+) \div (+) = +$ $\quad (-) \div (+) = -$ $\quad (+) \div (-) = -$ $\quad (-) \div (-) = +$

Division question	Related multiplication	Counter model	Number line model
$12 \div 3 = 4$	$12 \div 3 = ■$ is related to $■ \times 3 = 12$	12 red counters can be divided into 4 groups of 3 red counters or into 3 groups of 4 red counters.	0 3 6 9 12 0 4 8 12
$-12 \div (-3) = 4$	$-12 \div (-3) = ■$ is related to $■ \times (-3) = -12$	12 blue counters can be divided into 4 groups of 3 blue counters.	−12 −9 −6 −3 0 −12 −8 −4 0
$-12 \div 3 = -4$	$-12 \div 3 = ■$ is related to $■ \times 3 = -12$	12 blue counters can be divided into 3 groups of 4 blue counters.	−12 −9 −6 −3 0 −12 −8 −4 0
$12 \div (-3) = -4$	$12 \div (-3) = ■$ is related to $■ \times (-3) = 12$	Dividing a positive integer by a negative integer cannot be represented easily with counters or a number line.	

Q: How do you evaluate integer expressions that involve several operations?

A: Follow the same order of operations that you use with whole numbers and decimals.

For example,

$$\frac{48 \div [2 + (-10)]}{(-1)[-9 - (-6)]}$$
$$= \frac{48 \div (-8)}{(-1)(-9 + 6)}$$
$$= \frac{-6}{(-1)(-3)}$$
$$= \frac{-6}{3}$$
$$= -2$$

NEL

Practice Questions

(6.2) **1.** One day in October, the low temperature was $-9°C$ in Yellowknife, $6°C$ in Halifax, $-8°C$ in Whitehorse, and $0°C$ in Thunder Bay. What is the difference between the highest and lowest of these temperatures?

(6.2) **2.** Use a positive integer and a negative integer to make each equation true.

a) $\square + \square = -38$

b) $\square - \square = -38$

(6.2) **3.** Follow this sequence. Record each value as you go.

- Start with -83.
- Add -14.
- Subtract -36.
- Add 125.

(6.2) **4.** The depth of the Siberian Shelf in the Arctic Ocean varies from 20 m to 550 m. Use an integer to describe the range of its depth.

(6.4) **5.** The product of three consecutive integers is -720. What is the greatest of these three integers?

(6.6) **6.** Write a multiplication or division expression for each of the following.

a) $-38 + (-38) + (-38) + (-38)$

b) You lose \$4 eight times.

c)

d) Ryan walks -935 m at 85 m/min. (The negative sign represents west.) For how long has Ryan been walking?

e)

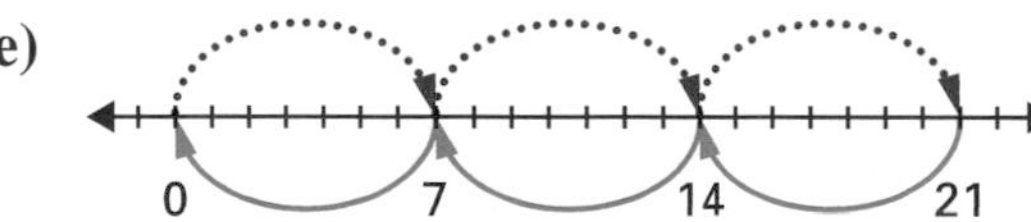

(6.6) **7.** What is the missing integer?

$-7 \times \square = -1421$

8. Calculate. (6.6)

a) -4×9

b) $0 \times (-100)$

c) $-16 - (-10)$

d) $25 - 32$

e) $-189 \div 9$

f) $-390 \div (-10)$

9. Yuri says, "When you divide two integers with the same sign, the answer is always positive. When you divide two integers with different signs, the answer is always negative." Is he correct? Explain. (6.6)

10. Rebecca is playing a game on a game board that has each integer from -30 to 30. She starts with a number and completes these three instructions, but not necessarily in this order: (6.6)

- Subtract -10.
- Divide by -3.
- Multiply by 2.

Rebecca ends with -8. Where might she have started?

11. Copy and complete each equation using $+, -, \times$, or $\div$. (6.7)

a) $-58 \;\square\; (-36) \;\square\; (-15) = -37$

b) $-4 \;\square\; (-3) \;\square\; 28 = 40$

c) $-4 \;\square\; (-3 \;\square\; 28) = -100$

12. Estimate. (6.7)

a) $9 \times (-3) + (-15) \div 3$

b) $-6 - (-8) \times 5 \div (-10)$

c) $(-45) \div 5 + 7 - (-12)$

d) $\dfrac{90 \div (-3)}{2 - (-4)(-2)}$

13. Melissa says, "When I combine integers using several operations, I always get the right answer if I do the operations from left to right." Use examples to explain whether she is right or wrong. (6.7)

Chapter Task

Mystery Integers

Select four integers. Do not tell anyone what they are. Make up a set of eight clues that will allow someone to guess the integers you chose. All eight clues must be necessary.

The clues must

- use all four operations somewhere in the eight clues
- include comparing integers

For example, suppose that your integers are -8, 7, 5, and -3. Here are three possible clues:

- The sum of the four integers is 1.
- If you order the integers from least to greatest, the product of the two middle integers is -15.
- If you subtract the least integer from the greatest integer, and divide the difference by 3, the quotient is 5.

Task Checklist

- ☑ Did your clues involve all four operations with integers?
- ☑ Does at least one of your clues require comparing integers?
- ☑ Did you use appropriate math language?
- ☑ Did you check to see that your clues worked?

? What eight clues can you write to describe your four integers?

A. The three clues above do not give enough information to figure out the integers. What five additional clues would give enough information?

B. Select any four integers of your own, and make up eight clues. Remember that all the clues must be necessary. It should not be possible to figure out all the integers with only some of the eight clues.

Cumulative Review
Chapters 4–6

Cross-Strand Multiple Choice

(4.2) **1.** Which algebraic expression describes the phrase "three times a number increased by one"?

A. $3n - 1$ **C.** $n + 3$
B. $3n + 1$ **D.** $n - 3$

(4.2) **2.** Which algebraic expression describes this pattern?

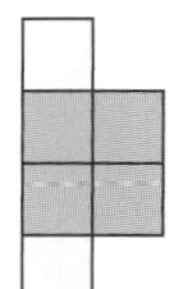
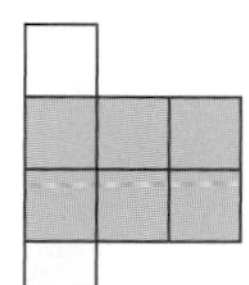
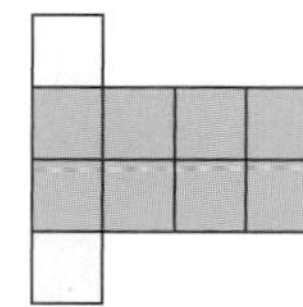

A. $2(n + 1)$ **C.** $2(n+1) + 2$
B. $2n + 6$ **D.** $4 + n$

(4.3) **3.** What is the value of the first three terms of the sequence described by the pattern rule $3n - 2$?

A. 1, 3, 4 **C.** 1, 3, 7
B. 4, 5, 7 **D.** 1, 4, 7

(4.3) **4.** What is the number of toothpicks needed for the 60th term of this sequence?

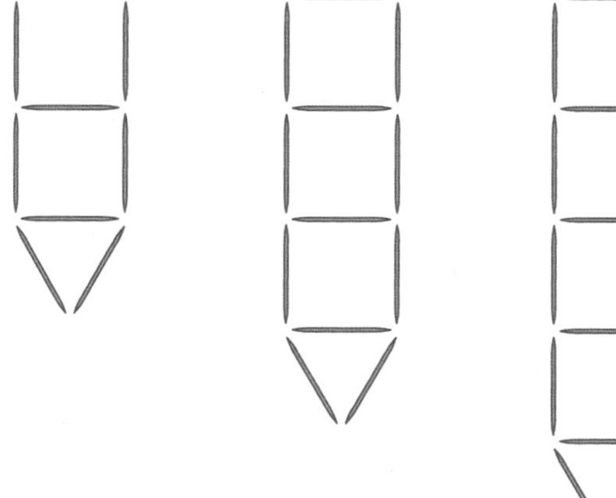

A. 186 **B.** 180 **C.** 189 **D.** 183

5. What is the circumference of this circle, to one decimal place? (5.3)

8.1 m

A. 25.4 m
B. 206.1 m
C. 50.9 m
D. 824.4 m

6. The diameter of the Canadian Gold Maple Leaf, which was minted between 1979 and 1982, is 3.00 cm. What is the area of one side, to two decimal places? (5.5)

A. 7.07 cm^2
B. 28.27 cm^2
C. 9.42 cm^2
D. 4.71 cm^2

7. What area is shaded blue? (5.5)

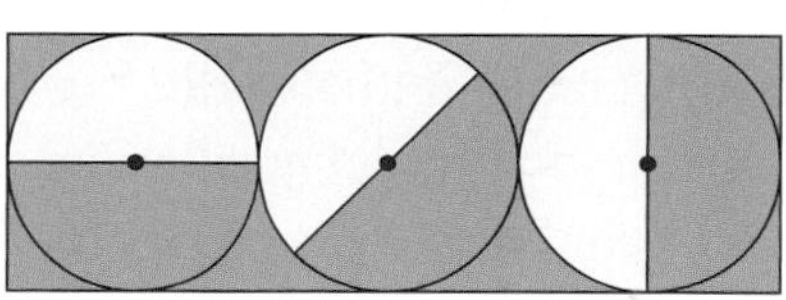

8 m

A. 75 m^2 **C.** 110 m^2
B. 142 m^2 **D.** 117 m^2

8. What is the result for $-14 - (-17)$? (6.2)

A. 3 **B.** -3 **C.** 31 **D.** -31

9. What is the result for $(-6)(-3)$? (6.4)

A. 2 **B.** -2 **C.** -18 **D.** 18

10. What is the result for $100 \div (-4)$? (6.6)

A. -25 **B.** 25 **C.** 400 **D.** -400

11. What is the result for $\frac{-36 - [1 - (-5)]}{(2)(-3)}$?

A. -5 **B.** 5 **C.** -7 **D.** 7 (6.7)

Cross-Strand Investigation

Some students are organizing an environmental awareness presentation at their school.

12. Amy researched information about containing an oil slick by placing a boom around it. Her presentation focused on a news report about an oil slick with a radius of 120 m.

a) What length of material, to the nearest metre, is needed for the boom? (Assume that the oil slick is a circle and that the boom fits it as closely as possible.)

b) Unless an oil slick is contained, it becomes thinner and spreads over a greater area. Suppose that this table shows how an oil slick would spread without a boom. Write an algebraic expression to describe the change in radius if this pattern continued.

Length of time (h)	Radius of oil slick (m)
1	122
2	124
3	126

c) Use your algebraic expression from part (b) to predict the radius of the oil slick after 24 h.

d) Predict the area of the oil slick after 24 h, without the boom.

13. Gary researched data about whooping cranes. In 1940, there were 22 whooping cranes in the world. For his presentation, Gary represented an increase in population as a positive integer and a decrease in population as a negative integer.

Whooping Crane World Population						
Year	1950	1960	1970	1980	1990	2000
Change in population	+12	−1	+23	+20	+70	+31

a) Based on Gary's data, in which decade did the population decrease? By how much did it decrease from a decade earlier?

b) What is the difference between the greatest 10-year increase and the least 10-year increase?

c) Estimate the mean 10-year change for the decades ending in 1970, 1980, 1990, and 2000.

d) Calculate the mean 10-year change for the decades ending in 1960 and 1970.

CHAPTER 7

Transformations

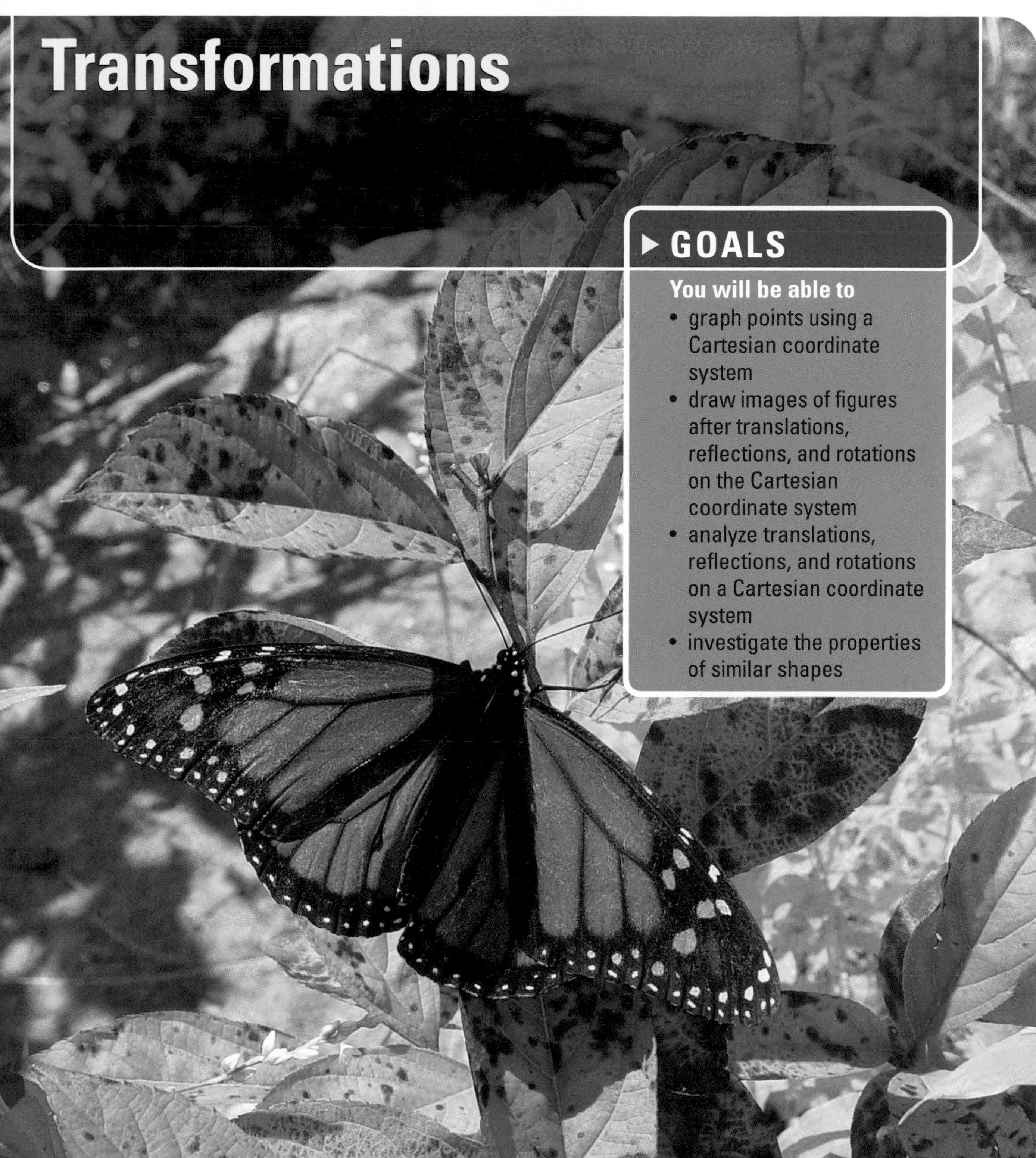

▶ GOALS

You will be able to

- graph points using a Cartesian coordinate system
- draw images of figures after translations, reflections, and rotations on the Cartesian coordinate system
- analyze translations, reflections, and rotations on a Cartesian coordinate system
- investigate the properties of similar shapes

Getting Started

You will need
- construction paper
- scissors
- tape

Tessellating Tiles

Maria's art class is studying the work of M.C. Escher that involves tessellations. She wants to create a tile that tessellates.

Symmetry Drawing E08
by M.C. Escher

? How can Maria make a tile that tessellates?

A. Cut out a square from a piece of construction paper.

B. Cut out a curved piece from the bottom of the square, as shown below. Translate this piece vertically to the top of the square. Tape it in place. Describe the translation using centimetre measurements.

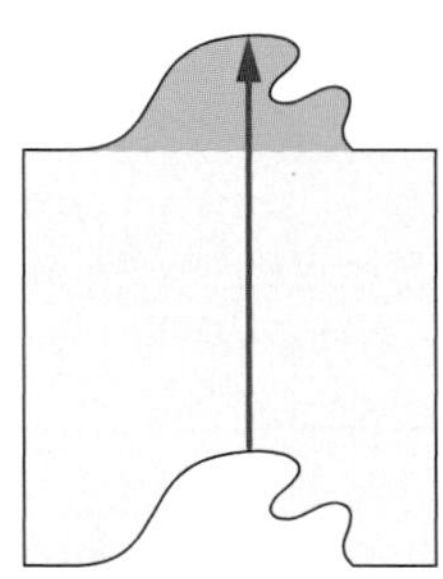

C. Show how a vertical, curved cut and a translation can be used to make the following shape from your shape in step B.

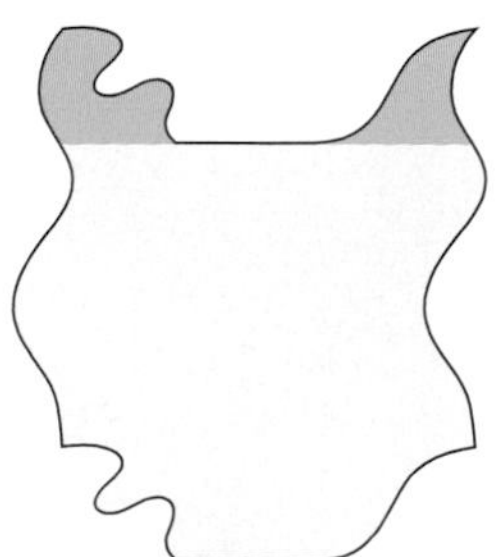

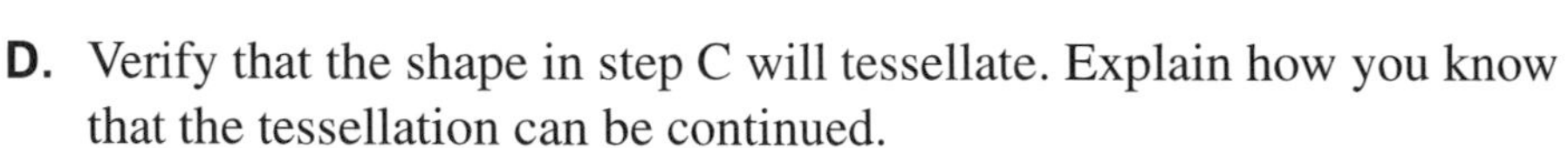

D. Verify that the shape in step C will tessellate. Explain how you know that the tessellation can be continued.

E. Make another tessellating shape, starting with a rectangle and ending with at least 10 curved or straight sides.

NEL

Do You Remember?

1. Name the coordinates of each point.

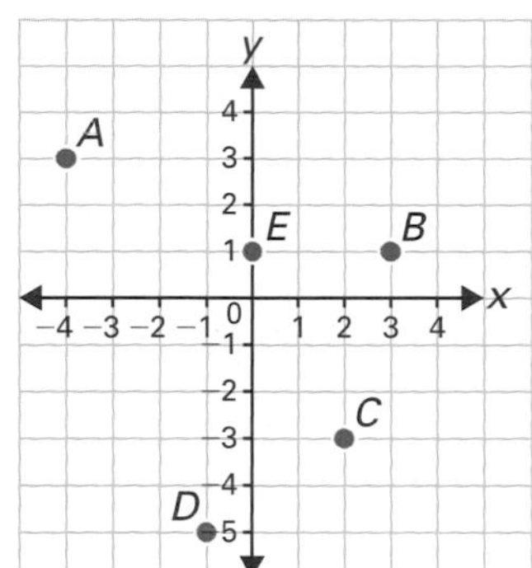

2. Plot the following points on a **Cartesian coordinate system**.
   $A(6, 5)$, $B(2, -4)$, $C(-5, -3)$, $D(-2, 5)$, $E(-3, 0)$, $F(0, 0)$

3. Use the points (15, 32), (20, −15), (18, −41), and (18, 27).
   a) Which point is farthest right?
   b) Which point is farthest left?
   c) Which point is highest up?
   d) Which point is lowest down?

4. Examine figures Q, R, and S. Which of these figures is not a **translation** of figure P? Explain.

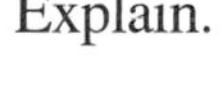

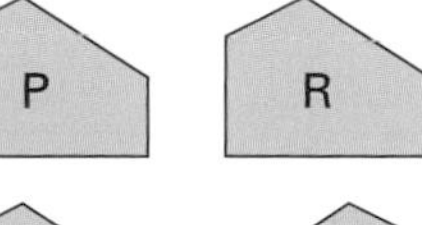

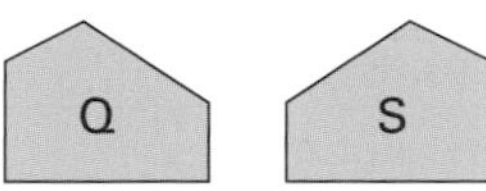

5. Examine figures B, C, D, and E. Which of these figures are not **reflections** of figure A? Explain.

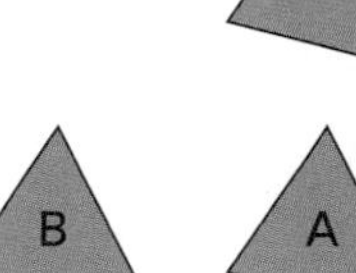

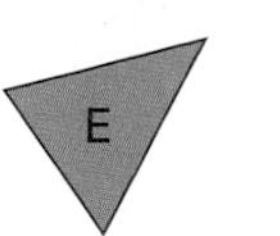

6. Examine figures W, X, Y, and Z. Which of these figures are not **rotations** of figure V?

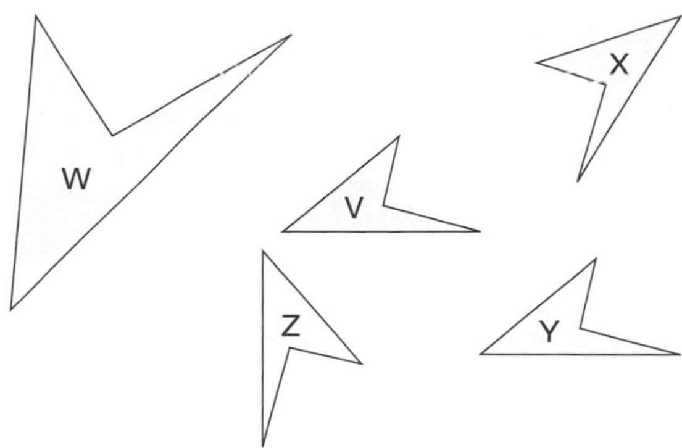

7. **a)** Which figure below is the result of a translation of figure A? Explain.

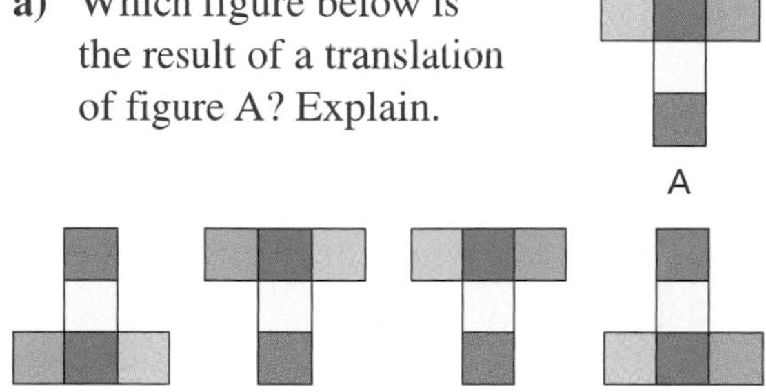

   b) Which figure in part (a) is the result of a rotation of figure A? Explain.
   c) Which figures in part (a) are the result of a reflection of figure A? Explain.

8. Examine figures L, M, N, and O. Which of these figures are similar to figure K?

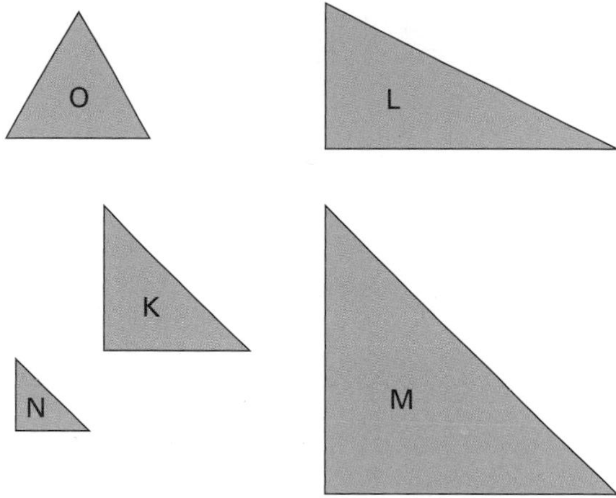

7.1 Coordinates of Points on a Grid

You will need
- grid paper
- a ruler
- dynamic geometr
  software (optiona

▶ **GOAL**

Graph points using the four quadrants of a Cartesian coordinate system.

Learn about the Math

Benjamin has been asked to paint a large maple leaf on a wall in the school cafeteria. He decides to draw a **Cartesian coordinate system** on a small picture of a maple leaf. Then he will copy key points from the small picture onto a large grid on the wall and draw the large maple leaf.

Cartesian coordinate system

a method for describing a location on a plane by identifying first the distance right or left from a vertical number line (the y-axis) and then the distance up or down from a horizontal number line (the x-axis); the axes intersect at the point (0, 0), which is called the origin; the location of a point is represented by an ordered pair of coordinates, (x, y)

quadrant

one of the four areas into which the x-axis and y-axis divide a Cartesian coordinate system

? How can you assign coordinates to points on a picture?

Benjamin placed grid paper over the maple leaf picture. Then he drew an x-axis and a y-axis on the grid.

"I marked the coordinates of vertices on my drawing. I started by marking points with integer coordinates, because these were easy to figure out. I noticed that the signs of the coordinates depended on what **quadrant** the point was in."

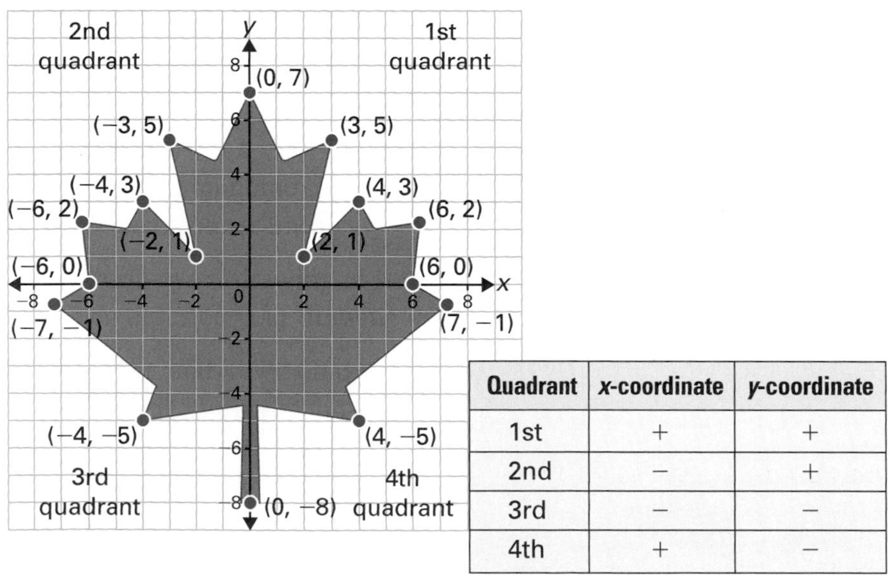

Quadrant	x-coordinate	y-coordinate
1st	+	+
2nd	−	+
3rd	−	−
4th	+	−

"I plotted the other vertices using the closest integer coordinates. I plotted all my points on the wall grid and then connected them with line segments. This gave me an outline that I could colour in."

Example 1: Using *The Geometer's Sketchpad*® to plot key points

Use dynamic geometry software to plot key points.

Hoshi's Solution

I used a scanner to copy the maple leaf picture. Then I copied the scanned image and pasted it into *The Geometer's Sketchpad*®.

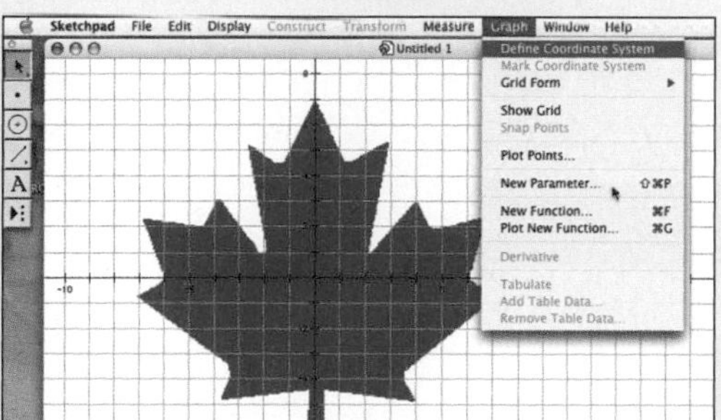

Next I used the **Graph: Define Coordinate System** command.

I moved the leaf picture and adjusted the grid scale to get as many integer coordinates for key points as possible.

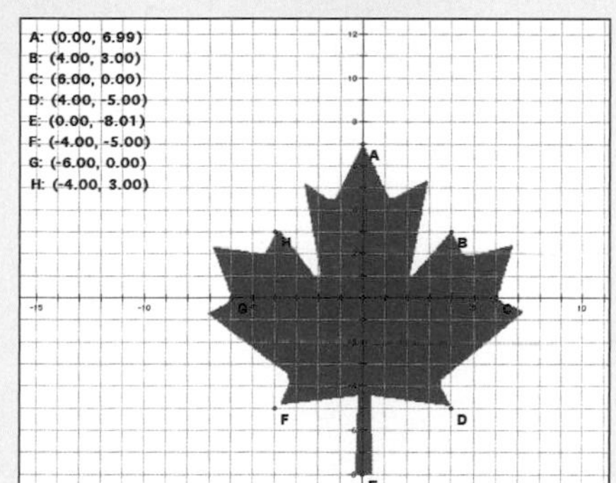

I set *The Geometer's Sketchpad*® to show labels for key points as I marked them with the "point" tool. The **Graph: Snap Points** command made it easy to mark points with integer coordinates.

After I selected all the points, I used **Measure: Coordinates** to show the ordered pair for each point. Some of the points had decimal coordinates. I rounded each decimal to the nearest integer.

Reflecting

1. What does the positive or negative sign of a coordinate tell you about the location of the point?
2. How can you locate a point if you know its coordinates on a Cartesian coordinate system?
3. How can you determine the coordinates of a point from its location on a Cartesian coordinate system?

Work with the Math

Example 2: Drawing a polygon using the coordinates of the vertices

a) Polygon *ABCD* has vertices *A*(−6, 1), *B*(0, 7), *C*(7, −2), and *D*(0, −8). Use the coordinates of the vertices to draw *ABCD*.

b) Determine the coordinates of one point inside and one point outside *ABCD*.

Solution

a)

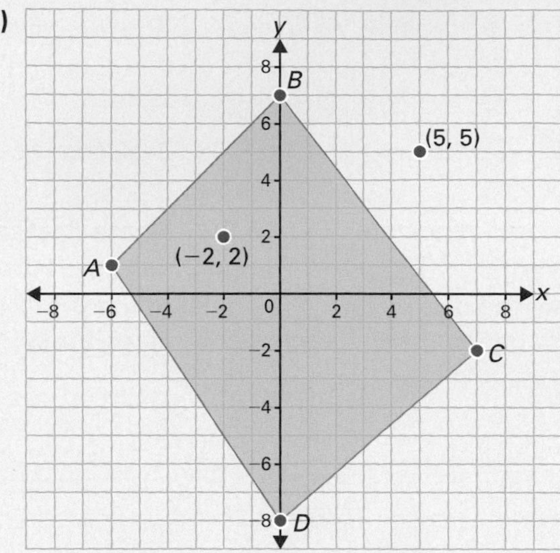

b) One possible point inside polygon *ABCD* is (−2, 2). One possible point outside the polygon is (5, 5).

A Checking

4. Name the coordinates of each point.

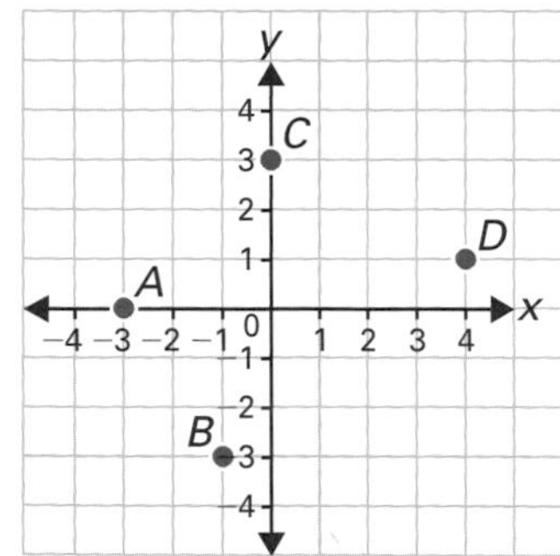

5. Plot the following points on a Cartesian coordinate system:
A(3, 0), *B*(−1, 1), *C*(0, 0), *D*(2, −3)

B Practising

6. Name the coordinates of each point.

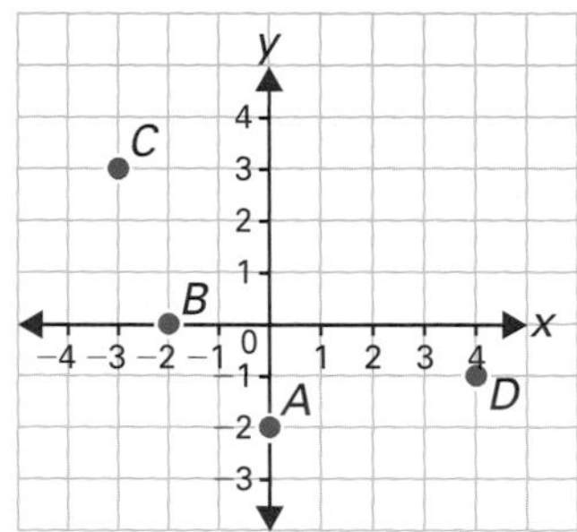

7. Plot the following points on a Cartesian coordinate system:

O (0, 0), the origin   *X* (−2, 4)
W (3, 5)   *Y* (2, −3)

8. Follow these instructions for each set of points below:

- Plot the points.
- Connect the points in order, and connect the last point to the first point.
- Name the polygon formed.

a) $A(-5, -1)$, $B(5, -1)$, $C(5, 5)$

b) $D(0, -4)$, $E(0, 4)$, $F(3, 0)$

c) $G(-3, -3)$, $H(-3, 2)$, $I(3, 2)$, $J(3, -3)$

d) $K(0, -2)$, $L(-5, 0)$, $M(1, 0)$, $N(5, -2)$

e) $P(-6, 4)$, $Q(-5, 6)$, $R(-3, 6)$, $S(-2, 4)$

f) $W(-4, 2)$, $X(0, 4)$, $Y(4, 2)$, $Z(0, 0)$

9. Name three points for each description.

a) to the right of $(-10, 0)$

b) below $(-1, -1)$

c) above and to the right of $(-4, 5)$

d) to the left of $(-3, 3)$

10. $(3, y)$ is below and to the right of $(x, -1)$. Use $<$ or $>$ to make each inequality true.

a) $3 \; \blacksquare \; x$ **b)** $-1 \; \blacksquare \; y$

11. Square *PQRS* has its top left corner at $P(3, 4)$ and its sides parallel to either the x-axis or the y-axis. List one set of possible coordinates for the other three vertices. Explain how you determined these coordinates. Draw the square.

12. Suppose that the sides of the square in question 11 were not parallel to either axis. List one set of possible coordinates for the other three vertices. Explain how you determined these coordinates.

13. Parallelogram *JKLM* has its bottom left corner at $J(-3, 4)$. List one set of possible coordinates for the other three vertices. Explain how you determined these coordinates. Draw the parallelogram.

14. $\triangle WXY$ is an isosceles triangle. The vertices of its base are $W(-2, -4)$ and $X(4, -4)$. List two possible ordered pairs for vertex Y. Explain how you determined these coordinates.

C Extending

15. Marisol wrote one set of numbers. Everton wrote another set of numbers by subtracting each of Marisol's numbers from 5.

a) Why can each of Everton's numbers be described as $5 - n$?

b) Create a table of values for $5 - n$, using integer values from 3 to -3 for n.

n	$5 - n$
3	
2	
1	

c) Plot the values in each row of your table of values as an ordered pair. Use n as the x-coordinate and $5 - n$ as the y-coordinate. Draw a line through the points.

d) Explain how the position of your line relates to Everton's calculations.

16. The point (a, b) has integer coordinates. Describe the possible positions of (a, b) for which the product $a \times b$ will be

a) positive **b)** negative **c)** zero

17. The point (a, b) has integer coordinates. Describe the possible positions of (a, b) for which the quotient $a \div b$ will be

a) positive **c)** zero

b) negative **d)** undefined

18. Three number sequences have general terms defined as $3n + 2$, $3n - 2$, and $-3n + 2$.

a) Complete a table of values for each rule using integer values from -3 to 3 for n.

b) Plot the points in each table of values. Draw a line through each set of points.

c) Describe the relationship among the positions of your lines.

7.2 Translations on a Coordinate System

You will need
- grid paper
- a ruler
- dynamic geometr[y] software (optiona[l])

▶ **GOAL**
Graph the results of a translation on a coordinate grid.

Learn about the Math

Hoshi made a flipbook to animate the movement of a boat. Her flipbook had pages that showed the original shape, the final **image**, and four in-between images. The in-between images broke the translation into five identical steps. The coordinate grid below shows Hoshi's original shape and final image.

image
a new shape that is created when a shape is transformed

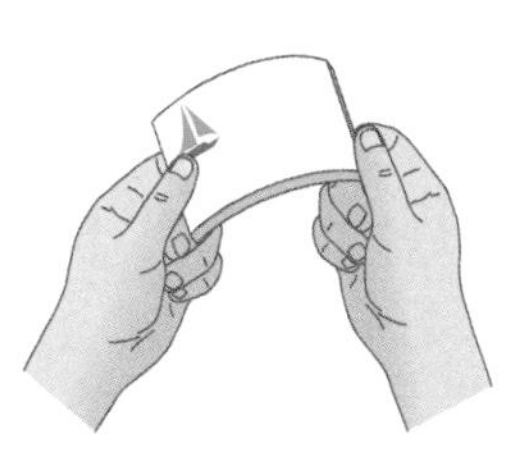

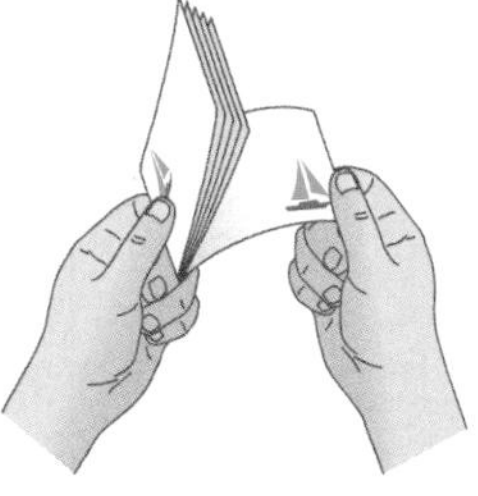
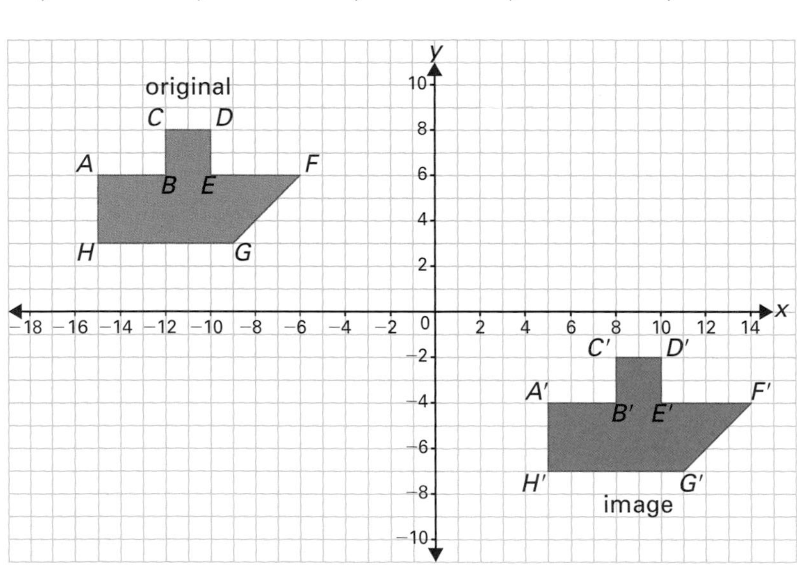

Communication Tip

The vertices of an image are often labelled using the same letters as the original shape, but with small marks read "prime" to show which vertices of the image match which vertices of the original shape. For example, *M* is transformed to *M′* (read "*M* prime"); when a second transformation is performed, *M′* is transformed to *M″*.

? What translation should Hoshi use to make each of the in-between images?

A. Make a copy of Hoshi's original shape and final image.

NEL

B. Label the coordinates of the vertices of Hoshi's original shape and final image.

C. Write the **translation vector** for the translation needed to shift each vertex of the original shape to its final image.

D. Write the translation vector for each of the five identical translations that can be put together to move the original shape to the final image.

E. Draw the image of the original shape after the first translation in step D. Mark the coordinates of each image vertex.

F. Repeat step E for the remaining translations from step D.

translation vector

an ordered pair of integers used to represent the horizontal and vertical moves that describe a translation; for example, [−2, 5] represents the translation "2 units left and 5 units up"

5

−2

Reflecting

1. How can you calculate the translation vector in step C, using the coordinates of the original shape and image?
2. How do the vectors for the in-between translations relate to the vector for the translation in step C?
3. How could you use the in-between translation vector in step D to calculate the coordinates of the vertices in steps E and F?

Communication Tip

Ordered pairs in square brackets represent a translation. Ordered pairs in round brackets represent the coordinates of a point.

Work with the Math

Example 1: Determining image coordinates on a grid

Determine the coordinates of the image of $\triangle ABC$ after the translation [−3, 5].

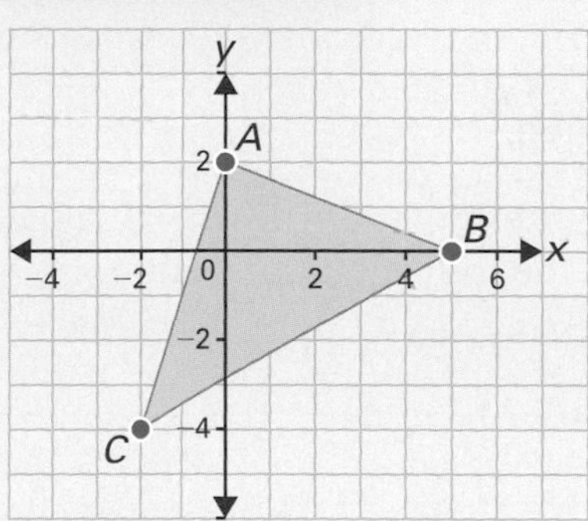

Chad's Solution

$A(0, 2)$, $B(5, 0)$, $C(-2, -4)$

$A(0, 2) \rightarrow A(0 + (-3), 2 + 5)$, or $A'(-3, 7)$

$B(5, 0) \rightarrow B(5 + (-3), 0 + 5)$, or $B'(2, 5)$

$C(-2, -4) \rightarrow C(-2 + (-3), -4 + 5)$, or $C'(-5, 1)$

I wrote the coordinates of each vertex.

I added the values from the translation vector to the coordinates of each point.

Example 2: Determining image coordinates using geometry software

Determine the coordinates of the image of $\triangle ABC$ after the translation [−3, 5]. $\triangle ABC$ has coordinates $A(0, 2)$, $B(5, 0)$, and $C(-2, -4)$.

Tran's Solution

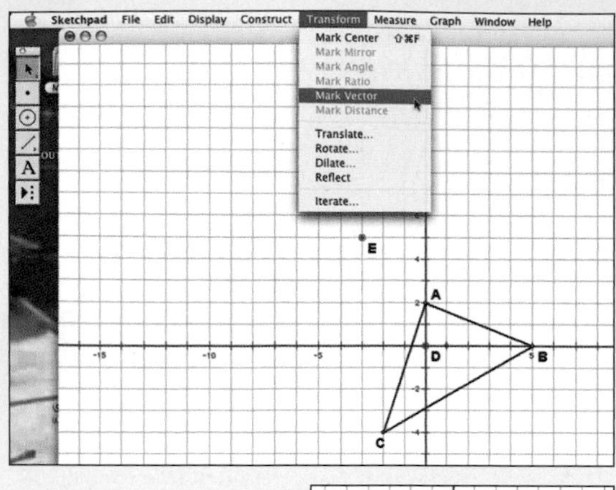

I drew $\triangle ABC$ by plotting points A, B, and C using the command **Graph: Plot Points ...** in *The Geometer's Sketchpad®*. Then I selected all three points and used **Construct: Segment** to construct the triangle.

I represented the translation [−3, 5] by plotting point $D(0, 0)$ as a starting point and then plotting $E(-3, 5)$. I selected D first and then E. I used **Transform: Mark Vector** to tell *The Geometer's Sketchpad®* to use segment DE for the translation.

I selected points A, B, and C and the segments joining them. Then I used **Transform: Translate** to apply the [−3, 5] transformation.

The Geometer's Sketchpad® automatically labelled the image vertices.

I read the image coordinates as $A'(-3, 7)$, $B'(2, 5)$, and $C'(-5, 1)$.

A Checking

4. Name the coordinates of the image of each point after the indicated translation.

a) (−2, 4) after [−3, 1]

b) (0, 7) after [2, −6]

5. a) Copy this shape. Draw its image after the translation [−2, 1].

b) Name the coordinates of the image vertices.

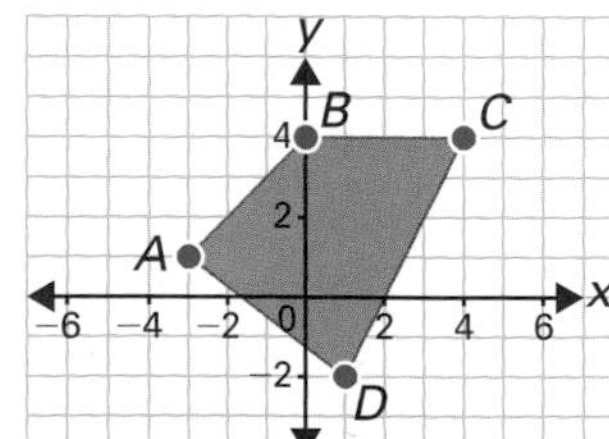

B Practising

6. Describe the translation that moved $JKLM$ to $J'K'L'M'$.

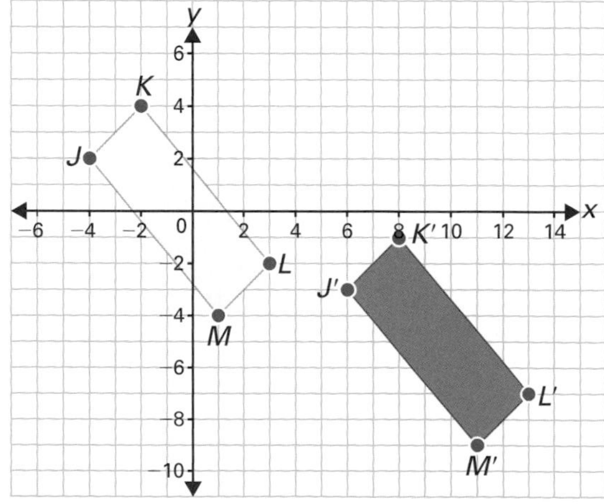

7. The coordinates of the vertices of $\triangle ABC$ are $A(1, -1)$, $B(3, 0)$, and $C(2, 4)$.

a) State the translation vector needed to move A to $A'(3, 4)$.

b) State the image of B and C under the same translation.

8. The coordinates of the vertices of $\triangle XYZ$ are $X(0, -4)$, $Y(0, 0)$, and $Z(3, 3)$.

a) Determine the coordinates of the image of $\triangle XYZ$ after the translation $[3, -2]$.

b) Determine the coordinates of the image of $\triangle XYZ$ after the translation $[-3, 6]$.

9. a) Write the translation vector needed to translate

i) $ABCD$ to $A'B'C'D'$

ii) $A'B'C'D'$ to $A''B''C''D''$

iii) $ABCD$ to $A''B''C''D''$

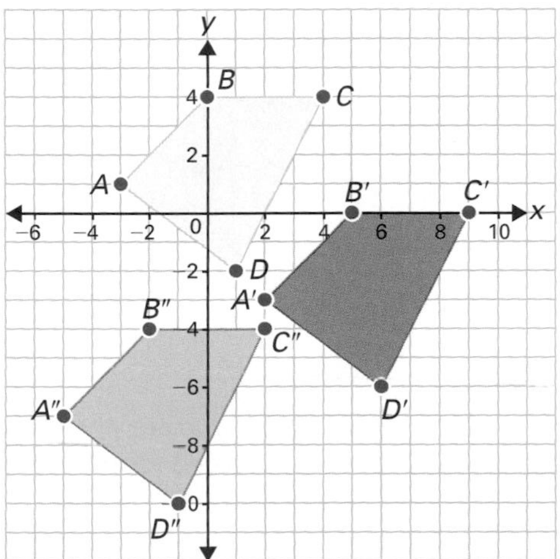

b) Show how you can use integer operations to explain the relationships among the translation vectors in part (a).

10. $\triangle DEF$ is transformed to $\triangle D''E''F''$ by applying the same translation two times. The coordinates of D are $(-5, -5)$. The vertices of the final image are at $D''(-1, -15)$, $E''(-6, -10)$, and $F''(4, -12)$.

a) Write the translation vector.

b) Write the coordinates of vertices E and F.

11. Suppose that you were given only the coordinates of the vertices of these two triangles without the diagram. How could you use the coordinates to show that $\triangle A'B'C'$ is *not* the image of $\triangle ABC$ after a translation?

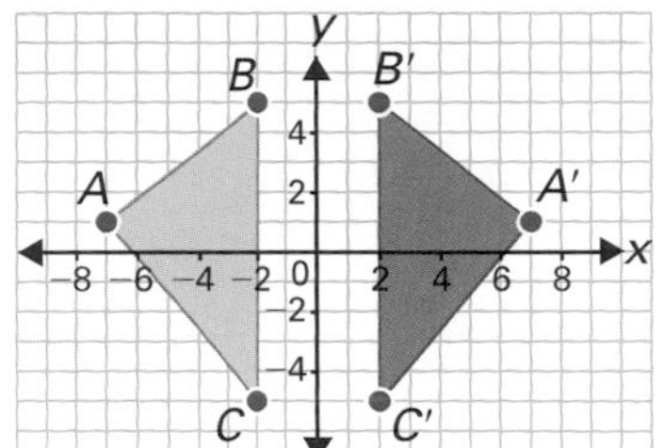

12. The coordinates of the vertices of $\triangle PQR$ are $P(-2, -1)$, $Q(2, 1)$, and $R(0, 4)$. Determine the coordinates of the image vertices after a translation that moves vertex P to vertex Q.

13. *PQRS* is a square with two vertices at $P(-2, 4)$ and $Q(4, 4)$.

a) State two possible sets of coordinates for the other two vertices.

b) Draw your two squares on grid paper.

c) Write the translation vector needed to move the upper square to cover the lower square.

C Extending

14. a) $\triangle ABC$ has vertices at $A(-2, 4)$, $B(-4, 1)$, and $C(2, 1)$. Draw $\triangle ABC$.

b) Draw $\triangle ABC$ after the translation $[2, 2]$.

c) Draw the triangle in part (b) after the translation $[-2, 1]$.

d) Use your drawings to determine the translation vector that will move your image triangle in part (c) back to the original triangle.

e) How can you use the translation vectors $[2, 2]$ and $[-2, 1]$ to determine the translation vector in part (d)?

7.3 Reflections and Rotations

You will need
- grid paper
- a protractor
- a compass
- a ruler

▶ **GOAL**

Graph the results of reflections and rotations on a coordinate grid.

Learn about the Math

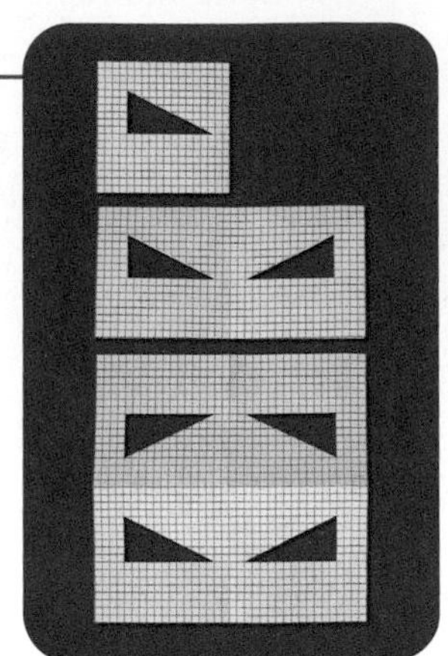

Chad and Toma are making stencil designs. First they fold square pieces of paper into fourths. Then they cut shapes in the folded paper.

Chad and Toma want to be able to draw similar designs on grid paper, so they can use coordinates to transfer the designs to a larger surface.

? How can you make designs using only reflections or only rotations?

Example 1: Determining image coordinates after a reflection

Determine the coordinates of the image of $\triangle ABC$ after a reflection in the x-axis, followed by a reflection in the y-axis.

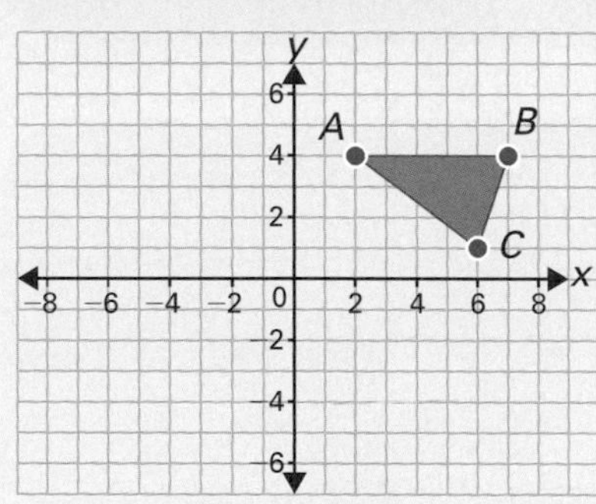

Chad's Solution

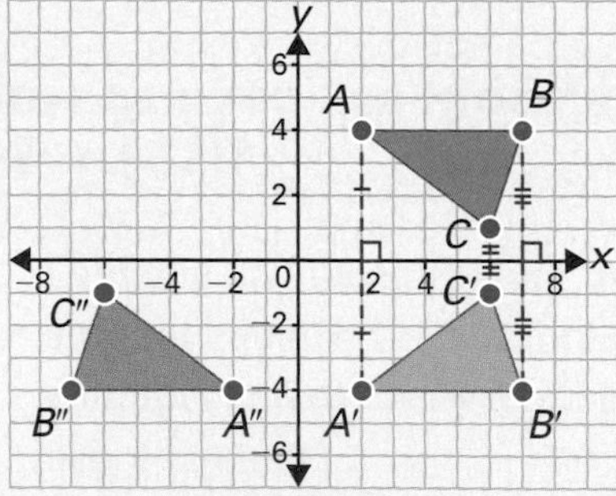

I plotted $\triangle ABC$. I know that the reflected image of each point in $\triangle ABC$ will be the same distance from the x-axis (the line of reflection), but on the other side. Point A is 4 units above the x-axis, so I plotted point A' directly below A, 4 units below the x-axis.

Point B is also 4 units above the x-axis, so I plotted B' directly below B, 4 units below the x-axis.

Point C is 1 unit above the x-axis, so I plotted C' 1 unit below the x-axis.

I joined the image points to form the image $\triangle A'B'C'$.

I followed the same process for reflecting in the y-axis. The image points are the same distance from the y-axis, but on the opposite side.

The coordinates of the image after a reflection in the x-axis are $A'(2, -4)$, $B'(7, -4)$, and $C'(6, -1)$.

The coordinates of the image after a reflection in the y-axis are $A''(-2, -4)$, $B''(-7, -4)$, and $C''(-6, -1)$.

Example 2: Determining image coordinates after a rotation

$\triangle ABC$ has vertices $A(2, 4)$, $B(7, 4)$, and $C(6, 1)$. Determine the coordinates of the image of $\triangle ABC$ after a rotation of 90° counterclockwise (ccw) about the origin, $O(0, 0)$.

Toma's Solution

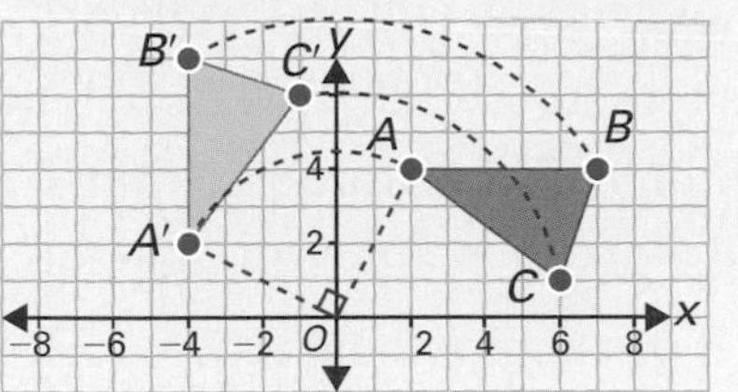

I plotted $\triangle ABC$. I drew a line segment from the origin to A. I measured a 90° angle in a counterclockwise direction from line segment OA and drew another line segment the same length from O to A'. A' is the same distance from O as A, but turned 90°.

I did the same thing to mark points B' and C'.

I joined the image points to form the image, $\triangle A'B'C'$.

The coordinates of the image are $A'(-4, 2)$, $B'(-4, 7)$, and $C'(-1, 6)$.

Reflecting

1. How do you determine the coordinates of a point after a reflection in the x-axis?
2. How do you determine the coordinates of a point after a reflection in the y-axis?
3. How do you determine the coordinates of a point after a 90° rotation about the origin? Do you think this would be true with rotations of 180° and 270° as well? Why?

Work with the Math

Example 3: Graphing reflections

$\triangle ABC$ has vertices $A(3, 1)$, $B(7, 3)$, and $C(6, 0)$. Plot the image of $\triangle ABC$ after a reflection in the line that passes through the origin and $(1, 1)$.

Solution

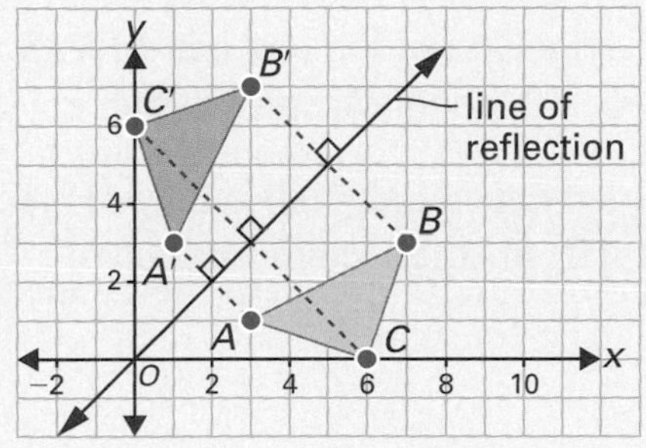

Plot $\triangle ABC$. Draw the line of reflection. Draw a line segment perpendicular to the line of reflection through point A. Plot A' on this line segment the same distance from the line of reflection as A. Repeat with the other two vertices. Join the image points.

The coordinates of the image vertices are $A'(1, 3)$, $B'(3, 7)$, and $C'(0, 6)$.

Example 4: Graphing rotations

ABCD has vertices *A*(1, 3), *B*(3, 7), *C*(6, 6), and *D*(3, 1). Plot the image of *ABCD* after a 180° ccw rotation.

Solution

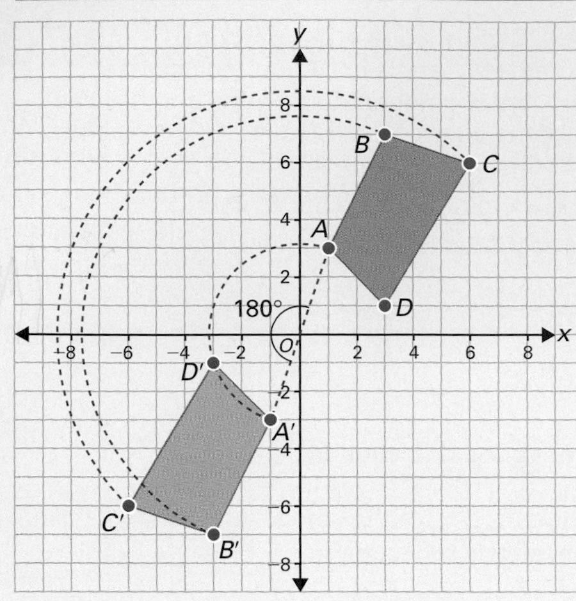

Plot *ABCD*. Draw a line from the origin (*O*) to *A*. Mark a rotation of 180° ccw from line segment *OA* to determine *A*′. Repeat for the other three vertices, and then join the image points.

The coordinates of the image vertices are *A*′(−1, −3), *B*′(−3, −7), *C*′(−6, −6), and *D*′(−3, −1).

A Checking

4. Reflect *ABCD* in the *x*-axis. Determine the coordinates of the image vertices.

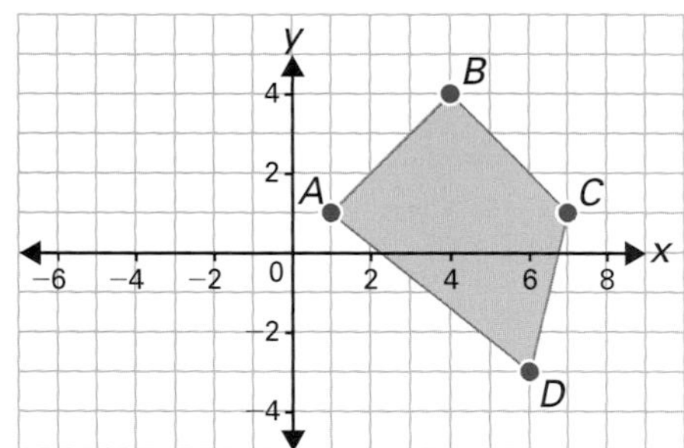

5. $\triangle ABC$ has coordinates $A(-6, 2)$, $B(-4, 0)$, and $C(-2, 5)$. Determine the coordinates of the image vertices after each reflection of $\triangle ABC$.

a) a reflection in the *y*-axis

b) a reflection in the line that passes through (0, 0) and (1, 1)

6. Determine the coordinates of the image vertices after each rotation of $\triangle ABC$.

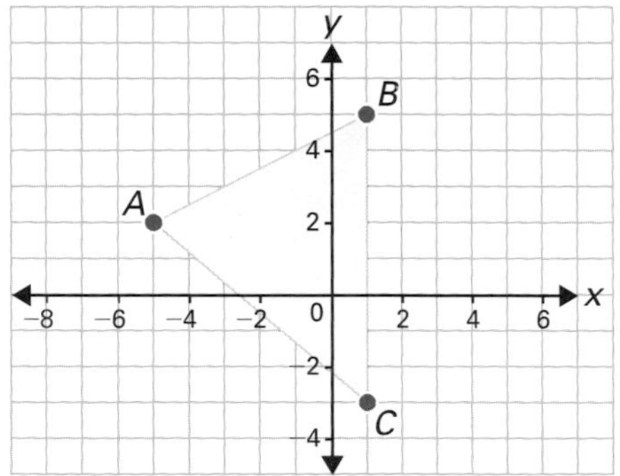

a) a rotation of 90° ccw about the origin

b) a rotation of 180° ccw about the origin

c) a rotation of 270° clockwise (cw) about the origin

B Practising

7. Draw the image of $\triangle ABC$ after each transformation. Determine the coordinates of the image vertices.

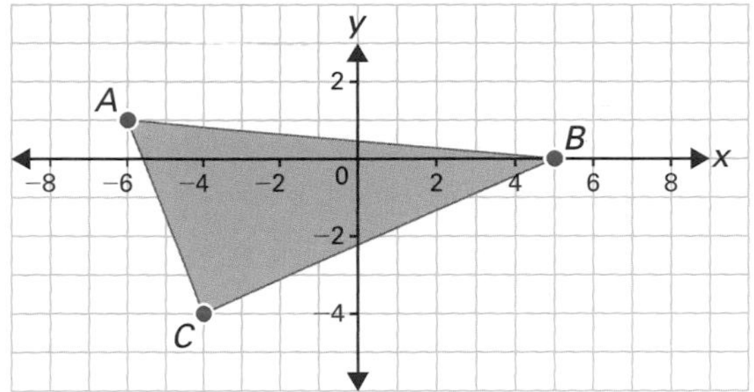

a) a reflection in the x-axis

b) a reflection in the y-axis

c) a reflection in the line that passes through (0, 0) and (1, 1)

d) a rotation of 90° ccw about the origin

e) a rotation of 180° ccw about the origin

8. $A(-4, 1)$, $B(1, 5)$, $C(4, -3)$, and $D(-2, -3)$ are the vertices of a quadrilateral. Determine the coordinates of the image vertices after each transformation of $ABCD$.

a) a reflection in the x-axis

b) a reflection in the y-axis

c) a rotation of 180° cw about the origin

d) a rotation of 270° cw about the origin

9. Draw a quadrilateral on grid paper. Show that the image vertices after a rotation of 180° about the origin are the same as the image vertices after a reflection in the y-axis followed by a reflection in the x-axis.

10. Fazel says that if you reflect a triangle in the x-axis and then in the y-axis, the image will be the same as if you did the reflections in the opposite order. Do you think he is right? Use the coordinates of three different triangles to support your opinion.

11. Use reflections in the x-axis and the y-axis to show that this shape has reflection symmetry.

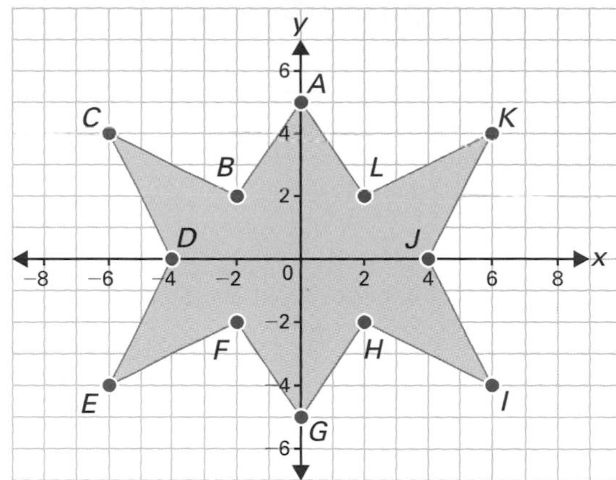

12. Use rotations to show that the shape in question 11 is the same as the shape you would get by turning it 180° about the origin.

C Extending

13. Point A has coordinates (x, y). Determine the coordinates of the image of A after each transformation.

a) a reflection in the x-axis

b) a reflection in the y-axis

c) a reflection in the line that passes through the origin and (2, 2)

d) a rotation of 90° cw about the origin

e) a rotation of 180° cw about the origin

f) a rotation of 270° cw about the origin

14. $\triangle A''B''C''$ is the image of $\triangle ABC$ after a reflection in the y-axis and one other reflection. Determine the position of the reflection line for the second reflection.

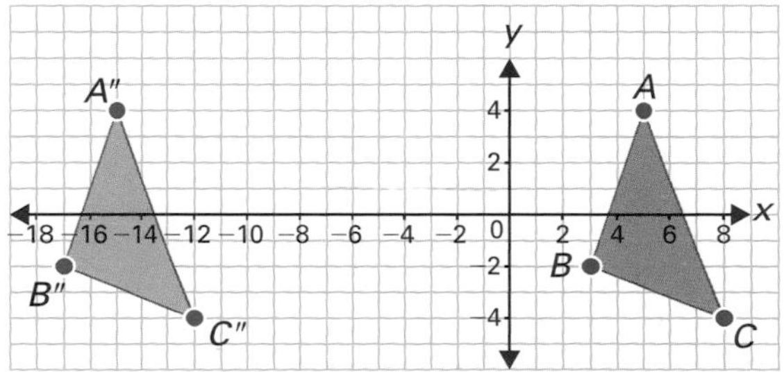

Mid-Chapter Review

Frequently Asked Questions

Q: What are quadrants?

A: Quadrants are areas into which the *x*-axis and *y*-axis divide the Cartesian coordinate system. There are four quadrants, as shown at the right.

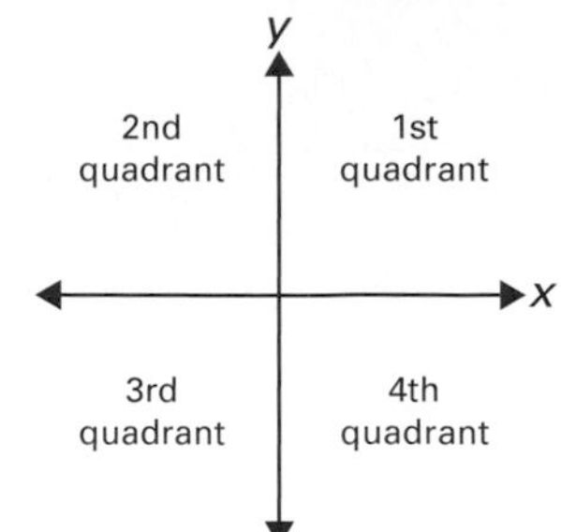

Q: How do you use the coordinates of a point to locate it on a graph?

A: The distance of a point from the *y*-axis is determined by its *x*-coordinate. The distance of a point from the *x*-axis is determined by its *y*-coordinate.

The sign and value of the coordinates indicate the quadrant or axis where the point is located.

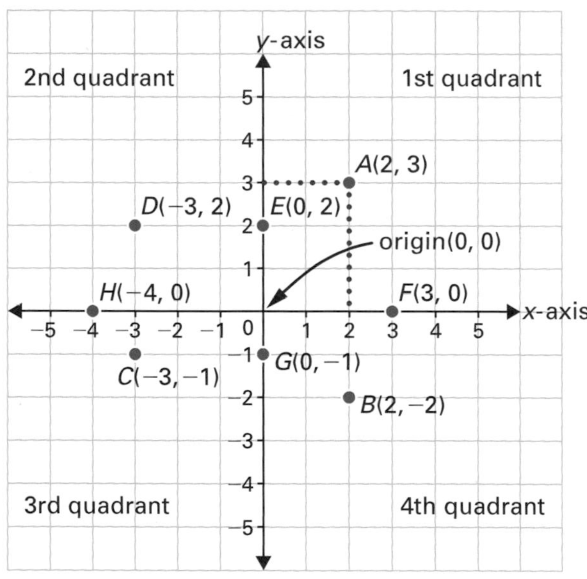

Example	Location	Signs of coordinates, (*x*, *y*)
A	1st quadrant	(+, +)
D	2nd quadrant	(−, +)
C	3rd quadrant	(−, −)
B	4th quadrant	(+, −)
F and *H*	*x*-axis	(*x*, 0)
E and *G*	*y*-axis	(0, *y*)

Q: How can you determine the coordinates of the image of a point after a transformation?

A1: You can apply the transformation and then determine the coordinates of the image by reading them from the coordinate grid.

A2: You can determine the coordinates of the image without plotting the point or the image. If point *A* has coordinates (*x*, *y*), the coordinates of its image can be determined as follows:

Transformation of *A*(*x*, *y*)	Coordinates of *A′*	Example
translation by [*a*, *b*]	(*x* + *a*, *y* + *b*)	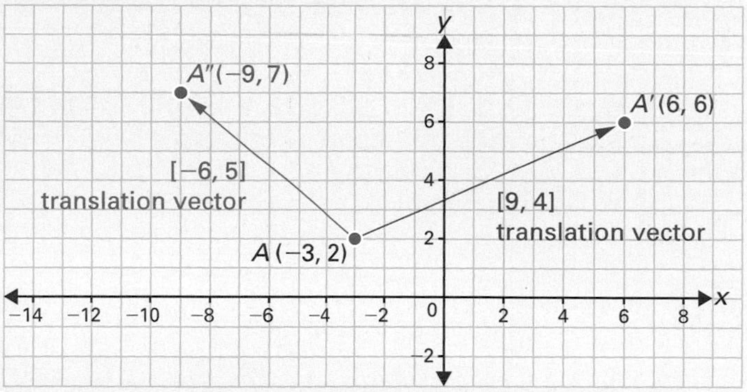 *A*″(−9, 7); *A*′(6, 6); [−6, 5] translation vector; *A*(−3, 2); [9, 4] translation vector
reflection in *x*-axis reflection in *y*-axis reflection in line that passes through (0, 0) and (1, 1)	(*x*, −*y*) (−*x*, *y*) (*y*, *x*)	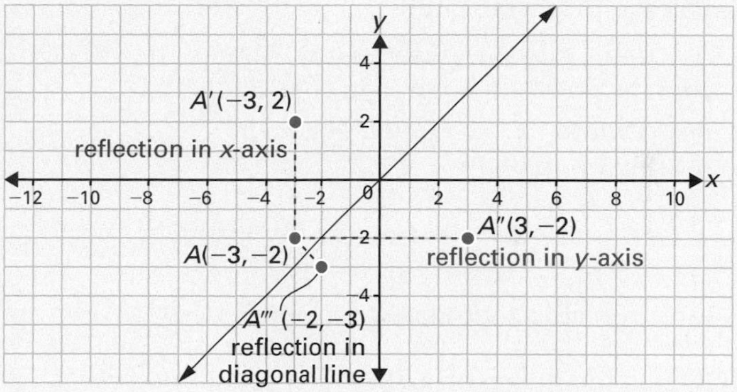 *A*′(−3, 2) reflection in *x*-axis; *A*(−3, −2); *A*″(3, −2) reflection in *y*-axis; *A*‴(−2, −3) reflection in diagonal line
rotation of 90° cw (or 270° ccw) rotation of 180° rotation of 270° cw (or 90° ccw)	(*y*, −*x*) (−*x*, −*y*) (−*y*, *x*)	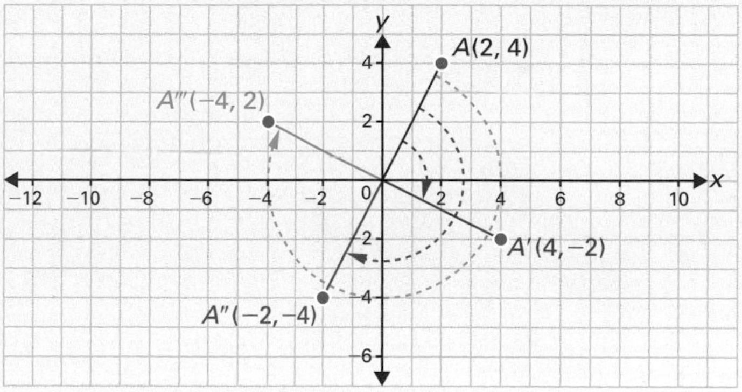 *A*(2, 4); *A*‴(−4, 2); *A*′(4, −2); *A*″(−2, −4)

Practice Questions

(7.1) **1. a)** Name the coordinates of each point.

b) State the quadrants that points B and C are in.

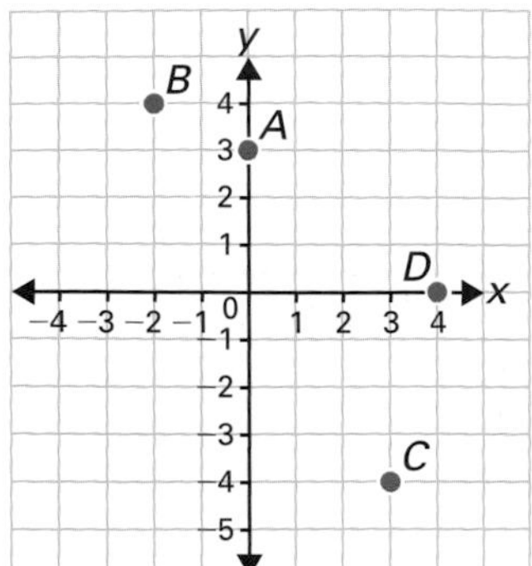

(7.1) **2.** Plot the following points:
$A(-2, 0)$, $B(0, 3)$, $C(7, 0)$, $D(5, -3)$
Join the points in order, and connect the last point to the first point. Name the resulting polygon.

(7.1) **3.** $\triangle GHI$ is an isosceles triangle. Two vertices are $G(-6, 3)$ and $H(-6, -5)$. Determine three possible coordinates for vertex I.

(7.2) **4.** Sketch the image of $ABCD$ after each translation.

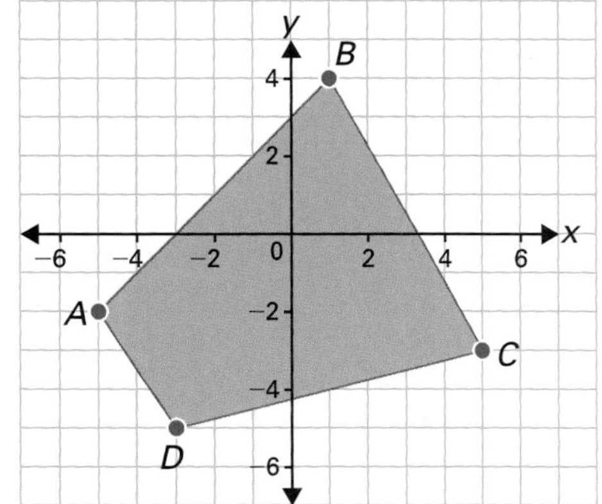

a) $[-2, 0]$

b) $[3, -1]$

c) $[-4, -5]$

5. a) Quadrilateral $ABCD$ in question 4 is translated again, moving B to D. State the vector that represents this translation.

b) State the coordinates of each image vertex after this translation. (7.2)

6. Describe the translation that moved $\triangle WXY$ to $\triangle W'X'Y'$. (7.2)

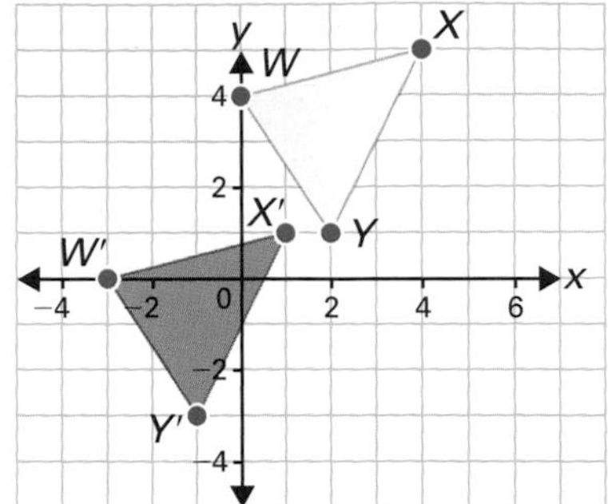

7. $\triangle ABC$ is translated according to the vector $[-3, -2]$. The vertices of the image are at $A'(1, 1)$, $B'(-3, -2)$, and $C'(5, 0)$. Determine the coordinates of the vertices of $\triangle ABC$. (7.2)

8. Perform each transformation on quadrilateral $ABCD$. Then sketch the image and state the coordinates of the image vertices. (7.3)

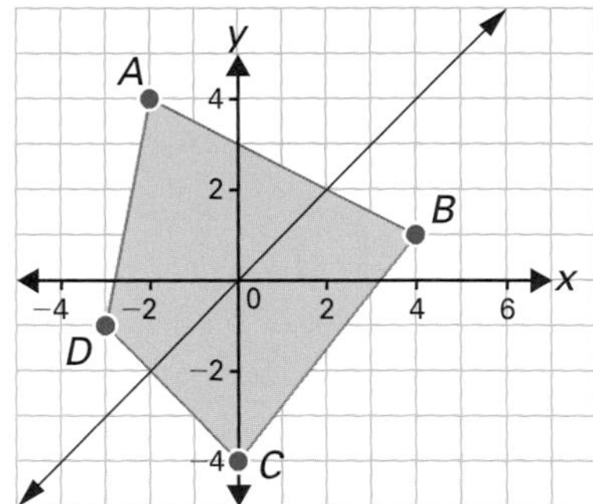

a) a reflection in the y-axis

b) a reflection in the x-axis

c) a reflection in the diagonal line

d) a rotation of 90° ccw about the origin

e) a rotation of 270° ccw about the origin

9. The vertices of $\triangle ABC$ are at $A(1, 1)$, $B(-1, 1)$, and $C(-3, 5)$. (7.3)

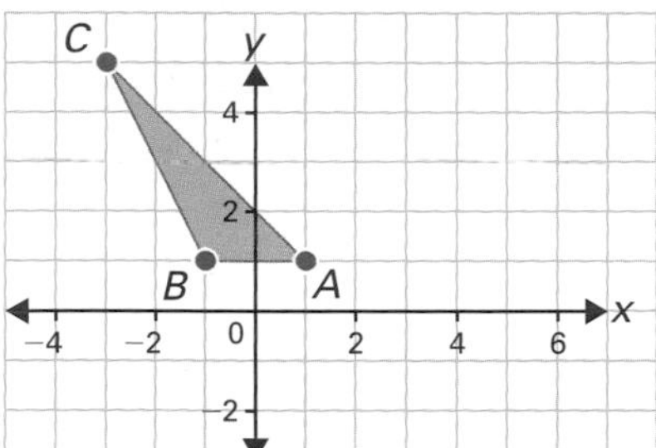

a) Determine the coordinates of the image vertices after a reflection in the x-axis followed by a reflection in the y-axis.

b) Show that when you apply the reflections in the opposite order, the coordinates of the final image vertices are the same.

c) Show that a rotation of 180° will result in the same image vertices.

10. Describe the rotation that moves $\triangle KLM$ to $\triangle K'L'M'$. (7.3)

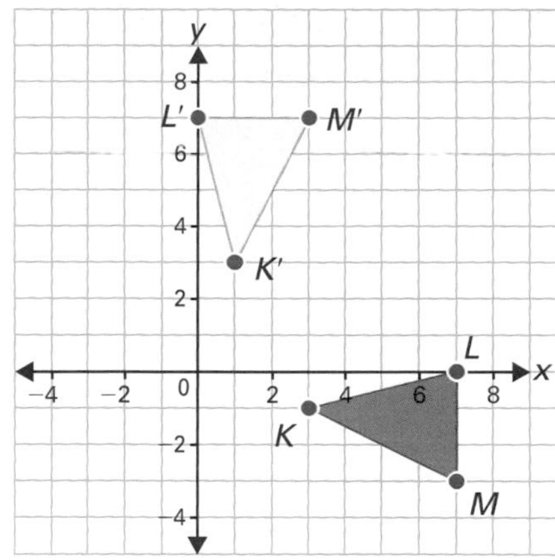

11. A shape in the third quadrant is rotated 90° cw about the origin and then reflected in the y-axis. In which quadrant is the final image? Explain. (7.3)

Mental Imagery

CUTTING AND FORMING SHAPES

Draw a 9-by-16 rectangle on grid paper. Cut the rectangle along the grid lines to form two congruent pieces. Then put together the two pieces to form a square.

You will need
- grid paper
- scissors

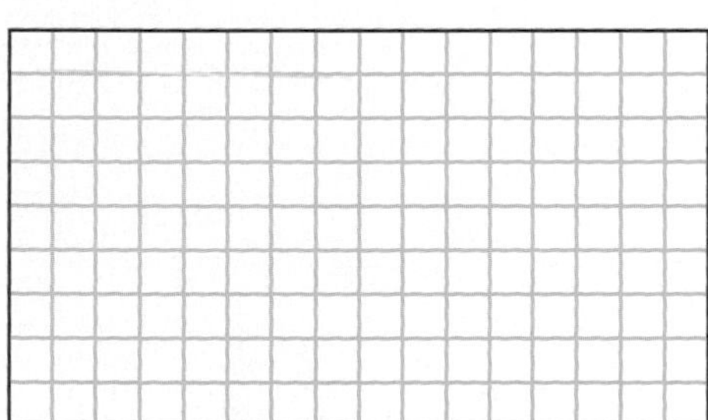

1. What is the area of each piece?

2. What are the dimensions of the square when the two pieces are put together? Explain your reasoning.

3. Draw your solution to this problem on grid paper.

7.4 Exploring Similar Shapes

You will need
- grid paper
- a ruler
- a protractor

or
- dynamic geometry software

▶ **GOAL**

Investigate the properties of similar shapes.

Explore the Math

Benjamin noticed that his original maple leaf picture and the enlargement he painted on the wall were **similar** shapes. He wondered how the measurements of the two shapes were related.

similar

identical in shape, but not necessarily the same size

? How do the measurements of similar shapes compare?

Choose Method 1 or Method 2 for your exploration.

Method 1: Using grid paper

A. Construct a triangle on a Cartesian coordinate system. Place its base on the *x*-axis and one vertex at the origin.

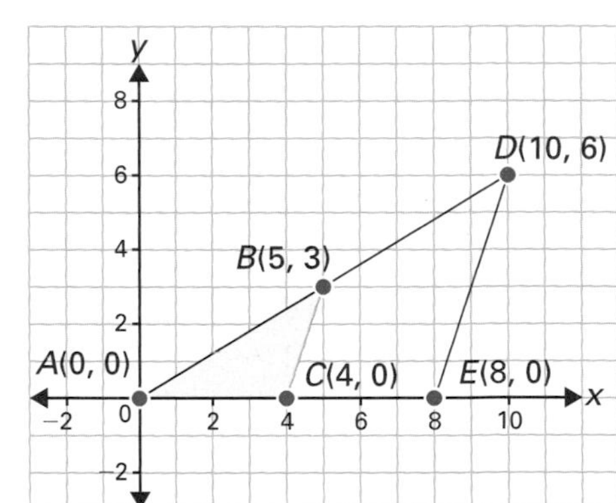

B. Extend the two sides of the triangle at the origin to twice their lengths. Mark the two new vertices.

C. Compare the coordinates of the vertices of the triangles.

D. Compare the side lengths and perimeters of the triangles.

E. Compare the areas of the triangles. ($A = bh \div 2$)

F. Compare the measures of the angles in the two triangles.

G. Repeat steps B to F, extending the side lengths of the triangle in step A to three times as long.

H. Repeat steps B to F using a triangle with side lengths half as long as the triangle in step A.

I. The diagram at the right shows steps A and B using a quadrilateral. Complete steps C to H for this quadrilateral.

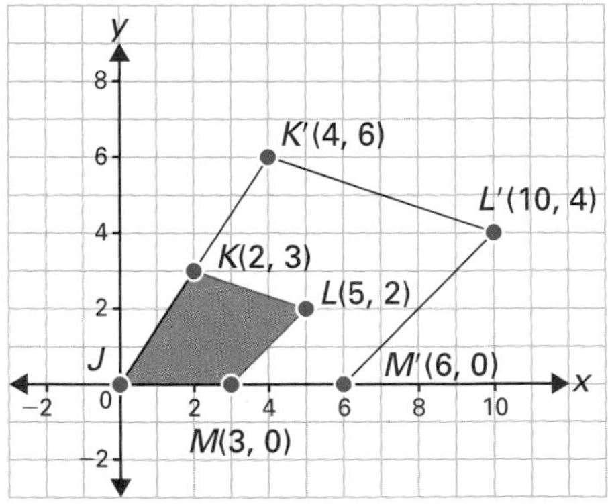

Method 2: Using *The Geometer's Sketchpad*®

A. Open a new sketch in *The Geometer's Sketchpad*®. Create a Cartesian coordinate system for the sketch. Plot three points as vertices of a triangle.

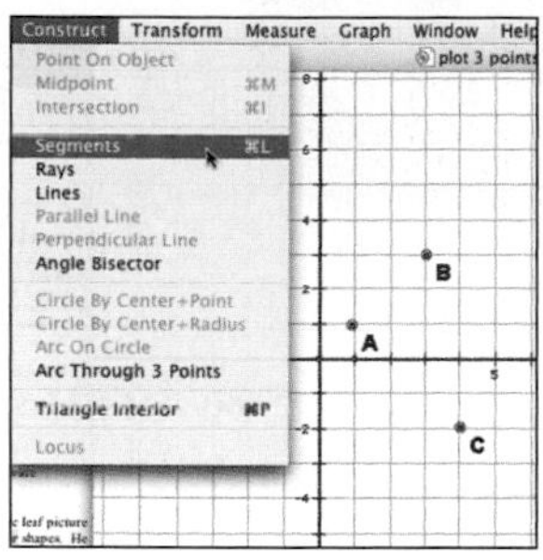

B. Select all three points, and use **Construct: Segments** to draw the triangle's sides.

C. Select the three vertex points, and use **Construct: Triangle Interior** to create a solid triangle interior.

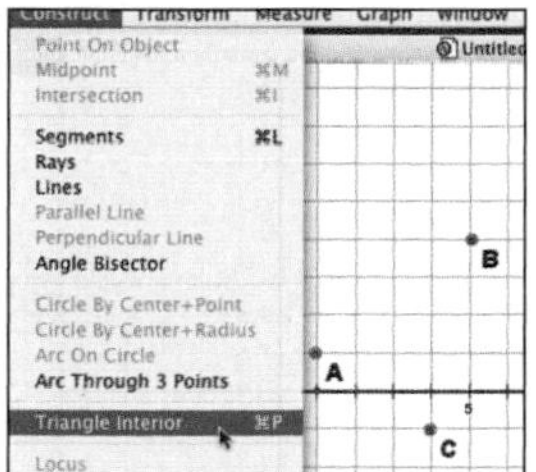

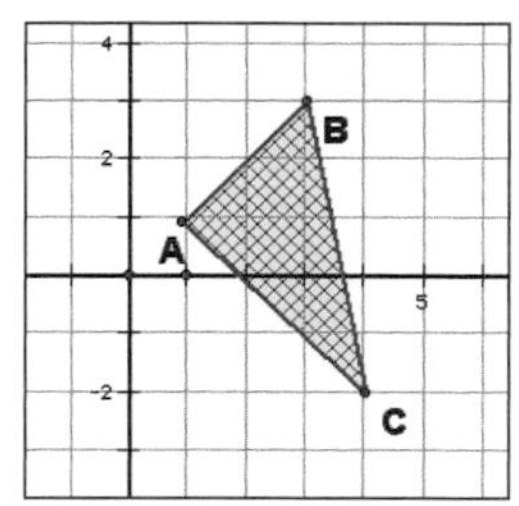

D. Select the origin, and perform **Transform: Mark Center**. This will cause all the enlargements and reductions to be centred at the origin.

E. Select the vertex points, the triangle sides, and the triangle interior. Perform **Transform: Dilate**. *The Geometer's Sketchpad®* will ask you to enter a scale factor. For example, using a ratio of 1:2 will create an image with sides half the length of the original. Click **Dilate**.

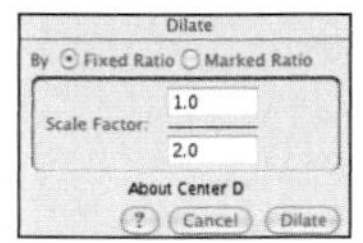

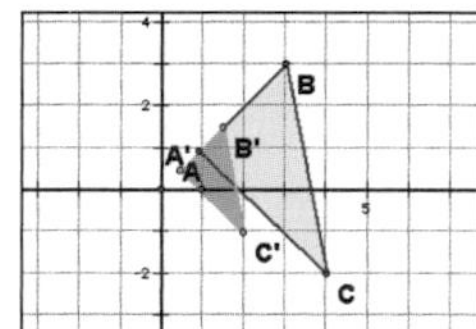

F. Use **Measure: Coordinates** to determine the coordinates for each vertex.

G. Use **Measure: Length** to measure each side length in both triangles.

H. Use **Measure: Angle** to measure each angle in the triangles.

I. Select the interiors of the two triangles. Use **Measure: Perimeter** and **Measure: Area** to determine the perimeter and area of each triangle.

J. Repeat steps E to I using two different scale factors. At least one scale factor should have the first term greater than the second.

K. Repeat steps A to J using a quadrilateral.

Reflecting

1. How do the coordinates of a point and its image compare when shapes are similar?

2. How do the measures of matching angles of similar figures compare?

3. How do the lengths and perimeters of similar figures compare?

4. How do the areas of similar figures compare?

You will need
- grid paper
- coloured pencils

7.5 Communicating about Transformations

▶ **GOAL**

Describe transformations of geometric figures.

Communicate about the Math

Maria performed several transformations on $\triangle ABC$. She drew a picture of her work and wrote an explanation of what she had done. She asked Tran to read her report to make sure that her explanation was clear.

? How can Maria improve her description?

Maria's Report

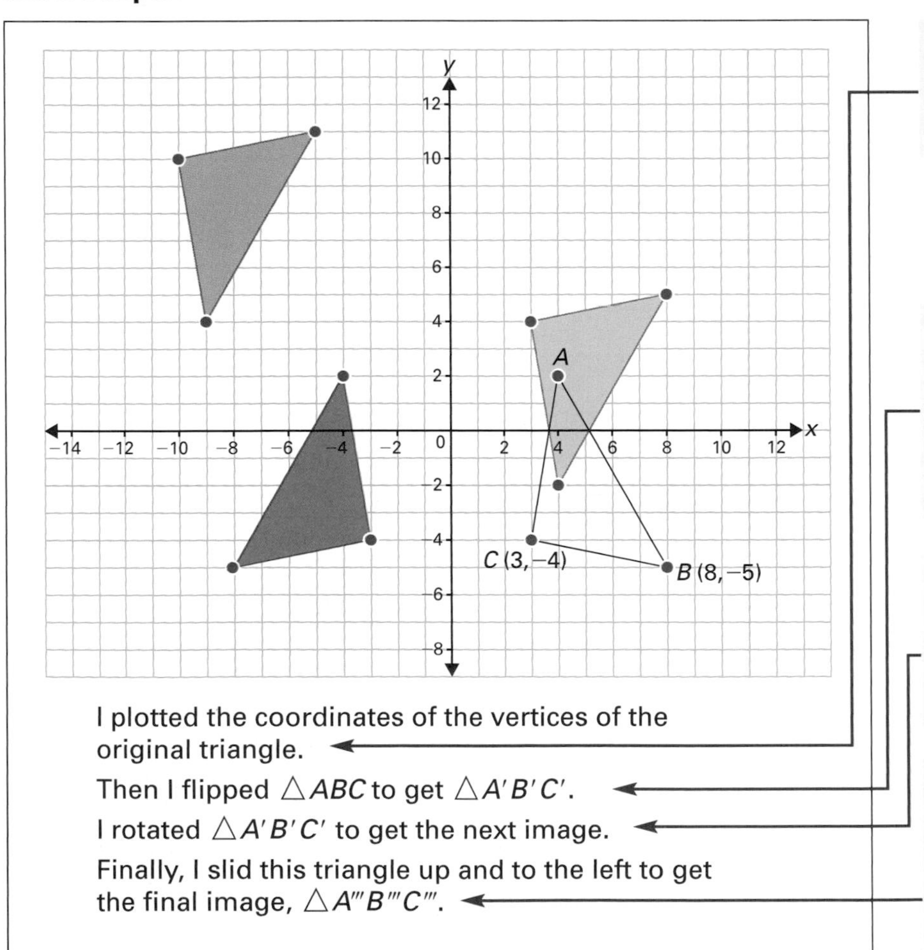

Tran's Questions

Why didn't you show all the coordinates of $\triangle ABC$?

What is the mirror line for the reflection? What are the coordinates of the image vertices?

What angle did you use for the rotation? Which triangle is the image?

How far did you translate the previous triangle in each direction?

NEL

A. Use the Communication Checklist to explain why Tran's questions could help Maria improve her description.

B. Improve Maria's drawing so that it clearly shows the effect of each transformation.

C. Rewrite Maria's description using Tran's ideas as well as your own. Explain how your changes improve Maria's description.

Communication Checklist

- ☑ Did you show all the necessary steps?
- ☑ Did you provide enough information for someone else to complete each step correctly?
- ☑ Did you use a drawing effectively?
- ☑ Did you use appropriate math language?

Reflecting

1. What points in the Communication Checklist did Tran use?
2. Why should Maria state the coordinates of the vertices of each image?
3. Why should Maria include accurate and detailed drawings with her report?

Work with the Math

Example: Comparing rotation images with reflection images

Reflecting $\triangle ABC$ in the *x*-axis and then in the *y*-axis has the same effect as rotating $\triangle ABC$ 180° about the origin. Explain how you know this is true.

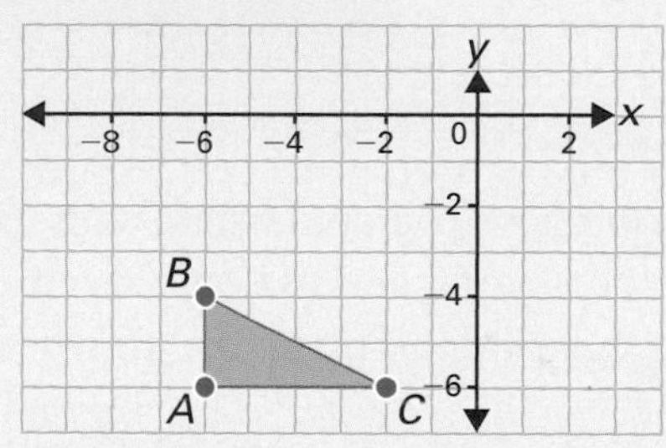

Hoshi's Solution

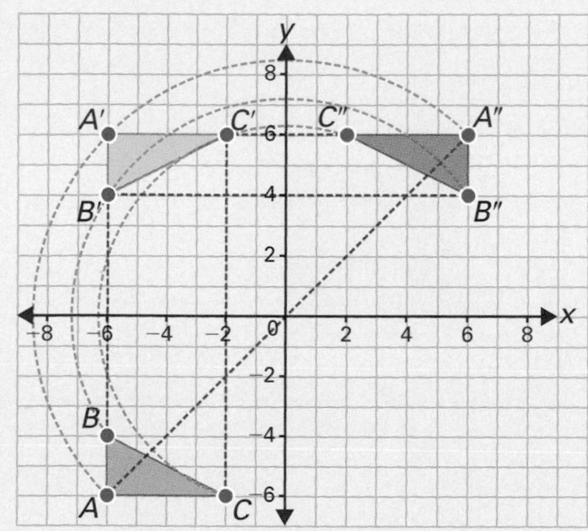

I reflected the blue triangle in the *x*-axis to get the green triangle. I reflected the green triangle in the *y*-axis to get the purple triangle.

Then I turned the blue triangle 180° clockwise around the origin. I landed on the purple triangle.

I think this seems reasonable since the two reflections take the triangle from quadrant 3 to quadrant 2 to quadrant 1, and the rotation takes the triangle from quadrant 3 to quadrant 1.

A Checking

4. Go back to $\triangle ABC$ with coordinates $A(-6, -6)$, $B(-6, -4)$, and $C(-2, -6)$. Explain how you know that reflecting $\triangle ABC$ in the y-axis and then in the x-axis has the same effect as rotating $\triangle ABC$ 180° about the origin.

B Practising

5. The following pinwheel design was made using four congruent quadrilaterals.

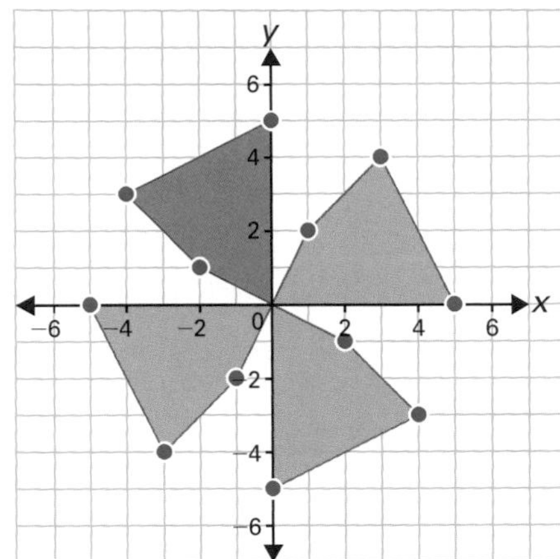

a) Describe how you could start with the red quadrilateral and use only rotations about the origin to make the pinwheel design.

b) Describe how you could start with the red quadrilateral and use a combination of reflections in the x-axis or y-axis and rotations to make the pinwheel design.

6. Taylor says that you can always get from one shape to a congruent shape using three reflections at most. Test Taylor's theory using three examples. Describe your transformations each time.

7. The blue pentomino tile is the starting shape for a tessellation on grid paper. Describe how transformations of the blue tile were used to create the other tiles in the tessellation.

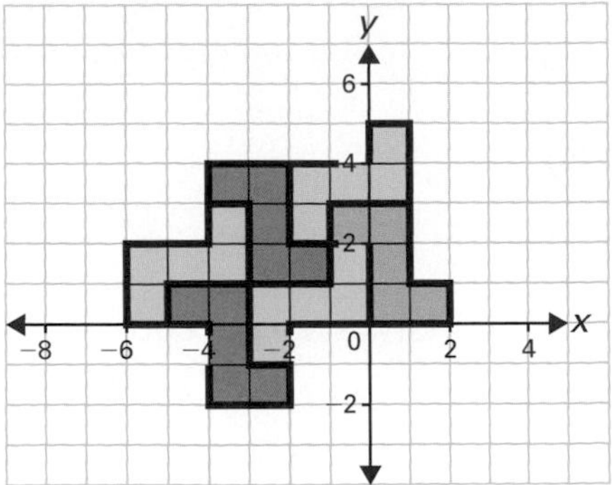

8. Describe the transformations needed to move each pentomino in diagram A to form the square in diagram B.

A.

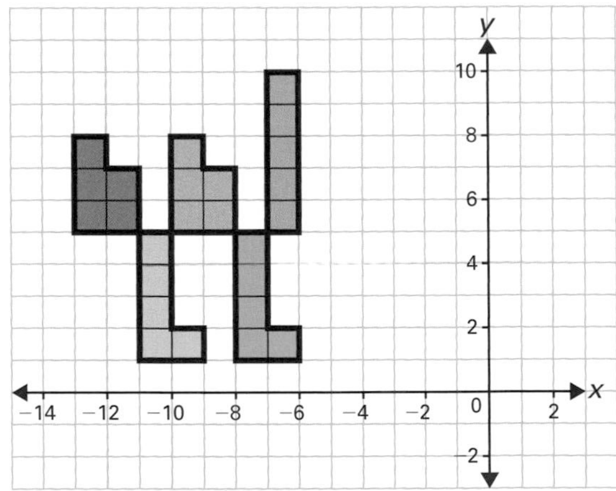

B.

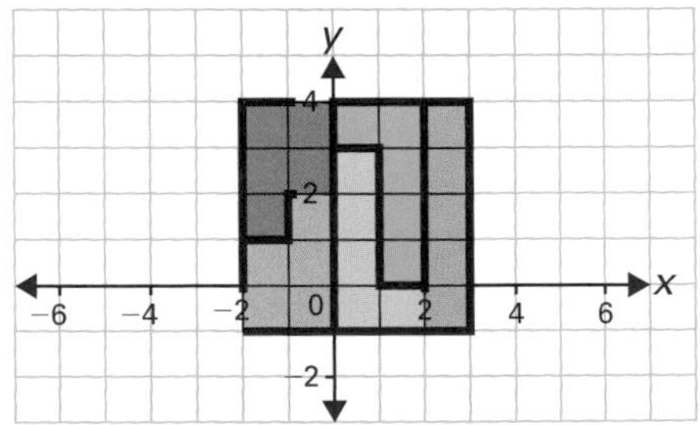

Curious Math

DISTORTION ART

Shapes that have been drawn on a grid using a Cartesian coordinate system can be distorted by distorting the grid. At the right is the letter Z, followed by four distortion images.

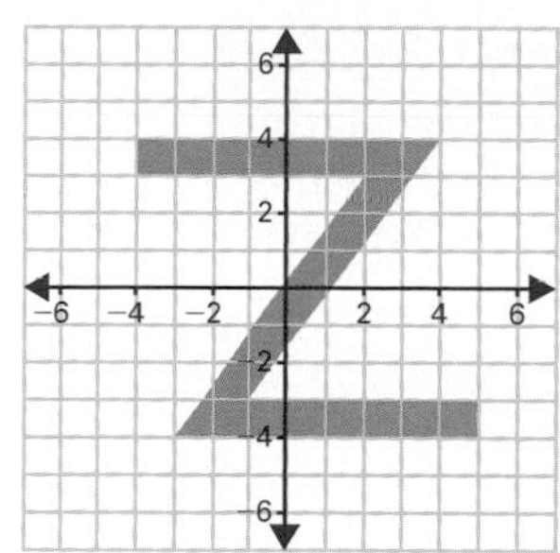

A.

B.

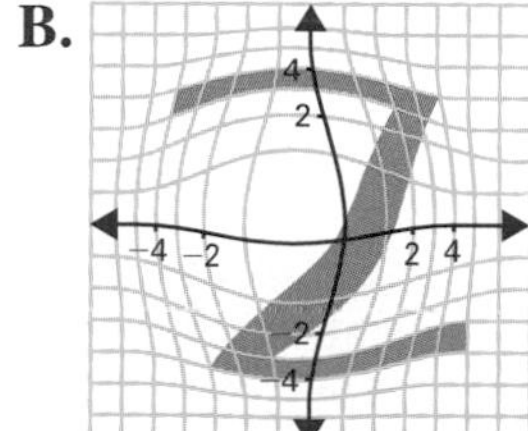

C.

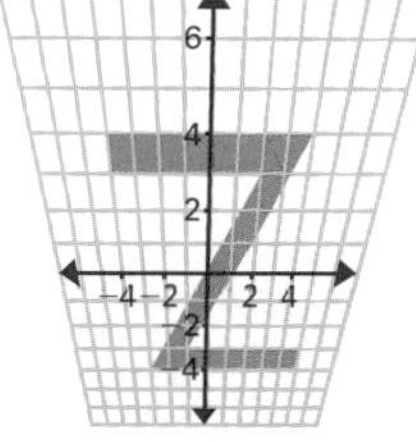

D.

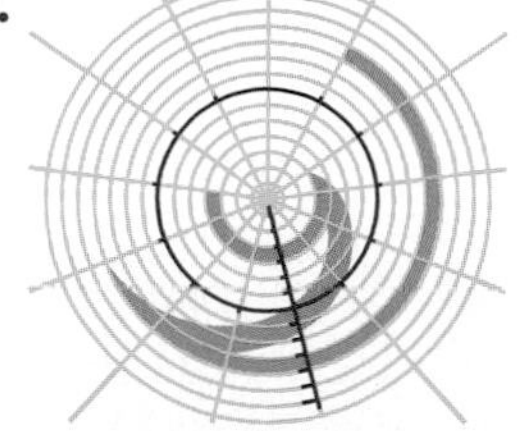

1. Describe how the Z was distorted in diagrams A and B. How does each distortion relate to the way the grid was distorted?

2. Place your eyes close to this page, below diagram C. What does the Z look like now? This type of grid distortion is used to make signs painted on road surfaces easier for drivers to read.

3. Describe the grid in diagram D. Find a cylindrical object about the size of a AA battery, and wrap some aluminum foil tightly around it. Stand the object at the centre of diagram D, and look at the reflection in the foil. Historically, this method was used to disguise pictures and documents.

4. Draw one of your initials on a grid, using a Cartesian coordinate system. Then create a distorted grid and plot your initial on it. You should be able to see some interesting effects.

Math Game COORDINATE RACING

In this game, players race around a racecourse, plotting points using translation vectors.

Number of players: 2 to 4

You will need
- grid paper
- a ruler
- coloured pencils

Rules

1. Create your own racecourse using the guidelines shown at the right.
2. Randomly select the order in which players mark their starting positions on the start/finish line. Use a different colour for each player.
3. All players begin the game with a [0, 0] translation vector. They take turns adding +1, −1, or 0 to the two parts of their previous translation vector. They do not have to add the same number to both parts.
4. Players move to their next position by using their new translation vector.
5. If a player goes off the racecourse, she or he must restart from the previous position, using [0, 0] as the translation vector on the next turn.
6. The game ends at the finish line.

The first three moves for players A and B are shown below.

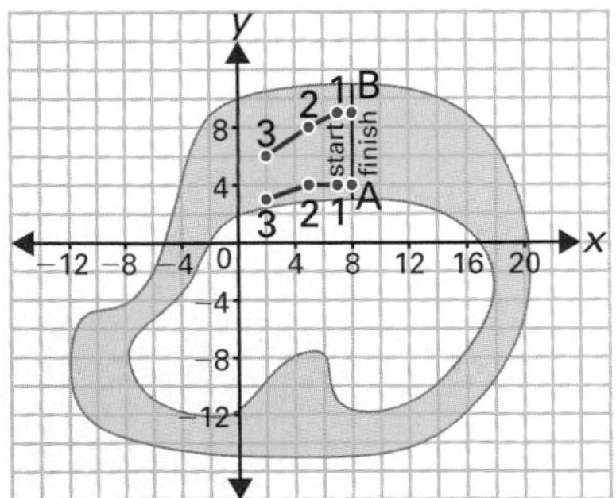

Racecourse

Use a Cartesian coordinate system on a grid. Your racecourse should

- be wide enough to contain at least two points with integer coordinates throughout its length
- vary in width
- include oportunities to turn left and right
- include a start/finish line that passes through several points with integer coordinates and is wide enough to allow each player to have a different starting position

Turn number	Player A	
	Translation vector	New position
start	[0, 0]	(8, 4)
1	[−1, 0]	(7, 4)
2	[−2, 0]	(5, 4)
3	[−3, −1]	(2, 3)

Turn number	Player B	
	Translation vector	New position
start	[0, 0]	(8, 9)
1	[−1, 0]	(7, 9)
2	[−2, −1]	(5, 8)
3	[−3,−2]	(2, 6)

Chapter Self-Test

1. The coordinates of the vertices of a triangle are $A(-2, 3)$, $B(0, 5)$, and $C(2, -7)$.
   a) Which point is the farthest left?
   b) Which point is the farthest up?
   c) Which point is horizontally between the other two points?
   d) Which point is vertically between the other two points?

2. Plot each point below. Connect the points in order, and connect the last point to the first point. Name the polygon formed.
   $A(-3, 4)$, $B(-3, -4)$, $C(5, 0)$

3. a) Write the vector for the translation that moved $ABCD$ to $A'B'C'D'$.

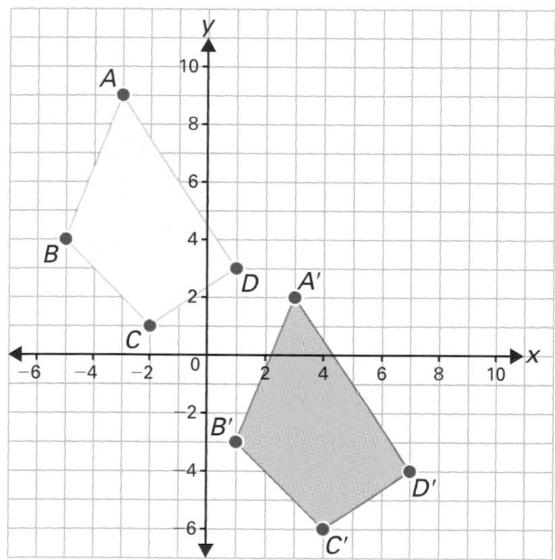

   b) Write the vector for the translation that would move vertex D to vertex A.
   c) Write the coordinates of each image vertex under the translation in part (b).

4. $ABCD$ is a parallelogram in which AB is parallel to CD. The coordinates of three vertices are $A(2, -3)$, $B(7, 0)$, and $C(-1, 6)$.
   a) State the coordinates of vertex D.
   b) Write the translation vector needed to move vertex A to vertex C.
   c) Determine the image coordinates after $ABCD$ is translated using the vector in part (b).

5. Determine the coordinates of the image of $\triangle ABC$ after each transformation.

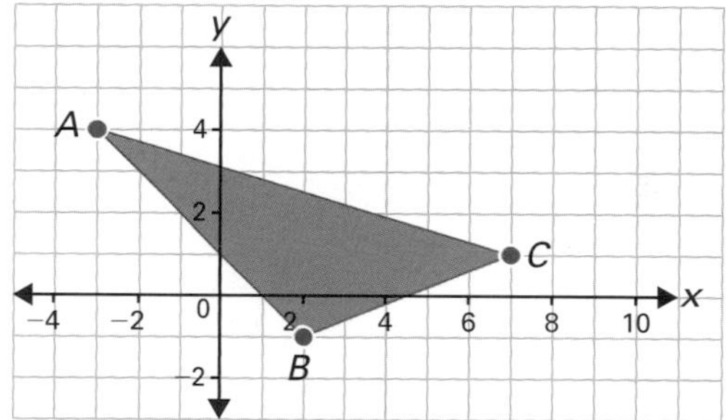

   a) a reflection in the x-axis
   b) a reflection in the y-axis
   c) a rotation of 90° ccw about the origin
   d) a rotation of 180° ccw about the origin

6. The vertices of square $ABCD$ are $A(1, 1)$, $B(2, 1)$, $C(2, 2)$, and $D(1, 2)$.
   a) Draw the square on a grid, using a Cartesian coordinate system. Draw a line segment from the origin through each vertex, and extend each line segment.
   b) Square $A'B'C'D'$ has sides that are twice the length of the sides of square $ABCD$ and a vertex on each extended line segment. What are the coordinates of the vertices of $A'B'C'D'$?

Chapter Review

Frequently Asked Questions

Q: How can you determine whether two polygons are similar?

A: Similar polygons are the same shape but different sizes. The matching angles in the two polygons must be the same size. The lengths of the matching sides must all be in the same ratio.

For example, $A'B'C'D'$ and $ABCD$ are similar because the matching angles are the same size and the lengths of the matching sides are in the ratio 2 : 1.

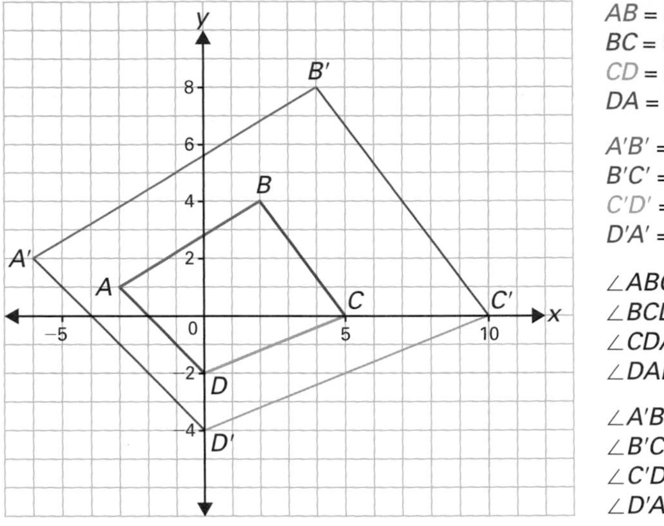

$AB = 5.8$ cm
$BC = 5.0$ cm
$CD = 5.4$ cm
$DA = 4.2$ cm

$A'B' = 11.6$ cm
$B'C' = 10.0$ cm
$C'D' = 10.8$ cm
$D'A' = 8.4$ cm

$\angle ABC = 96°$
$\angle BCD = 75°$
$\angle CDA = 113°$
$\angle DAB = 76°$

$\angle A'B'C' = 96°$
$\angle B'C'D' = 75°$
$\angle C'D'A' = 113°$
$\angle D'A'B' = 76°$

Q: How can you draw a polygon that is similar to another polygon?

A: Use grid paper and a ruler to draw line segments from the origin, (0, 0), through the vertices of the original polygon. Extend or shorten these line segments so that the ratio of each new line segment to the original is the same.

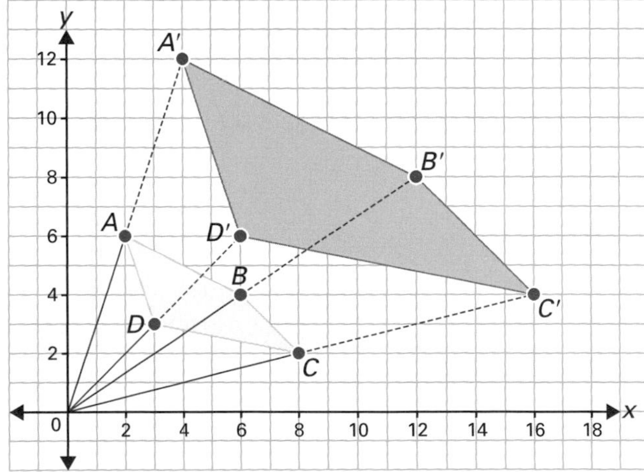

Practice Questions

(7.1) **1. a)** Name the coordinates of each point.

b) State the quadrant that each point is in.

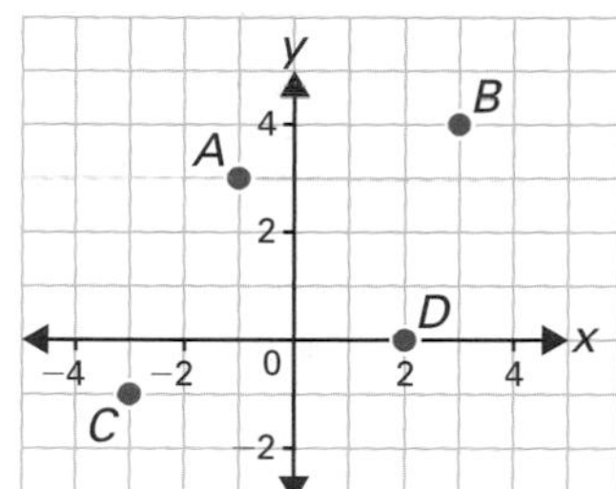

(7.1) **2.** *PQR* is an isosceles triangle. Its base is on the x-axis, and its upper vertex is on the y-axis. Vertex P is located at 5 on the x-axis. State two sets of possible coordinates for all three vertices.

(7.2) **3.** Sketch the image of *ABCD* after each translation, and state the coordinates of the image vertices.

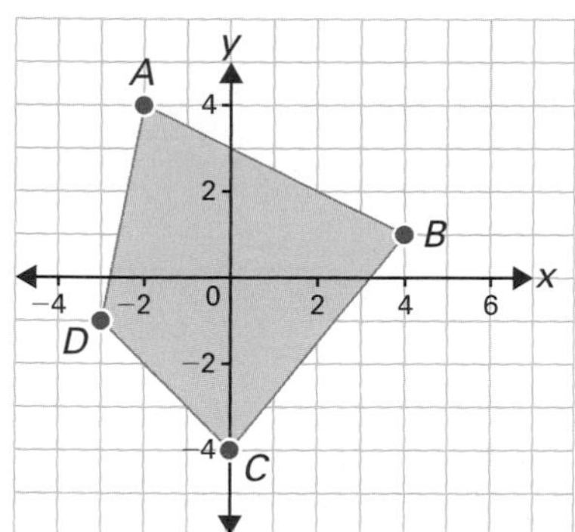

a) $[2, -5]$ **b)** $[-3, 2]$

(7.2) **4.** Go back to quadrilateral *ABCD* in question 3.

a) Determine the translation vector needed to shift vertex D to the origin.

b) Write the coordinates of each image vertex following the translation in part (a).

5. Sketch the image of the shape below after each transformation. State the coordinates of the images of vertices A and F. (7.3)

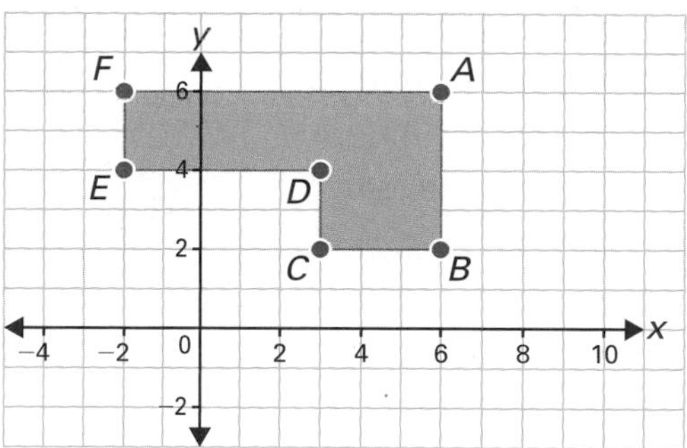

a) a reflection in the x-axis

b) a reflection in the y-axis

c) a rotation of 90° ccw about the origin

d) a rotation of 180° ccw about the origin

e) a rotation of 270° ccw about the origin

6. a) Draw $\triangle ABC$.

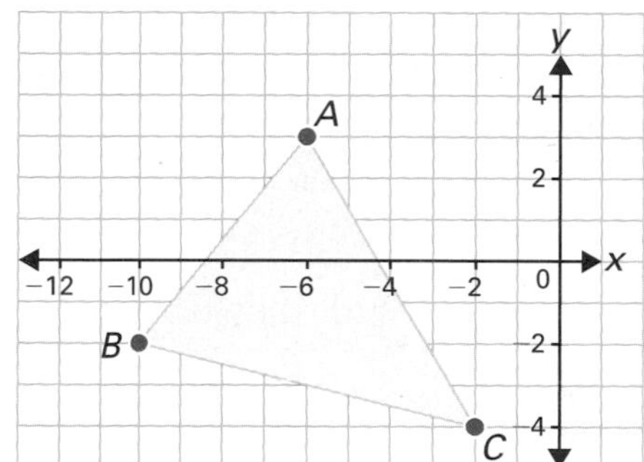

b) Construct $\triangle A'B'C'$ so that it is similar to $\triangle ABC$, with sides that are twice as long.

c) Construct a triangle that is similar to $\triangle ABC$, with sides that are half as long. (7.4)

Chapter Task

Animation

Animation is created by breaking the movement of a figure into a sequence of pictures. Each picture shows a small part of the change from the starting position to the final position.

As you saw in lesson 7.2, a flipbook can be used to create simple animation.

? How can you use transformations to create a flipbook?

A. Draw a figure on a grid, using a Cartesian coordinate system. Label the coordinates of each vertex or key point on your figure. Label at least three points.

B. Plan a sequence of transformations to perform on your figure. You must use
- at least one translation
- at least one reflection in the x-axis or y-axis
- at least one counterclockwise rotation of 90°, 180°, or 270° about the origin

C. Animate the sequence of transformations you planned in step B, using one page for each transformation. Draw each transformation on a grid, using a Cartesian coordinate system.

D. Choose three of the points you labelled in step A. Label the coordinates of the images of these points for each transformation.

E. On the back of each page of your flipbook, write a description of the transformation shown on that page.

Task Checklist

- ☑ Did you include all the required transformations?
- ☑ Did you correctly identify the coordinates of three vertices or key points on your original figure and its image after each transformation?
- ☑ Did you draw all the images correctly?
- ☑ Did you describe each transformation using appropriate math language?

CHAPTER 8

Equations and Relationships

GOALS

You will be able to

- represent relationships with equations
- model equations
- solve equations and verify the solutions
- use algebra and graphs to represent situations and solve problems

HARDCOVERS
$1.50 each

PAPERBACKS
$0.85 each

Getting Started

You will need
- coloured counter
- linking cubes
- grid paper
- a ruler

Understanding Number Tricks

Stefan created this number trick:

- Choose a number, any number.
- Add 4.
- Multiply by 2.
- Subtract your original number.
- Subtract 5.
- Subtract your original number again.

? How can you create your own number trick?

A. Kayley chose 3. Her results are shown in the chart below. Copy and continue the chart, for four different starting numbers. What do you notice about your final results?

Choose a number.	Add 4.	Multiply by 2.	Subtract the original number.	Subtract 5.	Subtract the original number to get the final result.
3	7	14	11	6	3

B. Kayley used cubes and counters to model the steps in Stefan's number trick. Copy and complete the chart by drawing cubes and counters.

Choose a number.	Add 4.	Multiply by 2.	Subtract the original number.	Subtract 5.	Subtract the original number to get the final result.
		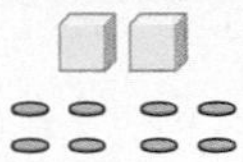			

C. How does the model in step B help you understand the number trick?

D. Add another row to your chart in step B. In this row, use the **variable** n to represent the starting number. Complete this row by writing an **algebraic expression** for each step in the number trick.

E. How do your algebraic expressions in step D help you to understand the number trick?

F. Make up your own number trick. Use models or algebraic expressions to show how it works.

NEL

Do You Remember?

1. Determine the value of each algebraic expression by substituting $n = 6$.

a) $3n + 5$ **c)** $6n - 2n + 8$

b) $2n + 4n - 6$ **d)** $0.5n + 1.5n$

2. Determine the value of each algebraic expression by substituting $a = 2.5$.

a) $4a + 2$ **c)** $2 \times 10a$

b) $3a - 0.5$ **d)** $4a \div 5$

3. Create an algebraic expression for each pattern rule.

a)

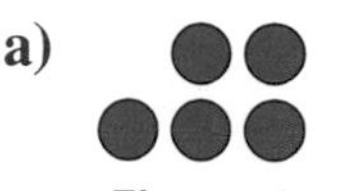
Figure 1

Figure 2

Figure 3

b)

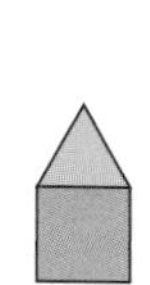
Figure 1

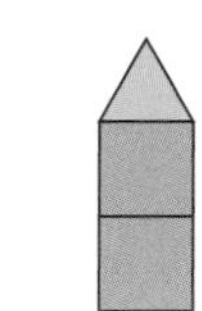
Figure 2

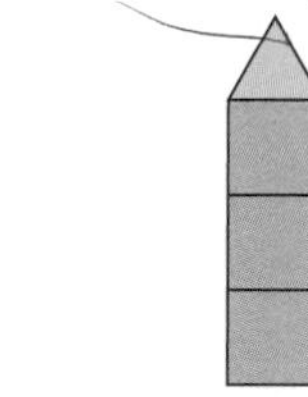
Figure 3

4. a) Copy and complete the table of values to show the number of counters needed for each figure in this pattern:

Figure number	Number of counters
1	3
2	7
3	11
4	
5	
6	

b) Draw a scatter plot using your table of values.

c) Use your scatter plot to determine the number of counters in the 10th figure.

5. a) Use the graph to determine the cost of 1.6 kg of nails.

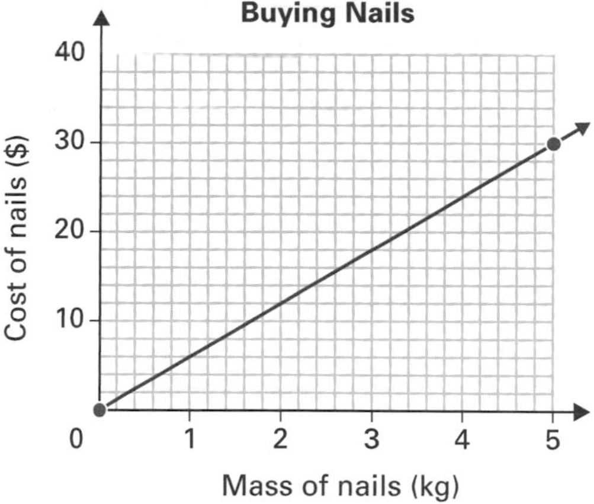

b) Use the graph to determine how many kilograms of nails you could buy for $24.

6. The pattern rule $3n + 5$ describes the number of counters needed to make figure n in this pattern. If a figure contains 41 counters, what figure number is it?

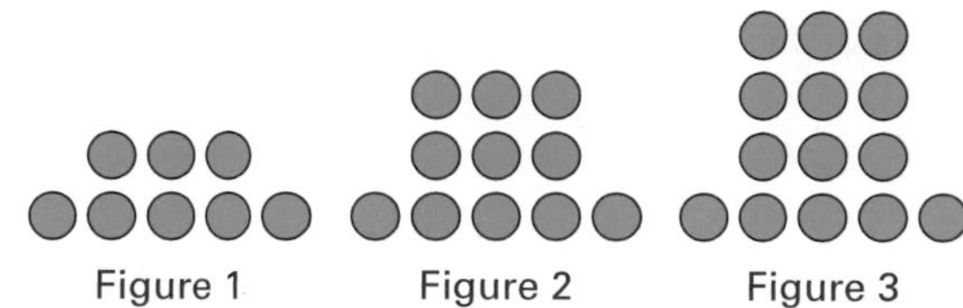

7. Determine which solution is correct.

a) $7t = 56$ $t = 49$ or $t = 8$

b) $3w + 3 = 39$ $w = 12$ or $w = 13$

c) $5a - 5 = 35$ $a = 7$ or $a = 8$

d) $11 = 2y - 7$ $y = 9$ or $y = 2$

8. Solve each equation.

a) $m + 2 = 21$ **c)** $4w + 2 = 18$

b) $5s = 10$ **d)** $4y - 2 = 18$

9. Solve each equation.

a) $3n - 2 = 13$ **c)** $2n - 3 = 31$

b) $3n - 2 = 67$ **d)** $8n - 7 = 9$

8.1 Solving Equations by Graphing

You will need
- grid paper
- a ruler
- coloured pencils

▶ **GOAL**

Use tables and graphs to solve equations.

Learn about the Math

Carina wants to determine the area of a garden. The garden is enclosed by 32 border tiles. The garden and border tiles are part of this pattern of squares.

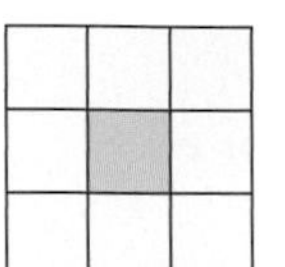
Figure 1

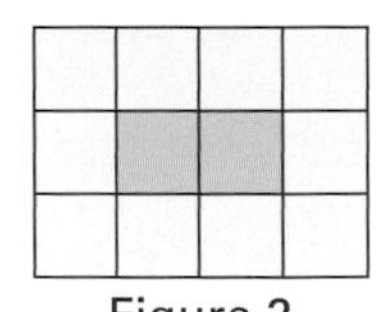
Figure 2

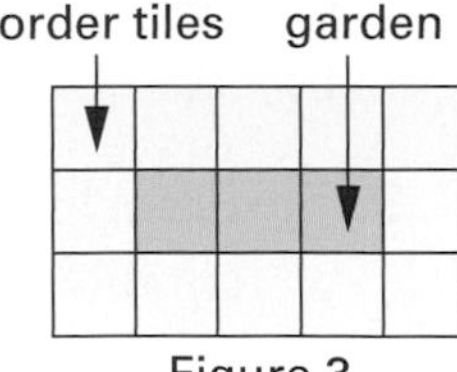

Figure 3

Carina used the variable n to represent the area of the garden. Since there are always six tiles on the left and right sides of the garden and $2n$ tiles directly above and below the garden, the number of border tiles is $2n + 6$.

Carina realized that $2n + 6$ and 32 both describe the number of border tiles. So, she wrote the **equation** $2n + 6 = 32$. The **solution to the equation** will tell her the area of the garden.

equation
a mathematical statement in which the value on the left side of the equal sign is the same as the value on the right side of the equal sign; for example, the equation $5n + 4 = 39$ means that 4 more than the product of 5 and a number equals 39

solution to an equation
the value of a variable that makes the equation true; for example, in the equation $5n + 4 = 39$, the value of n is 7 because $5(7) + 4 = 39$

? How can you determine the area of a garden surrounded by 32 border tiles?

A. Copy and complete the table of values using Carina's pattern rule.

B. Use the data in step A to draw a scatter plot. Put the area of the garden on the horizontal axis and the number of border tiles on the vertical axis. Connect the points to form a line, and extend it.

C. Use your graph to determine the area of the garden enclosed by 32 border tiles.

Area of garden (term number)	Number of border tiles (term value)
1	8
2	10
3	12
4	
5	
n	

Reflecting

1. Explain why it was reasonable to extend your graphed line in step B.

2. a) How did you use a graph to solve the equation $2n + 6 = 32$?
   b) How can you check your solution to make sure that it solves Carina's problem?

NEL

Work with the Math

Example: Using a graph to solve an equation

a) Determine an algebraic expression for this pattern:

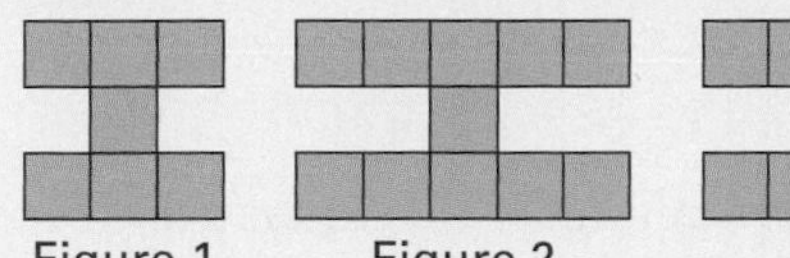

b) Create and solve an equation to determine the number of the figure with 39 tiles.

Rishi's Solution

a) Let n represent the figure number.

Figure number (term number)	Number of tiles (term value)
1	7
2	11
3	15
4	19
n	$4n + 3$

+4
+4
+4

I made a table of values to organize the data. I noticed that each figure has four more tiles than the previous figure. Since repeated addition is like multiplication, I know that the pattern rule includes $4n$.

I substituted the first few term numbers into the expression $4n$. The pattern rule must be $4n + 3$.

b) $4n + 3 = 39$

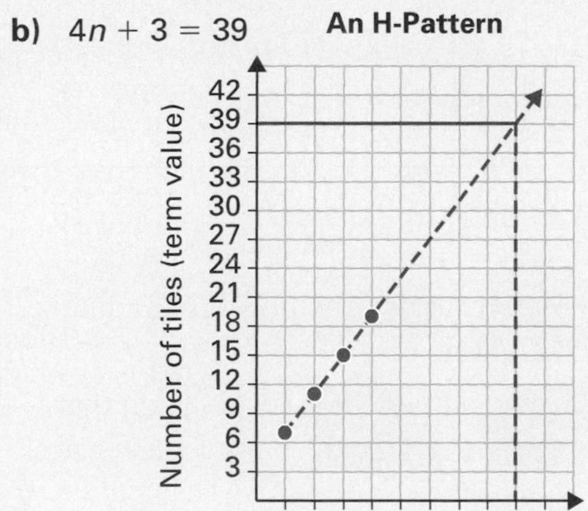

I needed to know the term number for a term value of 39. So, I had to solve the equation $4n + 3 = 39$.

I drew a graph using the data in the table. The plotted points formed a straight line, which I extended to show that the pattern continues.

I found 39 on the vertical axis. I drew a horizontal line until it touched my graphed line. Then I drew a vertical line from the intersection point to the horizontal axis. This meant that the solution to the equation is $n = 9$.

Figure 9 has 39 tiles.

Check: Left side | Right side

$4n + 3$ | 39

$= 4(9) + 3$

$= 36 + 3$

$= 39$ ✓

I checked my solution by substituting 9 for the variable n. The expressions on both sides of the equation were equal, so I knew that my solution was correct.

A Checking

3. Use the graph to determine the solution to the equation $2n + 3 = 17$.

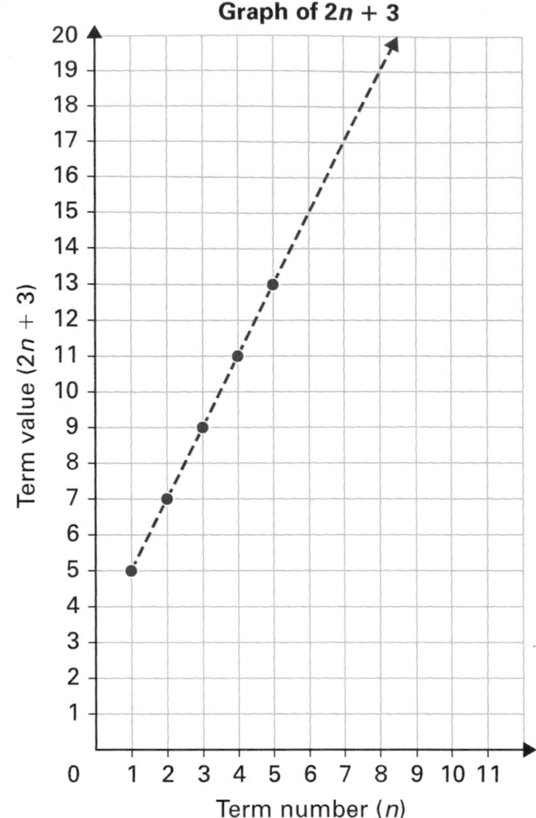

4. a) Make a table of values to represent this pattern of tiles.

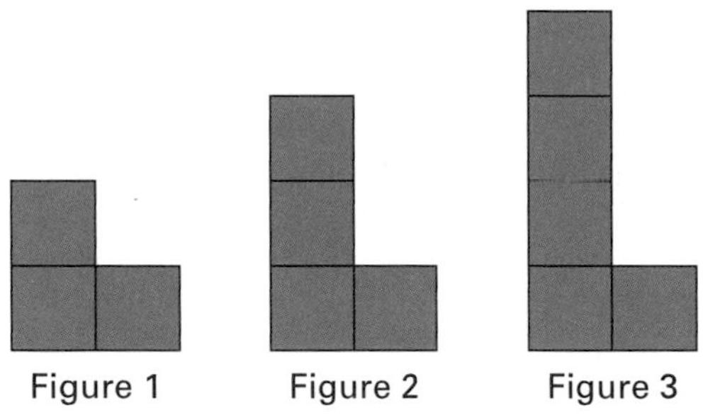

b) Write an algebraic expression for the pattern rule.

c) Create an equation to determine the number of the figure with 22 tiles.

d) Draw a graph to solve your equation in part (c).

B Practising

5. a) Make a table of values for this pattern.

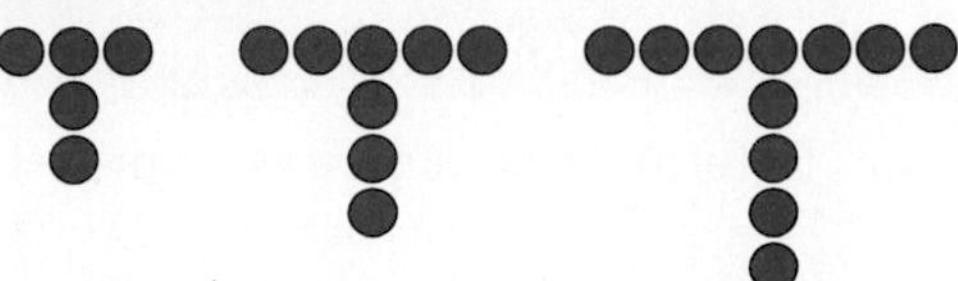

b) Write an algebraic expression for the pattern rule.

c) Create an equation to determine the number of the figure with 23 counters.

d) Draw a graph to solve your equation.

6. The graph shows the weekly balance in David's bank account, rounded to the nearest \$5.

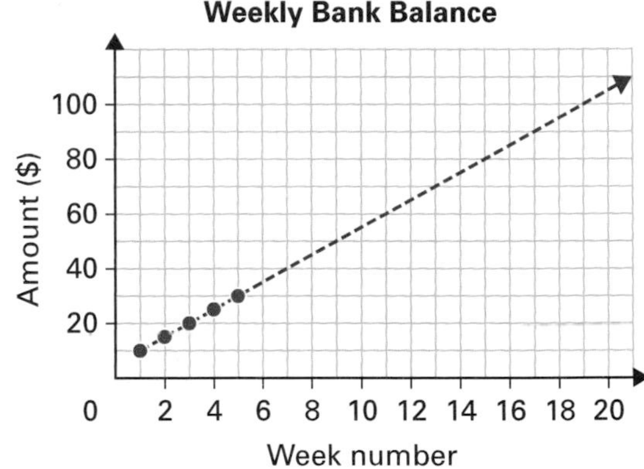

a) Make a table of values for the data in the graph.

b) Create an algebraic expression that represents David's bank balance after w weeks.

c) Write an equation to determine when his bank balance was \$60.

d) Use the graph to solve your equation in part (c). After how many weeks was David's bank balance \$60?

e) If the pattern continues, when will David's bank balance reach \$100?

f) If the pattern continues, what will his bank balance be at the end of 20 weeks?

7. a) Examine the following pattern. What is the number of the figure that you could make using 97 toothpicks?

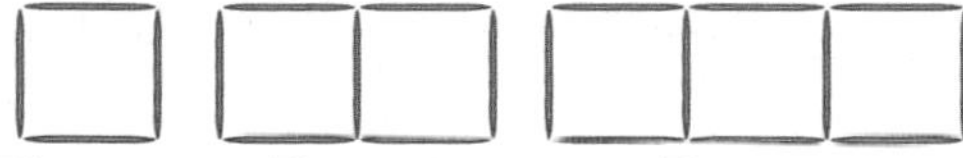

Figure 1 Figure 2 Figure 3

b) Examine the following pattern. What is the number of the figure that you could make using 97 toothpicks?

Figure 1

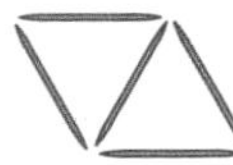

Figure 2

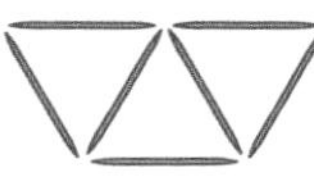

Figure 3

8. On the same set of axes, use three different colours to draw a graph for the three pattern rules below. Then use your graph to determine the solutions when the term value is 19. How do the equations and solutions compare?

a) $2n + 5$ **b)** $2n + 7$ **c)** $2n + 9$

9. On the same set of axes, use three different colours to draw a graph for the three pattern rules below. Then use your graph to determine the solutions when the term value is 15. How do the equations and solutions compare?

a) $2n + 3$ **b)** $3n + 3$ **c)** $4n + 3$

C Extending

10. Brooke used blue and yellow squares to represent a series of square ponds with border tiles.

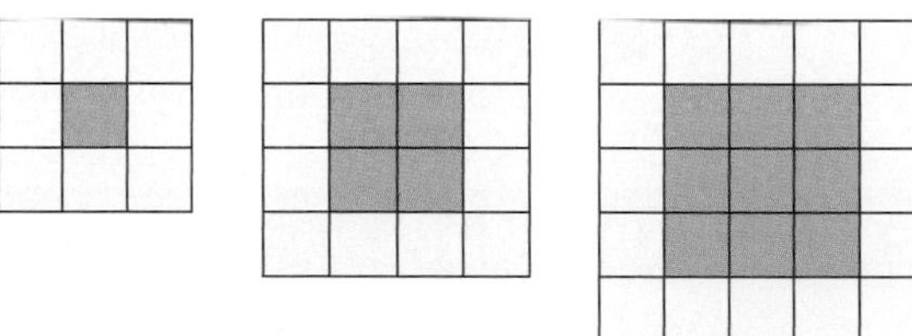

Figure 1 Figure 2 Figure 3

a) Copy and complete the table of values for the pond pattern.

Figure number	Area of pond	Number of border tiles
1	1	8
2		
3		
4		

b) Use the table of values to determine two algebraic pattern rules: one for the area of the pond and one for the number of border tiles.

c) On the same set of axes, use two different colours to create a graph from the table of values.

d) What are some differences between the pattern rules? What are some differences between the two lines on the graph?

e) Create and solve an equation to determine the number of the figure with 56 border tiles.

f) Create and solve an equation to determine the figure number for a pond area of 121.

8.2 Representing Pattern Relationships

You will need
- grid paper
- a ruler
- a calculator

▶ **GOAL**

Represent a pattern relationship using a chart, an equation, and a graph.

Explore the Math

Suppose that you have some $2 coins and $5 bills. The total value of the coins and bills is $100.

? Which combinations of $2 coins and $5 bills have a total value of $100?

A. Use a chart like the one above to list three combinations of $2 coins and $5 bills with a total value of $100.

B. Use your combinations in step A to make a graph.

C. Explain why there is no combination with exactly five $5 bills.

D. Explain why there is no combination with exactly four $2 coins.

E. Which other numbers of $5 bills and $2 coins are not possible? Why?

F. One combination has two more $5 bills than another combination. Compare the numbers of $2 coins in these combinations.

G. **a)** Write an algebraic expression that represents the value of the $2 coins. Use t to represent the number of $2 coins.

b) Write an algebraic expression that represents the value of the $5 bills. Use f to represent the number of $5 bills.

H. Write an equation that represents the combinations of $2 coins and $5 bills with a total value of $100.

I. Solve your equation for $t = 15$. Where is this solution located in your chart? Where is this solution located in your graph?

J. Use your chart, graph, or equation to determine all of the combinations of $2 coins and $5 bills that have a total value of $100.

Reflecting

1. How can a chart help you solve this problem?
2. How can a graph help you solve this problem?
3. How can an equation help you solve this problem?

Curious Math

A WINNING FORMULA FOR BILLIARDS

How many rebounds will a billiard ball make before it reaches a corner pocket?

For certain types of billiard shots, you can use the following formula to predict the number of rebounds:

Number of rebounds = length + width − 2

This winning formula only works if the following conditions are met:

- The billiard table must have no side pockets.
- The length and width of the table must be measured in whole numbers.
- The ball has to be hit from a corner at a 45° angle.
- Neither the original hit nor the sinking of the ball in the corner pocket is included when counting rebounds.

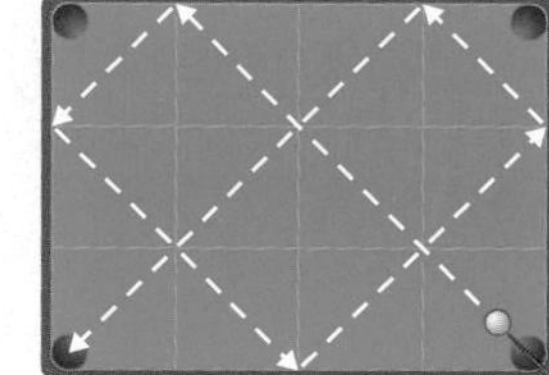

$$\begin{aligned}\text{Number of rebounds} &= l + w - 2\\ &= 4 + 3 - 2\\ &= 7 - 2\\ &= 5\end{aligned}$$

A. Draw models of the following four billiard tables on grid paper: 5 by 3, 6 by 4, 6 by 5, and 12 by 8.

B. For each billiard table in step A, use the formula to predict the number of rebounds a ball will make before it reaches a corner pocket. If the length and width have a ratio that is not in lowest terms, simplify it. (For example, simplify 6 : 4 to 3 : 2.)

Size of table	5 by 3	6 by 4	6 by 5	12 by 8
Number of rebounds				

C. Use a ruler to draw the path of the ball on each table.

D. Check your predictions by counting the number of rebounds before the ball reaches a corner pocket.

You will need
- a calculator

8.3 Creating and Evaluating Algebraic Expressions

▶ **GOAL**

Use algebraic expressions to represent calculations.

Learn about the Math

Maxine works at a swimming-pool store. She keeps a record of the amount of pH Plus powder that is sold. The powder comes in two sizes of containers: large (1.25 kg) and small (0.75 kg). The following table shows the number of containers sold on three days.

pH Plus Powder Sales

Day	Number of small (0.75 kg) containers	Number of large (1.25 kg) containers	Total mass
1	14	31	49.25 kg
2	19	42	
3	24	28	

? What algebraic expression can Maxine use to calculate the total mass of pH Plus powder that was sold?

A. Explain how Maxine calculated the total mass (in kilograms) of powder that was sold on day 1.

B. If the variable s represents the number of small containers sold, describe what value the algebraic expression $0.75s$ represents.

C. Write an algebraic expression that represents the mass (in kilograms) of powder sold in large containers daily. Use the variable l.

D. Use your results in steps B and C to write an algebraic expression for the total mass of powder sold on day 1 in both sizes of containers. Evaluate your expression using the values for day 1 in the table.

E. Use your algebraic expression to calculate the total mass of powder sold on day 2 and day 3.

Reflecting

1. Why did you need to use two variables to write an algebraic expression for the total mass of powder sold on each day?
2. How did you use the variables to create your algebraic expression?
3. How was using an algebraic expression helpful for calculating the total mass of powder sold on each day?

Work with the Math

Example: Creating and evaluating an algebraic expression

During a garage sale, hardcover books sold for $1.50 and paperback books sold for $0.85.

a) Write an algebraic expression that represents the total income from all the used books that were sold during the sale.

b) Evaluate your expression if 8 hardcover books and 15 paperback books were sold.

Carina's Solution

a) The variable *h* tells how many hardcover books were sold. The variable *p* tells how many paperback books were sold.

I decided which letters to use for the variables.

My expression for the total income is $1.50h + 0.85p$.

I wrote an expression to represent the total value of the books sold. I multiplied each variable by the price of this type of book.

b) The total income for books was

$1.50(8) + 0.85(15)$
$= 12.00 + 12.75$
$= 24.75$

The total income for books was $24.75.

I used brackets to show when I substituted a number for a variable. I substituted 8 for *h* and 15 for *p* because these were the numbers of books sold. Then I evaluated the expression.

A Checking

4. Luca sells muffins and juice boxes at the school snack bar. Muffins are $1.50 each and juice boxes are $1.25 each.
   a) Write an algebraic expression for the total income Luca received from the sale of muffins and juice boxes.
   b) One day, Luca sold 30 muffins and 40 juice boxes. Use your expression to calculate his total income that day.

5. Calculate the value of each expression.
   a) $7c - 4$, when $c = 5$
   b) $(h + 2) \times 2.5$, when $h = 5$
   c) $2r + 3s$, when $r = 1.2$ and $s = 2.3$
   d) $a + 5b - 2$, when $a = -5$ and $b = 7$
   e) $(5m - n) \div p$, when $m = 5$, $n = 9$, and $p = 4$

B Practising

6. Calculate the value of each expression.
   a) $8b + 6$, when $b = 5$
   b) $p + 1.5 \times 3$, when $p = 2.5$
   c) $10n - m$, when $n = 3.5$ and $m = 3.4$
   d) $5x - 6y + 8$, when $x = -1$ and $y = -2$
   e) $3p + 4q - 8$, when $p = -3$ and $q = 2$

7. a) Write an algebraic expression that represents the total value of any combination of dimes, nickels, and quarters.
   b) Evaluate the expression if there are 21 dimes, 23 nickels, and 25 quarters.

8. Two hoses are being used to fill a swimming pool. Water is pumped through the first hose at a rate of 22 L/min and through the second hose at a rate of 18 L/min. Write an algebraic expression for each situation.
   a) the amount of water pumped through the first hose after t minutes
   b) the amount of water pumped through the second hose after t minutes
   c) the total amount of water pumped into the pool from both hoses after t minutes
   d) How much water has been pumped into the pool after 2.5 h?

9. A school long-jump team is competing at the Aberfoyle international track meet. Kurt jumps an average of 4.6 m, and Jared jumps an average of 4.4 m. Each boy's score is the sum of the lengths of his jumps. The team score is the sum of the scores of both boys.

   a) Write an algebraic expression that represents Kurt's score if he jumps k times.
   b) Write an algebraic expression that represents Jared's score if he jumps j times.
   c) Use your results in parts (a) and (b) to write an algebraic expression for the team score.
   d) Evaluate your expression in part (c) to determine the team score if Kurt jumps 5 times and Jared jumps 4 times.

10. A geography test has 6 questions worth 3 marks each and 16 questions worth 2 marks each. Write an algebraic expression for each situation.
    a) the number of marks that Amy earns from 3-mark questions if she gets t correct
    b) the number of marks that Amy earns from 2-mark questions if she gets w correct
    c) the total number of marks that Amy earns on the test
    d) Determine Amy's mark on the test if she answers 5 three-mark questions and 13 two-mark questions correctly.

11. A box of apples has a mass of 17.5 kg. A box of pears has a mass of 15.5 kg.

a) Write an algebraic expression for the total mass of a boxes of apples and p boxes of pears.

b) Use your expression to determine the total mass of a shipment of 32 boxes of apples and 41 boxes of pears.

12. a) Write an algebraic expression for the perimeter of the rectangle.

b) Write an algebraic expression for the area of the rectangle.

c) Evaluate your expressions in parts (a) and (b) if $l = 11.2$ m and $w = 8.4$ m.

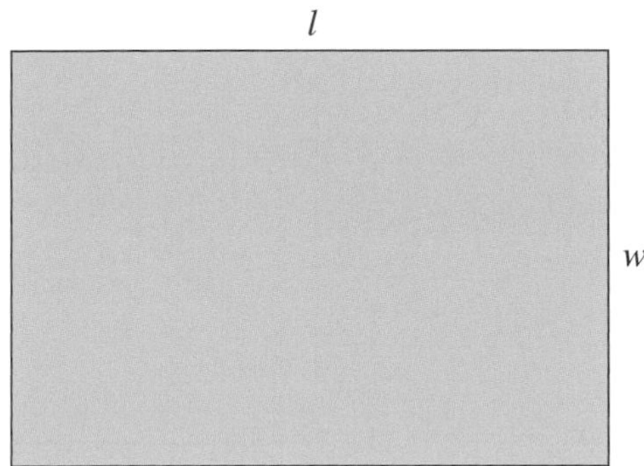

13. Nick works on a tree farm, bundling seedlings. His workweek is 40 h, and he can complete three bundles per hour. He needs to choose one of the following rates of pay:

i) \$8.75 per hour

ii) \$4.75 per hour plus \$1.35 per bundle

iii) \$2.75 per bundle

a) Write an algebraic expression that shows Nick's weekly earnings at each rate of pay.

b) Which rate of pay should Nick choose? Use your algebraic expressions to support your answer.

C Extending

14. Shannon works at a shoe store. She earns a commission of \$2.45 for each pair of shoes and \$2.85 for each pair of boots that she sells.

a) Create an algebraic expression for Shannon's total commission.

b) One day, Shannon sold eight pairs of shoes and seven pairs of boots. Calculate her commission on that day.

15. One square has a side length of s. Another square has a side length of t.

a) Write an algebraic expression that describes the sum of the areas of the two squares.

b) Evaluate your expression for various whole number values of s and t.

c) Does the resulting sum ever represent the area of a single square with a whole-number side length? Explain.

16. The length of a rectangle is 2 cm more than its width. Write an algebraic expression that describes each situation.

a) its width in terms of its length

b) its area in terms of its length

c) its area in terms of its width

d) Use your expressions in parts (b) and (c) to determine the area of the rectangle if its length is 10 cm.

17. To raise money, a school is selling containers of frozen cookie dough for \$4.25 each. The school pays \$2.50 for each container.

a) Write two different algebraic expressions that represent the profit from the sale of any number of containers of cookie dough.

b) Evaluate each expression for total sales of 174 containers.

Mid-Chapter Review

Frequently Asked Questions

Q: How can you use a graph to solve an equation such as $2x + 3 = 25$?

A: First, you create a table of values. In the left-hand column, record values of the variable x. In the right-hand column, record the value of the algebraic expression for each value of x.

Then plot your data from the table of values as a scatter plot.

To solve the equation, find the number on the vertical axis that is equal to the algebraic expression. Draw a horizontal line from this number all the way across. Where the horizontal line intersects your graphed line, draw a vertical line to determine the value of the variable x that solves the equation. For the equation $2x + 3 = 25$, the value of x is 11.

To solve $2x + 3 = 25$, create a table of values.

x	$2x + 3$
1	5
4	11
7	17

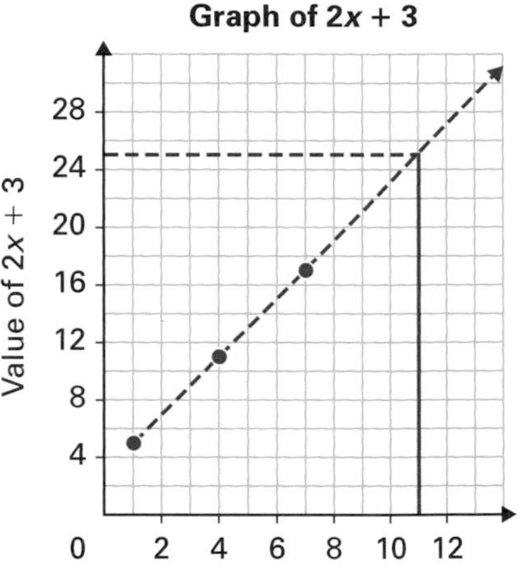

Q: How do you create an equation to solve a pattern problem?

A: First, you determine what quantity in the situation changes. Choose a letter, called a variable, to represent this quantity. One side of the equation you write will show the pattern rule using the variable. The other side will show the value of the expression.

For example, suppose that you have four equal bags of marbles and six extra marbles, for a total of 46 marbles. The variable m represents the number of marbles in each bag. So, an equation that represents this situation is $4m + 6 = 46$.

Q: How do you evaluate an algebraic expression?

A: First you substitute numbers for the variables. Then you use the rules for order of operations to calculate the result.

For example, you would evaluate the expression $5d - 3f$, when $d = 3.75$ and $f = 4.50$, as follows:

$$\begin{aligned} & 5d - 3f \\ &= 5(3.75) - 3(4.50) \\ &= 5.25 \end{aligned}$$

NEL

Practice Questions

(8.1) **1.** A factory produced the same number of golf carts each day for 15 days.

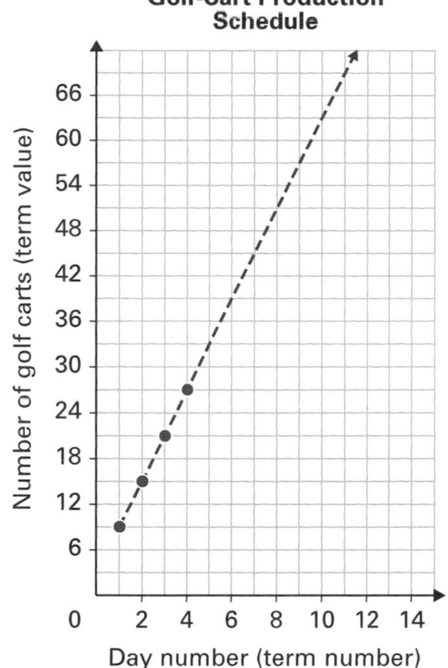

a) Create a table of values to record the data displayed in the graph.

b) Create an algebraic expression that represents the number of golf carts produced after n days.

c) Write an equation to determine when 51 golf carts were produced. Use the graph to solve your equation.

(8.1) **2. a)** Create a table of values to represent the pattern.

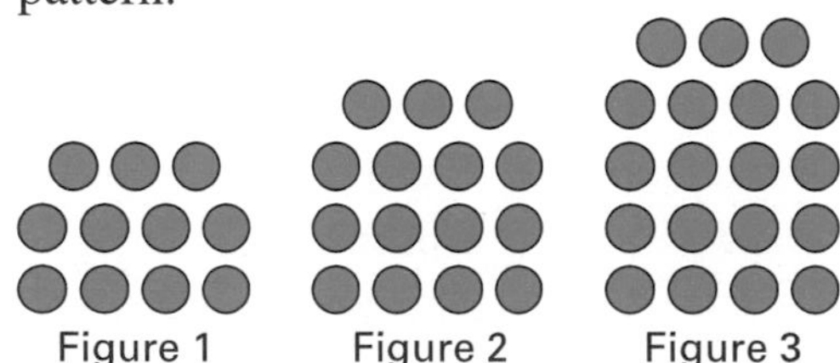

b) Use your table of values to write an algebraic expression for the pattern rule.

c) Create an equation to determine the number of the figure that has 63 counters.

d) Draw a graph to solve your equation.

3. Use the graph to solve each equation. (8.1)

a) $4n - 7 = 41$

b) $4n - 7 = 49$

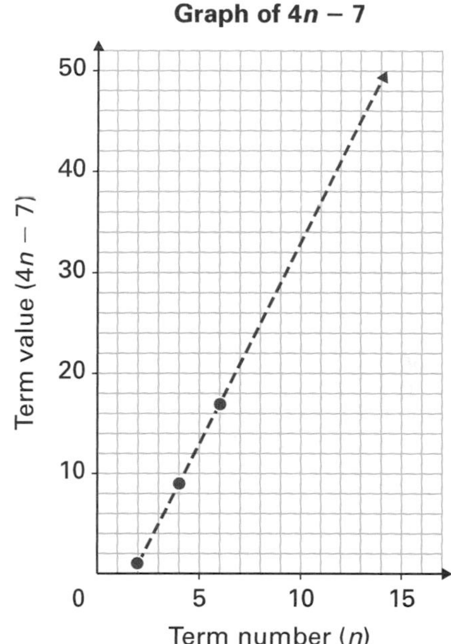

4. Calculate the value of each expression. (8.3)

a) $3m + 4$, when $m = 1.2$

b) $8n - 6$, when $n = -2$

c) $5m + 2n$, when $m = 1.2$, $n = 1.4$

d) $9n + 5 - 6m$, when $m = -3$, $n = -2$

5. Erin has a balance of \$182.73 in her savings account. She makes a deposit of \$12.50 in her account each week. (8.3)

a) Write an algebraic expression that represents the amount of money in Erin's savings account after n weeks.

b) Calculate how much money Erin will have in her account after eight weeks.

8.4 Solving Equations I

You will need
- a calculator
- grid paper
- a ruler

▶ **GOAL**
Solve equations using inspection, systematic trial, and graphing.

Learn about the Math

Rowyn is planning to mow lawns as a summer job. She wants to earn almost \$910 to buy a new guitar and amplifier. She needs to earn \$230 to pay for the lawn mower and about \$100 to pay for gasoline. She plans to charge \$15 per lawn.

? How many lawns does Rowyn need to mow to reach her goal?

Example 1: Solving an equation by inspection and systematic trial

Determine the number of lawns that Rowyn must mow to reach her goal.

Rowyn's Solution: Using inspection to estimate a solution

I'll use n to represent the number of lawns I need to mow.

$15n = 910 + 230 + 100$
$15n = 1240$
$n = 1240 \div 15$
$n \doteq 82.7$

I need to earn just over \$1200—about \$900 for the guitar and amp, and about \$300 for the lawn mower and gas. I can use the equation $15n = 1200$ to estimate.

$n = 1200 \div 15$, or about 80 lawns

I need to mow 83 lawns to reach my goal.
Check: $83 \times \$15 = \$1245$
This is more than enough.

Since 83 is close to my estimate of 80, my answer seems reasonable. I'll substitute to check.

Kito's Solution: Using systematic trial

n tells the number of lawns to be mowed.

Predict n.	Evaluate $15n$.
80	$15(80) = 1200$ (too low)
85	$15(85) = 1275$ (too high)
83	$15(83) = 1245$
82	$15(82) = 1230$

I used guess and test to determine the value of n.
I used a table to organize my guesses.
I started with 80, Rowyn's estimate.
I used a calculator to multiply.
$n = 83$ looked like it was the solution, but I had to check $n = 82$ to make sure.

Rowyn needs to mow 83 lawns.

Reflecting

1. How did Rowyn use the estimate in her solution?
2. How did Kito use the estimate in his solution?
3. How would Kito's solution have changed if he had started with 100 instead of 80?

Work with the Math

Example 2: Solving a problem by solving an equation

Gero opened a bank account. He deposited the same amount of money each week for two weeks. Then he used his bank card to buy a gift for $14. His new bank balance was $107. How much did Gero deposit each week?

Solution A: Using inspection

Use d to represent each deposit. The amount of money deposited after two weeks is $2d$. Once the withdrawal of $14 is made, the balance is $107. The equation for the problem is $2d - 14 = 107$.

$$2d - 14 = 107$$
$$2d = 121$$
$$d = 60.5$$

Gero deposited $60.50 each week.

Solution B: Using systematic trial

Guess and test to determine the value of d that makes $2d - 14$ equal to 107.

Estimate a value to start with.
$2d - 14 = 107$ is close to $2d = 110$.
So, d is about 55.

Predict d.	Evaluate $2d - 14$.	Is the answer 107?
55	$2(55) - 14 = 96$	No, it's too low.
60	$2(60) - 14 = 106$	It's still too low.
61	$2(61) - 14 = 108$	Now it's too high, but it's very close.
60.5	$2(60.5) - 14 = 107$	It's correct.

Gero deposited $60.50 each week.

Solution C: Using a graph

Create a table of values for the expression $2d - 14$. Use your table to draw a graph. Put the values of d on the horizontal axis and the values of $2d - 14$ on the vertical axis. Draw a horizontal line from 107 on the vertical axis to the graphed line. Draw a line down to the horizontal axis from this point. That's the solution.

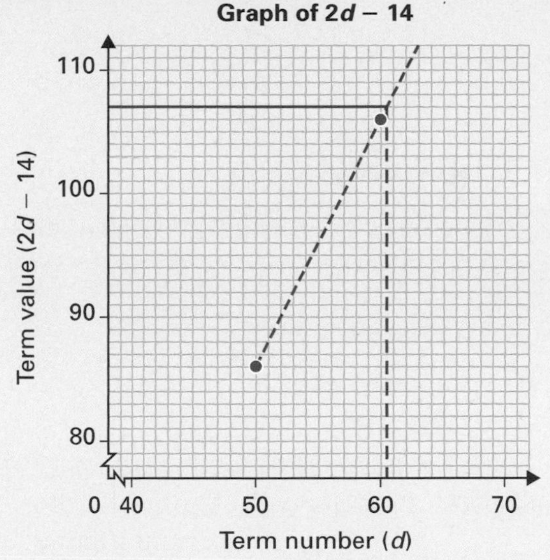

Gero deposited $60.50 a week.

A Checking

4. Rowyn can buy a used guitar and amplifier for \$425, instead of buying new ones. She can borrow a lawn mower, but she still needs about \$100 for gas. She charges \$15 per lawn.

   a) Draw a graph to show this situation. Put the number of lawns Rowyn might mow on the horizontal axis and the amount she will earn on the vertical axis.

   b) Write an equation that relates Rowyn's earnings to the number of lawns she mows.

   c) Solve your equation to determine how many lawns Rowyn needs to mow.

   d) Do you think your solution is correct? Explain.

5. Solve.

   a) $n + 7 = 13$
   b) $n + 3 = 5.5$
   c) $9.3 = 3n$
   d) $2n - 2.5 = 5.5$

B Practising

6. Repeat question 4 with Rowyn charging \$18 per lawn.

7. Estimate each solution.

   a) $29 = 3x$
   b) $129c = 387$
   c) $2a + 5.4 = 75$
   d) $5h - 1.2 = 8.3$
   e) $2p + 1.1 = 6.4$
   f) $4n - 5 = 21$

8. Some of the following solutions are correct, but some are not. If the solution is correct, verify it. If the solution is not correct, determine the correct solution.

   a) $3n - 3 = 42$ $\quad n = 13$
   b) $6m + 6 = -36$ $\quad m = -7$
   c) $t + 5.1 = 60$ $\quad t = 9$
   d) $18 = 5y + 3$ $\quad y = 3$
   e) $3x - 2.4 = 1.8$ $\quad x = 1.4$
   f) $5w - 4.3 = 10.7$ $\quad w = 2.6$

9. Solve each equation.

   a) $8 = b + 4$
   b) $4x + 2 = 6$
   c) $4n + 2 = 6.8$
   d) $2t + 2.25 = 10.75$
   e) $t - 0.23 = 4.6$
   f) $15n - 6.5 = 53.5$

10. Write an equation for each situation. Then solve your equation.

    a) A number is multiplied by 6, and the result is 48.

    b) When a number is doubled and 10 is subtracted, the result is 37.

    c) A number is multiplied by 7. Then 2.5 is added. The result is 58.5.

11. A school basketball team bought 20 new uniforms for \$918.85, including taxes. The taxes were \$119.85.

    a) Explain how the equation $20u + 119.85 = 918.85$ represents this situation.

    b) Calculate the cost of one uniform, before taxes.

12. A grocery store collects donated canned food for a food bank. The cans are packed in boxes that hold 24 cans. The store has collected 744 cans.

   a) Draw a graph to show this situation. Put the number of boxes on the horizontal axis and the number of cans on the vertical axis.

   b) Use your graph to estimate the number of boxes needed to hold 744 cans.

   c) Write an equation that relates the number of boxes needed to the number of cans.

   d) Solve your equation to determine the number of boxes needed.

   e) Compare your solution in part (d) with your estimate in part (b). Do you think your solution is correct? Explain.

13. Austin is filling shelves at a grocery store. With every carton of 12 cereal boxes, he can fill 60 cm of shelving. The rack has 10 m of shelving, but 2 m is already occupied with other products. Austin must use enough cereal boxes to fill the rack.

   a) Draw a graph to show this situation. Put the number of cartons used on the horizontal axis and the length of shelving filled with cereal boxes on the vertical axis.

   b) Use your graph to estimate the number of cartons Austin will use to fill the rack.

   c) Write an equation that relates the length of shelving filled to the number of cartons used.

   d) Solve your equation to determine the number of cartons Austin will use.

   e) Compare your solution in part (d) with your estimate in part (b). Do you think your solution is correct? Explain.

C Extending

14. The sum of three consecutive whole numbers is 36. Determine the numbers.

15. Madison and Daryl deliver flyers. Madison's weekly earnings are three times Daryl's weekly earnings. Together, they earn \$41.00. How much does each person earn per week?

16. In a gymnastics competition, Holly and Julia scored a total of 107 points. Holly scored 35 more points than one half of Julia's points. Write and solve an equation to determine who scored more points. What is the difference between their scores?

17. Solve.

   a) $3m + 4 = -14$

   b) $-3m + 4 = 13$

   c) $5t - 0.5 = -45.5$

8.5 Solving Equations II

You will need
- paper bags
- red and blue coloured counters
- a calculator

▶ **GOAL**

Solve equations by balancing.

Learn about the Math

Rishi places the same number of counters in three paper bags and has two left over. Then he asks Stefan how many counters are in each bag. Stefan's only clue is that the total number of counters on the left is the same as the total number of counters on the right, 17.

? How can you determine the number of counters in each bag?

Example 1: Solving an equation by balancing

Determine the number of counters that Rishi placed in each bag.

Stefan's Solution: Using inspection

n represents the number of counters in each bag.

I used a variable for the quantity I have to calculate.

$3n + 2 = 17$

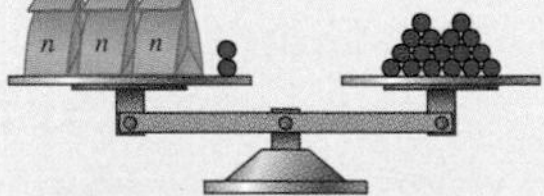

Then I wrote the equation.

$3n + 2 - 2 = 17 - 2$

If I take away two counters from each side, both sides still balance.

$3n = 15$

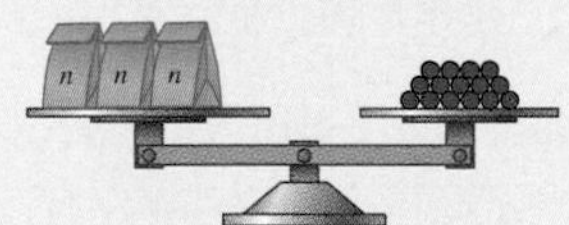

$3n \div 3 = 15 \div 3$

$n = 5$

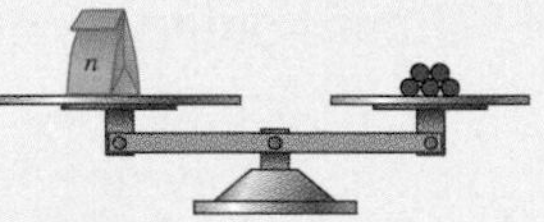

Since there are three bags on the left side, I divided the counters on the right side into three equal groups. Then I matched each bag on the left side with one of the groups of counters on the right side.

Each bag contains 5 counters.

Check: Left side	Right side
$3n + 2$ $= 3(5) + 2$ $= 17$ ✓	17

I checked my solution by substituting 5 into the original equation.

Example 2: Solving an equation that involves subtraction

Solve the equation $25 = 4n - 3$.

Kayley's Solution

$25 = 4n - 3$ means the same as $4n - 3 = 25$.

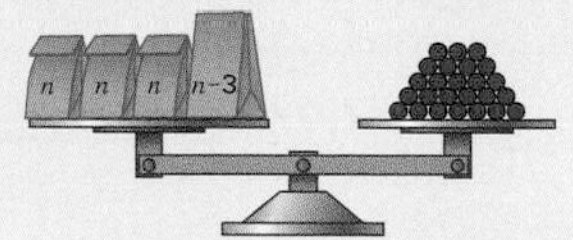

I turned the equation around. Then I modelled the equation using bags and counters on a balance. On the left side, there were four bags. Three of the bags had the same number of counters (they were full), but the fourth bag had three fewer counters.

$4n - 3 + 3 = 25 + 3$

$4n = 28$

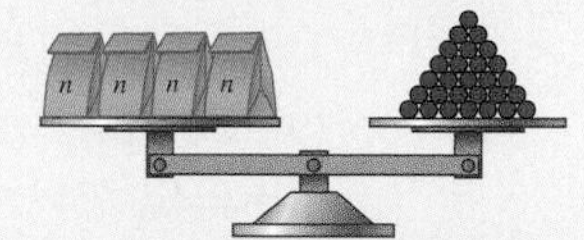

I added three counters to the fourth bag so that it had the same number of counters as the other three bags. On the right side, I added three counters to keep the balance.

$4n \div 4 = 28 \div 4$

$n = 7$

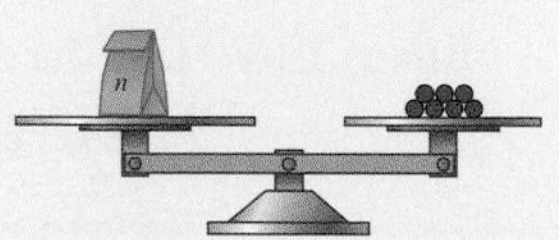

I divided the counters on the right side into four equal groups. Then I matched one bag on the left side with one of the groups of counters on the right side.

Check:

Left side	Right side
$4n - 3$	25
$= 4(7) - 3$	
$= 25$ ✓	

I checked my solution by substituting 7 into the original equation.

Reflecting

1. How is an equation like a pan balance? Does the variable have to be on the left side, or can it be on the right side?

2. Does adding or subtracting the same number of counters on both sides of a pan balance change the equation? Does it change the solution to the equation?

3. Why is grouping the counters on one side of a balance to match the number of bags on the other side like dividing both sides of an equation by the same amount? Why is this model helpful for solving an equation like $3n = 15$ or $4n = 28$?

4. How do you decide whether to add counters, subtract counters, or separate counters into groups when you are solving an equation represented by a balance model?

Work with the Math

Example 3: Solving an equation that involves decimals

Three full bags of sand all have the same mass. When 4.5 g of sand is removed from the third bag, the total mass of the three bags is 233.7 g. What is the mass of each full bag of sand?

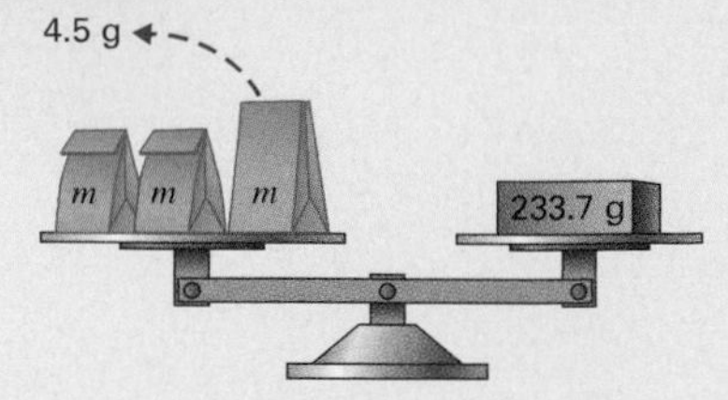

Solution

Let m represent the mass of sand in each bag.

$$3m - 4.5 = 233.7$$
$$3m - 4.5 + 4.5 = 233.7 + 4.5$$
$$3m \div 3 = 238.2 \div 3$$
$$m = 79.4$$

Each bag contains 79.4 g of sand.

Check: Left side	Right side
$3m - 4.5$	233.7
$= 3(79.4) - 4.5$
$= 233.7$ ✓

A Checking

5. a) Suppose that you double the number of counters on the left side. What must you do on the right side to keep the balance?

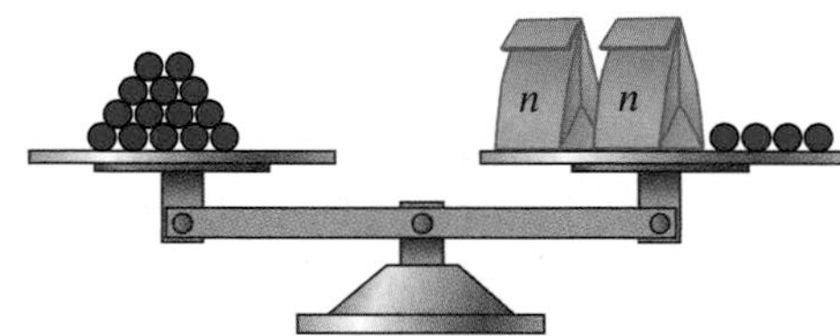

b) Suppose that you subtract four counters on the left side. What must you do on the right side to keep the balance?

6. Write an equation for the diagram. Solve your equation using a model or another diagram. Show your steps.

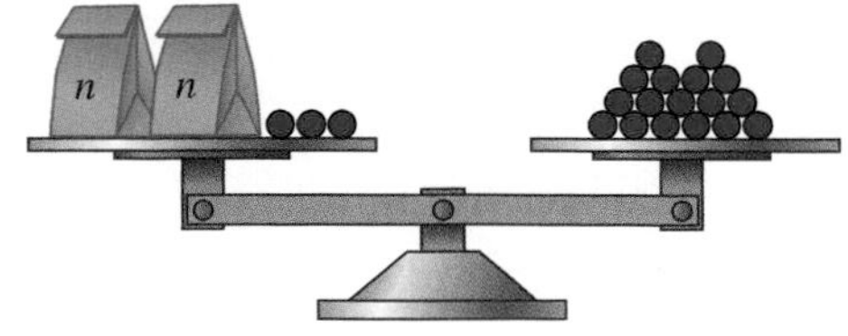

7. Solve each equation. Show your steps.

a) $t - 3 = 9$

b) $7 = a + 4$

c) $3b - 1 = 8$

d) $x \div 2 = 8$

B Practising

8. Write an equation for the diagram. Solve your equation. Show your steps.

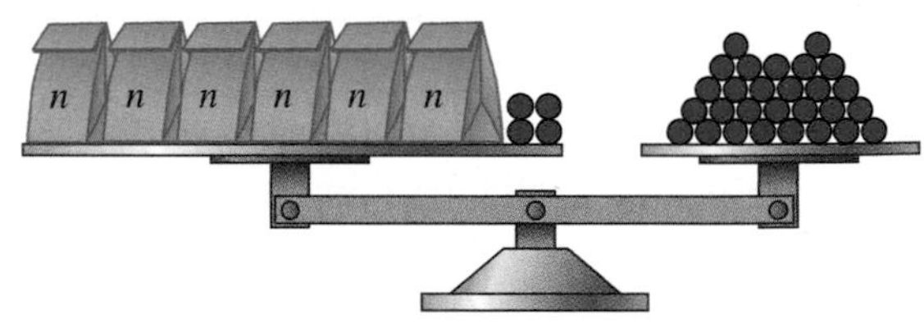

9. Solve each equation. Show your steps.

a) $2m - 3 = 31$

b) $5a + 15 = 75$

c) $n \div 8 - 123 = 37$

d) $214 = 6n + 19$

e) $10w - 145 = 955$

f) $n \div 4 + 7 = 13$

10. Solve.

a) $1.8 - u + 0.7$

b) $2t + 1.3 = 3.9$

c) $4n - 4.2 = 39.8$

d) $6x - 5.5 = 42.2$

e) $3n + 3.3 = 86.7$

f) $n \div 5 + 9 = 22$

11. Suppose that you have four bags of stones and four extra stones. In total, you have 28 stones. Each bag has the same number of stones. How many stones are in each bag?

12. Write an equation for each situation. Then solve your equation to find the number of stones in one bag. Each bag has the same number of stones.

a) Two bags of stones and six extra stones equals 66 stones.

b) When seven stones are removed from one of the bags, the three bags contain a total of 32 stones.

13. Solve.

a) $5x - 2 = 10$

b) $2n + 4.1 = 8.5$

c) $x \div 3 - 7 = 2$

d) $n \div 5 + 0.25 = 5.75$

14. Deborah bought three identical binders and received \$1.15 change from \$10. How much did each binder cost?

15. Farhan's grandfather bought two tickets to a charity hockey game. When a delivery charge of \$3.75 per order was added to the cost of the tickets, the total was \$31.65. What was the cost of each ticket?

16. At a butcher shop, meat is sold by mass. The bill for 4 kg of steak, plus a jar of barbecue sauce that cost \$3.79, was \$23.19. Determine the cost of 1 kg of steak.

17. Four identical bags of cement and a concrete block have a total mass of 98 kg. The concrete block has a mass of 8 kg. What is the mass of each bag of cement?

18. A grocery bag contains five apples, one pineapple, and one orange. The total mass of the fruit is 2.7 kg. The mass of the pineapple is 1.25 kg, and the mass of the orange is 0.2 kg. Create and solve an equation to determine the average mass of each apple.

C Extending

19. The diagram below models the integer equation $x + (-4) = 6$. Solve the equation.

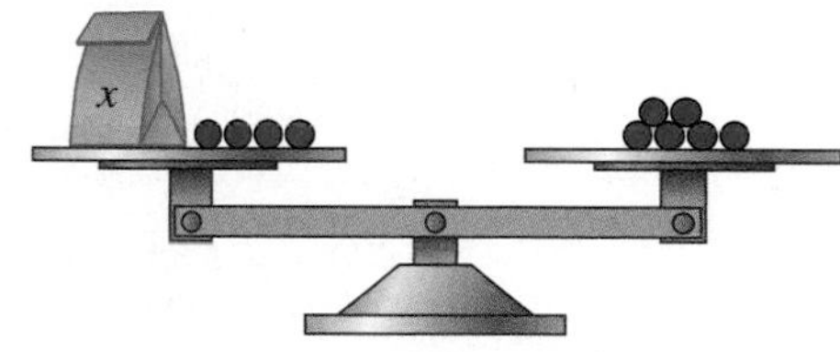

20. Use a model or a diagram to solve each integer equation.

a) $x + 6 = -4$

b) $2n + (-2) = 8$

c) $-2x - 5 = -23$

d) $3n - (-2) = 14$

e) $2n + (-2) = -6$

Mental Math

MULTIPLYING MIXED NUMBERS PART BY PART

To multiply a mixed number (a fraction greater than 1) by a whole number, you multiply the whole number first and then the fraction.

Bannock
4 1/2 cups flour
1/4 cup sugar
2 1/2 teaspoons baking powder
1/2 cup lard
1/2 teaspoon salt
2 3/4 cups cold water
1/2 cup raisins

Suppose that you want to make eight batches of bannock. You have to calculate the number of cups or teaspoons of each ingredient in eight batches.

To calculate the number of cups of flour, multiply the whole numberand then the fraction:

$$8 \times 4\frac{1}{2} = 8 \times 4 + 8 \times \frac{1}{2}$$

$$32 + 4 = 36$$

You need 36 cups of flour to make eight batches of bannock.

1. Calculate the number of cups or teaspoons of each ingredient in eight batches of bannock.

2. Multiply.

   a) $6 \times 1\frac{1}{3}$ b) $5 \times 2\frac{1}{2}$ c) $7 \times 2\frac{1}{3}$ d) $9 \times 2\frac{1}{4}$ e) $2 \times 5\frac{3}{4}$

Math Game

ALGE-SCRABBLE

In this game, you will create and solve equations to score points.

Number of players: 2 to 4

You will need

- a game board (a 20-by-20 grid of 2 cm squares)
- tiles (or counters) in four colours

Write on the tiles with a washable marker, so that you have

- at least 10 green tiles for each of the four basic operations ($+$, $-$, $\times$, $\div$)
- at least 10 blue tiles with variables
- at least 10 red tiles with = signs
- at least 50 yellow tiles with values from 1 to 25

Rules

1. Place the tiles with their blank sides facing up. Each player chooses 15 tiles—5 green tiles, 5 blue tiles, and 5 yellow tiles—at the beginning of his or her first turn. The red = tiles can be used whenever they are needed.
2. Players take turns placing tiles on the game board to form an equation with a variable, such as $3n + 2 = 20$.
3. Players score points equal to the value of the variable that solves their equation. For example, the equation $3n + 2 = 20$, which has a solution of $n = 6$, gives a score of 6 points.
4. At the end of each turn, players draw new tiles to replace the tiles used.
5. Players can use tiles that are already on the game board to build an equation, but the original value of the variable cannot change.
6. The game is finished after five rounds. The player with the highest score wins.

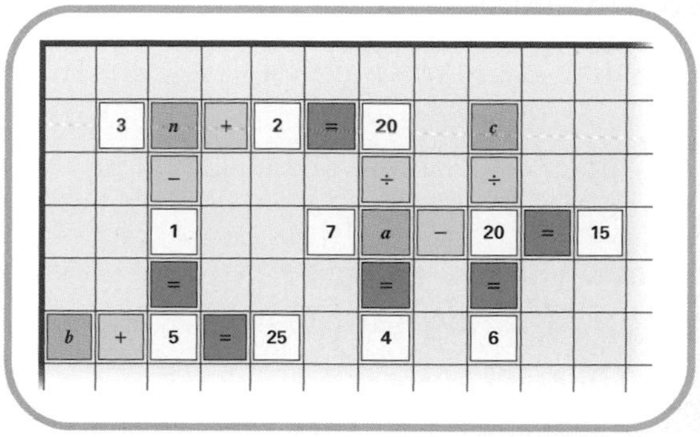

	3	n	+	2	=	20		c		
		−				÷		÷		
		1			7	a	−	20	=	15
		=				=		=		
b	+	5	=	25		4		6		

For example, for the game board above:

$3n + 2 = 20$	$n = 6$, so the player scores 6 points.
$n - 1 = 5$	$n = 6$, so the player scores 6 points.
$20 \div a = 4$	$a = 5$, so the player scores 5 points.
$7a - 20 = 15$	$a = 5$, so the player scores 5 points.
$b + 5 = 25$	$b = 20$, so the player scores 20 points.
$c \div 20 = 6$	$c = 120$, so the player scores 120 points.

Variation

If the game board includes double-value and triple-value squares, the variable tiles can be placed on these squares to score extra points.

8.6 Communicating about Equations

You will need
- a calculator

▶ **GOAL**

Describe how to create and solve problems.

Communicate about the Math

For a math assignment, Carina had to create a problem that could be represented by the equation $2n + 1 = 7$. Then she had to solve her problem and explain her solution.

Carina wrote the following problem, solution, and explanation. She asked Rowyn to look at her work and help her improve it before she handed it in.

? How can Carina improve her problem, solution, and explanation?

Carina's Problem and Solution	Carina's Explanation	Rowyn's Questions
Jason bought two burgers and a drink for \$1, and his total came to \$7. How much did each burger cost?	I wanted the total cost to be \$7. ←	Did the burgers and the drink cost \$1?
$2n + 1 = 7$	I don't need dollar signs in my equation. ←	I'm not sure what $2n$ represents. Does it represent "burgers" or "cost"?
$n = 3$	I know that two groups of 3 equals 6, so $n = 3$. ←	I can't tell how you knew that the answer is 3. How did you know that your answer makes sense?
It is \$3. ←		What is \$3?

Communication Checklist

- ☑ Did you explain how your equation represents the situation described in your problem?
- ☑ Did you clearly identify what quantity the variable represents?
- ☑ Are the steps in your solution complete and easy to follow?
- ☑ Did you check your solution?
- ☑ Did you write a concluding sentence to answer the question in the problem?

A. Do you think Rowyn's questions were helpful? Explain.

B. Rewrite Carina's work using the Communication Checklist. Explain how your changes improve her work.

Reflecting

1. How did Carina's choice of \$1 for the cost of a drink relate to the equation? How did her decision to determine the cost of two burgers relate to the equation?
2. Why do you need to show your steps in a logical order when solving an algebraic equation?
3. Which parts of the Communication Checklist did Carina cover well?

Work with the Math

Example: Interpreting and solving an equation

Create a problem that could be solved using the equation $3n + 1.5 = 27$. Then solve your problem and explain your solution.

Rishi's Solution

$3n$ represents the cost of 3 pizzas, 1.5 represents the delivery charge, and 27 represents the total cost.	I could let 27 represent a cost. Then n would represent the cost of one thing, and $3n$ would represent the cost of three things.
My problem: I ordered 3 pizzas. What is the cost of each pizza if the delivery charge is \$1.50 and the total bill is \$27.00?	The number 1.5 could represent \$1.50 tax, so $3n$ would represent the cost before tax. Or 1.5 could represent the delivery charge when ordering pizza.
My solution: n represents the cost of each pizza. $3n + 1.5 = 27$	I wrote the equation, explaining what the variable means. I don't need dollar signs in my equation. I used 1.5 and 27 instead of 1.50 and 27.00.
$3n + 1.5 - 1.5 = 27 - 1.5$ $3n = 25.5$ $n = 8.5$	I subtracted 1.5 from both sides of the equation so that I could see the cost of 3 pizzas. I divided both sides by 3 to get the cost of one pizza.
Check: Left side: $3n + 1.5 = 3(8.5) + 1.5 = 27$ ✓ Right side: 27	I checked my solution by substitution.
Each pizza costs \$8.50.	My concluding sentence answers the question asked in my problem.

A Checking

4. a) Create a problem that can be represented by the equation $2h + 1.50 = 5.50$.

b) Solve your problem.

c) Explain how you created your problem and how you solved it. Use the Communication Checklist to help you.

B Practising

5. Explain the solution to the equation below. Then create a problem that could be solved using the equation.

$12n - 6 = 48$
$n = 4.5$

6. Improve Mason's solution to the problem he created. Use the Communication Checklist to help you.

My Problem:

Mason's grandmother knits sweaters and sells them through the Internet. A customer ordered some identical sweaters but in different colours. The total cost of this customer's order was $60.75, after the shipping charge of $3.25 per order was added. If the cost of each sweater, including tax, was $28.75, how many sweaters did the customer buy?

My Solution:

Let s represent the number of sweaters.

The equation is
$s \times 28.75 + 3.25 = 60.75$.

I guessed that the answer was 2, and this number worked when I checked it.

7. Create a problem for the equation $4n + 7 = 55$. Then solve your problem and explain your solution. Use the Communication Checklist to help you.

8. Create a problem for the equation $5n + 1.39 = 8.89$. Explain how you created your problem.

9. Create a problem for the equation $6.5n + 5 = 31$. Then solve your problem and explain your solution. Use the Communication Checklist to help you.

10. Describe how to create and solve an equation for this problem.

A square back yard has an area of 144 m². Cedars are going to be planted on three sides of the yard. They will be planted every half metre, starting and ending next to the house. How many cedars will be planted?

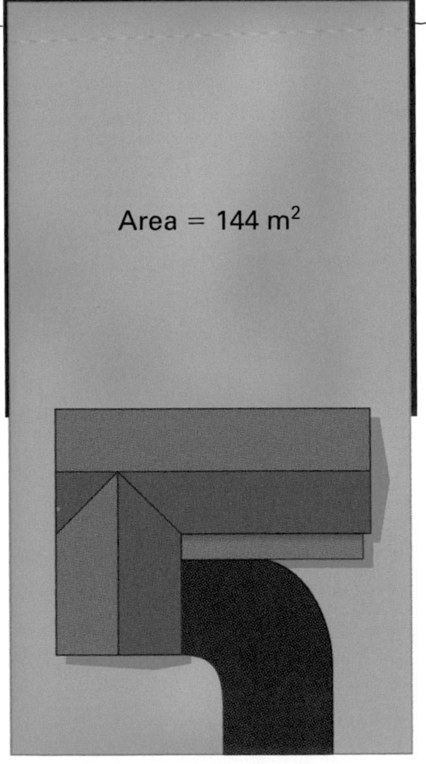

Chapter Self-Test

1. Use the following graph to solve the equation $3n + 7 = 52$.

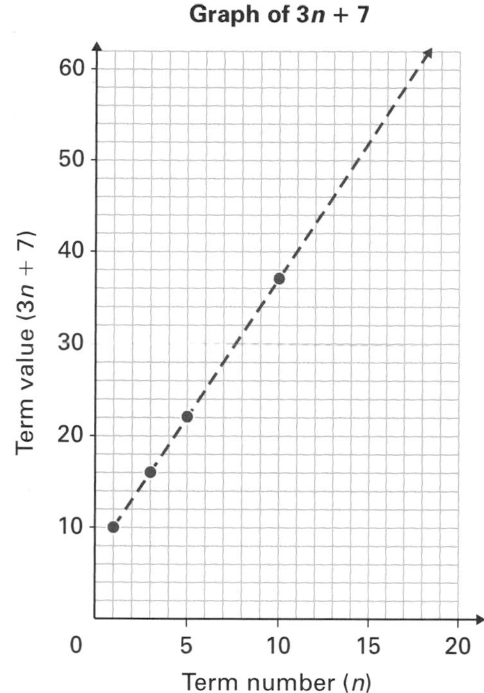

2. a) Create a table of values to represent this pattern.

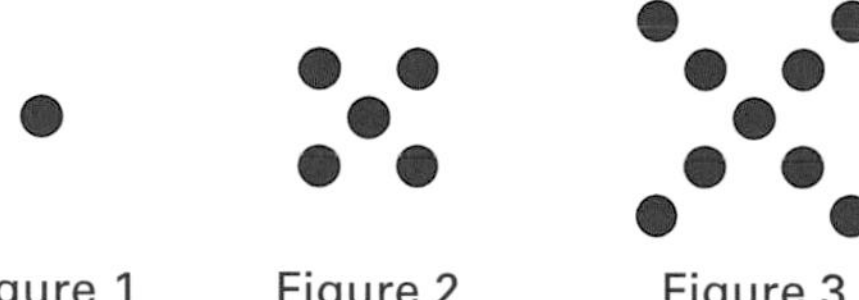

b) Write an algebraic expression for the pattern rule.

c) Create an equation to determine the number of the figure with 161 counters.

d) Solve your equation using any method you wish.

3. a) Evaluate the expression $7a + 8c$, when $a = 12.25$ and $c = 3.7$.

b) Evaluate the expression $-7a + 8c$, when $a = 3$ and $c = -2$.

4. Solve each equation.

a) $78 = 6x$

b) $6n + 5 = 41$

c) $4m - 11 = 45$

d) $2t = 208.5$

5. Determine each solution.

a) $n - 2 = 5$

b) $x - 6.1 = 12.2$

c) $t + 0.23 = 5.6$

d) $1.68h = 6.72$

e) $6p + 1 = 19$

f) $25n - 8.5 = 101.5$

6. Write an equation for each situation.

a) 7.1 added to a number equals 10.3.

b) A number is multiplied by 6, and the result is 48.6.

c) When a number is added to itself, the result is 49.

d) A number is tripled, and 2.5 is added. The result is 83.5.

7. Choose an appropriate variable for each situation. Then write and solve an equation.

a) If I doubled the money in my savings account, I would have \$150.62.

b) Three times the hourly wage plus \$7.65 in tips equals \$27.90.

8. Create an equation for the following problem. Use your equation to solve the problem.

Ying bought a jacket and some socks. The jacket cost \$39, and the socks cost \$2.50 per pair. Ying's bill for these items totalled \$51.50 before tax. How many pairs of socks did she buy?

Chapter Review

Frequently Asked Questions

Q: How can balancing be used to solve an equation?

A: An equation is like a pan balance that is level because the two sides are equal. As you make changes to an equation to solve it, you must make the same changes to both sides to keep the balance. For example, consider the equation $5x - 3 = 15$.

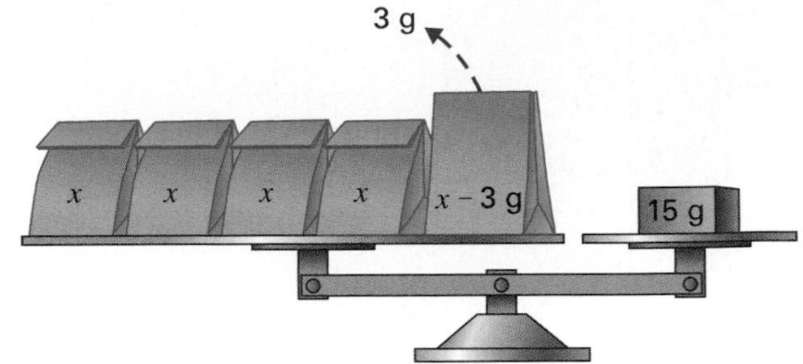

$5x - 3 = 15$	
$5x - 3 + 3 = 15 + 3$	Add 3 to both sides of the equation or balance.
$5x = 18$	Simplify. There are 5 bags on one side and 18 g on the other side.
$5x \div 5 = 18 \div 5$	Divide each side by 5 to determine the mass of one bag.
$x = 3.6$	Simplify.

The solution is $x = 3.6$.

Check: Left side	Right side
$5x - 3$	15
$= 5(3.6) - 3$	
$= 15$ ✓	

Q: How can you use an equation to solve a problem?

A: First decide what the variable represents. Then write an equation that represents the situation. Next, solve the equation using any method you wish (using a graph, inspection, systematic trial, or balancing). Finally, answer the question that was asked in the problem.

For example, consider this problem:

Two bags are filled with the same number of cubes, and there are 19 extra cubes. In total, there are 163 cubes. How many cubes are in each bag?

If n represents the number of cubes in each bag, the equation is $2n + 19 = 163$.

The solution to the equation is $n = 72$. This means that 72 cubes are in each bag.

NEL

Practice Questions

(8.1) **1. a)** Use the graph to solve $2n + 4 = 20$.

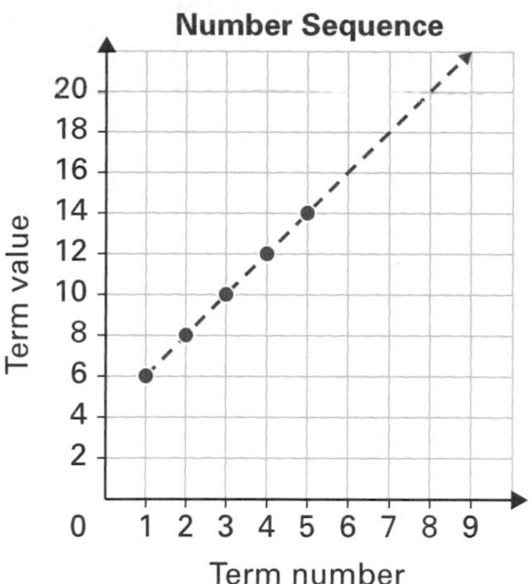

b) Write an equation for a term value of 12. Solve your equation.

(8.1) **2. a)** Create a table of values to represent this pattern.

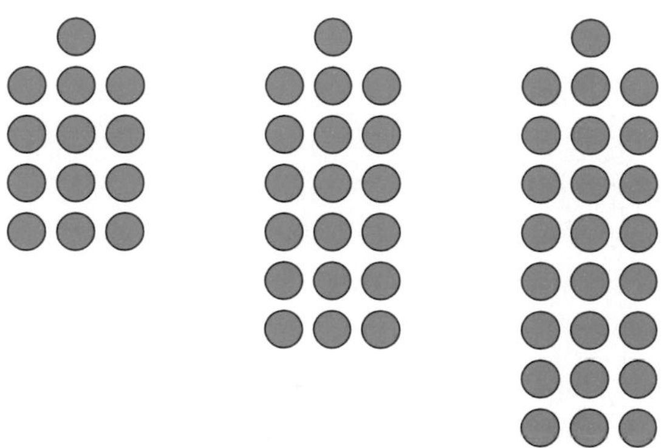

Figure 1 Figure 2 Figure 3

b) Write an algebraic expression for the pattern rule.

c) Draw a graph to determine the number of the figure that has 145 counters.

(8.3) **3.** Kyra has a summer job selling ice-cream bars. She is paid \$40 per day. She is also paid a commission of \$0.25 for each ice-cream bar she sells. Create and evaluate an algebraic expression to calculate how much Kyra can earn in one day if she sells 77 ice-cream bars.

4. Solve each equation. (8.4)

a) $2b + 4 = 14$

b) $5a + 2 = 10$

c) $n + 4.3 = 5.1$

d) $0.5x = 21 - 3$

e) $4t + 1 = 20$

f) $4m + 7 = 43.8$

5. Match each description with the correct equation below. Then solve the equation.

a) When 3.21 is added to a number, the sum is 16.05.

b) The product of 3.21 and a number is 16.05.

c) When a number is doubled and 3.21 is subtracted, the result is 16.05. (8.4)

$$3.21n = 16.05$$
$$2n - 3.21 = 16.05$$
$$n + 3.21 = 16.05$$

6. Create an equation for the following problem. Use your equation to solve the problem.

The members of a basketball team need to raise \$895 for new uniforms. They already have \$351 from food sales. To raise the remainder, they are planning a shoot-out challenge. If 34 teams sign up, how much must they charge per team to meet their goal? (8.4)

7. Create a problem for the equation $10.99t = 21.98$. Solve your problem. (8.5)

8. Write a problem for this situation. Then use an equation to solve the problem.

Edan buys two tickets to a concert. When the delivery charge of \$3.75 per order is added to the cost of the tickets, the total cost is \$54.75. (8.5)

Chapter Task

The Chocolate Equation

Michel wants to buy his mother handmade chocolates for Mother's Day. He has \$15.00 to spend. The price of each type of chocolate is given below.

Fudge centres: \$0.60 Nut clusters: \$0.75 Truffles: \$0.80

? How many chocolates can Michel buy with \$15.00?

A. Create and solve an equation for each type of chocolate to determine how many Michel can buy with \$15.00, if he buys only one type.

B. Michel decides to buy all three types of chocolates, instead of choosing just one type.

- **a)** If Michel buys the same number of all three types, how many can he buy and stay within his budget?
- **b)** Exactly how much will Michel spend?
- **c)** Write an algebraic expression that represents the total amount Michel will spend. Then substitute for the variables and evaluate your expression. How does this amount compare with your amount in part (b)?

C. Michel's final choice costs \$14.80. It is a combination of all three types of chocolates.

- **a)** Determine four possible combinations of chocolates he could have selected.
- **b)** Create and evaluate an algebraic expression to show that each of your combinations works.

Task Checklist

- ☑ Did you include a table of values?
- ☑ Did you write a clear algebraic solution for each equation?
- ☑ Did you check your solutions?

Math in Action

Entrepreneur

Kate Hennessy wanted to earn money for university, but there were few jobs near her home on Galiano Island, British Columbia. Her solution was to create her own business, doing something she loved—ocean kayaking. She decided to run an ocean-kayaking business each year from April to October.

Kate explains, "I had to estimate what money would come in and anticipate any costs. Subtracting my costs from the business income told me how much I'd have left to run my business, pay back the lenders, and earn money myself."

Problems, Applications, and Decision Making

Kate decided to apply for a bank loan to start her business. She created a cash flow spreadsheet to show her financial predictions.

Kate's Predicted Cash Flow

	A	B	C	D	E	F	G	H
1		April	May	June	July	August	September	October
2	Sales	900	2300	4200	6900	7800	3800	1100
3	Cash Borrowed	6000	4200	0	0	0	0	0
4	Total Cash In							
5	Equipment Purchases	6500	11000	200	200	200	0	0
6	Salaries	600	400	500	1600	1900	900	300
7	Equipment Rentals	40	45	90	190	210	0	0
8	Cash Withdrawals	0	250	250	300	200	900	3000
9	Loan Payments	0	120	120	120	120	120	3050
10	Total Cash Out							
11	Monthly Cash Flow							
12	Cumulative Cash Flow							

1. Explain what each numbered row in Kate's spreadsheet represents. Copy the spreadsheet.

2. Total Cash In includes Sales and Cash Borrowed. Enter a formula in cell B4 to represent the Total Cash In for April.

3. Total Cash Out includes Equipment Purchases, Salaries, Equipment Rentals, Cash Withdrawals, and Loan Payments. Enter a formula in B10 to represent the Total Cash Out for April.

4. Monthly Cash Flow is calculated by subtracting the Total Cash Out from the Total Cash In. Enter this formula in B11.

5. a) If the Total Cash Out was greater than the Total Cash In for a month, would the Monthly Cash Flow be positive or negative? Why?
   b) What would a Monthly Cash Flow of zero mean?

6. a) Kate's Cumulative Cash Flow can be calculated by adding the Monthly Cash Flow for the current month to the Cumulative Cash Flow for the previous month. Write a formula for B12 and C12 to show this.
   b) Kate's Cumulative Cash Flow for each month can be calculated by adding the Monthly Cash Flows up to, and including, the current month. Write a formula for B12 and C12 to show this.
   c) Enter the appropriate formulas in row 12.

7. a) Complete the spreadsheet.
   b) Kate's Cumulative Cash Flow for April is the same as her Monthly Cash Flow for April. Why?

8. Describe trends in Kate's cash flow. Suggest possible reasons for the trends.

9. Suppose that you are a bank loans officer. Would you lend Kate the money she needs? Explain how Kate's spreadsheet justifies your decision.

Kate ran her ocean-kayaking business from 1992 to 1997. Then, her brother James took over the business to pay for his university education. Kate began teaching in Taiwan and China, where she learned Mandarin. Kate then earned a Commonwealth Scholarship for a Master's degree in England at the University of London School of Oriental and African Studies. She went on to study for a Ph.D. in anthropology at the University of British Columbia. As well, she works with First Nations in British Columbia. She still finds time to kayak.

CHAPTER 9

Fraction Operations

▶ GOALS

You will be able to

- add and subtract fractions and mixed numbers
- multiply and divide fractions and mixed numbers
- relate decimal calculations to fraction calculations
- use order of operations with fractions
- solve problems that involve all four operations with fractions

Getting Started

You will need
- pattern blocks

Pattern Block Designs

Jordan made a design using pattern blocks.

? What fractions can you use to compare the different-coloured parts of Jordan's design?

A. Look at Jordan's design. If each yellow hexagon has an area of 1 unit, what is the area of the red block? What is the area of the blue block? What is the area of the green block?

B. The equation $3 - \frac{1}{2} = 2\frac{1}{2}$ describes the difference between the areas of two colours. Which two colours? How do you know?

C. Use equations with fractions and/or mixed numbers to describe each difference.

a) the difference between the area of the green blocks and the area of the blue block

b) the difference between the area of the yellow blocks and the area of all the blocks that are not yellow

c) the difference between the area of the yellow blocks and the area of the blue and green blocks

d) the difference between the area of the red block and the area of the green blocks

D. What other fraction comparisons can you make based on Jordan's design?

E. Make a new design, following these design rules. You must use
- a total of eight blocks
- at least one of each of these blocks

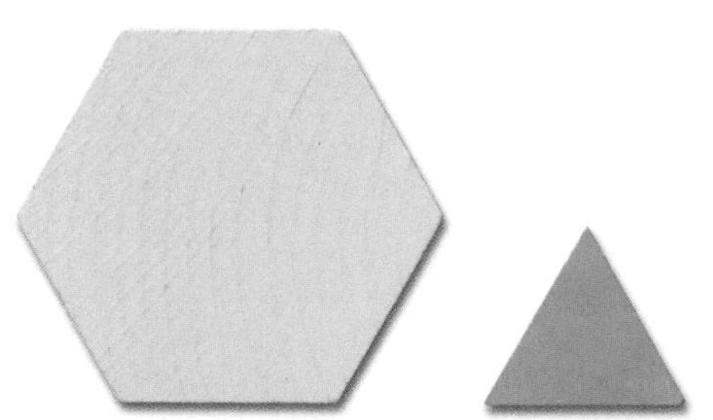

Repeat steps C and D for your design. If you cannot answer any of the questions, explain why.

Do You Remember?

1. Name two **equivalent fractions** for each fraction.

   a) $\frac{3}{8}$ c) $\frac{11}{2}$

   b) $1\frac{2}{3}$ d) $\frac{9}{12}$

2. Order these fractions from least to greatest.

   $\frac{3}{5}$ $\frac{3}{8}$ $\frac{6}{7}$ $\frac{12}{5}$

3. Write an addition equation to describe the fraction of the whole rectangle modelled by the blue and yellow parts.

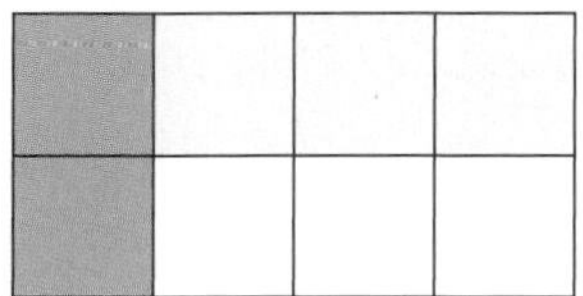

4. For each diagram, write an equation involving fraction subtraction to describe how much more is yellow than red.

   a)

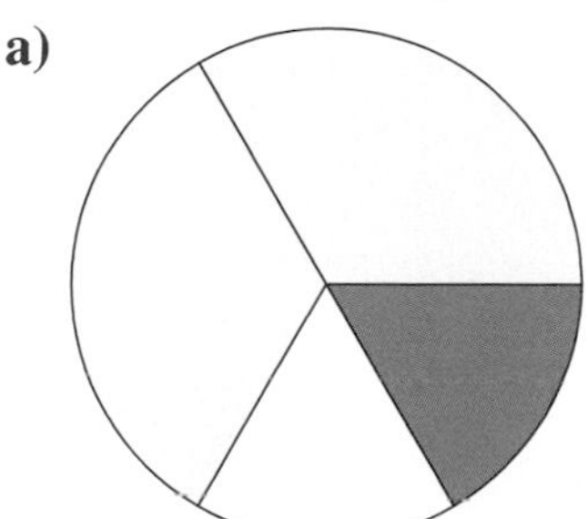

   b)

5. Use a number line, like the one below, to model each calculation.

   0 1 2

   a) $\frac{3}{5} + \frac{1}{3}$ b) $4 \times \frac{2}{5}$

6. This grid shows how you might add $\frac{1}{3} + \frac{1}{2}$.

Step 1

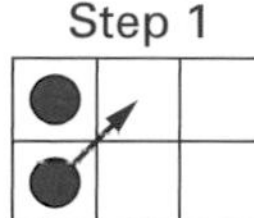

Step 2

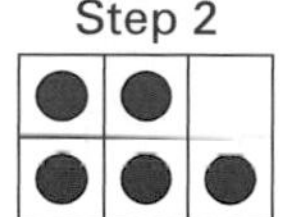

   Model each calculation on a grid, and record your result.

   a) $\frac{3}{5} + \frac{1}{4}$ c) $3 \times \frac{3}{5}$

   b) $\frac{2}{5} - \frac{1}{4}$ d) $2 \times \frac{9}{10}$

7. Determine the missing value in each equation.

   a) $\frac{3}{5} + \blacksquare = 1\frac{1}{2}$

   b) $\blacksquare + \frac{1}{2} = 1\frac{2}{3}$

   c) $\frac{5}{8} + \blacksquare = 2$

8. Copy and complete the chart to show how repeated addition relates to multiplication.

Repeated addition	Multiplication	Result
$\frac{2}{3} + \frac{2}{3} + \frac{2}{3} + \frac{2}{3}$		
	$3 \times \frac{5}{8}$	

9. Aaron bought 3 pizzas, each with 12 slices. He and his friends ate $1\frac{2}{3}$ of the pizzas.

   a) How many slices were left?

   b) How many pizzas were left?

10. Thea poured 7 glasses of juice. Each glass was $\frac{2}{3}$ full. How many glasses could she completely fill with the same amount of juice?

9.1 Adding and Subtracting Fractions Less Than 1

You will need
- fraction strips

▶ **GOAL**
Add and subtract fractions less than 1.

Learn about the Math

This graph represents the recent destinations of Canadians who travelled within Canada.

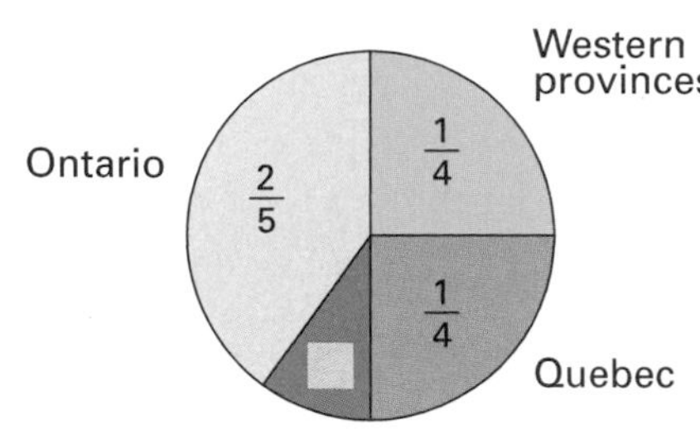

? What fraction of Canadians who travelled within Canada went to the Atlantic provinces?

A. List the fractions that represent the trips to Ontario, Quebec, and the western provinces. Order them from least to greatest.

B. Calculate the fraction that represents the sum of all the trips to Ontario, Quebec, and the western provinces. Use a fraction strip model.

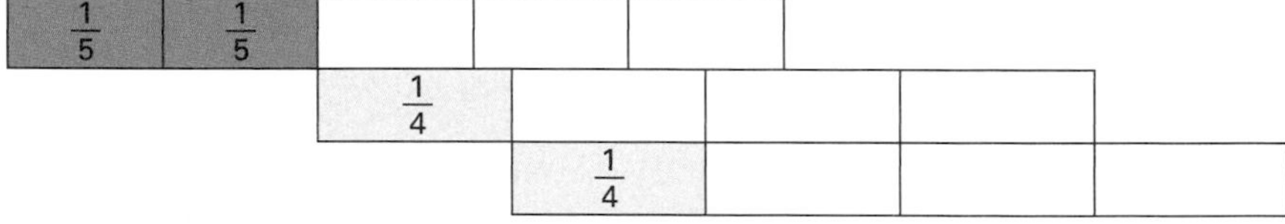

C. Show how to add the fractions without the fraction strip model.

D. Explain why the fraction representing trips to the Atlantic provinces can be calculated as $\frac{1}{2} - \frac{2}{5}$. Refer to the circle graph.

E. Write a different equation that you could use to determine the fraction representing trips to the Atlantic provinces. Solve your equation. Explain why your equation works.

Reflecting

1. In step B, you might have added the fractions for Quebec and the western provinces first. Why would this be easier than adding the fractions for Ontario and Quebec first?
2. Which denominator did you choose in step C to add the three fractions? Why did you choose this denominator?
3. Why does a common denominator make adding or subtracting fractions easier?

Work with the Math

Example 1: Subtracting with a number line model

Marlie has $\frac{2}{3}$ cup of flour. She uses $\frac{1}{6}$ cup for a recipe. How much flour does she have left?

Sheree's Solution

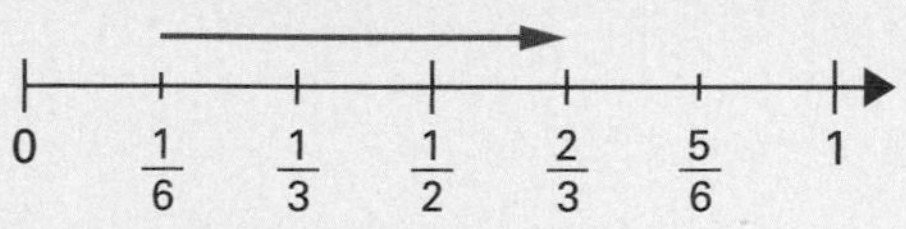

To see how much flour would be left, I drew a number line. I needed to figure out the distance from $\frac{1}{6}$ to $\frac{2}{3}$.

$$\frac{2}{3} - \frac{1}{6} = \frac{3}{6}$$
$$= \frac{1}{2}$$

The distance is $\frac{3}{6}$. In lowest terms, this is $\frac{1}{2}$.

Marlie has $\frac{1}{2}$ cup of flour left.

Communication Tip

When a fraction is written as an equivalent fraction with a numerator and a denominator that are lower numbers, we say that the equivalent fraction is in lower terms. If there is no way to write a fraction in even lower terms, we say that the fraction is in lowest terms, or simplest form. Some people call this simplifying. For example, $\frac{12}{24}$ can be written as $\frac{6}{12}$ in lower terms or as $\frac{1}{2}$ in lowest terms.

Example 2: Adding and subtracting fractions with a grid model

Jay discovered that $\frac{3}{4}$ of the students in his class were born in Sudbury and $\frac{1}{7}$ were born in Toronto. What fraction of the students were born in other places?

Teo's Solution

I used two steps to solve this problem. First I added $\frac{3}{4}$ and $\frac{1}{7}$ to show students who were born in Sudbury and Toronto. Then I subtracted from 1 whole to determine the fraction of students born in other places.

$$\frac{3}{4} = \frac{21}{28}$$

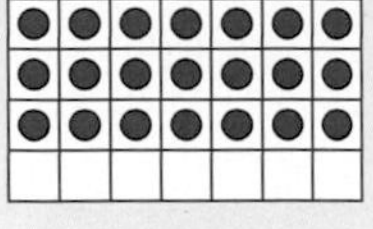

I used a 4-by-7 rectangle to show fourths as rows and sevenths as columns. I filled 3 of the 4 rows to show $\frac{3}{4}$.

$$\frac{1}{7} = \frac{4}{28}$$

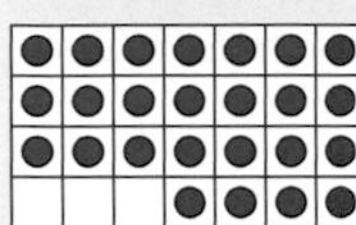

Then I moved three counters to make space to fill one column to show $\frac{1}{7}$.

$$\frac{3}{4} + \frac{1}{7} = \frac{21}{28} + \frac{4}{28}$$
$$= \frac{25}{28}$$

$$1 - \frac{25}{28} = \frac{3}{28}$$

So, $\frac{3}{28}$ of the students were not born in Sudbury or Toronto.

A Checking

4. Add or subtract using a model.

a) $\frac{3}{6} + \frac{2}{3}$ **b)** $\frac{7}{8} - \frac{3}{4}$

5. Calculate each sum or difference using equivalent fractions.

a) $\frac{3}{7} - \frac{1}{4}$ **b)** $\frac{2}{5} + \frac{5}{12}$

6. At a school party, $\frac{2}{3}$ of the students are wearing T-shirts and $\frac{1}{5}$ are wearing long-sleeved shirts. Which fraction is greater? By how much is it greater?

B Practising

7. Two fractions with different denominators are being added using this grid model. Identify the fractions, and explain your reasoning.

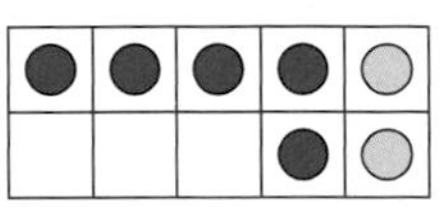

8. How much greater is the first shaded fraction than the second shaded fraction?

$\frac{1}{7}$	$\frac{1}{7}$	$\frac{1}{7}$	$\frac{1}{7}$	$\frac{1}{7}$	$\frac{1}{7}$	$\frac{1}{7}$

$\frac{1}{2}$	$\frac{1}{2}$

9. Complete the equation.

$\frac{2}{3} + \frac{3}{5} = \frac{■}{15} + \frac{■}{15}$

10. Draw a model to show each calculation. Then determine the sum or difference.

a) $\frac{2}{3} + \frac{1}{6}$
b) $\frac{1}{2} + \frac{3}{5}$
c) $\frac{1}{2} - \frac{3}{7}$
d) $2 - \frac{3}{4}$

11. Four students added $\frac{3}{4} + \frac{5}{6}$ and got these answers: $\frac{38}{24}$, $1\frac{14}{24}$, $1\frac{7}{12}$, and $\frac{19}{12}$.

a) Are they all correct? How do you know?
b) Which answer is in simplest form?

12. Add or subtract using equivalent fractions.

a) $\frac{2}{3} + \frac{3}{7}$
b) $\frac{3}{5} + \frac{4}{7}$
c) $\frac{3}{4} + \frac{7}{9}$
d) $\frac{3}{4} - \frac{1}{3}$
e) $\frac{3}{4} - \frac{2}{5}$
f) $\frac{5}{8} - \frac{1}{6}$

13. How much more of the container must be filled so that only $\frac{1}{4}$ is empty?

14. This circle graph shows the number of sports programs that students participate in.

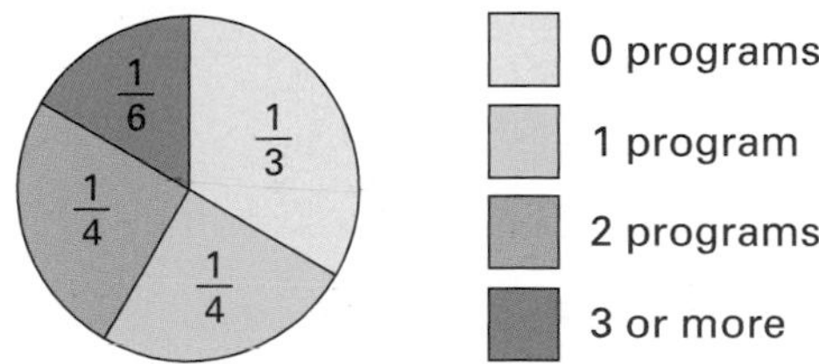

a) What fraction of students participate in one or more programs?
b) What fraction of students participate in more than one program?

15. A pail of water was $\frac{1}{4}$ full. Kassia added some water until the pail was $\frac{2}{3}$ full. How much water did she add? Express your answer as a fraction of the total capacity of the pail.

16. Calculate the value of each expression.

a) $n + n$, when $n = \frac{7}{8}$
b) $a - b$, when $a = \frac{5}{6}$ and $b = \frac{1}{12}$

17. Which answer is closest to $\frac{1}{2}$? How close is it?

A. $\frac{3}{4} - \frac{2}{10}$
B. $\frac{4}{5} - \frac{1}{3} + \frac{1}{15}$
C. $\frac{1}{3} + \frac{1}{5} + \frac{1}{10}$
D. $\frac{2}{9} + \frac{1}{6} + \frac{1}{3}$

18. Describe a situation in which you might add $\frac{1}{3} + \frac{1}{4} + \frac{1}{2}$.

19. Use each digit from 1 to 4 once to make this equation true.

$\frac{■}{6} + \frac{■}{5} + \frac{■}{■} = \frac{49}{30}$

C Extending

20. About $\frac{1}{3}$ of Canadians regularly read news online. Another 12% rarely read news online. What fraction of Canadians never read news online?

How often do you read news online?
- ☐ regularly
- ☐ rarely
- ☐ never

21. This year, $\frac{3}{5}$ of the students in Fiona's class are girls. Fiona notices that $\frac{2}{3}$ of these girls wear braces. Only $\frac{1}{2}$ of the boys wear braces. What fraction of all the students in Fiona's class wear braces?

9.2 Adding and Subtracting Fractions Greater Than 1

You will need
- fraction models (such as pattern blocks, grids and counters, and number lines)

▶ **GOAL**
Solve problems by adding or subtracting mixed numbers and improper fractions.

Learn about the Math

Reilly is using his grandmother's recipes to make cookies. He has enough white sugar to make four batches of chocolate cookies.

Chocolate Cookies

2 cups unsalted butter
$1\frac{1}{3}$ cups white sugar
1 cup brown sugar
2 large eggs
4 tablespoons melted chocolate

Cherry Cookies

3/4 c. dried cherries
1/4 c. orange juice
1/2 c. butter or margarine
1/2 c. packed light brown sugar
1/2 c. white sugar
1 egg
1 teaspoon vanilla

? How much white sugar is left over if Reilly makes seven batches of cherry cookies instead of four batches of chocolate cookies?

Example 1: Adding using pattern blocks

Calculate the amount of white sugar Reilly needs for

a) four batches of chocolate cookies

b) seven batches of cherry cookies

Reilly's Solution

a) $1\frac{1}{3} + 1\frac{1}{3} + 1\frac{1}{3} + 1\frac{1}{3} = 4\frac{4}{3}$, or $5\frac{1}{3}$

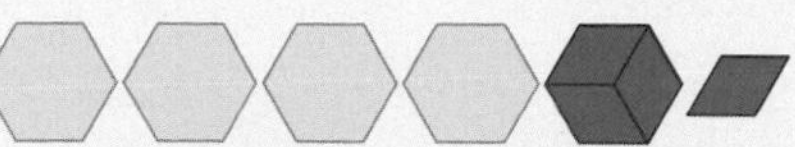

I need $5\frac{1}{3}$ cups of white sugar to make four batches of chocolate cookies.

I added four $1\frac{1}{3}$ cup measures to calculate the number of cups of white sugar in four batches of chocolate cookies.

There are 4 whole cups and 4 one third cups. That's $4 + \frac{4}{3}$, or $4 + 1 + \frac{1}{3}$.

b) $7 \times \frac{1}{2} = \frac{7}{2}$, or $3\frac{1}{2}$

I need $3\frac{1}{2}$ cups of white sugar to make seven batches of cherry cookies.

I need $7 \times \frac{1}{2}$ cups of sugar to make seven batches of cherry cookies.

It takes 2 halves to make a whole. So $\frac{7}{2}$, or 7 halves, is 3 sets of 2 halves and another half.

NEL

Example 2: Subtracting using equivalent fractions

Calculate the amount of white sugar left over if Reilly makes seven batches of cherry cookies instead of four batches of chocolate cookies.

Tamara's Solution

Reilly needed $5\frac{1}{3}$ cups of white sugar for the chocolate cookies and $3\frac{1}{2}$ cups for the cherry cookies.

I estimated that the difference will be about about $5 - 3 = 2$.

$$5\frac{1}{3} - 3\frac{1}{2} = 5\frac{2}{6} - 3\frac{3}{6}$$

I subtracted using equivalent fractions with a common denominator of $3 \times 2 = 6$.

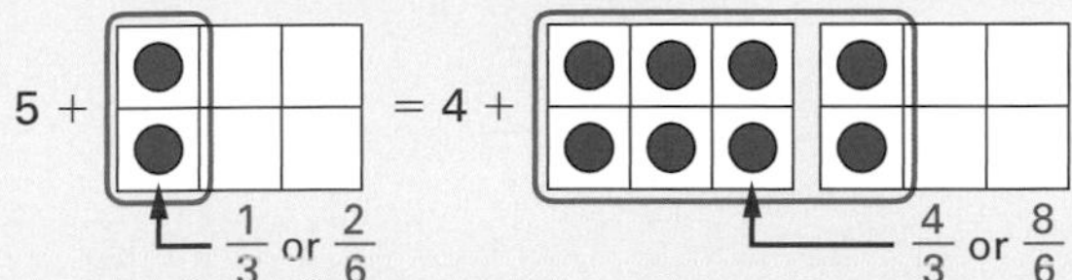

I had to subtract $\frac{3}{6}$ from $\frac{2}{6}$, but $\frac{2}{6} < \frac{3}{6}$. So, I regrouped one of the 5 wholes to get more sixths. Then I had 4 wholes and $\frac{8}{6}$ instead of 5 wholes and $\frac{2}{6}$.

$$5\frac{2}{6} - 3\frac{3}{6} = 4\frac{8}{6} - 3\frac{3}{6}$$
$$= 1\frac{5}{6}$$

I represented the fraction parts using grids and subtracted.

$1\frac{5}{6}$ cups of white sugar will be left over.

$1\frac{5}{6}$ makes sense since it's almost 2.

Manuel's Solution

$$5\frac{1}{3} - 3\frac{1}{2} = \frac{16}{3} - \frac{7}{2}$$
$$= \frac{32}{6} - \frac{21}{6}$$
$$= \frac{11}{6}\text{, or } 1\frac{5}{6}$$

I subtracted using improper fractions.

To subtract halves from thirds, I used equivalent fractions with a denominator of $3 \times 2 = 6$. This let me calculate the difference by comparing.

I subtracted the numerators to compare the number of sixths. The difference is 11 sixths.

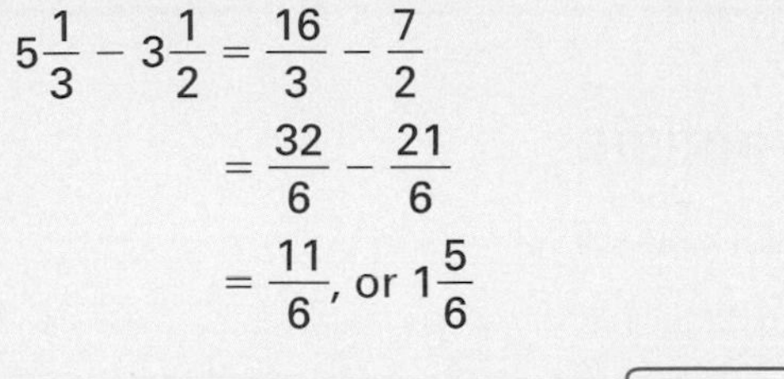

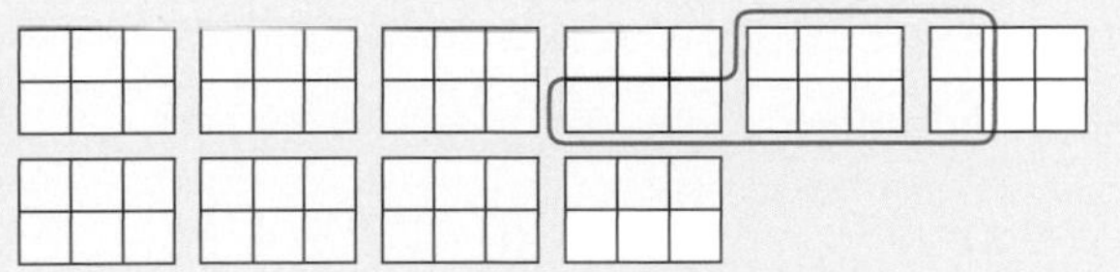

$1\frac{5}{6}$ cups of white sugar will be left over.

Reflecting

1. What other models could Reilly, Tamara, and Manuel have used?
2. Why was the result in both examples a fraction with a denominator of 6?
3. Why is it easier to estimate a difference using mixed numbers rather than improper fractions?

Work with the Math

Example 3: Adding and subtracting mixed numbers

Caleb combined $1\frac{1}{2}$ cans of yellow paint with $2\frac{3}{4}$ cans of blue paint. He used $3\frac{2}{5}$ cans to paint his room. How much paint was left over?

Solution A:
Using mixed numbers

$$1\frac{1}{2} + 2\frac{3}{4} = 1\frac{2}{4} + 2\frac{3}{4}$$
$$= 3\frac{5}{4}$$
$$= 4\frac{1}{4}$$

$$4\frac{1}{4} - 3\frac{2}{5} = 4\frac{5}{20} - 3\frac{8}{20}$$
$$= 3\frac{25}{20} - 3\frac{8}{20}$$
$$= \frac{17}{20}$$

$\frac{17}{20}$ cans were left over.

Solution B:
Using improper fractions

$$1\frac{1}{2} + 2\frac{3}{4} = \frac{3}{2} + \frac{11}{4}$$
$$= \frac{6}{4} + \frac{11}{4}$$
$$= \frac{17}{4}$$

$$\frac{17}{4} - 3\frac{2}{5} = \frac{17}{4} - \frac{17}{5}$$
$$= \frac{85}{20} - \frac{68}{20}$$
$$= \frac{17}{20}$$

$\frac{17}{20}$ cans were left over.

Solution C:
Using a TI-15 calculator

1 [n] 2 [+] 3 [n] 4 [+] 1 [+] 2 [=]

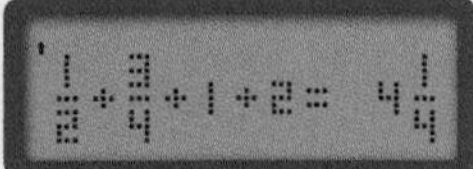

4 [+] 1 [n] 4 [−] 3 [−] 2 [n] 5 [=]

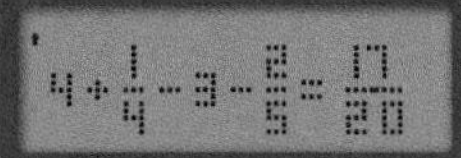

$\frac{17}{20}$ cans were left over.

A Checking

4. Reilly has exactly enough white sugar for five batches of cherry cookies. He decides to make five batches of chocolate cookies instead. How much more white sugar does he need?

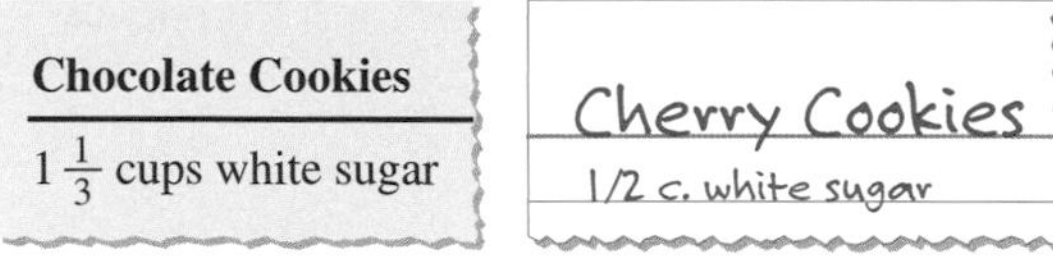

5. Model and solve.

a) $2\frac{1}{4} + 2\frac{2}{3}$ **b)** $2\frac{1}{4} - 1\frac{5}{8}$

6. Calculate.

a) $5\frac{7}{8} + 2\frac{5}{6}$ **b)** $10\frac{1}{5} - 7\frac{5}{6}$

B Practising

7. Model and solve.

a) $3\frac{1}{2} + 2\frac{4}{5}$ **b)** $2\frac{3}{5} - \frac{3}{4}$

8. Calculate.

a) $1\frac{2}{5} + 3\frac{4}{5}$

b) $5\frac{1}{3} + 3\frac{3}{5}$

c) $\frac{9}{2} + \frac{8}{3}$

d) $2\frac{2}{3} + 4\frac{4}{5}$

e) $2\frac{3}{4} + 5\frac{1}{6}$

f) $2\frac{1}{5} + \frac{7}{3} + 5\frac{1}{2}$

9. Calculate.

a) $4\frac{2}{5} - 2\frac{4}{5}$

b) $5\frac{3}{7} - 3\frac{1}{4}$

c) $\frac{21}{4} - \frac{22}{5}$

d) $\frac{38}{5} - 3\frac{1}{2}$

10. Jasleen goes to bed 3 h after dinner. Yesterday, she spent $1\frac{1}{2}$ h on her homework and $\frac{2}{3}$ h on the telephone after dinner. How much time did she have left before bedtime?

11. Jeff painted $1\frac{3}{4}$ walls in the computer room. How many walls does he still have to paint if the computer room has 4 walls?

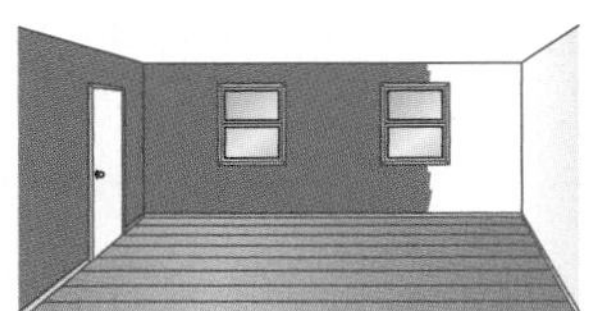

12. Mei used a number line to model each calculation. Explain how you know that her model is correct.

a) $2\frac{1}{3} + 3\frac{1}{6} = 5\frac{1}{2}$

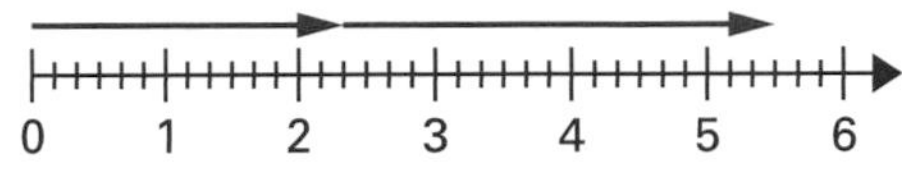

b) $3\frac{1}{4} - 1\frac{1}{2} = 1\frac{3}{4}$

0 1 2 3 4 5 6

13. Which difference is greater?

a) $5\frac{1}{3} - 4\frac{1}{2}$ b) $6\frac{1}{2} - 3\frac{2}{9}$

14. This week, Anita spent $3\frac{1}{2}$ h practising the piano. She also spent $6\frac{1}{4}$ h at soccer practice and $4\frac{1}{3}$ h on the telephone.

a) How much time, in total, did Anita spend on the piano and at soccer?

b) How much more time did Anita spend at soccer than on the phone?

15. Describe a situation in which you might calculate $3\frac{1}{4} - 1\frac{1}{2}$.

16. Aviv cut out the ads on 5 pages of a newspaper. He discovered that when he put the ads together, they filled $1\frac{1}{3}$ pages. How many pages would the non-advertising parts of these pages fill if Aviv put them together?

17. Kevin added two mixed numbers, $4\frac{\blacksquare}{\blacksquare}$ and $3\frac{\blacksquare}{\blacksquare}$. What could the whole number part of the answer be? Why?

18. Jeff added two fractions. Lydia subtracted the same two fractions. Jeff's answer was $\frac{3}{4}$ greater than Lydia's. What could the fractions be?

19. To calculate $7\frac{1}{8} - 2\frac{2}{3}$, Lee added $\frac{1}{3}$ to $4\frac{1}{8}$. Why do you think that Lee did this?

C Extending

20. Each car on a commuter train holds 20 people. On a particular morning, 5 cars were 90% full and 3 cars were 65% full. If the people were rearranged to fill as many cars as possible, how many cars would be filled?

21. A large popcorn bag holds four times as much as a small popcorn bag. At the end of a party, $3\frac{1}{3}$ small bags and $2\frac{1}{4}$ large bags were left.

a) How many small bags would the leftover popcorn fill?

b) How many large bags would the leftover popcorn fill?

22. Use each of the digits 1, 2, 4, 5, 8, and 9 once to create the greatest possible value of the following expression. The mixed numbers have to be in proper form, without being renamed.

$$\blacksquare\frac{\blacksquare}{3} - \blacksquare\frac{\blacksquare}{6} + 7\frac{\blacksquare}{\blacksquare}$$

9.3 Exploring Fraction Patterns

▶ **GOAL**

Analyze fraction patterns that involve addition and subtraction.

Explore the Math

The students in Jordan's class are creating fraction pattern puzzles. This is the beginning of Jordan's puzzle.

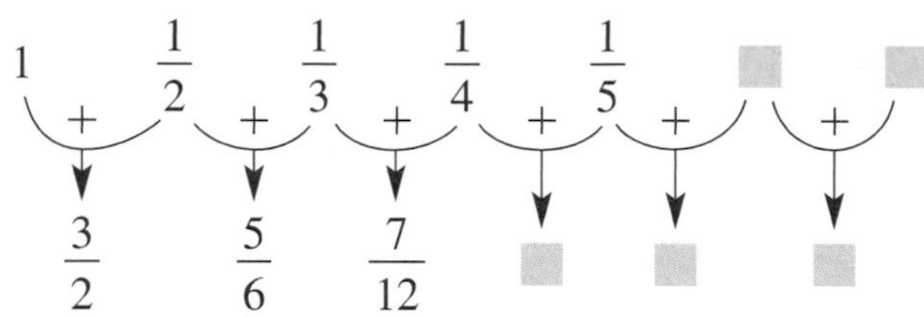

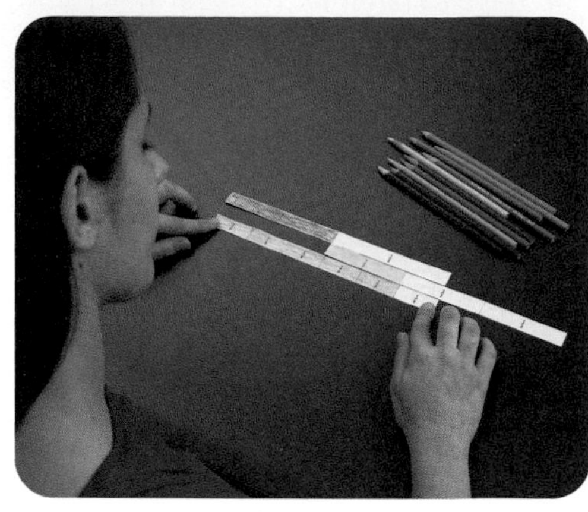

? How can you predict the values in a fraction pattern puzzle?

A. Extend the pattern to fill in the missing numbers in Jordan's puzzle. Do the values of the fractions in each row increase or decrease?

B. Describe the pattern in each row in words.

C. Predict the 20th fraction in each row.

D. Write an algebraic expression to describe the *n*th term in each row.

E. Repeat steps A to D with Manuel's fraction pattern puzzle, shown below.

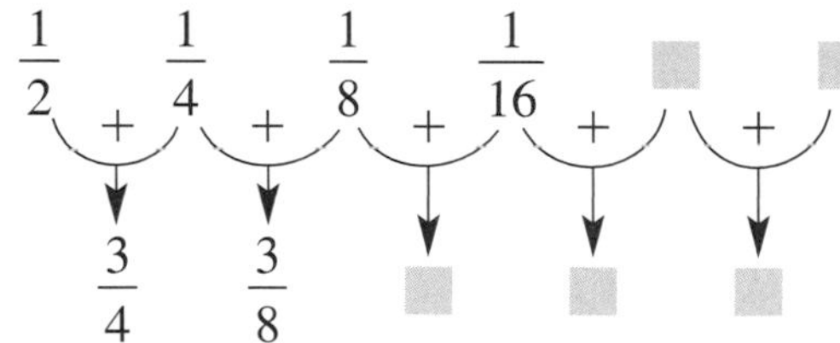

F. Repeat steps A to D with Sheree's fraction pattern puzzle.

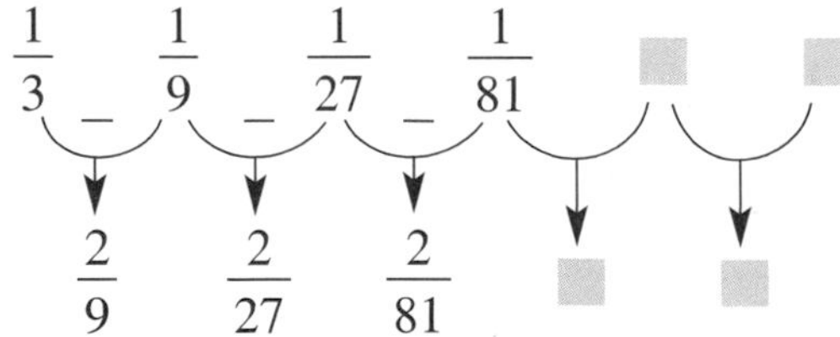

Reflecting

1. Why were the numerators in the second row of Jordan's pattern all odd, while the denominators were all even?

2. How are Manuel's and Sheree's patterns similar?

3. Why does each pattern work the way it does?

Mental Imagery

COMPARING NEGATIVE RATIONALS

Fractions and their equivalent decimals are **rational numbers**. The set of rational numbers also includes negatives. On a number line, each negative fraction or negative decimal is placed the same distance to the left of 0 as its positive opposite is to the right of 0. For example, $-\frac{4}{5}$ (or -0.8) is placed at position A since $\frac{4}{5}$ (or 0.8), its opposite, is at position B. The two positions are symmetrical about 0.

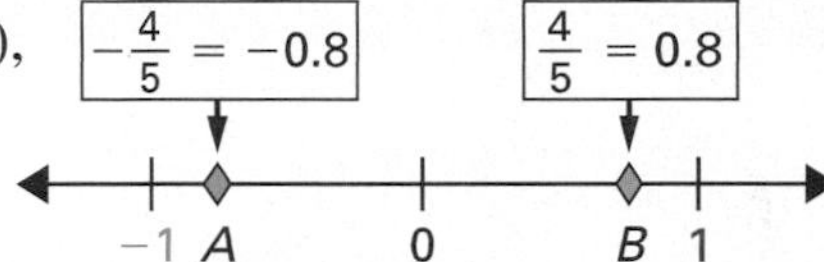

The number line below shows that $\frac{3}{8} < \frac{1}{2}$, so $\frac{3}{8}$ is closer to 0 than $\frac{1}{2}$.

This makes $-\frac{3}{8}$ closer to 0 than $-\frac{1}{2}$, so $-\frac{1}{2} < -\frac{3}{8}$.

$-\frac{1}{2} < -\frac{3}{8}$ since $+\frac{1}{2} > +\frac{3}{8}$

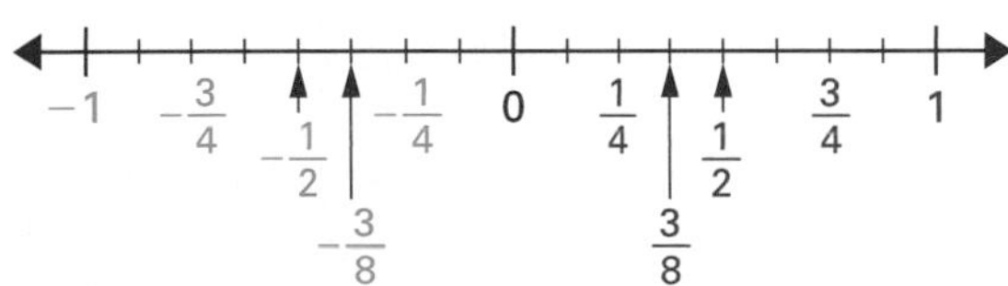

1. Which is less?

   a) $-\frac{3}{5}$ or $-\frac{2}{3}$

   b) $-\frac{2}{3}$ or $\frac{2}{5}$

   c) 0.7 or -0.6

   d) -1.5 or $-\frac{2}{8}$

2. Name three values for each ■ to make the inequality true.

   a) $-\frac{■}{5} < -\frac{1}{2}$

   b) $-2\frac{■}{4} < -\frac{4}{5}$

   c) $-\frac{2}{■} < -\frac{2}{5}$

   d) $-■.3 < -2.4$

9.4 Fractions of Fractions

You will need
- fraction strips
- coloured pencils
- scissors

▶ **GOAL**

Represent one fraction as part of another fraction.

Learn about the Math

Teo is playing a fraction game with his friends. The game board is a fraction strip tower. Each player picks a card and covers sections of fraction strips.

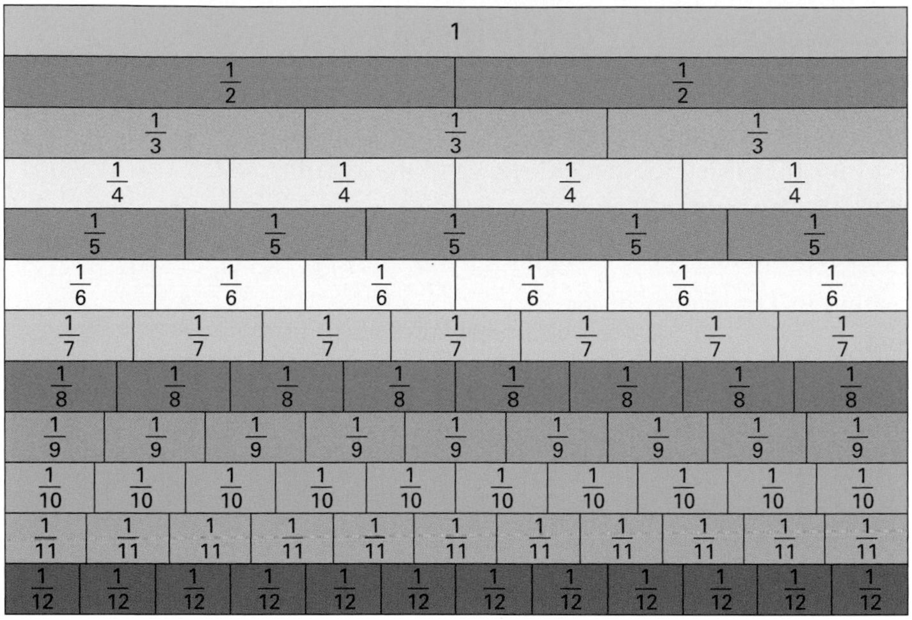

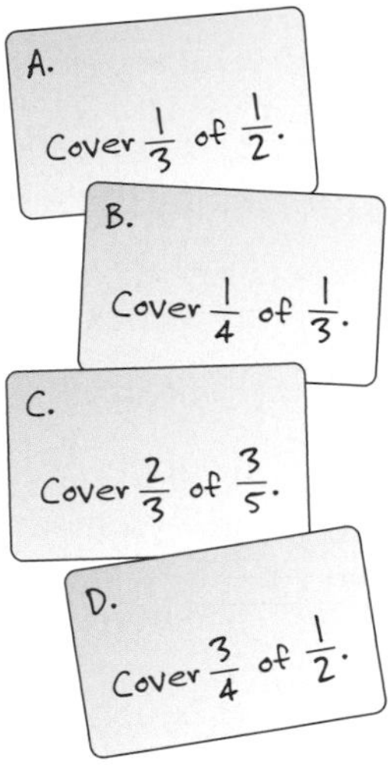

1

$\frac{1}{2}$ $\frac{1}{2}$

$\frac{1}{3}$ $\frac{1}{3}$ $\frac{1}{3}$

$\frac{1}{4}$ $\frac{1}{4}$ $\frac{1}{4}$ $\frac{1}{4}$

$\frac{1}{5}$ $\frac{1}{5}$ $\frac{1}{5}$ $\frac{1}{5}$ $\frac{1}{5}$

$\frac{1}{6}$ $\frac{1}{6}$ $\frac{1}{6}$ $\frac{1}{6}$ $\frac{1}{6}$ $\frac{1}{6}$

$\frac{1}{7}$ $\frac{1}{7}$ $\frac{1}{7}$ $\frac{1}{7}$ $\frac{1}{7}$ $\frac{1}{7}$ $\frac{1}{7}$

$\frac{1}{8}$ $\frac{1}{8}$ $\frac{1}{8}$ $\frac{1}{8}$ $\frac{1}{8}$ $\frac{1}{8}$ $\frac{1}{8}$ $\frac{1}{8}$

$\frac{1}{9}$ $\frac{1}{9}$ $\frac{1}{9}$ $\frac{1}{9}$ $\frac{1}{9}$ $\frac{1}{9}$ $\frac{1}{9}$ $\frac{1}{9}$ $\frac{1}{9}$

$\frac{1}{10}$ $\frac{1}{10}$ $\frac{1}{10}$ $\frac{1}{10}$ $\frac{1}{10}$ $\frac{1}{10}$ $\frac{1}{10}$ $\frac{1}{10}$ $\frac{1}{10}$ $\frac{1}{10}$

$\frac{1}{11}$ $\frac{1}{11}$ $\frac{1}{11}$ $\frac{1}{11}$ $\frac{1}{11}$ $\frac{1}{11}$ $\frac{1}{11}$ $\frac{1}{11}$ $\frac{1}{11}$ $\frac{1}{11}$ $\frac{1}{11}$

$\frac{1}{12}$ $\frac{1}{12}$ $\frac{1}{12}$ $\frac{1}{12}$ $\frac{1}{12}$ $\frac{1}{12}$ $\frac{1}{12}$ $\frac{1}{12}$ $\frac{1}{12}$ $\frac{1}{12}$ $\frac{1}{12}$ $\frac{1}{12}$

A. Cover $\frac{1}{3}$ of $\frac{1}{2}$.

B. Cover $\frac{1}{4}$ of $\frac{1}{3}$.

C. Cover $\frac{2}{3}$ of $\frac{3}{5}$.

D. Cover $\frac{3}{4}$ of $\frac{1}{2}$.

? What cards can you make to cover $\frac{1}{8}$?

A. Suppose that Teo picks card A. Which fraction strip section can he cover? How does the fraction tower show that this is the right fraction strip?

B. Suppose that Teo picks card B. How do you know that the section he covers has to be shorter than the $\frac{1}{3}$ section?

C. Suppose that Teo picks card C. Why can he cover sections in the same strip as the $\frac{3}{5}$ section?

D. Suppose that Teo picks card D. Which fraction strip can he use? How many of the sections in this strip can he cover?

E. Make up at least three cards that Teo can use to cover $\frac{1}{8}$.

Reflecting

1. When might $\frac{1}{2}$ of one fraction be greater than $\frac{3}{4}$ of another fraction?
2. Can there be more than one way to describe a section of a fraction strip as a fraction of another fraction? Use examples to support your answer.
3. How can you use a fraction strip model to describe a fraction of a fraction? Use an example to explain.

Work with the Math

Example 1: Relating fractions using fraction strips

Use fraction strips to show $\frac{1}{2}$ of $\frac{1}{3}$.

Jordan's Solution

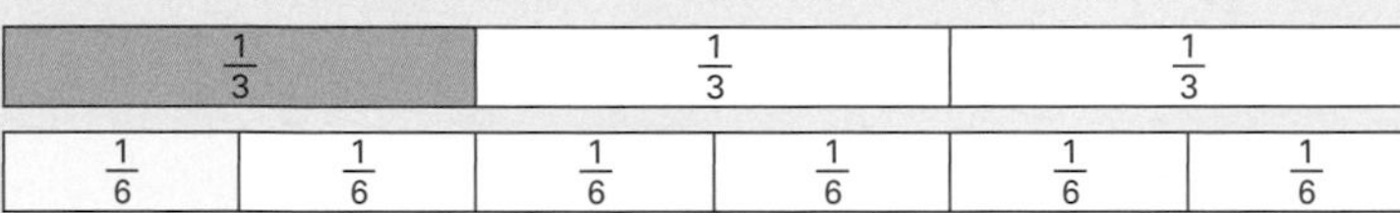

First I found the strip in the tower that $\frac{1}{3}$ is in.

Then I looked for a strip with twice as many sections so that I could show $\frac{1}{2}$ of $\frac{1}{3}$.

$\frac{1}{2}$ of $\frac{1}{3} = \frac{1}{6}$

Example 2: Relating fractions using equivalent representations

Use fraction strips to show $\frac{2}{3}$ of $\frac{2}{5}$.

Manuel's Solution

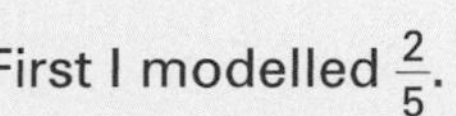

First I modelled $\frac{2}{5}$.

Since I wanted to show $\frac{2}{3}$ of $\frac{2}{5}$, I divided each fifth into 3 equal smaller sections.

$$\frac{2}{5} = \frac{2 \times 3}{5 \times 3} = \frac{6}{15}$$

Then I coloured $\frac{2}{3}$ of each fifth.

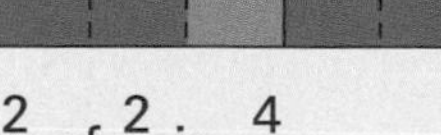

$\frac{2}{3}$ of $\frac{2}{5}$ is $\frac{4}{15}$.

A Checking

Use the fraction strip tower.

1

$\frac{1}{2}$ $\frac{1}{2}$

$\frac{1}{3}$ $\frac{1}{3}$ $\frac{1}{3}$

$\frac{1}{4}$ $\frac{1}{4}$ $\frac{1}{4}$ $\frac{1}{4}$

$\frac{1}{5}$ $\frac{1}{5}$ $\frac{1}{5}$ $\frac{1}{5}$ $\frac{1}{5}$

$\frac{1}{6}$ $\frac{1}{6}$ $\frac{1}{6}$ $\frac{1}{6}$ $\frac{1}{6}$ $\frac{1}{6}$

$\frac{1}{7}$ $\frac{1}{7}$ $\frac{1}{7}$ $\frac{1}{7}$ $\frac{1}{7}$ $\frac{1}{7}$ $\frac{1}{7}$

$\frac{1}{8}$ $\frac{1}{8}$ $\frac{1}{8}$ $\frac{1}{8}$ $\frac{1}{8}$ $\frac{1}{8}$ $\frac{1}{8}$ $\frac{1}{8}$

$\frac{1}{9}$ $\frac{1}{9}$ $\frac{1}{9}$ $\frac{1}{9}$ $\frac{1}{9}$ $\frac{1}{9}$ $\frac{1}{9}$ $\frac{1}{9}$ $\frac{1}{9}$

$\frac{1}{10}$ $\frac{1}{10}$ $\frac{1}{10}$ $\frac{1}{10}$ $\frac{1}{10}$ $\frac{1}{10}$ $\frac{1}{10}$ $\frac{1}{10}$ $\frac{1}{10}$ $\frac{1}{10}$

$\frac{1}{11}$ $\frac{1}{11}$ $\frac{1}{11}$ $\frac{1}{11}$ $\frac{1}{11}$ $\frac{1}{11}$ $\frac{1}{11}$ $\frac{1}{11}$ $\frac{1}{11}$ $\frac{1}{11}$ $\frac{1}{11}$

$\frac{1}{12}$ $\frac{1}{12}$ $\frac{1}{12}$ $\frac{1}{12}$ $\frac{1}{12}$ $\frac{1}{12}$ $\frac{1}{12}$ $\frac{1}{12}$ $\frac{1}{12}$ $\frac{1}{12}$ $\frac{1}{12}$ $\frac{1}{12}$

4. Which section of the fraction strip tower shows each value?

a) $\frac{2}{3}$ of $\frac{3}{7}$ **b)** $\frac{1}{3}$ of $\frac{2}{3}$

5. Arrange these values in order from least to greatest.

a) $\frac{2}{3}$ of $\frac{9}{10}$

b) $\frac{3}{5}$ of $\frac{5}{9}$

c) $\frac{1}{2}$ of $\frac{6}{7}$

6. This picture models a fraction of a fraction. Complete the sentence: ▒ of ▒ is ▒.

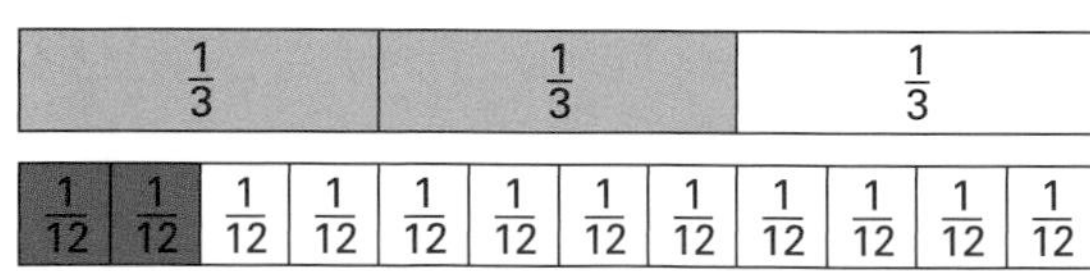

B Practising

7. Each picture models a fraction of a fraction. Complete this sentence for each picture: ▒ of ▒ is ▒.

a)

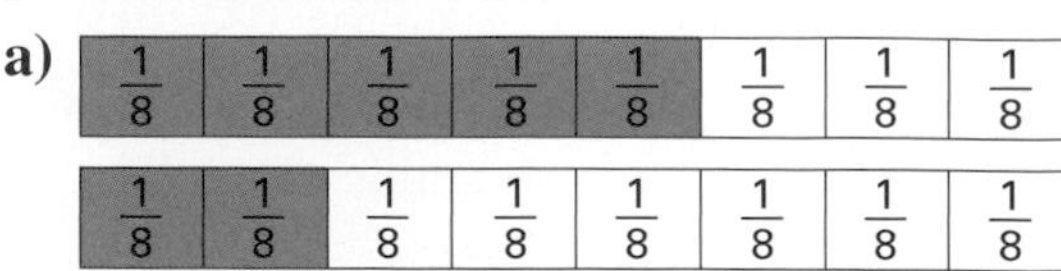

b)

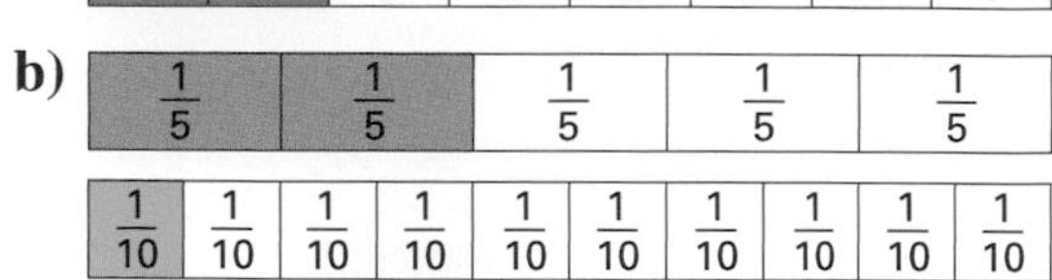

c)

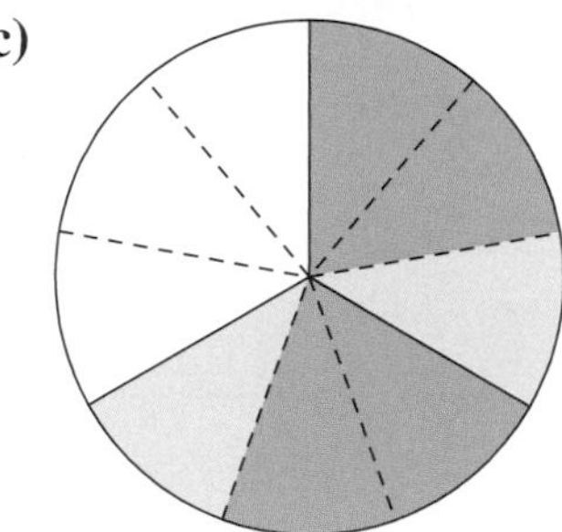

8. What section of the fraction strip tower shows each value?

a) $\frac{1}{2}$ of $\frac{1}{6}$ **d)** $\frac{5}{6}$ of $\frac{1}{2}$

b) $\frac{1}{3}$ of $\frac{1}{4}$ **e)** $\frac{3}{4}$ of $\frac{4}{9}$

c) $\frac{1}{6}$ of $\frac{1}{2}$ **f)** $\frac{4}{5}$ of $\frac{1}{2}$

9. a) How does this picture show that $\frac{1}{2}$ of $\frac{3}{4}$ is $\frac{3}{8}$?

$\frac{1}{4}$ $\frac{1}{4}$ $\frac{1}{4}$ $\frac{1}{4}$

$\frac{1}{8}$ $\frac{1}{8}$ $\frac{1}{8}$ $\frac{1}{8}$ $\frac{1}{8}$ $\frac{1}{8}$ $\frac{1}{8}$ $\frac{1}{8}$

b) Draw a picture to show $\frac{3}{4}$ of $\frac{1}{2}$.

c) What do you notice?

10. Sketch an appropriate fraction strip, and shade the fraction $\frac{4}{11}$. Then use your sketch to show each expression.

a) $\frac{1}{4}$ of $\frac{4}{11}$ b) $\frac{1}{2}$ of $\frac{4}{11}$

11. How does this picture show that $\frac{2}{3}$ of $\frac{1}{2}$ is $\frac{1}{3}$?

$\frac{1}{2}$ (shaded)			$\frac{1}{2}$		
$\frac{1}{6}$	$\frac{1}{6}$	$\frac{1}{6}$	$\frac{1}{6}$	$\frac{1}{6}$	$\frac{1}{6}$

12. What is the missing fraction in each sentence?

a) $\frac{3}{8}$ is $\frac{3}{5}$ of ■.

b) $\frac{2}{3}$ is ■ of $\frac{3}{4}$.

c) ■ is $\frac{1}{4}$ of $\frac{2}{5}$.

13. Explain how you know that $\frac{2}{3}$ of $\frac{4}{5}$ is the same as each expression below.

a) twice as much as $\frac{1}{3}$ of $\frac{4}{5}$

b) twice as much as $\frac{2}{3}$ of $\frac{2}{5}$

c) four times as much as $\frac{1}{3}$ of $\frac{2}{5}$

14. Which is easier to determine, $\frac{1}{6}$ of $\frac{6}{7}$ or $\frac{1}{6}$ of $\frac{5}{7}$? Why?

15. About $\frac{2}{5}$ of the students in a school were invited to participate in a special video-conferencing program. Only $\frac{1}{3}$ of these students brought in their permission forms by the first day of the program. What fraction of the students were permitted to participate in the first day of the program?

16. Write each fraction as a fraction of another fraction (not 1).

a) $\frac{1}{5}$ b) $\frac{2}{8}$ c) $\frac{5}{12}$ d) $\frac{3}{7}$

17. Describe a situation in which you might calculate $\frac{3}{4}$ of $\frac{8}{10}$.

C Extending

18. Draw a circle. Show that $\frac{1}{2}$ of $\frac{1}{2}$ of $\frac{1}{2}$ is $\frac{1}{8}$.

19. Each fraction below is $\frac{2}{3}$ of another fraction. What is the other fraction?

a) $\frac{2}{9}$ b) $\frac{2}{7}$ c) $\frac{1}{4}$ d) $\frac{6}{15}$

20. Draw a picture to show that $\frac{2}{3}$ of $1\frac{1}{2}$ is 1.

21. About $\frac{3}{4}$ of the students in Ms. Erskine's class use instant messaging every day. About 60% of these students are girls.

a) What fraction of the whole class are the girls who use instant messaging?

b) How many students do you think are in the class? Why?

22. Why might using a diagram to calculate $\frac{1}{3}$ of $\frac{3}{5}$ be better than multiplying 0.333 33… by 0.6?

9.5 Multiplying Fractions

You will need
- fraction strips
- grid paper
- coloured pencils

▶ **GOAL**

Multiply two fractions less than 1.

Learn about the Math

About $\frac{1}{10}$ of Canadians who are 12 and older downhill ski. About $\frac{2}{5}$ of these skiers are between the ages of 12 and 24.

? What fraction of the Canadian population between the ages of 12 and 24 downhill ski?

Example 1: Using a fraction strip model

The fraction of Canadians between the ages of 12 and 24 who downhill ski is $\frac{2}{5}$ of $\frac{1}{10}$. What fraction is this?

Jordan's Solution

$\frac{1}{10}$	$\frac{1}{10}$	$\frac{1}{10}$	$\frac{1}{10}$	$\frac{1}{10}$	$\frac{1}{10}$	$\frac{1}{10}$	$\frac{1}{10}$	$\frac{1}{10}$	$\frac{1}{10}$

I used fraction strips to model $\frac{2}{5}$ of $\frac{1}{10}$.

I divided $\frac{1}{10}$ into 5 equal sections and coloured 2 of the sections.

I divided each $\frac{1}{10}$ the same way to determine the size of each section.

I made $5 \times 10 = 50$ sections. Only 2 sections were coloured.

So, $\frac{2}{5}$ of $\frac{1}{10}$ is $\frac{2}{50}$.

$\frac{2}{50} = \frac{1}{25}$ since every 2 sections of $\frac{1}{50}$ can be combined to make 1 section of $\frac{1}{25}$.

$$\frac{2}{5} \text{ of } \frac{1}{10} = \frac{2}{50}$$
$$= \frac{1}{25}$$

About $\frac{1}{25}$ of Canadians between the ages of 12 and 24 downhill ski.

Example 2: Using a grid model to determine a fraction of a fraction

Calculate $\frac{2}{5} \times \frac{1}{10}$.

Sheree's Solution

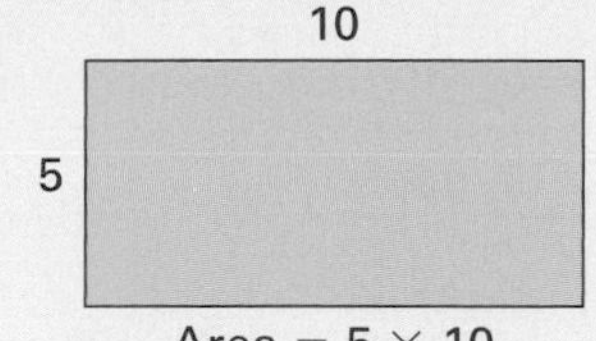

To calculate the area of a rectangle, you multiply the two dimensions. The area of a rectangle 5 units wide and 10 units long is 5 × 10. So, $\frac{2}{5} \times \frac{1}{10}$ must be the area of a rectangle that is $\frac{2}{5}$ of a unit wide and $\frac{1}{10}$ of a unit long.

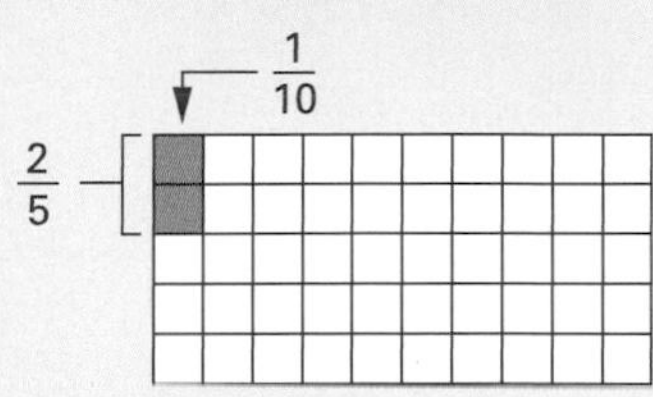

I used a 5-by-10 grid to help me see the fifths and tenths. There are 5 × 10 or 50 sections.

The purple rectangle is $\frac{1}{10}$ wide and $\frac{2}{5}$ long. It is $\frac{2}{50}$ of the whole.

$\frac{2}{50}$ can be written in simplest form as $\frac{1}{25}$.

$$\frac{2}{5} \times \frac{1}{10} = \frac{2 \times 1}{5 \times 10}$$
$$= \frac{2}{50}$$
$$= \frac{1}{25}$$

Reflecting

1. Calculating $\frac{2}{5}$ of $\frac{1}{10}$ is the same as calculating $\frac{2}{5} \times \frac{1}{10}$. How does Sheree's solution show this?
2. How can you use a model to determine the numerator and denominator of a product?
3. Write a rule for multiplying two fractions less than 1.

Work with the Math

Example 3: Multiplying fractions less than 1

About $\frac{2}{3}$ of the students in Windham Ridge School are in Grades 7 and 8. About $\frac{5}{8}$ of these students are girls. What fraction of the students in the school are girls in Grades 7 and 8?

Solution A: Using fraction strips

This model shows $\frac{5}{8}$ of $\frac{2}{3}$. Divide $\frac{2}{3}$ into 8 equivalent sections, and colour 5 of the sections.

$\frac{1}{3}$	$\frac{1}{3}$	$\frac{1}{3}$

$\frac{1}{12}$	$\frac{1}{12}$	$\frac{1}{12}$	$\frac{1}{12}$	$\frac{1}{12}$	$\frac{1}{12}$	$\frac{1}{12}$	$\frac{1}{12}$	$\frac{1}{12}$	$\frac{1}{12}$	$\frac{1}{12}$	$\frac{1}{12}$

$$\frac{5}{8} \times \frac{2}{3} = \frac{5}{12}$$

So, $\frac{5}{12}$ of the students are girls in Grades 7 and 8.

Solution B: Using an area model

Colour a 3-by-8 rectangle to show $\frac{5}{8}$ by $\frac{2}{3}$.

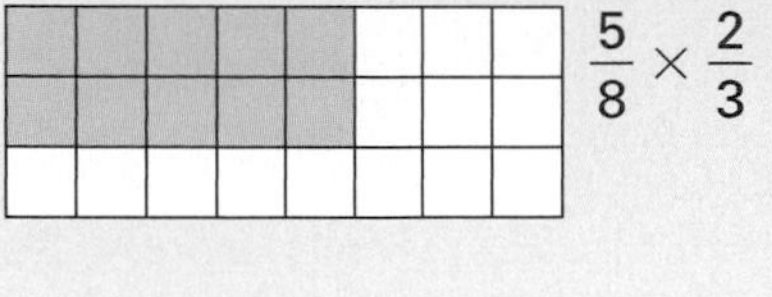

$$\frac{5}{8} \times \frac{2}{3} = \frac{5 \times 2}{8 \times 3} = \frac{10}{24} = \frac{5}{12}$$

So, $\frac{5}{12}$ of the students are girls in Grades 7 and 8.

A Checking

4. What multiplication expression does each model represent?

a)

$\frac{1}{4}$	$\frac{1}{4}$	$\frac{1}{4}$	$\frac{1}{4}$

$\frac{1}{12}$	$\frac{1}{12}$	$\frac{1}{12}$	$\frac{1}{12}$	$\frac{1}{12}$	$\frac{1}{12}$	$\frac{1}{12}$	$\frac{1}{12}$	$\frac{1}{12}$	$\frac{1}{12}$	$\frac{1}{12}$	$\frac{1}{12}$

b)

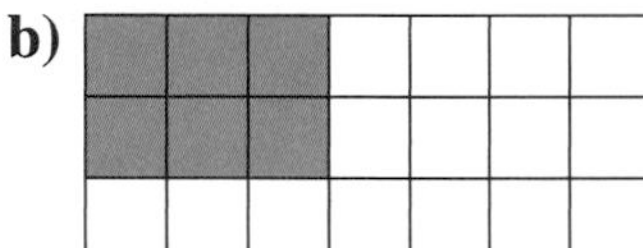

5. Draw a model for $\frac{3}{4} \times \frac{2}{5}$. Use your model to determine the product.

6. About $\frac{2}{11}$ of Canadian downhill skiers are from British Columbia. Recall that about $\frac{1}{10}$ of Canadians downhill ski. What fraction of all Canadians are downhill skiers from British Columbia?

B Practising

7. What multiplication expression does each model represent?

a)

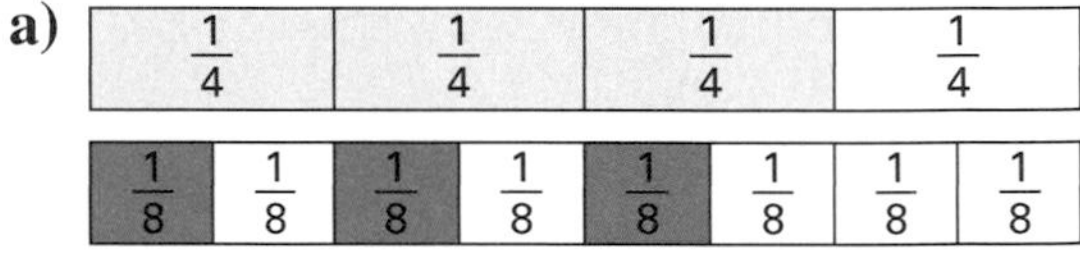

b)

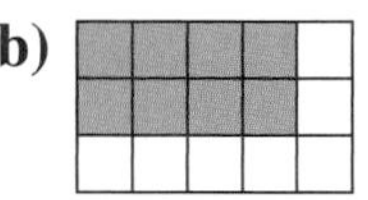

c)

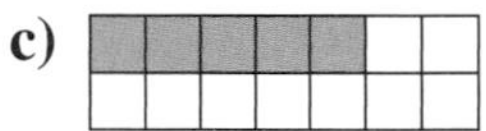

8. Draw a model for each multiplication expression. Determine the product.

a) $\frac{1}{2} \times \frac{3}{8}$

b) $\frac{4}{5} \times \frac{1}{3}$

c) $\frac{1}{6} \times \frac{2}{5}$

d) $\frac{3}{4} \times \frac{2}{6}$

9. Match each expression with its product.

a) $\frac{5}{6} \times \frac{7}{10}$

b) $\frac{3}{8} \times \frac{4}{9}$

c) $\frac{2}{6} \times \frac{9}{10}$

d) $\frac{4}{7} \times \frac{14}{15}$

$\frac{1}{6}$	$\frac{8}{15}$
$\frac{3}{10}$	$\frac{7}{12}$

10. Matthew's bed takes up $\frac{1}{3}$ of the width of his bedroom and $\frac{3}{5}$ of the length. What fraction of the area of the floor does Matthew's bed take up?

11. Jessica is awake $\frac{2}{3}$ of the day. She spends $\frac{5}{8}$ of this time at home.

a) What fraction of the day is Jessica awake at home?

b) How many hours is Jessica awake at home?

12. a) Complete this pattern, and continue it for three more products.

$4 \times \frac{1}{2} = \blacksquare$

$2 \times \frac{1}{2} = \blacksquare$

$1 \times \frac{1}{2} = \blacksquare$

$\frac{1}{2} \times \frac{1}{2} = \blacksquare$

b) How does this pattern explain the product of $\frac{1}{2} \times \frac{1}{2}$?

13. a) Draw a picture to show that $\frac{2}{5} \times \frac{3}{8} = \frac{6}{40}$.

b) List two other pairs of fractions with a product of $\frac{6}{40}$.

14. Daniel said that $\frac{a}{b} \times \frac{c}{d} = \frac{\blacksquare}{\blacksquare}$. Complete the missing fraction, and explain your thinking.

15. a) Recall that $a^2 = a \times a$ and $a^3 = a \times a \times a$. Calculate each power for $a = \frac{2}{3}$.

i) a^2 ii) a^3 iii) a^4

b) Why does a higher power of $\frac{2}{3}$ result in a lower product?

16. How does the product of two fractions less than 1 compare with the two fractions being multiplied? Is the product greater than, less than, or equal to each fraction? How do you know?

17. a) Calculate 0.4×0.3.

b) Rename each decimal as a fraction, and multiply. What do you notice?

C Extending

18. More than $\frac{3}{4}$ of Americans eat ice cream at least once a month. About $\frac{3}{10}$ of these people eat vanilla ice cream.

a) What fraction of Americans eat vanilla ice cream at least once a month?

b) According to recent statistics, there are about 300 million Americans. About how many of them eat vanilla ice cream at least once a month?

19. a) What is the probability of landing in the red A section?

b) Why does it make sense that the probability is $\frac{1}{2} \times \frac{1}{3}$?

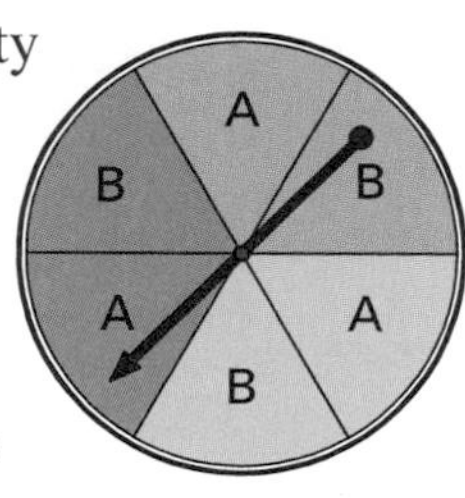

20. What is the value of a in $\frac{2}{7} \times \frac{a}{a+2} = \frac{2}{9}$?

21. What is the product of $\frac{1}{2} \times \frac{2}{3} \times \frac{3}{4} \times \frac{4}{5} \times \ldots \times \frac{99}{100}$?

Mid-Chapter Review

Frequently Asked Questions

Q: How do you add two fractions less than 1?

A: You can use equivalent fractions with the same denominator and add the numerators, or you can use a model. These methods work for all fractions, both greater than 1 and less than 1. Sometimes, you have to simplify the result.

For example, add $\frac{1}{2}$ and $\frac{1}{6}$.

$$\frac{1}{2} + \frac{1}{6} = \frac{3}{6} + \frac{1}{6}$$
$$= \frac{4}{6}$$
$$= \frac{2}{3}$$

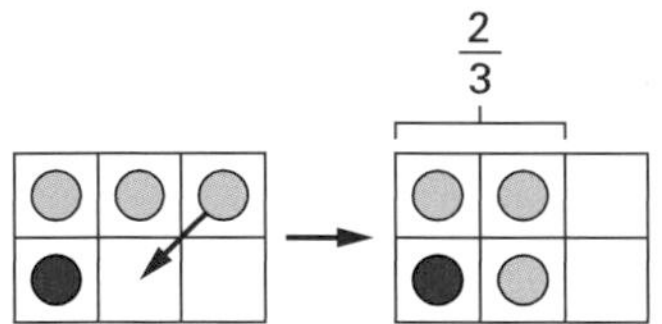

For example, add $\frac{4}{3}$ and $\frac{7}{6}$.

$$\frac{4}{3} + \frac{7}{6} = \frac{8}{6} + \frac{7}{6}$$
$$= \frac{15}{6}$$
$$= 2\frac{3}{6}$$
$$= 2\frac{1}{2}$$

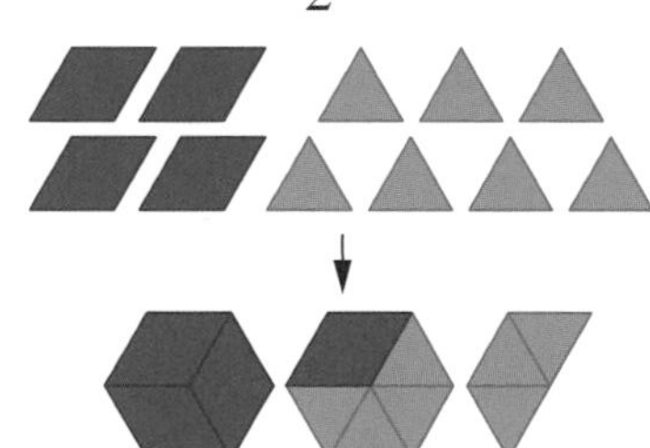

Q: How do you subtract two fractions less than 1?

A: You can use equivalent fractions with the same denominator and subtract the numerators, or you can use a model. These methods work for both proper and improper fractions. For example, calculate $\frac{3}{5} - \frac{1}{3}$.

$$\frac{3}{5} - \frac{1}{3} = \frac{9}{15} - \frac{5}{15}$$
$$= \frac{4}{15}$$

$\frac{1}{5}$	$\frac{1}{5}$	$\frac{1}{5}$	$\frac{1}{5}$	$\frac{1}{5}$

$\frac{1}{3}$	$\frac{1}{3}$	$\frac{1}{3}$

$\frac{1}{15}$	$\frac{1}{15}$	$\frac{1}{15}$	$\frac{1}{15}$	$\frac{1}{15}$	$\frac{1}{15}$	$\frac{1}{15}$	$\frac{1}{15}$	$\frac{1}{15}$	$\frac{1}{15}$	$\frac{1}{15}$	$\frac{1}{15}$	$\frac{1}{15}$	$\frac{1}{15}$	$\frac{1}{15}$

For example,

$$\frac{9}{4} - \frac{5}{3} = \frac{27}{12} - \frac{20}{12}$$
$$= \frac{7}{12}$$

Q: How do you add or subtract mixed numbers?

A1: Use a model to show addition or subtraction.

$3\frac{1}{2} - 2\frac{3}{5} = \frac{9}{10}$ $\quad 3\frac{1}{2} + 2\frac{3}{5} = 6\frac{1}{10}$

0 1 2 3 4 5 6

A2: Add or subtract the whole number parts and the fraction parts separately. Regroup when necessary.

$$3\frac{1}{2} + 2\frac{3}{5} = 3\frac{5}{10} + 2\frac{6}{10}$$
$$= 5\frac{11}{10}$$
$$= 6\frac{1}{10}$$

$$3\frac{1}{2} - 2\frac{3}{5} = 3\frac{5}{10} - 2\frac{6}{10}$$
$$= 2\frac{15}{10} - 2\frac{6}{10}$$
$$= \frac{9}{10}$$

Q: How can you multiply two fractions less than 1?

A1: You can model one fraction and then divide it into the appropriate number of sections to show the fraction of it. For example, to show $\frac{2}{3}$ of $\frac{6}{7}$, you can model $\frac{6}{7}$ and divide each of the 6 sevenths into thirds. Then, to show $\frac{2}{3}$, you colour 2 of each third.

$\frac{1}{7}$	$\frac{1}{7}$	$\frac{1}{7}$	$\frac{1}{7}$	$\frac{1}{7}$	$\frac{1}{7}$	$\frac{1}{7}$

$\frac{2}{3}$ of $\frac{6}{7}$ is $\frac{12}{21}$, or $\frac{4}{7}$.

A2: You can determine the area of a rectangle.

For example, to model $\frac{2}{3} \times \frac{2}{5}$, create a rectangle that is $\frac{2}{5}$ of a unit in length and $\frac{2}{3}$ of a unit in width.

$$\frac{2}{3} \times \frac{2}{5} = \frac{4}{15}$$

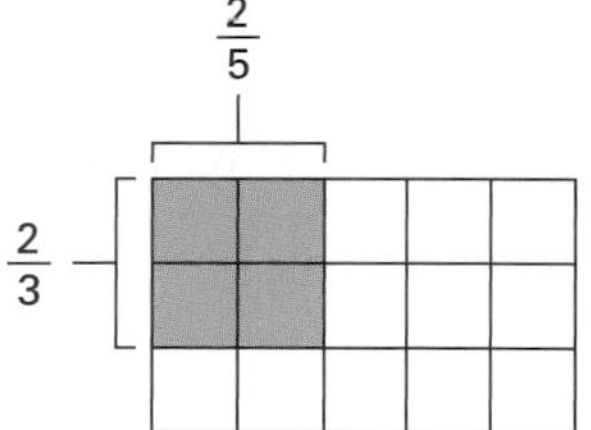

A3: Multiply the numerators, and multiply the denominators.

$$\frac{a}{b} \times \frac{c}{d} = \frac{a \times c}{b \times d}$$

For example,

$$\frac{2}{3} \times \frac{2}{5} = \frac{2 \times 2}{3 \times 5}$$
$$= \frac{4}{15}$$

Practice Questions

(9.1) **1. a)** What is the sum of $\frac{1}{2}$ and $\frac{1}{3}$?

b) How much greater is $\frac{2}{3}$ than $\frac{1}{6}$?

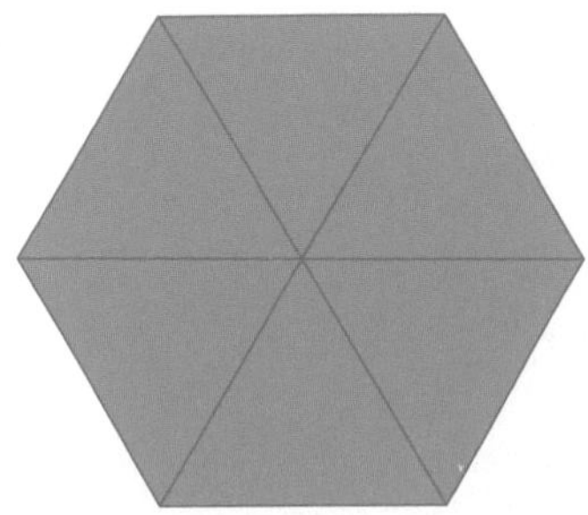

(9.1) **2.** Draw a model to show each calculation. Then determine the sum or difference.

a) $\frac{3}{4} + \frac{5}{6}$ **b)** $\frac{3}{8} - \frac{1}{6}$

(9.1) **3.** Estimate whether each sum is less than 1 or greater than 1.

a) $\frac{1}{3} + \frac{1}{4}$ **d)** $\frac{2}{3} + \frac{3}{5}$

b) $\frac{5}{8} + \frac{5}{8}$ **e)** $\frac{5}{6} + \frac{1}{10}$

c) $\frac{5}{8} + \frac{5}{10}$ **f)** $\frac{3}{4} + \frac{2}{5}$

(9.1) **4.** Calculate.

a) $\frac{5}{8} + \frac{1}{4}$ **d)** $\frac{3}{8} - \frac{1}{5}$

b) $\frac{7}{10} - \frac{1}{3}$ **e)** $\frac{7}{9} - \frac{5}{7}$

c) $\frac{1}{5} + \frac{1}{9} + \frac{1}{3}$ **f)** $\frac{7}{10} - \frac{1}{11}$

(9.1) **5.** What fraction addition is shown in each picture? Calculate the sum.

a)

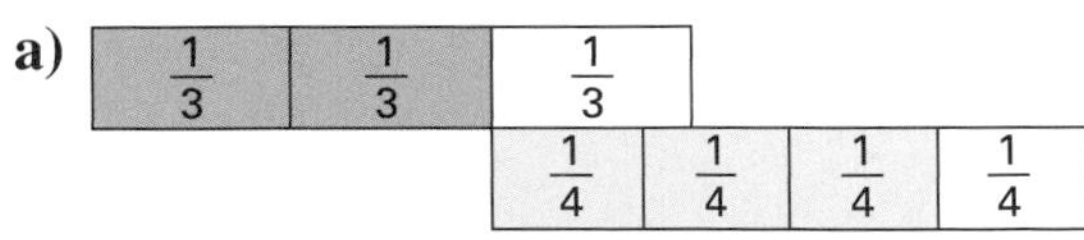

b)

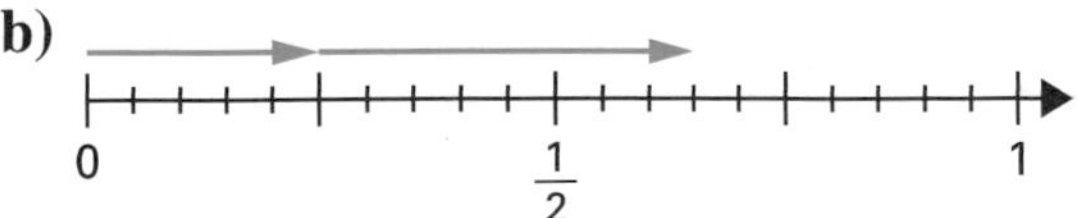

6. Calculate. (9.1)

a) $\frac{1}{2} + \frac{7}{12}$ **d)** $\frac{9}{10} - \frac{3}{4}$

b) $\frac{2}{3} + \frac{2}{5}$ **e)** $\frac{5}{9} + \frac{5}{6}$

c) $1 - \frac{5}{8}$ **f)** $1 - \frac{6}{15}$

7. a) List three pairs of fractions that have a sum of $\frac{3}{5}$.

b) List three pairs of fractions that have a difference of $\frac{3}{5}$. (9.1)

8. Julie added three fractions and got $\frac{7}{8}$ as her answer. List four sets of fractions she might have added. (9.1)

9. Stephen completed $\frac{1}{3}$ of his project on Tuesday night and $\frac{1}{4}$ on Wednesday night. How much of his project is left to complete? (9.1)

10. Create a problem to go with this calculation. Solve your problem. (9.1)

$1 - \frac{11}{12} = \blacksquare$

11. Franca is training to become a hospital aide. The first training session she attends is $3\frac{1}{2}$ days long. The second session is $1\frac{3}{4}$ days long. How long, in total, is her training? (9.2)

12. Estimate each sum or difference. (9.2)

a) $5\frac{2}{5} + 4\frac{3}{4}$ **d)** $1\frac{3}{4} - 1\frac{2}{3}$

b) $\frac{3}{5} + 2\frac{1}{2}$ **e)** $3\frac{1}{4} - 2\frac{3}{10}$

c) $1\frac{3}{10} + 3\frac{3}{4}$ **f)** $7\frac{1}{5} - 4\frac{5}{6}$

(9.2) **13.** Calculate.

a) $6\frac{2}{3} + 2\frac{1}{12}$

b) $4\frac{1}{3} + 1\frac{4}{9}$

c) $3\frac{1}{3} + 2\frac{3}{5}$

d) $3\frac{5}{6} - \frac{1}{2}$

e) $3\frac{7}{12} - 1\frac{1}{4}$

f) $1\frac{5}{6} - \frac{3}{4}$

(9.2) **14.** Sometimes the sum of two mixed numbers is a whole number. Give an example.

(9.2) **15.** How does the following model show that $4 - 1\frac{2}{3} = \frac{1}{3} + 2$?

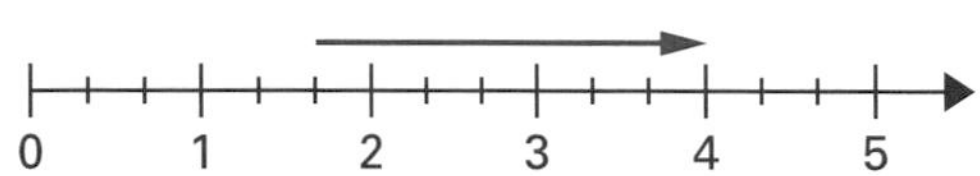

(9.3) **16. a)** Continue this pattern for three more differences.

$1 - \frac{1}{2} = \frac{1}{2}$

$\frac{1}{2} - \frac{1}{4} = \frac{1}{4}$

$\frac{1}{4} - \frac{1}{8} = \frac{1}{8}$

b) Which difference will have an answer that is less than $\frac{1}{1000}$? Explain.

(9.4) **17.** Draw a picture to show $\frac{2}{3}$ of $\frac{3}{8}$.

(9.4) **18.** Draw a picture to show that $\frac{1}{3}$ of $\frac{3}{5}$ is the same as $\frac{2}{3}$ of $\frac{3}{10}$.

(9.4) **19.** What is the missing fraction in each sentence?

a) $\frac{1}{4}$ of $\frac{2}{7}$ is ■.

b) $\frac{3}{5}$ is ■ of $\frac{4}{5}$.

c) ■ of $\frac{3}{4}$ is $\frac{3}{12}$.

20. Draw a model for each multiplication. Use your model to determine the product. (9.5)

a) $\frac{1}{3} \times \frac{1}{6}$

b) $\frac{3}{7} \times \frac{4}{5}$

21. What fraction multiplication does each model represent? (9.5)

a)

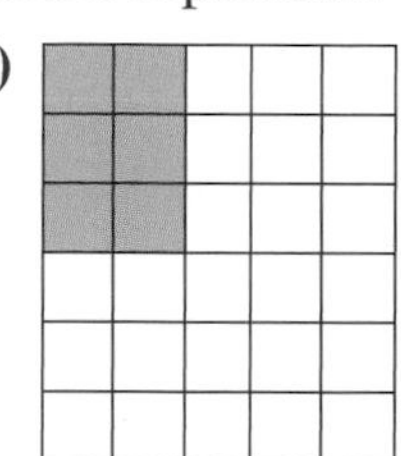

b)

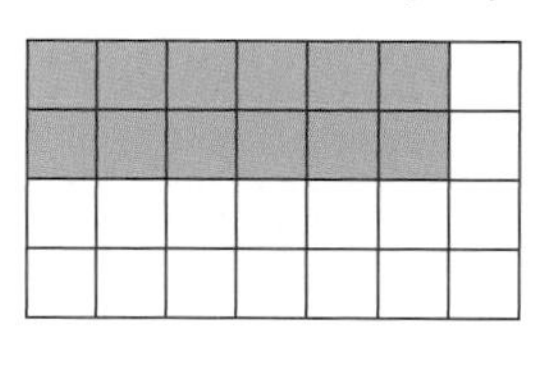

c)

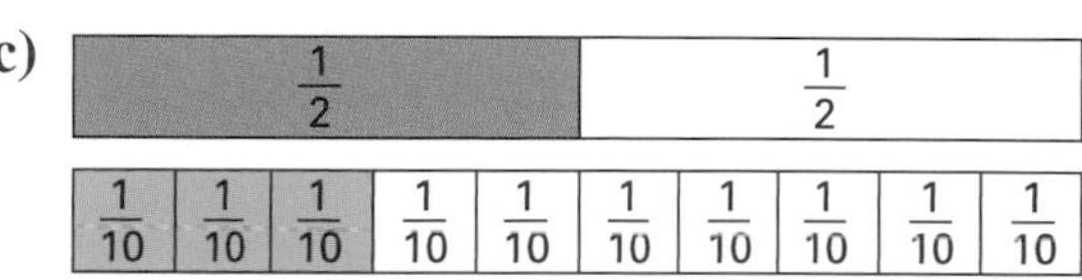

22. Calculate each product. (9.5)

a) $\frac{1}{7} \times \frac{1}{8}$

b) $\frac{2}{5} \times \frac{3}{11}$

c) $\frac{5}{6} \times \frac{3}{4}$

d) $\frac{2}{9} \times \frac{1}{6}$

e) $\frac{3}{10} \times \frac{4}{5}$

f) $\frac{9}{10} \times \frac{9}{10}$

23. If you multiply $\frac{2}{8}$ by another fraction, can the denominator be 20? Explain. (9.5)

24. Kyle multiplied a fraction less than 1 by $\frac{3}{7}$. Could the answer be $\frac{3}{5}$? Explain. (9.5)

25. How much greater is the first product than the second product? (9.5)

a) $\frac{2}{7} \times \frac{2}{5}$ than $\frac{1}{7} \times \frac{3}{5}$

b) $\frac{3}{8} \times \frac{4}{9}$ than $\frac{1}{8} \times \frac{2}{3}$

c) $\frac{3}{5} \times \frac{2}{3}$ than $\frac{1}{5} \times \frac{1}{4}$

26. Describe a situation in which you might multiply $\frac{2}{3} \times \frac{3}{5}$. (9.5)

9.6 Multiplying Fractions Greater Than 1

You will need
- grid paper
- fraction strips
- coloured pencils

▶ **GOAL**

Multiply mixed numbers and improper fractions.

Learn about the Math

A large popcorn bag holds $2\frac{1}{2}$ times as much as a small popcorn bag. Manuel has $1\frac{1}{2}$ large bags of popcorn. He is pouring the popcorn into small bags to share. He knows that he can multiply $2\frac{1}{2}$ by $1\frac{1}{2}$ to determine the number of small bags he can fill. He estimates that he can fill about 4 small bags.

? **How many small bags will the popcorn fill?**

Example 1: Using the rule for multiplying fractions

How many small bags will the popcorn from $1\frac{1}{2}$ large bags fill?

Tamara's Solution

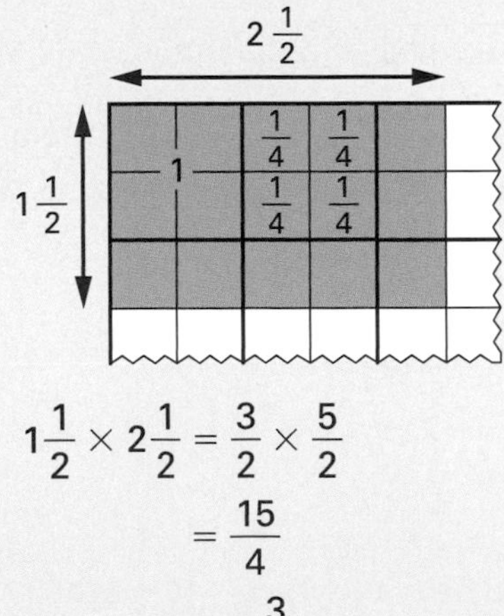

$$1\frac{1}{2} \times 2\frac{1}{2} = \frac{3}{2} \times \frac{5}{2}$$
$$= \frac{15}{4}$$
$$= 3\frac{3}{4}$$

The popcorn will fill $3\frac{3}{4}$ small bags.

To model the problem, I coloured a rectangle with a width of $1\frac{1}{2}$ units and a length of $2\frac{1}{2}$ units on a grid.

$1\frac{1}{2} = \frac{3}{2}$ and $2\frac{1}{2} = \frac{5}{2}$, so the rectangle is 3 grid squares by 5 grid squares.

Each grid square in the rectangle is $\frac{1}{4}$ of a square with an area of 1. Since each grid square has an area of $\frac{1}{4}$, the total area is $\frac{15}{4}$, or $3\frac{3}{4}$.

Example 2: Multiplying using models

Calculate $1\frac{1}{2} \times 2\frac{1}{2}$.

Manuel's Solution: Adding partial areas

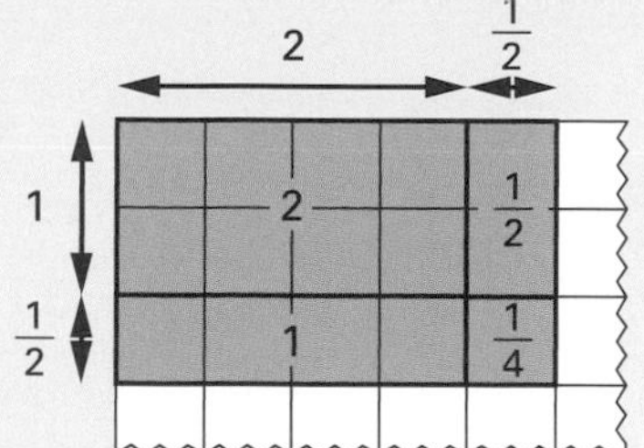

I drew a rectangle that was $2\frac{1}{2}$ units long and $1\frac{1}{2}$ units wide. I divided the rectangle into smaller rectangles.

The area of a 1-by-2 rectangle is $1 \times 2 = 2$ units.

The area of a 1-by-$\frac{1}{2}$ rectangle is $1 \times \frac{1}{2} = \frac{1}{2}$ unit.

The area of a $\frac{1}{2}$-by-2 rectangle is $\frac{1}{2} \times 2 = 1$ unit.

The area of a $\frac{1}{2}$-by-$\frac{1}{2}$ rectangle is $\frac{1}{2} \times \frac{1}{2} = \frac{1}{4}$ unit.

The total area is

$2 + 1 + \frac{1}{2} + \frac{1}{4} = 3\frac{3}{4}$.

The popcorn will fill $3\frac{3}{4}$ bags.

This makes sense since $3\frac{3}{4} = \frac{15}{4}$ and the coloured squares show 15 fourths.

Teo's Solution: Using fraction strips

$$2 \times 2\frac{1}{2} = 2 \times 2 + 2 \times \frac{1}{2}$$
$$= 4 + 1$$
$$= 5$$

I estimated the number of bags to be $2 \times 2\frac{1}{2}$, which is 5. My answer should be less than 5 since $1\frac{1}{2} \times 2\frac{1}{2}$ is less than $2 \times 2\frac{1}{2}$.

To calculate $1\frac{1}{2} \times 2\frac{1}{2}$, I had to model $1\frac{1}{2}$ groups of $2\frac{1}{2}$. So, first I modelled $2\frac{1}{2}$ fraction strips. Then I modelled $\frac{1}{2}$ of $2\frac{1}{2}$ fraction strips. To model $\frac{1}{2}$ of $2\frac{1}{2}$, I divided each whole into fourths.

$\frac{1}{2}$ of $2\frac{1}{2} = \frac{5}{4}$, or $1\frac{1}{4}$

Then I calculated the total of the coloured strips.

$$1\frac{1}{2} \times 2\frac{1}{2} = 2\frac{1}{2} + 1\frac{1}{4}$$
$$= 3\frac{3}{4}$$

The popcorn will fill $3\frac{3}{4}$ small bags.

Reflecting

1. How do you think Manuel arrived at his estimate of 4 small bags?

2. Suppose that Manuel had only $\frac{3}{4}$ of a large bag of popcorn. How would each student change his or her solution to calculate the number of small bags the popcorn would fill?

3. How is each solution like multiplying fractions less than 1? How is each solution different from multiplying fractions less than 1?

Work with the Math

Example 3: Multiplying two mixed numbers

Multiply $3\frac{1}{3} \times 2\frac{1}{3}$.

Solution A:
Adding partial areas

Calculate the area of the rectangle by calculating the four partial areas and then adding.

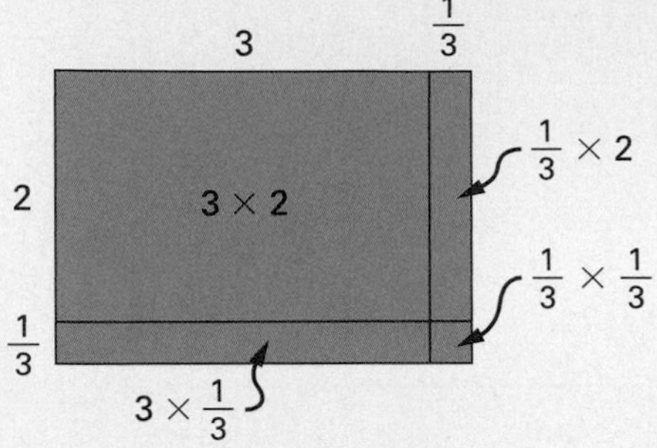

$$3\frac{1}{3} \times 2\frac{1}{3} = 6 + \frac{2}{3} + \frac{3}{3} + \frac{1}{9}$$
$$= 6 + \frac{6}{9} + 1 + \frac{1}{9}$$
$$= 7\frac{7}{9}$$

Solution B:
Using the rule for multiplying fractions

Express the mixed numbers as improper fractions. Then multiply the numerators and multiply the denominators.

$$3\frac{1}{3} \times 2\frac{1}{3} = \frac{10}{3} \times \frac{7}{3}$$
$$= \frac{10 \times 7}{3 \times 3}$$
$$= \frac{70}{9}$$
$$= 7\frac{7}{9}$$

A Checking

4. Estimate each product.

a) $\frac{5}{8} \times 6\frac{1}{2}$ **b)** $7\frac{2}{9} \times 6\frac{3}{4}$

5. Show each multiplication using a different model. Determine the product.

a) $2\frac{2}{3} \times 1\frac{4}{5}$ **b)** $\frac{1}{2} \times 4\frac{4}{7}$

6. Calculate each product.

a) $\frac{2}{9} \times 4\frac{1}{4}$ **b)** $4\frac{2}{5} \times 3\frac{3}{5}$

7. Miriam is making $3\frac{1}{2}$ dozen cookies. If $\frac{2}{7}$ of the cookies have icing, how many dozen cookies have icing?

B Practising

8. Calculate each product.

a) $\frac{2}{3} \times 2\frac{1}{4}$ **d)** $\frac{3}{4} \times 2\frac{5}{6}$

b) $\frac{5}{8} \times 1\frac{1}{2}$ **e)** $\frac{5}{6} \times 1\frac{5}{7}$

c) $\frac{1}{5} \times 2\frac{2}{3}$ **f)** $\frac{2}{9} \times 1\frac{1}{6}$

9. Use a model to show each multiplication. Use at least two different models.

a) $\frac{4}{3} \times \frac{3}{2}$

b) $\frac{1}{4} \times 4\frac{4}{7}$

c) $2\frac{1}{5} \times 3\frac{1}{6}$

10. Calculate each product.

a) $2\frac{1}{4} \times 3\frac{1}{3}$

b) $1\frac{1}{2} \times 2\frac{1}{2}$

c) $1\frac{4}{5} \times 2\frac{2}{3}$

d) $3\frac{1}{5} \times 2\frac{1}{4}$

e) $3\frac{1}{6} \times 2\frac{2}{3}$

f) $1\frac{1}{6} \times 1\frac{1}{4}$

11. A muesli recipe requires $1\frac{1}{4}$ cups of oatmeal. How many cups of oatmeal do you need for each number of batches?

a) $2\frac{1}{2}$ batches

b) $3\frac{1}{3}$ batches

12. Zoë had $3\frac{1}{3}$ times as much money as her brother. She spent $\frac{2}{5}$ of her money on a new CD player. Now how many times as much money as her brother does Zoë have?

13. Tai calculated $3\frac{1}{3} \times 4\frac{3}{8}$. He multiplied the whole number parts together and then multiplied the fraction parts together. He got an incorrect product of $12\frac{3}{24}$.

a) Why would estimation not help Tai realize that he had made a mistake?

b) How could you show Tai that his answer is incorrect?

14. Andrea's bedroom is $1\frac{1}{3}$ times as long as Kit's bedroom and $1\frac{2}{3}$ times as wide. What fraction of the area of Kit's bedroom is the area of Andrea's bedroom?

15. The highest point in Alberta is Mount Columbia. Mount Columbia is about $4\frac{3}{5}$ times as high as the highest point in New Brunswick, Mount Carleton. Mount Carleton is about $5\frac{3}{4}$ times as high as the highest point in Prince Edward Island. Compare the height of Mount Columbia with the height of the highest point in Prince Edward Island.

16. a) Multiply $3\frac{4}{10}$ by $2\frac{3}{10}$.

b) Rename these two fractions as decimals, and multiply the decimals.

c) How was the decimal multiplication similar to the fraction multiplication?

17. Describe a situation in which you might multiply $3\frac{1}{2}$ by $2\frac{1}{3}$.

C Extending

18. The values of a, b, and c are all improper fractions. What could the values be?

$a \times b \times c = \frac{14}{3}$

19. David multiplied $3\frac{1}{5}$ by another mixed number. The product was a whole number. What are two possibilities for the mixed number?

9.7 Dividing Fractions I

You will need
- fraction strips

▶ **GOAL**

Divide fractions using models and using equivalent fractions with a common denominator.

Learn about the Math

Sheree exercises for $\frac{3}{4}$ of an hour several times a week.

? How many times does Sheree have to exercise if she wants to exercise for a total of 4 h every week?

A. Line up 4 whole fraction strips to show a total of 4 ones.

1	1	1	1

B. Line up enough $\frac{3}{4}$ strips to fit along the four whole strips from step A.

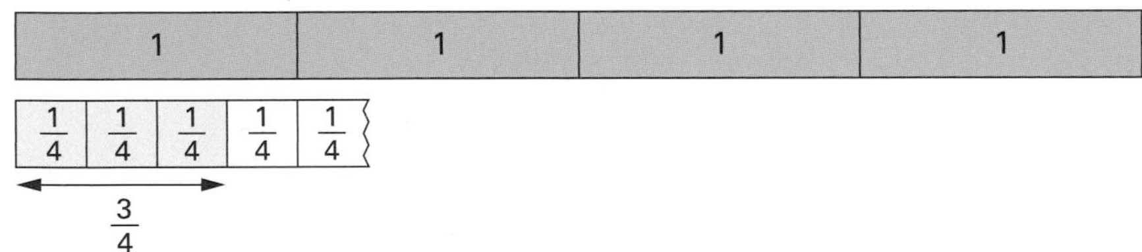

C. Divide each whole strip into 4 fourths.

D. How many times does the $\frac{3}{4}$ strip fit along the 4 whole strips?

E. How many times does Sheree have to exercise to achieve her goal of 4 h?

Reflecting

1. How did dividing each whole strip into fourths help you solve the problem?
2. Why does finding out how many $\frac{3}{4}$ strips fit along the length of 4 whole strips help you solve the problem?
3. How could you solve the problem using equivalent fractions for 4 and $\frac{3}{4}$, and then dividing the numerators?

Work with the Math

Example 1: Using a model to divide fractions

Calculate $\frac{4}{5} \div \frac{1}{3}$.

Reilly's Solution

$\frac{1}{5}$	$\frac{1}{5}$	$\frac{1}{5}$	$\frac{1}{5}$	$\frac{1}{5}$

$\frac{1}{3}$	$\frac{1}{3}$	$\frac{1}{3}$

To divide $\frac{4}{5}$ by $\frac{1}{3}$, I asked myself how many $\frac{1}{3}$s are in $\frac{4}{5}$. Since $\frac{1}{3} < \frac{4}{5}$, the answer must be greater than 1. I think a little more than 2 thirds will fit in.

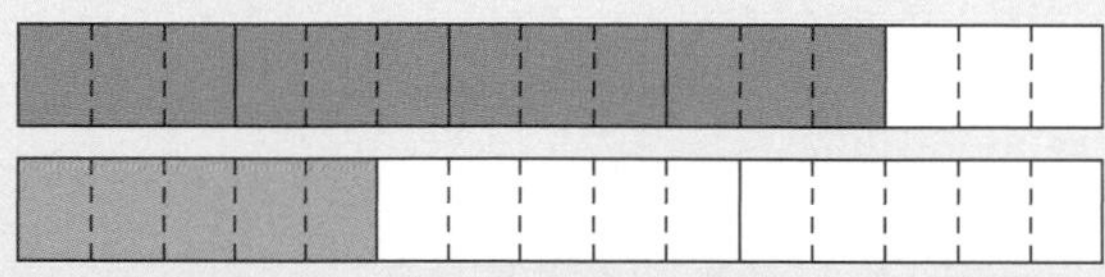

It would be easier if both fractions were fifteenths. Then I could count how many times the $\frac{1}{3}$ piece fits into $\frac{4}{5}$.

$$\begin{aligned}\frac{4}{5} \div \frac{1}{3} &= \frac{12}{15} \div \frac{5}{15} \\ &= \frac{12}{5} \\ &= 2\frac{2}{5}\end{aligned}$$

There are 12 fifteenths in $\frac{4}{5}$ and 5 fifteenths in $\frac{1}{3}$. I have to figure out how many times 5 goes into 12. I need 2 and $\frac{2}{5}$ of the thirds to get the length of $\frac{4}{5}$.

Example 2: Using common denominators to divide fractions

Calculate $\frac{1}{3} \div \frac{2}{5}$.

Manuel's Solution

To calculate $\frac{1}{3} \div \frac{2}{5}$, I need to find out how many $\frac{2}{5}$s fit into $\frac{1}{3}$. I can't fit an entire $\frac{2}{5}$ into $\frac{1}{3}$, so the answer must be less than 1. But I can fit most of $\frac{2}{5}$ into $\frac{1}{3}$, so the answer should be close to 1. I can solve the problem using a common denominator.

$$\begin{aligned}\frac{1}{3} \div \frac{2}{5} &= \frac{1 \times 5}{3 \times 5} \div \frac{2 \times 3}{5 \times 3} \\ &= \frac{5}{15} \div \frac{6}{15} \\ &= \frac{5}{6}\end{aligned}$$

A common denominator for $\frac{1}{3}$ and $\frac{2}{5}$ is $3 \times 5 = 15$.

I divided the numerators to determine how many 6 fifteenths fit into 5 fifteenths. The answer makes sense. It's less than 1, but close to 1.

A Checking

4. What division expression does this picture represent?

$\frac{1}{3}$			$\frac{1}{3}$			$\frac{1}{3}$		
$\frac{1}{9}$	$\frac{1}{9}$	$\frac{1}{9}$	$\frac{1}{9}$	$\frac{1}{9}$	$\frac{1}{9}$	$\frac{1}{9}$	$\frac{1}{9}$	$\frac{1}{9}$

5. Draw a fraction strip model to show the number of times $\frac{1}{4}$ fits into $\frac{7}{8}$.

6. Calculate.

a) $\frac{5}{8} \div \frac{3}{4}$ **b)** $2\frac{1}{2} \div \frac{2}{3}$

7. Craig needs to measure $3\frac{1}{3}$ cups. How many times must he fill a $\frac{1}{2}$ cup measuring cup?

B Practising

8. What division expression does each picture represent?

a)

$\frac{1}{4}$		$\frac{1}{4}$		$\frac{1}{4}$		$\frac{1}{4}$	
$\frac{1}{8}$	$\frac{1}{8}$	$\frac{1}{8}$	$\frac{1}{8}$	$\frac{1}{8}$	$\frac{1}{8}$	$\frac{1}{8}$	$\frac{1}{8}$

b)

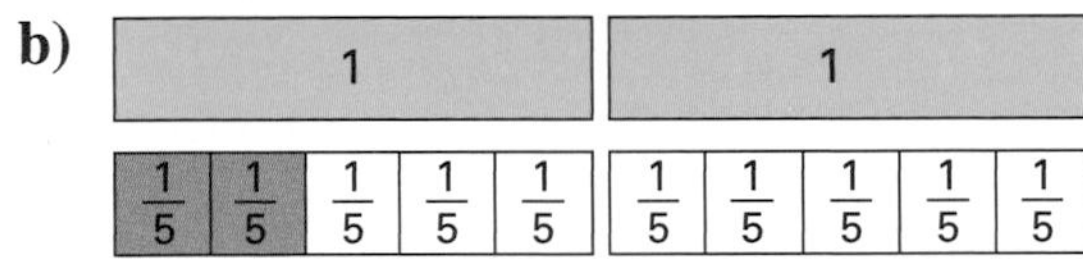

9. Calculate each quotient using equivalent fractions.

a) $5 \div \frac{1}{3}$ **c)** $2\frac{1}{2} \div \frac{3}{8}$

b) $1\frac{3}{4} \div \frac{5}{6}$ **d)** $\frac{3}{5} \div \frac{5}{6}$

10. Fredreka wrote $\frac{2}{5}$ of her report in 1 h. How much time will she need to complete the entire report at this rate?

11. Alana is cooking a turkey. It takes $4\frac{1}{2}$ h to cook. She checks it every 20 min, or $\frac{1}{3}$ h. How many times will she check it before it is cooked?

12. How can you calculate $\frac{3}{5} \div \frac{1}{2}$ using equivalent fractions with a common denominator?

13. Calculate.

a) $\frac{1}{4} \div \frac{5}{6}$ **c)** $\frac{3}{4} \div 6$

b) $\frac{4}{7} \div \frac{1}{10}$ **d)** $1\frac{1}{5} \div \frac{2}{5}$

14. Craig needs to measure $2\frac{3}{8}$ cups. How many times must he fill a $\frac{1}{3}$ cup measuring cup?

15. Does order matter in division of fractions? For example, is $\frac{2}{3} \div \frac{1}{5}$ the same as $\frac{1}{5} \div \frac{2}{3}$? Explain.

16. $\frac{16}{■} \div \frac{2}{■} = 8$. Explain why this is true no matter what the denominator is, as long as both denominators are the same.

17. How do you know that dividing by $\frac{1}{6}$ is the same as multiplying by 6?

18. Teo made a video that was $2\frac{1}{2}$ h long. He made it by clipping together sections that were each about $\frac{1}{3}$ h long.

a) About how many sections did Teo clip together?

b) How do you know that the sections were not all exactly $\frac{1}{3}$ h long?

C Extending

19. For each of the following, how can you predict that the first calculation will be double the second calculation?

a) $\frac{3}{4} \div \frac{1}{8}$ and $\frac{3}{4} \div \frac{1}{4}$

b) $\frac{6}{8} \div \frac{2}{3}$ and $\frac{3}{8} \div \frac{2}{3}$

20. One store offers a discount of 20% on a price. Another store offers a $\frac{1}{3}$ discount on the same price. What fraction of the higher sale price is the lower sale price?

21. One fraction divides into another fraction $3\frac{1}{4}$ times. List two possible pairs of fractions.

Curious Math

CONTINUED FRACTIONS

Fractions like the ones below are called **continued fractions**. They go on forever.

The continued fraction shown below is a famous number called the **golden ratio**. If you divide two consecutive terms from the Fibonacci sequence, you get values that are closer to this number.

Fibonacci sequence: 1, 1, 2, 3, 5, 8, 13, 21, 34, …

$$1 + \cfrac{1}{1 + \cfrac{1}{1 + \cfrac{1}{1 + 1 \ldots}}}$$

$$= 1 + \cfrac{1}{1 + \cfrac{1}{1 + \frac{1}{2}}}$$

$$= 1 + \cfrac{1}{1 + \cfrac{1}{\frac{3}{2}}}$$

$$= 1 + \cfrac{1}{1 + \frac{2}{3}}$$

$$= 1 + \cfrac{1}{\frac{5}{3}}$$

$$= 1 + \frac{3}{5}$$

$$= 1\frac{3}{5}$$

This is the same as the ratio of the 6th and 5th terms of the Fibonacci sequence.

To estimate the value, you can stop partway. You calculate your estimate by working up from the bottom.

1. a) Get a closer estimate by starting the fraction with two more steps.

   b) Show that this value is close to the ratio of the 10th and 9th terms of the Fibonacci sequence.

2. Estimate this continued fraction.

$$2 + \cfrac{2}{2 + \cfrac{2}{2 + \cfrac{2}{2 + 2 \ldots}}}$$

9.8 Dividing Fractions II

You will need
- fraction strips

▶ **GOAL**

Divide fractions using related multiplication.

Learn about the Math

Tamara has a large can of paint. Jordan has $\frac{7}{8}$ of a large can of paint. Each student is pouring paint into small cans that hold $\frac{2}{3}$ as much as a large can.

? How many small cans of paint will each student fill?

Example 1: Dividing a whole number by a fraction

How many small cans will Tamara fill with her large can of paint?

Tamara's Solution

The number of small cans I can fill from a large can is $1 \div \frac{2}{3}$.

I need to divide to find out how much of one thing fits into another.

The quotient will be more than 1 since I'm pouring the paint into smaller cans. I don't think it will fill 2 cans, though.

Tamara's 1 large can		
$\frac{1}{3}$	$\frac{1}{3}$	$\frac{1}{3}$
1 small can		$\frac{1}{2}$ small can

I decided to use fraction strips to model $1 \div \frac{2}{3}$.

I showed my large can of paint using a whole fraction strip.

I divided my whole strip into thirds and coloured two of the thirds to show the amount of paint a small can will hold.

$$1 \div \frac{2}{3} = \frac{3}{2}$$

I saw that my large can would fill $1\frac{1}{2}$ or $\frac{3}{2}$ small cans. This seems reasonable.

My large can of paint will fill $1\frac{1}{2}$ small cans.

Example 2: Dividing a fraction by a fraction

How many small cans will Jordan fill with her large can that is $\frac{7}{8}$ full?

Jordan's Solution

The number of small cans I can fill from $\frac{7}{8}$ of a large can is $\frac{7}{8} \div \frac{2}{3}$.

I need to divide the amount in the large can by the amount that fills each small can.

$$\frac{7}{8} \div \frac{2}{3} = \frac{7}{8} \times \frac{3}{2} = \frac{7 \times 3}{8 \times 2} = \frac{21}{16} = 1\frac{5}{16}$$

My can holds $\frac{7}{8}$ as much as Tamara's, so I should be able to fill $\frac{7}{8}$ as many small cans as Tamara. That's why I decided to multiply Tamara's answer by $\frac{7}{8}$.

Since $\frac{7}{8}$ is almost 1, I predict that the answer will be almost $\frac{3}{2}$.

$$\frac{7}{8} \times \frac{3}{2} = 1\frac{5}{16}$$

I can fill $1\frac{5}{16}$ small cans.

$1\frac{5}{16}$ is a bit less than $1\frac{1}{2}$, so it seems reasonable.

Reflecting

1. Why did Tamara and Jordan divide by $\frac{2}{3}$ to solve their problems?

2. The result when Tamara divided 1 by $\frac{2}{3}$ was the **reciprocal** of $\frac{2}{3}$. What happens when you multiply $\frac{2}{3}$ by its reciprocal?

reciprocal
the fraction that results from switching the numerator and denominator; for example, $\frac{4}{5}$ is the reciprocal of $\frac{5}{4}$

3. Every ratio can be described as a fraction. Why can you describe the ratio of the can sizes as any of the following?

   $3:2 \qquad 1:\frac{2}{3} \qquad \frac{3}{2}:1$

4. How can Jordan's strategy be used to show that a fraction divided by $\frac{2}{3}$ is the product of this fraction and $\frac{3}{2}$? Use examples to support your explanation.

Work with the Math

Example 3: Dividing a mixed number by a fraction

Tamara wants to pour $1\frac{7}{8}$ large cans of paint into small cans. Each small can holds $\frac{3}{5}$ as much paint as a large can. How many small cans will Tamara fill?

Solution A: Using fraction strips to divide

Estimate: Since $\frac{3}{5}$ is about $\frac{1}{2}$, Tamara will fill 3 or 4 small cans with the paint from $1\frac{7}{8}$ large cans. Do a simpler problem using 1 large can first.

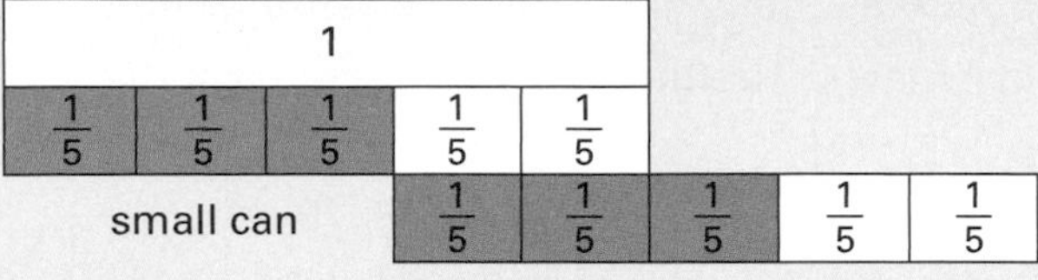

$1 \div \frac{3}{5} = \frac{5}{3}$, or $1\frac{2}{3}$ small cans

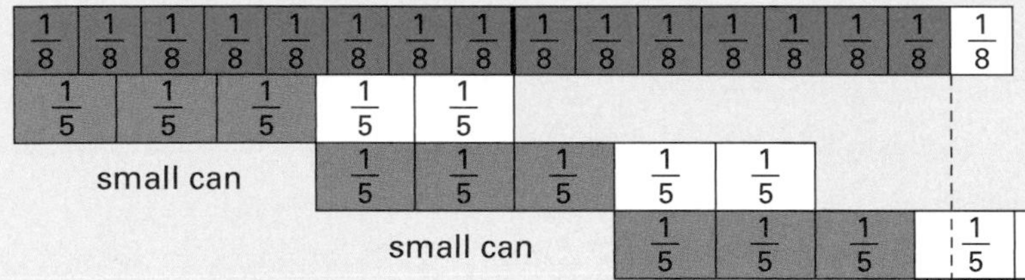

$1\frac{7}{8} \div \frac{3}{5} = 3\frac{1}{8}$

$\frac{3}{24} = \frac{1}{8}$ small can

Tamara will fill $3\frac{1}{8}$ small cans with paint.

Solution B: Using a common denominator

$$\begin{aligned}1\frac{7}{8} \div \frac{3}{5} &= \frac{15}{8} \div \frac{3}{5}\\ &= \frac{15 \times 5}{8 \times 5} \div \frac{3 \times 8}{5 \times 8}\\ &= \frac{75}{40} \div \frac{24}{40}\\ &= \frac{75}{24}\\ &= 3\frac{3}{24}\\ &= 3\frac{1}{8}\end{aligned}$$

Tamara will fill $3\frac{1}{8}$ small cans with paint.

Solution C: Multiplying by the reciprocal

$$\begin{aligned}1\frac{7}{8} \div \frac{3}{5} &= \frac{15}{8} \div \frac{3}{5}\\ &= \frac{15}{8} \times \frac{5}{3}\\ &= \frac{75}{24}\\ &= 3\frac{3}{24}\\ &= 3\frac{1}{8}\end{aligned}$$

Tamara will fill $3\frac{1}{8}$ small cans with paint.

NEL

A Checking

5. Calculate.

   a) $\frac{3}{8} \div \frac{1}{2}$ b) $\frac{7}{8} \div \frac{1}{3}$

6. Lynnsie has $1\frac{1}{2}$ large cans of paint. Each small can holds $\frac{3}{5}$ as much paint as a large can. How many small cans will Lynnsie be able to fill?

B Practising

7. Calculate.

   a) $\frac{3}{9} \div \frac{2}{9}$ d) $\frac{4}{5} \div \frac{2}{3}$

   b) $\frac{1}{2} \div \frac{1}{3}$ e) $\frac{1}{5} \div \frac{2}{5}$

   c) $\frac{4}{8} \div \frac{7}{8}$ f) $\frac{9}{20} \div \frac{3}{5}$

8. Why does it make sense that $\frac{7}{8} \div \frac{3}{4}$ is greater than $\frac{7}{8}$?

9. Which quotients are $1\frac{1}{4}$? How do you know?

   a) $\frac{5}{2} \div \frac{1}{2}$ c) $\frac{3}{5} \div \frac{3}{4}$

   b) $\frac{3}{4} \div \frac{3}{5}$ d) $5 \div 4$

10. a) Which quotients are greater than 1?

    i) $\frac{3}{5} \div \frac{2}{3}$ ii) $\frac{9}{2} \div \frac{5}{6}$ iii) $\frac{3}{7} \div \frac{1}{8}$

    b) How could you have predicted the answers to part (a) without calculating the quotients?

11. Which quotients are greater than 2? Calculate these quotients only.

    a) $\frac{5}{9} \div \frac{1}{4}$ c) $\frac{8}{9} \div \frac{3}{4}$

    b) $3\frac{1}{3} \div \frac{4}{5}$ d) $\frac{7}{8} \div \frac{1}{3}$

12. Timo says that you can divide $\frac{15}{16} \div \frac{3}{4}$ by calculating $\frac{15 \div 3}{16 \div 4}$.

    a) Do you agree with Timo?

    b) Does Timo's method work with other fractions?

13. Printers print at different rates. How many pages does each printer print per minute?

    a) 20 pages in $1\frac{1}{2}$ min

    b) 20 pages in $1\frac{1}{3}$ min

    c) 20 pages in $2\frac{1}{2}$ min

14. Miri filled $2\frac{1}{2}$ pitchers with $\frac{2}{3}$ of the punch she made. How many pitchers would she fill if she used all the punch she made?

15. Trevor takes $4\frac{1}{2}$ min to run once around a track. How many laps can he do in each time?

    a) 30 min b) 20 min c) 15 min

16. Describe a situation in which you might use each calculation.

    a) $\frac{9}{8} \div \frac{2}{3}$ b) $1\frac{2}{5} \div 2\frac{2}{3}$

17. How do you know $1\frac{2}{3} \div 3\frac{1}{2}$ has to be less than $\frac{1}{2}$, without calculating the quotient?

18. If Kyle divides $4\frac{2}{3}$ by a fraction less than 1, the answer is a whole number. List three possible fractions.

C Extending

19. Evaluate $\frac{3}{a} \div \frac{a}{3}$ for each value of a.

    a) $a = 4$ b) $a = 6$

20. The quotient of two fractions is the same as their sum. List three possible pairs of fractions.

9.9 Communicating about Multiplication and Division

▶ **GOAL**

Describe the relationship between multiplying and dividing decimals and multiplying and dividing fractions.

Communicate about the Math

Reilly explained how he multiplied 4.2 by 0.2 and got the answer 0.84. Then Manuel asked questions about Reilly's explanation to help Reilly improve it.

Reilly's Explanation

$$4.2 \times 0.2 = \frac{42}{10} \times \frac{2}{10}$$
$$= \frac{84}{100}$$

Whenever you multiply two decimal numbers, you count the total number of places after the decimal point. This tells you how many decimal places are in the answer.

Manuel's Questions

How do you know that $4.2 = \frac{42}{10}$?

Why did you decide to write the two decimals as fractions?

How do you know this rule?

How does writing the decimals as fractions help you explain this rule?

Are you sure this rule always works?

? How can you improve Reilly's explanation of how to multiply decimals?

A. How can you respond to Manuel's questions to improve Reilly's explanation?

B. What other questions could Manuel have asked?

Communication Checklist

- ☑ Did you explain each step of your calculations?
- ☑ Did you justify your conclusions?
- ☑ Did you use models to make your thinking clear?
- ☑ Did you use enough examples to support your thinking?

Reflecting

1. Which parts of the Communication Checklist did Reilly cover well? Which parts did Manuel cover in his questions?

2. How would you modify Reilly's explanation to explain why the rules for decimal operations are related to the rules for fraction operations?

NEL

Work with the Math

Example: Explaining the rule for dividing decimals

Explain how to determine the number of decimal places when dividing decimals.

Sheree's Solution

$8 \div 2 = 4$

$$0.8 \div 0.2 = \frac{8}{10} \div \frac{2}{10} = \frac{8}{2} = 4$$

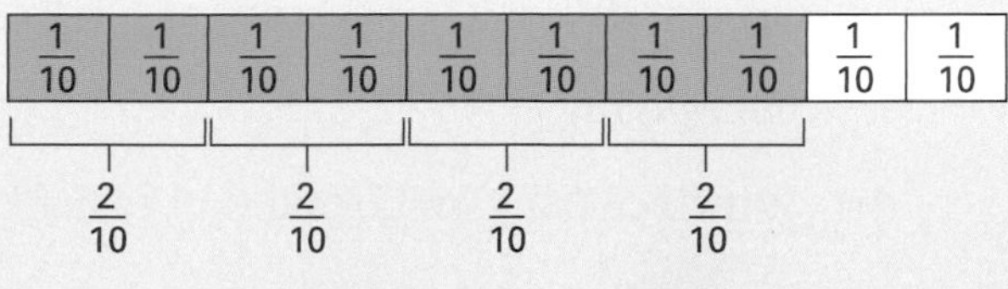

$$0.08 \div 0.02 = \frac{8}{100} \div \frac{2}{100} = \frac{8}{2} = 4$$

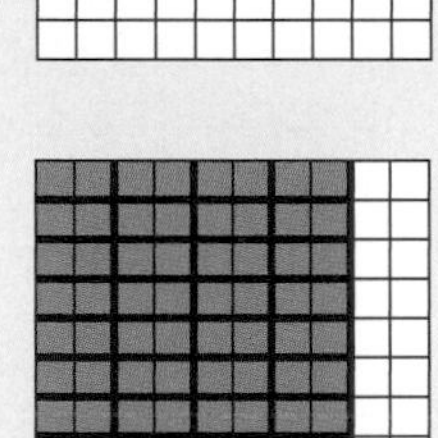

When two numbers have the same number of places after the decimal point, you can ignore the decimal point and just divide the numbers.

The examples show that the number of 2s in 8 is the same as the number of 2 tenths in 8 tenths and the same as the number of 2 hundredths in 8 hundredths. So, 8 ÷ 2 means how many sets of 2 of anything are in 8 of the same thing.

$$0.8 \div 0.02 = \frac{8}{10} \div \frac{2}{100} = \frac{80}{100} \div \frac{2}{100} = \frac{80}{2} = 40$$

When two numbers have different numbers of decimal places, you can rewrite one number as an equivalent decimal. Then both numbers will have the same number of decimal places. So, you can ignore the decimal point.

$$0.08 \div 0.2 = \frac{8}{100} \div \frac{2}{10} = \frac{8}{100} \div \frac{20}{100} = \frac{8}{20} = \frac{4}{10} = 0.4$$

It makes sense that not even one group of 2 tenths goes into 8 hundredths, so the answer should be less than 1. So, 0.4 makes sense.

A Checking

3. Complete Diane's explanation for calculating 1.2×3.55.

4. Explain how you know that 4.25×2.1 equals 42.5×0.21.

B Practising

5. Use words and these pictures to explain why $\frac{3}{5}$ of $\frac{2}{3}$ is the same as $\frac{2}{3}$ of $\frac{3}{5}$.

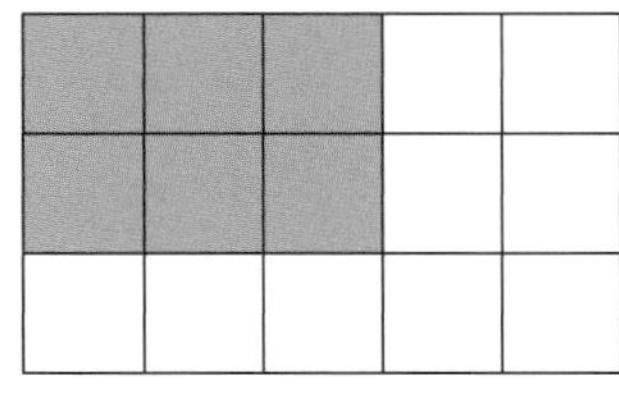

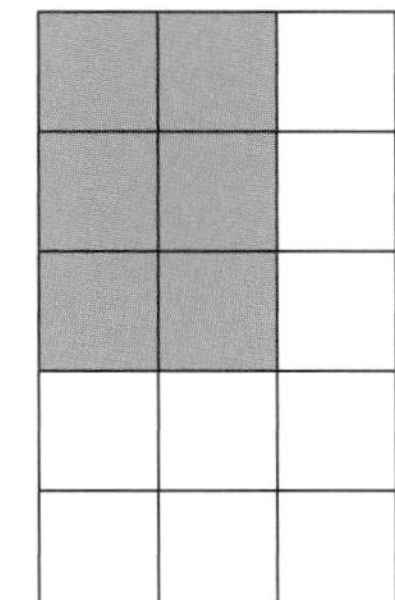

6. Explain why you can calculate $2 \div \frac{2}{3}$ using each method below. Use the Communication Checklist and the picture to help you.

a) Divide equivalent fractions with the same denominator.

b) Multiply 2 by 3 and then divide by 2.

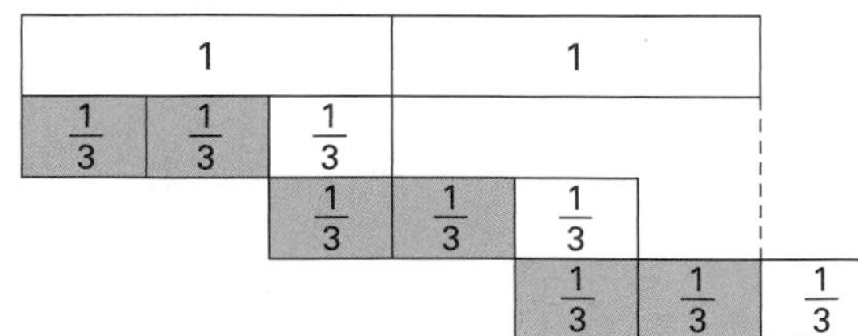

7. Fabienne said that she now understands why she needs to multiply the numerator and denominator of a fraction by the same amount to get an equivalent fraction. Explain her reasoning, shown below.

$$\frac{3}{5} \times 1 = \frac{3}{5}$$

$$1 = \frac{2}{2}$$

$$\frac{3}{5} \times \frac{2}{2} = \frac{3}{5}$$

$$\frac{3 \times 2}{5 \times 2} = \frac{3}{5}$$

8. a) Why can you calculate 60% of 1.5 by multiplying $\frac{3}{5} \times \frac{3}{2}$?

b) Which calculation do you find easier? Why?

9. How do you know that $3\frac{1}{2} \times 6\frac{1}{3}$ must be greater than 21 before you do the calculation?

10. Mereille showed that $\frac{6}{5} \times 10\frac{1}{2}$ equals $10\frac{1}{2} + 2\frac{1}{10}$. Complete her explanation.

> $\frac{6}{5} = 1\frac{1}{5}$, so $\frac{6}{5}$ of something is 1 of that thing and another fifth of it.

11. Explain why 3.2×1.5 can be written as a product with only one decimal place, not two.

12. Explain why $\frac{15}{8} \div \frac{5}{4}$ is half of $\frac{15}{8} \div \frac{5}{8}$.

13. Shakira says that $0.4 \div 0.08$ is $\frac{1}{10}$ of $4 \div 8$. Do you agree? Explain.

Math Game

TARGET $\frac{2}{3}$

In this game, you will roll a pair of dice twice to create two fractions. Then you will add, subtract, multiply, or divide your fractions to get an answer as close as possible to $\frac{2}{3}$.

Number of players: 2, 3, or 4

You will need
- a pair of dice

Rules

1. Roll the dice twice. Use the four numbers as the numerators and denominators of two fractions.

2. You can add, subtract, multiply, or divide the two fractions to get an answer as close as possible to $\frac{2}{3}$.
3. The player with the answer closest to $\frac{2}{3}$ gets a point.
4. Keep playing until one player has 10 points.

For example, suppose that Reilly rolls the following numbers:

$$\frac{2}{1} \div \frac{6}{4} = 2 \times \frac{4}{6}$$
$$= \frac{8}{6}$$
$$= 1\frac{2}{6}$$ This is not close enough.

$$\frac{2}{4} + \frac{1}{6} = \frac{2}{3}$$ Perfect!

9.10 Order of Operations

▶ **GOAL**

Understand the rules for order of operations, and apply them to fraction calculations.

Learn about the Math

Tamara and Teo are playing a math game called Target 1.

Rules for Target 1

1. Pick three fraction (F) cards.
2. Pick two operation (O) cards.
3. Put them in this order: F O F O F
4. Rearrange the cards to get a value as close as possible to 1.
5. The closest value gets 1 point.
6. The first player to get 5 points wins.

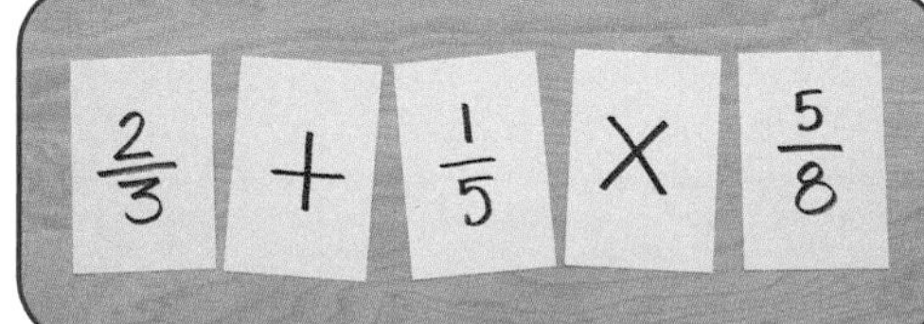

? How close to 1 can Tamara get with her cards?

A. Show how Tamara got $\frac{65}{120}$.

B. What would Tamara's answer be if she were to use the rules for the order of operations? Can she get any closer to 1 by rearranging her cards?

Reflecting

1. How could you use brackets to get the same answer as Tamara in step A?
2. What is the correct order of operations for Tamara's original calculation?

Work with the Math

Example: Calculating an expression with exponents and all operations

Calculate $\left(\frac{2}{3}\right)^2 - \frac{5}{6} \times \frac{1}{2} + \frac{3}{4} \div \frac{1}{3}$.

Reilly's Solution

I can use BEDMAS to remember the order of operations:
Perform operations in **B**rackets first.
Calculate **E**xponents next.
Divide and **M**ultiply from left to right.
Add and **S**ubtract from left to right.

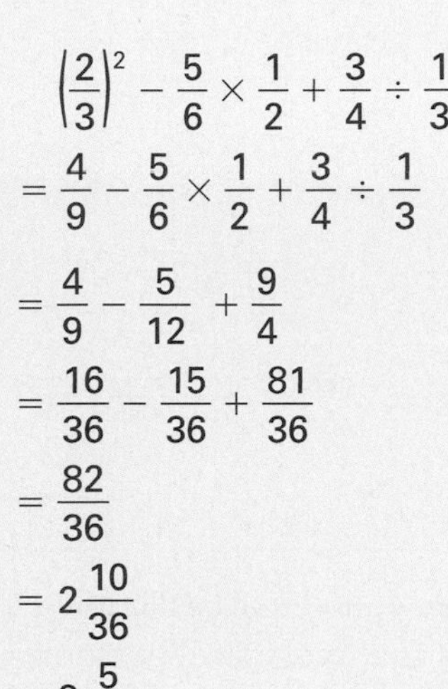

$$\left(\frac{2}{3}\right)^2 - \frac{5}{6} \times \frac{1}{2} + \frac{3}{4} \div \frac{1}{3}$$

So, the first operation I should do is $\left(\frac{2}{3}\right)^2$.

This is $\frac{2}{3} \times \frac{2}{3}$, or $\frac{4}{9}$.

$$= \frac{4}{9} - \frac{5}{6} \times \frac{1}{2} + \frac{3}{4} \div \frac{1}{3}$$

Next, I multiply and divide.

$$= \frac{4}{9} - \frac{5}{12} + \frac{9}{4}$$

Then I subtract and add. But first I need to find a good common denominator for 9, 12, and 4. I'll use 36. Then I can just subtract and add the numerators.

$$= \frac{16}{36} - \frac{15}{36} + \frac{81}{36}$$

$$= \frac{82}{36}$$

I can write $\frac{82}{36}$ as a mixed number and use $\frac{5}{18}$ as an equivalent fraction for $\frac{10}{36}$.

$$= 2\frac{10}{36}$$

$$= 2\frac{5}{18}$$

A Checking

3. Calculate using the rules for order of operations.

a) $3 + \frac{1}{2} \div \frac{2}{3} \times 8$ **b)** $\frac{2}{3} + \left(\frac{1}{6}\right)^2$

4. Suppose that Tamara picked these cards in the game Target 1:

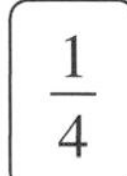

$\frac{2}{5}$ $\frac{3}{8}$ ÷

List three different ways that she could arrange the cards. Then calculate the value for each arrangement.

5. Suppose that Tamara picked these cards in Target 1:

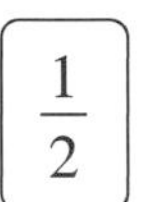

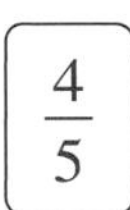

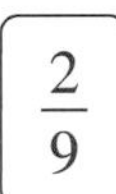

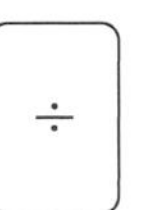

a) List three values greater than 0 that she could calculate, without using brackets, by placing the cards in different positions.

b) Are there other values she could calculate if she were allowed to use brackets?

B Practising

6. Calculate using the rules for order of operations.

a) $\frac{1}{2} - \frac{1}{3} \times \frac{1}{4} + \frac{1}{5} \div \frac{1}{6}$

b) $\left(\frac{1}{2} - \frac{1}{3}\right) \times \left(\frac{1}{4} + \frac{1}{5} \div \frac{1}{6}\right)$

c) $\left(\frac{1}{2} - \frac{1}{3} \times \frac{1}{4} + \frac{1}{5}\right) \div \frac{1}{6}$

d) $\left(\frac{1}{2} + \frac{1}{3} - \frac{1}{6}\right)^3 + \frac{2}{3} \times \frac{4}{5}$

e) $\frac{5}{4} \times \frac{1}{2} - \frac{2}{3} \div 2 + \frac{1}{2}$

f) $\left(\frac{2}{3} + \frac{1}{6}\right)^2$

7. Which expressions have the same value?

A. $\frac{2}{3} \div \frac{5}{7} \times \frac{3}{6} + \frac{1}{2}$

B. $\frac{2}{3} \div \left(\frac{5}{7} \div \frac{3}{6}\right) + \frac{1}{2}$

C. $\frac{2}{3} \div \frac{5}{7} \times \left(\frac{3}{6} + \frac{1}{2}\right)$

D. $\frac{2}{3} \div \left(\frac{5}{7} \times \frac{3}{6} + \frac{1}{2}\right)$

8. Calculate.

a) $\frac{6}{7} - \frac{3}{4} \times \left(\frac{3}{5} + \frac{2}{10}\right)$

b) $\frac{5}{8} \div \frac{1}{10} + \frac{1}{3}$

c) $\frac{5}{4} + 2\frac{1}{2} \times 3 \div \frac{2}{3}$

d) $\frac{3}{7} \div \frac{4}{5} + \frac{1}{5}$

e) $\frac{4}{9} + \frac{2}{3} \times \frac{4}{5} \div \frac{1}{10}$

f) $\frac{8}{9} \times \left(\frac{2}{5} + \frac{3}{7} \times \frac{1}{3} + \frac{3}{5}\right) \times 4$

9. What is the missing digit in the following equation?

$$\frac{5}{\blacksquare} + \left(\frac{3}{4} - \frac{2}{3}\right)^2 = \frac{1}{24}$$

10. Use two pairs of brackets to make the following equation true.

$$2 + \frac{1}{4} + \frac{1}{3} \times \frac{3}{7} - \frac{2}{5} \times \frac{3}{8} \div \frac{1}{10} + \frac{1}{5} = 1\frac{3}{4}$$

11. What values of a, b, and c will make the value of the expression below greater than $1\frac{1}{2}$? Determine two sets of possibilities with a, b, and c as proper fractions.

$a - b + c^2$

12. Which expressions have values less than 1?

A. $\frac{1}{2} + \left(\frac{1}{2}\right)^2 \times \frac{1}{2}$

B. $2 \div \frac{7}{10} \times \frac{1}{3}$

C. $\frac{7}{8} \times 1\frac{1}{4} \div \left(\frac{1}{4}\right)^2$

D. $2\frac{2}{3} \times \frac{1}{5} + \frac{1}{5}$

C Extending

13. The values of a, b, c, and d are fractions. Determine values that make each statement true.

a) $\frac{1}{2} \times a + b < \frac{1}{2} + a \times b$

b) $\frac{2}{3} \div c > \frac{2}{3} + c$

c) $3\frac{1}{2} \times d > d \div \frac{2}{3}$

14. Create an expression involving fractions and operation signs that results in a whole number only if the correct order of operations is used.

15. Determine the value of m or n to make the equation true.

a) $\frac{2}{m} \times \frac{3}{4} + \frac{1}{5} \div \frac{1}{2} = \frac{m}{5} \times \frac{1}{2} + \frac{m}{5}$

b) $\frac{4}{n} - \frac{1}{2} \times \frac{6}{n} \div \frac{2}{n} = 1 - \frac{1}{n}$

Chapter Self-Test

1. Calculate.

a) $\frac{1}{2}+\frac{3}{4}$

b) $\frac{2}{3}+\frac{1}{9}$

c) $\frac{3}{5}+\frac{1}{3}$

d) $\frac{7}{10}-\frac{2}{5}$

e) $\frac{1}{4}-\frac{1}{12}$

f) $\frac{2}{3}-\frac{1}{4}$

2. Order these expressions from least to greatest.

a) $\frac{3}{4}-\frac{1}{10}$

b) $\frac{1}{2}+\frac{1}{6}$

c) $\frac{5}{6}-\frac{1}{4}$

d) $\frac{3}{5}+\frac{1}{6}$

3. Draw a model that represents $3-1\frac{2}{5}$.

4. Calculate.

a) $1\frac{2}{5}+3\frac{4}{5}$

b) $\frac{3}{4}+5\frac{3}{8}$

c) $6\frac{3}{10}-1\frac{1}{5}$

d) $4\frac{1}{3}-2\frac{1}{2}$

5. Kevin bought 3 pizzas to share with his family. Together, they ate $1\frac{5}{12}$ pizzas on Monday and another $\frac{3}{4}$ of a pizza on Tuesday. How much pizza is left after Tuesday?

6. Use fraction strips to model and complete.

a) $\frac{2}{3}$ of $\frac{1}{4}$ is ■.

b) $\frac{1}{2}$ of $\frac{6}{9}$ is ■.

c) $1\frac{1}{5}$ of $\frac{5}{7}$ is ■.

7. Explain why multiplying a fraction by $\frac{5}{6}$ results in a value that is less than the original fraction.

8. Calculate.

a) $\frac{3}{5}\times\frac{5}{8}$

b) $\frac{2}{6}\times\frac{5}{6}$

c) $\frac{3}{7}\times\frac{1}{6}$

d) $\frac{5}{8}\times\frac{3}{7}\times\frac{1}{2}$

9. Draw a picture to show that $\frac{3}{4}\times\frac{4}{5}$ is $\frac{12}{20}$, or $\frac{3}{5}$.

10. Describe a situation in which you would multiply $\frac{1}{2}\times\frac{3}{4}$.

11. Show two ways to calculate $1\frac{2}{3}\times 2\frac{1}{4}$.

12. Calculate.

a) $\frac{3}{5}\times 5\frac{1}{2}$

b) $\frac{7}{10}\times 6\frac{3}{4}$

c) $1\frac{2}{5}\times 1\frac{3}{4}$

d) $\frac{2}{9}\times 5\frac{1}{3}$

13. a) Draw a picture to show that $\frac{3}{4}\div\frac{5}{8}$ is $1\frac{1}{5}$.

b) Use a multiplication equation to show that $\frac{3}{4}\div\frac{5}{8}=1\frac{1}{5}$.

14. Calculate.

a) $\frac{4}{5}\div\frac{2}{5}$

b) $\frac{5}{8}\div\frac{1}{5}$

c) $\frac{1}{5}\div\frac{5}{8}$

d) $3\frac{1}{2}\div 1\frac{1}{4}$

15. The product of 3.4×4.1 has a digit in the hundredths place, but not in the thousandths place. Use fraction operations to explain why.

16. Calculate.

a) $\frac{2}{3}-\frac{1}{4}\times\frac{5}{6}\div 2$

b) $\left(\frac{2}{3}-\frac{1}{4}\right)\times\left(\frac{5}{6}\div 2\right)$

c) $\frac{2}{3}-\left(\frac{1}{2}\right)^2\times\frac{5}{6}\div 2$

Chapter Review

Frequently Asked Questions

Q: How can you multiply two mixed numbers?

A1: You can use an area model to multiply two mixed numbers. For example, suppose that you wanted to calculate the area of a rectangle that is $1\frac{1}{3}$ units long and $2\frac{1}{2}$ units wide. There are 4×5 squares, each with an area of $\frac{1}{6}$. So, the total area is $\frac{20}{6} = \frac{10}{3}$, or $3\frac{1}{3}$.

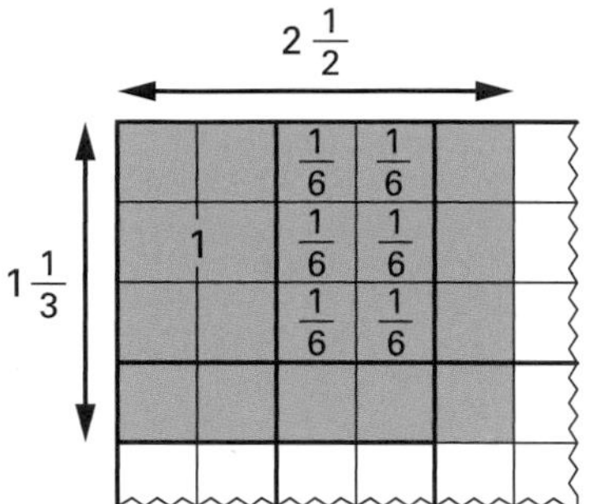

A2: You can write each mixed number as an improper fraction. Then you multiply the numerators to get the numerator of the product and multiply the denominators to get the denominator of the product.

$$\begin{aligned} 1\frac{1}{3} \times 2\frac{1}{2} &= \frac{4}{3} \times \frac{5}{2} \\ &= \frac{20}{6} \\ &= 3\frac{2}{6} \\ &= 3\frac{1}{3} \end{aligned}$$

You can check if your answer is reasonable by estimating. Since $1 \times 2\frac{1}{2} = 2\frac{1}{2}$, it is reasonable that the answer is a bit more than 3.

Q: How can you divide two fractions?

A1: You can determine the number of times the divisor fits into the dividend using fraction strips and a common denominator.

$$2\frac{2}{3} \div \frac{5}{6} = \frac{8}{3} \div \frac{5}{6}$$
$$= \frac{16}{6} \div \frac{5}{6}$$
$$= \frac{16}{5}, \text{ or } 3\frac{1}{5}$$

$\frac{1}{3}$	$\frac{1}{3}$	$\frac{1}{3}$	$\frac{1}{3}$	$\frac{1}{3}$	$\frac{1}{3}$	$\frac{1}{3}$	$\frac{1}{3}$	$\frac{1}{3}$

$\frac{1}{6}$	$\frac{1}{6}$	$\frac{1}{6}$	$\frac{1}{6}$	$\frac{1}{6}$	$\frac{1}{6}$	$\frac{1}{6}$	$\frac{1}{6}$	$\frac{1}{6}$	$\frac{1}{6}$	$\frac{1}{6}$	$\frac{1}{6}$	$\frac{1}{6}$	$\frac{1}{6}$	$\frac{1}{6}$	$\frac{1}{6}$	$\frac{1}{6}$	$\frac{1}{6}$	$\frac{1}{6}$	$\frac{1}{6}$

A2: You can multiply by the reciprocal. For example,

$$2\frac{2}{3} \div \frac{5}{6} = \frac{8}{3} \div \frac{5}{6}$$
$$= \frac{8}{3} \times \frac{6}{5}$$
$$= \frac{48}{15}$$
$$= \frac{16}{5}, \text{ or } 3\frac{1}{5}$$

Q: In what order do you perform a series of fraction calculations?

A: Use the rules for the order of operations:

Perform the operations in **B**rackets first.
Calculate **E**xponents next.
Divide and **M**ultiply from left to right.
Add and **S**ubtract from left to right.

For example,

$$\frac{3}{2} - \frac{2}{5} \div \frac{1}{5} \times \left(\frac{3}{8} + \frac{1}{8}\right)^2 + \frac{2}{3}$$
$$= \frac{3}{2} - \frac{2}{5} \div \frac{1}{5} \times \left(\frac{1}{2}\right)^2 + \frac{2}{3}$$
$$= \frac{3}{2} - \frac{2}{5} \div \frac{1}{5} \times \frac{1}{4} + \frac{2}{3}$$
$$= \frac{3}{2} - 2 \times \frac{1}{4} + \frac{2}{3}$$
$$= \frac{3}{2} - \frac{1}{2} + \frac{2}{3}$$
$$= 1\frac{2}{3}$$

Practice Questions

(9.1) **1.** Sketch a model and calculate.

a) $\frac{3}{5} + \frac{2}{7}$

b) $\frac{3}{5} - \frac{2}{7}$

(9.1) **2. a)** Calculate the sum of $\frac{3}{5}$ and $\frac{2}{3}$.

b) Calculate the difference of $\frac{3}{5}$ and $\frac{2}{3}$.

c) How much greater is the sum than the difference?

(9.1) **3.** Calculate.

a) $\frac{5}{8} + \frac{1}{3}$

b) $\frac{3}{4} + \frac{5}{6}$

c) $\frac{2}{5} + \frac{1}{7}$

d) $\frac{2}{5} - \frac{1}{10}$

e) $\frac{5}{9} - \frac{2}{7}$

f) $\frac{7}{8} - \frac{2}{3}$

(9.1) **4.** Jake mowed about $\frac{3}{5}$ of the school lawn yesterday. He mowed another $\frac{1}{4}$ of the lawn this morning. How much is left to mow?

(9.2) **5.** Sketch a model, and calculate the answer.

a) $2\frac{1}{5} + 3\frac{3}{5}$

b) $2\frac{4}{5} + 3\frac{1}{2}$

c) $8 - 2\frac{1}{3}$

d) $7\frac{3}{10} - 2\frac{1}{4}$

(9.2) **6.** $\frac{a}{b}$ is a fraction. The sum of $\frac{a}{b}$ and $\frac{b}{a}$ is close to 2. List two possible values for $\frac{a}{b}$.

(9.2) **7.** Calculate.

a) $2\frac{1}{5} + 3\frac{1}{6}$

b) $5\frac{1}{2} - 3\frac{1}{3}$

c) $8 - 1\frac{3}{5}$

d) $6\frac{1}{4} - 3\frac{5}{6}$

8. A recipe calls for $1\frac{2}{3}$ cups of flour and $\frac{3}{4}$ cup of sugar. These are the only dry ingredients. What is the total measure of the dry ingredients? (9.2)

9. a) Continue this addition pattern to get three more terms in each row. (9.3)

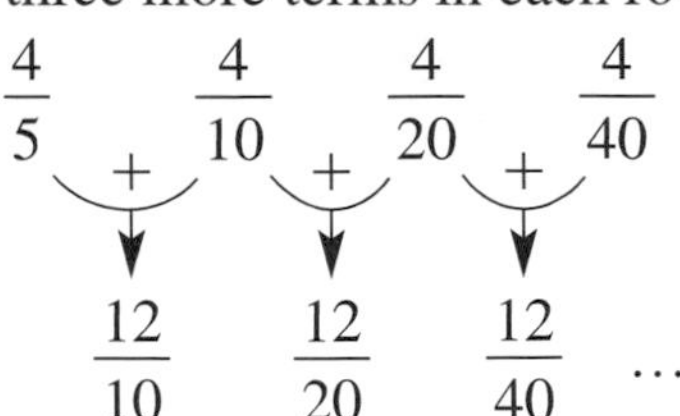

b) What is the 10th number in the 2nd row?

c) Why does it make sense that all the numerators in the 2nd row are 12?

10. What is the value of each expression? (9.4)

a) $\frac{1}{5}$ of $\frac{1}{2}$

b) $\frac{3}{8}$ of $\frac{8}{9}$

c) $\frac{2}{3}$ of $\frac{6}{8}$

d) $\frac{4}{6}$ of $\frac{1}{2}$

11. What is the missing fraction in each sentence? (9.4)

a) $\frac{2}{5}$ is $\frac{2}{3}$ of ■.

b) $\frac{3}{8}$ is $\frac{3}{4}$ of ■.

c) $\frac{2}{12}$ is $\frac{1}{4}$ of ■.

d) $\frac{5}{12}$ is $\frac{1}{2}$ of ■.

12. What is the missing fraction in each sentence? (9.4)

a) ■ of $\frac{1}{2}$ is $\frac{1}{8}$.

b) ■ of $\frac{5}{6}$ is $\frac{1}{12}$.

c) ■ of $\frac{4}{9}$ is $\frac{1}{3}$.

d) ■ of $\frac{5}{7}$ is $\frac{3}{7}$.

13. Sketch a model for this calculation. (9.5)

$\frac{3}{4} \times \frac{2}{5} = \frac{6}{20}$

(9.5) **14.** Which products are greater than $\frac{1}{2}$?

A. $\frac{3}{4} \times \frac{5}{6}$

B. $\frac{1}{6} \times \frac{7}{8}$

C. $\frac{3}{9} \times \frac{8}{9}$

D. $\frac{3}{5} \times \frac{2}{3}$

(9.5) **15.** How much greater is the first product than the second product?

a) $\frac{3}{4} \times \frac{5}{6}$ than $\frac{1}{4} \times \frac{5}{6}$

b) $\frac{3}{4} \times \frac{5}{6}$ than $\frac{3}{4} \times \frac{1}{2}$

(9.5) **16.** Calculate.

a) $\frac{2}{9} \times \frac{2}{7}$

b) $\left(\frac{3}{5}\right)^2$

c) $\left(\frac{2}{3}\right)^3$

d) $\frac{5}{8} \times \frac{2}{3}$

e) $\frac{1}{5} \times \frac{5}{7}$

f) $\frac{3}{7} \times \frac{2}{5}$

(9.5) **17.** About $\frac{3}{4}$ of the students in the drama club are girls. About $\frac{3}{4}$ of these girls are in Grade 8. What fraction of the students in the drama club are Grade 8 girls?

(9.6) **18.** Eileen used to be on the phone $3\frac{1}{2}$ times as much as her sister every day. As a New Year's resolution, she decided to cut down to about $\frac{2}{5}$ of the time she used to be on the phone. About how many times as much as her sister is Eileen now on the phone?

(9.6) **19.** Calculate.

a) $\frac{3}{7} \times 3\frac{1}{2}$

b) $\frac{2}{5} \times 1\frac{3}{5}$

c) $1\frac{1}{3} \times 1\frac{2}{3}$

d) $\frac{5}{6} \times 6\frac{12}{25}$

e) $2\frac{3}{4} \times 3\frac{3}{4}$

f) $3\frac{1}{5} \times 6\frac{3}{8}$

20. Sketch a model to show $\frac{5}{6} \div \frac{1}{3} = 2\frac{1}{2}$. (9.7)

21. Explain how you know that $\frac{4}{6} \div \frac{3}{6}$ has the same quotient as $\frac{4}{5} \div \frac{3}{5}$. (9.7)

22. Calculate. (9.7)

a) $\frac{5}{6} \div \frac{1}{6}$

b) $\frac{5}{8} \div \frac{1}{4}$

c) $\frac{5}{6} \div \frac{1}{4}$

d) $\frac{3}{8} \div \frac{2}{9}$

23. What fraction calculation can you use to determine the number of quarters in $4.50? (9.7)

24. Pia used $\frac{2}{3}$ of her sugar to make $\frac{3}{4}$ of a batch of cookies. How much of her sugar would she need to make the whole batch? (9.8)

25. Choose two fractions to make each statement true. (9.8)

a) The sum is greater than the product.

b) The sum is less than the product.

c) The quotient is greater than the sum.

26. Use fractions to explain why 4.5×0.5 equals 2.25. (9.9)

27. Which expression has the greatest value? How do you know? (9.10)

A. $\frac{4}{5} \times \frac{2}{3} - \frac{1}{5} \times \frac{5}{8}$

B. $\frac{4}{5} \times \left(\frac{2}{3} - \frac{1}{5}\right) \times \frac{5}{8}$

C. $\left(\frac{4}{5} \times \frac{2}{3} - \frac{1}{5}\right) \times \frac{5}{8}$

28. Where can you place brackets to make this equation true? (9.10)

$$\frac{3}{5} + \frac{1}{4} \div \frac{2}{3} + \frac{1}{3} = \frac{193}{120}$$

Chapter Task

Parts of Canada

? How can you use fraction calculations to compare the parts of Canada?

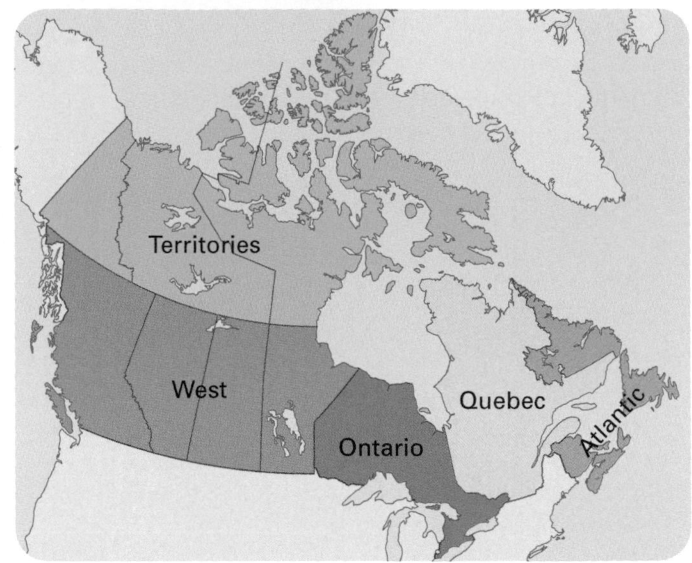

A. Use the map and the given populations to complete the chart below. Use the map to estimate the land area. Round the populations to estimate the fractions.

Region	Atlantic	Quebec	Ontario	West	Territories
Approximate fraction of land area of Canada		$\frac{1}{6}$	$\frac{1}{9}$		
Approximate fraction of population of Canada					

Populations in 2004	
Atlantic	2 367 000
Quebec	7 451 000
Ontario	12 178 000
West	8 552 000
Territories	99 000

B. Matthew noticed that the land area of Ontario is about $\frac{2}{3}$ of the land area of Quebec. Use fraction operations to compare the regions of Canada in at least five different ways. Make sure that

- one comparison involves three operations
- one comparison involves two operations
- each of the four operations is used somewhere

C. Which calculations did you perform using mental math? Why?

D. Describe at least two comparisons that involve several calculations. What do you need to know about the rules for order of operations to perform these calculations?

Task Checklist

- ☑ Did you use the given populations correctly to calculate the fractions?
- ☑ Did you check that the fractions in each row add to 1?
- ☑ Did you use all the operations in your comparisons?
- ☑ Did you perform all the calculations correctly?
- ☑ Did you explain your thinking clearly?

Cumulative Review
Chapters 7–9

Cross-Strand Multiple Choice

(7.1) **1.** What are the coordinates of the point in quadrant 4?

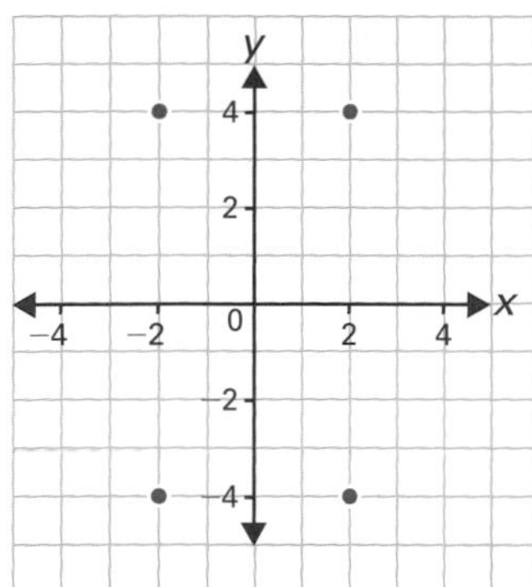

A. (2, −4) **C.** (−2, 4)
B. (2, 4) **D.** (−2, −4)

Use $\triangle ABC$ to answer questions 2 and 3.

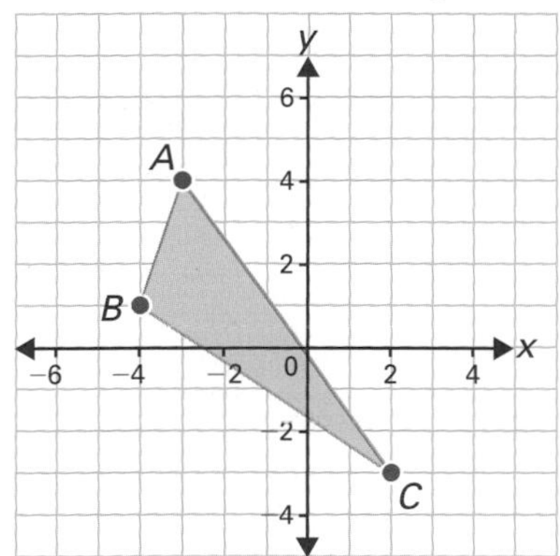

(7.3) **2.** What is the image of *A* after a reflection in the *x*-axis?

A. (−3, −4) **C.** (3, −4)
B. (3, 4) **D.** (4, −3)

(7.3) **3.** What is the image of *A* after a rotation of 270° clockwise about the origin?

A. (4, 3) **C.** (−3, −4)
B. (3, −4) **D.** (−4, −3)

4. When the number of players signing up for a sport is multiplied by 7, and 3 players leave, there are 60 players left. Which equation represents this situation? (8.4)

A. $3 - 7n = 60$ **C.** $7n - 3 = 60$
B. $7n + 3 = 60$ **D.** $n - 21 = 60$

5. What is the solution for the equation $2x + 7 = 13$? (8.4)

A. $x = 3$ **C.** $x = 6.5$
B. $x = 10$ **D.** $x = 4$

6. What is the solution for the equation $4t - 2.8 = 62.8$? (8.5)

A. $t = 15$ **C.** $t = 12.9$
B. $t = 16.4$ **D.** $t = 15.7$

7. Toma went out for $4\frac{1}{2}$ h. She spent $2\frac{2}{3}$ h watching a movie and the rest of the time riding her bike. How much time did Toma spend riding her bike? (9.2)

A. $1\frac{1}{6}$ h **C.** $2\frac{5}{6}$ h
B. $1\frac{5}{6}$ h **D.** $2\frac{2}{3}$ h

8. Rishi has $\frac{3}{4}$ of a bag of peanuts. Sheree has $2\frac{1}{2}$ times as much. How many bags of peanuts does Sheree have? (9.6)

A. $6\frac{1}{2}$ **B.** $3\frac{3}{4}$ **C.** $\frac{3}{10}$ **D.** $1\frac{7}{8}$

9. What is the value of $\frac{3}{4} + \frac{4}{5} \times \frac{2}{3} \div \frac{1}{5}$? (9.10)

A. $5\frac{1}{6}$ **B.** $3\frac{5}{12}$ **C.** $17\frac{2}{9}$ **D.** $\frac{31}{45}$

Cross-Strand Investigation

Confederation Bridge joins Prince Edward Island and New Brunswick over the Northumberland Strait. It is the longest bridge over ice-covered waters in the world.

10. a) Confederation Bridge is 11.00 m wide. Each direction has a lane for traffic and a 1.75 m emergency shoulder. The two traffic lanes are equal in width. Write and solve an equation to determine the width of each traffic lane.

b) Approximately 11 000 m of Confederation Bridge is over water. There are 44 piers to support the bridge, creating 43 spaces between the piers. Write and solve an equation to determine the mean distance, to the nearest metre, between the centre of one pier to the centre of the next pier.

c) Last week, Joe spent $1\frac{1}{3}$ h crossing Confederation Bridge. Each crossing took $\frac{1}{6}$ of an hour. How many round trips did he make?

d) In 1 h, 788 automobiles, 19 recreational vehicles, 68 trucks, 21 motorcycles, and 23 buses went through the tollbooth on Confederation Bridge. Write and solve an algebraic expression to determine the total amount of money collected from these vehicles.

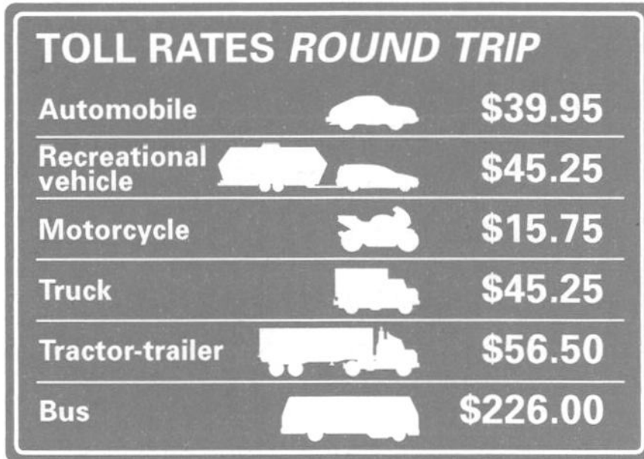

TOLL RATES *ROUND TRIP*	
Automobile	$39.95
Recreational vehicle	$45.25
Motorcycle	$15.75
Truck	$45.25
Tractor-trailer	$56.50
Bus	$226.00

e) Lyle tallied the number of vehicles that crossed Confederation Bridge in 1 h. He found that $\frac{3}{4}$ of the vehicles were automobiles and $\frac{1}{5}$ were trucks. What fraction describes the number of vehicles that were not automobiles or trucks?

f) The trucks that are used to maintain the bridge are parked in the positions shown. Describe one reflection followed by another reflection that could move the red truck to the position of the green truck. Give two possible answers.

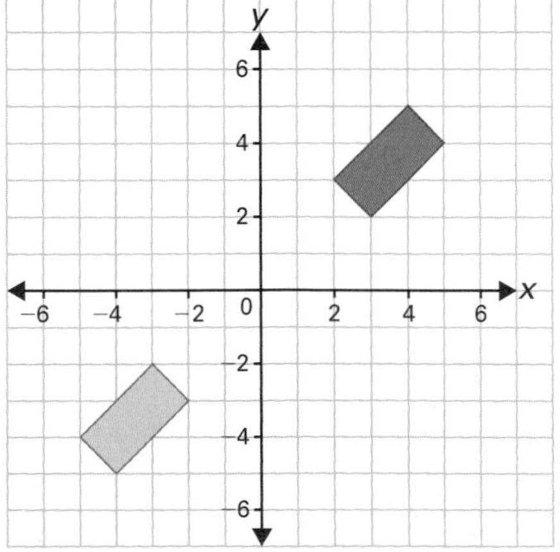

CHAPTER 10

Angles and Triangles

▶ GOALS

You will be able to

- construct circles, triangles, and quadrilaterals, and describe their properties
- investigate, describe, and use the relationships between angles of intersecting lines
- investigate, describe, and use the Pythagorean relationship for right triangles
- create and solve problems that involve lines, angles, and right triangles

Getting Started

You will need
- a protractor
- a ruler
- a calculator

Determining Location

Hikers can get lost in a new environment, so they are encouraged to carry rescue equipment. If they have a cell phone, rescue personnel may be able to track their location using the signal from the phone.

? What information do rescuers need to locate a hiker?

A. A lost hiker calls rescue personnel. They pinpoint her signal to be between the east tower and west tower, which are 6 km apart. They determine that the signal comes from the north and reaches the east tower at an angle of 60° to the line between the east tower and west tower. The signal reaches the west tower at an angle of 50° to the same line.

Draw a scale diagram of this situation. Start with a horizontal line, and use 1 cm to represent 1 km. What 2-D shape have you drawn?

B. Give directions for someone to locate the hiker, starting at the east tower.

C. Another lost hiker calls and says that he remembers passing a tower when he was walking north. He is now walking east. The phone signal comes to the east tower at a 30° angle from north. Why can the rescuers not determine exactly where he is?

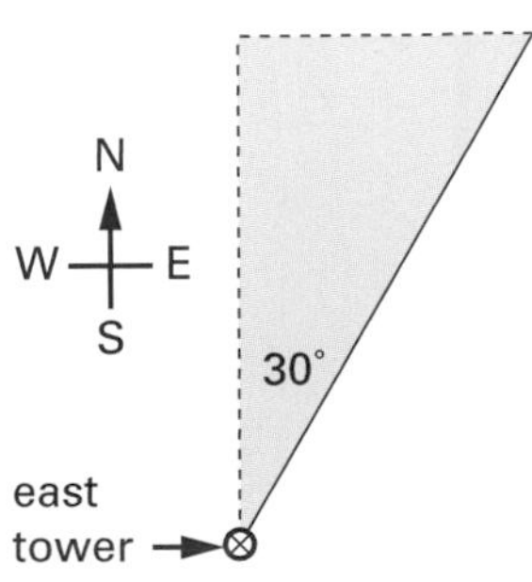

D. What other information might the rescuers need to locate the second hiker?

Do You Remember?

1. Determine each square root. Use a calculator when necessary. Round to one decimal place.

   a) $\sqrt{64}$ c) $\sqrt{49}$ e) $\sqrt{24}$
   b) $\sqrt{9}$ d) $\sqrt{10}$ f) $\sqrt{2}$

2. Measure the sides and angles in each triangle, using a ruler and a protractor.

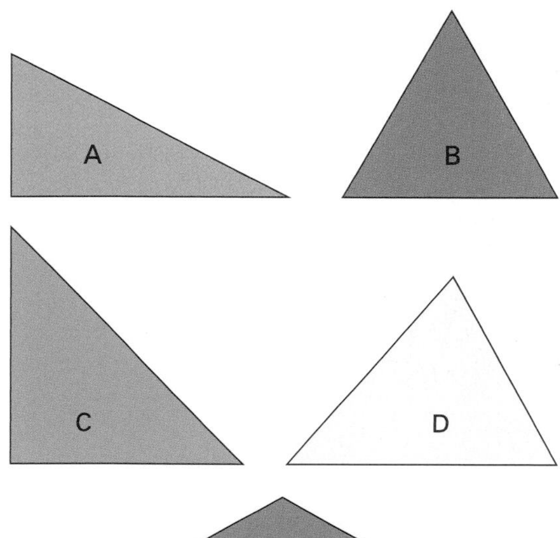

   Then select all the words that describe each triangle from the list below.

   isosceles equilateral right
   acute obtuse scalene

3. Which angles in each triangle are equal?

   a)

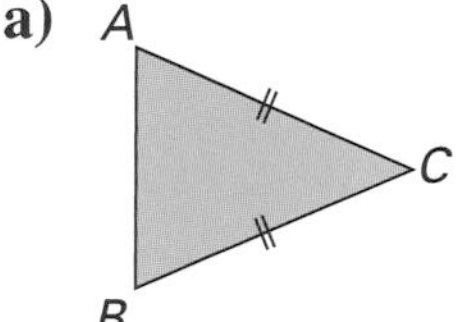

   b)

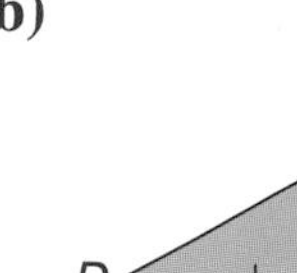

4. Use the letters to identify the **parallel** and **perpendicular** sides in each quadrilateral.

   a) b) c)

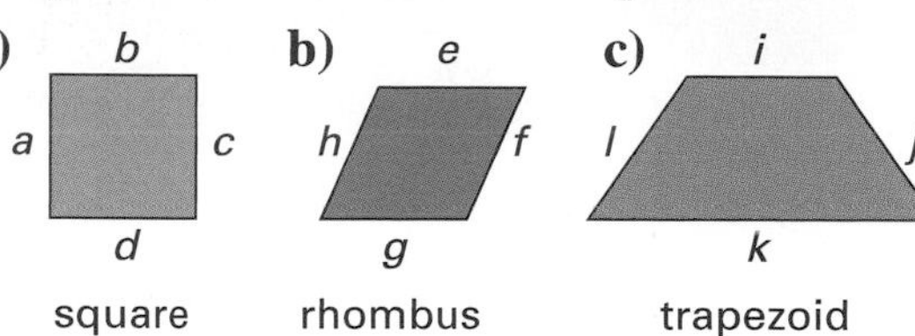

5. These pattern block tessellations show congruent regular polygons. Determine the measures of $\angle 1$ and $\angle 2$, without measuring.

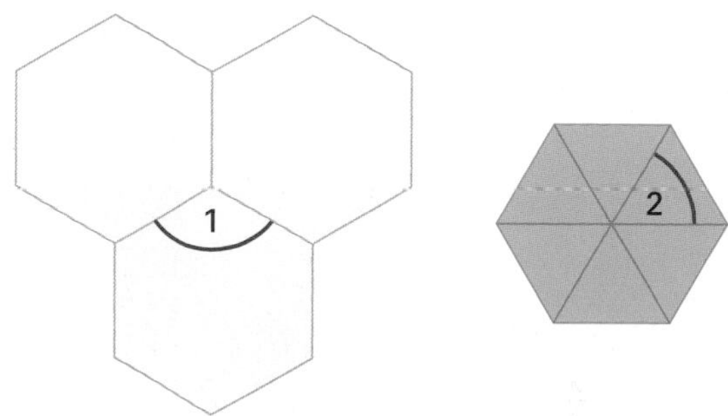

6. $\triangle ABC$ is **similar** to $\triangle DEF$.

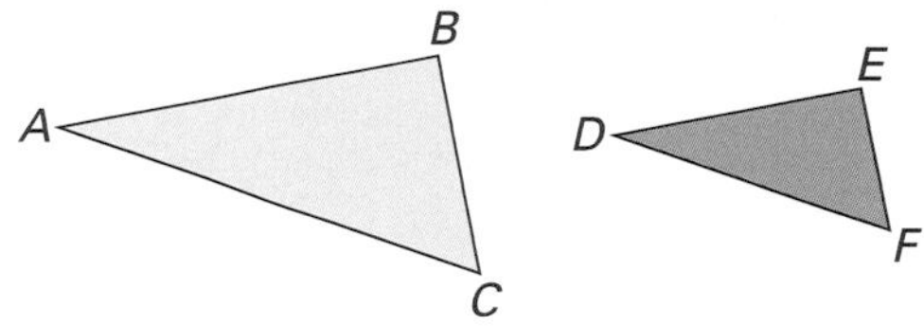

   a) Which angle has the same measure as $\angle A$?

   b) Which other pairs of angles are equal?

7. Draw a triangle that fits each description. Draw a second triangle if possible.

   a) a triangle with a 90° angle and a 4 cm side

   b) a triangle with a 3 cm side between 30° and 70° angles

   c) a triangle with a 5 cm side and 40° and 60° angles

10.1

Exploring Points on a Circle

You will need
- a protractor
- a ruler
- a compass
- coloured pencils

▶ **GOAL**
Locate the centre of a circle, given three points on the circle.

Explore the Math

Three houses are going to be built at the end of a street in a new subdivision. For safety, a streetlight will be placed in a position that is **equidistant** from the three houses. The diagram below shows the positions of the houses.

equidistant
the same distance

? Where should the streetlight be placed?

A. On a large piece of paper, draw a diagram like the one below. Use a labelled point to represent each house location.

Y •

X •

• Z

B. Mark three points that are equidistant from points X and Y. Use any method you wish. (Check by measuring, and adjust the points if necessary.)

C. Draw a line that passes through all three points you found in step B.

D. Pick two other points on your line. Show that each point is also equidistant from X and Y.

E. Join XY. How do you know that your line is the **perpendicular bisector** of XY?

F. Repeat steps B to E using points X and Z or Y and Z. What do you notice?

G. Place the point of your compass on the point where your lines intersected in step F. Draw a circle that passes through point X. What other points does it pass through?

H. Where should the streetlight be placed?

Reflecting

1. How did you find the points that were equidistant from X and Y in step B?

2. What is the relationship between the endpoints of a line segment and any point on the perpendicular bisector of the line segment?

3. Suppose that you were asked to draw a circle through any three given points. What would you do?

perpendicular bisector

a line that intersects a line segment to form two 90° angles and divides this line segment into two equal lengths

perpendicular bisector

A B

Communication Tip

In a diagram, perpendicular lines are indicated by a little square.

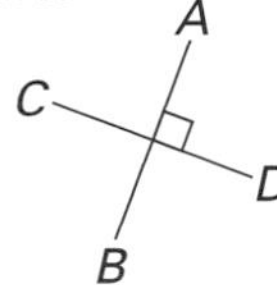

In writing, perpendicular lines are indicated by the symbol $\perp$. For example, $AB \perp CD$.

10.2 Intersecting Lines, Parallel Lines, and Transversals

You will need
- a protractor
- a ruler
- scissors
- a compass

▶ **GOAL**
Identify and apply the relationships between the measures of angles formed by intersecting lines.

Learn about the Math

The picture shows that Thomson Street is parallel to Queen Street. It also shows that King Street crosses both of these streets at an angle that is not 90°. There are three cyclists in the picture. Anneli and Norah will be turning onto Queen Street. David will be turning onto Thomson Street.

? How are the angles formed by intersecting streets related?

A. In your notebook, draw and label a large diagram like the one below. Then trace your diagram on a piece of paper, and cut out the four angles.

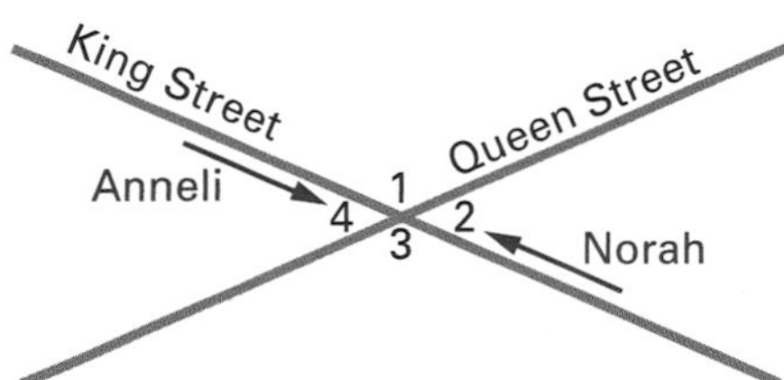

B. The following diagram shows what happens if both Norah and Anneli turn right. Compare the **opposite angles**, ∠2 and ∠4. (Place one cut angle on top of the other, or measure the angles in your drawing.) What do you notice?

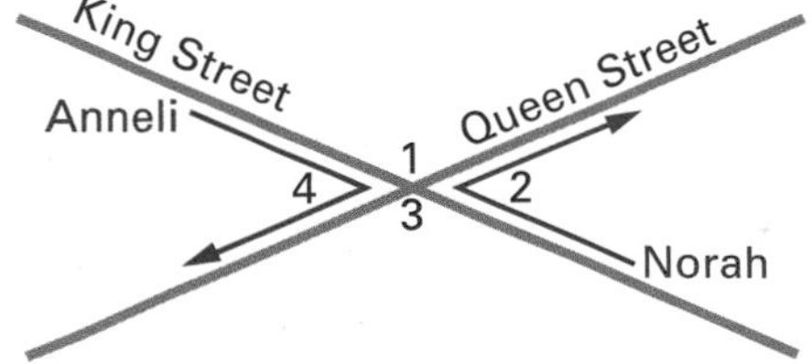

opposite angles
non-adjacent angles that are formed by two intersecting lines

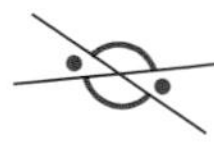
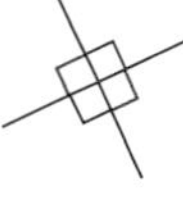

C. This diagram shows what happens if Norah turns right and Anneli turns left. Compare the **adjacent angles**, ∠2 and ∠1. (Place one cut angle on top of the other, or measure the angles in your drawing.) What do you notice?

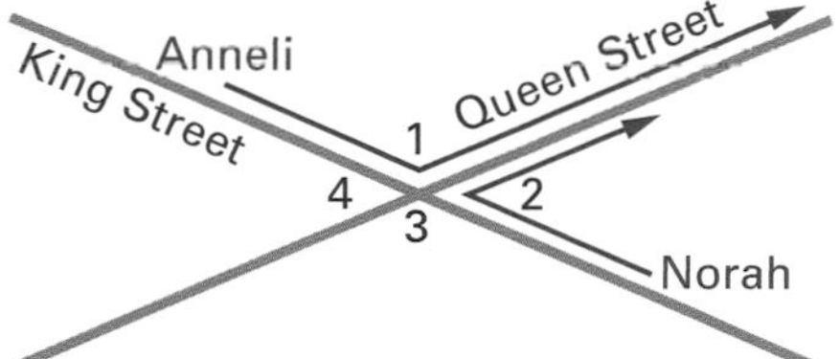

adjacent angles

angles that share a common vertex and a common arm

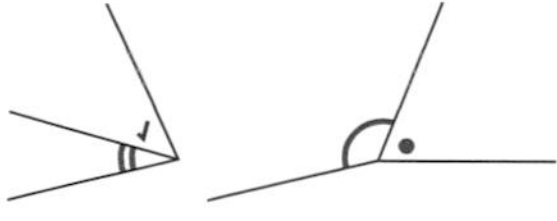

D. How do you know that ∠1 and ∠2 form a **straight angle**? (Place your cut angles together, or measure the angles in your drawing.) Why are these angles **supplementary angles**?

straight angle

an angle that measures 180°

supplementary angles

two angles whose sum is 180°

E. Draw another line on your diagram from step A to represent Thomson Street. How can you make sure that this line is parallel to the line that represents Queen Street? Label the eight angles that are formed by the intersecting lines.

F. The line that represents King Street is a **transversal**. It crosses the two parallel lines that represent Queen Street and Thomson Street. Which of the eight angles formed have the same measure as ∠8?

transversal

a straight line that intersects two or more lines

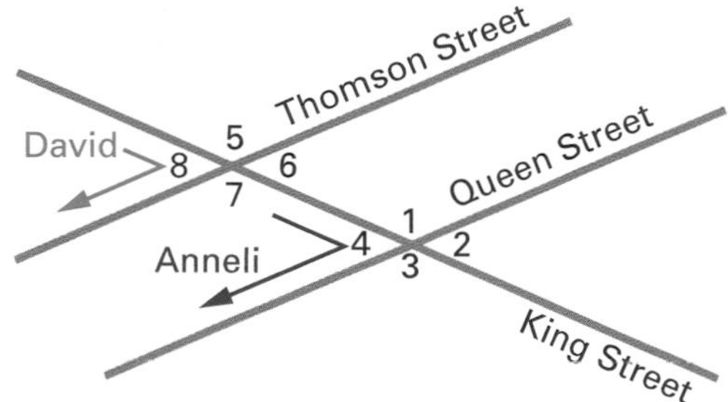

corresponding angles

matching angles that are formed by a **transversal** and two parallel lines

G. The diagram above shows what happens if both Anneli and David turn right. Compare the **corresponding angles**, ∠4 and ∠8. What do you notice?

Reflecting

1. Two lines intersect, and you know the measure of one angle. How can you determine the measures of the other three angles?
2. a) How do you know that ∠1 and ∠6 are supplementary angles?
   b) What other pairs of non-adjacent angles are supplementary?
3. A transversal intersects two parallel lines, and you know the measure of one angle. How can you determine the measures of the other seven angles?

Communication Tip

In a diagram, parallel lines are indicated with matching numbers of arrowheads on the lines.

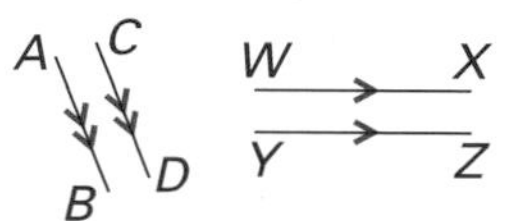

In writing, parallel lines are indicated by the symbol ∥. For example, *AB* ∥ *CD*.

Work with the Math

Example: Identifying angle relationships

What is the relationship between ∠2 and ∠8?

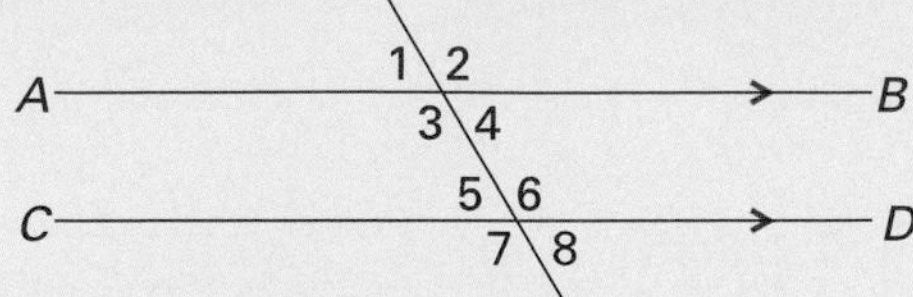

Denis's Solution: Measuring angles using a protractor

∠2 = 120° and ∠8 = 60°

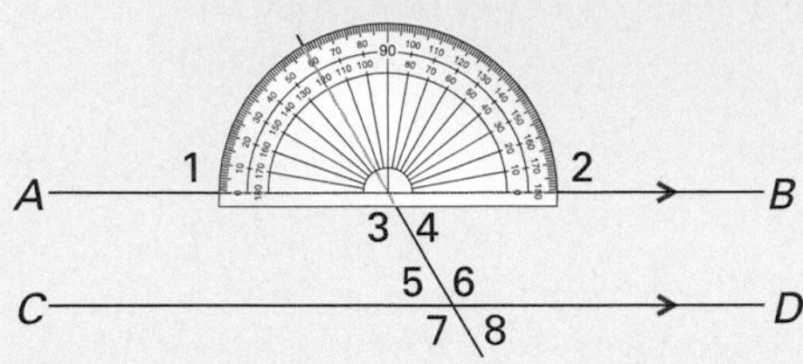

I saw that ∠2 is bigger than ∠8. When I measured the angles, I found that they add up to 180°.

So, ∠2 and ∠8 are supplementary angles.

Eva's Solution: Using angle relationships

In the diagram, ∠4 = ∠8.

∠2 + ∠4 = 180°

So, ∠2 + ∠8 = 180°

A transversal that crosses parallel lines forms corresponding angles. These corresponding angles are equal.

I know that ∠2 and ∠4 form a straight angle, so they are supplementary angles.

So, ∠2 and ∠8 must also be supplementary angles.

A Checking

4. What is the measure of the marked angle?

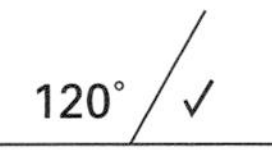

5. a) What is the measure of the marked angle?

b) What is the measure of each unmarked angle?

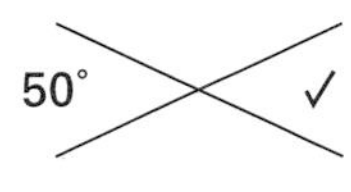

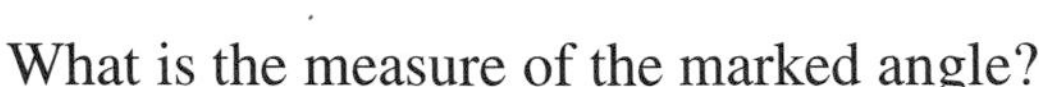

6. What is the measure of the marked angle?

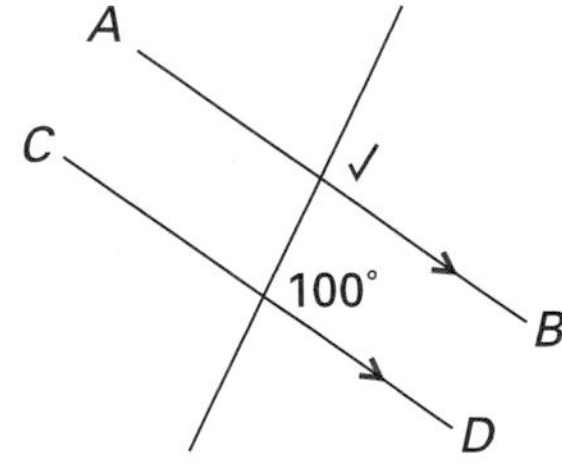

B Practising

7. What are the measures of ∠*a*, ∠*b*, ∠*c*, and ∠*d*? How do you know?

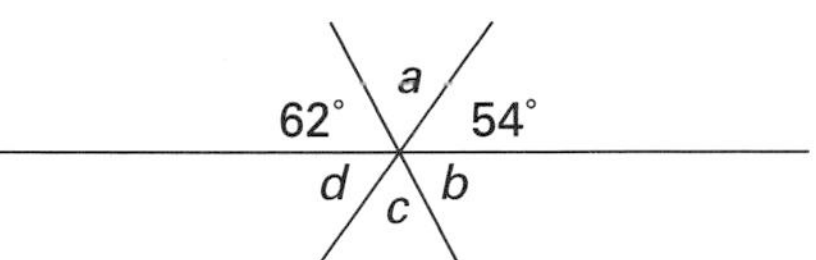

8. Which of ∠5, ∠6, ∠7, and ∠8 are supplementary to ∠1? How do you know?

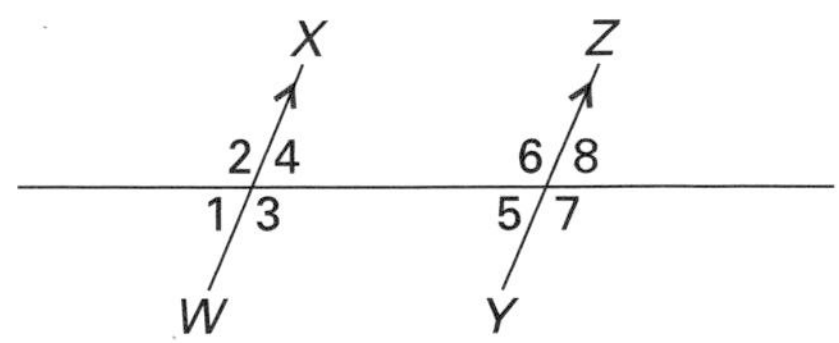

NEL

9. Draw a diagram in which $XY \parallel CD$. Then draw a transversal that crosses both lines at a 60° angle. Label the angles with numbers. Which pairs of angles in your diagram are corresponding angles?

10. Draw a diagram in which $JK \perp MN$. Label the angles with numbers. Which angles are supplementary angles?

11. Measure $\angle a$ and $\angle c$. Then determine the measures of $\angle 1$, $\angle 2$, and $\angle 3$ without measuring. Explain your reasoning.

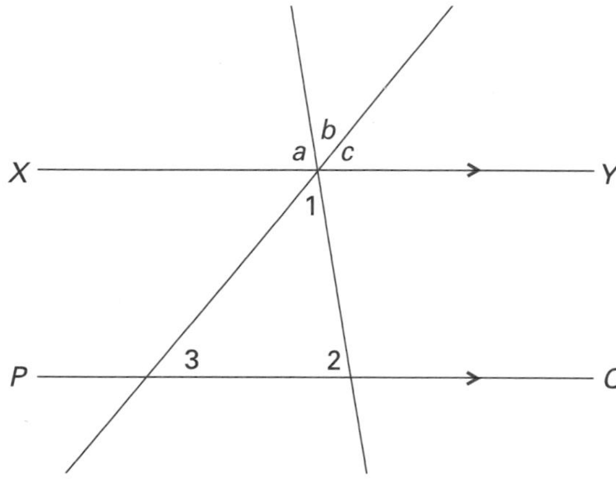

12. The shaded shape is a parallelogram.

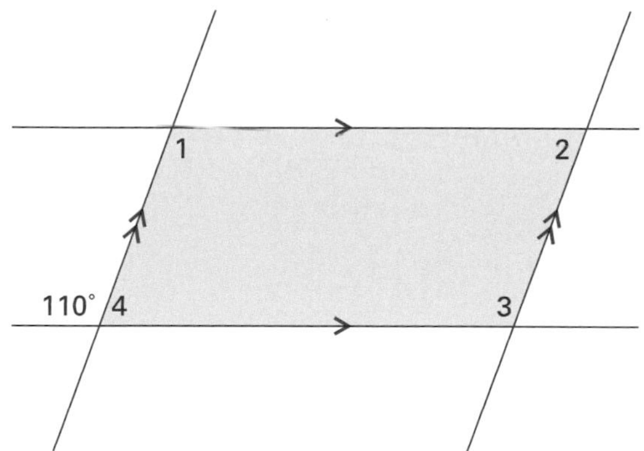

a) What are the measures of $\angle 1$, $\angle 2$, $\angle 3$, and $\angle 4$?

b) Which angles in the parallelogram are supplementary?

C Extending

13. Some people use letter shapes that are formed by intersecting lines and transversals to help them remember the angle relationships.

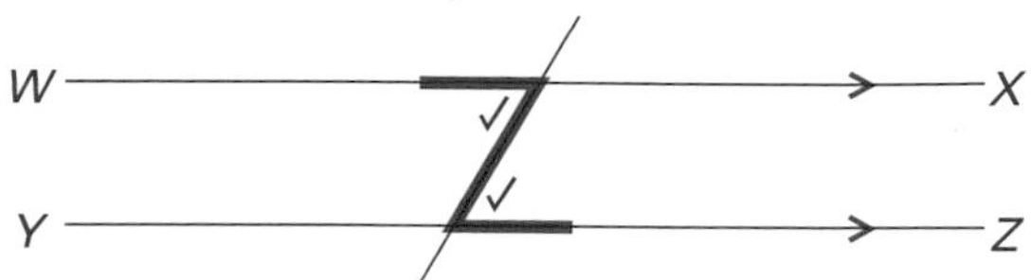

a) The diagram above shows a Z design. What is the relationship between the marked angles?

b) There are also C and F designs in the diagram above. Draw a diagram to show each design. Describe the relationships between the angles.

14. a) Draw the following group of rectangles on grid paper: a 3-by-1 rectangle, a 3-by-2 rectangle, a 3-by-3 rectangle, a 3-by-4 rectangle, and a 3-by-5 rectangle. Then draw the diagonals in each rectangle.

b) Describe what happens to the measure of the angles created by the diagonals as the rectangles get wider.

15. This diagram shows a transversal that crosses two non-parallel lines.

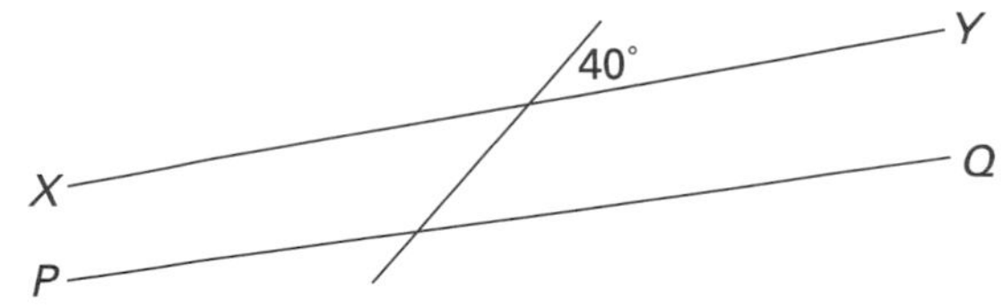

a) What angle measures do you know without measuring? What are these angle measures?

b) What angle measures do you *not* know without measuring?

10.3 Angles in a Triangle

You will need
- a protractor
- a ruler
- scissors

▶ **GOAL**
Determine the sum of the angles in a triangle.

Learn about the Math

Maria's family is building a solar house. The back of the house will get the most sunlight. Maria read that the best roof angle for collecting solar energy is 50°. The front of the roof will have a smaller angle.

To finish constructing the roof, the builder needs to know the measure of the top angle. Maria says that she can calculate this, so that no one has to climb up and measure it.

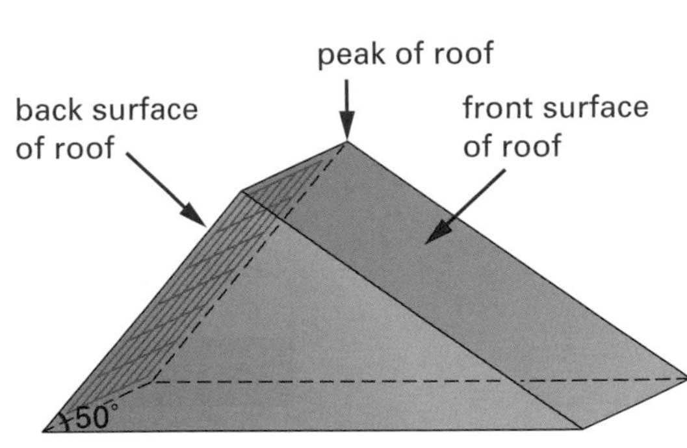

? How can Maria determine the measure of the angle at the peak without measuring it?

A. Draw two congruent triangles, each with a 50° angle. Cut out your triangles.

B. Tear off two of the corners of one triangle. Place the corners so that all three vertices meet at one point, without gaps. What do you notice?

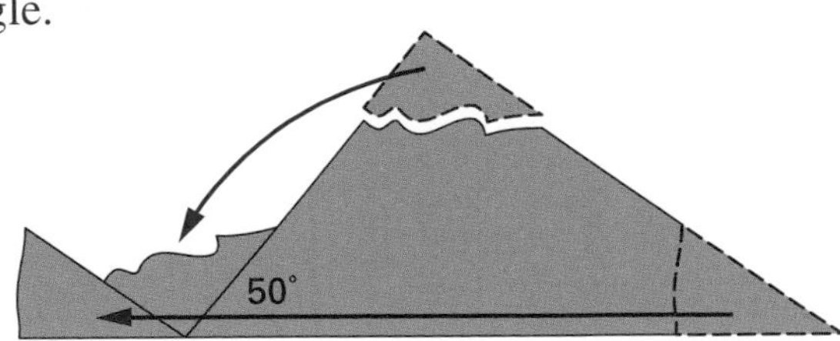

C. Fold in the vertices of the second triangle so that they meet at the base to form a rectangle. What do you notice about how the angles fold together?

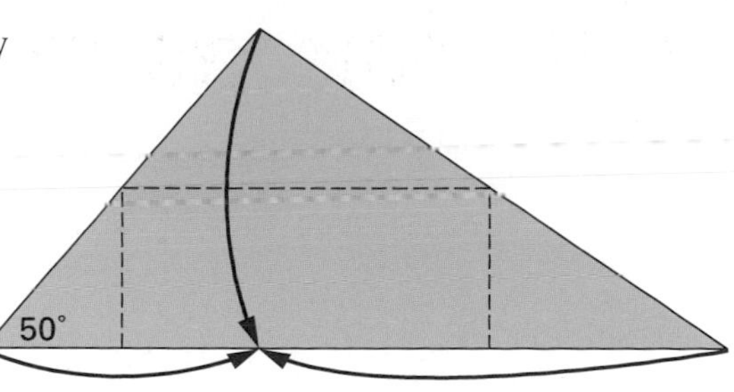

D. Repeat steps A to C for three triangles with different angles. What do you notice?

E. If the angle at the front of the house measures 35°, what is the angle at the peak?

Reflecting

1. What did you discover about the measures of the angles in a triangle?

2. How did knowing the measure of a straight angle help you answer the questions in steps B and C?

Work with the Math

Example: Determining angle measures

What are the measures of $\angle a$ and $\angle b$?

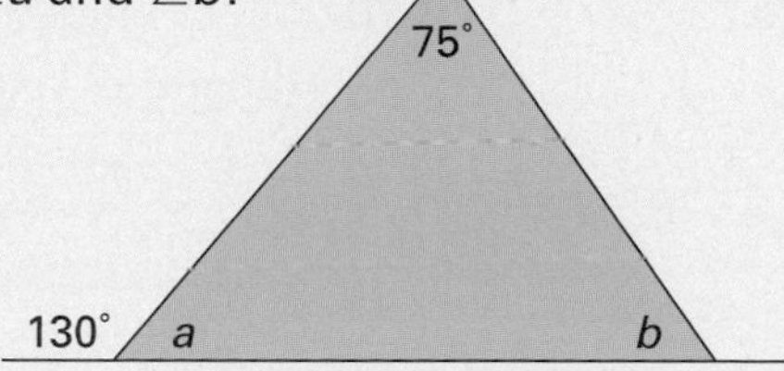

Nathan's Solution

$\angle a = 180° - 130°$
$= 50°$

$\angle a$ is 50° because $\angle a$ and the 130° angle make a straight angle.

$\angle b = 180° - (50° + 75°)$
$= 55°$

The sum of the measures of the angles in a triangle is 180°.

A Checking

3. What is the measure of $\angle x$?

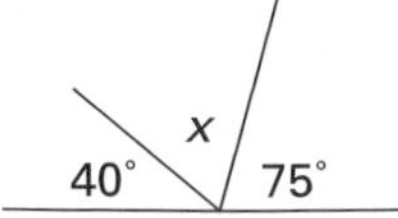

4. Calculate the missing angle measures.

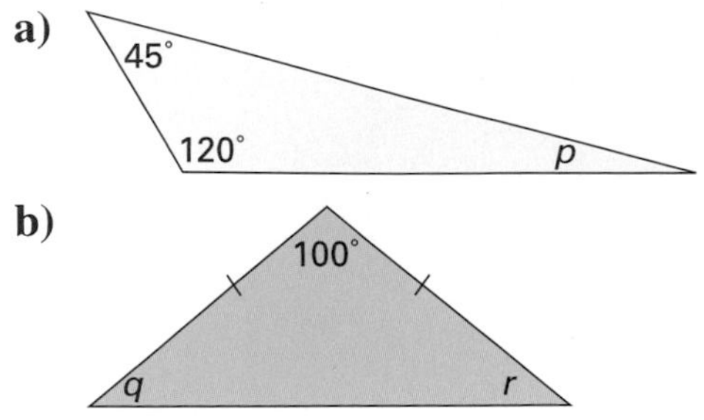

5. The sum of two angles in a triangle is 110°. What is the measure of the third angle?

B Practising

6. Calculate the missing angle measures.

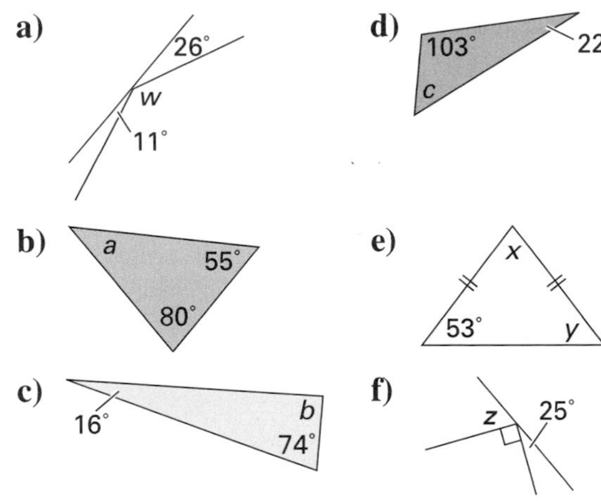

7. Can each group of angles be the angles in a triangle? Explain.

a) 50°, 40°, 80°
b) 75°, 65°, 60°
c) 64°, 64°, 52°
d) 13°, 16°, 161°

8. Connor is planning an orienteering course in the shape of a triangle. One of the angles is 130°. Give three possible pairs of angle measures. Then draw your three triangles.

9. Determine which numbered angle has the same measure as each lettered angle.

a) $\angle a$
b) $\angle b$
c) $\angle c$

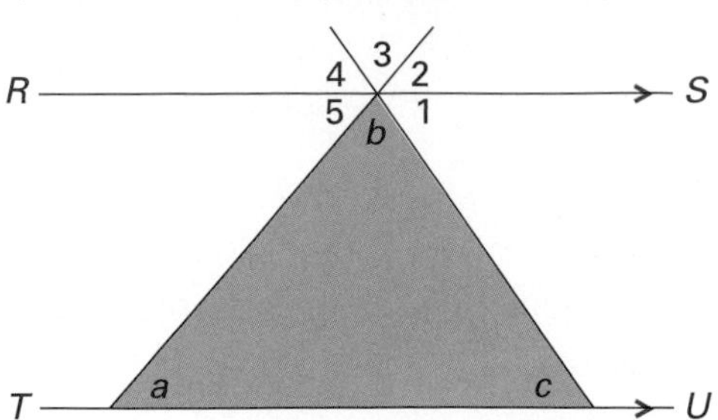

10. The roof of a solar house is elevated by an angle of 50° at the front and by an angle of 40° at the back.

a) What is the measure of the angle at the peak?
b) What kind of triangle do these angles create? Explain why.

11. a) A piece of stained glass is cut into a triangle. The sum of two of its angles is 70°. Can this triangle be an acute triangle? Why or why not?

b) Make up a problem like the one in part (a). Then solve your problem.

12. What kind of triangle is shown in the diagram? Explain how you know.

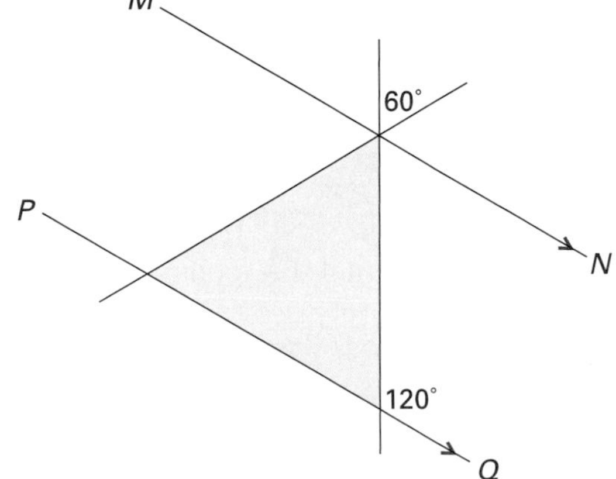

13. One angle in a triangle is 55°.

a) How do you know that there is no 140° angle in the triangle?

b) Why can you not be sure that one of the other angles measures 30°?

14. Gabriela measured and labelled the 120° and 110° angles in this diagram.

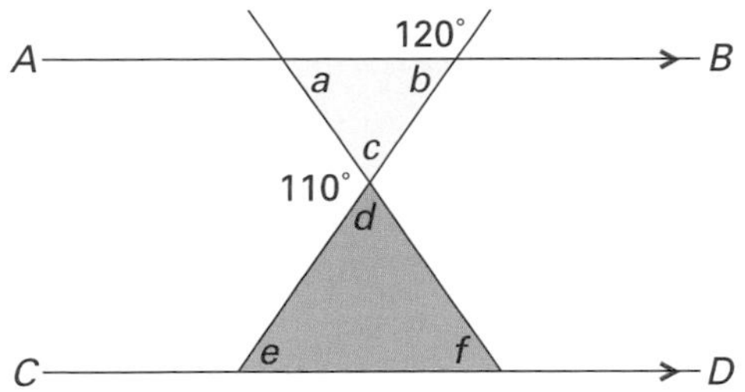

a) What are the measures of the angles inside the two triangles? How do you know?

b) How do you know that the two triangles are similar triangles?

15. Triangles are used to provide strength in structures. Sketch two different triangles you see in this photo. Estimate the measures of the angles in each triangle, and explain your thinking.

C Extending

16. a) Copy quadrilateral $ABCD$. Join A to C.

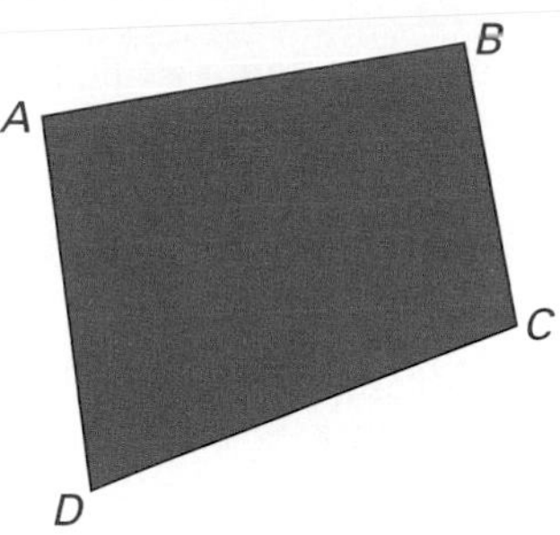

b) What new shapes were formed when you joined A to C?

c) Use these shapes to determine the sum of the measures of the interior angles in the quadrilateral, without measuring.

17. a) Copy the pentagon, hexagon, and heptagon shown below.

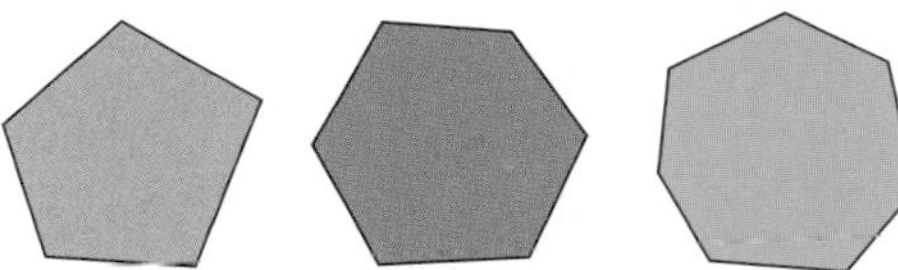

Divide each shape into triangles by drawing diagonals from one vertex.

b) Use what you know about triangles to determine the sum of the interior angles in each shape.

18. Think about how you folded the vertices of the triangle in step C on page 345. How did this show that the area of a triangle is $\frac{1}{2} \times$ base $\times$ height?

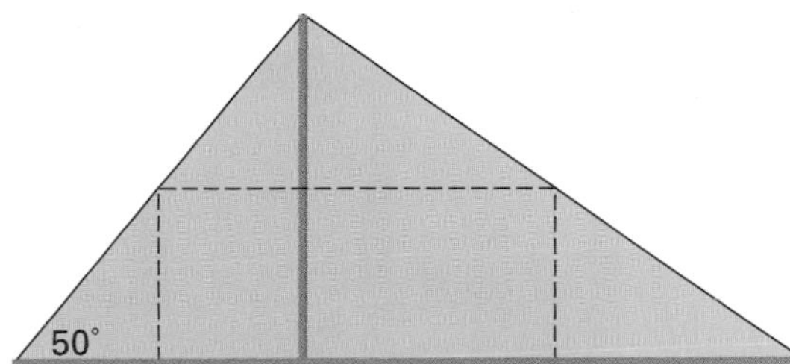

10.4 Exploring Quadrilaterals

You will need
- a ruler
- a protractor
- cardboard
- scissors

▶ **GOAL**
Determine some angle properties of quadrilaterals.

Explore the Math

Ken wants to create an animation sequence that shows a triangle being transformed into different types of quadrilaterals.

? How can you create quadrilaterals using transformations of triangles?

A. Choose a scalene triangle or an isosceles triangle to use for this exploration. The diagrams below show some examples of each type of triangle.

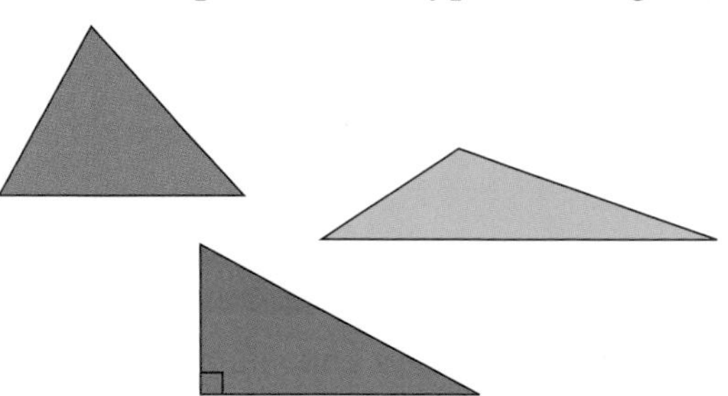

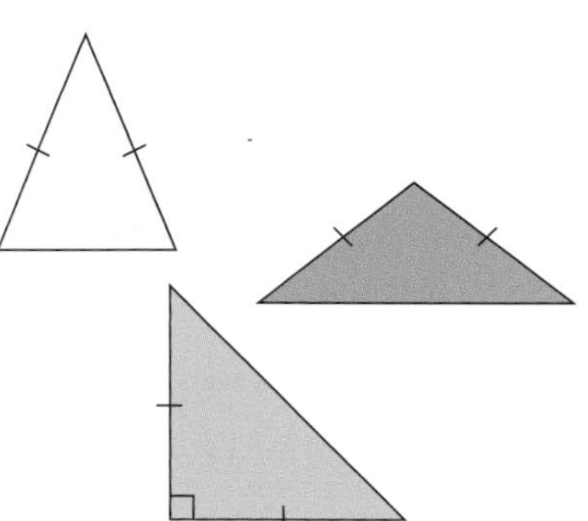

B. Draw your triangle on cardboard, using a ruler and protractor, and then cut it out. Trace around your triangle.

C. **a)** Reflect your triangle about one of its sides to create a quadrilateral. Trace around the image.

b) What is the name of the quadrilateral made with your original triangle and its image? How do you know?

c) One diagonal of the quadrilateral is drawn. Draw the other diagonal to intersect the first diagonal. Measure the angles at which the diagonals meet. What do you notice?

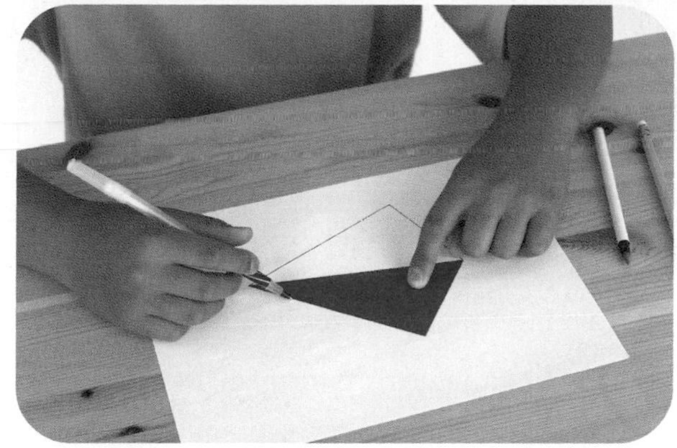

D. Repeat steps B and C for other types of triangles.

E. **a)** Determine the **midpoint** of one side of your original triangle.

b) Rotate your triangle 180° about the midpoint of the side, and trace around the image.

c) What is the name of the quadrilateral made with your original triangle and its image? How do you know?

d) Draw the other diagonal in your quadrilateral. Measure the angles at which the diagonals meet. What do you notice?

F. Repeat step E for different types of triangles.

G. Calculate the sum of the angles in each of your quadrilaterals.

H. What observances can you make about angles in the various quadrilaterals you created?

midpoint

the point on a line segment that divides the line segment into two equal parts

Reflecting

1. Why do you get a quadrilateral when you rotate or reflect a triangle and combine the triangle with its image?

2. What types of quadrilaterals can you get? Why?

3. Summarize, in a chart, what you learned about how the diagonals of quadrilaterals intersect.

4. What else did you observe about your quadrilaterals? Include this in your chart.

Mid-Chapter Review

Frequently Asked Questions

Q: What is the relationship between the angles that are formed by two intersecting lines?

A: Four angles are formed.

There are two pairs of equal opposite angles: $\angle 2 = \angle 4$ and $\angle 1 = \angle 3$.

As well, there are four pairs of supplementary angles (angles that form a straight line): $\angle 1$ and $\angle 2$, $\angle 2$ and $\angle 3$, $\angle 3$ and $\angle 4$, and $\angle 4$ and $\angle 1$.

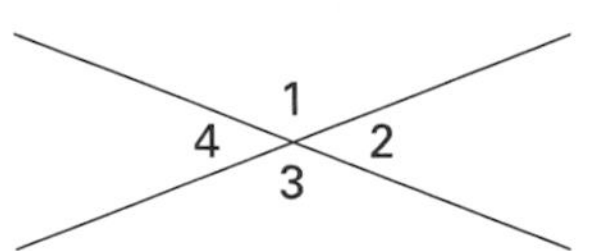

Q: What is the relationship between the angles that are formed by a transversal crossing two parallel lines?

A: Eight angles are formed.

There are four pairs of equal corresponding angles: $\angle 1 = \angle 5$, $\angle 4 = \angle 8$, $\angle 2 = \angle 6$, and $\angle 3 = \angle 7$.

The angles in each pair are in the same positions relative to the transversal.

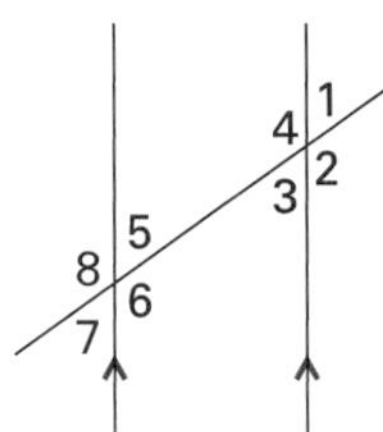

Q: What is the sum of the angle measures in a triangle?

A: The sum of the angle measures in a triangle is 180°.

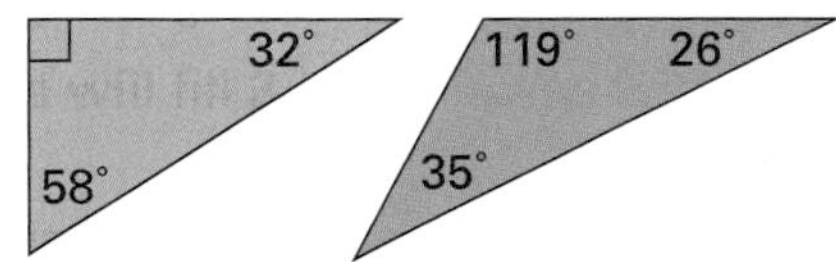

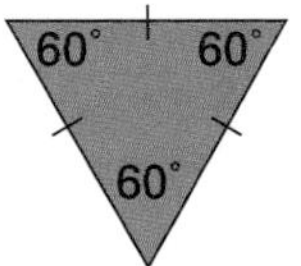

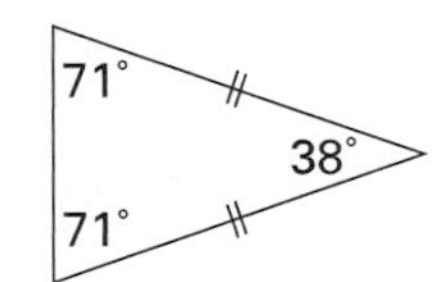

Q: What do you know about the angle at which diagonals meet in a quadrilateral?

A: Whenever a quadrilateral is created by reflecting a triangle about one of its sides, the diagonals of the resulting kite or rhombus meet at 90°. The angle sum in a quadrilateral is always 360°, since a quadrilateral is made up of two triangles with angle sums of 180°.

Whenever a quadrilateral is created by rotating a triangle about the midpoint of one of its sides, the diagonals only intersect at 90° if the original triangle was isosceles and a rhombus is created.

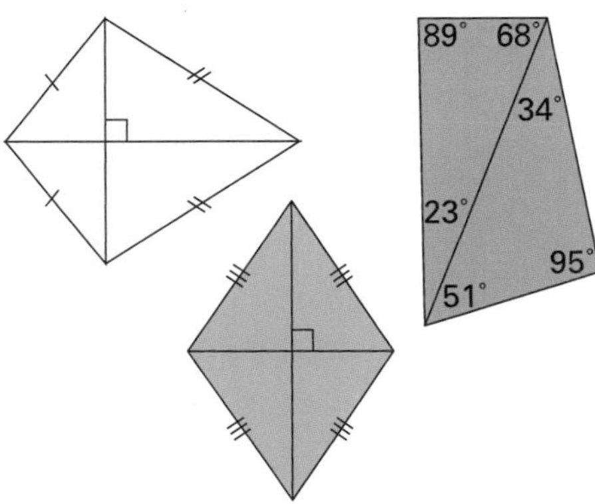

Practice Questions

(10.1) **1. a)** Draw a triangle with a 5.0 cm side between 30° and 70° angles.

b) Draw a circle that passes through all the vertices of the triangle you drew.

c) What is the radius of the circle, rounded to one decimal place?

(10.2) **2. a)** This diagram shows floor tiles that are the shape of a rhombus. One of the interior angles is 75°. What are the measures of ∠1, ∠2, and ∠3? How do you know?

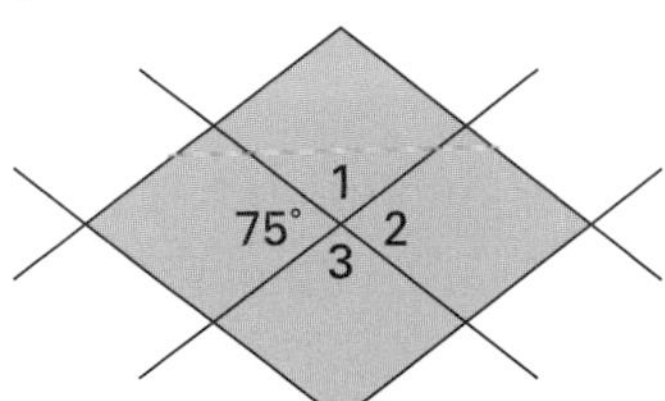

b) Make up a problem like the one in part (a). Then solve your problem.

(10.2) **3.** The following diagram shows where a road intersects two parallel streets. At one intersection, ∠2 measures 120°. What are the measures of ∠7 and ∠8 at the other intersection? How do you know?

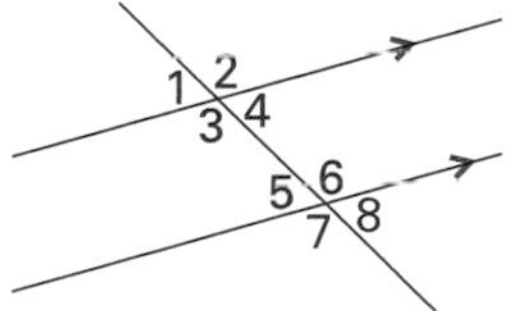

(10.2) **4.** A straight road crosses two parallel railway tracks. The angle between the road and the first track is 95°. What is the angle between the road and the second track? Why?

(10.3) **5.** Use the triangle you drew in question 1. What is the measure of the angle that is not 30° or 70°?

6. Lanny measured the angles in a triangular pennant. She said that they measured 11°, 90°, and 80°. (10.3)

a) How do you know that Lanny made a mistake?

b) If Lanny made a small mistake when measuring one of the angles, what could the measurements be? Give three possible combinations.

7. Calculate the missing angle measure in each triangle. Then classify the triangle as acute, right, or obtuse, and as scalene, isosceles, or equilateral. (10.3)

a) 40° angle, 50° angle, ▒ angle

b) 50° angle, 65° angle, ▒ angle

c) 7° angle, 124° angle, ▒ angle

d) two 88° angles, ▒ angle

8. What are the measures of ∠*a*, ∠*b*, and ∠*c*? (10.3)

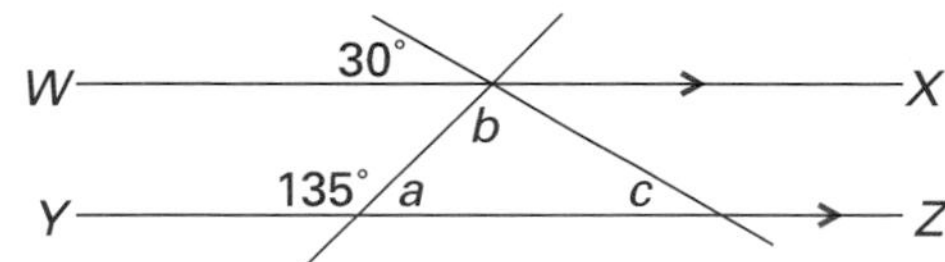

9. The angle at the top of this kite measures 88°. The angle at the bottom measures 50°. (10.4)

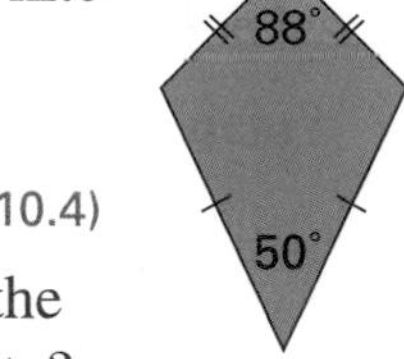

a) What is the sum of all the interior angles in the kite?

b) Copy the kite, and draw the diagonals. What is the measure of the angle at which the diagonals intersect?

10. Draw two pairs of parallel lines to form parallelogram *ABCD*, so that $AB \parallel DC$ and $AD \parallel BC$. When do the diagonals of parallelograms intersect at 90°? (10.4)

10.5 Exploring Right Triangles

You will need
- 0.5 cm grid paper
- a protractor
- scissors
- a ruler
- a calculator

▶ **GOAL**

Relate the lengths of the sides of right triangles.

Explore the Math

In regulation baseball, the distance between adjacent bases is 90 feet. This is about 27 m. Suppose that the right fielder catches the ball while standing on the foul line, 10 m from first base. Then the right fielder throws the ball to second base.

? How can you calculate the distance that the right fielder throws the ball, without measuring?

A. Draw a diagram like the one above, on 0.5 cm grid paper. Let one grid unit represent 1 m. The red line, which is called the **hypotenuse**, shows the path of the ball.

B. Measure the angles in the triangle. Which two angles are **complementary angles**?

C. Using 0.5 cm grid paper, cut out two squares to fit on the two short sides of the triangle.

D. Determine the area of each square by counting grid squares. (*Hint:* Remember that each grid unit represents 1 m.)

E. Use a ruler to measure the hypotenuse to the nearest tenth of a centimetre. Using 0.5 cm grid paper, cut out a square with that side length. Estimate the area of the square.

F. Square the length of the hypotenuse to calculate a more precise value for the area of the largest square.

G. Describe how the area of the largest square seems to compare with the sum of the areas of the two smaller squares.

hypotenuse

the longest side of a right triangle; the side that is opposite the right angle

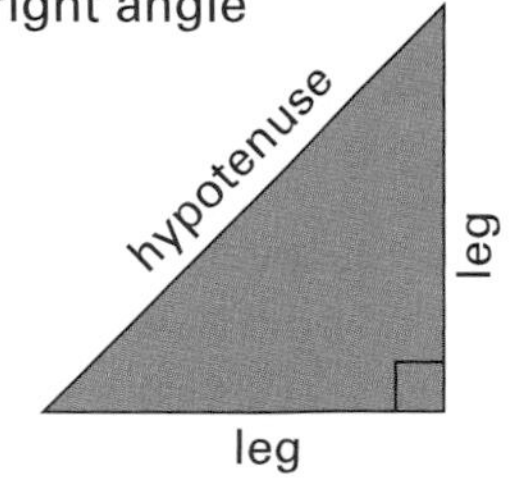

complementary angles

two angles whose sum is 90°

H. How does the distance that the right fielder throws the ball relate to the sum of the areas of the smaller squares?

Reflecting

1. Why are the two non-right angles in a right triangle always complementary?

2. What did you learn when you compared the areas of the squares on the three sides of the right triangle?

3. How does the length of the hypotenuse relate to the lengths of the other two sides of a right triangle?

Curious Math — DISSECTING SQUARES

You will need
- a ruler
- a protractor

The area of the square on the hypotenuse of a right triangle is equal to the sum of the areas of the squares on the other two sides. Did you know that you can cut and rearrange the squares to show this?

A. Draw a right triangle, using a ruler and a protractor. Label the sides of your triangle a, b, and c, where c is the side that is opposite the right angle.

B. Draw squares on the sides of your triangle.

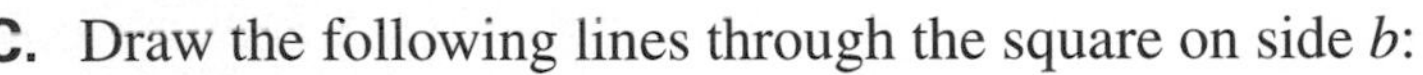

C. Draw the following lines through the square on side b:
- a line that extends one side of the square on c through the square on b
- a line that is parallel to side c and passes through the vertex opposite side c

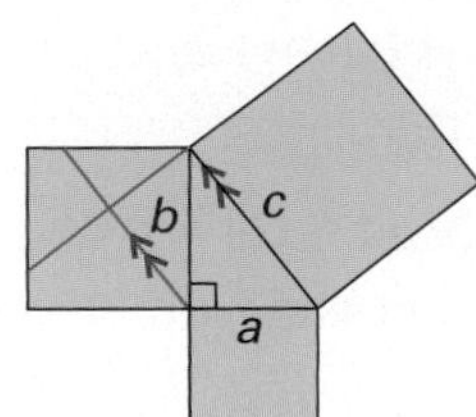

D. Cut out all three squares. Then cut the square from side b along the blue lines.

E. Fit square a and the pieces of square b into square c. What do you notice? (*Hint:* Do not rotate the pieces.)

F. Try drawing other right triangles and dissecting the squares. What do you notice?

10.6 Applying the Pythagorean Theorem

You will need
- a ruler
- a calculator

▶ **GOAL**

Use the Pythagorean theorem to solve problems.

Learn about the Math

A roofer has a ladder that is 12.0 m long. The roofer needs to tar a flat roof that is 10.0 m above the ground. Safety standards suggest that the top of the ladder must extend at least 1 m above the top of the wall. Also, the foot of the ladder must be at least 1 m from the base of the wall for every 3 m of ladder.

? What calculation will show whether the roofer can safely use the ladder to climb onto the roof?

You can use the relationship between the legs and hypotenuse of a right triangle, which you explored in the previous lesson:

The sum of the areas of the squares on the legs of a right triangle is equal to the area of the square on the hypotenuse.

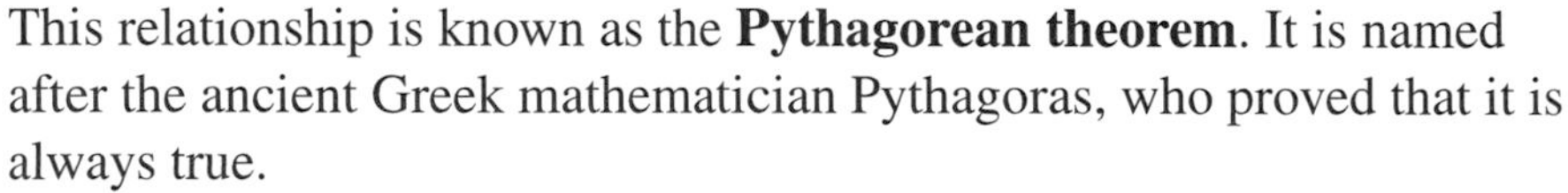

This relationship is known as the **Pythagorean theorem**. It is named after the ancient Greek mathematician Pythagoras, who proved that it is always true.

An equation for the Pythagorean theorem is $\boldsymbol{a^2 + b^2 = c^2}$, where a and b represent the legs of a right triangle and c represents the hypotenuse.

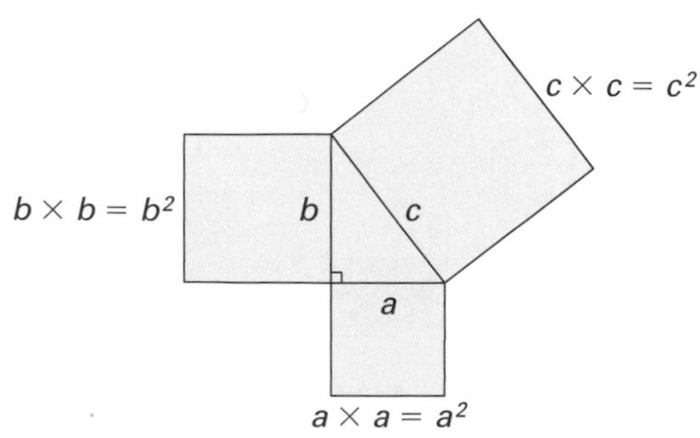

Example 1: Using the Pythagorean theorem

Can the roofer safely use the 12.0 m ladder to climb onto the 10.0 m roof? Explain.

Susan's Solution

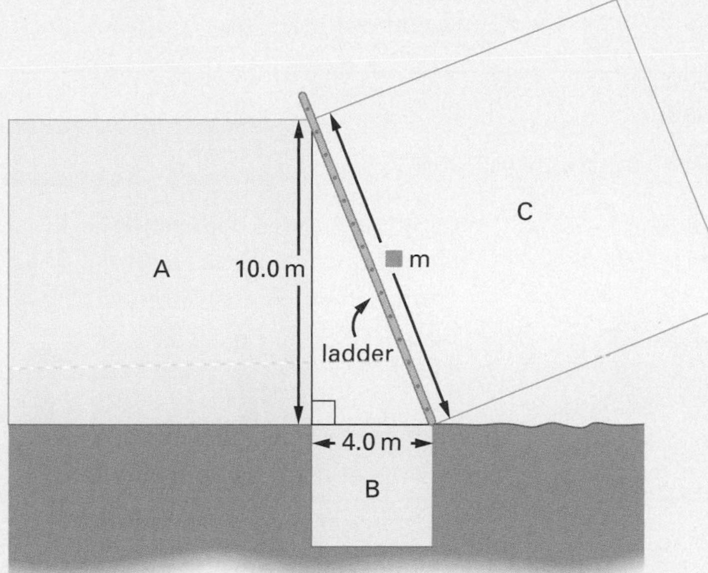

I drew a diagram of the situation. I knew that the foot of the ladder would have to be at least 4.0 m from the base of the wall because $12 \div 3 = 4$. (For every 3 m of ladder, the ladder must be 1 m from the base of the wall.)

I decided to calculate how long the ladder should be in order to reach from the ground to the top of the wall.

Area of square A is $10.0 \text{ m} \times 10.0 \text{ m} = 100.0 \text{ m}^2$.

Area of square B is $4.0 \text{ m} \times 4.0 \text{ m} = 16.0 \text{ m}^2$.

I found the areas of square A and square B on the right triangle.

Area of square C = Area of square A + Area of square B

So, Area of square C = 116.0 m^2

The area of square C is equal to the sum of the areas of squares A and B.

The hypotenuse should be $\sqrt{116.0 \text{ m}^2}$. This is about 10.8 m.

To be safe, the ladder must be at least 10.8 m. The ladder is 12.0 m long, so it's safe.

To find the length of the hypotenuse, I thought "What number multiplied by itself gives an answer of 116.0?" I calculated the square root of 116 using my calculator.

Reflecting

1. How did Susan use the Pythagorean theorem to solve this problem?

2. What other way could Susan have solved this problem?

Work with the Math

Example 2: Calculating the height of a right triangle

Erik is flying a kite. Calvin is directly under the kite. Erik and Calvin are 60 m apart, and the string is 100 m long. How high is the kite above Calvin?

Solution

Draw a diagram to represent the problem.

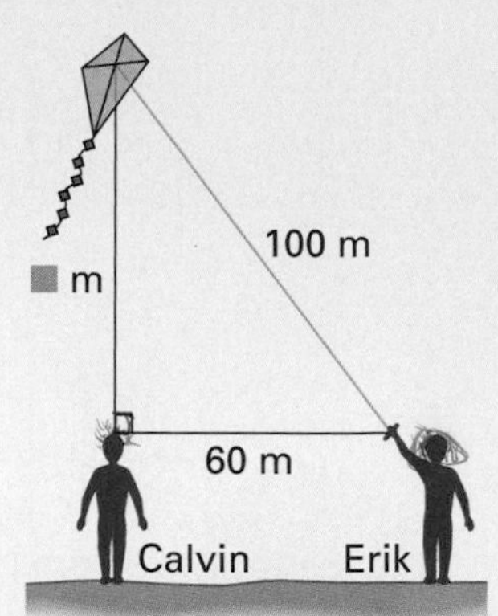

Use the Pythagorean theorem to create an equation with the missing term. Then calculate.

$$\blacksquare^2 + 60^2 = 100^2$$
$$\blacksquare^2 + 3600 = 10\,000$$
$$\blacksquare^2 = 6400$$
$$\blacksquare = \sqrt{6400}$$
$$\blacksquare = 80$$

The kite is 80 m above Calvin.

A Checking

3. What is the length of the third side in each right triangle?

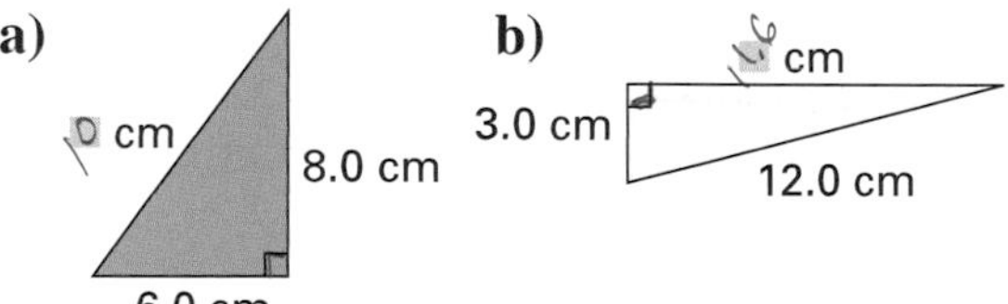

B Practising

4. Calculate the length of the unknown side in each right triangle.

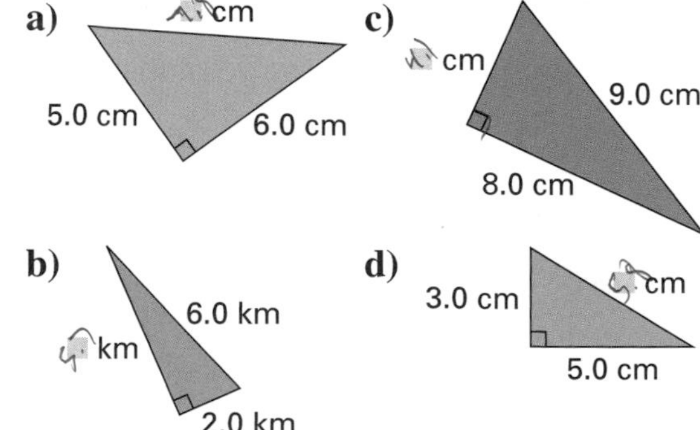

5. A right triangle has two sides that are each 7 cm long.

a) Draw the triangle. Label the complementary angles.

b) Can there be more than one triangle that fits this description?

c) Can one of the 7 cm sides be the hypotenuse? Why or why not?

6. Refer to the triangle you drew in question 5.

a) In which range of measurements is the length of the hypotenuse?

A. between 7 cm and 8 cm
B. between 8 cm and 9 cm
C. between 9 cm and 10 cm
D. between 10 cm and 11 cm

b) How did you estimate this?

7. The jib sail of a yacht is a right triangle that is attached to the mast and the prow. The sail is 15 m high, and the mast is 4 m from the prow. How long is the forestay?

8. A cable car travels 2236 m to climb a mountain that is 1000 m high. It then travels 1414 m to descend 1000 m on the other side of the mountain. A tunnel goes straight through the mountain, from the starting point to the endpoint of the cable car's journey. How long is the tunnel?

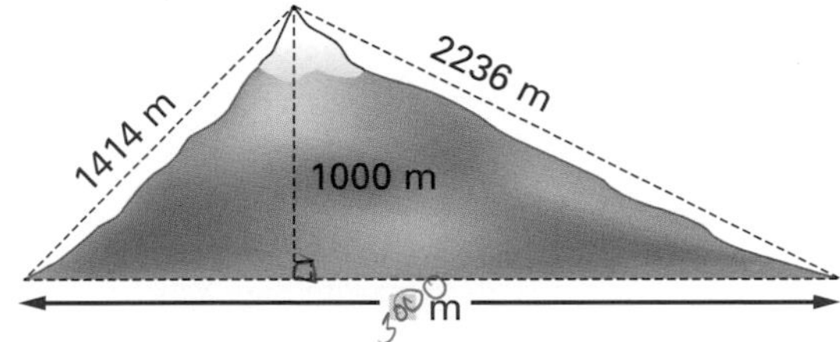

9. A wheelchair ramp must be 12 m long for every metre of height.

a) What is the length of a ramp that rises 2.0 m?

b) How long does this ramp extend along the ground? Round your answer to one decimal place.

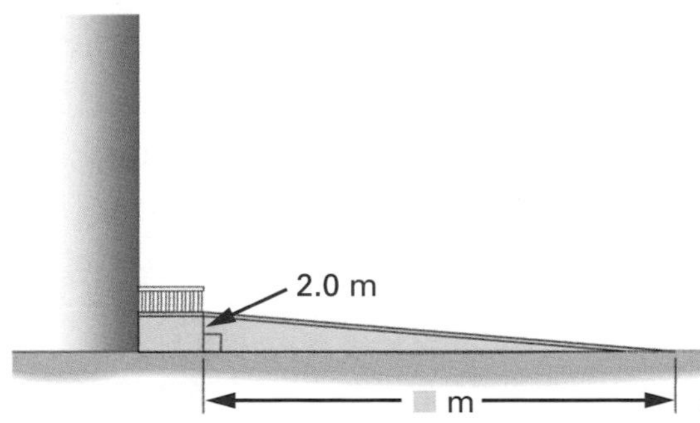

10. The height of an equilateral triangle is also the perpendicular bisector of its base. Determine the area of an equilateral triangle that has 6.0 cm sides.

11. An airplane travels about 1500 km in a straight line between Toronto and Winnipeg. However, the plane must climb to 10 000 m during the first 200 km. Then it must descend 10 000 m during the final 300 km.

a) How much distance do the climb and descent add to the flight?

b) The airplane averages a speed of 600 km/h. Do climbing and descending 10 000 m add hours, minutes, or seconds to the flight? Explain.

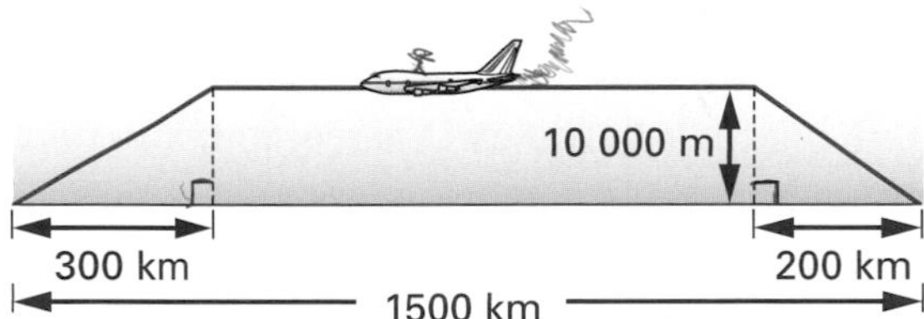

C Extending

12. Determine whether or not this is a right triangle. Justify your conclusion.

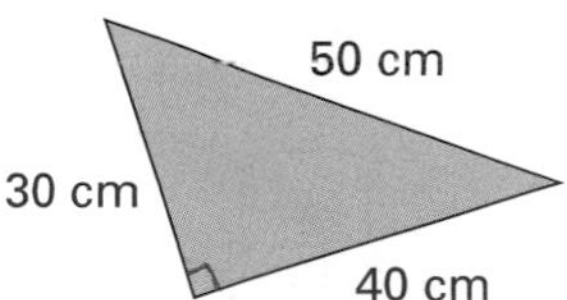

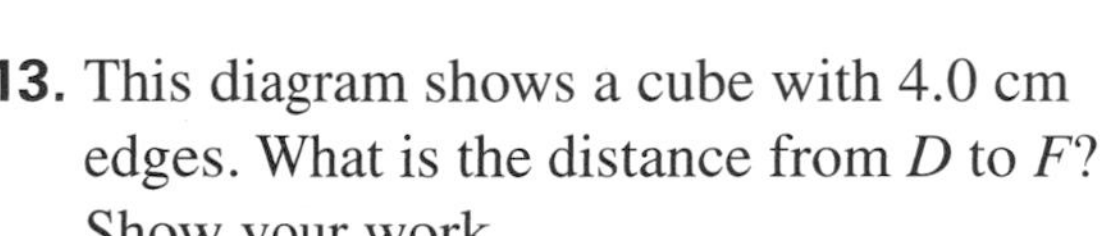

13. This diagram shows a cube with 4.0 cm edges. What is the distance from *D* to *F*? Show your work.

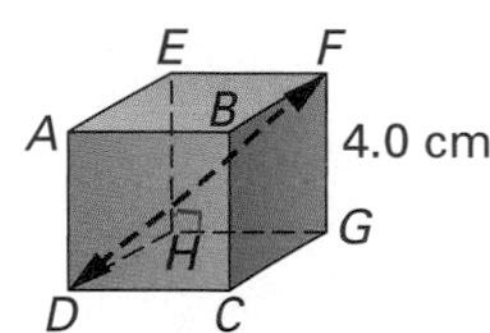

You will need
• a calculator

10.7 Solve Problems Using Logical Reasoning

▶ **GOAL**
Use logical reasoning to solve problems.

Learn about the Math

On this city map, the blue lines show major roads. Notice the following:

- One angle measure is given.
- All lettered streets are parallel to each other.
- All numbered avenues are parallel to each other.
- Queen Street is perpendicular to King Street.
- 1st Avenue is perpendicular to A Street.
- Queen Street crosses 3rd Avenue halfway between C and D Streets.
- King Street crosses D Street halfway between 1st and 2nd Avenues.

Problem: A car starts at one of the labelled red dots (school, pool, library, or mall). It travels less than 1 km and crosses a street. After travelling 1.8 km, it turns right at an angle of 56°. Then, 4 km later, it turns right, travels 5 km, turns left, and travels 1.2 km to its destination.

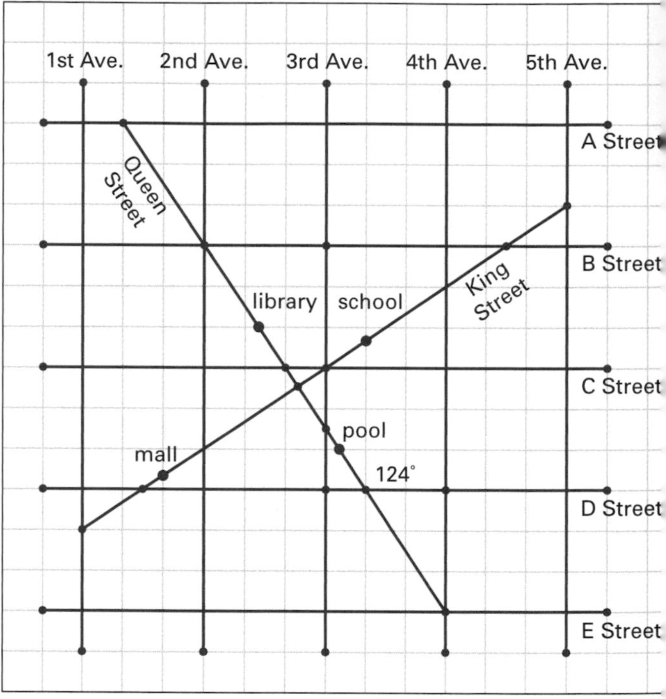

Scale: 1 unit = 1 km

? Where did the car start and end?

1 Understand the Problem

Annika understands that she needs to determine the path of the car from one of the red dots and end up at a different red dot after following the directions.

2 Make a Plan

Annika plans to eliminate some starting and ending locations by using only the first and last pieces of information in the problem.

3 Carry Out the Plan

First, Annika determines which of the four locations are less than 1 km from an intersection.

"If I draw a line from the school perpendicular to 3rd Avenue, the distance is 1 km. The road to the intersection is the hypotenuse of a right triangle. So, it must be more than 1 km from the intersection.

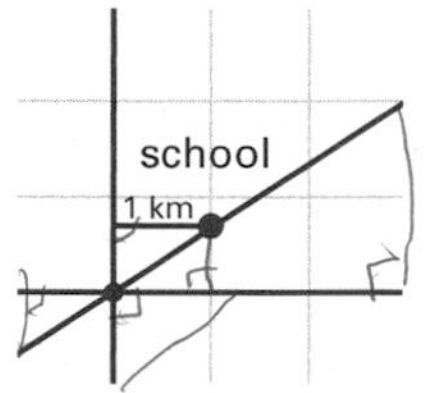

"I can use the same logic to show that the library is more than 1 km from the closest intersection.

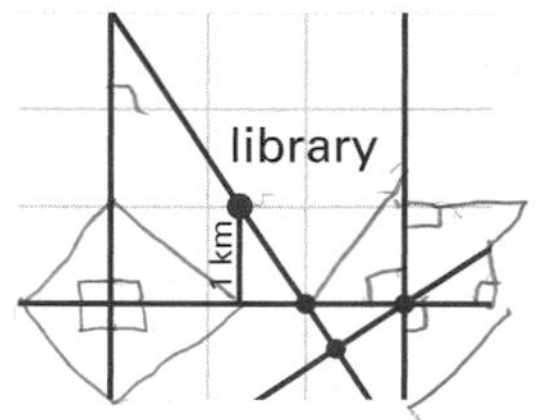

"The only possible starting points are the mall and the pool."

Next, Annika determines the possible ending locations.

"I'll look for places where the car can travel 5 km between intersections. The possibilities are

- along 2nd Avenue from B Street to King Street
- along 4th Avenue from D Street to King Street
- along C Street from 1st Avenue to Queen Street

"I followed all these routes. I found that only when travelling along C Street can you turn left and go a little over 1 km to a red dot. The ending location must be the library.

"I'll work backward from the library to find the starting location. A distance of 1.2 km takes the car back to C Street. Turning right (opposite of turning left because I'm going backward) takes the car onto C Street. Then 5 km takes the car to 1st Avenue. Turning left and travelling 4 km takes the car to King Street. Turning left at a 56° angle onto King Street and travelling 1.8 km takes the car to the mall.

"The car started at the mall and ended at the library."

4 Look Back

Annika followed the directions starting at the mall. The car ended at the library.

Reflecting

1. Why is it reasonable to assume that the library is 1.2 km from the intersection of C Street and Queen Street?

2. Looking back, Annika said that the key piece of information she used was the car travelling 5 km between two intersections. Why did this help her eliminate so many possibilities?

3. Annika could have calculated all the angles and distances on the map and tested all the routes. How did logical reasoning reduce her work?

Work with the Math

Example: Eliminating possibilities by using a table

Three people are in a room. Use the following clues to figure out their names and occupations.

Clue 1: Their first names are Anna, Peter, and Roger.

Clue 2: Two of the last names are Pavan and Attwell.

Clue 3: One person's first and last names begin with the same letter as her or his occupation.

Clue 4: One person is an architect.

Clue 5: The person whose last name is Davis is a pilot.

Clue 6: Roger is not a singer.

Ken's Solution

1 Understand the Problem

I need to figure out which combination works for each person.

2 Make a Plan

I'll make a chart of all the combinations and mark the combinations that don't work.

3 Carry Out the Plan

From clues 1 to 4, either Anna Attwell could be the architect or Peter Pavan could be the pilot. But from clue 5, Davis is the pilot. So, Anna Attwell must be the architect. (From this, I can complete the first row and the third and fifth columns in my chart.)

From clue 6, Roger is not the singer. So, he must be Roger Davis, the pilot. From this, I can complete the rest of the chart. Peter Pavan is the singer.

	Pavan	Attwell	Davis	architect	pilot	singer
Anna	X	yes	X	yes	X	X
Peter	yes	X	X	X	X	yes
Roger	X	X	yes	X	yes	no

4 Look Back

I checked to make sure that my answer works with the clues that were given.

A Checking

4. The hypotenuse in a right scalene triangle is 7.0 cm. What must be the length of one of the legs?

   A. 8.0 cm **C.** 5.5 cm

   B. 4.95 cm **D.** 7.0 cm

B Practising

5. Five students are walking in single file. Devon is not second. Wendy is just behind Devon. Hannah is just behind Kathryn, who is not third. Gregory is neither first nor last. Who is third? How do you know?

6. Suppose that you know the measure of the angle with a check mark. Can you determine the measures of all the angles marked with dots? Why or why not?

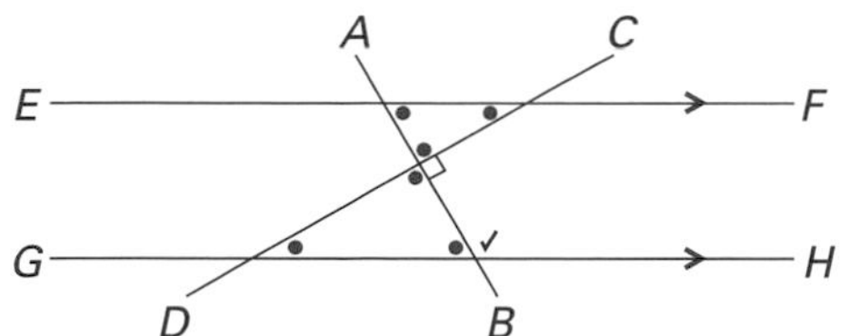

7. How many bananas weigh the same as one cantaloupe?

2 cantaloupe = 1 grapefruit + 1 banana

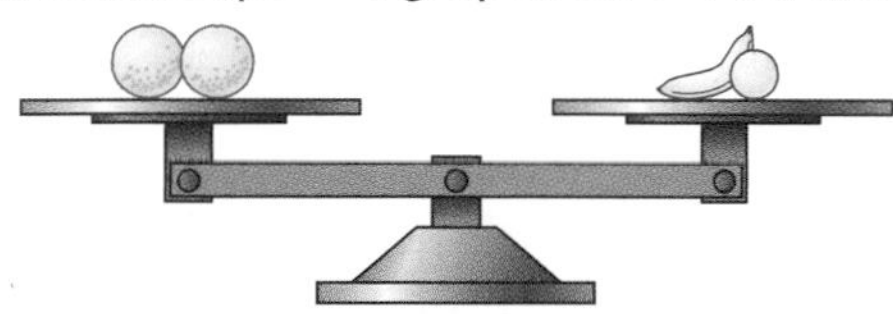

1 grapefruit = 5 bananas

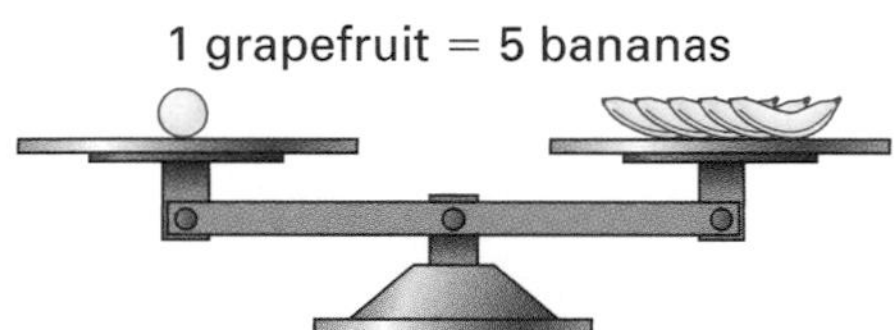

8. Draw three triangles. Each triangle should fit at least two of the following criteria. Explain your thinking.
   - The side lengths you can choose from are 3 cm, 4 cm, 4 cm, 4 cm, 5 cm, 5 cm, 5 cm, 5 cm, and 7 cm.
   - One triangle is acute.
   - One triangle is obtuse.
   - One triangle is a right triangle.
   - One triangle is an equilateral triangle.
   - One triangle is isosceles, but not equilateral.
   - One triangle is scalene.

9. All the marked sides of the polygons are 4 cm. Explain how to order the polygons from least to greatest area.

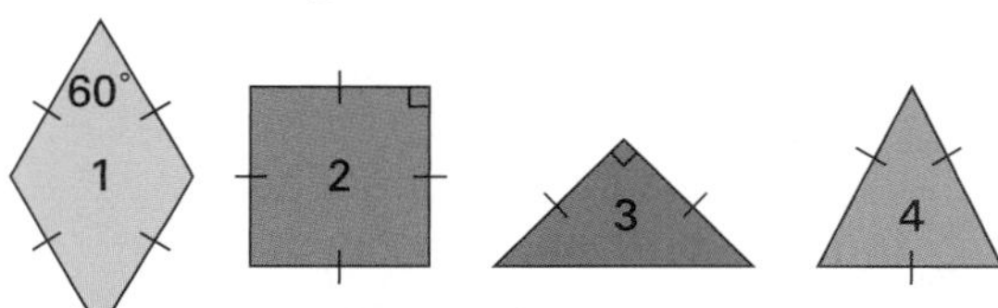

Mental Math

SQUARING NUMBERS THAT END IN 5

You can square a two-digit number that ends in 5 by calculating the area of a square. To calculate 25^2, for example, think of the area of a 25-by-25 square.

To square 25, first square 20, then double 100 (which is 5×20), and then square 5. Add the four areas to get the total area.

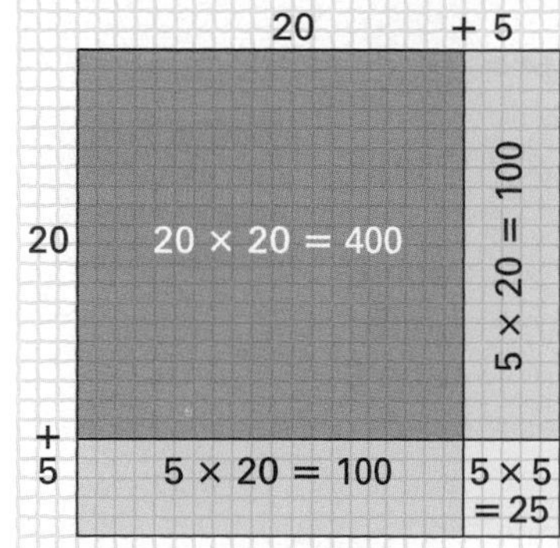

$$\begin{array}{rl} & 20 \times 5 \\ \times & 20 \times 5 \\ \hline & 400 \quad 20^2 \\ & 100 \quad 5 \times 20 \\ & 100 \quad 5 \times 20 \\ & 25 \quad 5 \times 5 \\ \hline & 625 \end{array}$$

1. Use this mental math strategy to calculate each square.
   a) 15^2 b) 45^2 c) 75^2
2. Use your answers to question 1 to calculate each square.
   a) 1.5^2 b) 3.5^2 c) 5.5^2 d) 7.5^2 e) 9.5^2 f) 8.5^2

Math Game

NEEDLE IN A HAYSTACK

This game is similar to the classic Battleship game. Players try to find a needle in their opponent's "haystack," or grid.

Number of players: 2 (or 2 teams)

You will need
- 1 cm grid paper
- a ruler
- a calculator

Rules

1. Each player needs two 10-by-10 game grids.

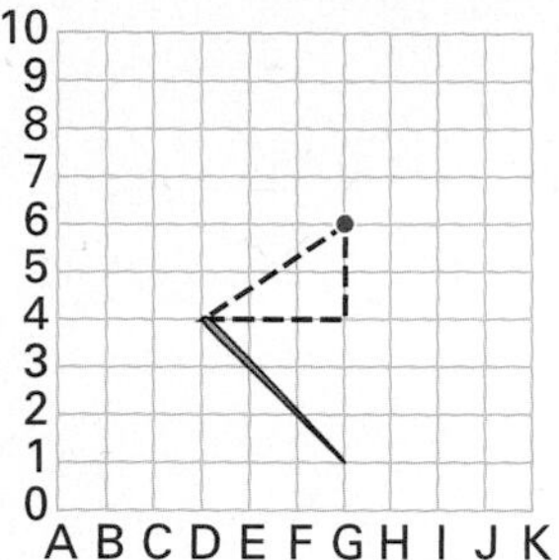

2. Each player "hides" a needle on grid 1. The needle must cross four adjacent grid points. It can be vertical, horizontal, or diagonal.

3. Player A begins by choosing a point on his or her grid 2 (for example, G6) and recording the guess.

4. Player B records the guess on her or his grid 1 and either announces a "hit" (if it is one of the intersection points on the needle) or a "miss" (if it is not on the needle).

If it is a hit, player B does *not* have to tell player A any information about where the hit occurred on the needle.

If it is a miss, player B *must* tell player A how far the guess was from the top of the needle. In the example, the distance is the hypotenuse of a right triangle that has 3 cm and 2 cm legs. The distance is calculated using the Pythagorean theorem, as follows:

$$3^2 + 2^2 = c^2$$
$$c = \sqrt{9 + 4}$$
$$= \sqrt{13}$$
$$\doteq 3.6 \text{ cm}$$

5. Players can use any method they choose to record hits and misses.

6. A player who records a hit continues to guess until he or she misses. Then the turn goes to the opponent to guess.

7. The winner is the first player to find all the intersection points on his or her opponent's needle.

Chapter Self-Test

1. Explain how you can find the centre of a circle if you are given three points on the circumference. Use a drawing to support your answer.

2. What are the measures of $\angle a$, $\angle b$, and $\angle c$? How do you know?

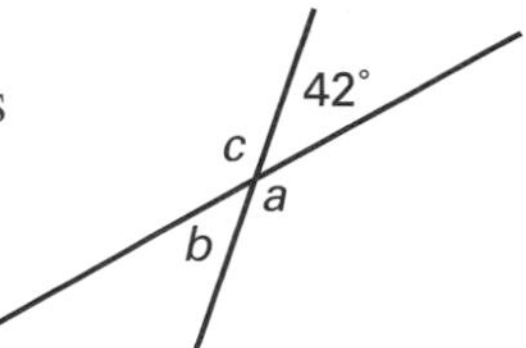

3. Draw a triangle that has two complementary angles. Label the measure of each angle.

4. The shaded shape in the diagram is a trapezoid.

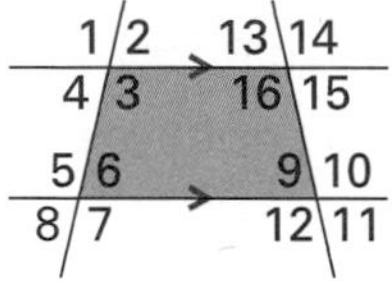

   a) How many pairs of corresponding angles are in the diagram?
   b) Which angles inside the trapezoid are supplementary?
   c) What is the sum of the interior angles of the trapezoid?

5. What are the measures of $\angle a$, $\angle b$, $\angle c$, and $\angle d$?

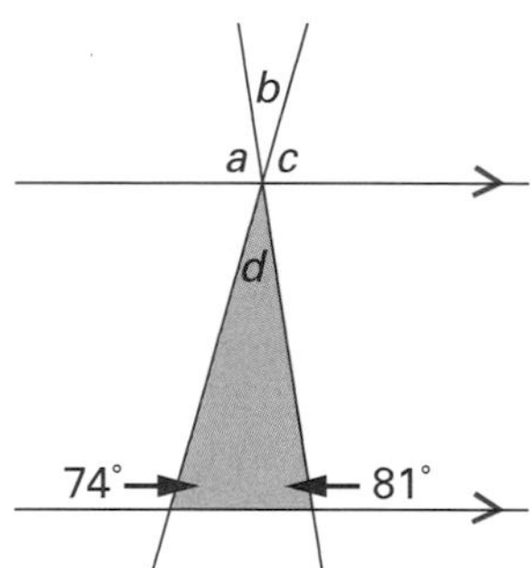

6. One angle in a triangle measures 98°. Another angle measures 37°.
   a) What is the measure of the third angle?
   b) How did you determine your answer in part (a)?
   c) Classify the triangle.

7. An isosceles triangle has one angle that is 94°.
   a) Draw the triangle. Label the measures of all the angles.
   b) Reflect the triangle about its sides. What types of quadrilateral did you draw?
   c) What are the measures of the angles at which the diagonals meet in each case?

8. Calculate the length of the unknown side in each right triangle, to one decimal place.

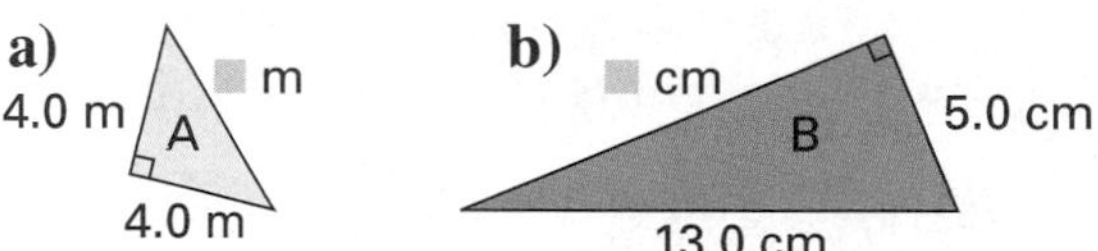

9. Draw a right triangle that has the 90° angle between 6 cm and 8 cm sides. What is the length of the third side? How do you know without measuring?

10. When travelling along King Street or Queen Street, the distance between any two parallel streets is always about 1.42 km.

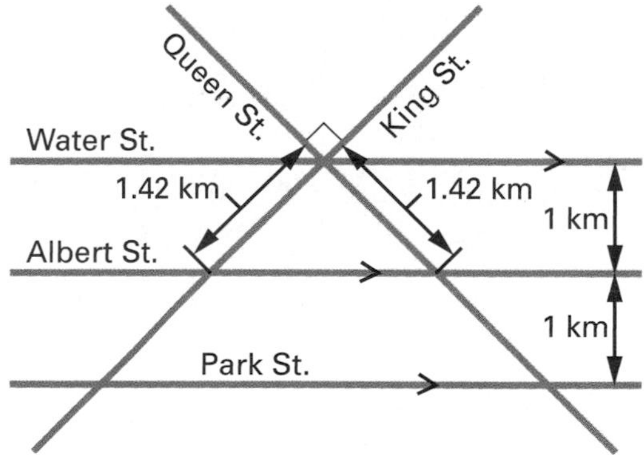

How much greater is the distance along Park Street from King Street to Queen Street than the distance along Albert Street from King Street to Queen Street?

Chapter Review

Frequently Asked Questions

Q: What does the Pythagorean theorem say about the areas of the squares on the sides of a right triangle?

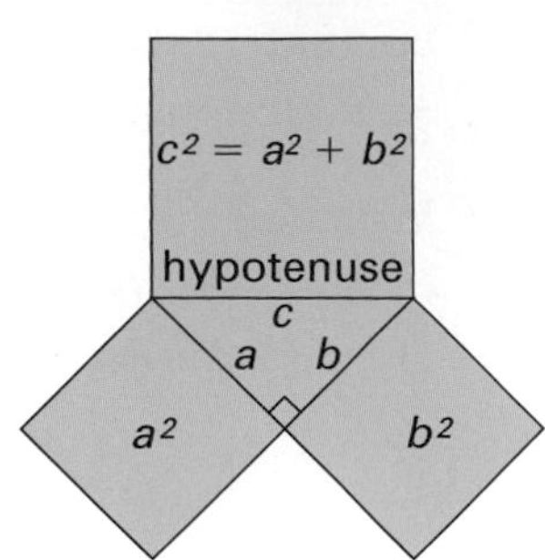

A: The Pythagorean theorem states that the sum of the areas of the squares on the two shorter sides of a right triangle is equal to the area of the square on the hypotenuse. The Pythagorean theorem can be written in algebraic terms as $a^2 + b^2 = c^2$, where a, b, and c represent the lengths of the sides of the right triangle and c represents the hypotenuse.

Q: If you know the lengths of two sides in any right triangle, can you always calculate the length of the third side?

A: Yes. You can use an equation for the Pythagorean theorem, $a^2 + b^2 = c^2$.

For example, you can calculate the length of the hypotenuse of triangle A like this:

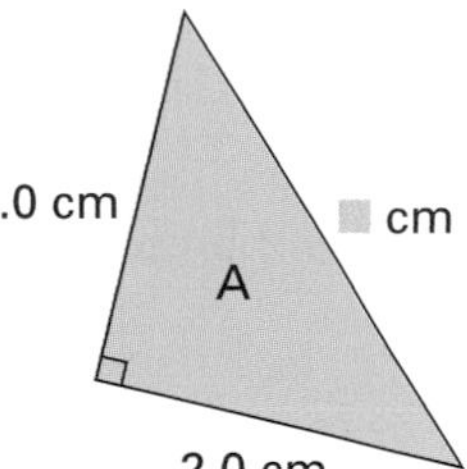

$$c^2 = 2.0^2 + 2.0^2$$
$$= 8.0$$
$$c = \sqrt{8.0}$$
$$\doteq 2.8$$

The hypotenuse is about 2.8 cm.

You can calculate the length of the shorter leg of triangle B.

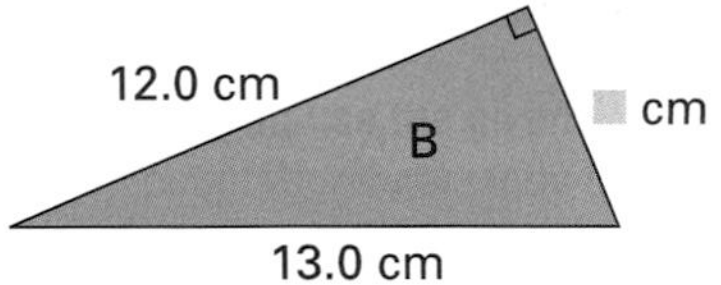

$$a^2 + 12.0^2 = 13.0^2$$
$$a^2 + 144.0 = 169.0$$
$$a^2 = 25.0$$
$$a = \sqrt{25.0}$$
$$a = 5.0$$

The shorter leg is 5.0 cm.

You can calculate the length of the longer leg of triangle C.

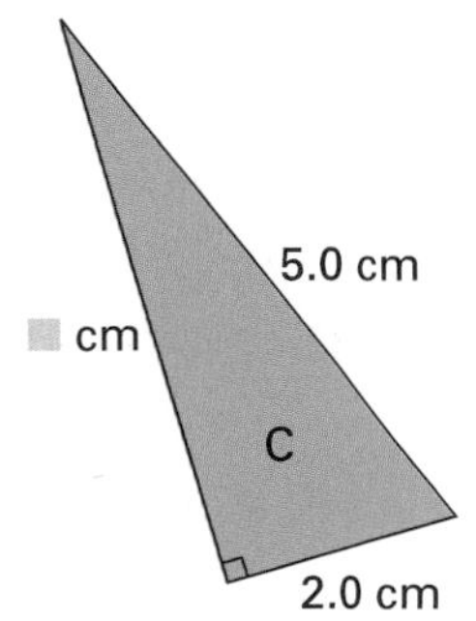

$$2.0^2 + b^2 = 5.0^2$$
$$4.0 + b^2 = 25.0$$
$$b^2 = 21.0$$
$$b = \sqrt{21.0}$$
$$b = 4.6$$

The longer leg is about 4.6 cm.

NEL

Practice Questions

(10.2) **1. a)** Which angles are equal?

b) What name is used to describe these angles?

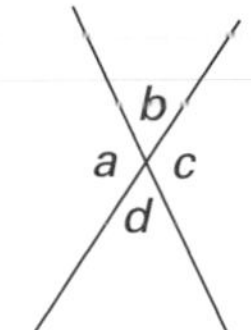

(10.2) **2.** If $AB \parallel CD$ and $\angle 1 = 82°$, what are the measures of the other seven angles?

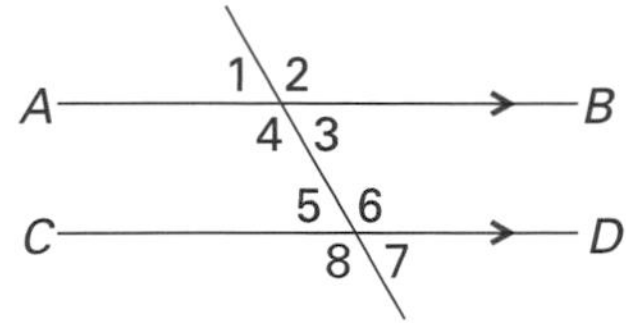

(10.2) **3.** Which angles are supplementary to $\angle a$? How do you know?

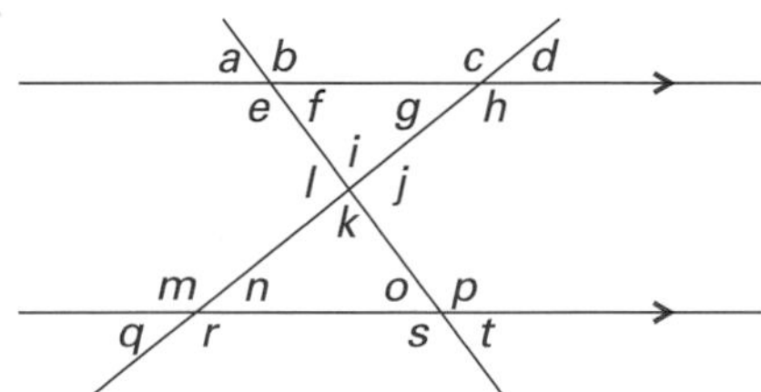

(10.3) **4.** What is the measure of the marked angle?

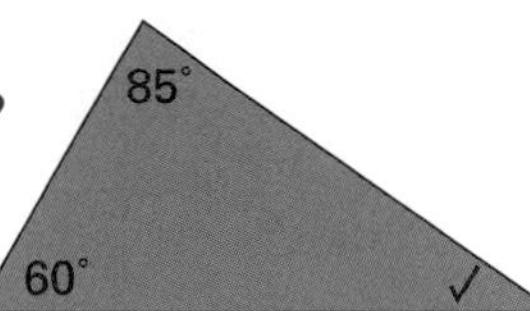

(10.4) **5. a)** Is this a right triangle? Explain how you know.

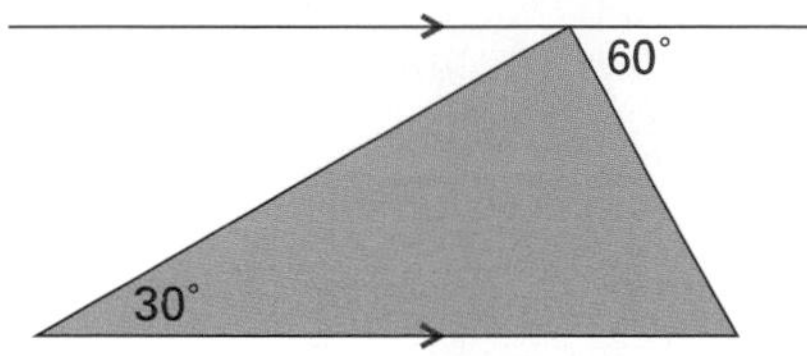

b) If you rotate the triangle 180° about the midpoint of its longest side, what type of quadrilateral is formed?

c) How can you use your answer to part (b) to predict whether or not the diagonals will meet at a 90° angle?

6. A square that is drawn on the hypotenuse of a right triangle has an area of 25 cm². What are possible lengths of the legs? Explain your thinking. (10.5)

25 cm²

7. Draw each shape. Then determine the missing value, without measuring. (10.6)

a) an acute angled triangle with a 50° angle, a 45° angle, and an angle that measures ■

b) a right triangle with a 4.0 cm side, a 7.0 cm side, and a hypotenuse that measures ■ cm

c) an isosceles triangle with two 6.0 cm sides that have a 150° angle in between, and equal angles that measure ■

d) a parallelogram made of two right triangles, both with a 12° angle and an angle that measures ■

8. Two cyclists start at the same location. Cyclist A travels 5.5 km, turns left 90°, and travels 3.4 km. Cyclist B travels 3.4 km, turns right 90°, and travels 5 km. (All distances are in straight lines.) (10.6)

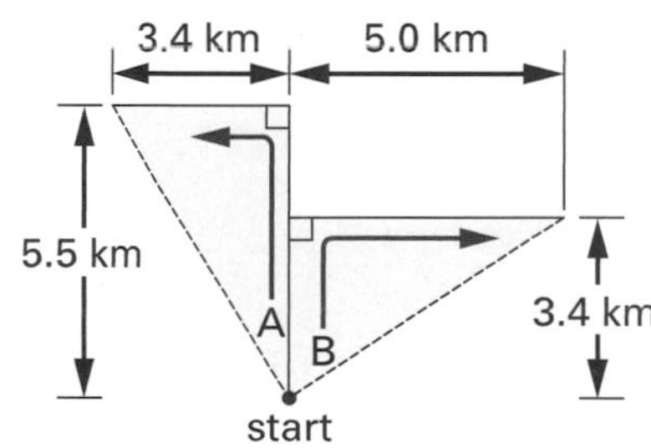

a) If both cyclists turn and ride directly back to the start in a straight line, who will have farther to ride?

b) What calculations do you have to make to determine the answer to part (a)?

c) Why was it important to know that the cyclists turned at an angle of 90°?

Chapter Task

Transmission Towers

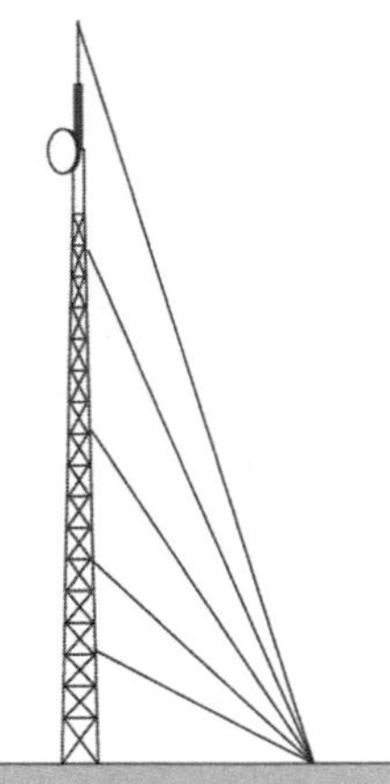

Imagine that you are an engineer. You are designing a radio transmission tower that will be 100 m high. It will be supported by cables, called guy wires, as follows:

- The guy wires will be anchored on the ground at three equally spaced locations in a circle around the tower.
- The distance of the anchor points from the base of the tower will be one quarter the height of the tower.
- There will be five guy wires from each anchor point. The guy wires will be attached to five points on the tower at 20 m intervals, going up.

? How much guy wire do you need to support the tower?

A. Draw a diagram as if you were looking down at the base of the tower. Show the location of the three anchor points. Explain how you know that the anchor points are equally spaced around the tower, and that they are all the same distance from the base of the tower.

B. How far are the anchor points from the base of the tower?

C. Draw a side view of the tower, showing all the guy wires from one anchor point.

D. Calculate the total amount of guy wire needed. Each guy wire requires 2 m at each end to attach it to the tower and the base. Round your answer to the closest metre. Show all your work.

Task Checklist

- ☑ Did you draw your diagrams accurately?
- ☑ Did you show all the steps you used?
- ☑ Did you explain your thinking?
- ☑ Did you check your answers?

Math in Action

Theatre Technician

Patrick Brennan, a theatre technician, tells about the connection between mathematics and theatre: "I like applying technology in an artistic way. I work with theatre designers and directors to come up with technical solutions to make their designs possible."

Problems, Applications, and Decision Making

Patrick explains, "A theatre technician helps with designing and building props."

1. For one play, Patrick built a train track on a ramp. Plywood for the top of the ramp is sold in sheets that measure 1.22 m by 2.44 m. Patrick used the 1.22 m side for the width of the top.

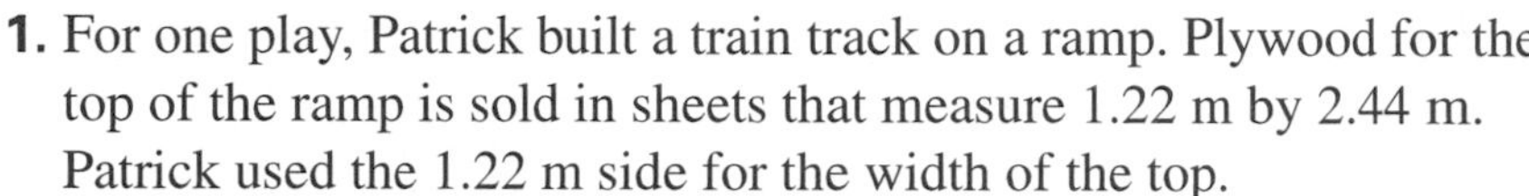

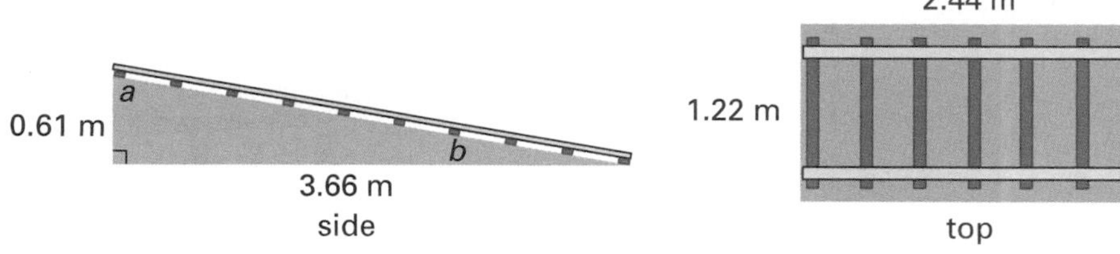

   a) How many sheets of plywood did Patrick need to buy for the top of the ramp?

   b) Patrick needed 1.40 m² of plywood to build another prop. Did he have enough left over, after building the top of the ramp? Explain.

   c) Patrick measured $\angle a$, which was 81°. $\angle b$ was difficult to measure on the stage. Show how Patrick might have calculated its measure.

2. Patrick is going to paint the stage floor for a performance. He sketched the diagram shown at the right, which has two parallel line segments and a transversal. One angle measures 54°. To tape the design on the floor, Patrick needs to know the other angle measures. Copy the diagram, and determine the unknown angle measures without using a protractor. How do you know these angle measures?

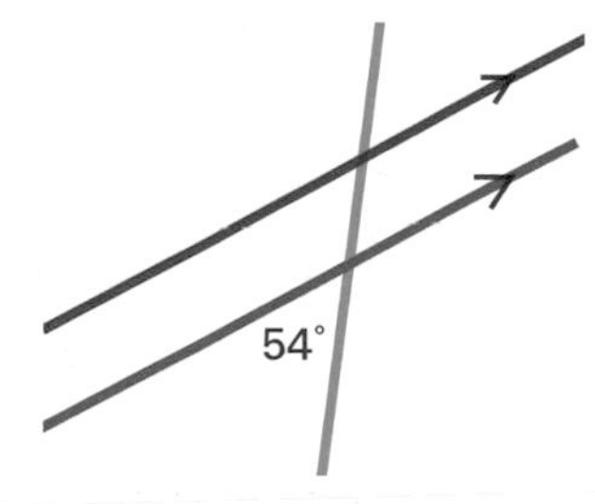

"We apply our knowledge of angles and measurement to help us safely construct the scenic elements," says Patrick.

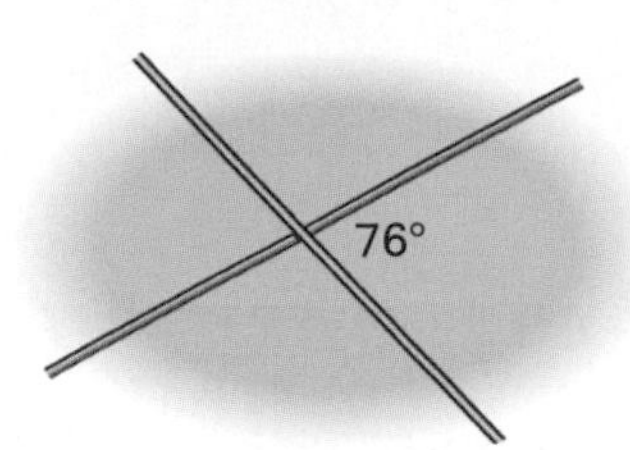

3. A piece of scenery needs to be hung with two intersecting guy wires. For safety, each of the four angles must be within 15° of a right angle. If one angle is 76°, will the scenery be hung safely? Explain.

4. The director wants the spotlight to shine equally on three dancers. This means that the centre of the light circle must be equidistant from the three dancers. Sketch a stage and mark a position for each dancer. Draw a circle that passes through the three positions. Mark the centre for the light circle.

Advanced Applications

Sometimes a design is painted on heavy canvas instead of on the stage floor. During performances, this floor cloth adds decoration to the stage. It may also provide guidance for the dancers.

"The McMaster Urban Dance Company tours dance festivals. They need a touring floor cloth. It will be rolled out for each production," explains Patrick.

5. Patrick paints the parallel blue line segments with $\angle a$ equal to $\angle b$. The length of the red transversal is 2.05 m. The dancers need to know the distance between the parallel line segments. What is the distance?

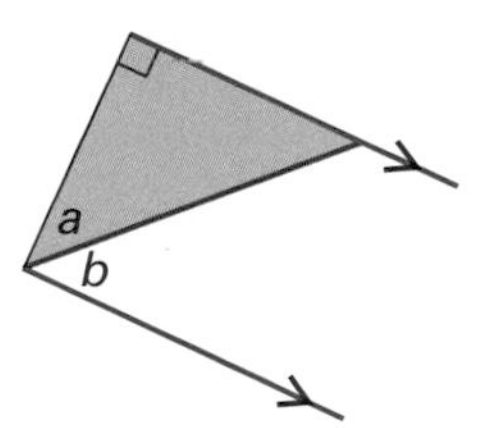

"Technicians use their knowledge of angles to make sure that the performers are properly lit," says Patrick.

6. A spotlight that is shining vertically down onto a stage has different lens barrels. Depending on which lens barrel is used, the beam angle can be 20°, 30°, 40°, or 50°. Patrick wants the angle where the light meets the stage (marked in red) to be as close as possible to 73°, but not greater than 73°.

a) Which lens barrel should he choose? Explain.

b) What will be the angle where the light meets the stage?

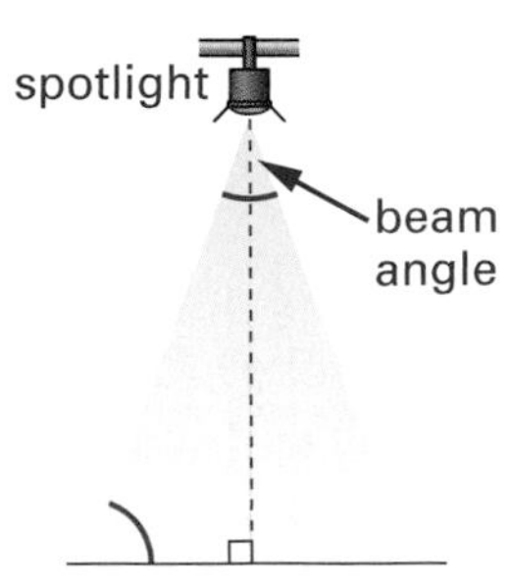

CHAPTER 11

Geometry and Measurement Relationships

▶ GOALS

You will be able to

- develop and apply formulas to calculate the surface area and volume of a cylinder
- solve problems that involve the surface area and volume of a cylinder
- investigate the properties of Platonic solids
- determine how the number of faces, edges, and vertices of a polyhedron are related (Euler's formula)

KILBEAR POINT

Getting Started

You will need
- a calculator
- centimetre grid paper

Designing a Juice Container

Hoshi and Tran are designing a container to hold 1 L of juice. They decide to try the shape of a triangular prism.

? What dimensions can Hoshi and Tran use for the juice container?

A. What is the least possible volume, in cubic centimetres, for the container? ($1 \text{ cm}^3 = 1 \text{ mL}$)

B. About 10% of the space in the container will be empty. How many cubic centimetres do Hoshi and Tran need for the total volume of the container?

C. If the container is 10 cm deep, what must the area of the triangular base be?

D. What dimensions could Hoshi and Tran use for the triangular base?

Do You Remember?

1. What unit (centimetres, square centimetres, cubic centimetres, litres, or millilitres) would you use to measure each of the following?
   a) the quantity of fuel in a car's gas tank
   b) the length of trim on a blanket
   c) the amount of paint to cover a playhouse
   d) the space inside a storage box

2. Draw a net for each prism using centimetre grid paper. Calculate the surface area of each prism to the nearest square centimetre.

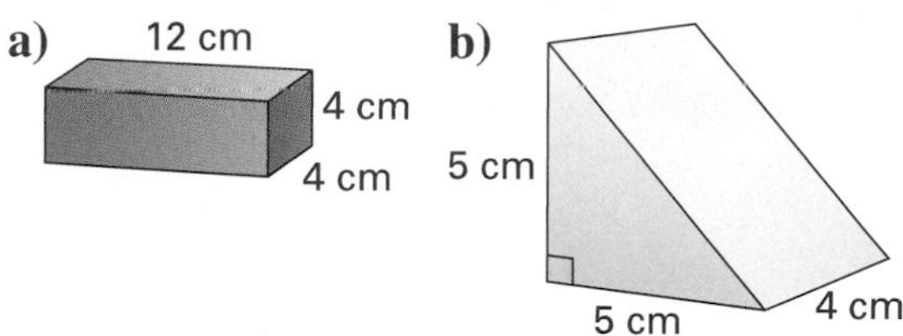

3. Sarah is covering the faces of this wooden box with fabric for a gift. How much fabric will she need to cover the box?

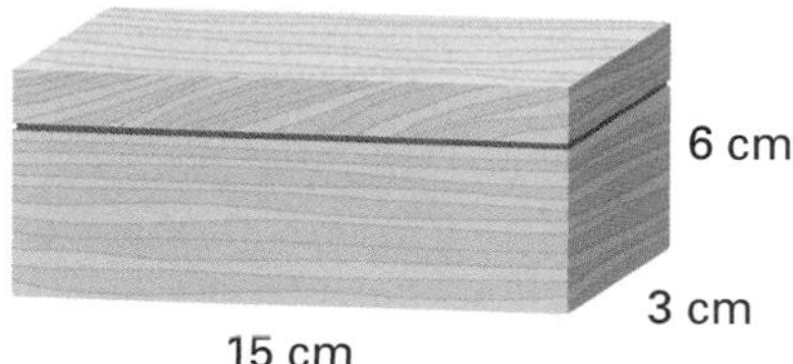

4. Calculate the area and circumference of each circle.

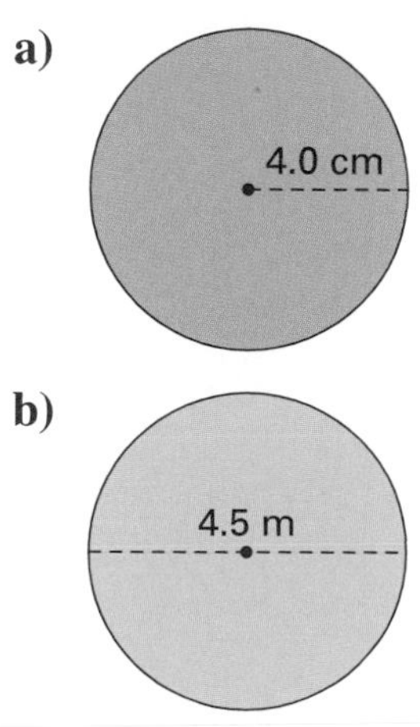

5. Calculate the volume of each prism.

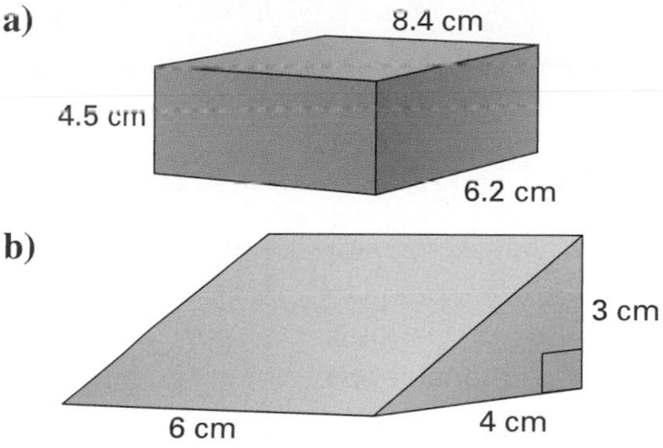

6. How much water would you need to fill each prism in question 5? ($1 \text{ cm}^3 = 1 \text{ mL}$)

7. List the number of edges, faces, and vertices on each prism.

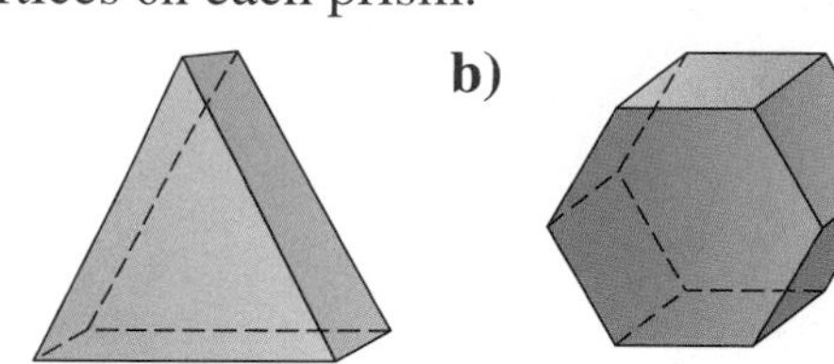

8. Centimetre cubes need to be packed in a box that has a volume of 36 cm^3. Sketch three possible boxes that are rectangular prisms.

9. Think of this cement traffic barrier as a rectangular prism with a trapezoidal prism on top.

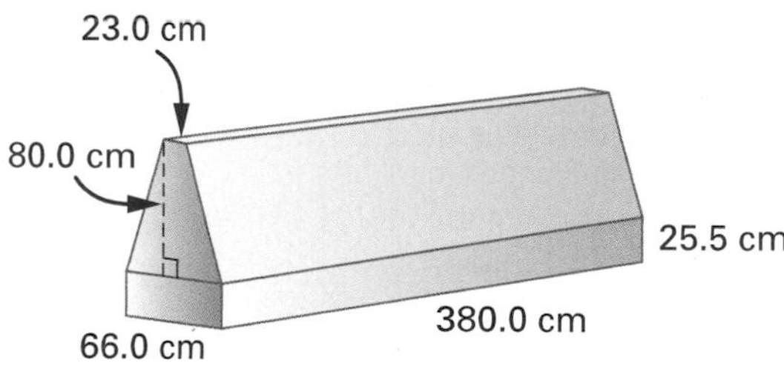

   a) What is the area of the base of each prism?
   b) What is the volume of each prism?
   c) What is the total volume of the cement needed to make the traffic barrier?

11.1 Exploring Cylinders

You will need
- paper
- scissors
- a calculator

▶ **GOAL**

Explore the relationship between the dimensions of a cylinder and the dimensions of its net.

Explore the Math

Maria and Benjamin are playing a game at their school math fair. They are shown a lid for a cylindrical container and four labels. To win a prize, they have to choose the label that matches the lid. They can ignore any overlap on the labels.

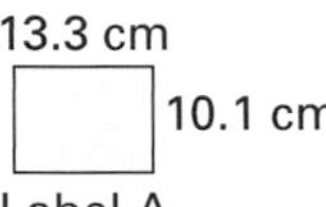

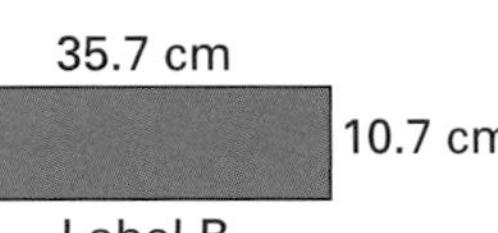

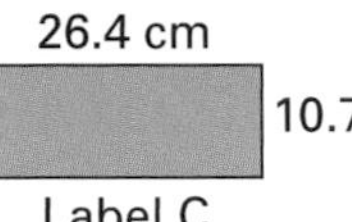

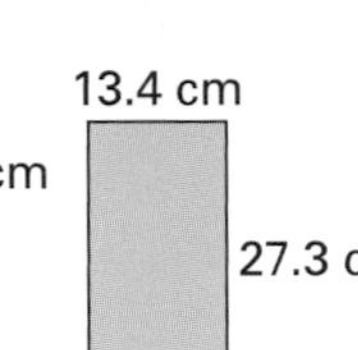

? How can you use the size of a lid to predict the width of the label?

A. Cut out paper models of the lid and the rectangular labels.

B. Use the rectangles to construct cylinders without bases.

C. Find the cylinder that matches the lid. Make a net for this cylinder.

D. Estimate the radius, circumference, and area of the lid.

E. Which measurement of the lid—the radius, circumference, or area—does the width of the label match?

F. Compare the widths of the labels with the measurement of the lid you selected in step E. Which label goes with the lid?

Communication Tip

The curved side of a cylinder has height and width. When the curved side is unrolled into a rectangle, the height of the cylinder becomes the length of the rectangle.

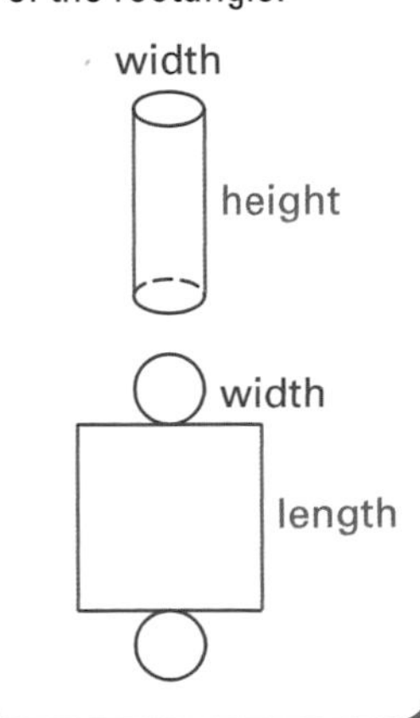

Reflecting

1. How did you know which label went with the lid?
2. How would the labels for two cylinders with the same height but different diameters compare?
3. If you knew the height and radius of a cylinder, how would that help you draw its net?

Curious Math

NETS OF CONES

The net for a cone provides clues that tell you how flat the cone will be when it is constructed.

You will need
- a compass
- scissors
- a ruler
- a protractor
- tape

Cone A

Cone B

Cone C

Net X

Net Y

Net Z

A. Draw three circles, each with a radius of 8 cm. Cut out your circles.

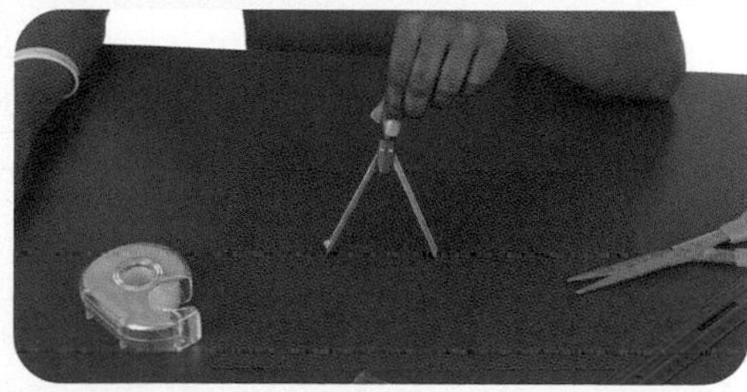

B. Cut out a section of one circle, along two radii of the circle, to create a net for a bottomless cone. Measure the angle.

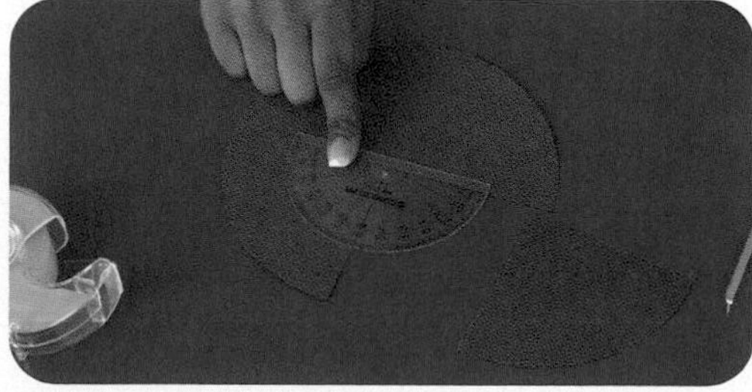

C. Tape together the cut edges to make the cone.

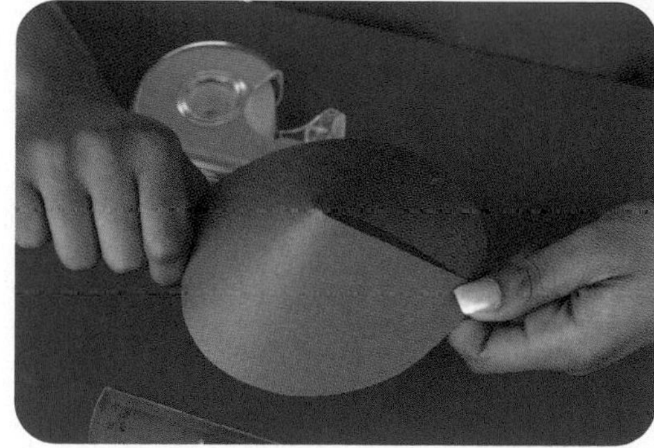

D. Repeat steps B and C to make two different-sized nets and cones.

E. What relationship do you notice between the angles of your nets and the flatness of your cones?

F. Which net (X, Y, or Z) goes with which cone (A, B, or C)?

11.2 Surface Area of a Cylinder

You will need
- a calculator
- centimetre grid paper
- a ruler
- a compass

▶ **GOAL**
Develop and apply a formula for calculating the surface area of a cylinder.

Learn about the Math

Toma and Maria are wrapping tea lights to sell for a school fundraiser. They are wrapping the tea lights in stacks of five.

? How much paper do Toma and Maria need to wrap each stack of tea lights?

Example 1: Estimating surface area with grid paper

Use a net to estimate the amount of wrapping paper that Toma and Maria need to wrap each stack of five tea lights.

Toma's Solution

I imagined unwrapping the package and laying the paper flat. I traced the circular base and top of the cylinder on grid paper.

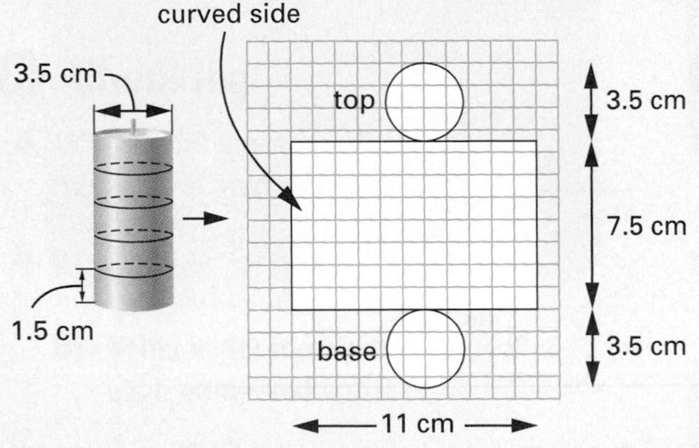

The height of each tea light is 1.5 cm, so the height of the curved side is $5 \times 1.5 \text{ cm} = 7.5 \text{ cm}$.

The width of the curved side is the same as the circumference of the base. The diameter of the base is 3.5 cm, so the circumference is $3.5 \text{ cm} \times \pi \doteq 11 \text{ cm}$.

I counted the squares in the net. There are about 10 squares in each circle. There are about $7.5 \times 11 \doteq 83$ squares in the curved side (rectangle). Each square has an area of 1 cm^2.

Total surface area = area of base + area of top + area of curved side
$\doteq 10 \text{ cm}^2 + 10 \text{ cm}^2 + 83 \text{ cm}^2$
$\doteq 103 \text{ cm}^2$

Toma and Maria need about 103 cm^2 of wrapping paper for each stack of tea lights.

NEL

Example 2: Calculating surface area using a formula

Calculate the amount of wrapping paper that Toma and Maria need to wrap each stack of five tea lights.

Maria's Solution

The base and top of each stack are congruent faces, so they have the same area. I just need to determine the area of one face, and then I can double it.

The diameter is 3.5 cm, so the radius is 3.5 cm $\div$ 2 $\doteq$ 1.8 cm.

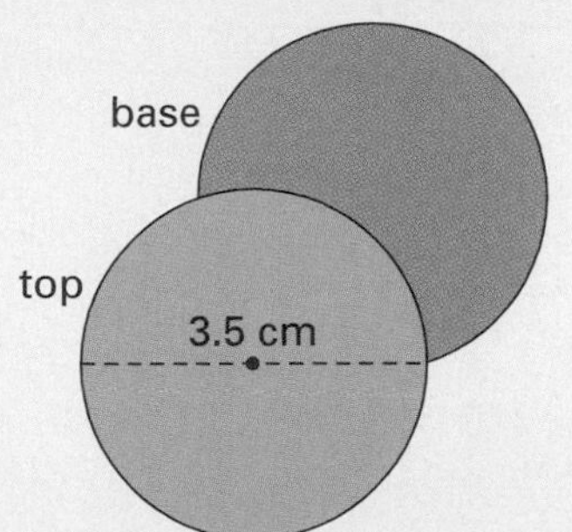

Area of top and base $= 2 \times \pi r^2$

$\doteq 2 \times \pi \times (1.8\text{ cm})^2$

2×π×1.8^2=
20.35752043

The area of the top and base is 20.4 cm². I rounded to one decimal place because this is how the radius is given in the problem.

If I laid out the curved side of the package, it would form a rectangle. Its width would be equal to the circumference of the base. Its length would be equal to the height of the package. So, its area is equal to the circumference of the base multiplied by the height of the package.

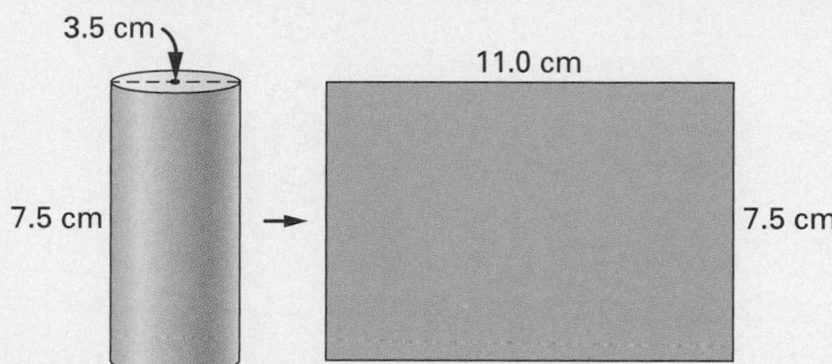

Area of curved surface

= circumference of base × height

$= \pi d \times$ height

$= (\pi \times 3.5\text{ cm}) \times 7.5\text{ cm}$

π×3.5×7.5=
82.46680716

The area of the curved surface is 82.5 cm².

Total surface area = area of top and base + area of curved surface

$\doteq 20.4\text{ cm}^2 + 82.5\text{ cm}^2$

$\doteq 102.9\text{ cm}^2$

Toma and Maria need 102.9 cm² of wrapping paper for each stack of tea lights.

Reflecting

1. What part of the net for a cylinder is affected by the height of the cylinder?

2. What part of the net for a cylinder is affected by the size of the base?

3. Write a formula to calculate the surface area of a cylinder.

Work with the Math

Example 3: Calculating surface area using a formula

Calculate the surface area of this cylinder.

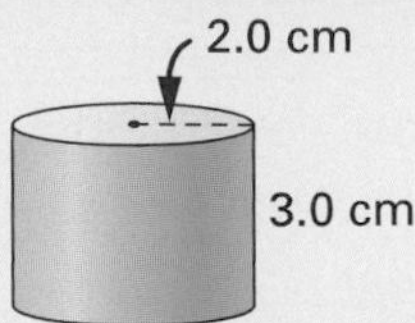

Solution

Surface area of cylinder = area of base and top + area of curved surface

Sketch the faces, and calculate the area of each face.

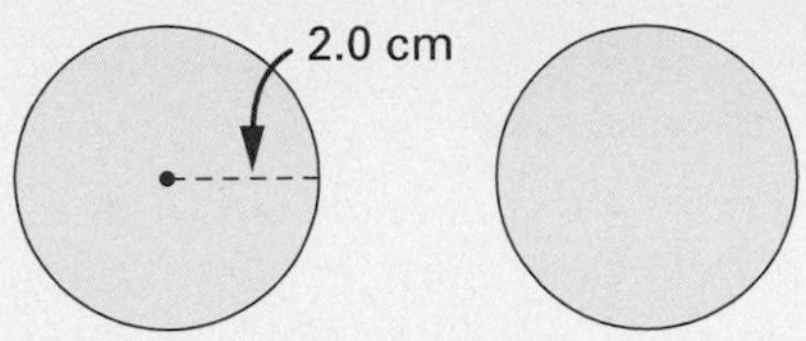

Area of base and top = 2 × area of base

$= 2 \times \pi r^2$

$\doteq 2 \times 3.14 \times (2.0 \text{ cm})^2$

$\doteq 25.1 \text{ cm}^2$

3.0 cm

12.6 cm

Width of rectangle = circumference of circle

$= 2\pi r$

$\doteq 2 \times 3.14 \times 2.0 \text{ cm}$

$\doteq 12.6 \text{ cm}$

Area of curved surface = area of rectangle

= length × width

$\doteq 3.0 \text{ cm} \times 12.6 \text{ cm}$

$\doteq 37.8 \text{ cm}^2$

Surface area of cylinder = area of base and top + area of curved surface

$\doteq 25.1 \text{ cm}^2 + 37.8 \text{ cm}^2$

$\doteq 62.9 \text{ cm}^2$

The surface area is 62.9 cm^2.

A Checking

4. Calculate the surface area of each cylinder.

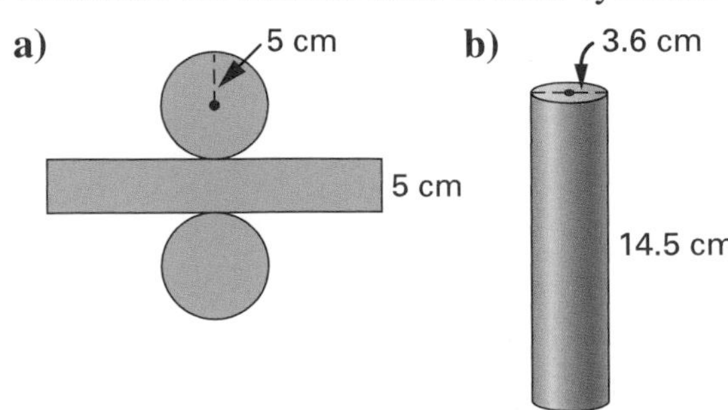

B Practising

5. Use each net to determine the surface area of the cylinder.

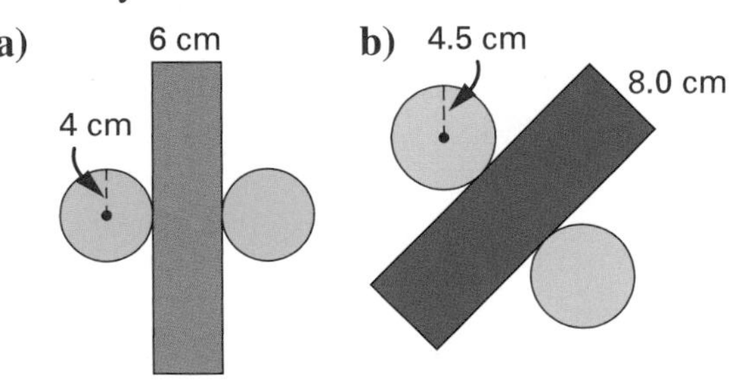

6. Three cylinders have bases that are the same size. The area of the base is 10.0 cm^2. Determine the surface area of each cylinder, given its height.

a) 8.0 cm **b)** 6.5 cm **c)** 9.4 cm

7. Calculate the surface area of each cylinder.

a) **c)**

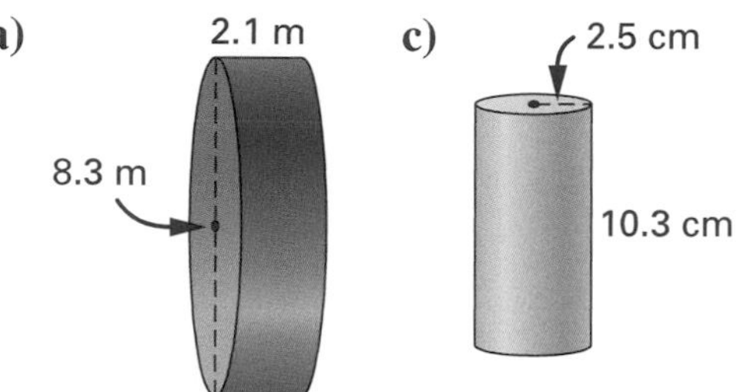

b)

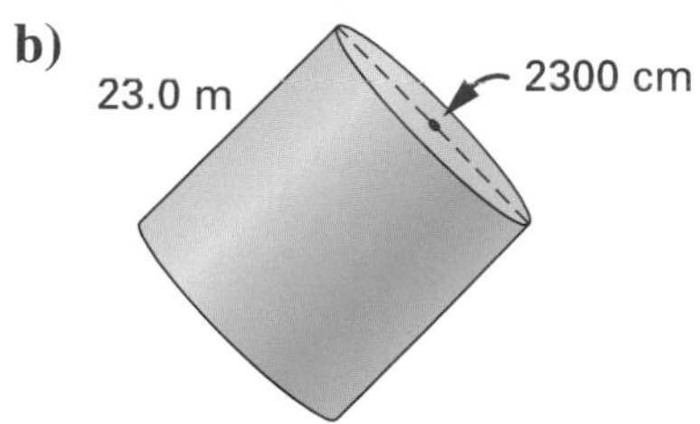

8. Describe how you would determine the surface area of a potato-chip container that is shaped like a cylinder.

9. **a)** This railway car is 3.2 m in diameter and 17.2 m long. Calculate its surface area.

b) Estimate the cost of painting the outside of the railway car, if a can of paint covers an area of 40 m^2 and costs $35.

10. Explain why two cylinders that are the same height can have different surface areas.

11. "Anik" is the name of a series of Canadian communications satellites. The first Anik, shown here, was launched in 1972. It was a cylindrical shape, 3.5 m high and 190 cm in diameter. All satellites are wrapped with insulation because the instruments inside will not work if they become too cold or hot. What was the approximate area of the insulation used to wrap the first Anik?

12. A games shop sells marbles in clear plastic cylinders. Four marbles fit across the diameter of the cylinder, and 10 marbles fit from the base to the top of the cylinder. Each marble has a diameter of 2 cm. What is the area of the plastic that is needed to make one cylinder?

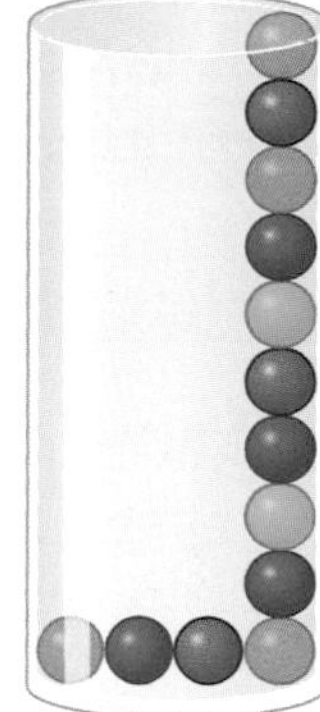

C Extending

13. Gurjit has a CD case that is a cylindrical shape. It has a surface area of 603 cm^2 and a height of 10 cm. What is the area of the circular lid of the CD case?

11.3 Volume of a Cylinder

You will need
- centimetre grid paper
- a compass
- centimetre linking cubes
- a calculator

▶ **GOAL**
Develop and apply a formula for calculating the volume of a cylinder.

Learn about the Math

Guess which jar holds the most jellybeans, and win the jar!

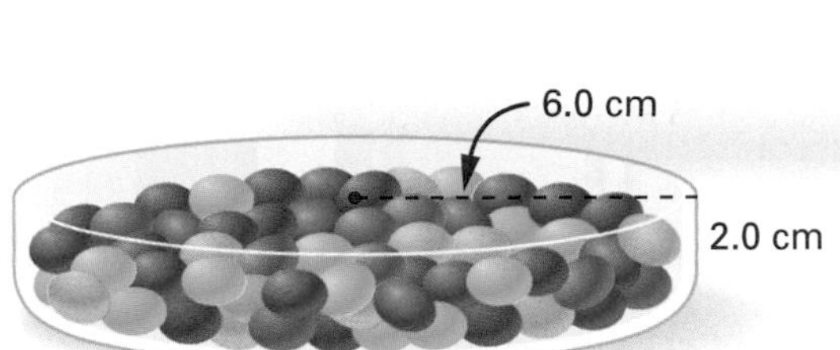

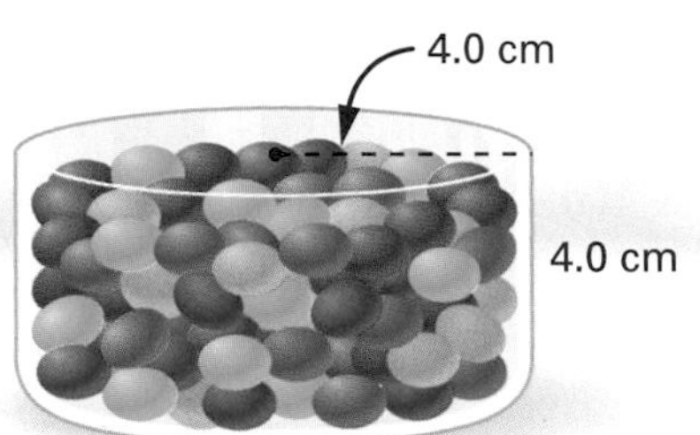

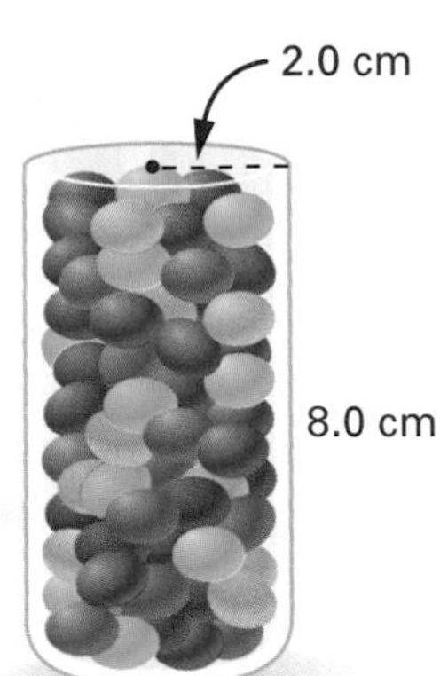

Benjamin says, "The jar with the greatest volume holds the most jellybeans. One jellybean has a volume of about 1 cm^3. If I can calculate the volume of each jar, I can estimate the number of jellybeans it holds. I'll use models of the jars to estimate their volumes.

I know that the bottom of each jar is a circle. I'll estimate the number of centimetre cubes that will cover the bottom. I'll stack centimetre cubes to determine the number of layers."

? Which jar holds the most jellybeans?

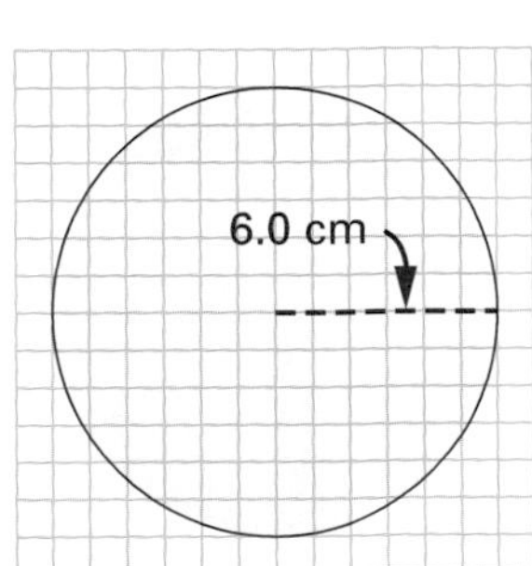

A. On centimetre grid paper, draw a circle with a radius of 6.0 cm to model the base of the first jar. Estimate the area of the base.

B. Stack centimetre cubes to model the height of the jar. How many layers of cubes will fit inside the jar?

C. Estimate the volume of the first jar.

D. Repeat steps A to C for the other two jars.

E. Which jar holds the most jellybeans? Explain your answer.

Reflecting

1. Why do both the radius of a cylinder and its height matter when you are estimating its volume?
2. How does Benjamin's strategy show how to use the area of the base of a cylinder to determine the volume of the cylinder?
3. Write a formula for calculating the volume of a cylinder.

Work with the Math

Example 1: Calculating volume using radius

Calculate the volume of this cylinder.

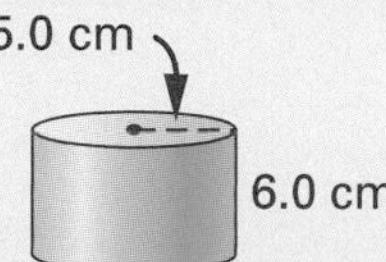

Hoshi's Solution

Volume of cylinder = area of base × height
$= \pi r^2 \times$ height
$\doteq 3.14 \times (5.0\text{ cm})^2 \times 6.0\text{ cm}$
$\doteq 471.0\text{ cm}^3$

The volume of a cylinder is calculated like the volume of a prism: area of base × height.

I calculated the volume using the formula and 3.14 for π.

The volume of the cylinder is 471.0 cm^3.

Example 2: Estimating volume using diameter

Estimate which cylinder has the greater volume.

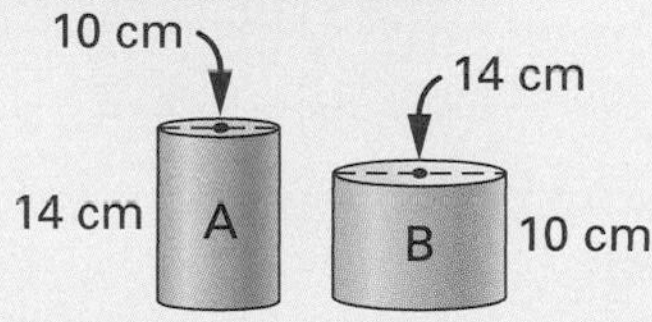

Chad's Solution

Cylinder A

The diameter of cylinder A is 10.0 cm, so the radius is $10.0 \div 2 = 5.0$ cm.

For an estimate, I can use rounded measurements for easier mental math.

Volume of cylinder A = area of base × height
$= \pi r^2 \times$ height
$= \pi \times (5\text{ cm})^2 \times 14\text{ cm}$
$\doteq \pi \times 25\text{ cm}^2 \times 16\text{ cm}$
$\doteq \pi \times 400\text{ cm}^3$

Cylinder B

The diameter of cylinder B is 14.0 cm, so the radius is 7.0 cm.

Volume of cylinder B = area of base × height
$= \pi r^2 \times$ height
$= \pi \times (7\text{ cm})^2 \times 10\text{ cm}$
$\doteq \pi \times 50 \times 10\text{ cm}$
$\doteq \pi \times 500\text{ cm}^3$

Cylinder B has the greater volume.

A Checking

4. Estimate the volume of each cylinder.

a)

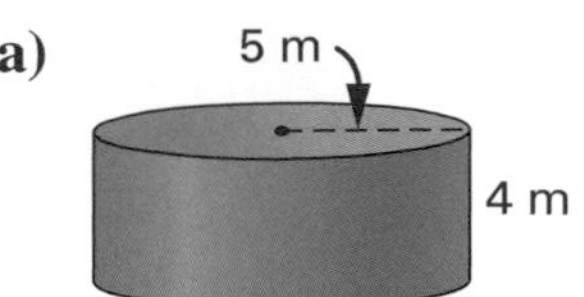

b)

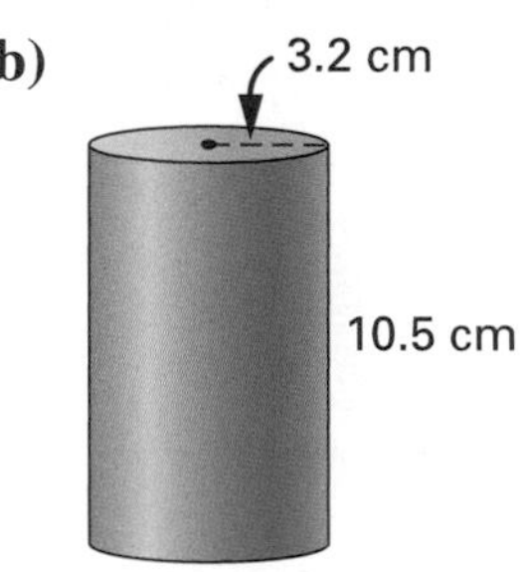

5. Calculate the volume of each cylinder.

a)

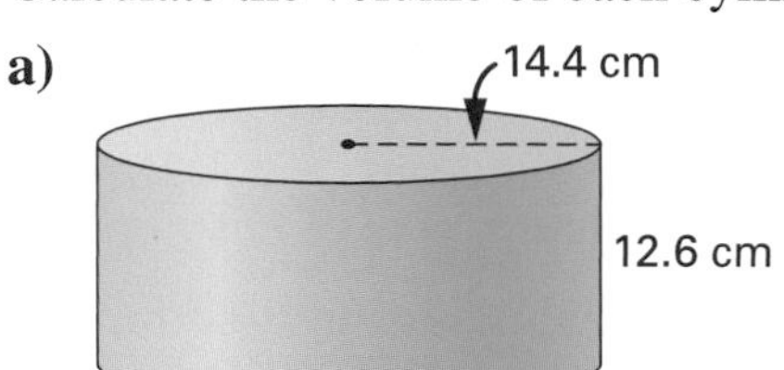

b)

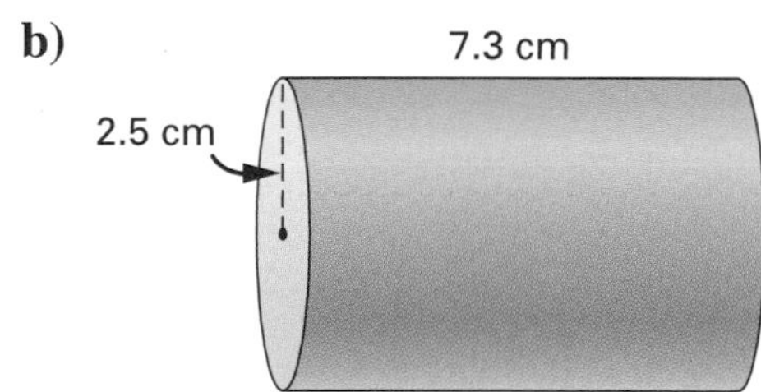

B Practising

6. Estimate the volume of each cylinder.

a)

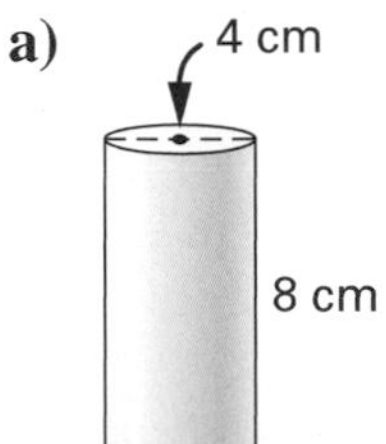

b)

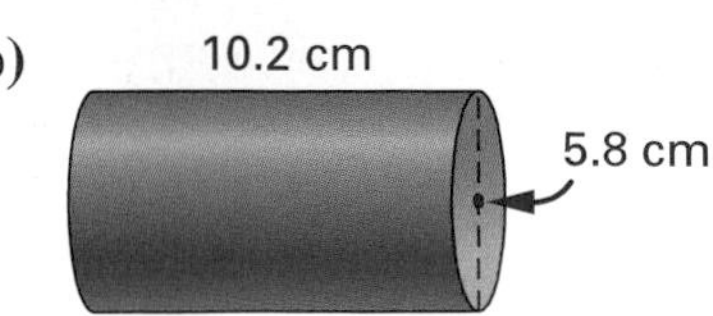

7. a) Determine the volume of Mandy's mug.

b) About how many millilitres of liquid will it hold?

8. Calculate the volume of each cylinder.

a)

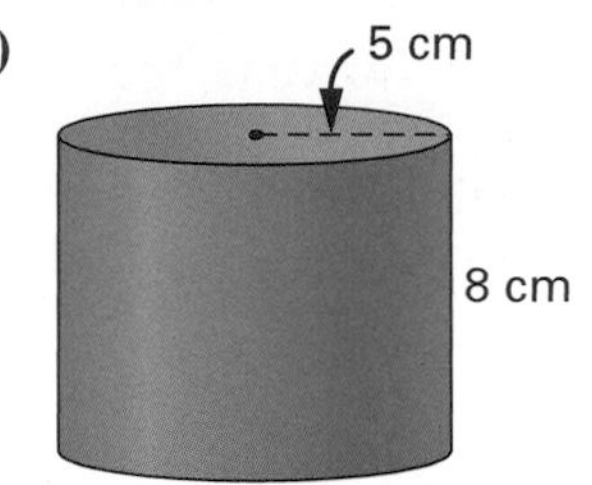

b)

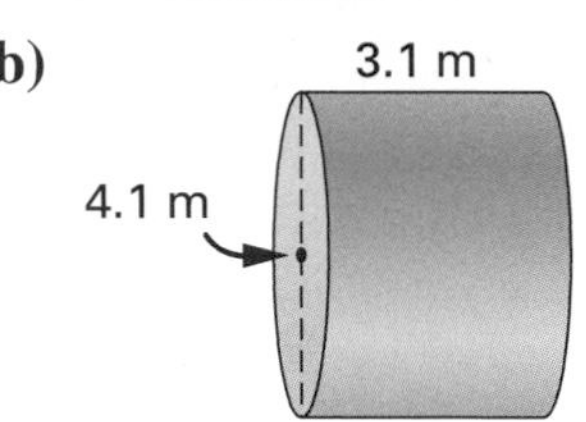

9. Cosmo's family has a pool like this.

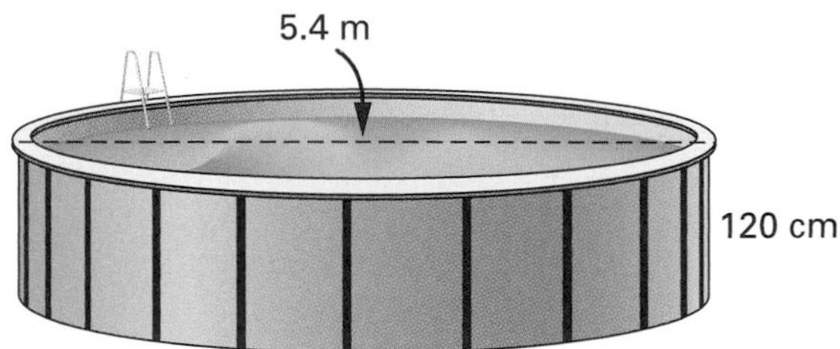

a) What is the volume of the pool?

b) How many litres of water will the pool hold?

c) How long will it take to fill the pool at a rate of 50 L/min?

10. Tennis balls are sold in cylinders. Each cylinder has a height of about 22 cm and a diameter of about 7 cm. Estimate the volume of the cylinder.

11. A cylindrical candle is sold in a gift box that is a square-based prism. What is the volume of empty space in the box?

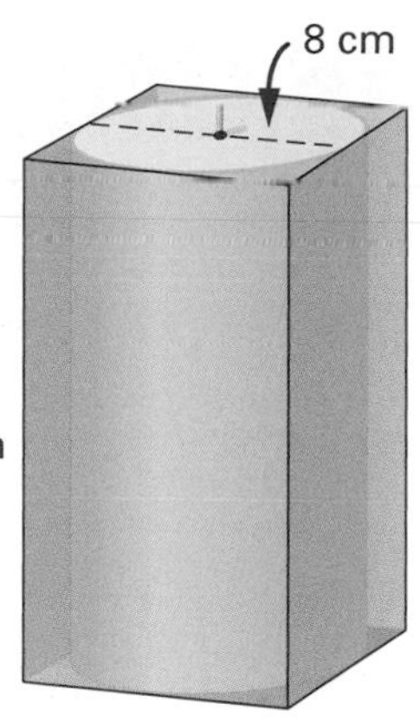

12. Copy and complete this chart for cylinders.

Radius of base	Diameter of base	Height	Volume
4 cm		11 cm	
	12.0 m	5.0 m	
3.5 cm			307.7 cm³
		2.0 m	226.1 m³

13. The area of the base of a cylinder is 50.2 cm². The volume of the cylinder is 502.4 cm³. Determine the height of the cylinder.

14. A lipstick tube has a volume of 25.1 cm³ and a diameter of 2.0 cm. What is the height of the tube?

15. The volume of each cylinder below is 0.3040 m³. Solve for the unknown measure.

a)

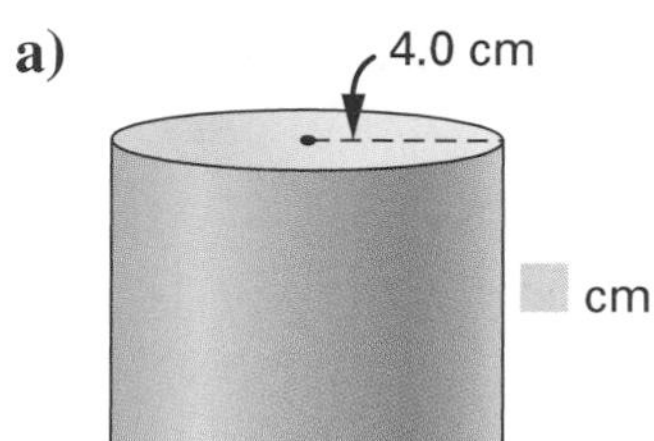

b)

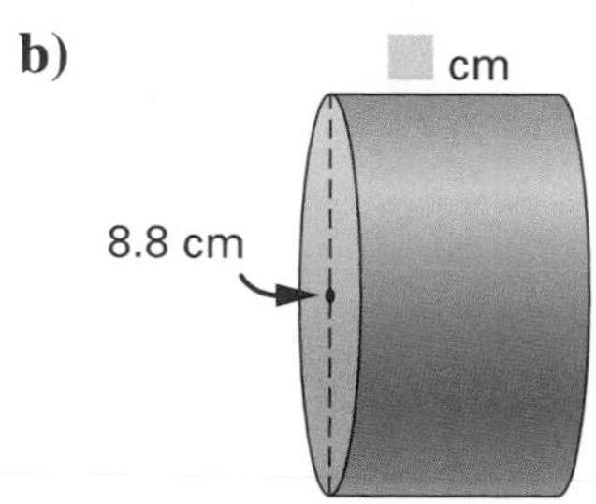

16. Which container holds more, the cylinder or the triangular prism? Justify your answer.

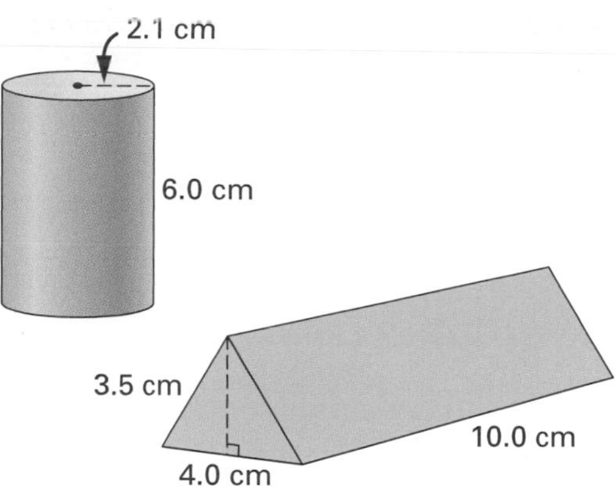

17. Which holds more, a cylinder with a height of 10.0 cm and a diameter of 7.0 cm or a cylinder with a height of 7.0 cm and a diameter of 10.0 cm? Explain your answer.

C Extending

18. These two metal cans both hold the same quantity of soup.

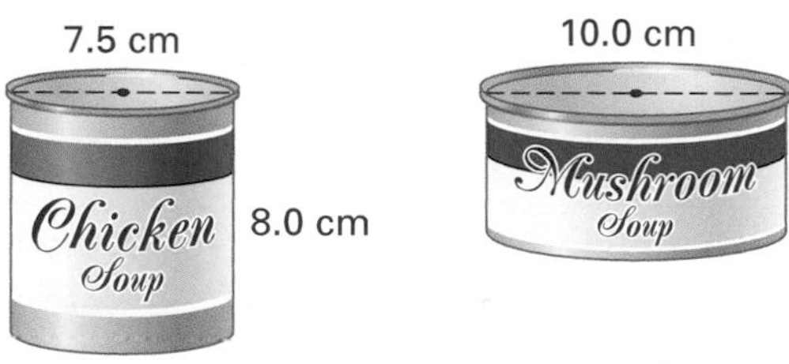

a) What is the height of the can of mushroom soup? Show your solution.

b) Which can uses more metal? Explain.

19. Suppose that the radius of a cylinder is the same as its height. What would happen to the volume of the cylinder if its radius were doubled and the height stayed the same?

20. These two containers each hold 1 L of liquid. What might their dimensions be?

11.4 Solve Problems Using Diagrams

You will need
- a calculator

▶ **GOAL**
Use diagrams to solve measurement problems.

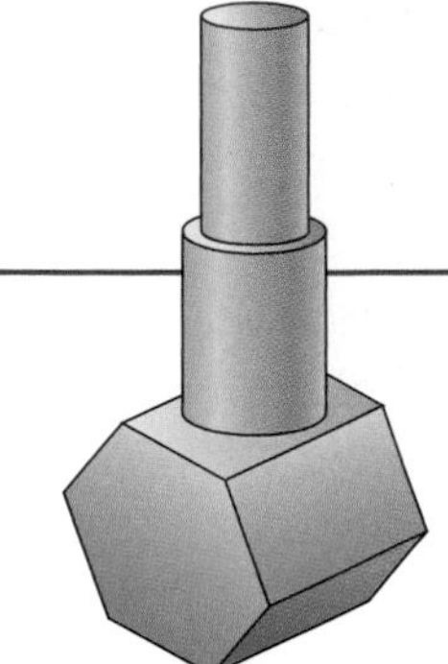

Learn about the Math

For a babysitting course, Toma is designing a toy that will be filled with water.

? How many millilitres of water will Toma's toy hold?

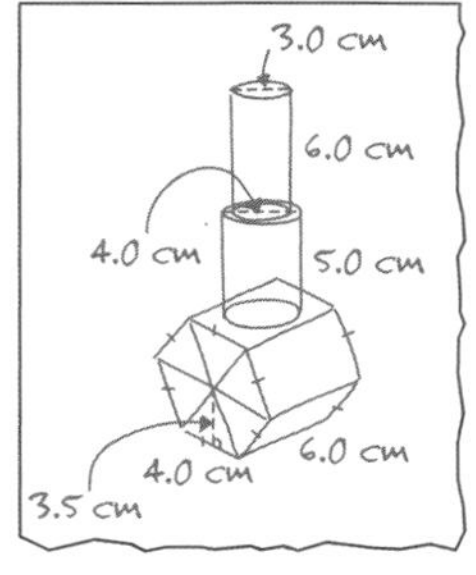

1 Understand the Problem
To determine the number of millilitres of water the toy will hold, Toma needs to determine its volume in cubic centimetres. (1 mL = 1 cm^3)

2 Make a Plan
Toma will use diagrams and a formula to determine the volume of each of the three figures that make up the toy. Then she will add the three volumes.

3 Carry Out the Plan

Figure	Area of base of figure	Volume of figure
top	Area of base of top figure $= \pi r^2$ $= \pi \times (1.5\text{ cm})^2$ $\doteq 7.1\text{ cm}^2$	Volume of top figure = area of base × height $\doteq 7.1\text{ cm}^2 \times 6.0\text{ cm}$ $\doteq 42.6\text{ cm}^3$
middle	Area of base of middle figure $= \pi r^2$ $= \pi \times (2.0\text{ cm})^2$ $\doteq 12.6\text{ cm}^2$	Volume of middle figure = area of base × height $\doteq 12.6\text{ cm}^2 \times 5.0\text{ cm}$ $\doteq 63.0\text{ cm}^3$
bottom	The area of the base of the bottom figure is the area of six triangles. Area of one triangle $= \frac{1}{2}$ base × height $= \frac{1}{2}(4.0\text{ cm}) \times 3.5\text{ cm}$ $= 7.0\text{ cm}^2$ Area of six triangles $= 6 \times 7.0\text{ cm}^2$ $= 42.0\text{ cm}^2$	Volume of bottom figure = area of base × height $= 42.0\text{ cm}^2 \times 6.0\text{ cm}$ $= 252.0\text{ cm}^3$

$$\text{Total volume of toy} \doteq 42.6 \text{ cm}^3 + 63.0 \text{ cm}^3 + 252.0 \text{ cm}^3$$
$$\doteq 357.6 \text{ cm}^3$$

The volume of Toma's toy is about 358 cm^3. Since 1 cm^3 = 1 mL, the toy will hold about 358 mL of water.

4 Look Back

Toma estimates that the top two cylinders are smaller than a 4 cm by 4 cm by 11 cm square prism that has a volume of 176 cm^3. She thinks the bottom is smaller than a 6 cm cube that has a volume of 216 cm^3.

Her toy volume calculation is less than 176 cm^3 + 216 cm^3 = 392 cm^3, so her answer is reasonable.

Reflecting

1. How did the strategy of using diagrams help Toma solve this problem?

2. How did using diagrams to compare the sizes of the figures help Toma check her answer?

Work with the Math

Example: Using a tree diagram to determine probability

Maria and Tran are playing a game with two standard dice. To win the game, they need to roll a sum of 8. What is the probability of rolling a sum of 8?

Tran's Solution

1 Understand the Problem

I have to determine the number of different ways that I can roll a sum of 8 and compare this number with the number of possible outcomes.

2 Make a Plan

I'll draw a tree diagram to list all the possible outcomes. Then I'll count the number of outcomes that give a sum of 8.

3 Carry Out the Plan

Roll 1	1	2	3	4	5	6

Roll 2	1 2 3 4 5 6	1 2 3 4 5 6	1 2 3 4 5 6	1 2 3 4 5 6	1 2 3 4 5 6	1 2 3 4 5 6
Sum	2 3 4 5 6 7	3 4 5 6 7 8	4 5 6 7 8 9	5 6 7 8 9 10	6 7 8 9 10 11	7 8 9 10 11 12

There are 36 possible outcomes. The probability of rolling a sum of 8 is $\frac{5}{36}$.

4 Look Back

I see a pattern in the sums. In each group, they increase by 1. So, I'm sure that my diagram shows all the possible combinations.

A Checking

3. Sketch the prisms that make up this cabin. Then calculate the volume and surface area of the whole cabin.

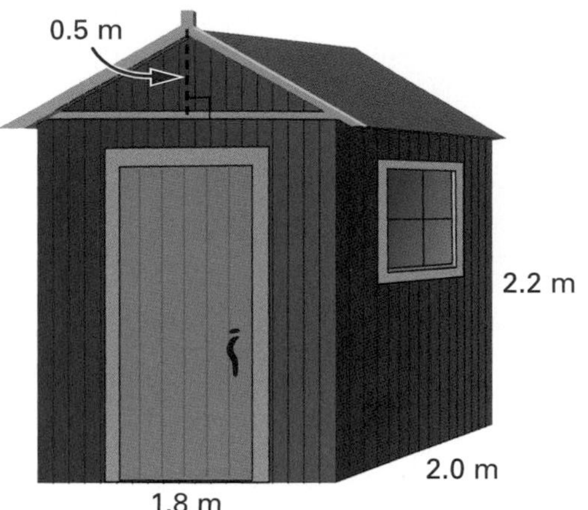

B Practising

4. Sketch the prisms that make up this skateboard ramp. Then calculate the volume and surface area of the whole skateboard ramp.

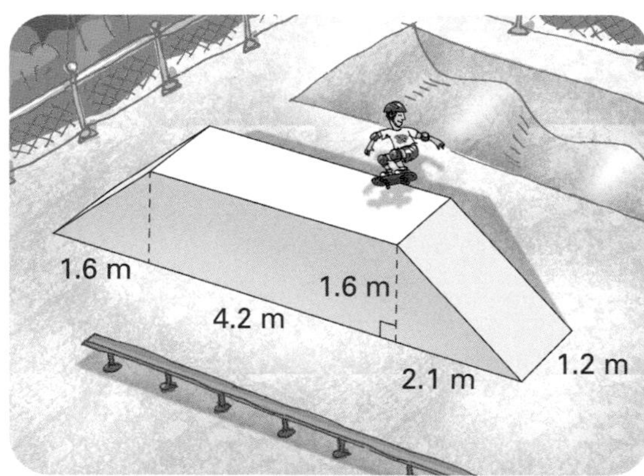

5. Perdita has a red shirt, a black shirt, a yellow shirt, and a white shirt. She also has a pair of white shorts, a pair of red shorts, and a pair of blue shorts.
   a) Determine the number of different outfits that Perdita could wear.
   b) What is the probability that she will wear at least one piece of clothing that is red?

6. Erik rolls two standard dice. Determine the probability that the sum will be 6, 7, or 8.

7. Fritz is making a stained-glass window. It consists of a rectangle that is 0.5 m wide by 2.5 m long, with a semicircle above the rectangle.
   a) Sketch an outline of the window. Label the dimensions.
   b) How much glass does Fritz need?

8. To copy a poster, Sohel reduces each dimension by 70%. The width of the original poster is 0.4 m. What is the width of the reduced copy?

9. How many squares are in figure 100?

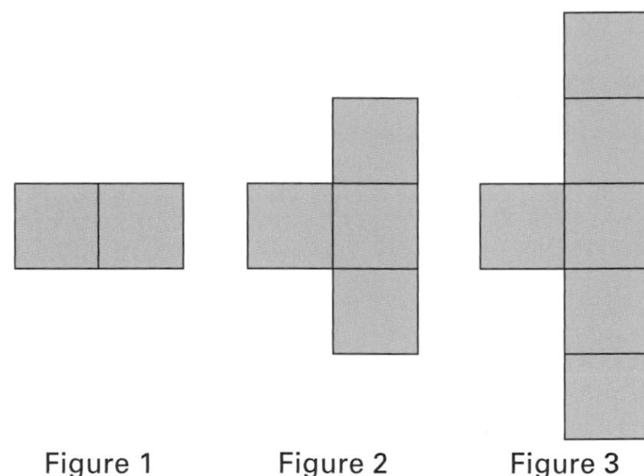

Figure 1 Figure 2 Figure 3

10. How many different ways can 360 players in a marching band be arranged in a rectangle?

11. A city park is a square with 600 m sides. Diane started walking from a point 150 m south of the northwest corner, straight to a point 150 m north of the southwest corner. How far did she walk?

12. James is estimating the amount of paint he needs for the walls of his 3.4 m by 2.6 m bedroom. His bedroom is 2.7 m high. One litre of paint covers about 10 m^2. About how much paint does James need?

Mental Imagery

CALCULATING SURFACE AREA OF CUBE STRUCTURES

Use nine linking cubes to build this shape.

You will need
- linking cubes

Each linking cube has a surface area of 6 square units. So, the total surface area of nine unattached cubes is $9 \times 6 = 54$ square units. In your shape, however, some of the cubes are attached to each other. Therefore, the surface area of your shape is less than 54 square units.

1. How many pairs of faces are attached to each other?

2. How can you use your answer to question 1 to calculate the surface area of your shape?

3. Build each shape below, and calculate its surface area.

a)

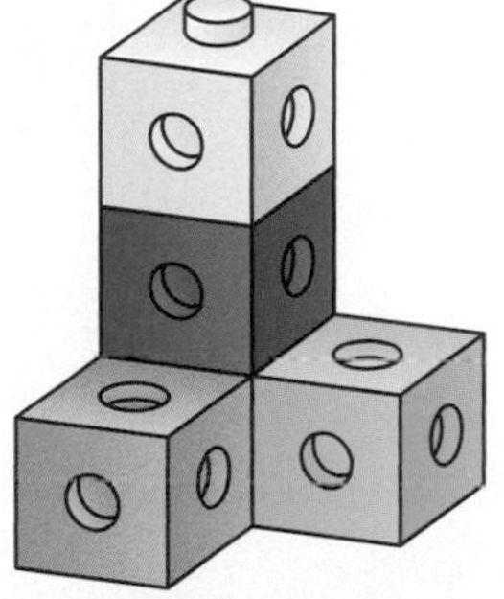

b)

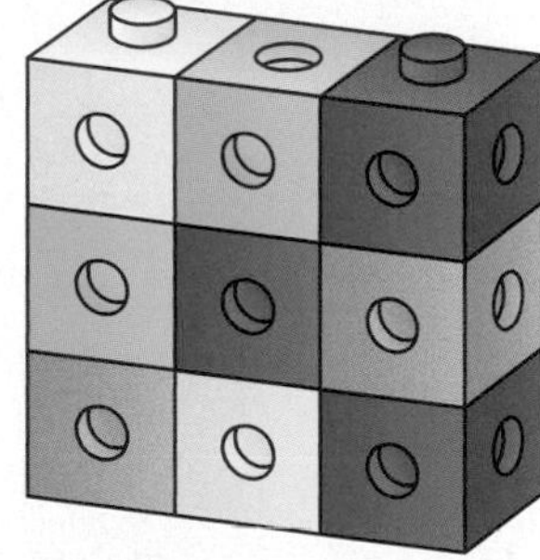

c)

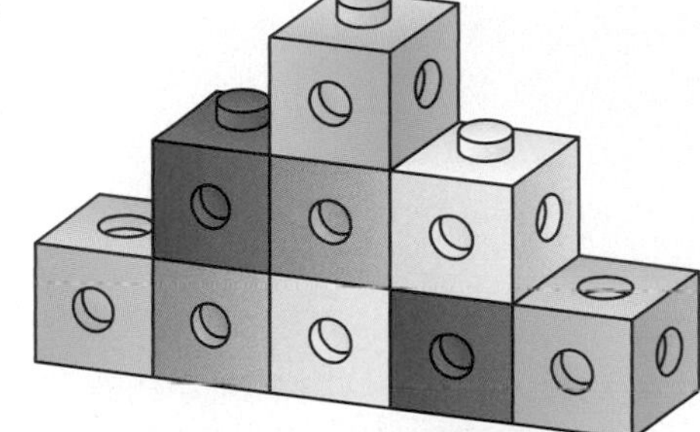

d)

Mid-Chapter Review

Frequently Asked Questions

Q: How do you calculate the surface area of a cylinder?

A: Sketch a net of the cylinder. The surface area is the sum of the areas of the faces. Like the base and top of a rectangular prism, the base and top of a cylinder are congruent. Therefore, they have the same area. Calculate the area of the base, and double it. Add this to the area of the curved surface.

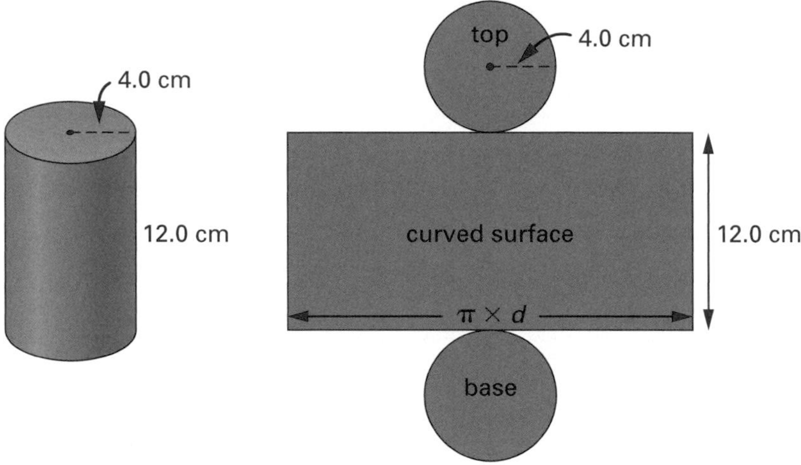

$$\begin{aligned}\text{Surface area} &= 2 \times \text{area of base} + \text{area of curved surface}\\ &= 2 \times \pi r^2 + (\pi d \times h)\\ &= 2 \times \pi \times (4.0\text{ cm})^2 + (\pi \times 8.0\text{ cm} \times 12.0\text{ cm})\\ &\doteq 402.1\text{ cm}^2\end{aligned}$$

Q: How do you calculate the volume of a cylinder?

A: The base of a cylinder is a circle. Calculate the volume of a cylinder in the same way you would calculate the volume of a prism—multiply the area of the base by the height.

$$\begin{aligned}\text{Volume} &= \text{area of base} \times \text{height}\\ &= \pi r^2 \times h\\ &= \pi \times (4.0\text{ cm})^2 \times 12.0\text{ cm}\\ &\doteq 603.2\text{ cm}^3\end{aligned}$$

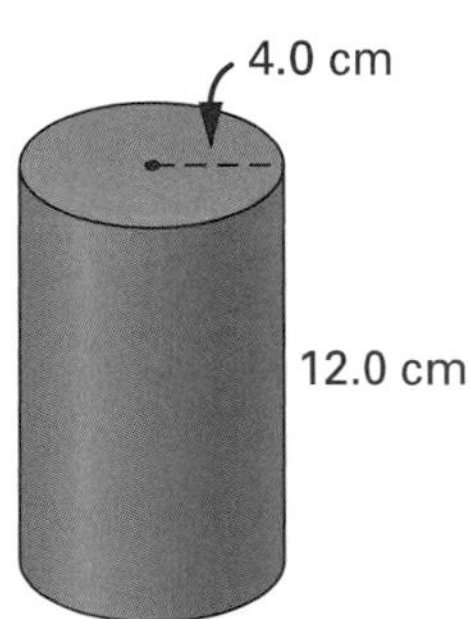

Practice Questions

(11.2) **1.** Sketch a net for each cylinder, and label its dimensions. Then calculate the surface area.

	Item	Radius of base (cm)	Height of cylinder (cm)
a)	potato-chip container	4	8
b)	coffee can	7.5	15.0
c)	CD case	8.5	20.5
d)	oil barrel	25.0	80.0

(11.2) **2.** Karim is painting a design on a cylindrical barrel. The height of the barrel is 1.2 m. The radius of its base is 0.3 m. What area will the paint have to cover? (Remember to include the bottom and lid of the barrel.)

(11.2) **3.** Write step-by-step instructions for determining the surface area of an empty paper-towel roll.

(11.2) **4.** Determine the surface area of each tin.

a) **b)**

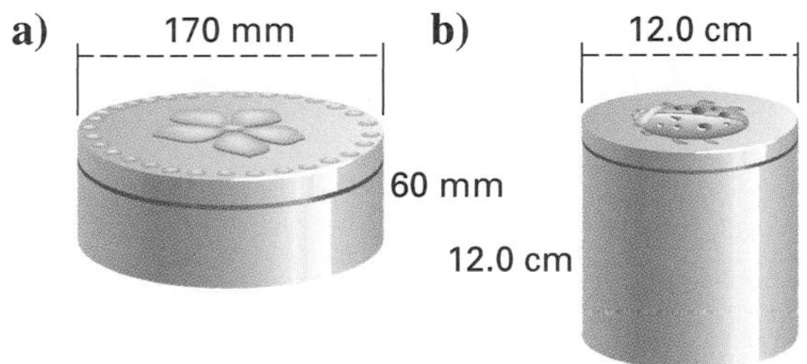

(11.2) **5.** A cylindrical candle has a radius of 6 cm and a height of 20 cm. How much waxed paper will Jake need to wrap the candle?

(11.3) **6.** Determine the volume of a cylinder that is 20 cm high and has the radius or diameter below.

a) radius 13 cm

b) radius 6.5 cm

c) diameter 20 cm

7. Deirdre is buying birdseed for the class bird feeder. The bird feeder is a cylinder with a diameter of 25 cm and a height of 45 cm. How many millilitres of seed should she buy? (11.3)

8. Determine the volume of this figure. Explain what you did. (11.3)

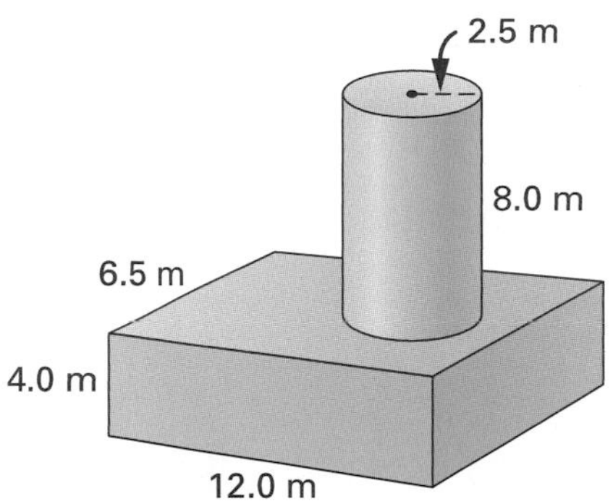

9. A soup can has a radius of 4 cm and a height of 11 cm. There are 24 cans in one case. How many litres of soup are in one case? (11.3)

10. The height of each cylinder in a set of food-storage containers is 30 cm. The radius of the largest container is 10 cm. The volume of the smallest container is $\frac{1}{3}$ the volume of the largest container. The volume of the middle-sized container is $\frac{2}{3}$ the volume of the largest container. What is the volume of each container? (11.4)

11.5 Exploring the Platonic Solids

▶ **GOAL**

Investigate properties of the Platonic solids.

You will need
- congruent equilateral triangles
- congruent squares
- congruent regular pentagons
- congruent regular hexagons
- tape
- a protractor

Explore the Math

A Platonic solid is a **polyhedron** with faces that are all congruent **regular polygons**. The same number of faces meet at all the vertices.

polyhedron

a 3-D shape that has polygons as its faces

There are only five Platonic solids.

tetrahedron

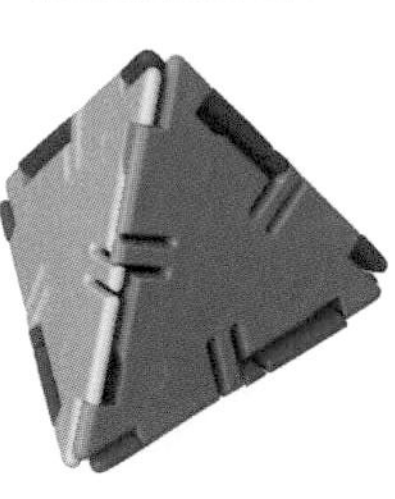

cube

octahedron

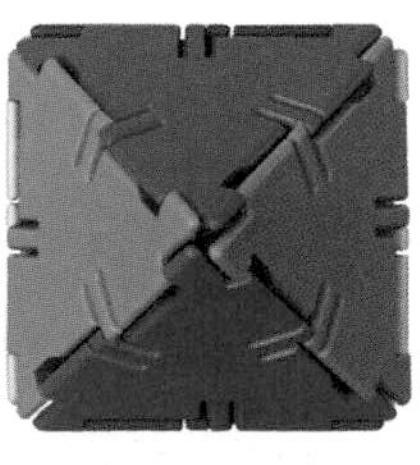

dodecahedron

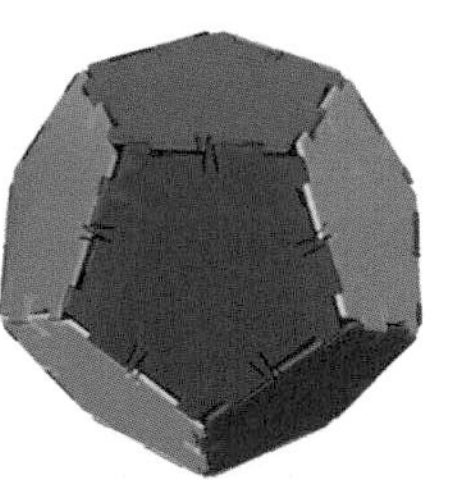

icosahedron

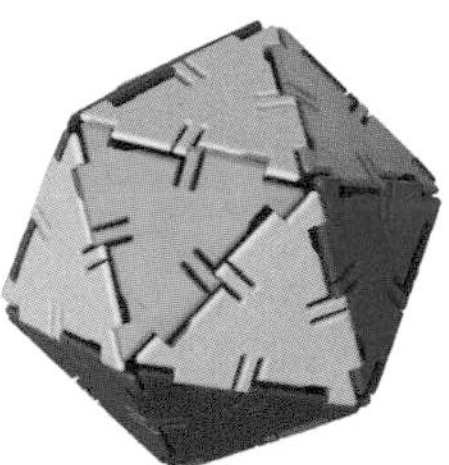

? Why are there only five Platonic solids?

A. Look at the five Platonic solids. What shapes are the faces? How many faces meet at each vertex?

B. A Platonic solid can have faces that are equilateral triangles. What is the measure of the interior angles of an equilateral triangle?

C. Using only equilateral triangles, draw the nets for as many polyhedrons as you can. Make sure that the same number of triangles meet at each vertex. Cut out and fold your nets to make sure that they work.

D. For each polyhedron you made, how many faces meet at each vertex? What is the sum of the angles at each vertex?

E. What is the least number of equilateral triangles you can join at a vertex and still fold the net to make a Platonic solid? What is the greatest number?

F. Repeat steps B to E using only squares.

G. Repeat steps B to E using only regular pentagons.

H. Copy and complete the following chart.

	Face information			
Platonic solid	**Polygon**	**Measure of interior angles on one face**	**Number of faces at each vertex**	**Sum of angles at each vertex**
tetrahedron	equilateral triangle			
cube	square			
octahedron	equilateral triangle			
dodecahedron	regular pentagon			
icosahedron	equilateral triangle			

I. Explain why you cannot use any other regular polygons as the faces of a Platonic solid. Explain why you cannot use any more of the regular polygons you have already used.

Reflecting

1. Why does a Platonic solid look the same no matter which vertex you position at the top?

2. Refer to your chart. Look at the measures of the interior angles in each Platonic solid and the number of faces. How does the measure of the interior angles determine the number of faces that can join at a vertex?

3. A Platonic solid cannot be made from regular polygons that have more than five sides. How can you use the measures of the interior angles of regular polygons to show this is true?

11.6 Polyhedron Faces, Edges, and Vertices

You will need
- pipe cleaners or straws
- modelling clay

▶ **GOAL**
Determine how the number of faces, edges, and vertices of a polyhedron are related.

Learn about the Math

Toma and Benjamin noticed that whenever you make a 2-D polygon, the number of vertices is the same as the number of edges. They wondered whether the number of faces, vertices, and edges of 3-D polyhedrons are related.

? What pattern links the number of faces, edges, and vertices of a polyhedron?

Benjamin tried building an unusual polyhedron first. "I'll start building it from the top. The number of vertices and number of edges are the same, and there is one face."

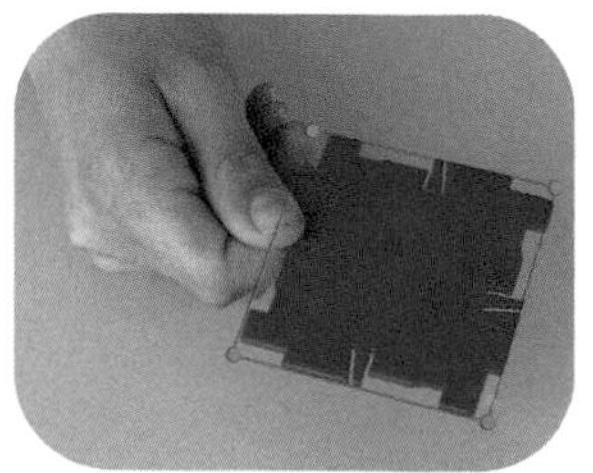

Part built	Number of faces	Number of vertices	Number of edges
top	1	4	4

"Next, I'll add squares. For each square, I add one new face, two new vertices, and three new edges. The total number of new faces and new vertices is equal to the number of new edges.

"Now I'll add triangles. For each triangle, I add one new face and one new edge, but no new vertices. Again, the total number of new faces and vertices is the same as the number of new edges."

Part built	Number of faces	Number of vertices	Number of edges
top	1	4	4
4 new squares	4 more	8 more	12 more
4 new triangles	4 more	0 more	4 more

A. Construct the parts that Benjamin constructed. Add the next set of squares. Explain why the number of edges is 1 less than the total number of faces and vertices.

B. Add the bottom of the polyhedron. Explain why you have added no new edges or vertices, but one new face.

C. Why is the number of edges 2 less than the total number of faces and vertices?

D. Choose one of the following shapes. Compare the number of edges with the total number of faces and vertices. What do you observe?

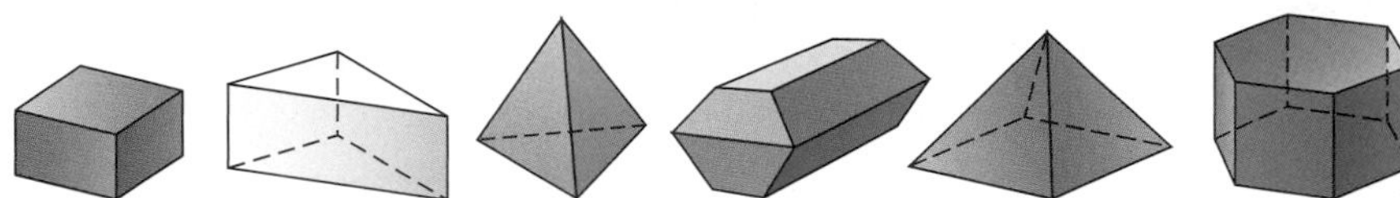

E. Compare your results with the results of students who chose different shapes. What do you notice?

Reflecting

1. The relationship you described in step C is called Euler's formula (pronouced "oiler"). Explain why it can be written as $F + V - E = 2$, where F is the number of faces, V is the number of vertices, and E is the number of edges of the shape.

2. How does Euler's formula allow you to predict the number of edges, faces, or vertices of a shape if you know two of these values?

Work with the Math

Example 1: Checking whether a polyhedron is possible

Is it possible to make a polyhedron with 6 faces, 7 vertices, and 10 edges?

Tran's Solution

$F + V - E = 2$	I used Euler's formula. If it is possible to make a polyhedron like this, the result should be 2 when I substitute the values into Euler's formula.
$F + V - E = 6 + 7 - 10$ $= 3$	I substituted the values into the formula. The result is 3, not 2, so it is not possible to make such a polyhedron.

Example 2: Using Euler's formula to determine a missing value

If a polyhedron has 10 faces and 18 edges, how many vertices should it have?

Benjamin's Solution

$F + V - E = 2$	I used Euler's formula.
$10 + V - 18 = 2$	I substituted 10 for the number of faces and 18 for the number of edges.
$V - 8 = 2$	
$V - 8 + 8 = 2 + 8$	I used balancing to solve the equation.
$V = 10$	The polyhedron should have 10 vertices.

A Checking

3. A student used 10 pipe cleaners to make the edges of a polyhedron. If the polyhedron has 6 vertices, how many faces must it have?

4. Show that Euler's formula works for a tetrahedron.

B Practising

5. Show that Euler's formula works for the other four Platonic solids: a cube, an octahedron, a dodecahedron, and an icosahedron.

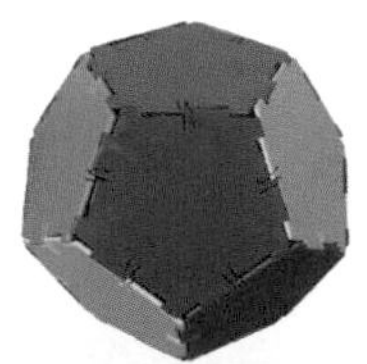

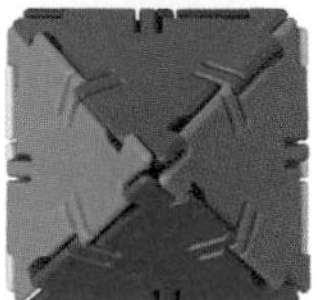

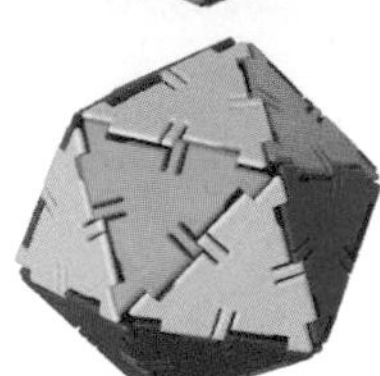

6. Copy and complete the chart for some polyhedrons.

Number of faces	Number of edges	Number of vertices
	9	5
6	12	
6		7
20	30	
16		10
	12	6

7. The following crystals and gemstones have been cut to form polyhedrons. Show that Euler's formula works for each polyhedron.

a)

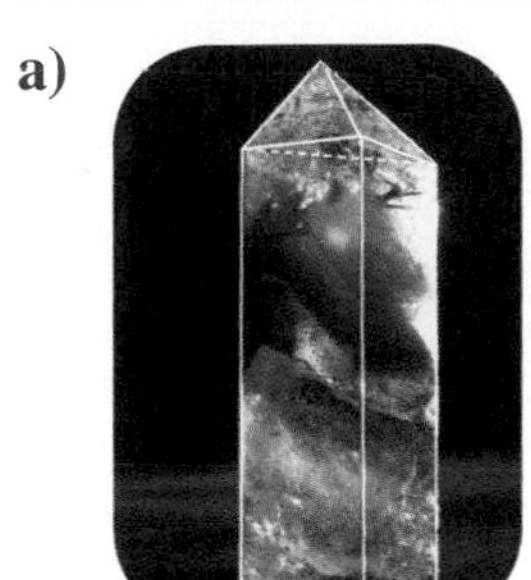

b)

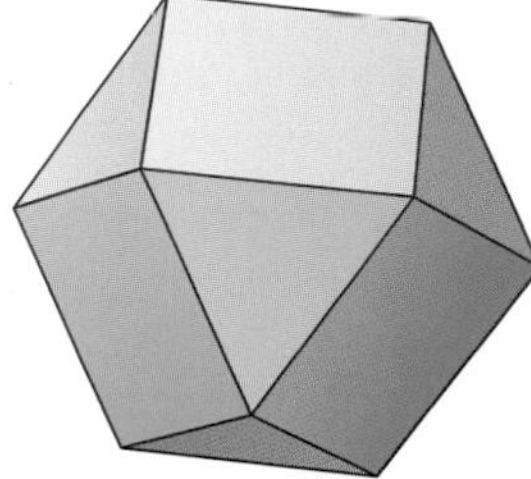

8. Show that Euler's formula works for this cuboctahedron.

9. Make a cube using modelling clay. Cut the corners off the cube. Show that Euler's formula works for the new shape.

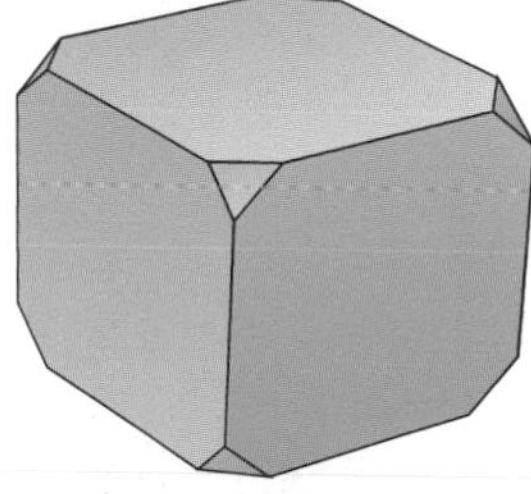

10. Make another cube using modelling clay. Then make a pyramid on each face of the cube. Show that Euler's formula works for this polyhedron.

11. Imagine that you drilled a rectangular hole through a cube. Does Euler's formula work for the new shape?

12. **a)** Construct a triangular prism.

b) How many faces does the prism have?

c) How many edges does the prism have?

d) How many vertices does the prism have?

e) Show that Euler's formula works for the prism.

13. Repeat question 12 using a pentagonal pyramid.

C Extending

14. Make a cube using modelling clay. Mark a point in the centre of each face. Imagine that you joined these points with string inside the cube to form a polyhedron. Show that Euler's formula works for this polyhedron.

15. A prism has a base with n sides.

a) How many faces does the prism have?

b) How many edges does the prism have?

c) How many vertices does the prism have?

d) Show that Euler's formula works for the prism.

16. A pyramid has a base with n sides.

a) How many faces does the pyramid have?

b) How many edges does the pyramid have?

c) How many vertices does the pyramid have?

d) Show that Euler's formula works for the pyramid.

Math Game

THE VOLUMIZER GAME!

In this game, you will calculate the volume of a cylinder using a radius given on a card and a height obtained by rolling a die or spinning a spinner.

Number of players: 2 or more

You will need
- index cards
- a die or spinner
- a calculator

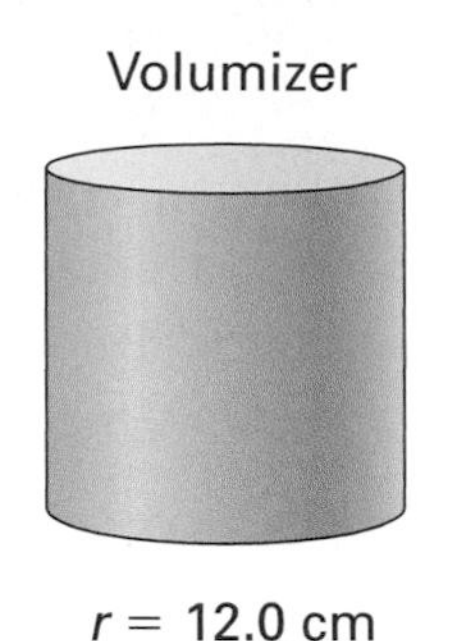

Rules

1. To create a deck of Volumizer cards, use about 20 blank index cards. On each card, sketch a cylinder and label the radius of the base in centimetres.
2. To play the game, each player
   - selects a Volumizer card from the pile
   - rolls the die or spins the spinner
   - calculates the volume of the cylinder, using the number on the die or spinner as the height of the cylinder in centimetres

   All players take their turns at the same time. Players may check each other's calculations.
3. The player who has the cylinder with the greatest volume keeps the card. The other players return their cards to the deck.
4. The game is finished when the number of cards left in the pile is less than the number of players.
5. The player with the most cards at the end of the game is the winner.

Chapter Self-Test

1. Draw a net for the paper needed to wrap each candle. Label the dimensions.

2. Which parts of this net of a cylinder are equal to the circumference of the base?

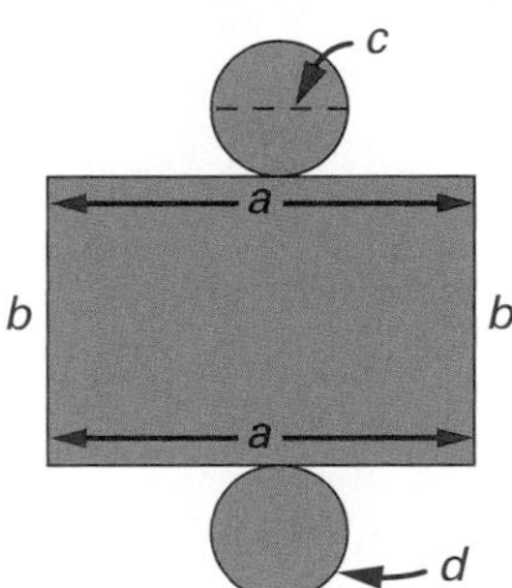

3. Calculate the surface area and volume of each cylinder.

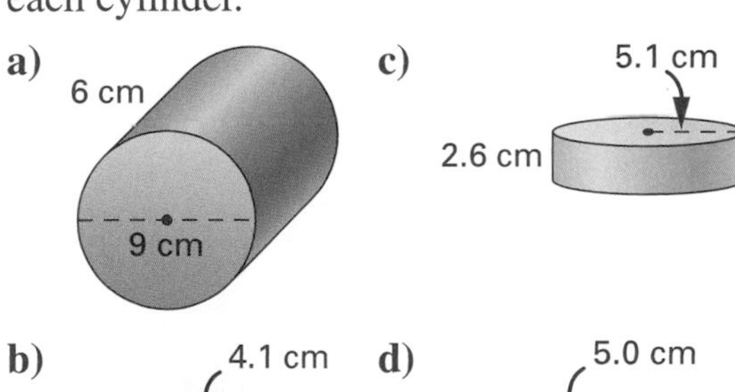

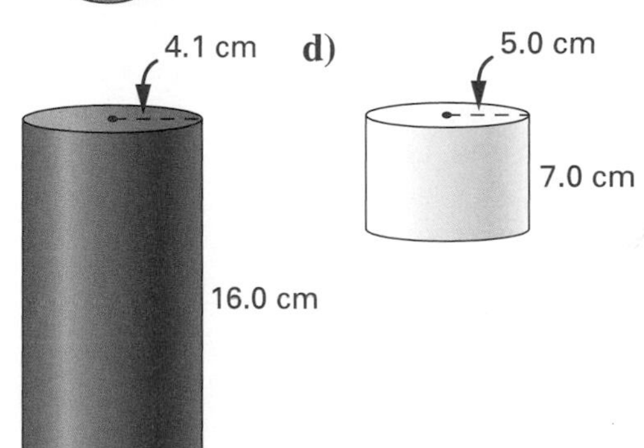

4. This railway car is 320 cm in diameter and 17.2 m long. Calculate its volume.

5. Suppose that you increase the height of this cylinder by 10 cm. By how much does the volume increase?

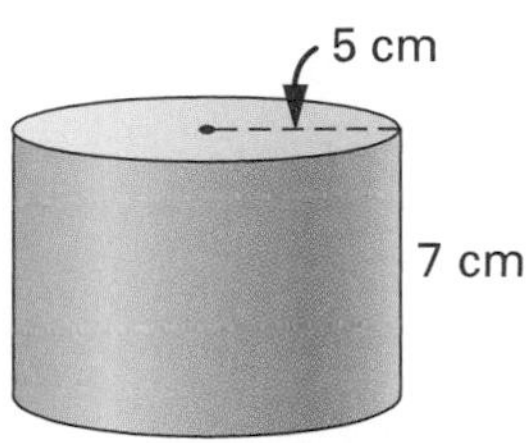

6. No more than three congruent squares can meet at each vertex of a Platonic solid. Explain why.

7. A soccer ball is a polyhedron made from 20 regular hexagons and 12 regular pentagons. It has 60 vertices. Determine the number of edges on a soccer ball.

Chapter Review

Frequently Asked Questions

Q: What is a Platonic solid?

A: A Platonic solid is a polyhedron with faces that are all congruent regular polygons. The same number of faces meet at all the vertices in a Platonic solid. The five Platonic solids are shown below.

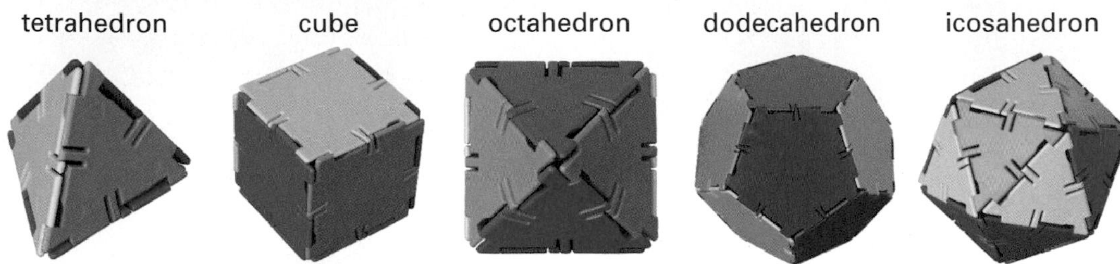

Q: Why are there only five Platonic solids?

A: The total of the interior angles that meet at each vertex of a Platonic solid must be less than 360°. At least three faces must meet at each vertex.

Regular polygons with more than five sides have angles that measure at least 120°. When you build a polyhedron, at least three faces have to meet at each vertex to make the polyhedron 3-D. If you tried to use the faces of polygons with more than five sides as the faces of a polyhedron, the sum of the angles that meet at each vertex would be at least 360°. This is not possible.

Q: How are the number of edges, vertices, and faces of a polyhedron related?

A: The relationship among the number of edges, vertices, and faces can be represented using the equation $F + V - E = 2$, where F is the number of faces, E is the number of edges, and V is the number of vertices. This equation is known as Euler's formula.

For example, the following cube has 6 faces, 8 vertices, and 12 edges.

$$F + V - E = 2$$
$$6 + 8 - 12 = 2$$

Practice Questions

(11.2) **1.** Calculate the surface area of this cylinder.

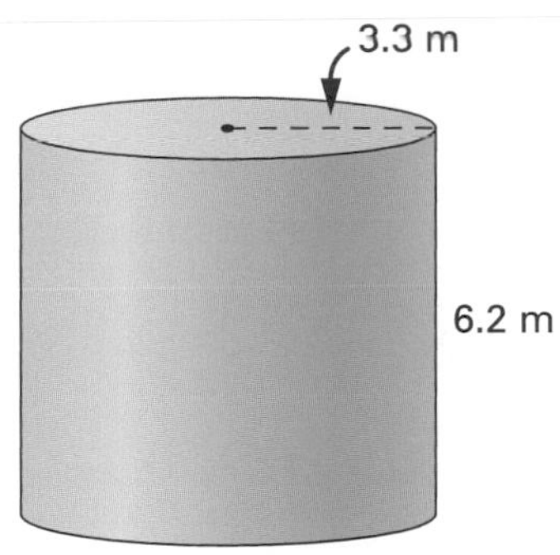

(11.3) **2.** Calculate the volume of the cylinder in question 1.

3. Mohammed is choosing a bass drum to buy for his band. The "Bashmaster" is 71.1 cm in diameter and 35.6 cm high. The "Crash" is 91.5 cm in diameter and 66.0 cm high. The "Boomalot" is 81.3 cm in diameter and 45.7 cm high.

(11.2) **a)** Which drum has the greatest surface area? Justify your answer.

(11.3) **b)** Which drum has the greatest volume in cubic centimetres? Justify your answer.

4. A glass in the shape of a cylinder is 10.0 cm high and has a diameter of 3.5 cm. How many millilitres of juice will the glass hold if it is filled to the top? (11.3)

5. What might be the dimensions of a cylindrical container that holds 750 mL of juice? (11.3)

6. Sketch a shape made up of a cylinder and a triangular prism that has a total volume between 100 cm^3 and 200 cm^3. (11.4)

7. Why is it impossible to have a Platonic solid in which six or more equilateral triangles meet at each vertex? (11.5)

8. Show that Euler's formula works for a pentagonal prism. (11.6)

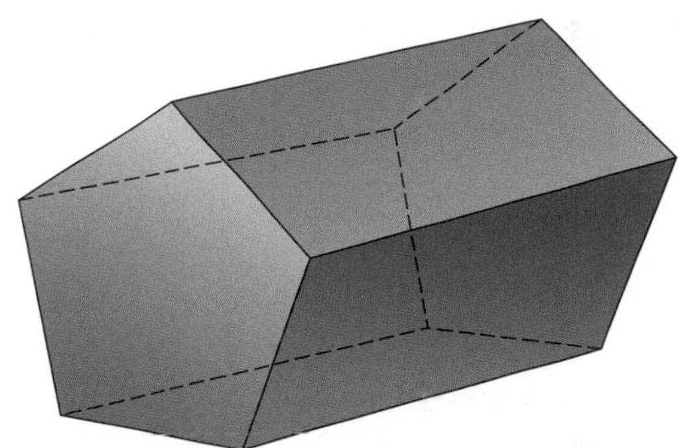

9. A polyhedron has 9 edges and 6 vertices.

a) Calculate the number of faces.

b) Sketch the polyhedron. (11.6)

10. A polyhedron has 6 faces and 6 vertices. Calculate the number of edges. (11.6)

11. A polyhedron has 8 faces and 12 edges. Calculate the number of vertices. (11.6)

Chapter Task

Storage Capacity of a Silo

In this task, you will design a silo that can be used to store corn for animal feed. The outside of the silo will be painted to make it rust resistant and more attractive.

Keep in mind:

- The paint comes in 3.8 L cans. Each can covers an area of 40 m^2 and costs $35, including taxes.
- In 2003, corn for animal feed was sold for about $120 per tonne.

? How can you design a silo and report on the costs?

A. Sketch the silo you recommend. Show its diameter and height.

B. Calculate the surface area of your silo.

C. Calculate the cost to cover your silo with one coat of paint.

D. What is the volume of the corn that can be stored in your silo?

E. What mass of corn can be stored in your silo? Use the height of the corn in your silo and the following table to estimate the mass of the corn. (1 t = 1000 kg)

Height of corn (m)	Mass (kg) of 1 m^3 of corn
9	570
12	610
15	660
18	700
21	740
24	770

F. Estimate the value of the corn that can be stored in your silo.

G. Prepare a written report that shows your calculations and explains your thinking.

Task Checklist

- ☑ Did you show all your steps?
- ☑ Did you explain your thinking?
- ☑ Did you draw and label your diagram neatly and accurately?
- ☑ Did you use appropriate math vocabulary?

CHAPTER 12

Probability

▶ GOALS

You will be able to

- calculate and compare theoretical and experimental probabilities
- use tree diagrams and organized lists to solve probability problems
- choose and design models to simulate real-life events

Getting Started

Which Is More Likely?

? Are you more likely to get a sum of 8 or a difference of 2 when you roll two dice?

A. Copy and complete this table to show all the possible sums when you roll two dice.

+	1	2	3	4	5	6
1						
2						
3						
4						
5						
6						

B. How many sums are in your table?

C. How many of these sums are 8?

D. Calculate the **theoretical probability** of rolling a sum of 8 with two dice.

E. Create another table to show all the possible differences when you roll two dice. Always record the positive difference.

F. Calculate the theoretical probability of rolling numbers that are 2 apart.

G. Suppose that you actually rolled two dice several times. Would you expect the **experimental probability** to be the same as the theoretical probability? Explain.

H. Which is more likely—a sum of 8 or a difference of 2?

Do You Remember?

1. Mario rolled a die 30 times and recorded the number of 6s. He displayed his results as a **broken-line graph**.

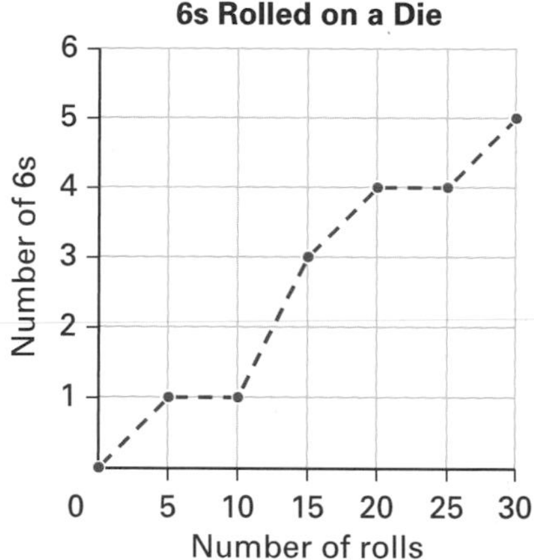

   a) After 15 rolls, how many 6s had Mario rolled?
   b) For which group of rolls can you be certain that no 6s were rolled?
   c) Describe the trend for the broken-line graph.
   d) Calculate the experimental probability of rolling a 6 for the 30 rolls.

2. One card is drawn at random from a standard deck of 52 playing cards. Copy and complete the table to determine the probability of each event using three different forms.

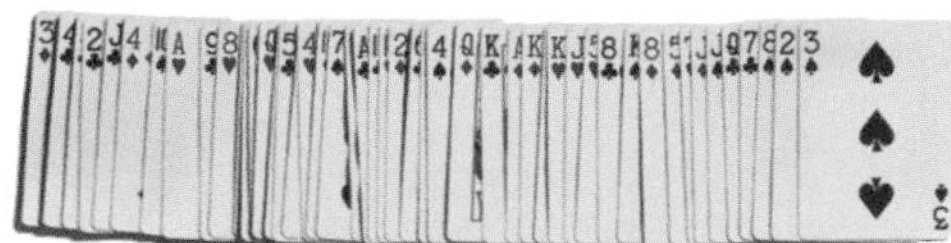

Event	Fraction form of probability	Decimal form of probability	Percent form of probability
4			
number card greater than 5			
red			

3. Mark tossed a coin 100 times and got 43 Tails.
   a) What is Mark's experimental probability of getting Heads?
   b) What is the theoretical probability of getting Heads?
   c) Suppose that you tossed a coin 100 times. About how many Heads would you expect to get?

4. Ruth tosses a coin and spins this spinner. Use a **tree diagram** to determine each probability.

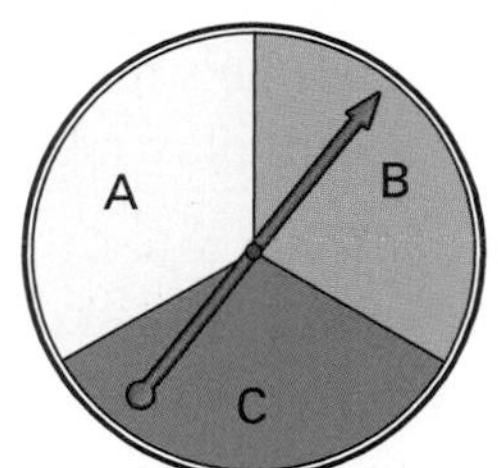

   a) *P*(Heads and A)
   b) *P*(Tails, and either B or C)
   c) *P*(either Heads or Tails, and B)

5. The probabilities of three different events are $\frac{2}{3}$, 0.68, and 70%. Which event is most likely?

6. a) The probability of an event is 1. What do you know about the event?
   b) The probability of another event is 0. What do you know about this event?

7. If one score of 39 is changed to 40, how will this histogram change?

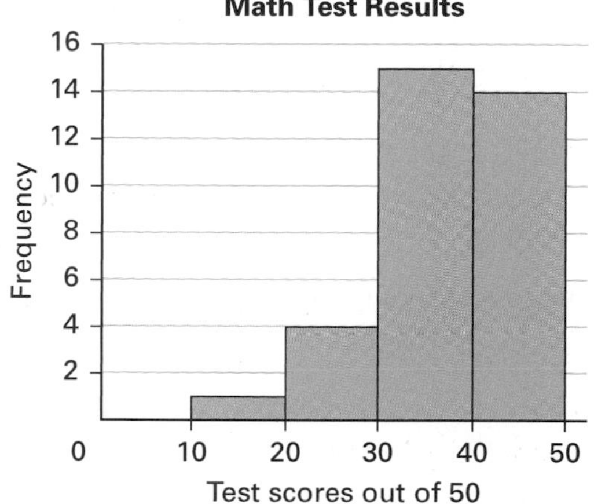

12.1 Exploring Theoretical and Experimental Probabilities

You will need
- blank cards
- a calculator

▶ **GOAL**
Compare expected probability with the results of an experiment.

Explore the Math

Stefan and Kito are playing cards. Stefan has won six games in a row. He claims that he has won because he's really good at guessing what card Kito will play next.

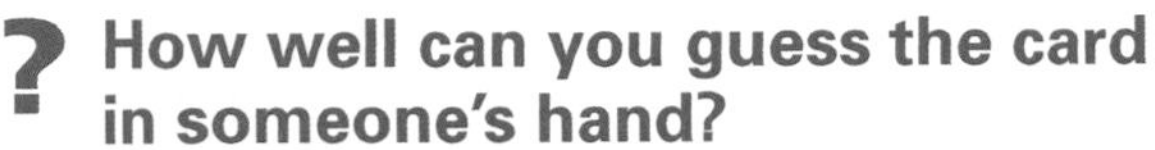

? How well can you guess the card in someone's hand?

A. Work with a partner. Get four blank cards, and draw a simple symbol on each.

B. Sit back to back. Pick a card at random without letting your partner see it.

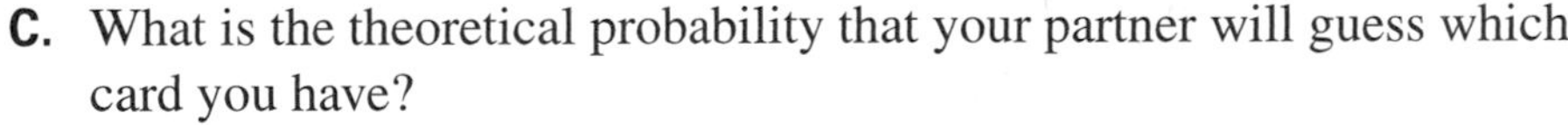

C. What is the theoretical probability that your partner will guess which card you have?

D. Have your partner guess which card you have. Record the result in a table like the one below. Continue for 20 trials.

Trial	Correct	Incorrect	Fraction of total guesses correct	Approximate percent of total guesses correct (%)
1	✓		$\frac{1}{1}$	100
2		✓	$\frac{1}{2}$	50
3	✓		$\frac{2}{3}$	67

E. Switch roles with your partner so that you are guessing the card. Repeat steps B and D.

F. Copy the graph shown, and create a broken-line graph to display your results.

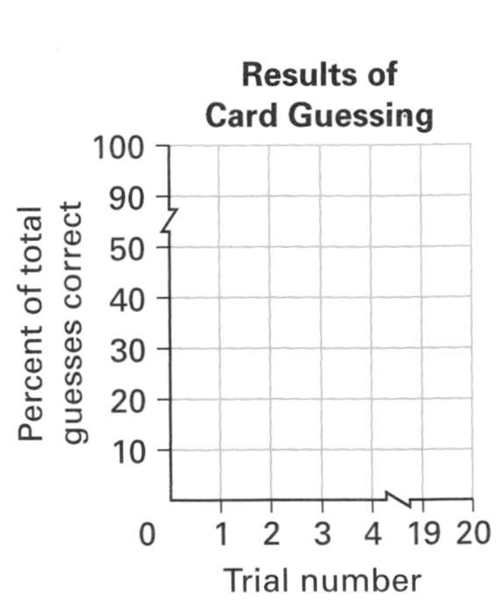

G. Describe what your graph shows about your results.

H. Calculate your overall percent correct. Use the class data to draw a histogram that shows how many students fell in each "percent correct" interval.

Reflecting

1. Compare the percent correct for your 20 trials with the percent correct for the class data. How do these percentages compare with the theoretical probability you calculated in step C?
2. How does the shape of your histogram relate to the theoretical probability you calculated in step C?

Mental Math — ESTIMATING PERCENTS

In 300 spins of this spinner, the number 1 occurred 63 times. The experimental probability of spinning a 1 is $\frac{63}{300}$. Here are two different methods you can use to estimate $\frac{63}{300}$ as a percent:

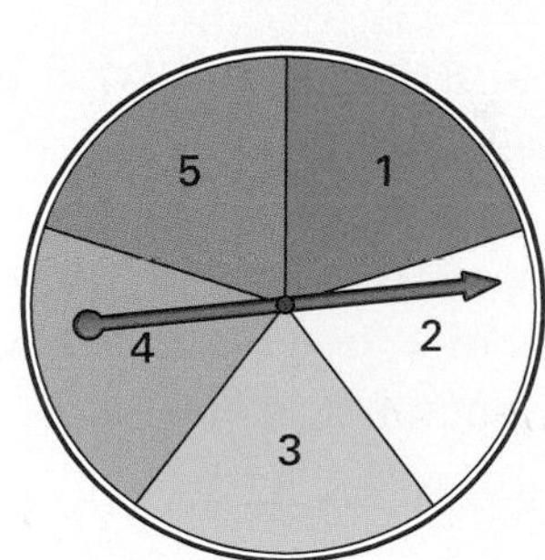

Method 1

10% of 300 is 30.

So, 20% of 300 is $2 \times 30 = 60$.

This is close to 63.

$\frac{63}{300}$ is close to 20%.

Method 2

$\frac{63}{300}$ is close to $\frac{60}{300}$.

$$\frac{60}{300} \overset{\div 3}{=} \frac{20}{100} = 20\%$$

$\frac{63}{300}$ is close to 20%.

Check:
If you divide 63 by 300 on a calculator, you get 0.21, or 21%. So, 20% is a good estimate.

1. Estimate each fraction as a percent. Then use a calculator to check your estimate.

a) $\frac{7}{15}$ **b)** $\frac{23}{99}$ **c)** $\frac{185}{300}$ **d)** $\frac{95}{500}$ **e)** $\frac{148}{200}$ **f)** $\frac{33}{300}$

12.2 Theoretical and Experimental Probabilities

You will need
- a spinner
- blocks and a bag

▶ **GOAL**
Calculate and compare theoretical and experimental probabilities.

Learn about the Math

Rowyn and Kayley are designing a nutrition game for their health class. They need a way for players to select a number from 0 to 9 randomly.

Rowyn suggests that they use the last digit of food prices in store flyers. Kayley and Rowyn wonder if the digits in food prices are random.

? Do the numbers 0 to 9 appear with equal probability in different place values in food prices?

A. Suppose that the numbers 0 to 9 were equally likely to be the last digit of a food price. What is the theoretical probability of having each number, from 0 to 9, as the last digit?

$1.4**9** $0.6**8** $2.2**5**

B. Record the frequency of each number, from 0 to 9, as the last digit in the list of food prices shown. Calculate the experimental probability for each number.

C. Which numbers were least likely to be the last digit of a price? Which number was the most likely?

D. Compare the theoretical probabilities you calculated in step A with the experimental probabilities you calculated in step B. Is this what you expected? Explain.

E. Calculate the experimental probabilities for the numbers 0 to 9 in the other two place values in the food prices. Write your answers in decimal form.

F. How do the probabilities you calculated in step A compare with the probabilities you calculated in step E?

G. Do all the numbers from 0 to 9 appear with equal probability in each position in the food prices?

$9.49
$8.99
$7.96
$6.99
$5.99
$4.00
$5.00
$3.99
$2.98
$1.49
$1.79
$1.67
$0.99
$0.99
$0.89
$0.57
$1.88
$0.25
$0.39
$4.49
$3.27
$0.45
$0.69
$6.79
$5.89
$9.45
$4.99
$3.29
$3.00
$2.99
$0.85
$2.77
$0.59
$0.79
$0.97
$0.95
$1.00
$1.47
$2.17
$3.45

Reflecting

1. Why might you expect the numbers 0 to 9 to appear with equal probability in some place values but not in others?

2. What convinced you that the numbers 0 to 9 did not appear with equal probability in all the place values in the food prices? In your answer, consider the difference between the theoretical probabilities you calculated in step A and the experimental probabilities you calculated in steps B and E.

Work with the Math

Example: Comparing theoretical and experimental probabilities

Does each number from 0 to 9 appear with equal probability in different positions in a telephone area code?

Rishi's Solution

YT, NT, NU — 867
BC — 250, 604
AB — 403, 780
SK — 306
NS, PE — 902
MB — 204
ON — 289, 416, 519, 613, 647, 705, 807, 905
NB — 506
NL — 709
QC — 418, 450, 514, 819

I used the area codes for Canada as my data.

Digit	First position Freq.	First position Prob.	Second position Freq.	Second position Prob.	Third position Freq.	Third position Prob.
0	0	$\frac{0}{22}$	10	$\frac{10}{22}$	3	$\frac{3}{22}$
1	0	$\frac{0}{22}$	6	$\frac{6}{22}$	0	$\frac{0}{22}$
2	3	$\frac{3}{22}$	0	$\frac{0}{22}$	1	$\frac{1}{22}$
3	1	$\frac{1}{22}$	0	$\frac{0}{22}$	2	$\frac{2}{22}$
4	4	$\frac{4}{22}$	1	$\frac{1}{22}$	3	$\frac{3}{22}$
5	3	$\frac{3}{22}$	2	$\frac{2}{22}$	2	$\frac{2}{22}$
6	3	$\frac{3}{22}$	1	$\frac{1}{22}$	3	$\frac{3}{22}$
7	3	$\frac{3}{22}$	0	$\frac{0}{22}$	3	$\frac{3}{22}$
8	3	$\frac{3}{22}$	2	$\frac{2}{22}$	1	$\frac{1}{22}$
9	2	$\frac{2}{22}$	0	$\frac{0}{22}$	4	$\frac{4}{22}$

If the numbers are equally likely, the theoretical probability is 10% for each number in each position. So, I would expect each number about two times out of 22.

The experimental probabilities are very different from this. I'm convinced that the numbers are not equally likely, especially in the second position.

A Checking

3. Calculate the theoretical probability of each event when rolling a die.
   a) $P(6)$
   b) $P(\text{even})$
   c) $P(\text{less than } 3)$

4. Elaine spun this spinner 80 times and graphed her results.

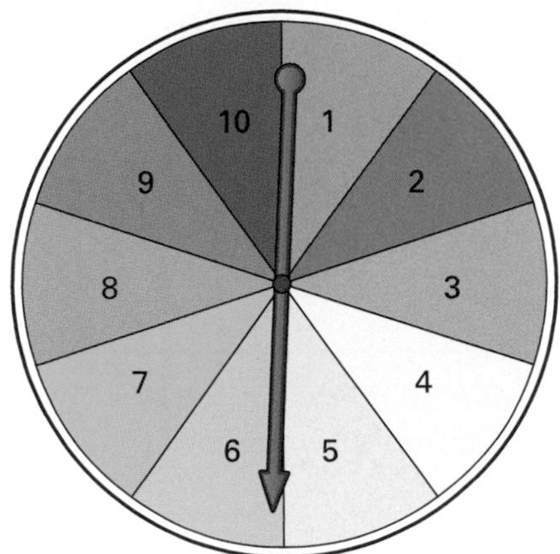

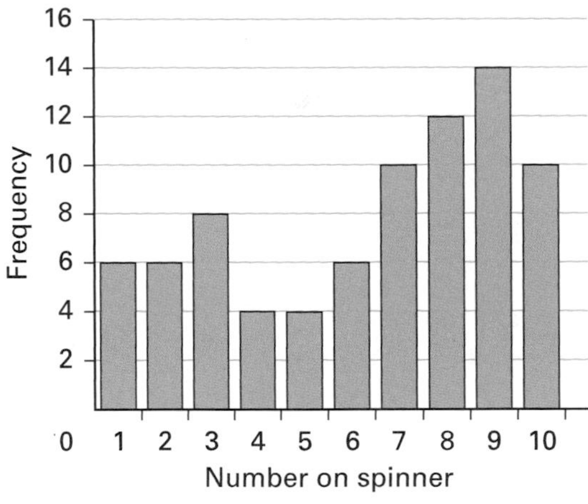

   a) The experimental probability of spinning a 3 is $\frac{8}{80}$, or $\frac{1}{10}$. Which numbers had greater experimental probabilities?
   b) What is the theoretical probability of spinning each number?

B Practising

5. Calculate the theoretical probability of each event, using one of the four items below.

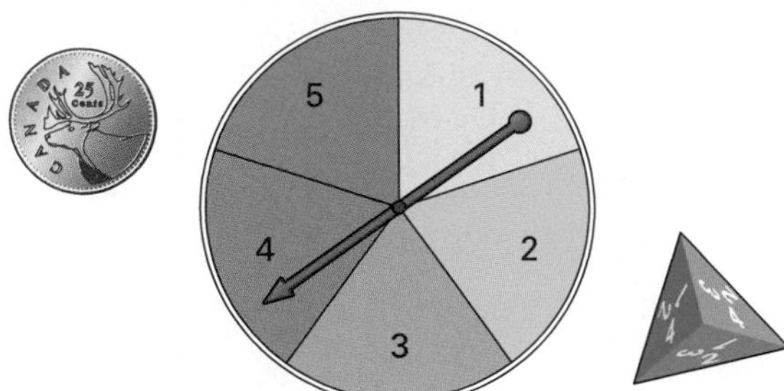

   a) tossing Tails
   b) spinning a 4
   c) drawing a black card
   d) rolling an even number
   e) spinning an odd number
   f) drawing a red card less than 9
   g) rolling a number greater than 1

6. a) Conduct an experiment to calculate the experimental probability of spinning an odd number with the spinner shown in question 5. Complete 20 trials.
   b) Calculate the theoretical probability of spinning an odd number with the spinner shown in question 5.
   c) Was the experimental probability close to the theoretical probability? Explain your answer.

7. Charmain rolled a 12-sided die (with the numbers 1 to 12) 48 times. These are her experimental probabilities.

- $P(\text{odd number}) = \frac{18}{48}$
- $P(\text{greater than } 8) = \frac{16}{48}$
- $P(9) = \frac{12}{48}$

a) Which experimental probability matches the theoretical probability exactly?

b) Which experimental probability is farthest from the theoretical probability?

8. There are 10 red marbles and 6 green marbles in a bag. Alex will choose one marble without looking. Calculate these theoretical probabilities.

a) *P*(green)

b) *P*(purple)

c) *P*(red or green)

9. Why might experimental probability be different from theoretical probability?

10. Place 6 blue blocks, 4 red blocks, and 2 green blocks in a bag.

a) What is the theoretical probability of taking out each colour of block from the bag without looking?

b) Take out a block, record its colour, and replace it. Continue until you have completed 10 trials. Determine the experimental probability of taking out each colour of block.

c) Repeat part (b), but complete 20 trials.

d) Were the experimental probabilities for 10 trials or for 20 trials closer to the theoretical probabilities? Did you expect this? Explain.

11. A bag contains 25 blue marbles, 10 red marbles, 10 yellow marbles, and 5 purple marbles.

a) Calculate each probability below, if you take out one marble without looking.
   i) *P*(purple)
   ii) *P*(blue)
   iii) *P*(red)

b) How many times would you expect to take out a blue marble if you completed 500 trials? What if you completed 75 trials? Explain.

12. A block was pulled from each box five times and replaced. A black block was pulled two times from box A, four times from box B, and three times from box C.

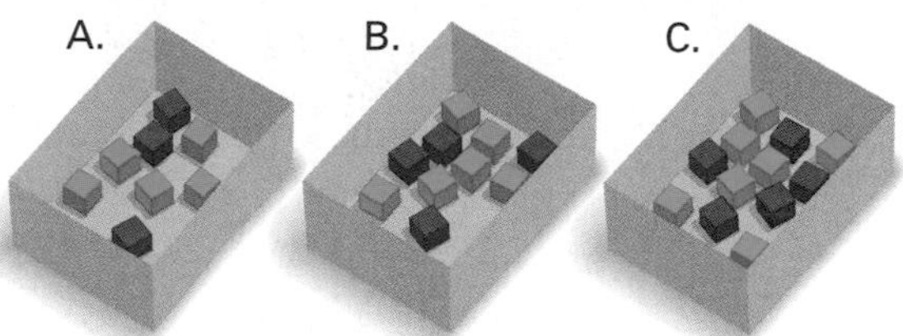

a) Calculate the experimental probability of pulling a black block from each box.

b) Calculate the theoretical probability of pulling a black block from each box.

c) For which box was the experimental probability closest to the theoretical probability?

C Extending

13. Describe an event that involves dice and has a theoretical probability of $\frac{5}{6}$. Conduct an experiment to compare the experimental probability with $\frac{5}{6}$.

14. David says that the probability of catching a cold is $\frac{1}{2}$ because there are two possible outcomes, catching a cold and not catching a cold. Is he correct? Explain.

12.3 Calculating Probabilities

▶ **GOAL**

Use tree diagrams and organized lists to calculate probabilities.

Learn about the Math

Carina, Kito, Rowyn, and Rishi are standing in line for the Drop Zone ride at Canada's Wonderland.

? If the ride operator loads them randomly, what is the probability that Rishi will sit between Rowyn and Carina?

favourable outcome

a desired result when calculating a probability; for example, the result that Rishi will sit between Rowyn and Carina

A. Use a tree diagram to show all the possible seating arrangements.

B. Use your tree diagram to determine all the possible outcomes and all the **favourable outcomes**.

C. Calculate the probability that Rishi will sit between Rowyn and Carina.

D. What is the probability of the **complementary event** "Rishi will not sit between Rowyn and Carina"?

complementary events

two events that have no outcome(s) in common but account for all possible outcomes of an experiment. The sum of the probabilities of complementary events is 1; for example, tossing Heads and tossing Tails are complementary events

Reflecting

1. How did you know that your tree diagram covered all the possible seating arrangements?
2. How did you know that the denominator of the probability in fraction form is 24?
3. Explain how you used your tree diagram to calculate the probability that Rishi will sit between Rowyn and Carina.
4. Explain how you determined the probability in step D.

Work with the Math

Example 1: Using an organized list to calculate probability

Monica selected math, geography, science, and English for her first semester of high school. She will have the same teacher for geography and English, so she will not have to change classrooms if these subjects are back to back. What is the probability of geography and English being back to back?

Stefan's Solution

EMSG	MSGE	SEGM	GEMS
EMGS	MSEG	SEMG	GESM
EGMS	MGSE	SGEM	GMES
EGSM	MGES	SGME	GMSE
ESMG	MESG	SMEG	GSEM
ESGM	MEGS	SMGE	GSME

I used an organized list to make sure that I looked at all the possibilities.

There are four possible subjects for period 1, so each of the four columns starts with a different subject.

There are three possibilities for period 2, because one subject was already in period 1.

There are two possibilities left for period 3, because two subjects are already in periods 1 and 2.

There is only one possibility left for period 4, because three subjects are already in periods 1, 2, and 3.

From my list, I can see that 12 of the 24 possible schedules are favourable. The probability of English and geography being back to back is $\frac{12}{24}$, or $\frac{1}{2}$.

Example 2: Using a tree diagram to calculate probability

Suppose that you toss a coin and then roll a six-sided die.

a) What is the probability of getting Heads and an even number?

b) What is the probability of not getting Heads and an even number?

Kayley's Solution

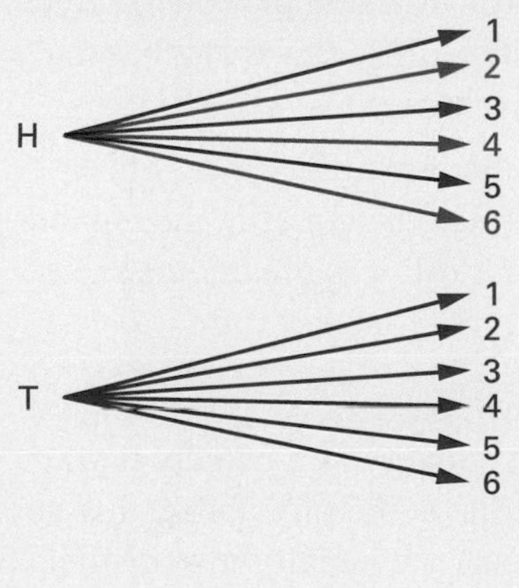

I listed all the possibilities in a tree diagram.

The 12 branches represent 12 equally likely outcomes.

a) Three of the branches start with Heads and end in an even number, so three outcomes are favourable.

$P(\text{H and even}) = \frac{3}{12}$, or $\frac{1}{4}$

b) Not getting Heads and an even number and the event in part (a) are complementary events.

$P(\text{not H and even}) + P(\text{H and even}) = 1$

$P(\text{not H and even}) + \frac{1}{4} = 1$

$P(\text{not H and even}) = \frac{3}{4}$

A Checking

5. Use the tree diagram you made in step A on page 408 to calculate each theoretical probability.

a) *P*(Rowyn beside Rishi)

b) *P*(Rowyn not beside Rishi)

c) *P*(either Rowyn or Carina, but not both, on the outside)

B Practising

6. Suppose that you roll the die and spin the spinner.

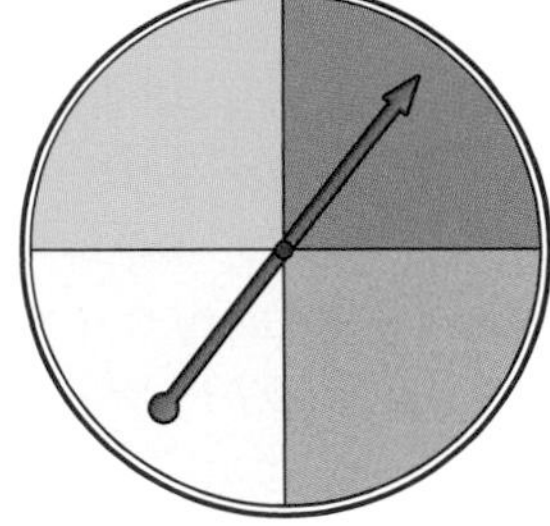

Use an organized list to determine the probability of each event.

a) *P*(3 and yellow)

b) *P*(anything except 3 and yellow)

c) *P*(number $>$ 3 and purple)

7. a) Create a tree diagram to show all the possible outcomes for tossing three coins.

b) What is the probability of getting one Tail?

c) What is the probability of getting two or three Tails?

d) What is the probability of not getting any Heads?

8. How does a tree diagram give you the denominator of the fraction form of a probability? How does an organized list give you the denominator?

9. Calculate the probability of having three boys in a family with three children.

10. Kaycee has won a contest. To determine the amount of her prize, she must spin this spinner twice. She will receive the sum of her two spins.

a) Create a tree diagram to show all the possible outcomes.

b) What is the probability that Kaycee will receive more than the minimum amount but less than the maximum amount?

c) What is the probability that Kaycee will receive more than $500?

11. Anthony, Peter, Francis, and Christopher are in a race. The first three to finish will receive ribbons. Which is more probable—that both Anthony and Peter will receive ribbons, or that Peter will finish ahead of Francis and Christopher?

C Extending

12. Deanna and Carol are playing a game. They roll a die twice and add the numbers they roll. A sum of 5 scores a point.

a) What is the probability of rolling a sum of 5?

b) Deanna rolled a sum of 5 on her first turn. List the different ways that she could have done this.

c) What is the probability that, when Deanna rolled a sum of 5, the number on the first roll was greater than the number on the second roll?

13. To play a new board game, you roll a die. Every fourth square has a penalty if you land on it. What is the probability that you will get at least one penalty in your first two rolls of the die?

Curious Math

FACTORIALS!

In lesson 12.3, you used a tree diagram to determine the 24 different ways for four students to sit on a ride.

There were four possibilities for the first seat. ⟶ 4

$\times$

Only three possibilities were left for the second seat. ⟶ 3

$\times$

Only two possibilities were left for the third seat. ⟶ 2

$\times$

Only one possibility was left for the fourth seat. ⟶ 1

You can use factorial notation to write this product:

$4! = 4 \times 3 \times 2 \times 1$

$= 24$

So, 4 factorial is 24.

Factorial notation works for other numbers, too. The number of possible orders for three different things is $3! = 3 \times 2 \times 1$.
The number of possible orders for five different things is $5! = 5 \times 4 \times 3 \times 2 \times 1$.
The number of possible orders for n different things is $n!$

1. Write each expression as a factorial.

a) $8 \times 7 \times 6 \times 5 \times 4 \times 3 \times 2 \times 1$

b) $12 \times 11 \times 10 \times 9 \times 8 \times 7 \times 6 \times 5 \times 4 \times 3 \times 2 \times 1$

2. Evaluate each factorial.

a) $3!$ **b)** $6!$ **c)** $2! \times 5!$ **d)** $1!$

3. How many different ways can seven students be arranged in a line?

4. How many different ways can the letters in "MATH ROCKS" be arranged?

5. There are 10 different CDs on a shelf. How many different ways can they be arranged?

Mid-Chapter Review

Frequently Asked Questions

Q: How do experimental and theoretical probabilities compare?

A: The greater the number of trials in an experiment, the closer the theoretical and experimental probabilities should be. The values will not likely be exactly the same, but they should be close.

For example, Ashley wondered whether the numbers 0 to 9 are equally likely to appear in the last position in a business telephone number. If all the numbers are equally likely, the theoretical probability of a business telephone number ending in 1 should be $\frac{1}{10}$. Ashley looked at 100 numbers in the yellow pages of her telephone book. She found 22 numbers that ended in a 1, for an experimental probability of $\frac{22}{100}$, or $\frac{11}{50}$.

Because the experimental and theoretical probabilities were so different, Ashley decided that the numbers 0 to 9 could not be equally likely in the last position in a business telephone number.

Q: How can you use a tree diagram to calculate a probability?

A: The number of branches tells you the number of equally likely possible outcomes. The denominator of the fraction form of the probability is the number of branches. The numerator is the number of branches that represent favourable outcomes.

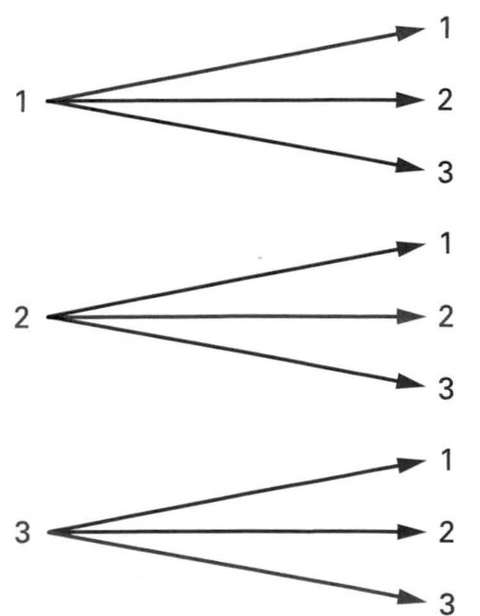

For example, two spins of this spinner can be represented by a tree diagram with nine branches, or nine possible outcomes.

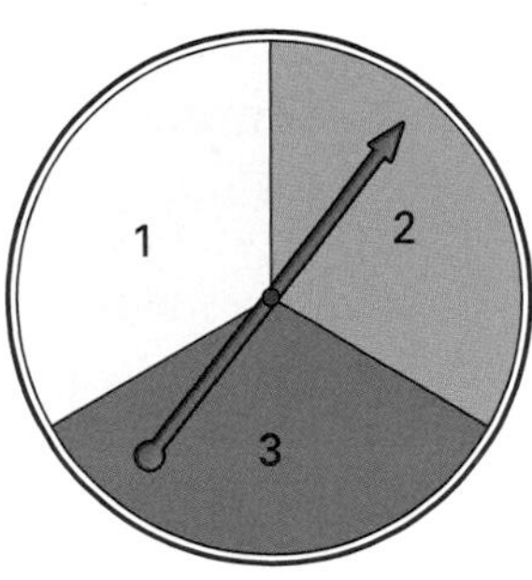

What is the probability that the second spin is the same as the first spin?

There are three branches that represent favourable outcomes.

P(both spins the same) $= \frac{3}{9}$, or $\frac{1}{3}$

Practice Questions

(12.2) **1.** What is the theoretical probability of each event?

a) drawing a queen from a standard deck of 52 cards

b) rolling a 1 using a standard die

c) spinning a 9 with this spinner

d) drawing a black card from a standard deck of 52 cards

(12.2) **2. a)** Perform an experiment to determine the experimental probability of rolling a 1 using a standard die. Complete 10 trials.

b) Repeat part (a), but complete 30 trials.

c) How do your experimental probabilities compare with the theoretical probability you calculated in question 1(b)?

(12.2) **3.** Both Rick and Dominique spun this spinner 18 times, for a total of 36 spins. Choose the fraction that matches each probability.

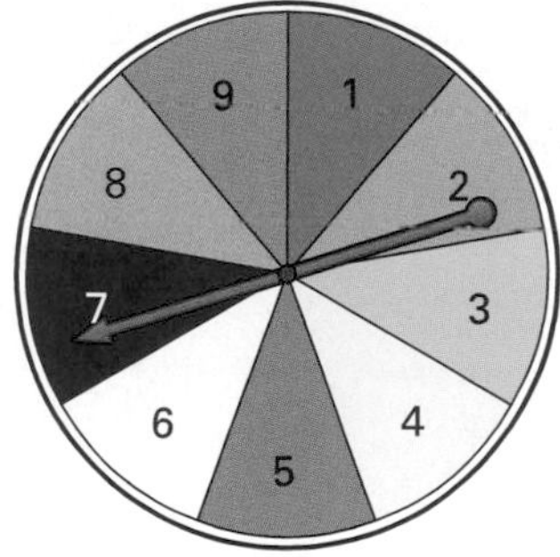

$\frac{14}{18}$	$\frac{5}{9}$
$\frac{1}{9}$	$\frac{9}{18}$

a) the theoretical probability of spinning an odd number

b) the theoretical probability of spinning purple

c) an unexpected experimental probability of spinning blue

d) an experimental probability of spinning an even number

4. Jeff rolled a die 600 times. Mary rolled a die 6 times. In which case is it more likely that the experimental probability of rolling a 1 was closest to $\frac{1}{6}$? Why? (12.2)

5. a) Suppose that you are going to roll a four-sided die (with numbers 1 to 4) and a standard six-sided die. Create a tree diagram or an organized list to show all the possible outcomes.

b) Calculate each theoretical probability.

i) P(sum of 2)

ii) P(sum of 3 or 4)

iii) P(sum of neither 3 nor 4) (12.3)

6. Suppose that you roll a 12-sided die (with numbers 1 to 12) and spin this spinner. Which is more likely—rolling an even number and spinning A, or rolling a number that is not a multiple of 3 and not spinning C? (12.3)

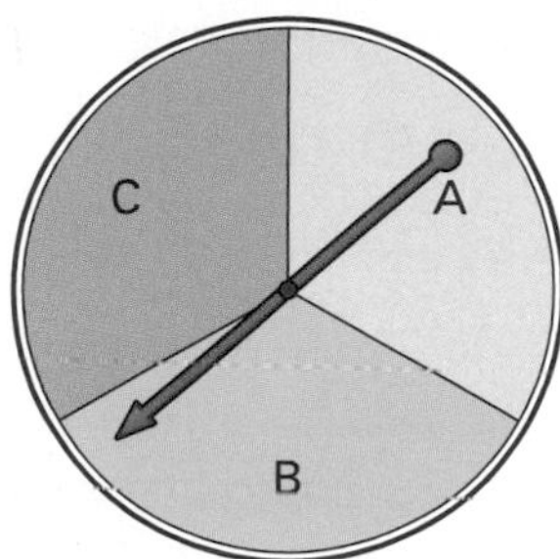

7. Judy has three pairs of pants: a blue pair, a black pair, and a brown pair. She has four shirts: one blue, one pink, one white, and one green. She also has three jackets: one black, one white, and one navy blue. (12.3)

a) Use a tree diagram to show all the possible outfits Judy could wear.

b) What is the probability that at least one outfit will include something black?

c) What is the probability that an outfit will not include something blue?

12.4 Solve Problems Using Organized Lists

▶ **GOAL**
Use an organized list to solve a problem.

Learn about the Math

Carina wants to buy a drink and a snack on the way to her next class. She knows that she has five coins in her locker, but she cannot remember whether they are quarters, dimes, or loonies. Depending on what the coins are, she may not be able to buy both the drink and the snack.

? What is the probability that Carina will be able to buy only one item?

1 Understand the Problem

- Carina has five coins.
- She has loonies, dimes, and/or quarters.
- There may be more than one of some types of coins.
- There may be none of some types of coins.
- If the total value of the coins is at least $2.00, but less than $4.00, Carina will be able to buy only one item.

2 Make a Plan

Carina decides to write all the possible combinations of coins in an organized list. This will help her see what combinations have a value of at least $2.00 but less than $4.00.

3 Carry Out the Plan

Loonies	Quarters	Dimes	Total value	Summary of possible outcomes
5	0	0	$5.00	with five loonies, one combination
4	1	0	$4.25	with four loonies, two combinations
4	0	1	$4.10	
3	2	0	$3.50 ✓	with three loonies, three combinations
3	1	1	$3.35 ✓	
3	0	2	$3.20 ✓	
2	3	0	$2.75 ✓	with two loonies, four combinations
2	2	1	$2.60 ✓	
2	1	2	$2.45 ✓	
2	0	3	$2.30 ✓	
1	4	0	$2.00 ✓	with one loonie, five combinations
1	3	1	$1.85	
1	2	2	$1.70	
1	1	3	$1.55	
1	0	4	$1.40	
0	5	0	$1.25	with no loonies, six combinations
0	4	1	$1.10	
0	3	2	$0.95	
0	2	3	$0.80	
0	1	4	$0.65	
0	0	5	$0.50	

Carina checks off the combinations with a total value of at least $2.00 but less than $4.00. The probability of being able to buy only one item is $\frac{8}{21}$.

4 Look Back

Carina sees a pattern in her table, so she feels confident that she did not miss or repeat any combinations.

Reflecting

1. How did using an organized list help Carina solve her problem?

2. What other methods could Carina have used to solve her problem?

Work with the Math

Example: Making an organized list to solve a problem

Kayley threw three darts at the target and hit three different colours. In how many ways can her score be greater than 30?

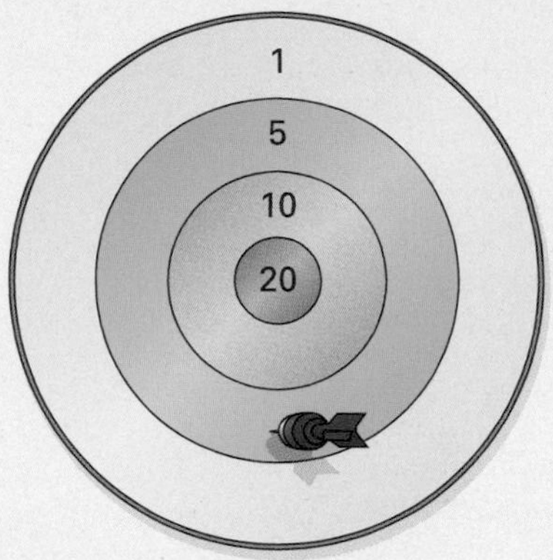

Rishi's Solution

1 Understand the Problem

This is the information I know:

- Kayley threw three darts.
- All three darts hit the target.
- Each dart earned a different score.
- Four different scores are possible: 20, 10, 5, and 1.

2 Make a Plan

I'll make an organized list of all the possible outcomes. I'll start with a score of 20 and then list 10, then 5, and finally 1. I'll look for scores greater than 30.

3 Carry Out the Plan

Dart 1	20	20	20	20	20	20	10	10	10	10	10	10	5	5	5	5	5	5	1	1	1	1	1	1
Dart 2	10	10	5	5	1	1	20	20	5	5	1	1	20	20	10	10	1	1	20	20	10	10	5	5
Dart 3	5	1	10	1	10	5	5	1	20	1	20	5	10	1	20	1	20	10	10	5	20	5	20	10
Score	(35)	(31)	(35)	26	(31)	26	(35)	(31)	(35)	16	(31)	16	(35)	26	(35)	16	26	16	(31)	26	(31)	16	26	16

There are 12 ways for Kayley's score to be greater than 30.

4 Look Back

I'm sure that I considered all the possible combinations because of the patterns I see in my list. For the first dart, each score appears six times. For the second dart, the other three scores appear in pairs. For the third dart, the two remaining scores are the possible scores.

A Checking

3. John has four jobs to do every day. For variety, he chooses slips of paper from a jar each morning to decide in which order he will do the jobs. What is the probability that John will unload the dishwasher after taking out the garbage?

B Practising

4. Alex bought a guitar pick for 25¢. He paid the exact amount, so he received no change.
   a) List the combinations of coins that Alex could have used to pay for the guitar pick.
   b) What is the least number of coins that Alex could have used?
   c) What is the greatest number of coins that Alex could have used?
   d) Could he have paid for the guitar pick using seven coins?

5. Robert and Frank were shooting baskets. They scored 3 points for a long shot, 2 points for a regular basket, and 1 point for a free throw.
   a) List the ways that Robert could have scored 12 points.
   b) Are there more ways to score 12 points with a free throw or without a free throw? How many more or less?

6. Rachel is trying to remember the combination for her lock. This is what she remembers:
   - There are three numbers in the combination.
   - The numbers may be 1, 2, 3, or 4.
   - No number is used twice.
   - The sum of the numbers may be even.

   a) Use an organized list to determine all the possible combinations with an even or odd sum.
   b) How many of the combinations have an even sum?
   c) What is the theoretical probability of the combination having an even sum?

7. To play "POETS in a Bag," players take turns selecting four of the five cards in a bag without looking, shuffling the cards, and laying them out. Players score a point if the letters on the cards spell a word.

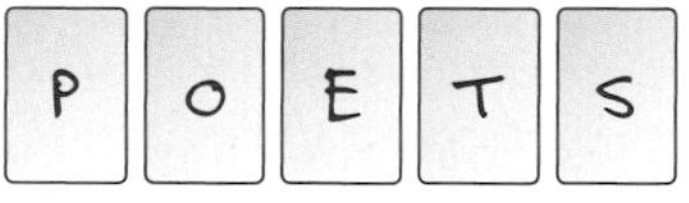

   a) On Kumar's turn, the E was left in the bag. What is the probability that Kumar will score a point?
   b) Calculate the probability of scoring a point for a different set of four letters.
   c) In one round of the game, each player chose a different set of four cards to shuffle and play. What is the greatest number of people who could have been playing?
   d) Describe a strategy to determine the four cards that give the greatest probability of scoring a point.

8. Create a problem that can be solved using an organized list. Provide a complete solution to your problem.

12.5 Using Simulations to Determine Probability

You will need
- a spinner

▶ **GOAL**

Choose a model to determine the probability of a real-life event.

Learn about the Math

Yan has a batting average of 0.250. Kelly has a batting average of 0.333. Both students hope to get at least three hits in the next five times they are up to bat. They decide to use a **simulation** to determine the probability of getting three or more hits in five times at bat.

simulation
an experiment that models an actual event

? What is the probability that Yan will get three or more hits in five times at bat?

Example 1: Simulating using a spinner

Determine each experimental probability.

a) Yan getting at least three hits in the next five times he is up to bat.

b) Yan getting less than three hits in the next five times he is up to bat.

Kito's Solution

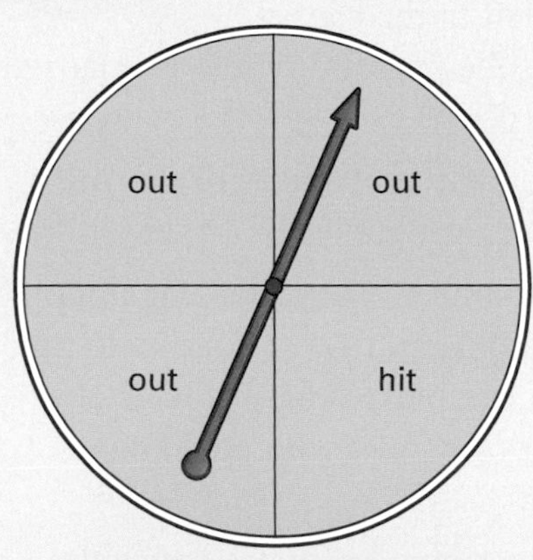

Three or more hits in five spins	Less than three hits in five spins
||	𝍸 𝍸 𝍸 |||

Yan's batting average is 0.250, or $\frac{1}{4}$. For every four times at bat, he usually gets one hit and three outs.

I used five spins of a spinner with four equal parts to model Yan's next five times at bat. I recorded whether or not there were three or more hits. I repeated the five spins 20 times.

a) The experimental probability of Yan getting three or more hits is $\frac{2}{20}$, or $\frac{1}{10}$.

b) The experimental probability of Yan getting less than three hits is $\frac{18}{20}$, or $\frac{9}{10}$.

Example 2: Simulating using a four-sided die

Determine the experimental probability of Yan getting at least three hits in the next five times he is up to bat.

Rowyn's Solution

With a 0.250 batting average, Yan has a 25% chance of getting a hit and a 75% chance of getting out.

For the simulation, I chose a tetrahedral die since it has four faces. I rolled the die five times for each trial. The numbers 1, 2, and 3 represented outs. The number 4 represented a hit.

Three or more hits	Less than three hits
3	33

After 36 trials, I calculated the experimental probability of getting three or more hits to be $\frac{3}{36}$, or $\frac{1}{12}$.

Reflecting

1. Explain why each simulation is appropriate for the situation.
2. Why would a standard six-sided die not be as good a model for the situation?

Work with the Math

Example 3: Simulating using labelled cards

Determine the experimental probability of Kelly getting at least three hits in the next five times she goes to bat.

Carina's Solution

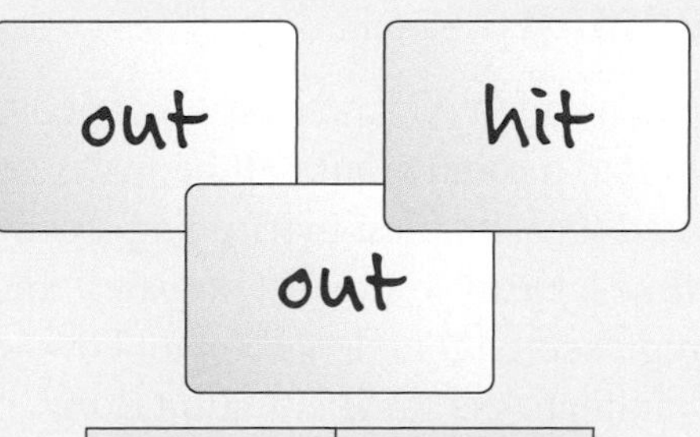

I made these three cards because Kelly's batting average is 0.333, or $\frac{1}{3}$. I put the cards in a bag.

Then I drew a card from the bag five times and replaced the card. I recorded whether or not there were three or more hits.

Three or more hits	Less than three hits
4	20

After 24 trials, I calculated the experimental probability to be $\frac{4}{24}$, or $\frac{1}{6}$, or about 16.7%.

A Checking

3. Which model(s) could be used to simulate the experimental probability for each situation below?

A. 

C. 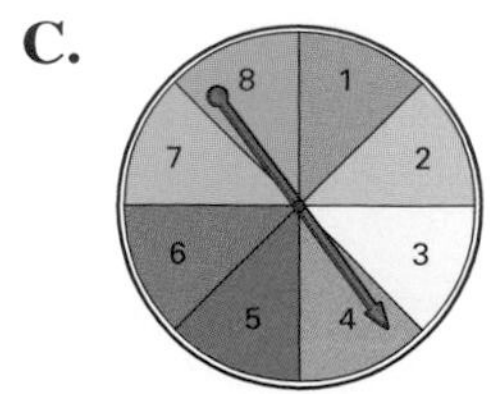

B. 

D. 

a) If six runners in a race have equal ability, the tallest runner will win the race.

b) The week that your name is drawn in a weekly prize draw will be the week of your birthday.

c) It will rain tomorrow if the forecast is a 50% chance of rain.

d) You will find a prize in your cereal box if there is a prize in every eighth box.

B Practising

4. Which spinner(s) could be used to simulate the experimental probability for each situation?

A. 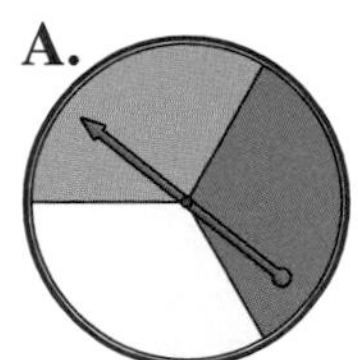

B. 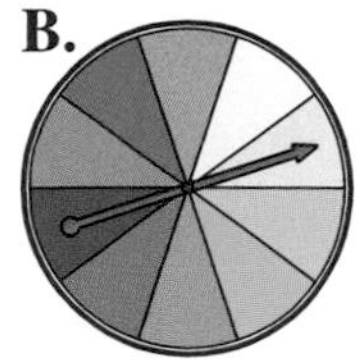

C. 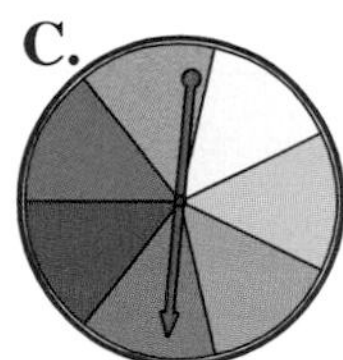

a) You have volunteered to help out one day at a weeklong summer festival. What is the probability that the day assigned to you will be Wednesday if the days are assigned randomly?

b) In a game of chance that is played in pairs, you can win, lose, or tie with equal likelihood. What is the probability that you will win three games in a row?

c) According to a poll, two of the candidates for mayor each have 30% of the votes. The third candidate has 40% of the votes. What is the probability that the third candidate will win the election?

5. Which model(s) could be used to determine the probability of each event? Justify your choices.

A. 

B. 

C. 

a) You will select the only red jellybean in a bag of 26 jellybeans.

b) You will score $\frac{10}{10}$ on a true/false quiz by guessing.

c) A family with four children has all girls.

d) The next three days will be rainy if a 30% chance of rain is forecast for all three days.

C Extending

6. Francine wondered if the next three people to walk into a room would all be male. She simulated this situation by flipping a coin three times. Heads represented males, and Tails represented females. Explain how you could simulate the same situation using each model below.

a) dice

b) playing cards

c) a spinner

d) a bag of marbles

12.6 Designing a Probability Model

You will need
- a probability model (like the models on this page)

▶ **GOAL**
Design a probability model to simulate a real-life event.

Explore the Math

Rishi and Carina are planning a school track and field day for the first Thursday in June. If it rains, the event will be on Friday. According to the weather forecast, there is an 80% chance of rain on Thursday and a 40% chance of rain on Friday. Rishi and Carina wonder if they should choose different days for the event.

? What is the probability of getting rain on both Thursday and Friday?

A. Design a simulation to model the probability of getting rain on both Thursday and Friday. Write out the steps.

B. Perform your simulation, and record your results.

C. Use your results in step B to calculate the experimental probability of getting rain on both days.

D. Compare your answer in step C with your classmates' answers. What do you think the experimental probability of getting rain on both days is likely to be?

E. Do you think Rishi and Carina should choose different days? Explain.

Reflecting

1. Why is a simulation a good strategy for solving this problem?
2. What characteristics of your model make it appropriate for the situation?
3. What other models would also be appropriate?

Math Game

ON A ROLL

The goal of this game is to be the first player to make 10 correct predictions.

Number of players: 2 to 4

You will need
- two dice

Rules

1. One player rolls two dice and calculates the product of the numbers rolled.
2. All the players predict whether the product of the next roll will be greater than, less than, or equal to this product.
3. Each player scores 1 point for a correct prediction.
4. Players take turns rolling the dice and calculating the product. The game continues until a player has 10 points.

Roll	Result of roll	Product	My score	My prediction for next roll
1		12		greater
2		15	1	equal
3		1	1 + 0 = 1	greater

Chapter Self-Test

1. Explain the difference between experimental probability and theoretical probability. Give an example to show the difference.

2. After six rolls of a standard die, the experimental probability of rolling a 3 is $\frac{2}{6}$. What do you expect will happen to the experimental probability if the die is rolled 90 more times? Explain.

3. Two four-sided dice (each with numbers 1 to 4) are rolled.

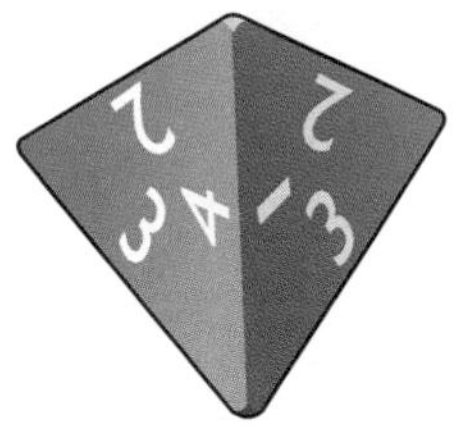

   a) Use a tree diagram or an organized list to show all the possible outcomes.
   b) What is the total number of outcomes?
   c) What is the theoretical probability that the sum of the numbers rolled will be 8?

4. Adele, Dennis, and Marie are siblings. The sum of their ages is 30. Marie is the eldest, and Adele is the youngest. None of the siblings are older than 15 or younger than 5. No two are the same age. List all the combinations of ages they could be.

5. Shad has 29¢ in his pocket. He could have any combination of pennies, nickels, dimes, and quarters.
   a) How many different combinations of coins are possible?
   b) How many combinations have fewer nickels than dimes?

6. Which model would you use to determine each probability?

   A. 

   B.  

   C. 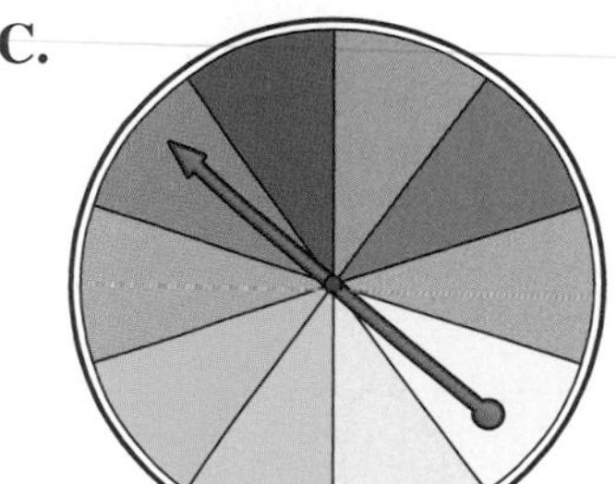

   D. 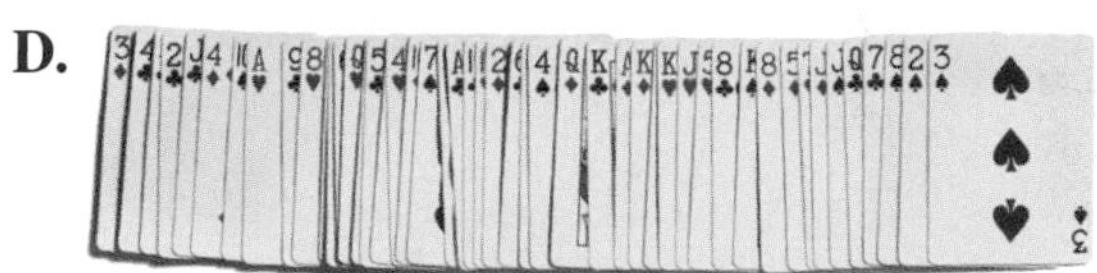

   a) Two field-hockey teams are equally matched. What is the probability that the same team will win all of the next four games they play against each other?
   b) To qualify to win a trip to Orlando, you must guess the week of the trip. What is the probability that you will qualify?
   c) There is a 30% chance of snow on each of the next three days. What is the probability of getting snow on one of these days?

7. Joan plays on a soccer team. She can usually score on a penalty kick 6 times out of 10. Describe a simulation that you could use to determine the probability of Joan scoring on her next three penalty kicks. Explain why your simulation is appropriate.

Chapter Review

Frequently Asked Questions

Q: How can you use an organized list to calculate probability?

A: An organized list shows all the possible outcomes. Therefore, it allows you to see the favourable outcomes easily. For example, suppose that you have several toonies, loonies, and quarters in your pocket. If you pull out any two coins, what is the probability that you will have enough money to pay for an item that costs $2.25?

Toonies	Loonies	Quarters	Total
2	0	0	$4.00 ✓
1	1	0	$3.00 ✓
1	0	1	$2.25 ✓
0	2	0	$2.00
0	1	1	$1.25
0	0	2	$0.50

There are six possible outcomes and three favourable outcomes. The probability is $\frac{3}{6}$, or $\frac{1}{2}$.

Q: How can you choose an appropriate model for a simulation?

A: A simulation is an experiment that models an actual event. You should choose a model with the required characteristics for the situation. For example, if an event has six possible outcomes that are equally likely, you could use a six-sided die. If an event has two possible outcomes that are equally likely, you could use a coin.

How you use a model depends on what you are simulating. For example, suppose that you were asked to predict the likelihood of seven sunny days in a row in a city where it is sunny 50% of the time, rainy 20% of the time, and cloudy 30% of the time. You could use a spinner with 10 equal sections. In five of the sections, you could write "sunny," in two of the sections you could write "rainy," and in the other three sections you could write "cloudy." One trial would be seven spins of the spinner. Each spin would represent the weather for one day.

Practice Questions

(12.2) **1. a)** Create a tree diagram to show all the possible outcomes for one spin of the spinner and one toss of the coin.

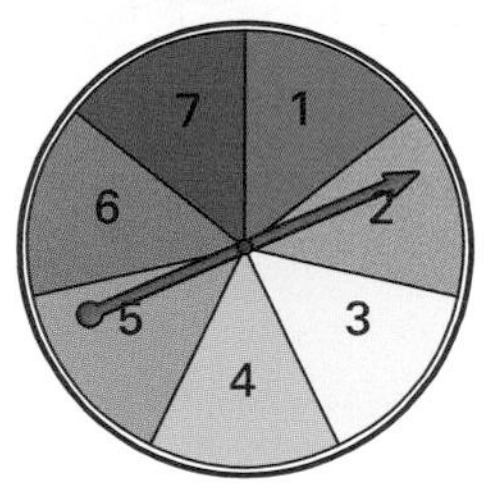

b) Calculate each theoretical probability.

i) P(7 and H)

ii) P(odd and T)

iii) P(neither 5 nor 6, and H)

iv) P(3 or 4, and T)

v) P(2, and H or T)

(12.3) **2.** Suppose that you choose one card and spin the spinner once. Calculate each theoretical probability below.

a) P(greater than 7, and C)

b) P(not greater than 7, and C)

c) P(not an ace, and A or B)

d) P(an ace, and B or C)

(12.3) **3.** Calculate the following theoretical probabilities for a family with four children.

a) P(two girls and two boys)

b) P(not two girls and two boys)

c) P(the youngest and oldest are boys)

d) P(at least two girls)

4. Asif, Sean, Bill, Francis, and Andrew are running against each other in a 100 m race. They all have an equal chance of winning. (12.4)

a) Show the possible orders for the first three runners crossing the finish line.

b) What is the probability of Andrew being one of the first three runners to cross the finish line? Assume that there will not be a tie.

5. Suppose that you have dimes, nickels, and pennies. (12.4)

a) What is the greatest number of coins you could use to pay for an item that costs 45¢?

b) In how many ways could you pay for the item using fewer pennies than nickels?

6. Which model would you use to answer each probability question below? (12.5)

A.

B.

C.

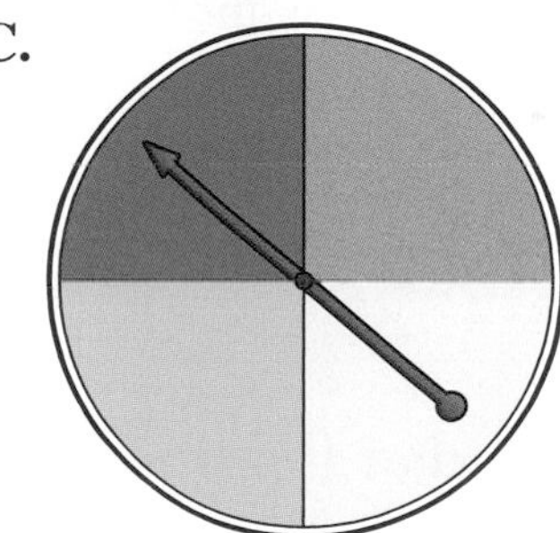

a) Each question on a multiple-choice quiz has four choices. What is the probability that you will get at least six answers right if you choose your answers randomly?

b) Sanjay, Rita, and Kieran are equally skilled at a trivia game. What is the probability that a "best of seven series" will end in four games?

Chapter Task

Free Throw

In practice, Rishi has the following free-throw accuracy:

- From 5 m, he is able to sink the ball 50% of the time.
- From 10 m, he is able to sink the ball half as often as from 5 m.
- From 15 m, he is able to sink the ball half as often as from 10 m.

In the tryouts for the school team, Rishi will get one shot from each distance.

? How can you predict the probability that Rishi will sink all three shots?

A. Predict the probability that Rishi will sink all three shots.

B. Design a simulation to model Rishi's chances of sinking all three shots. Explain why your choice is appropriate.

C. Use your simulation to calculate the experimental probability that all three shots will go in.

D. Compare your predicted probability with the experimental probability. Which do you think would be the more likely result if you did the simulation again?

Task Checklist

- ☑ Did you explain why you thought your prediction was reasonable?
- ☑ Did you justify the model you chose for your simulation?
- ☑ Did you perform enough trials in your simulation to be confident about your results?
- ☑ Did you support your choice of which probability would be the more likely result if you did the simulation again?

Cumulative Review
Chapters 10–12

Cross-Strand Multiple Choice

(10.2) **1.** Which two angles are supplementary angles?

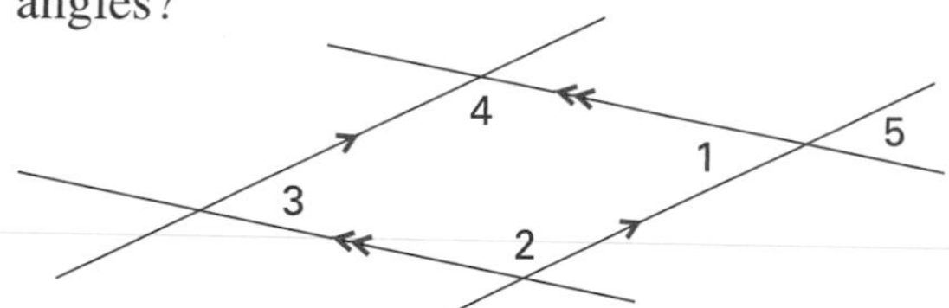

A. ∠3 and ∠1 **C.** ∠2 and ∠4
B. ∠1 and ∠5 **D.** ∠2 and ∠3

(10.2) **2.** What is the measure of the checked angle?

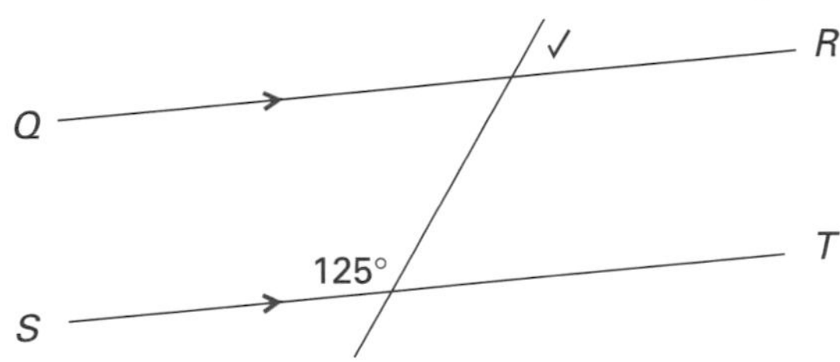

A. 125° **B.** 55° **C.** 65° **D.** 135°

(10.3) **3.** In △*JKL*, ∠*J* = 43° and ∠*L* = 71°. What is the measure of ∠*K*?

A. 19° **B.** 77° **C.** 114° **D.** 66°

(10.6) **4.** Selena walked 4550 m west and then 2865 m north. How far is she from where she started, to the nearest metre?

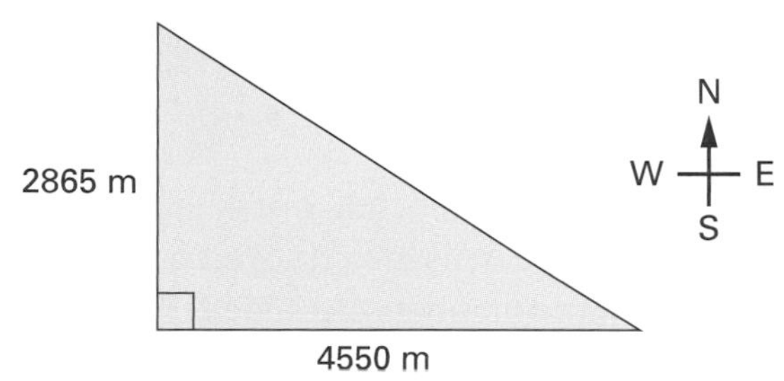

A. 3470 m **C.** 5377 m
B. 7365 m **D.** 5335 m

5. A cable, 11.3 m long, joins the top of a flagpole to an anchor that is 4.2 m from the base of the flagpole. How high is the flagpole, to the nearest tenth of a metre? (10.6)

A. 10.5 m **C.** 12.1 m
B. 15.5 m **D.** 7.1 m

Use this cylinder to answer questions 6 and 7.

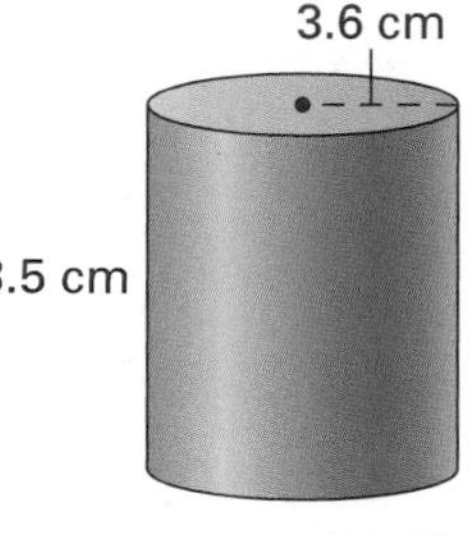

6. What is the surface area of the cylinder, rounded to the nearest square centimetre? (11.2)

A. 178 cm^2 **C.** 369 cm^2
B. 274 cm^2 **D.** 233 cm^2

7. What is the volume of the cylinder, rounded to the nearest cubic centimetre? (11.3)

A. 692 cm^3 **C.** 220 cm^3
B. 110 cm^3 **D.** 346 cm^3

8. The volume of a cylinder is 9.5 m^3, rounded to the nearest tenth of a cubic metre. Which diagram shows the cylinder? (11.3)

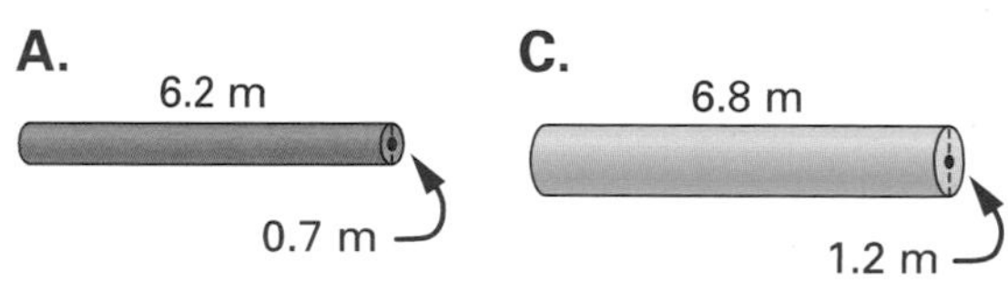

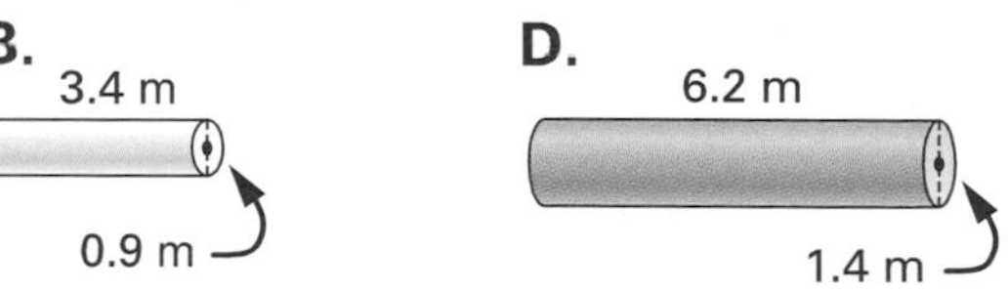

(11.5) **9.** Which statement about Platonic solids is not true?

- **A.** There are only five Platonic solids.
- **B.** All the faces of a Platonic solid are congruent.
- **C.** The faces of all Platonic solids, except the cube, are triangles.
- **D.** The same number of faces meet at each vertex.

(11.6) **10.** A polyhedron has 18 edges and 12 vertices. How many faces does the polyhedron have?

A. 10 **B.** 8 **C.** 12 **D.** 6

(11.6) **11.** A 12-sided die has 30 edges. How many vertices does the die have?

A. 18 **B.** 15 **C.** 20 **D.** 16

(12.1) **12.** Which of the following cannot represent the probability of an event?

A. $\frac{1}{14}$ **B.** 0 **C.** $\frac{8}{7}$ **D.** $\frac{20}{21}$

(12.2) **13.** As the number of trials increases, how is the experimental probability of an event likely to relate to its theoretical probability?

- **A.** The difference becomes greater.
- **B.** The difference stays exactly the same.
- **C.** The difference becomes less.
- **D.** The difference stays almost the same.

(12.2) **14.** What is the theoretical probability of drawing a red ace from a standard deck of 52 cards?

A. $\frac{1}{26}$ **B.** $\frac{1}{52}$ **C.** $\frac{1}{4}$ **D.** $\frac{1}{13}$

15. Katerina is going to roll these dice. What is the probability that the sum will be 7? (12.3)

A. $\frac{1}{36}$ **B.** $\frac{1}{12}$ **C.** $\frac{1}{48}$ **D.** $\frac{1}{4}$

16. Two six-sided dice are rolled. The probability of rolling a sum of 5 is $\frac{1}{9}$. What is the probability of not rolling a sum of 5? (12.3)

A. $\frac{1}{9}$ **B.** $\frac{7}{9}$ **C.** $\frac{2}{3}$ **D.** $\frac{8}{9}$

17. Which model is not appropriate for this probability situation? (12.5)

Kevin is driving through a small village. At each intersection, he has three choices of direction: right, left, and straight. Only one of these choices leads to where he wants to go. What is the probability that Kevin will choose the correct direction at the next two intersections?

A.

C.

B.

D.

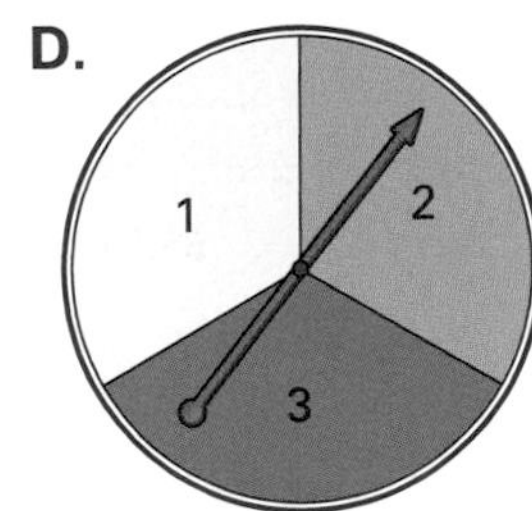

18. Four balls, numbered 1 to 4, are placed in a bag. Three balls are removed one at a time. The three numbers are added. What sum is not possible? (12.5)

A. 9 **B.** 5 **C.** 7 **D.** 6

Cross-Strand Investigation

To celebrate the 100th anniversary of Confederation, Montreal hosted the 1967 World's Fair, commonly called Expo 67. The theme of Expo 67 was "man and his world."

19. a) Part of the Canadian pavilion, shown at the right, was an inverted square pyramid, called a *Katimavik*, which means "meeting place" in the language of the Inuit. Each side of the square was about 75 m. What was the length of one diagonal?

b) The U.S. pavilion, shown below, was a dome, or three-quarter sphere, made with two layers of steel frames enclosing transparent panels. The outer frame was made of equilateral triangles with 2.4 m sides. The inner frame was made of regular hexagons with 1.5 m sides. What was the height of each triangular panel? What was the area of each triangular panel?

c) What was the measure of each angle in a triangular panel of the U.S. pavilion? What was the measure of each angle in a hexagonal panel of the U.S. pavilion?

d) The roof of the German pavilion was supported by a net made with many kilometres of steel strands. Each strand was a cylinder with a diameter of 12 mm. What was the volume of a strand that was 1000 m long, to the nearest thousandth of a cubic metre?

e) Expo 67 had four mobile television units and three mobile radio units. Both Hilda and Luis went to one mobile television unit and one mobile radio unit. What is the probability that they went to the same two units?

f) Kayo saw the films *Polar Life*, *Canada 67*, *A Time to Play*, and *A Place to Stand*. If she saw each film only once, what is the probability that she saw *Canada 67* just before she saw *A Place to Stand*?

Review of Essential Skills from Grade 7

Chapter 1: Number Relationships

Factors and Multiples

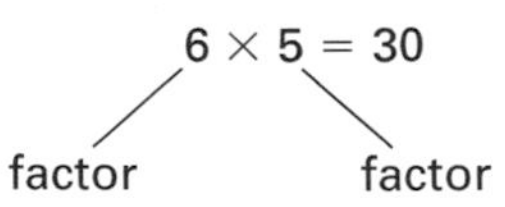

A **factor** is one of the numbers you multiply in a multiplication operation. The factors of 30 are 1, 2, 3, 5, 6, 10, 15, and 30.

A **common factor** is a number that divides into two or more other numbers with no remainder. For example, 2 is a common factor of 8 and 12. The **greatest common factor** (GCF) is the greatest whole number that divides into two or more other whole numbers with no remainder. For example, 5 is the GCF of 10 and 25.

A **common multiple** is a number that is a multiple of two or more given numbers. For example, 6, 12, and 24 are common multiples of 2 and 3. The **least common multiple** (LCM) is the least whole number that has two or more given numbers as factors. For example, 24 is the LCM of 3 and 8.

1. List all the factors of each number.

a) 24 **b)** 35 **c)** 64 **d)** 100

2. Use your answers to question 1 to determine the common factors and GCF of each pair of numbers.

a) 24 and 64 **b)** 35 and 100

3. Which numbers are multiples of 4?

20 38 300 128

4. List five common multiples of 3 and 5.

5. Determine the LCM for each set of numbers.

a) 2 and 3 **b)** 3, 6, and 9

Prime and Composite Numbers

A number with only two different factors, 1 and itself, is a prime number. For example, $7 = 7 \times 1$, so 7 is a **prime number**.

A number with more than two factors is a **composite number**. For example, $10 = 10 \times 1$ and $10 = 5 \times 2$, so 10 is a composite number.

The number 1 is neither prime nor composite, since $1 = 1 \times 1$.

6. a) List all the prime numbers from 1 to 15.

b) List all the composite numbers from 1 to 15.

7. Is an odd number always a prime number? Explain.

Powers

A numerical expression that shows repeated multiplication is called a **power**. The power 4^3 is a shorter way of writing $4 \times 4 \times 4$.

A power has a **base** and an **exponent**.

3 is the exponent of the power.

$4^3 = 64$

4 is the base of the power.

8. Use a power to represent each multiplication. Calculate.

a) $2 \times 2 \times 2 \times 2$ **b)** $5 \times 5 \times 5$ **c)** 7×7 **d)** $12 \times 12 \times 12$

9. Express each number as a power.

a) 25 **b)** 8 **c)** 81 **d)** 1000

10. a) Represent the area of this shape as a power.

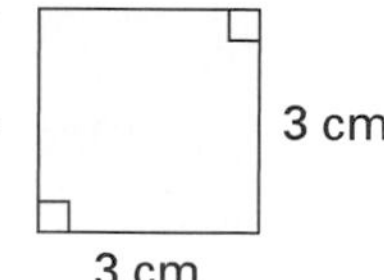

b) Represent the volume of this cube as a power.

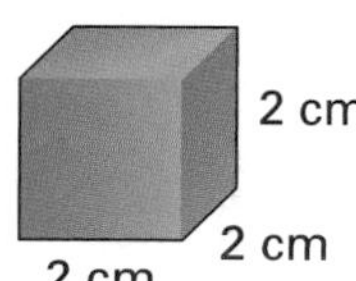

Square Roots

The product of a whole number multiplied by itself is a **perfect square**. For example, 49 is a perfect square because $49 = 7 \times 7$.

A **square root** is a number that, when multiplied by itself, equals the original number. The square root of 49 is represented as $\sqrt{49}$. $\sqrt{49} = 7$ because 7×7 or $7^2 = 49$.

11. List all the perfect squares from 1 to 100.

12. Determine each square root.

a) $\sqrt{64}$ **b)** $\sqrt{121}$ **c)** $\sqrt{16}$ **d)** $\sqrt{625}$

13. Calculate the dimensions of a square that has an area of 144 cm^2.

Order of Operations

Rules for the Order of Operations ("BEDMAS")

Brackets
Exponents
Divide and **M**ultiply from left to right.
Add and **S**ubtract from left to right.

For example,

$$\begin{aligned} & (6 + 3)^2 \div (3 \times 9) \\ &= 9^2 \div 27 \\ &= 81 \div 27 \\ &= 3 \end{aligned}$$

14. Evaluate each expression.

a) $3 \times 5 - 2 + 6$ **b)** $12 - 8 \div 2^2$ **c)** $(12 + 13) \div 5 - 3$

Chapter 2: Proportional Relationships

Fractions and Decimals

A **proper fraction** is a part of a whole. The **numerator** shows how many parts of a given size the fraction represents. The **denominator** tells how many parts the whole set has been divided into.

$\frac{3}{4}$ ← numerator (3), ← denominator (4)

A **decimal** is a way of writing a fraction with a denominator that is a multiple of 10.

For example,

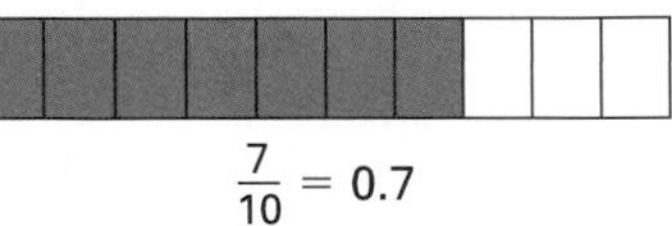

$\frac{7}{10} = 0.7$

A fraction can be written as a decimal by first expressing it as an **equivalent fraction** with a denominator of 10, 100, 1000, … and then representing it using the place value system.

For example,

$$\frac{6}{25} \overset{\times 4}{=} \frac{24}{100} \text{ and } \frac{24}{100} = 0.24$$

A decimal can be written as a fraction by using a denominator of 10, 100, 1000, …. The denominator used depends on the number of decimal places.

For example,

$$0.225 = \frac{225}{1000} \text{ and } \frac{225}{1000} \overset{\div 25}{=} \frac{9}{40}$$

1. Express each fraction as a decimal.

a) $\frac{9}{10}$ **b)** $\frac{1}{2}$ **c)** $\frac{1}{4}$ **d)** $\frac{3}{5}$ **e)** $\frac{3}{4}$ **f)** $\frac{13}{20}$ **g)** $\frac{11}{25}$

2. Express each decimal as a fraction.

a) 0.8 **b)** 0.65 **c)** 0.25 **d)** 0.3 **e)** 0.75 **f)** 0.44 **g)** 0.45

3. Arrange the following numbers in order from least to greatest.

a) $\frac{1}{2}, \frac{3}{4}, \frac{2}{5}, \frac{7}{10}, \frac{22}{25}, \frac{1}{4}$ **b)** 0.7, 0.35, 0.03, 0.1, 0.82, 0.75

Multiplying with Decimals

To multiply two decimal numbers without using a calculator, you can multiply either factor by a power of 10 to get a whole number, multiply this whole number by the other factor, and then divide your result by the same power of 10.

For example, calculate 0.4×3.28.
$0.4 \times 10 = 4$
$4 \times 3.28 = 13.12$
$13.12 \div 10 = 1.312$

Therefore, $0.4 \times 3.28 = 1.312$.
It makes sense that 4 tenths of 3.28 is one tenth of 4 times 3.28.

4. Calculate.

a) 0.3×4.7 **b)** 0.06×2.19 **c)** 0.265×2.48 **d)** 1.32×2.006

Dividing with Decimals

To divide one decimal by another without using a calculator, you can multiply the divisor by a power of 10 to get a whole number, multiply the dividend by the same power of 10, and then divide.

For example, calculate $83.5 \div 2.5$.
$2.5 \times 10 = 25$
$83.5 \times 10 = 835$
$835 \div 25 = 33.4$

Therefore, $83.5 \div 2.5 = 33.4$.
It makes sense that the number of 25 tenths (2.5) in 835 tenths (83.5) is the number of 25 ones in 835.

5. Calculate the following.

a) $14.56 \div 0.5$ **b)** $1300.512 \div 0.2$ **c)** $33.32 \div 3.2$ **d)** $517.5 \div 2.4$

Ratios

A **ratio** is a way to compare two or more numbers. For example, in a group of 7 boys and 9 girls, the ratio of boys to girls is 7 : 9, or 7 to 9, or $\frac{7}{9}$.

Equivalent ratios represent the same comparison. The ratios 7 : 9, 14 : 18, and 35 : 45 are equivalent ratios.

In any proportion, the number that you can multiply or divide each term in a ratio by to get the equivalent term in the other ratio is called the **scale factor**. The scale factor can be either a whole number or a decimal.

For example, $\frac{7 \times 5}{9 \times 5} = \frac{35}{45}$, so 5 is the scale factor.

A number sentence that relates two equivalent ratios is called a **proportion**.

For example, $\frac{7}{9} = \frac{35}{45}$ is a proportion.

6. Express each comparison as a ratio.

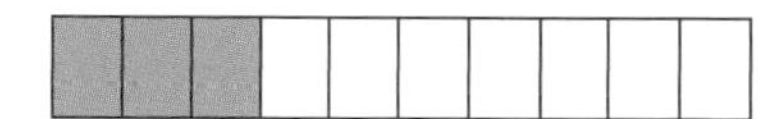

a) the number of blue squares to the number of white squares

b) the number of blue squares to the total number of squares

c) the number of white squares to the total number of squares

7. Which ratios are equivalent to 15 : 35?

5 : 7 18 : 42 9 : 21 3 : 7 $\frac{6}{14}$ $\frac{12}{30}$

8. Determine the missing number in each proportion.

a) $\frac{4}{9} = \frac{■}{81}$ **b)** $\frac{24}{9} = \frac{8}{■}$ **c)** $\frac{9}{■} = \frac{63}{49}$ **d)** $\frac{■}{3} = \frac{14}{21}$

Rates

A **rate** is a comparison of two quantities measured in different units. Unlike ratios, rates include units. For example, if Sarah ran 5 km in 2 h, then she ran at the equivalent rate of 2.5 km/h.

9. Write two equivalent rates for each comparison.

a) 6 goals in 3 games

b) 4 km jogged in 30 min

c) 36 km on 3 L of gas

10. Write a proportion for each situation, and determine the missing term.

a) In 2 h, you can earn \$15.00. In 8 h, you can earn \$■.

b) Six boxes contain 90 markers. One box contains ■ markers.

Percents

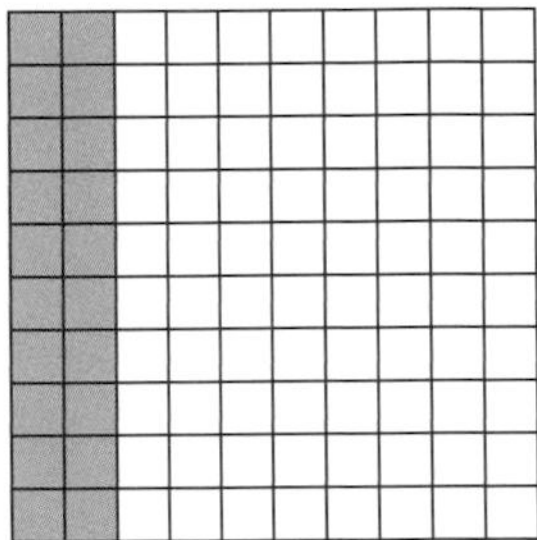

A **percent** is a special ratio that compares a number to 100 using the % symbol. For example, 20 of the 100 squares are shaded. Therefore, 20% of the whole is shaded.

$\frac{20}{100} = 0.2$ or 20%

11. What percent of the circle is shaded?

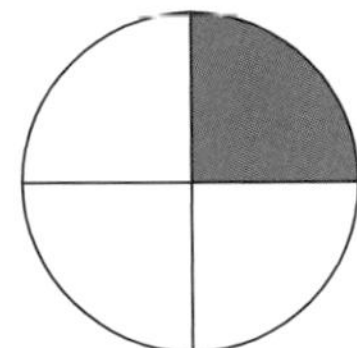

12. Copy and complete the chart.

Fraction	Ratio	Decimal	Percent
$\frac{1}{4}$		0.25	
	4:20		20%
	6:8	0.75	

13. Complete each calculation.

a) $\frac{3}{5} = \frac{■}{100} = ■\%$ b) $\frac{21}{25} = \frac{■}{100} = ■\%$

14. Write each fraction as a percent.

a) $\frac{19}{20}$ b) $\frac{1}{5}$ c) $\frac{13}{25}$ d) $\frac{7}{10}$

15. Calculate.

a) 25% of 36 b) 15% of 160 c) 30% of ■ = 24 d) 10% of ■ = 14

Chapter 3: Collecting, Organizing, and Displaying Data

Reading and Drawing Graphs

Before answering any questions about the information in a graph, you need to understand the parts of the graph:

- what type of graph it is (for example, a pictograph, bar graph, histogram, line graph, scatter plot, or circle graph)
- what the title tells you about the information in the graph
- what the labels on the axes mean
- what the units for the scales are
- what the legend (if there is one) tells you

1. a) What type of graph is shown?

b) How much was the profit from CD sales in September?

c) How much was the profit from CD sales in November?

d) What is the difference between the profits from DVD sales in October and December?

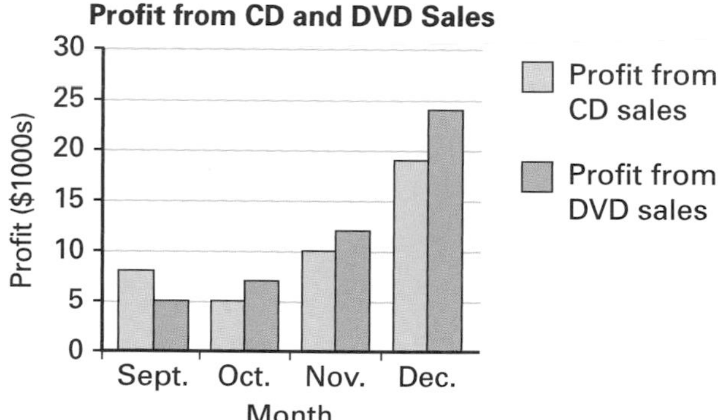

2. a) What type of graph is shown?

b) What distance was travelled in the first 30 min?

c) How long did it take to complete the 135 km trip?

d) What happened between 30 and 40 min?

e) Write the rate that compares the total distance travelled to the total time.

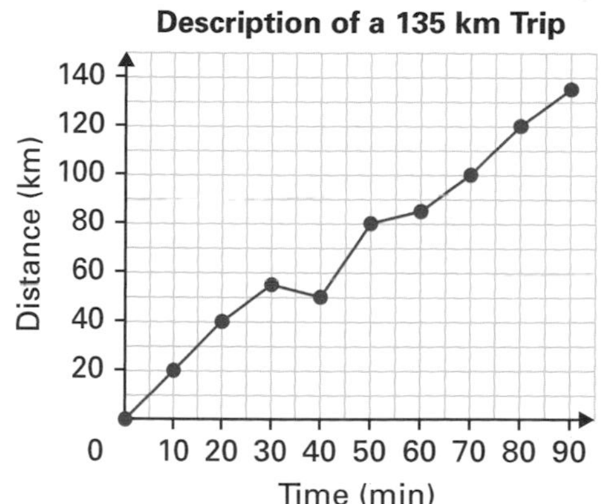

3. a) What type of graph is shown?

b) How many books does each symbol represent?

c) How many books were checked out of the library in January?

d) In which months was the same number of books checked out?

e) How many books, on average, are checked out of the library each month?

Books Checked Out of Library

Month	Books checked out
September	📖📖📖📖📖
October	📖📖📖📖📖
November	📖📖📖
December	📖📖📖📖
January	📖📖📖📖📖📖📖

📖 = 100 books

4. Last week, Joe recorded the daily high temperatures as shown.
   a) What type of graph would you use to display Joe's data? Why?
   b) Draw this graph.

Day	Temperature (°C)
Monday	15
Tuesday	17
Wednesday	21
Thursday	19
Friday	23
Saturday	23
Sunday	20

Scatter Plots

A **scatter plot** is a graph designed to show a relationship between two variables on a coordinate grid.

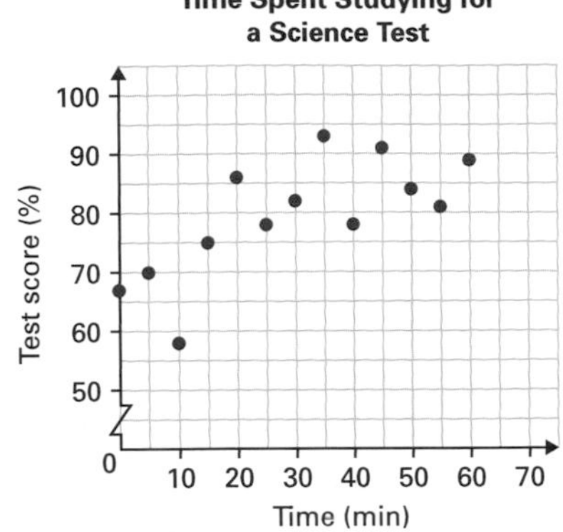

5. a) What quantity is represented on the horizontal axis of this scatter plot?
   b) What quantity is represented on the vertical axis of this scatter plot?
   c) Does this scatter plot show a relationship between the two quantities? If so, explain what it is. If not, explain why not.

6. a) Create a scatter plot for the data in this table.
   b) Describe the relationship that your scatter plot shows.

Winning Times in Women's Olympic 100 m Sprint

Year	1928	1932	1936	1948	1952	1956	1960	1964	1968
Time (s)	12.2	11.9	11.5	11.9	11.65	11.82	11.18	11.49	11.08

Year	1972	1976	1980	1984	1988	1992	1996	2000	2004
Time (s)	11.07	11.08	11.06	10.97	10.54	10.82	10.94	10.75	10.93

Sample and Population

The total number of individuals or items is called the **population**.

A **sample** is a part of a population that is used to make predictions about the whole population.

A **census** is used to count and question an entire population.

Mean, Median, and Mode

The **mean** of a set of numbers is a description of the average number in the set. It is calculated by dividing the sum of the set of numbers by the number of numbers in the set.

The middle number in a set of ordered numbers is the **median**. When there is an even number of numbers, the median is the mean of the two middle numbers.

The number that occurs most often in a set of numbers is the **mode**. There may be more than one mode, or there might be no mode.

7. Determine the mean, median, and mode of each set of data.

a) 4, 9, 5, 9, 6, 8, 9, 11 **b)** 2, 3, 6, 12, 6, 1, 3, 6, 4

8. These marks were scored by 20 students on a test.

a) Determine the mean, median, and mode of this set of data.

b) Create a sample of this set of data. Determine the mean, median, and mode of your sample.

80%	69%	72%	88%	90%	45%
58%	92%	73%	66%	100%	78%
67%	50%	59%	82%	90%	84%
40%	75%				

Stem-and-Leaf Plots

A **stem-and-leaf plot** organizes numerical data based on place values. The digits that represent the greater values are the stems. The other digits are the leaves.

For example, a basketball team scores these points in 14 games: 129, 108, 114, 125, 132, 107, 97, 127, 108, 124, 117, 94, 99, 108

To put the points in a stem-and-leaf plot, first put them in increasing order: 94, 97, 99, 107, 108, 108, 108, 114, 117, 124, 125, 127, 129, 132

Enter the scores in the stem-and-leaf plot. Use an appropriate interval for the stem. The stem-and-leaf plot of the scores is shown.

Basketball Scores

Stem	Leaf
9	4 7 9
10	7 8 8 **8**
11	4 7
12	4 5 7 9
13	2

This number represents the score 108.

9. a) Based on the data shown, how many students wrote the test?

b) What was the lowest score? What was the highest score?

c) How many students scored above 90%?

Math Test Scores (out of 50 points)

Stem	Leaf
3	5 6 8
4	0 2 2 4 5 5 7 8 9
5	0 0 0

10. Determine the mean, median, and mode of the data in the stem-and-leaf plot in question 9.

11. The heights, in centimetres, of Arjun's classmates are shown.

a) Display the heights in a stem-and-leaf plot.

b) What is the median height?

146	129	155	162	138	170	158	154
133	156	163	174	160	135	147	152
166	168	157	146	157	164		

Chapter 4: Patterns and Relationships

Pattern Rules for Sequences

A **sequence** is a list of things that are in a logical order or follow a pattern. For example, the sequence 1, 3, 5, 7, 9, … is the list of odd numbers. Each item or number in a sequence is called a **term**. In the sequence 1, 3, 5, 7, 9, …, the third term is 5. This sequence follows a pattern that can be described using an addition rule: "Start at 1. Add 2 to each term to get the next number in the sequence."

1. Describe the pattern rule for each sequence. Write the next three terms.

a) 3, 8, 13, 18, 23, … **b)** 2, 4, 8, 16, 32, 64, … **c)** 100, 96, 92, 88, 84, …

2. The pattern rule for a sequence is "Start with 7. Double the term number, and subtract 5 to get the next term in the sequence." Write the first five numbers in the sequence.

3. The student council held a bake sale to raise money for the United Way. In the first hour, the students sold $120 worth of baked goods. Each hour after that, they sold half of the previous hour's sales. The sale lasted for 6 h.

a) What were their sales in the second, third, and fourth hours?

b) What were their total sales?

Tables of Values and Scatter Plots

A **table of values** is an orderly arrangement of facts, usually set up in vertical and horizontal columns for easy reference.

A **scatter plot** is a graph designed to show a relationship between two variables on a coordinate grid. For example, the values in the following table of values are plotted on the scatter plot at the right.

Term number	Picture	Term value
1		2
2		6
3		10
4		14

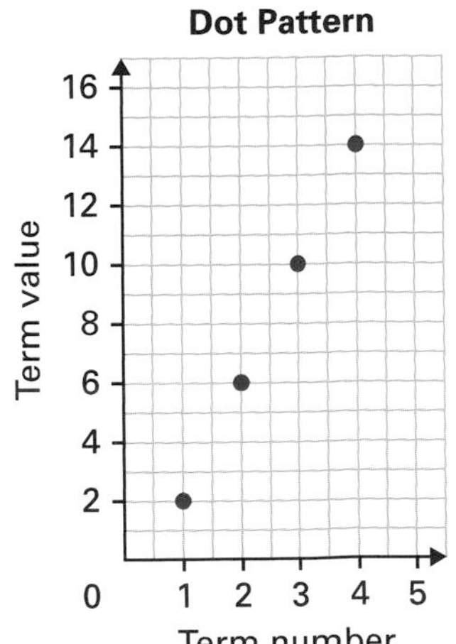

The pattern rule is the same in both the table of values and the scatter plot: "Start with 2, and add 4 to each term."

4. Maria and Vlad used counters to show a sequence of triangular numbers. They made the following table of values.

a) What are the fifth, sixth, and seventh triangular numbers? Explain how you know.

b) Write the pattern rule that uses an "adding on" strategy to describe how you could calculate any triangular number in this sequence.

c) Calculate the 10th triangular number.

Term number (figure number)	Picture	Term value (number of counters)
1		1
2		3
3		6
4		10

5. a) Use a table of values to predict the number of squares you would need to build the sixth figure in this sequence.

b) Explain the pattern rule.

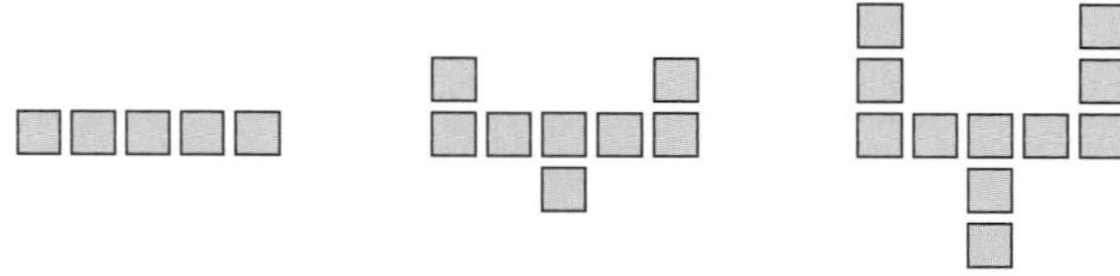

6. Create a scatter plot for the table of values. Use your scatter plot to determine the missing values in the table.

Term number	Term value
3	11
4	14
5	17
■	20
■	23
10	■
15	47

7. a) These figures are the first four figures in a sequence. Make a table of values to show the number of triangles of each colour used to build each figure.

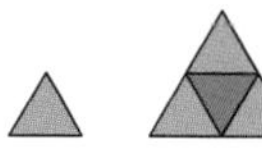 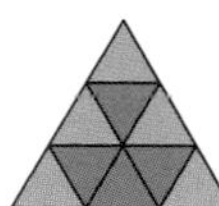 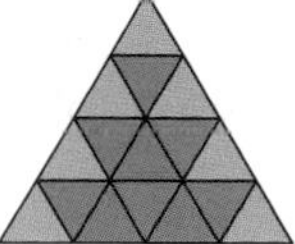

b) Draw a scatter plot to show the relationship between the red triangles in each figure and the term number.

c) Draw a scatter plot to show the relationship between the blue triangles in each figure and the term number.

Chapter 5: Measurement of Circles

Expressing Measurements in Different Units

The **metre** is the base unit for linear measurements in the metric system.

1 km (kilometre)	1 hm (hectometre)	1 dam (decametre)	1 m (metre)	1 dm (decimetre)	1 cm (centimetre)	1 mm (millimetre)
1000 m	100 m	10 m	1 m	$\frac{1}{10}$ or 0.1 m	$\frac{1}{100}$ or 0.01 m	$\frac{1}{1000}$ or 0.001 m

To rewrite a smaller unit using a larger unit, divide by the appropriate power of 10. For example, rewrite 32 mm using centimetres.
32 mm ÷ 10 = 3.2 cm

To rewrite a larger unit using a smaller unit, multiply by the appropriate power of 10. For example, rewrite 32 m using centimetres.
32 m × 10^2 = 3200 cm

1. Rewrite each measurement using millimetres.

a) 52 cm = ▒ mm **c)** 71 cm = ▒ mm
b) 68 cm = ▒ mm **d)** 73 m = ▒ mm

2. Rewrite each measurement using centimetres.

a) 70 mm = ▒ cm **c)** 6 km = ▒ cm
b) 105 dm = ▒ cm **d)** 317 m = ▒ cm

3. Rewrite each measurement using metres.

a) 7 km = ▒ m **c)** 62 mm = ▒ m
b) 79 cm = ▒ m **d)** 872 cm = ▒ m

4. Rewrite each measurement using kilometres.

a) 345 m = ▒ km **c)** 205 m = ▒ km
b) 8000 m = ▒ km **d)** 26 m = ▒ km

Perimeter

The distance around a 2-D shape is called its **perimeter**. To calculate the perimeter of a shape, add the lengths of all the sides of the shape.

5. Determine the perimeter of each shape.

a)

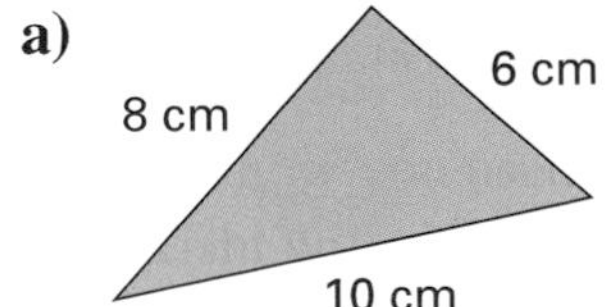

b)

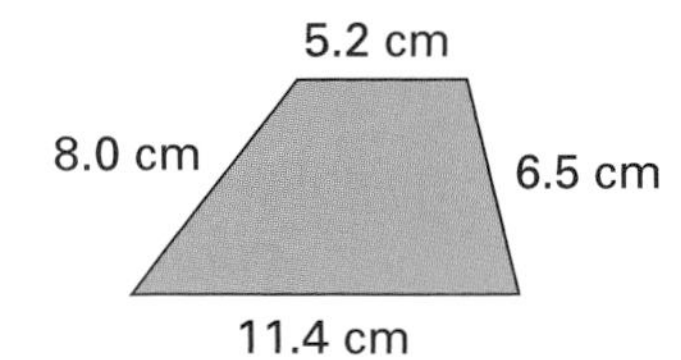

6. Tony needs to build a dog pen for his puppy. The pen will be a rectangle, with sides measuring 5 m and 8 m. How much fencing does he need?

Area

The number of square units needed to cover the surface of a shape is its **area**.

Area Formulas

Shape	Diagram	Formula
triangle	h, b	$A = (b \times h) \div 2$
square	s	$A = s^2$
rectangle	w, l	$A = l \times w$
parallelogram	h, b	$A = b \times h$
trapezoid	a, h, b	$A = (a + b) \times h \div 2$

7. What is the area of each shape, in square units?

a) 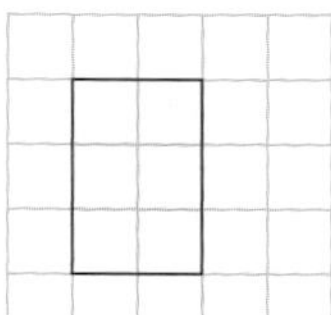

b) 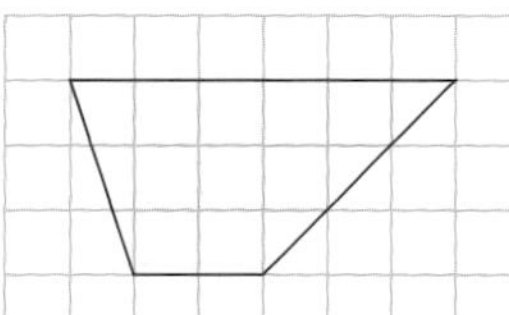

8. Calculate the area of each shape.

a) 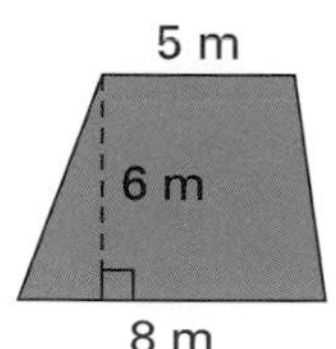

b) 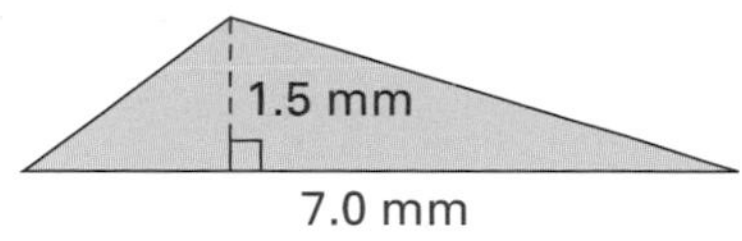

Chapter 6: Integer Operations

Comparing and Ordering Integers

The set of **integers** consists of all positive and negative whole numbers, including 0:

$\ldots, -3, -2, -1, 0, 1, 2, 3, \ldots$

You can compare integers by placing them on a number line. For example, $-3 < -1$, because -3 is to the left of -1 on a number line. This can also be written as $-1 > -3$.

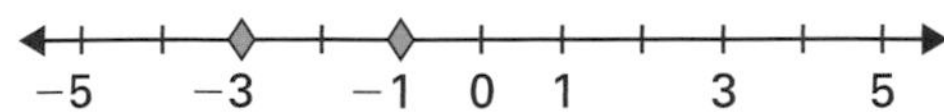

Opposite integers are the same distance away from 0 on a number line. For example, -5 and 5 are opposite integers.

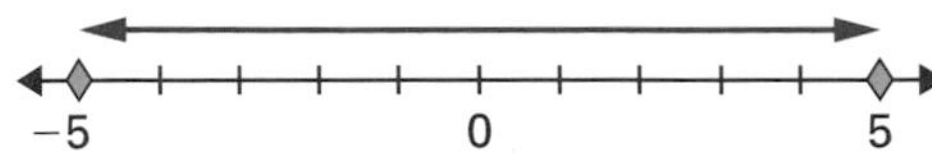

1. Identify the integer that each letter on the number line represents.

A B C D E

−10 −5 0 5 10

2. Draw a number line, and mark each of the following integers on it. Then list the integers from least to greatest.

$9, -3, 7, 0, -5, -8, 3, -2$

3. Use $<$ or $>$ to make each statement true.

a) -18 ■ -13 **d)** -9 ■ 5

b) 12 ■ -6 **e)** -22 ■ -24

c) 11 ■ 23 **f)** 16 ■ -16

Adding Integers and the Zero Principle

Integer addition uses the **zero principle**. The zero principle shows that the sum of any two opposite integers is 0. For example, the sum of $(+1)$ and (-1) is 0.

Integer addition can be modelled on a number line.
Use a line pointing to the right to represent a positive integer.
Use a line pointing to the left to represent a negative integer.

For example, calculate $(-6) + (+4)$.
Start at 0 on a number line. Draw a line that is 6 units long and points to the left. This represents -6.
Then, starting at the point where the first line ends, draw a line that is 4 units long and points to the right. This represents $+4$. The second line ends at -2 on the number line. So, $(-6) + (+4) = -2$. Note that the overlap of the lines becomes 0, based on the zero principle.

Integer addition can also be modelled with coloured counters, using red for positive and blue for negative. For example, calculate $(-6) + (+4)$. Use 6 blue counters to represent -6 and 4 red counters to represent $+4$.

Use the zero principle: a red counter and a blue counter together are called a zero pair because their sum is 0. Circle all the zero pairs. Since the sum of all the zero pairs is 0, you can remove these counters.

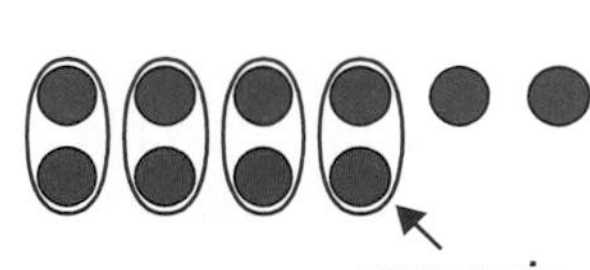

There are 2 blue counters remaining. This represents -2, so $(-6) + (+4) = -2$.

4. Write the addition represented by each model, and calculate the sum.

a) 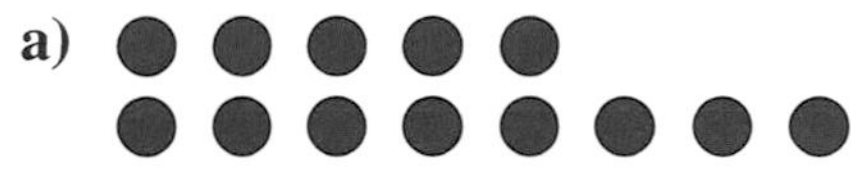

b) 

c) 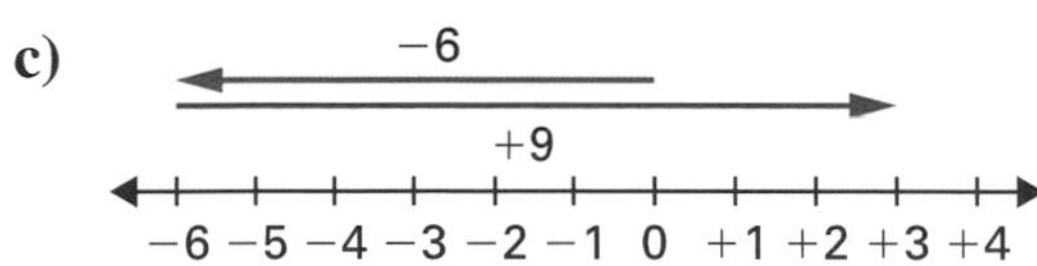

d)

5. Add using a model.

a) $(-6) + (+10)$
b) $(-3) + (-7)$
c) $(+15) + (-12)$
d) $(-3) + (-8) + (+11)$
e) $(-16) + (+16)$
f) $(-23) + (-37)$
g) $(+25) + (-32)$
h) $(-25) + (-18) + (+41)$

Subtracting Integers

Integer subtraction can be modelled using a number line. On the number line, locate the position of the second number in the subtraction. Draw a line from this number to the position of the first number in the subtraction. The length and direction of the line gives you the answer.

For example, calculate $(-3) - (-5)$.

+2

−6 −5 −4 −3 −2 −1 0 +1

The line begins at −5 and continues to −3. The line is 2 units long, and it goes to the right. So, $(-3) - (-5) = +2$.

Integer subtraction can also be modelled using counters. Add enough zero pairs (a red counter and a blue counter) to complete the subtraction. The counters that remain after the subtraction represent the answer.

For example, calculate $(-3) - (-5)$.

Start with 3 blue counters and 5 blue counters.
Add 2 zero pairs to the 3 blue counters.
Now you can subtract the blue counters.
There are 2 red counters remaining. So, $(-3) - (-5) = +2$.

6. Write the subtraction represented by each model, and calculate the difference.

a)

b)

c)

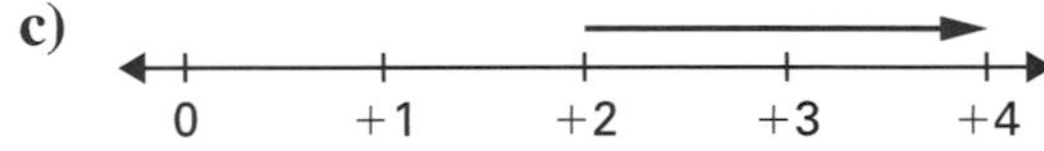

d)

−3 −2 −1 0 +1 +2 +3 +4

e)

−3 −2 −1 0 +1

7. Subtract using a model.

a) $(+5) - (-3)$

b) $(-6) - (-4)$

c) $(+7) - (+12)$

d) $(-12) - (+6)$

e) $(-15) - (-15)$

f) $(-26) - (+24)$

g) $(+37) - (+42)$

h) $(-42) - (-12)$

Chapter 7: Transformations

Location on a Grid

A Cartesian coordinate grid is a method for describing location as the distance from a horizontal number line (the x-axis) and a vertical number line (the y-axis). The x- and y-axes intersect at (0, 0), called the origin.

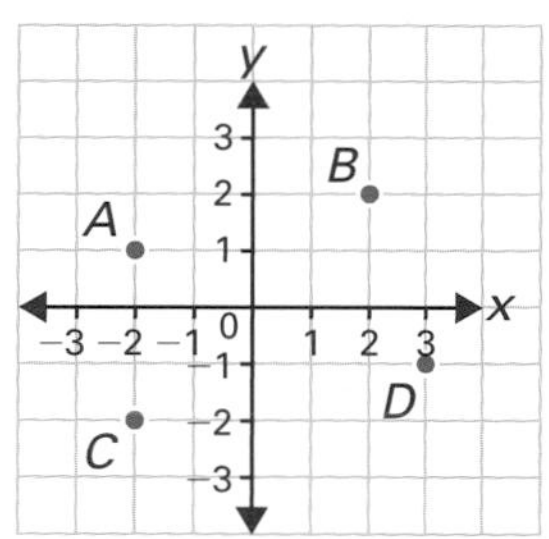

The location of a point is represented by an ordered pair of coordinates, (x, y). The coordinates of the points on this grid are $A(-2, 1)$, $B(2, 2)$, $C(-2, -2)$, and $D(3, -1)$.

Transformations

A 2-D shape can go through various kinds of transformations, including translations, rotations, and reflections. The new shape that is created when a shape is transformed is called the **image**. The image is always the same size as the original shape. The vertices of the image are often labelled using the same letters as the vertices of the original shape, but with primes. A'(read "A prime") is the image of A.

Translations

A **translation** is the result of a 2-D shape sliding in a straight line to a new position. The shape can slide up, down, sideways, or on a slant. The shape looks the same after a translation. Only the location changes.

This is a translation of $\triangle ABC$ 4 units to the right.

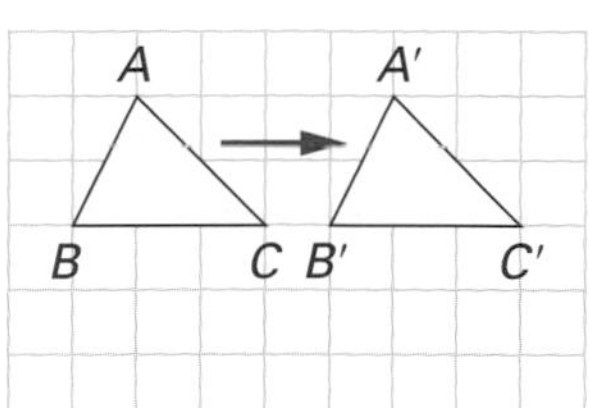

This is a translation of $\triangle ABC$ 4 units to the right and 2 units down.

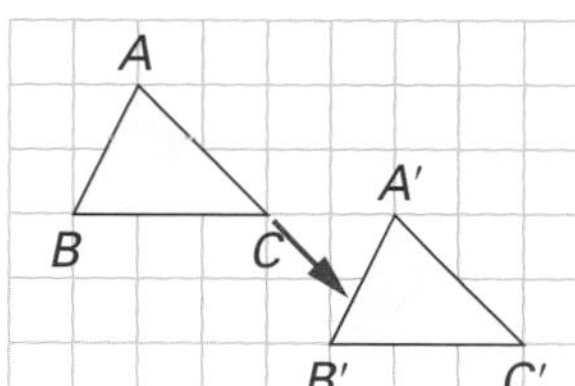

This is not a translation of $\triangle ABC$, because the shape looks different.

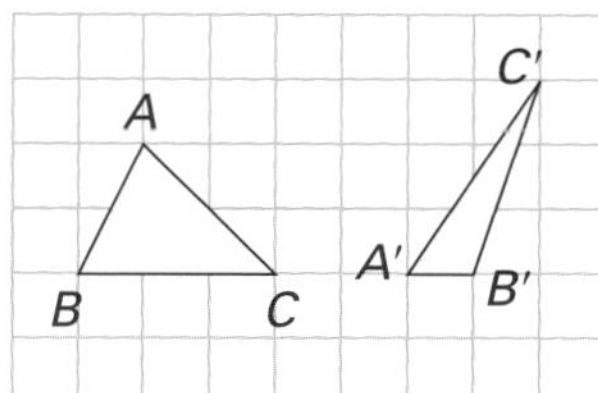

1. Which shape is a translation of A?

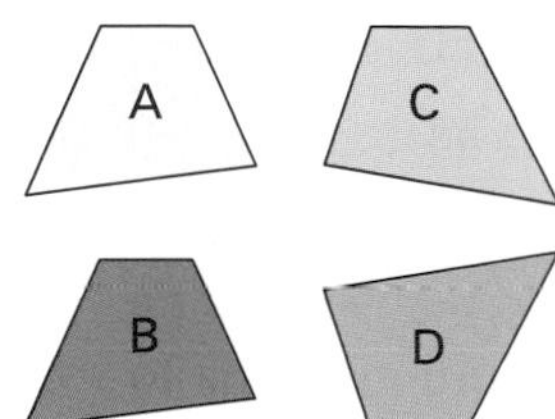

2. Describe the translation of $\triangle DEF$ to $\triangle D'E'F'$ in terms of how many units up, down, to the left, or to the right $\triangle DEF$ moved.

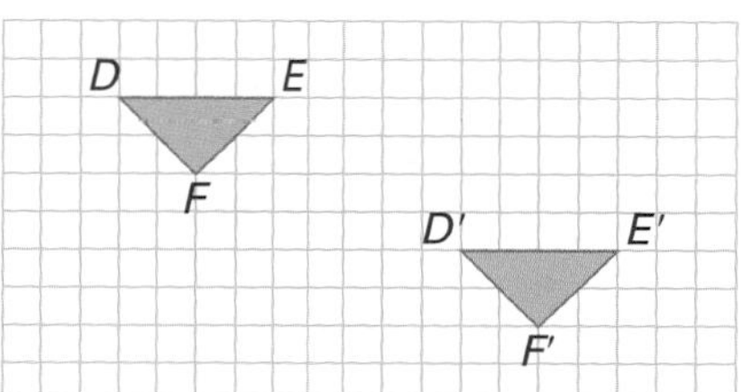

3. Copy parallelogram *ABCD* onto grid paper. Draw its image after a translation 2 units to the right and 3 units down.

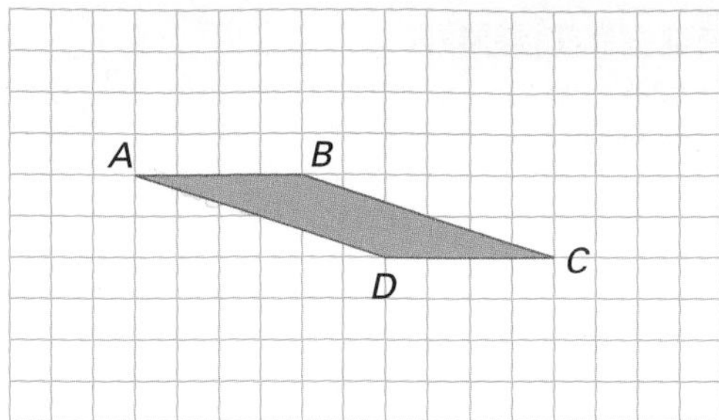

Rotations

A **rotation** occurs when each point in a shape moves about a fixed point, called the **centre of rotation**, through the same angle. In this rotation, for example, $\triangle ABC$ moves 90° clockwise through a centre of rotation.

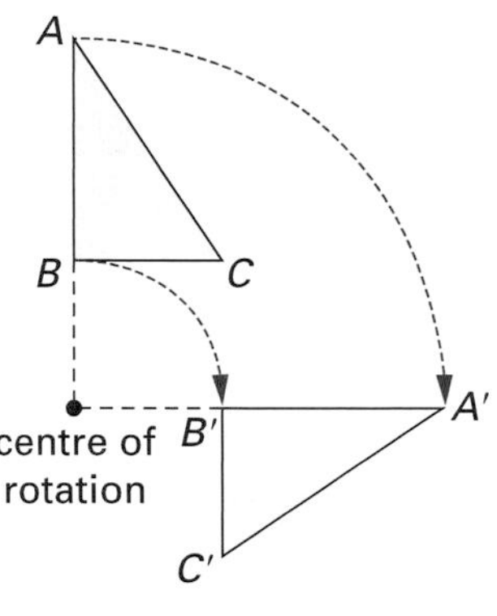

4. Which shape is not a rotation of A?

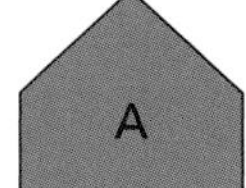

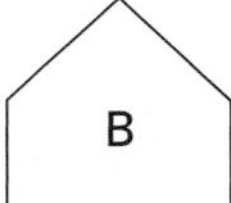

D

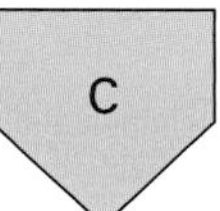

5. Describe the rotation of rectangle *ABCD* to rectangle *A′B′C′D′* in terms of how many degrees and in which direction *ABCD* was rotated.

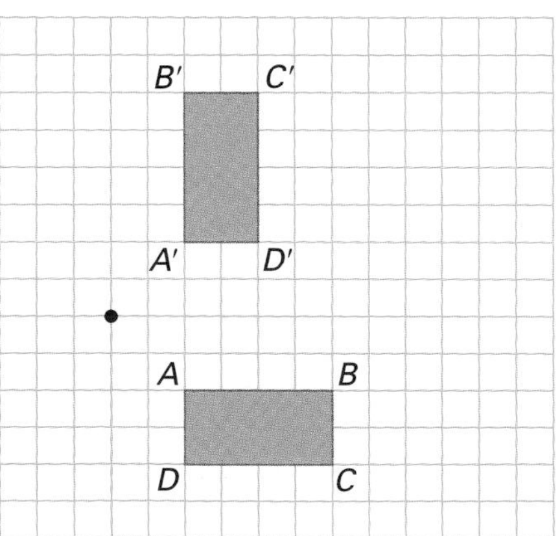

6. Copy square *PQRS* onto grid paper. Draw its image after a rotation of 180° about the centre of rotation.

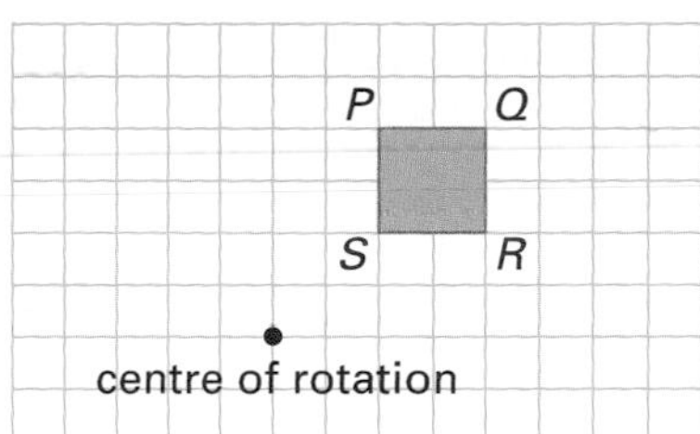

Reflections

A **reflection** is the result of a flip of a 2-D shape over a line of reflection. Each point in the shape is flipped to the opposite side of the line of reflection, but stays the same distance from the line. This is a reflection of $\triangle ABC$ in a vertical line of reflection.

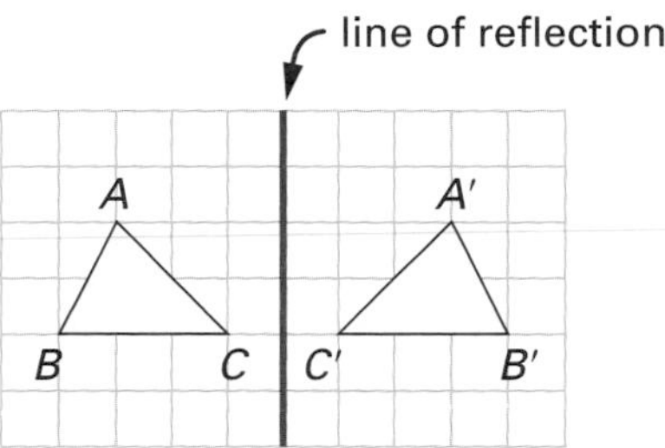

7. Which shape is a reflection of A?

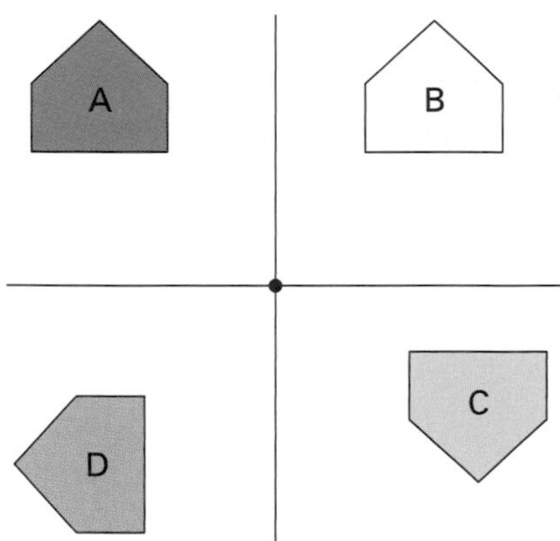

8. Copy *PQRS* onto grid paper. Draw its image after a reflection in the line *LR*.

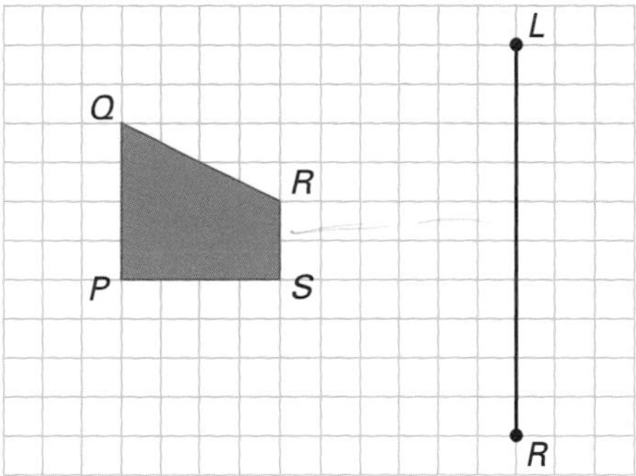

Similarity and Congruence

Two shapes that are the same shape are **similar**. Two shapes that are the same size and shape are **congruent**.

9. a) Identify the congruent shapes.

b) Identify the similar shapes.

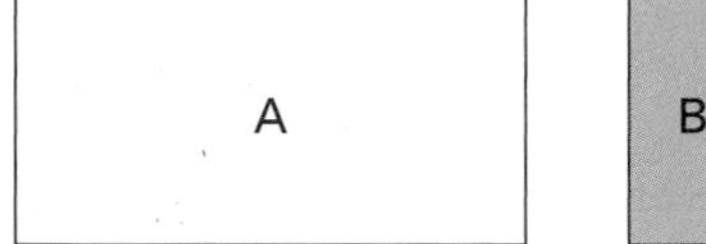

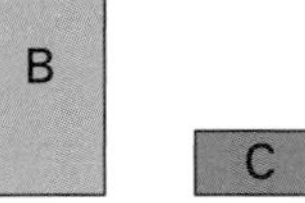

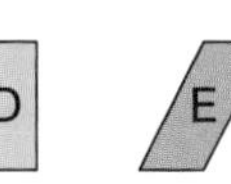

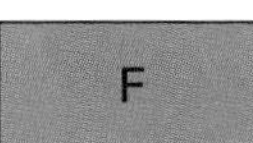

Chapter 8: Equations and Relationships

Algebraic Expressions

An **algebraic expression** is the result of applying arithmetic operations to numbers and variables. For example, in the formula for the area of a rectangle, $A = l \times w$, the **variables** A, l, and w represent the area, length, and width of the rectangle. The algebraic expression $l \times w$ shows the calculation.

1. a) What stays the same and what changes in this sequence?

Figure 1 Figure 2

Figure 3

b) Describe the sequence in words.

c) Write an algebraic expression that describes the total number of counters in each term of this sequence.

2. a) Describe, in words, the sequence 1, 4, 9, 16, 25, ….

b) Write an algebraic expression that describes how to calculate each term in this sequence using its term number.

3. The algebraic expression $3b + 2$ represents a pattern rule. Draw possible figures for the first three terms in the pattern.

4. Evaluate each expression for $c = 6$ and $d = 2$.

a) $8c$ **b)** $2d - 9$ **c)** $c^2 + d$

5. Write an algebraic expression for each phrase.

a) the cost of a number of hot dogs that are \$2 each

b) the length of a line that increases by 6 units every time

c) the total value of a number of quarters and dimes

Solving Equations by Inspection

An **equation** is a mathematical statement that two expressions are equal. For example, $5x + 3 = 8$.

The **solution to an equation** is the value of the variable that makes the equation true. One way to solve an equation is by inspection, which means by examining it carefully.

For example, solve $5b - 2 = 13$. If you add 2 to both sides, then $5b$ must equal 15. Since $5 \times 3 = 15$, then $b = 3$.

When you solve an equation, check the solution by substituting it into the equation to see if it makes the equation true.

The equation is true when $b = 3$, so this solution is correct.

Check:

Left side	Right side
$5b - 2$	13
$= 5(3) - 2$	
$= 13$ ✓	

6. Use inspection to solve each equation. Check your solution.

a) $n + 5 = 9$ **d)** $2x + 4 = 10$

b) $c - 6 = 4$ **e)** $5v - 2 = 48$

c) $6p = 54$ **f)** $9s - 4 = 68$

7. To rent a lawn mower, a company charges a fixed rate of \$5, plus \$2 per day.

a) Write an equation that describes the cost (c) of renting a lawn mower for a certain number of days (d).

b) Write an equation that represents the number of days you can rent a lawn mower for \$25.

c) Solve your equation and check your solution.

Solving Equations by Systematic Trial

To solve an equation by systematic trial, you need to predict the solution. Substitute your prediction into the equation, and calculate the result. If the result is too low, then increase your prediction. If the result is too high, then decrease your prediction. Repeat this process until you have the correct solution.

For example, solve $8k - 12 = 108$ using systematic trial.

Predict k.	Evaluate $8k - 12$.	Is it equal to 108?
20	$8(20) - 12 = 160 - 12$ $= 148$	No, it's too high.
12	$8(12) - 12 = 96 - 12$ $= 84$	No, it's too low.
15	$8(15) - 12 = 120 - 12$ $= 108$	I've solved it!

8. Use systematic trial to determine the value of the variable in each equation.

a) $c - 25 = 45$ **c)** $5 + 4c = 61$

b) $12d = 156$ **d)** $88 = 4g - 8$

9. The formula for the area of a triangle is $A = (b \times h) \div 2$.

a) Determine the value of b in centimetres, if $A = 12\text{ cm}^2$ and $h = 4\text{ cm}$.

b) Determine the value of h in centimetres, if $A = 26\text{ cm}^2$ and $b = 13\text{ cm}$.

Chapter 9: Fraction Operations

Modelling Fractions

A variety of models can be used to represent fractions.

For example, each model represents the fraction $\frac{3}{8}$.

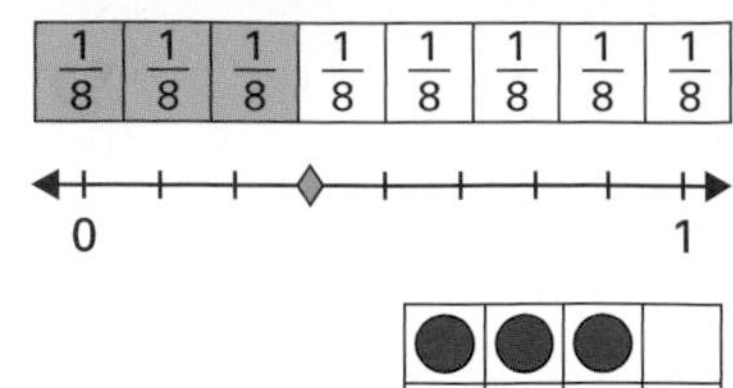

Adding Fractions

To add fractions, the fractions need to have the same denominator. If necessary, rename the fractions so that they have a common denominator. A **common denominator** is a common multiple of the two denominators. The numerator of the answer is the sum of the numerators. The denominator of the answer is the common denominator.

For example, add $\frac{2}{5} + \frac{1}{10}$ using fraction strips. Represent each fraction with a fraction strip. Align the end of one shaded region with the beginning of the other shaded region.

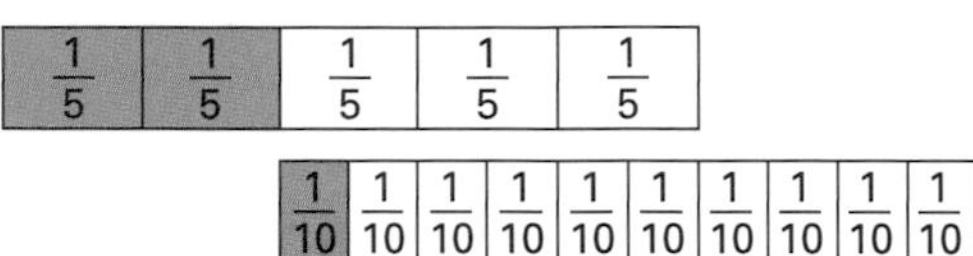

To get a common denominator, rename the $\frac{2}{5}$ fraction strip as $\frac{4}{10}$. The fraction strips show that $\frac{2}{5} + \frac{1}{10} = \frac{5}{10}$, or $\frac{1}{2}$.

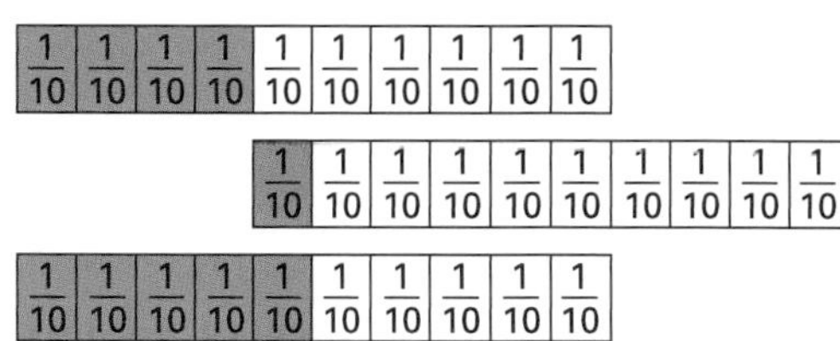

Now add $\frac{2}{3} + \frac{1}{6}$ using number lines. Use a number line marked in sixths. Rename $\frac{2}{3}$ as $\frac{4}{6}$. Draw arrows to show that $\frac{4}{6} + \frac{1}{6} = \frac{5}{6}$.

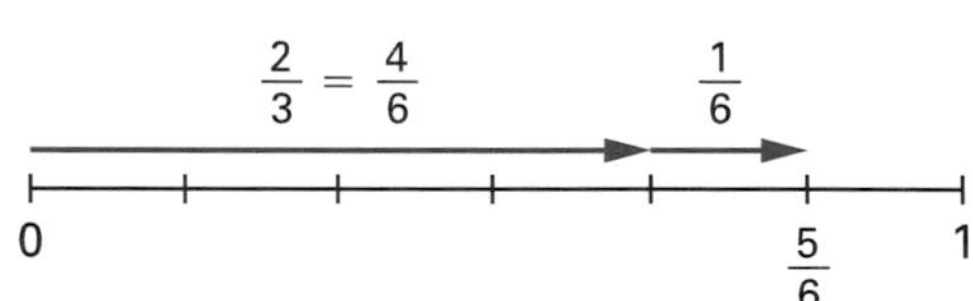

1. Write the fraction addition, and calculate the sum.

a) 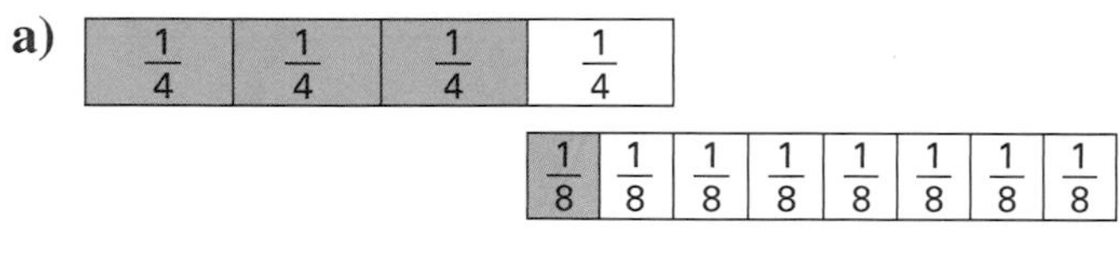

b) 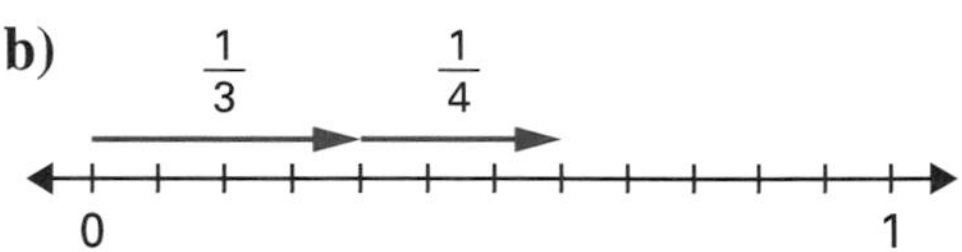

2. Add using a model.

a) $\frac{2}{5} + \frac{3}{5}$ b) $\frac{7}{8} + \frac{3}{8}$ c) $\frac{3}{4} + \frac{1}{2}$ d) $\frac{2}{5} + \frac{3}{4}$

3. Mark has $\frac{3}{8}$ of a tank of gas. He adds another $\frac{1}{2}$ of a tank of gas. Is his tank full? Explain.

Subtracting Fractions

To subtract fractions, use a common denominator. The numerator of the answer is the difference between the numerators. The denominator of the answer is the common denominator.

For example, subtract $\frac{2}{5} - \frac{1}{10}$ using fraction strips.

Represent each fraction with a fraction strip. Align the ends of the fraction strips.

$\frac{1}{5}$	$\frac{1}{5}$	$\frac{1}{5}$	$\frac{1}{5}$	$\frac{1}{5}$

$\frac{1}{10}$	$\frac{1}{10}$	$\frac{1}{10}$	$\frac{1}{10}$	$\frac{1}{10}$	$\frac{1}{10}$	$\frac{1}{10}$	$\frac{1}{10}$	$\frac{1}{10}$	$\frac{1}{10}$

Rename the $\frac{2}{5}$ fraction strip as $\frac{4}{10}$. The two fraction strips show that the difference between $\frac{2}{5}$ and $\frac{1}{10}$ is $\frac{3}{10}$.

$\frac{1}{10}$	$\frac{1}{10}$	$\frac{1}{10}$	$\frac{1}{10}$	$\frac{1}{10}$	$\frac{1}{10}$	$\frac{1}{10}$	$\frac{1}{10}$	$\frac{1}{10}$	$\frac{1}{10}$

$\frac{1}{10}$	$\frac{1}{10}$	$\frac{1}{10}$	$\frac{1}{10}$	$\frac{1}{10}$	$\frac{1}{10}$	$\frac{1}{10}$	$\frac{1}{10}$	$\frac{1}{10}$	$\frac{1}{10}$

Subtract $\frac{7}{4} - \frac{2}{3}$ using a number line.

Use a number line marked in 12ths. Rename $\frac{7}{4}$ as $\frac{21}{12}$, and rename $\frac{2}{3}$ as $\frac{8}{12}$. There are 13 spaces between $\frac{8}{12}$ and $\frac{21}{12}$. Each space is $\frac{1}{12}$, so $\frac{21}{12} - \frac{8}{12} = \frac{13}{12}$.

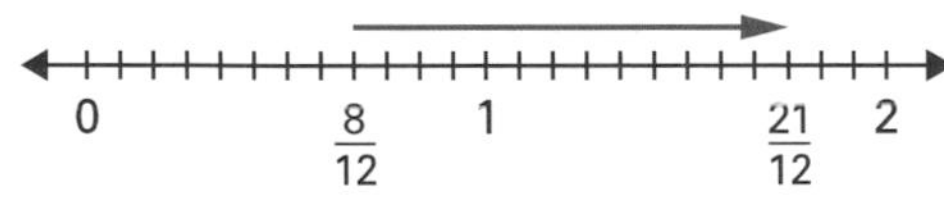

4. Write the fraction subtraction, and calculate the difference.

a)

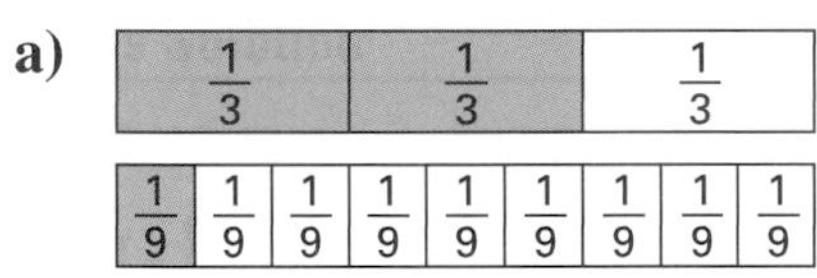

b)

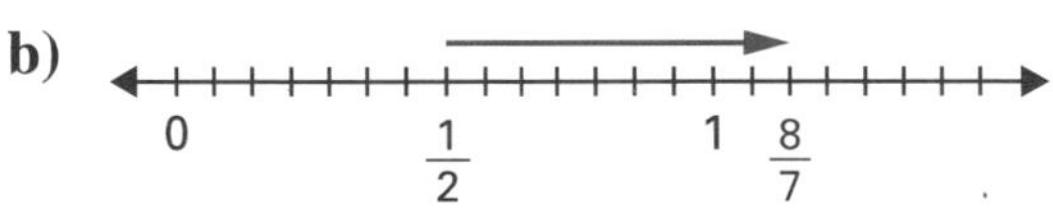

5. Subtract using a model.

a) $\frac{4}{5} - \frac{3}{5}$ **b)** $\frac{7}{8} - \frac{5}{8}$ **c)** $\frac{3}{4} - \frac{1}{2}$ **d)** $\frac{3}{4} - \frac{1}{5}$

6. Sarah's pitcher of juice is $\frac{7}{8}$ full. She pours out a full glass. The glass holds $\frac{1}{4}$ of a full pitcher. How full is Sarah's pitcher now?

Adding Mixed Numbers

A **mixed number** is made up of a whole number and a fraction, such as $3\frac{1}{4}$. To add mixed numbers, add the whole numbers and fractions separately.

For example, calculate $2\frac{2}{3} + 1\frac{1}{2}$ using a grid and counters.

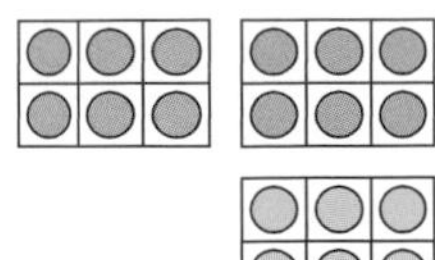

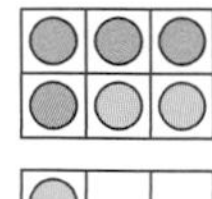

The common denominator for $\frac{2}{3}$ and $\frac{1}{2}$ is 6, so each rectangle has 6 squares. First add the whole numbers.

$2 + 1 = 3$

To add the fractions, rename them with a common denominator.

$$\frac{2}{3} + \frac{1}{2} = \frac{4}{6} + \frac{3}{6}$$
$$= \frac{7}{6}, \text{ or } 1\frac{1}{6}$$

To get the final answer, add the whole number and fraction sums.

$3 + 1\frac{1}{6} = 4\frac{1}{6}$

Calculate $2\frac{2}{3} + 1\frac{1}{2}$ using fraction strips.

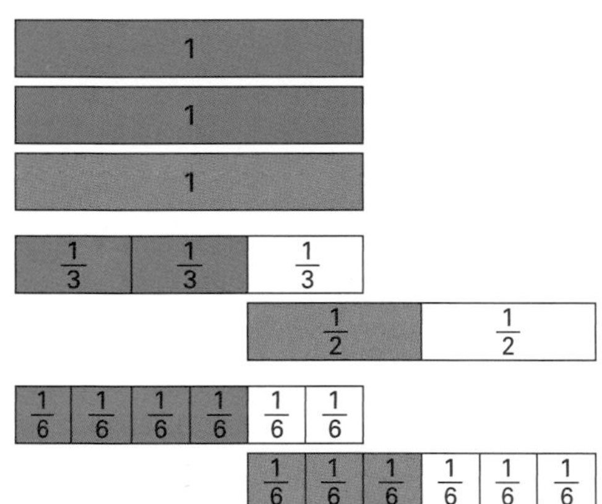

Add the whole numbers. $2 + 1 = 3$

Make a $\frac{2}{3}$ fraction strip and a $\frac{1}{2}$ fraction strip. Since 6 is the common denominator for $\frac{2}{3}$ and $\frac{1}{2}$, divide the fraction strips into sixths.

Rename the fractions and add.

$\frac{4}{6} + \frac{3}{6} = \frac{7}{6}$, or $1\frac{1}{6}$

To get the final answer, add the whole number and fraction sums.

$3 + 1\frac{1}{6} = 4\frac{1}{6}$

7. Write the addition of mixed numbers, and calculate the sum.

a) 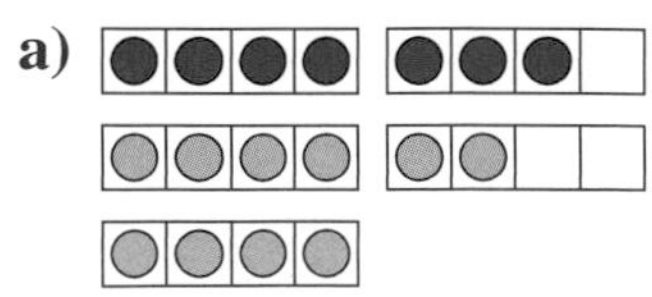

b) 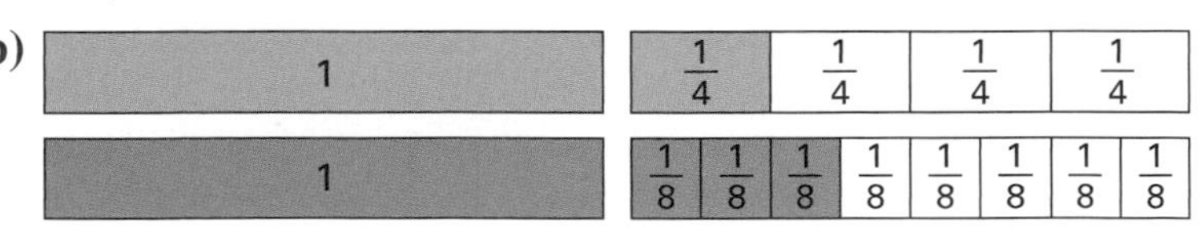

8. Add using a model.

a) $1\frac{2}{3} + 5\frac{1}{3}$ **b)** $5\frac{1}{2} + 3\frac{1}{4}$ **c)** $2\frac{3}{8} + 2\frac{1}{4}$

Subtracting Mixed Numbers

Calculate $5 - 1\frac{3}{10}$ using a number line.

$1\frac{3}{10} + n = 5$ Determine how much you need to add to $1\frac{3}{10}$ to get to 5. Use a number line divided into 10ths.

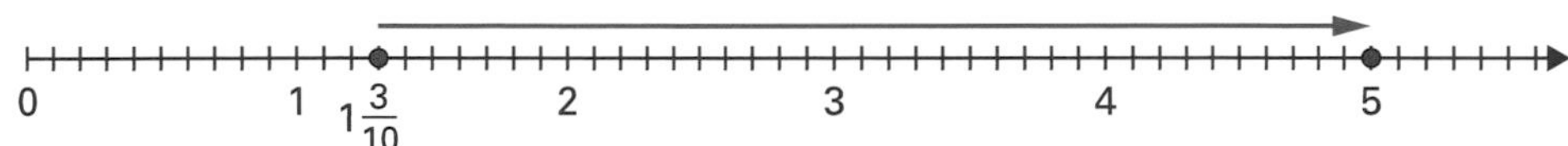

The distance from $1\frac{3}{10}$ to 2 is $\frac{7}{10}$. The distance from 2 to 5 is 3.
Therefore, the total distance is $\frac{7}{10} + 3$, or $3\frac{7}{10}$. So, $5 - 1\frac{3}{10} = 3\frac{7}{10}$.

Calculate $5 - 1\frac{3}{10}$ using fraction strips.
Represent each number with fraction strips. Line up the fractions to compare the numbers. Then figure out the difference.

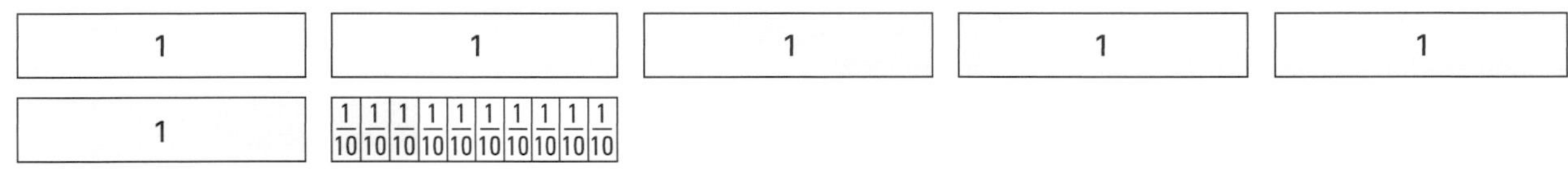

The difference is $3\frac{7}{10}$, so $5 - 1\frac{3}{10} = 3\frac{7}{10}$.

9. Write the subtraction, and calculate the answer.

a)

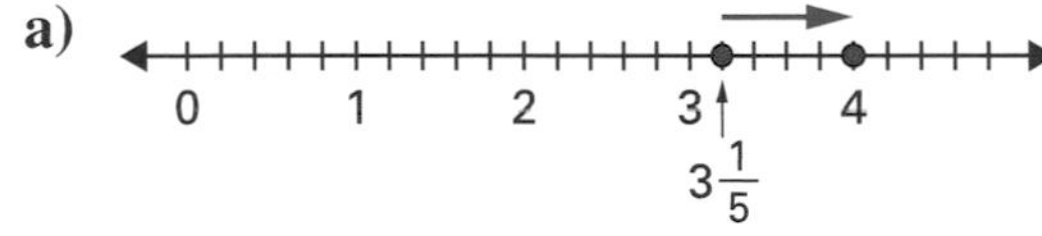

b)

10. Subtract using a model.

a) $5 - \frac{1}{3}$ **b)** $6 - 3\frac{3}{4}$ **c)** $6 - 2\frac{1}{5}$

11. Phil's class ordered 6 large pizzas. His class ate $4\frac{7}{8}$ of the pizzas. How much is left?

Multiplying a Whole Number by a Fraction

Multiply $4 \times \frac{5}{12}$ using grids and counters.

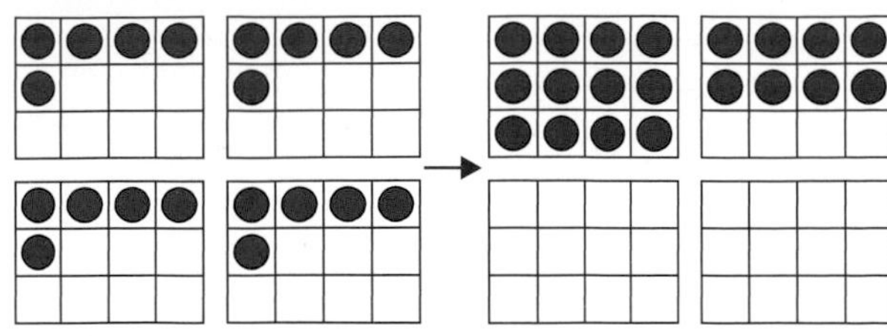

The denominator is 12, so use 3-by-4 rectangles. Show 4 sets of $\frac{5}{12}$. Move 7 counters to fill the empty squares in one rectangle. Move the remaining counters to fill as many squares as possible in another rectangle. The counters fill $1\frac{8}{12}$ squares. Therefore, $4 \times \frac{5}{12} = 1\frac{8}{12}$, or $1\frac{2}{3}$.

Multiply $5 \times \frac{1}{6}$ using fraction strips.

$5 \times \frac{1}{6}$ means 5 sets of $\frac{1}{6}$.

Put five $\frac{1}{6}$ strips together.

Together, they make $\frac{5}{6}$.

This shows that $5 \times \frac{1}{6} = \frac{5}{6}$.

Multiply $4 \times \frac{5}{2}$ using a number line.

$4 \times \frac{5}{2}$ is 4 sets of $\frac{5}{2}$. Use a number line marked in halves.
Draw 4 arrows. Each arrow shows $\frac{5}{2}$.
The arrows show that $4 \times \frac{5}{2} = \frac{20}{10}$, or 10.

12. Write the multiplication question, and calculate the answer.

a)
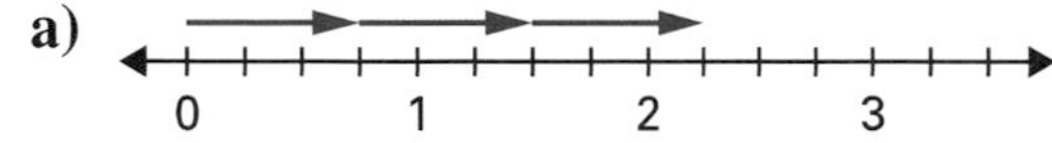

b)
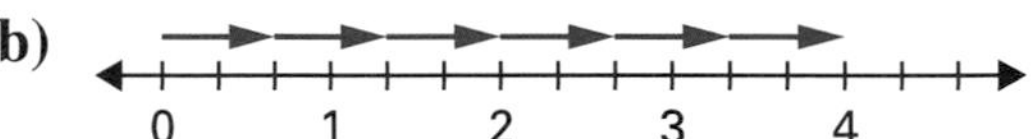

13. Multiply using a model.

a) $3 \times \frac{1}{2}$ **b)** $6 \times \frac{3}{4}$ **c)** $4 \times \frac{3}{8}$

14. Every school day, Akiko has a music class that lasts $\frac{3}{4}$ of an hour. There are 20 school days in a month. How many hours of music lessons does Akiko have each month?

Chapter 10: Angles and Triangles

Measuring and Constructing Angles

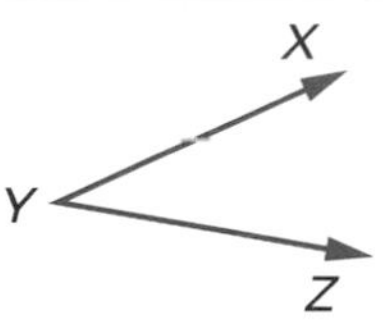

An angle is formed where two rays intersect at a point called the **vertex**. It is the amount of "turn," in degrees, that is needed to turn one ray onto the other. When naming an angle, the letter that represents the vertex is placed in the middle of the letter sequence, or it can be used on its own. For example, this angle can be called ∠*XYZ*, ∠*ZYX*, or ∠*Y*.

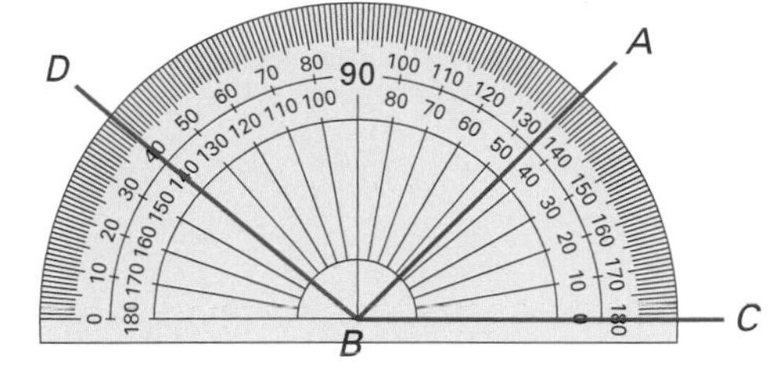

A protractor can be used to measure and construct angles. To measure an angle, place the 0° line of the protractor along one ray, with its centre over the vertex. Look at the scale on the edge to see how many degrees the angle is. For example, ∠*ABC* is 45° and ∠*DBC* is 140°.

To construct an angle, start by drawing one ray. Then place the 0° line of the protractor along the ray, with its centre at the start of the ray. On the scale of the protractor, locate the degree that you want the angle to be. Mark a dot on the paper at this degree. Then draw a line from the start of the first ray through this dot.

Angles of different measurements have different names.

Angle measurement	Name of angle
less than 90°	acute
90°	right
between 90° and 180°	obtuse
180°	straight
between 180° and 360°	reflex

1. Measure each angle using a protractor.

a)

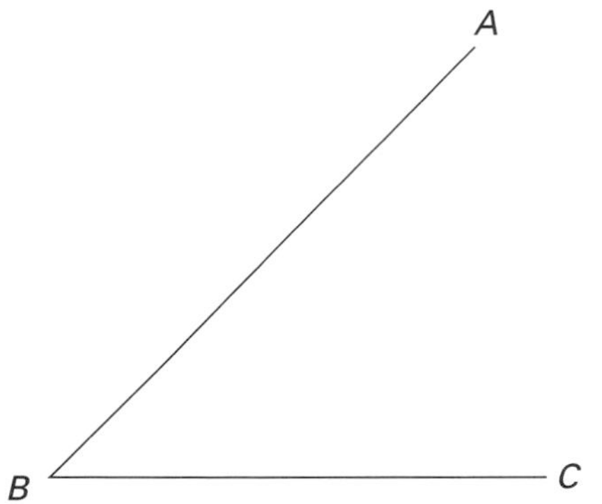

b)

2. Name each type of angle in question 1.

3. Use a protractor to construct each angle.

a) 30° **b)** 150° **c)** 85° **d)** 210°

Classifying Triangles and Quadrilaterals

Triangles can be named based on their angles.

Name of triangle	Description	Example
acute triangle	All angles are less than 90°.	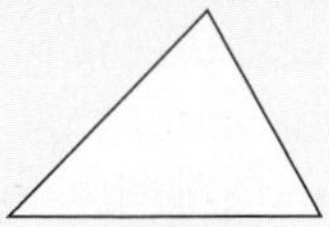
equilateral triangle	All angles are 60°.	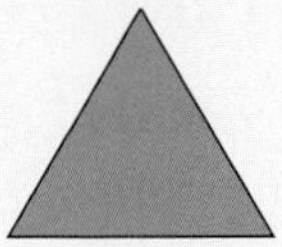
obtuse triangle	One angle is greater than 90°.	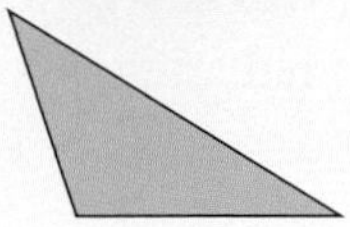
right triangle	One angle is 90°.	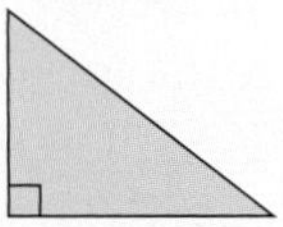

Triangles can also be named based on the lengths of their sides.

Name of triangle	Description	Example
equilateral triangle	All sides are equal lengths.	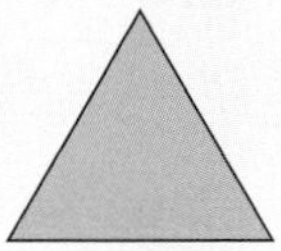
isosceles triangle	Two sides are equal lengths.	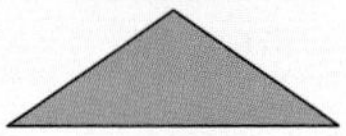
scalene triangle	No sides are equal.	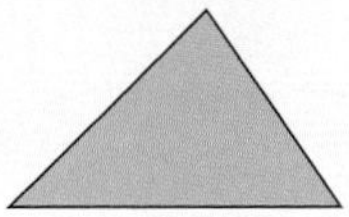

4. Name each triangle based on their angles and lengths of sides.

a)

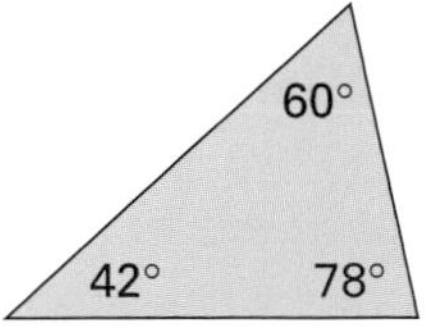

b)

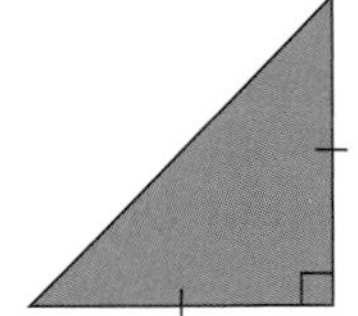

c)

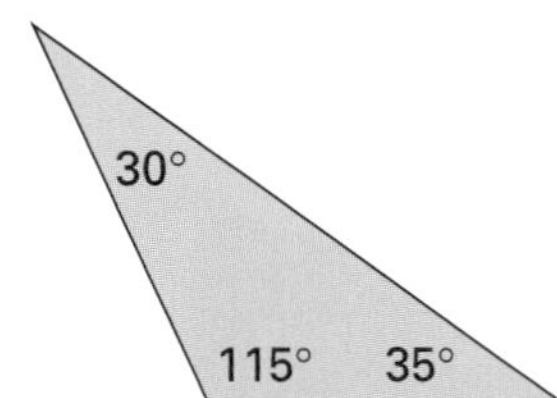

Quadrilaterals are named based on the characteristics of their angles and sides. The following flow chart will help you identify quadrilaterals.

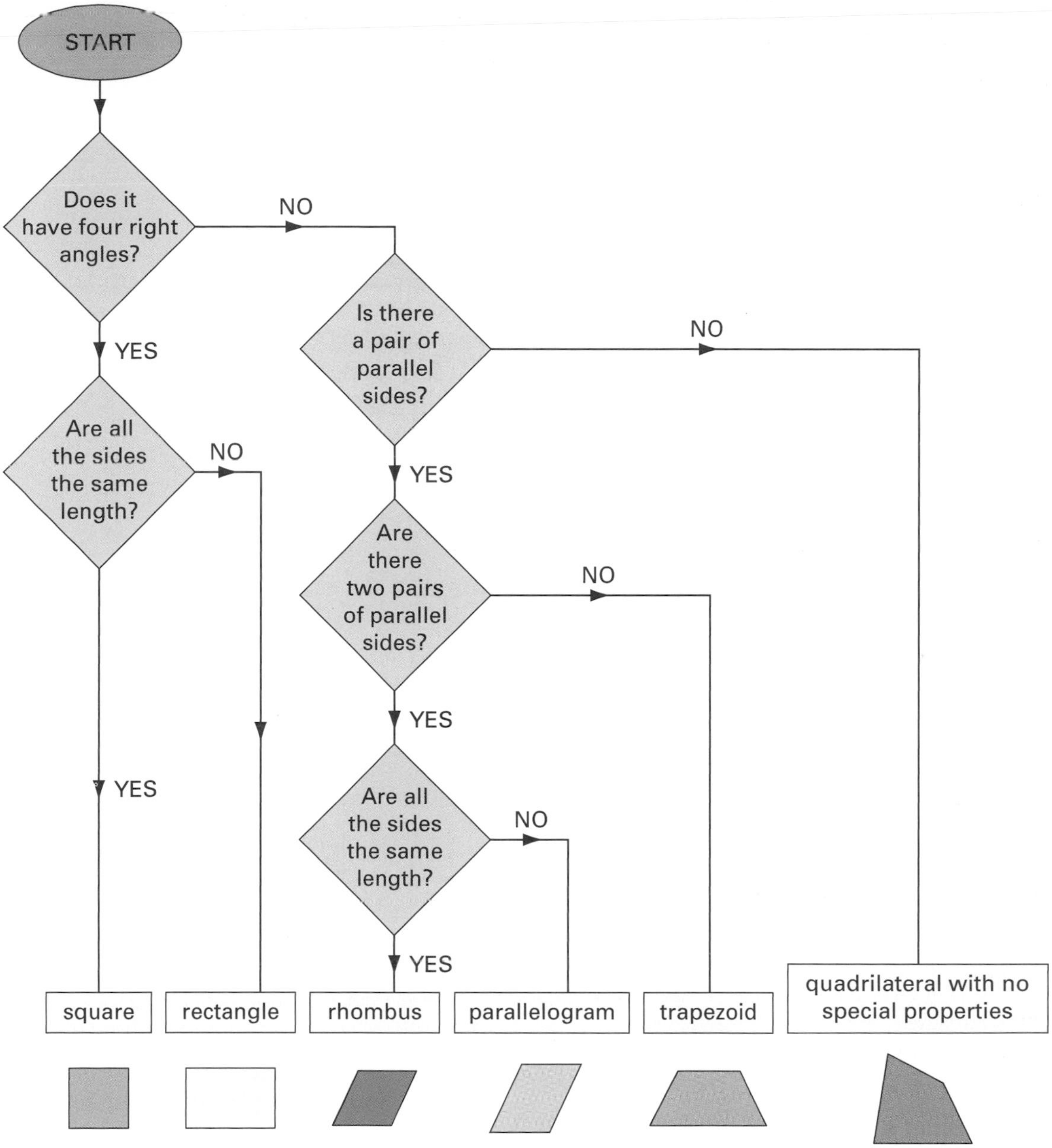

START

- Does it have four right angles?
  - YES → Are all the sides the same length?
    - YES → square
    - NO → rectangle
  - NO → Is there a pair of parallel sides?
    - NO → quadrilateral with no special properties
    - YES → Are there two pairs of parallel sides?
      - NO → trapezoid
      - YES → Are all the sides the same length?
        - YES → rhombus
        - NO → parallelogram

square	rectangle	rhombus	parallelogram	trapezoid	quadrilateral with no special properties

5. Name each quadrilateral.

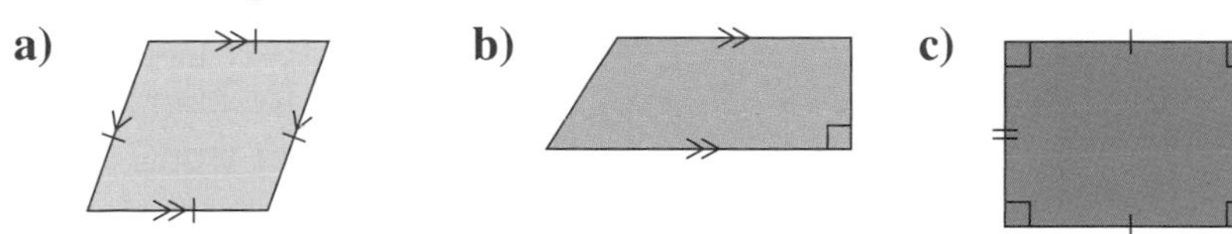

Chapter 11: Geometry and Measurement Relationships

Surface Area

The surface area of a 3-D object is the total area of all the faces of the object, including the base.

You can use a net to determine the surface area of an object. A **net** is a 2-D pattern that can be folded to create a 3-D shape.

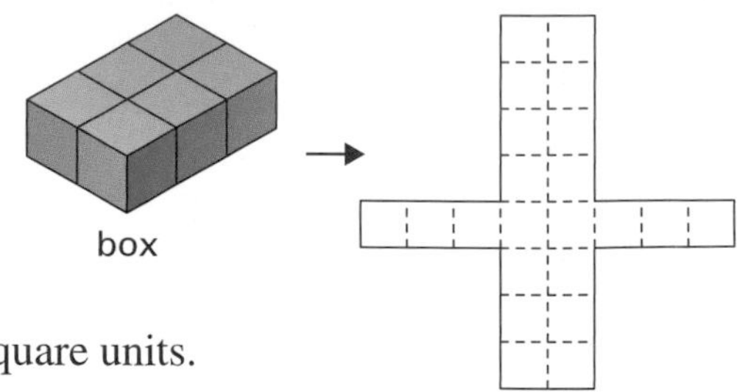

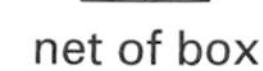

For example, the surface area of the box at the right is 22 square units.

To determine the surface area of a prism, calculate the areas of the top and bottom, and the areas of each rectangular side face. Then add the areas.

1. Use this net to determine the surface area of the folded-up prism.

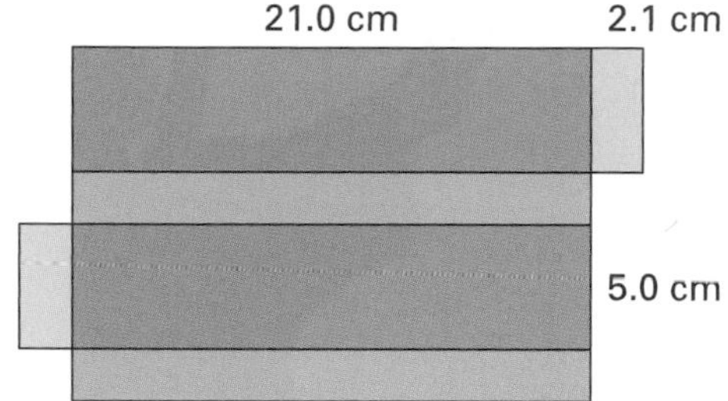

2. Sketch a net of each prism. Then calculate the surface area of the prism.

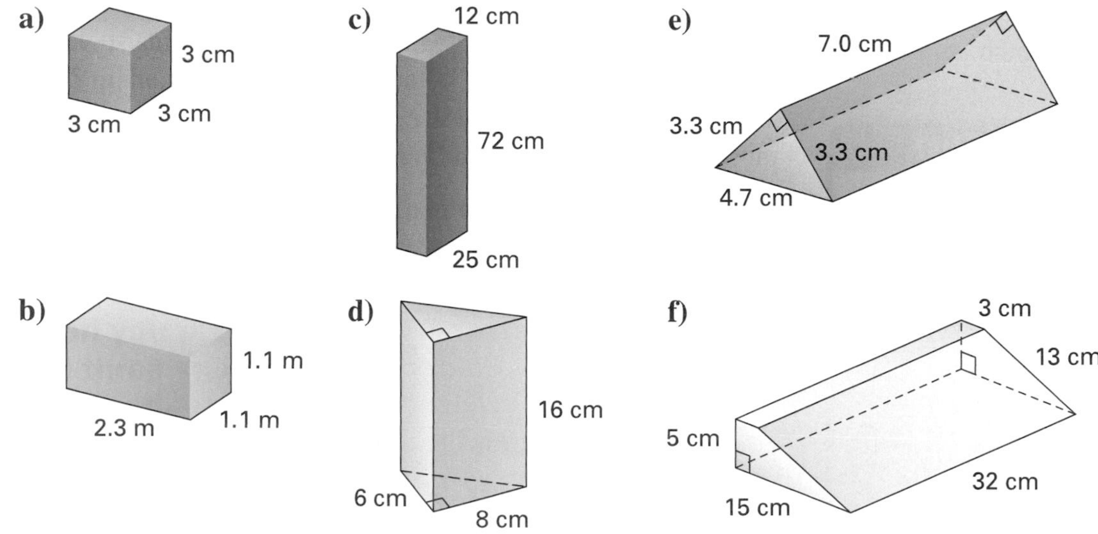

Volume

The volume of a 3-D object is the total amount of space that is occupied by the object.

For example, the volume of this box is 6 cubes.

To determine the volume of a prism, multiply the area of the base by the height of the prism.
Volume = (area of base) × (height)

3. Calculate the volume of each prism. Note that A represents the area of the base of the prism.

a)

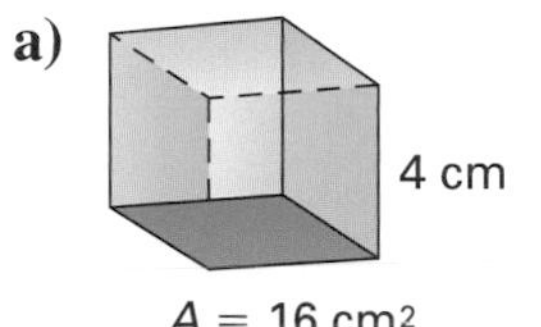

c)

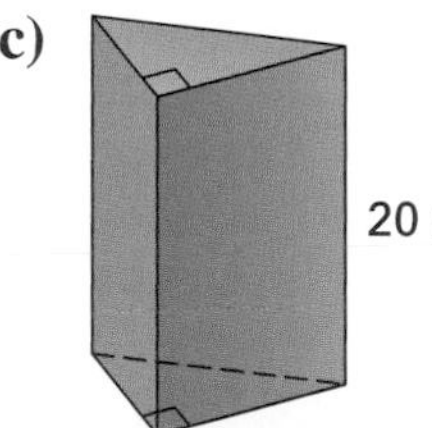

e)

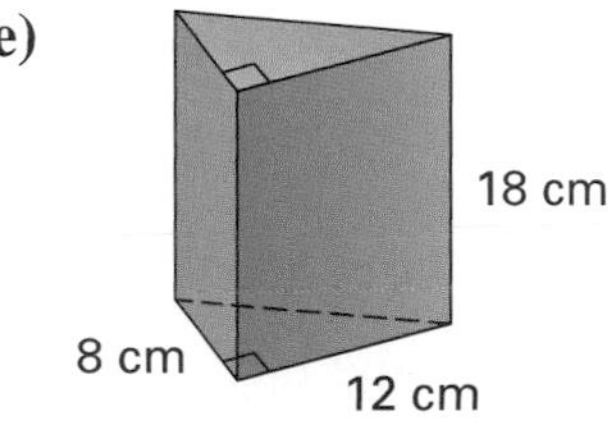

b)

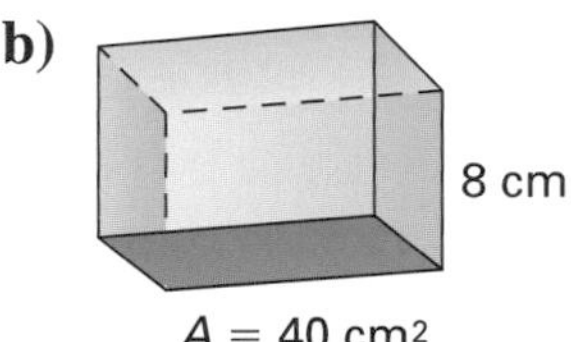

d)

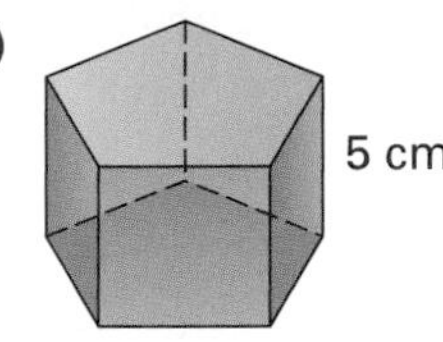

f)

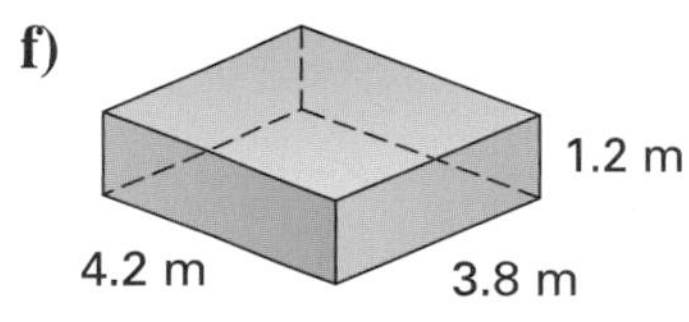

4. Use each net to determine the volume of the folded-up prism.

a)

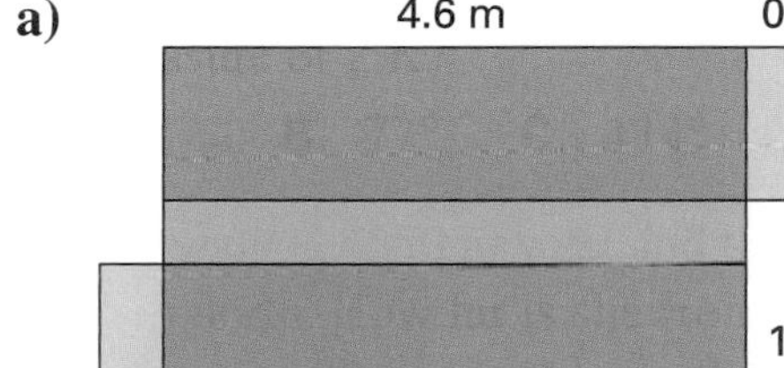

b)

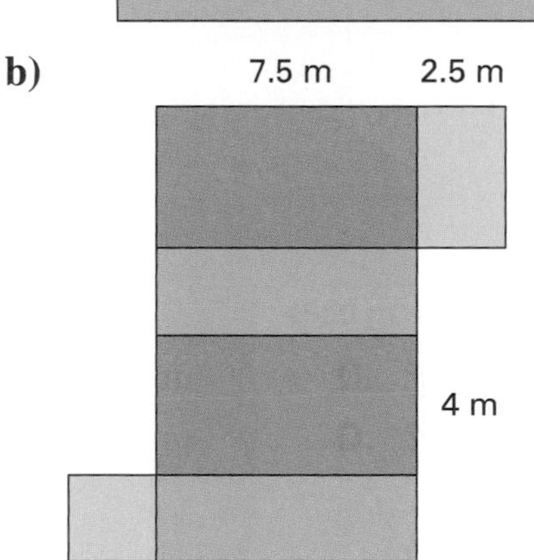

Chapter 12: Probability

Probability

Probability is a number between 0 and 1 that tells the likelihood of something happening. Sometimes you can conduct an experiment, such as tossing a coin or spinning a spinner, to determine probability.

A **possible outcome** is a single result that can occur in a probability experiment. For example, getting Heads when tossing a coin is a possible outcome.

The **favourable outcome** is the desired result in a probability experiment. For example, if you spin a coloured spinner to see how often the red section comes up, then red is the favourable outcome.

An **event** is a set of one or more outcomes for a probability experiment. For example, if you roll a cube with the numbers 1 to 6, the event of rolling an even number has the outcomes 2, 4, or 6.

The **experimental probability** of an event is the measure of the likelihood of the event, based on data from an experiment. It is calculated using this ratio:

$$\frac{\text{number of trials in which event occurred}}{\text{total number of trials in the experiment}}$$

The **theoretical probability** of an event is the measure of the likelihood of the event, calculated using this ratio:

$$\frac{\text{number of favourable outcomes for the event}}{\text{total number of possible outcomes}}$$

The probability of an event can be expressed as a fraction, a decimal, or a percent. The probability of an event is often written as $P(\text{X})$, where X is a description of the event. For example, if $P(\text{H})$ represents the probability of tossing a coin and getting Heads, then $P(\text{H}) = \frac{1}{2}$ or 0.5 or 50%.

1. Nesrine conducted an experiment in which she tossed two quarters together 50 times. The following chart shows her results.

Event	Number of occurrences
both coins Heads	10
one coin Heads and the other Tails	25
both coins Tails	15

a) Determine Nesrine's experimental probability for each event.

b) Determine the theoretical probability of each event.

c) Which experimental probability is the same as the theoretical probability?

2. Determine the theoretical probability of each event for the following situations. Write the probability as a fraction, a decimal, and a percent.

a) Alok spins a spinner numbered from 1 to 10. The 10 sections of the spinner are equal.
   i) P(spinning 5)
   ii) P(spinning a multiple of 3)
   iii) P(spinning a prime number)
   iv) P(spinning 11)

b) Ellen rolls a 20-sided die numbered from 1 to 20.
   i) P(rolling a 15)
   ii) P(rolling an even number)
   iii) P(rolling a number divisible by 5)

c) Paul selects one coin.

   i) P(dime)
   ii) P(copper coloured coin)
   iii) P(silver coloured coin)

Tree Diagrams

A **tree diagram** is a way to record and count all the possible combinations of events. For example, the tree diagram at the right shows all the possible outcomes of a three-child family.

This tree diagram shows that there are eight possible outcomes. You can use it to determine probabilities.

For example,
$P(\text{all 3 children are boys}) = \frac{1}{8}$

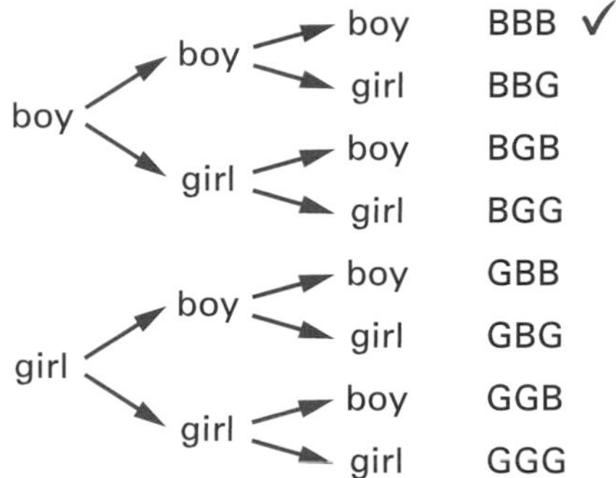

3. Use the tree diagram at the right to determine each probability.

a) P(3 girls)
b) P(1 boy and 2 girls)
c) P(at least 1 girl)
d) P(all boys or all girls)

4. Indira spins the spinner shown and rolls a die.

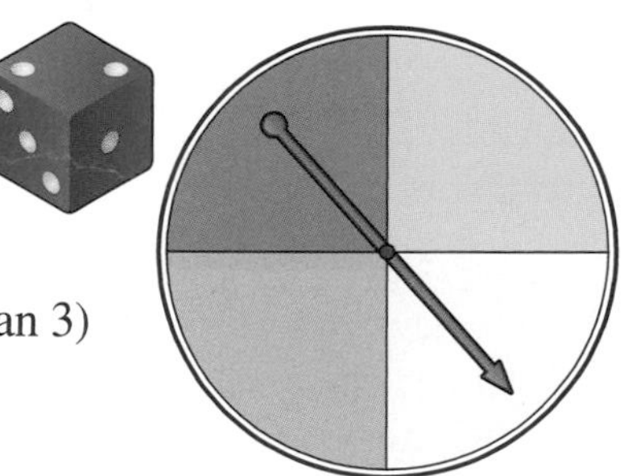

a) Create the tree diagram that shows all the possible outcomes for one spin and one roll.
b) Determine each probability below.
   i) P(the spinner is red and the die is 5)
   ii) P(the spinner is green and the die is even)
   iii) P(the spinner is orange or yellow and the die is greater than 3)
   iv) P(the spinner is not red and the die is a multiple of 2)
c) Explain why P(the spinner is yellow and the die is 7) = 0.

5. Bill rolls a pair of dice and calculates the sum of the two numbers.

a) List all the possible sums.
b) Draw a tree diagram that shows all the possible outcomes.
c) Determine the probability that Bill will toss a sum of 7.

Glossary

Instructional Words

C

calculate: Figure out the number that answers a question; compute

clarify: Make a statement easier to understand; provide an example

classify: Put things into groups according to a rule and label the groups; organize into categories

compare: Look at two or more objects or numbers and identify how they are the same and how they are different (e.g., Compare the numbers 6.5 and 5.6. Compare the size of the students' feet. Compare two shapes.)

conclude: Judge or decide after reflection or after considering data

construct: Make or build a model; draw an accurate geometric shape (e.g., Use a ruler and a protractor to construct an angle.)

create: Make your own example

D

describe: Tell, draw, or write about what something is or what something looks like; tell about a process in a step-by-step way

determine: Decide with certainty as a result of calculation, experiment, or exploration

draw: 1. Show something in picture form (e.g., Draw a diagram.)
2. Pull or select an object (e.g., Draw a card from the deck. Draw a tile from the bag.)

E

estimate: Use your knowledge to make a sensible decision about an amount; make a reasonable guess (e.g., Estimate how long it takes to cycle from your home to school. Estimate how many leaves are on a tree. What is your estimate of 3210 + 789?)

evaluate: 1. Determine if something makes sense; judge
2. Calculate the value as a number

explain: Tell what you did; show your mathematical thinking at every stage; show how you know

explore: Investigate a problem by questioning, brainstorming, and trying new ideas

extend: 1. In patterning, continue the pattern
2. In problem solving, create a new problem that takes the idea of the original problem farther

J

justify: Give convincing reasons for a prediction, an estimate, or a solution; tell why you think your answer is correct

M

measure: Use a tool to describe an object or determine an amount (e.g., Use a ruler to measure the height or distance around something. Use a protractor to measure an angle. Use balance scales to measure mass. Use a measuring cup to measure capacity. Use a stopwatch to measure the time in seconds or minutes.)

model: Show or demonstrate an idea using objects and/or pictures (e.g., Model addition of integers using red and blue counters.)

P

predict: Use what you know to work out what is going to happen (e.g., Predict the next number in the pattern 1, 2, 4, 7, ….)

R

reason: Develop ideas and relate them to the purpose of the task and to each other; analyze relevant information to show understanding

NEL

relate: Describe how two or more objects, drawings, ideas, or numbers are similar

represent: Show information or an idea in a different way that makes it easier to understand (e.g., Draw a graph. Make a model.)

S

show (your work): Record all calculations, drawings, numbers, words, or symbols that make up the solution

sketch: Make a rough drawing (e.g., Sketch a picture of the field with dimensions.)

solve: Develop and carry out a process for finding a solution to a problem

sort: Separate a set of objects, drawings, ideas, or numbers according to an attribute (e.g., Sort 2-D shapes by the number of sides.)

V

validate: Check an idea by showing that it works

verify: Work out an answer or solution again, usually in another way; show evidence of

visualize: Form a picture in your head of what something is like; imagine

Mathematical Words

A

adjacent angles: Angles that share a common **vertex** and a common arm

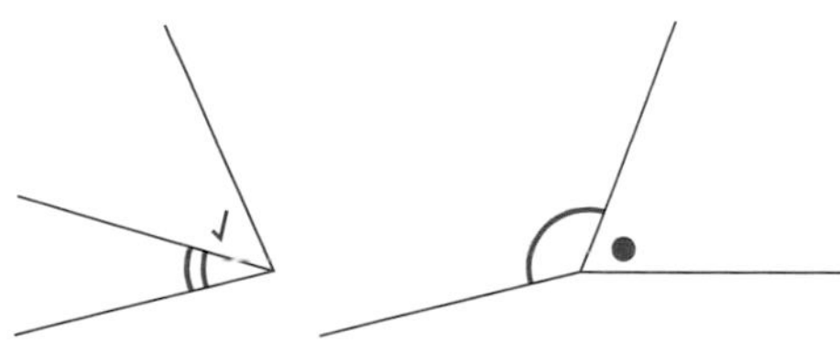

algebraic equation: An **equation** that includes **algebraic expressions** (e.g., $3x + 5 = 8$)

algebraic expression: A combination of one or more **variables**; it may include numbers and operation signs (e.g., $8x + 2y^2 - 9$)

arc: A section of the **circumference** of a **circle** that lies between two ends of a **chord** (each chord creates two arcs); the length of this section

area: The number of square units needed to cover a surface

B

base: 1. The face that determines the name and the number of edges of a **prism** or **pyramid**
2. In a 2-D shape, the line segment that is **perpendicular** to the height
3. The number that is used as a factor in a **power** (e.g., In the power 5^3, 5 is the base.)

BEDMAS: A made-up word used to recall the **order of operations**, standing for **B**rackets, **E**xponents, **D**ivision, **M**ultiplication, **A**ddition, **S**ubtraction

C

capacity: The amount that a container will hold. Common units are millilitres or litres. Note that 1 mL is equivalent to 1 cm^3.

Cartesian coordinate system: A method for describing a location on a plane by identifying first the distance right or left from a vertical number line (the y-axis) and then the distance up or down from a horizontal number line (the x-axis); the axes intersect at the point (0, 0), which is called the origin; the location of a point is represented by an ordered pair of coordinates, (x, y)

census: A survey of all the people in a population (e.g., A census would involve asking everyone who is going to the Fun Fair what flavour of ice cream they prefer.)

centre of rotation: A fixed point around which other points in a shape rotate in a clockwise (cw) or counterclockwise (ccw) direction; the centre of rotation may be inside or outside the shape

chord: A line segment that joins any two points on the **circumference** of a **circle**; the length of this line segment

circle: The set of all the points in a plane that are the same distance, called the **radius** (r) from a fixed point called the centre. The formula for the area of a circle is $A = \pi r^2$.

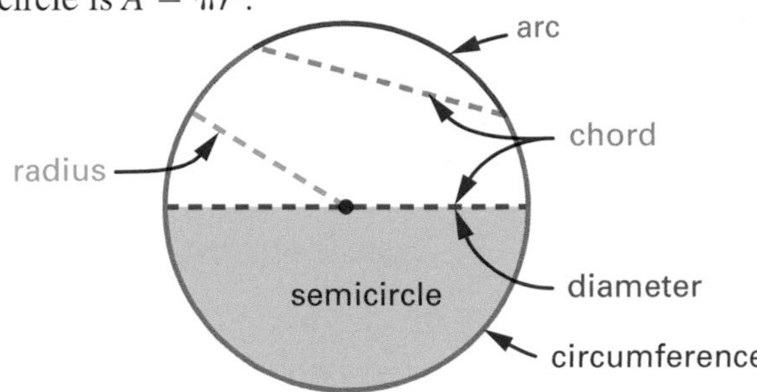

circumference: The boundary of a **circle**; the length of this boundary. The formula to calculate the length is $C = 2\pi r$, where r is the **radius**, or $C = \pi d$, where d is the **diameter**.

common denominator: A common multiple of the denominators of two or more fractions (e.g., 12 is a common denominator of $\frac{1}{2}$ and $\frac{1}{3}$.)

common factor: A number that divides into two or more other numbers with no remainder

common multiple: A number that is a **multiple** of two or more given numbers (e.g., 12, 24, and 36 are common multiples 4 and 6.)

complementary angles: Two angles whose sum is 90°

complementary events: Two events that have no outcome(s) in common but account for all possible outcomes of an experiment. The sum of the probabilities of complementary events is 1; for example, tossing Heads and tossing Tails are complementary events

composite number: A number with more than two **factors** (e.g., 12 is a composite number with the factors 1, 2, 3, 4, 6, and 12.) (Compare to **prime number**.)

congruent: Identical in size and shape

continued fractions: **Fractions** like this one

$$1 + \cfrac{1}{1 + \cfrac{1}{1 + \cfrac{1}{1 + 1 \ldots}}}$$

corresponding angles: Matching angles that are formed by a **transversal** and two **parallel** lines

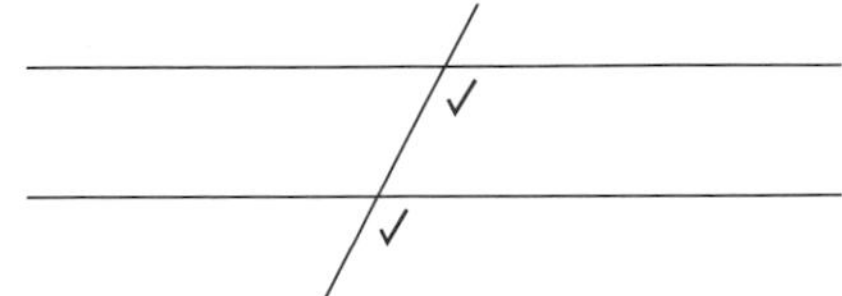

cylinder: A three-dimensional figure with two congruent, parallel, circular faces and one curved surface

D

data: Information gathered in a survey, in an experiment, or by observing (e.g., Data can be in words like a list of students' names, in numbers like quiz marks, or in pictures like drawings of favourite pets.) Note that the word *data* is plural, not singular.

denominator: The number in a **fraction** that represents the number of parts in the whole set, or the number of parts the whole set has been divided into (Also see **numerator**.) (e.g., In $\frac{4}{5}$, the fractional unit is fifths.)

$\frac{4}{5}$ ⟵ denominator

diameter: A line segment that joins two points on a **circle** and passes through the centre; the length of this line segment

divisibility rule: A way to determine whether one number is a **factor** of another number without actually dividing

E

equation: A mathematical statement in which the value on the left side of the equal sign is the same as the value on the right side of the equal sign (e.g., The equation $5n + 4 = 39$ means that 4 more than the product of 5 and a number equals 39.)

equidistant: The same distance (e.g., All points on a circle are equidistant from the centre.)

equivalent fractions: Fractions that represent the same part of a whole or set (e.g., $\frac{2}{4}$ is equivalent to $\frac{1}{2}$; $\frac{2}{4} = \frac{1}{2}$)

event: A set of one or more outcomes for a probability experiment (e.g., If you roll a cube with the numbers 1 to 6, the event of rolling an even number has the outcomes 2, 4, or 6.)

expanded form: A way of writing a number that shows the value of each digit as a **power** of 10 (e.g., 1209 in expanded form is $1 \times 10^3 + 2 \times 10^2 + 9 \times 1$.)

experimental probability: The observed probability of an event based on **data** from an experiment; calculated using the expression

$$\frac{\text{number of trials in which desired event was observed}}{\text{total number of trials in experiment}}$$

exponent: The number that tells how many equal **factors** are in a **power**

F

factor: One of the numbers you multiply in a multiplication operation

$$2 \times 6 = 12$$

(2 and 6 are each labelled "factor")

favourable outcome: A desired result when calculating a probability (e.g., The result a spinner will stop on green, instead of red.)

Fibonacci sequence: A special sequence of numbers in which each number is the sum of the two numbers before it: 1, 1, 2, 3, 5, 8, 13, …

G

golden ratio: A famous ratio equal to this **continued fraction**

$$1 + \cfrac{1}{1 + \cfrac{1}{1 + \cfrac{1}{1 + 1 \ldots}}}$$

greatest common factor (GCF): The greatest **whole number** that divides into two or more other whole numbers with no remainder (e.g., 4 is the greatest common **factor** of 8 and 12.)

H

histogram: A graph with bars that show frequencies of data organized into **intervals**; the intervals line up side by side, without gaps, on the number line

hypotenuse: The longest side of a right triangle; the side that is opposite the right angle

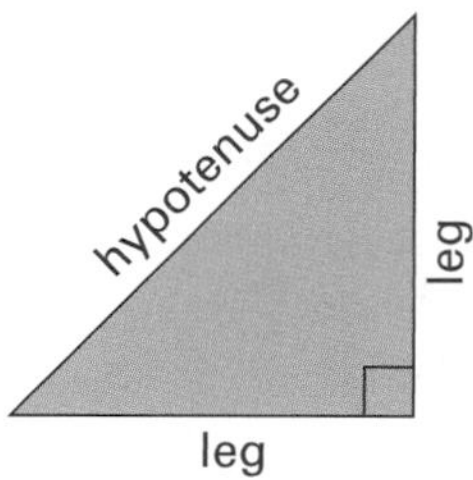

I

image: A new shape that is created when a shape is moved by a **transformation**

improper fraction: A fraction in which the **numerator** is greater than the **denominator** $\left(\text{e.g., } \frac{5}{4}\right)$

integers: All positive and negative **whole numbers**, including zero. … −3, −2, −1, 0, 1, 2, 3, …

interior angle: One of the angles inside a polygon (e.g., A square has four interior angles.)

interval: The space between two values (e.g., 0−10 represents the interval from 0 to 10 inclusive.)

irrational number: A number that cannot be represented as a terminating or repeating decimal (e.g., π, $\sqrt{5}$)

L

least common multiple (LCM): The least **whole number** that has two or more given numbers as factors (e.g., 12 is the least common multiple of 4 and 6.)

M

mean: The average; the sum of a set of numbers divided by the number of numbers in the set

median: The middle value in a set of ordered data (e.g., When there is an odd number of numbers, the median is the middle number. When there is an even number of numbers, the median is the mean of the two middle numbers.)

metre (m): A unit of measurement for length (e.g., 1 m is about the distance from a doorknob to the floor.); 1000 mm = 1 m; 100 cm = 1 m; 1000 m = 1 km

midpoint: The point on a line segment that divides the line segment into two equal parts

mixed number: A number made up of a **whole number** and a **fraction** (e.g., $5\frac{1}{7}$)

mode: The number that occurs most often in a set of data; there can be more than one mode or there might be no mode

multiple: The product of a **whole number** and any other whole number (e.g., When you multiply 10 by the whole numbers 0 to 4, you get the multiples 0, 10, 20, 30, and 40.)

N

net: A 2-D pattern you can fold to create a 3-D shape

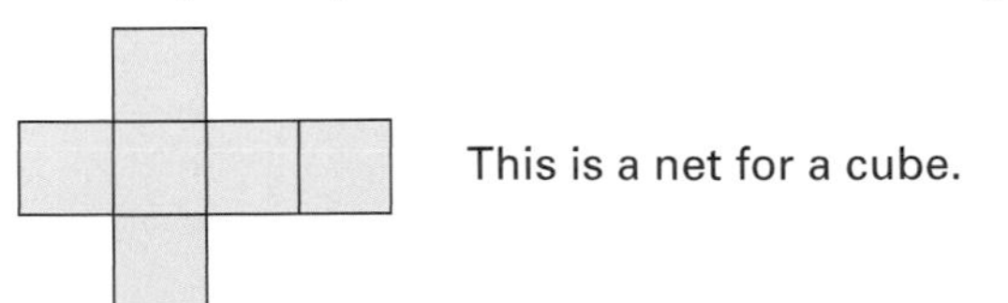

numerator: The number in a **fraction** that shows the number of parts of a given size the fraction represents. (Also see **denominator**.)

$\frac{1}{7}$ ← numerator

O

opposite angles: Non-adjacent angles that are formed by two intersecting lines

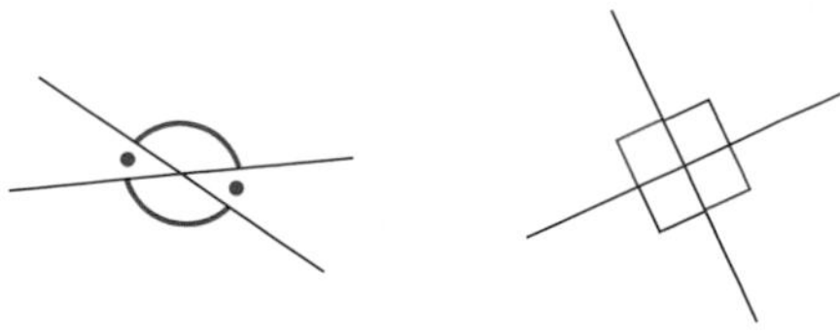

opposite integers: Two **integers** that are the same distance away from zero (e.g., +6 and −6 are opposite integers.)

order of operations: Rules describing what sequence to use when evaluating an expression:
1. Evaluate within brackets.
2. Calculate exponents and square roots.
3. Multiply or divide from left to right.
4. Add or subtract from left to right.

P

parallel: Always the same distance apart (e.g., Railway tracks are parallel to each other.)

percent: A special **ratio** that compares a number to 100 using the symbol %

perfect number: A number is perfect if all of its **factors**, other than the number itself, add up to the number (e.g., The factors of 6 are 1, 2, 3, and 6; since 6 = 1 + 2 + 3, 6 is a perfect number.)

perimeter: The distance around a shape

perpendicular: At a right angle (e.g., The base of a triangle is perpendicular to the height of the triangle.)

perpendicular bisector: A line that intersects a line segment to form two 90° angles and divides this line segment into two equal lengths

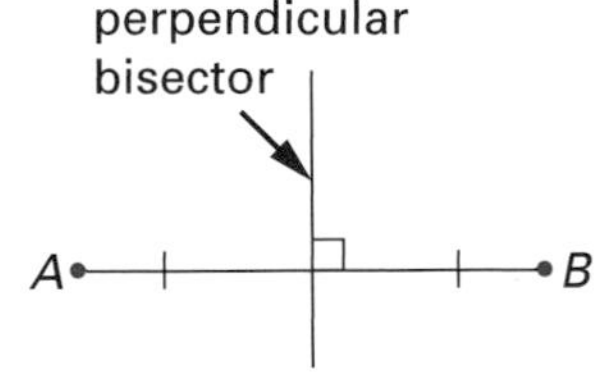

π (pi): The number of times the **diameter** of a circle divides the **circumference**; its value is 3.141 592 654 … or about 3.14, rounded to two decimal places

polygon: A closed 2-D shape with straight sides, such as a triangle, square, or pentagon

polyhedron: A 3-D shape that has **polygons** as its faces

population: The total number of individuals or objects that fit a particular description

possible outcome: A single result that can occur in a probability experiment (e.g., Getting Heads when tossing a coin is a possible outcome.)

power: A numerical expression that shows repeated multiplication (e.g., The power 5^3 is a shorter way of writing $5 \times 5 \times 5$.); a power has a **base** and an **exponent**: the exponent tells the number of equal factors there are in a power

3 is the exponent of the power.

$5^3 = 125$

5 is the base of the power.

prime factorization: The representation of a **composite number** as the product of its prime **factors** (e.g., The prime factorization of 24 is $2 \times 2 \times 2 \times 3$, or $2^3 \times 3$.); usually, the **prime numbers** are written in order from least to greatest

prime number: A number with only two factors, 1 and itself (e.g., 17 is a prime number since its only factors are 1 and 17.) (Compare to **composite number**.)

prism: A 3-D shape with opposite **congruent bases**; the other faces are parallelograms

probability: A number from 0 to 1 that shows how likely it is that an event will happen

proper fraction: A fraction in which the **denominator** is greater than the **numerator** $\left(\text{e.g., } \frac{1}{7}, \frac{4}{5}, \frac{29}{40}\right)$

proportion: A number sentence that shows two equivalent **ratios** (e.g., 1 : 2 : 3 = 3 : 6 : 9)

pyramid: A 3-D shape with a polygon for a base; the other faces are triangles that meet at a single **vertex**

Pythagorean theorem: The relationship between the lengths of the legs and **hypotenuse** of a right angle triangle; the theorem states that the sum of the areas of the squares on the legs of a right triangle is equal to the area of the square on the hypotenuse; an equation for the Pythagorean theorem is $a^2 + b^2 = c^2$, where a and b represent the lengths of the legs of a right triangle and c represents the length of the hypotenuse

Q

quadrant: One of the four areas into which the x-axis and y-axis divide a **Cartesian coordinate system**

R

radius (pl. radii): A line segment that goes from the centre of a **circle** to its **circumference**; the length of this line segment

rate: A comparison of two quantities measured in different units; unlike **ratios**, rates include units

ratio: A comparison of two or more quantities with the same units (e.g., If the heights of three students are 164 cm, 175 cm, and 180 cm, the ratio of their heights can be written as 164 : 175 : 180.)

rational number: A number that can be expressed as a fraction in which the denominator is not 0

reciprocal: The fraction that results from switching the **numerator** and **denominator** $\left(\text{e.g., } \frac{4}{5} \text{ is the reciprocal of } \frac{5}{4}.\right)$

reflection: A transformation in which a 2-D shape is flipped; each point in the shape flips to the opposite side of the line of reflection, but stays the same distance from the line

regular polygon: A polygon with all sides equal and all angles equal

repeating decimal: A **decimal** in which a block of one or more digits eventually repeats in a pattern (e.g., $\frac{25}{99} = 0.252\,525\,252\ldots$; $\frac{1}{7} = 0.142\,857\,142\,857\ldots$.)

representative sample: A **sample** from a **population** such that the properties of the sample reasonably reflect the properties of the population

rotation: A **transformation** in which each point in a shape moves about a fixed point through the same angle

rule for order of operations: See **order of operations**

S

sample: A part of a **population** that is used to make predictions about the whole population

scale factor: A number that you can multiply or divide each term in a **ratio** by to get the equivalent terms in another ratio; it can be a **whole number** or a **decimal**. The scale factor here is 5.

$$\frac{2}{3} = \frac{10}{15} \text{ or } \frac{2 \times 5}{3 \times 5} = \frac{10}{15}$$

(× 5 applied to numerator and denominator)

scatter plot: A graph that attempts to show a relationship between two variables by means of points plotted on a coordinate grid

scientific notation: A way of writing a number as a **decimal** between 1 and 10, multiplied by a power of 10 (e.g., 70 120 is written as 7.012×10^4.)

number between 1 and 10

7.012×10^4

power of 10

semicircle: One half of a **circle**

sequence: A list of things that are in a logical order or follow a predictable pattern or example (e.g., The sequence 1, 3, 5, 7, 9, … shows the odd numbers in order.)

similar: Identical in shape, but not necessarily the same size (e.g., These rectangles are similar.)

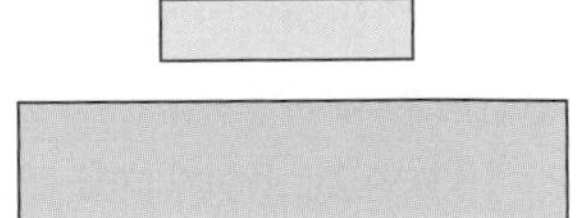

These rectangles are similar.

simulation: An experiment that models an actual **event** (e.g., repeatedly flipping a coin to find the probability that all four children in a family are girls)

solution to an equation: The value of a **variable** that makes the equation true (e.g., In the equation $5n + 4 = 39$, the value of n is 7 because $5(7) + 4 = 39$.)

speed: The **rate** at which a moving object changes position with time (e.g., A sprinter who runs 100 m in 10 s has an average speed of 100 m/10 s = 10 m/s.)

square number: An **integer** that is a perfect square of another integer (e.g., 1 is the square of 1, 4 is the square of 2, 9 is the square of 3, and so on.)

square root: One of two equal **factors** of a number (e.g., The square root of 100 is represented as $\sqrt{100}$ and is equal to 10 because 10×10 or $10^2 = 100$.)

stem-and-leaf plot: An organization of numerical data into categories based on place values; the most significant digits are the stems and the least significant digits are the leaves (e.g., The circled leaf in this stem-and-leaf plot represents the number 258.)

Stem	Leaves
24	1 5 8
25	2 2 3 4 7 ⑧ 9
26	0 3
27	
28	8

straight angle: An angle that measures 180°

supplementary angles: Two angles whose sum is 180°

T

table of values: An orderly arrangement of facts set out for easy reference; for example, an arrangement of numerical values in vertical and horizontal columns

term: Each number or item in a **sequence** (e.g., In the sequence 1, 3, 5, 7, …, the third term is 5.)

terminating decimal: A **decimal** that is complete after a certain number of digits, with no repetition (e.g., $\frac{29}{40} = 0.725$)

tessellation: An arrangement of plane figures that are the same shape and size over a plane (in all directions), without gaps or overlapping

theoretical probability: How likely an **event** is to occur, expressed as a number from 0 (will never happen) to 1 (certain to happen); calculated using the expression: $\frac{\text{number of favourable outcomes}}{\text{total number of possible outcomes}}$ $\left(\text{e.g., } P(\text{rolling a 4 on a six-sided die}) = \frac{1}{6}.\right)$

transformation: The result of moving a shape according to a rule; transformations include **translations**, **rotations**, and **reflections**

translation: A **transformation** that is the result of a slide; the slide must be along straight lines: left or right, up or down, or on a slant

translation vector: An ordered pair of **integers** used to represent the horizontal and vertical moves that describe a translation (e.g., [−2, 5] represents the translation "2 units left and 5 units up.")

transversal: A straight line that intersects two or more lines

tree diagram: A way to record and count all combinations of **events** (e.g., This tree diagram shows all the three-digit numbers that can be made from the digits 1, 2, and 3, if 1 must be the first digit and each digit is used only once.)

1 → 2 → 3 (123)
1 → 3 → 2 (132)

U

unit rate: A **rate** in which the second term is 1 (e.g., 60 km/h is a unit rate because it compares the distance travelled (60 km) to 1 h of time.)

V

variable: A letter or symbol, such as *a*, *b*, *x*, or *n*, that represents a number (e.g., In the formula for the area of a rectangle, the variables *A*, *l*, and *w* represent the area, length, and width of the rectangle.)

vertex (pl. vertices): The point at the corner of an angle or shape (e.g., A cube has eight vertices. A triangle has three vertices. An angle has one vertex.)

volume: The amount of space occupied by an object

W

whole numbers: The counting numbers that begin at 0 and continue forever; 0, 1, 2, 3, …

Z

zero principle: Two **opposite integers**, when added, give a sum of zero (e.g., $(-1) + (+1) = 0$)

Answers

Slight variations in answers may occur due to rounding and/or the value of π used in calculations.

Chapter 1, p. 1

Getting Started, p. 3

1. a) 1, 2, 3, 6 **b)** e.g., 36, 72, 108

2. a) no **b)** 2000 **c)** 2400

3. a) composite; factors: 1, 2, 3, 4, 6, 8, 12, 16, 24, 48
b) prime
c) composite; factors: 1, 2, 3, 4, 6, 9, 12, 18, 36
d) composite; factors: 1, 2, 3, 4, 5, 6, 8, 10, 12, 15, 20, 24, 30, 40, 60, 120

4. a) 4230 can be divided by 2 because it ends in an even number; it can be divided by 5 and 10 because the last digit is 0, which means the number is a multiple of 10.
b) yes **c)** divisible by 2 and 3

5. a) 4096 balloons
b) 8^4, base is 8, exponent is 4

6. a) $2^5 = 32$ **b)** $10^3 = 1000$

7. 8^2, 4^3, or 2^6

8.

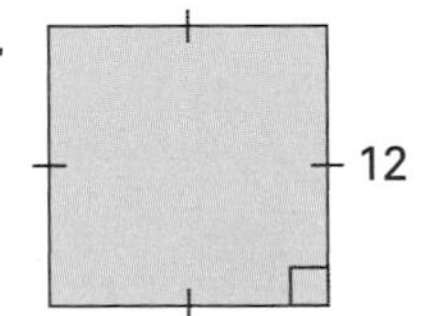

length of side $= \sqrt{144}$
$= 12$

area = 144 m²

9. a) 1 **b)** 5 **c)** 9 **d)** 8 **e)** 10 **f)** 6

10. a) 18 cm **b)** 2.8 m **c)** 730 g

11. a) $\neq$ **b)** $=$

1.1 Identifying Prime and Composite Numbers, pp. 6–7

3. 71, 73, 79

4. a) 163
b) e.g., I tried the prime factors of 2, 3, 5, 7, 11 and none were factors. I didn't need to try numbers 13 or greater because $13 \times 13 > 163$. Thus, the number is prime.

5. a) prime
b) composite: 1, 5, 25
c) prime
d) composite: 1, 2, 3, 4, 6, 8, 12, 16, 24, 48
e) prime
f) composite: 1, 3, 9, 11, 33, 99
g) composite: 1, 7, 23, 161
h) composite: 1, 3, 9, 19, 57, 171

10. a)

1	(2)	(3)	4	(5)	6
(7)	8	9	10	(11)	12
(13)	14	15	16	(17)	18
(19)	20	21	22	(23)	24
25	26	27	28	(29)	30
(31)	32	33	34	35	36
(37)	38	39	40	(41)	42
(43)	44	45	46	(47)	48
49	50	51	52	(53)	54
55	56	57	58	(59)	60

b) For example, they are one more or one less than a multiple of 6.

14. 30 students

15. There are no square prime numbers because square numbers have at least three factors: 1, the square root, and the number itself.

17. 3

18. e.g., Substituting 41 gives a value of 41^2 or 41×41, which has three factors and is not a prime number.

19. a) 31 marbles
b) e.g., 61, 91, 121 marbles

20. 420

21. a) The sum of the factors, other than the number itself, is 1, which is not a prime number.
b) $1 + 2 + 4 + 8 + 16 + 31 + 62 + 124 + 248 = 496$
c) 28

22. your partner

23. your partner

1.2 Prime Factorization, pp. 10–11

5. a) $3^2 \times 13$ **c)** $2^2 \times 5 \times 11$
b) 3×7^2 **d)** $2 \times 3^3 \times 5$

6. a) 1048222131
b) e.g., 2 divides an even number

7. a) $2^2 \times 5^2$ **e)** $2^2 \times 103$
b) $2 \times 3 \times 17$ **f)** $3 \times 5 \times 137$
c) $2^6 \times 5$ **g)** 2^9
d) 3×5^3 **h)** $3 \times 5^2 \times 7^2$

8. a) There are composite numbers at the ends of some branches.
b) $1755 = 3^3 \times 5 \times 13$ and $2180 = 2^2 \times 5 \times 109$

14. a) 35 is a factor.
b) 8 is a factor.
c) 10 is a factor, so the last digit is 0.

15. a) 2 is not a factor of both.
b) 5 and 7 are factors of both.
c) e.g., 15 is a factor.

16. a) e.g., $456 \times 1001 = 456\,456$
b) e.g., 456
c) $7 \times 11 \times 13$

17. a) e.g., $17 \times 19 = 323$; factors: 1, 17, 19, 323
b) e.g., $23 \times 47 = 1081$; factors: 1, 23, 47, 1081
c) 4 factors

18. a) e.g., $7 \times 11 \times 13 = 1001$; 1, 7, 11, 13, 77, 91, 143, 1001
b) e.g., $5 \times 19 \times 31 = 2945$; 1, 5, 19, 31, 95, 155, 589, 2945
c) 8 factors

19. 16 factors

20. All statements are true.

1.3 Common Factors and Common Multiples, pp. 14–15

4. a) GCF: 30, LCM: 840
b) GCF: 12, LCM: 1260

5. a) e.g., 10; 6 **b)** e.g., 1680, 3780

6. a) e.g., 2, 3, 6; 240, 480, 720
b) e.g., 2, 4, 8; 64, 128, 192
c) e.g., 2, 4, 8; 96, 192, 288
d) e.g., 2, 4, 8; 41 472, 82 944, 124 416

7. a) GCF: 26, LCM: 1326
b) GCF: 8, LCM: 96

9. a) GCF: 16, LCM: 960
b) GCF: 55, LCM: 275
c) GCF: 24, LCM: 144
d) GCF: 40, LCM: 600

10. a) GCF: 120, LCM: 1440

12. a) GCF: 8, LCM: 240
b) GCF: 40, LCM: 1200
c) GCF: 1, LCM: 20 200
d) GCF: 512, LCM: 3072

16. 78 and 22; 45 and 55; 12 and 88

17. a) $a = 30$ **b)** $b = 35$

18. GCF: 4, LCM: 192

1.4 Calculating Powers, p. 18

3. a) 16 384
b) about 5.378
c) about 0.329

4. a) 3^3 **b)** about 2800 m

9. a) B, since $2 \times 2^{51} = 2^{52}$, the point must be at half of the distance.
b) The new line will be twice as long as the given line.

11. $96.00

13. a) $0.1^2 = 0.01$, $0.1^3 = 0.001$, $0.1^4 = 0.0001$, $0.1^5 = 0.000\,01$
b) e.g., The number of digits after the decimal is equal to the exponent.
c) $0.1^6 = 0.000\,001$

1.5 Expanded Form and Scientific Notation, pp. 22–23

4. a) standard form **c)** expanded form
b) scientific notation

5.

Standard form	Expanded form	Scientific notation
360	$3 \times 10^2 + 6 \times 10$	3.6×10^2
3600	$3 \times 10^3 + 6 \times 10^2$	3.6×10^3
36 000	$3 \times 10^4 + 6 \times 10^3$	3.6×10^4
360 000	$3 \times 10^5 + 6 \times 10^4$	3.6×10^5

6. 6.13×10^3

13. 1.0×10^6

17. a) e.g., about 5.55×10^8 beats
b) e.g., about 8.4×10^7 times
c) e.g., about 2.8×10^9 bits

18. the first prize

19. a) about $60.1 billion **b)** $\$6.01 \times 10^{10}$

Mid-Chapter Review, p. 25

1. a) even number
b) last digit is 5
c) sum of digits is divisible by 3
d) even number

2. 127

3. a) 2 is not a factor because 247 is not even; 3 is not a factor because the sum of the digits is not divisible by 3; 5 is not a factor because the last digit is neither 0 nor 5.
b) 7, 11, and 13
c) 13 is another factor so 247 is a composite number.

4. a) $2 \times 3 \times 5$ **c)** $3 \times 5 \times 11$
b) 3×5^2 **d)** $2 \times 3 \times 11 \times 17$

5. a) $2 \times 3 \times 5 \times 7$ **c)** $2^3 \times 3^3$
b) $2^2 \times 7^2$ **d)** $2 \times 5 \times 7 \times 13$

6. 2, 7, 14; e. g., 280, 560, 840

7. a) 6 **b)** 120

8. a) 243 **b)** 64 **c)** 0.0016 **d)** 3.375

9. a) 125 DVDs **b)** 5^3

10.

Standard form	Expanded form	Scientific notation
456	$4 \times 10^2 + 5 \times 10 + 6 \times 1$	4.56×10^2
10 309	$1 \times 10^4 + 3 \times 10^2 + 9 \times 1$	1.0309×10^4
45 000	$4 \times 10^4 + 5 \times 10^3$	4.5×10^4
123 123	$1 \times 10^5 + 2 \times 10^4 + 3 \times 10^3 + 1 \times 10^2 + 2 \times 10 + 3 \times 1$	$1.231\ 23 \times 10^5$

11. a) $1 \times 10^4 + 2 \times 10^3 + 5 \times 10^2$; 1.25×10^4
b) $3 \times 10^7 + 2 \times 10^6$; 3.2×10^7
c) $2 \times 10^8 + 3 \times 10^7$; 2.3×10^8
d) $1 \times 10^{10} + 3 \times 10^9 + 8 \times 10^8$; 1.38×10^{10}

1.6 Square Roots, pp. 30–31

3. a) e.g., 3.9 **c)** e.g., 7.1
b) e.g., 17.3 **d)** e.g., 11.1

4. a) no, 6.481 **c)** yes, 31
b) yes, 12 **d)** no, 45.299

5. a) about 11 cm **b)** about 16 cm

9. Since 71 is between 64 and 81, and since $\sqrt{64} = 8$ and $\sqrt{81} = 9$, $\sqrt{71}$ must be between 8 and 9.

15. The answer is always 1.

16. 2025

18. e.g., 121, 11; 484, 22; and 10 201, 101

20. 390 625

21. a) e.g., $42 = 2 \times 3 \times 7$, $48 = 2^4 \times 3$, $63 = 3^2 \times 7$
b) e.g., $42^2 = 1764 = 2^2 \times 3^2 \times 7^2$
$48^2 = 2304 = 2^8 \times 3^2$
$63^2 = 3969 = 3^4 \times 7^2$
c) The exponent of each factor in the prime factorization of the square is twice the exponent of the same factor in the prime factorization of the square root. Divide each exponent in the prime factorization of the square by 2, and calculate the product of the resulting prime factors.
d) 153

22. c) The answer is 1 less than the chosen number.

1.8 Order of Operations, pp. 36–37

4. a) 13.25 **c)** 57.1
b) 164.64 **d)** 145 173.954

5. e.g., a) 2.5^2 is less than 9, 3.5 + 16 is 19.5, and 19.5 − 9 will be just over 10; so an answer of 13.25 is reasonable.

6. a) 55.875 **c)** 31 187.56
b) 3208.313 **d)** 2 172 860.254

8. e.g., about 149 beats/min

9. a) average: about 159 beats/min, high: about 200 beats/min
b) e.g., average: about 180 beats/min, high: about 220 beats/min

10. a) correct **c)** incorrect **e)** incorrect
b) incorrect **d)** correct **f)** correct

11. a) 2 **b)** 6.804 **c)** 770 **d)** 31.248

13. c) 25 **d)** 20.44

14. The square root was not applied correctly, and the operations have not been carried out in the correct order.

15. a) Answer would be the same; 54.72
b) Answer would not be the same; 58.8
c) Answer would not be the same; 400

16. a) about 10 km
b) about 66 km
c) about 4 km to 5 km

17. **a)** 65 536 **c)** same
b) 65 536 **d)** $5^8 = 390\ 625$

18. **a)** $(3.75 - 1.5)^2 \div 2$ **b)** $7 \times \sqrt{12.25 \div 0.25}$

1.9 Communicating about Number Problems, p. 40

3. e.g., Manuel could include more explanation about each calculation. There are 1000 mL in 1 L, so he divided the number of millilitres by 1000 to get the number of litres. Similarly, he divided the number of litres by 1000 to get the number of kilolitres. He multiplied by 60 because there are 60 min in an hour and by 24 because there are 24 h in a day and by 365 because there are 365 days in a year.

8. e.g., My Problem: An estimated 19.5 million vehicle tires are discarded every year in Canada. At present, 62% of discarded tires are sent to landfills. If the width of an average tire is about 60 cm, how long a line, in kilometres, would the tires in the landfill reach each year if placed side by side? (7200 km)

Chapter Self-Test, p. 41

1. 143 has more than 2 factors: 1, 11, 13, 143. So, it must be a composite number.

2. 3^6 is a multiple of 3, so it can't be prime.

3. **a)** $2^3 \times 3^2 \times 5$ **c)** $2^4 \times 5 \times 7$
b) 5×7^2 **d)** $2^2 \times 3^4 \times 5$

4. **a)** 2, 3, 6, 9, 18
b) e. g., 108, 216, 324
c) GCF: 18, LCM: 108

5. **a)** $1 \times 1 \times 144$, $1 \times 2 \times 72$, $1 \times 3 \times 48$, $1 \times 4 \times 36$, $1 \times 6 \times 24$, $1 \times 8 \times 18$, $1 \times 9 \times 16$, $1 \times 12 \times 12$, $2 \times 2 \times 36$, $2 \times 3 \times 24$, $2 \times 4 \times 18$, $2 \times 6 \times 12$, $2 \times 8 \times 9$, $3 \times 3 \times 16$, $3 \times 4 \times 12$, $3 \times 6 \times 8$, $4 \times 4 \times 9$, $4 \times 6 \times 6$
b) 1 by 1 by the prime number

6. **a)** $2^3 = 8$, $20^3 = 8000$, $200^3 = 8\ 000\ 000$, $2000^3 = 8\ 000\ 000\ 000$
b) e.g., Each power begins with an 8, followed by a number of zeros; the number of zeros equals the exponent times the number of zeros in the base.
c) 8 000 000 000 000

7. **a)** 4 **b)** 1.3

8. the first amount

9. about 8.06×10^9; $8 \times 10^9 + 0 \times 10^8 + 5 \times 10^7 + 8 \times 10^6 + 0 \times 10^5 + 4 \times 10^4 + 4 \times 10^3 + 6 \times 10^2 + 5 \times 10 + 1 \times 1$

10. **a)** 145 000 **c)** 48 880
b) 96 000 000 **d)** 5 670 000 000 000

11. about 3160 km

12. **a)** 4.472 **b)** 18.574 **c)** 27.839 **d)** 45

13. **a)** 17.44 **c)** 13.5 **e)** 4096
b) 34.2 **d)** 15 597.512 **f)** 21.8

Chapter Review, p. 43

1. 1579

2. **a)** 5×47 **c)** $2 \times 3 \times 7 \times 29$
b) $2^2 \times 3^2 \times 13$ **d)** $2^2 \times 3^2 \times 5^2 \times 7^2$

3. **a)** all the rectangles
b) e.g., 8 cm by 9 cm and 12 cm by 18 cm
c) If the dimensions of the rectangle are factors of the dimensions of the square, the rectangle will cover the square.

4. **a)** 0.6561 m **b)** 0.9^4 **c)** three more people

5. 2.56×10^{11} L

6. **a)** $1 \times 10^5 + 6 \times 10^4$, 1.6×10^5
b) $2 \times 10^6 + 2 \times 10^5 + 4 \times 10^4$, 2.24×10^6
c) $1 \times 10^8 + 4 \times 10^7 + 5 \times 10^6$, 1.45×10^8
d) $2 \times 10^{10} + 3 \times 10^9$, 2.3×10^{10}

7. about 41

8. **a)** 5.916 **b)** 22.361 **c)** 13 **d)** 8.367

9. 27

10. **a)** 21.25 **c)** 1252.098
b) 15.776 **d)** 4.995

11. Plan 150 costs $119 per month; Plan 400 costs $60 per month. Plan 400 is a better choice.

Chapter 2, p. 45

Getting Started, p. 47

1. **a)** 8:17 **b)** $\frac{8}{25}$ **c)** 68%

2. e.g., 6:16, 9:24, 12:32

3. **a)** scale factor 2, missing term 8
b) scale factor 5, missing term 35
c) scale factor 5, missing term 9
d) scale factor 2, missing term 7

4. **a)** 0.25 **b)** 0.5 **c)** 0.1 **d)** 0.2

5.

Ratio	Decimal	Percent
$\frac{3}{5}$	0.6	60%
$\frac{19}{25}$	0.76	76%
$\frac{41}{100}$	0.41	41%

6. a) 60% **b)** 40%
7. a) 14 **b)** 84% **c)** 90
8. a) 0.6 **b)** 32.2 **c)** 56.3 **d)** 0.52 **e)** 1.76 **f)** 2.45
9. \$11.88
10. 60
11. \$10.29
12. $18 = 2 \times 3 \times 3$

18
9 × 2
3 × 3 × 2

13. a) $2 \times 2 \times 5$ **b)** $2 \times 2 \times 3 \times 3$ **c)** $2 \times 2 \times 2 \times 3 \times 5$
14. a) 28 m **b)** 16 cm

2.1 Expressing Fractions as Decimals, p. 50

4. a) $0.\overline{5}$ **b)** $0.\overline{134\,56}$
5. a) $\frac{5}{16}$ **b)** $\frac{7}{11}$
6. a) terminates **b)** repeats **c)** repeats **d)** terminates
11. a) $<$ **b)** $=$ **c)** $>$ **d)** $>$ **e)** $<$
12. a) $\frac{1}{8}$, 0.35, $0.\overline{39}$, $\frac{5}{7}$, $\frac{9}{10}$
b) $\frac{27}{50}$, $\frac{5}{9}$, 0.56, $0.\overline{56}$, $0.5\overline{6}$
13. a) $\frac{13}{80}$ **b)** $\frac{7}{90}$ **c)** $\frac{3}{11}$ **d)** $\frac{13}{198}$
14. a) $0.\overline{6}$ **b)** $0.\overline{1}$ **c)** $0.0\overline{3}$
d) Since $\frac{1}{2} = 0.5$, $\frac{1}{2} + \frac{1}{3} = 0.8\overline{3}$.
15. e.g., $\frac{1}{60}$, $\frac{1}{110}$, $\frac{1}{130}$, $\frac{1}{300}$, $\frac{1}{700}$, and $\frac{1}{900}$. The denominators are all multiples of the prime numbers 3, 7, 11, and 13.

2.2 Multiplying and Dividing Decimals, pp. 54–55

3. a) 3.72 **b)** 4.5 **c)** 57.1849 **d)** 2436
4. a) 16.2 **b)** 44.028 **c)** 8.2 **d)** 14.28
5. \$41.49
10. a) \$64.00 **b)** \$8.00/h **c)** 1.35 times as much
13. \$3.00
14. \$2260.36
15. \$291.96
16. 203.8 cm^2

2.4 Ratios, pp. 60–61

4. 8 kg of cement, 24 kg of sand, 32 kg of gravel
5. a) $2:3 = 10:15$ **b)** $2:5:8 = 6:15:24$ **c)** $7:3:5 = 56:24:40$ **d)** $2:5:9 = 6:15:27$
6. a) 12 boys and 18 girls
b) 40% boys and 60% girls
8. $7\frac{1}{2}$ cups of mix, $3\frac{3}{4}$ cups of milk
9. 1125 g of raisins, 750 g of peanuts, and 125 g of cashews
11. Costas \$700, Sheila \$300
12. 40 kg of oats and 110 kg of barley
13. 1 kg of red blocks, 0.6 kg of green blocks, and 0.4 kg of yellow blocks
14. a) 1:12 **b)** 90%
c) 0.5 L of cashews, 1.5 L of marshmallows, and 18 L of chocolate ice cream
15. $5\frac{1}{4}$ cups of flour, 3 cups of sugar, and 1 cup of milk
16. a) 132 g each of cereal and pretzels and 66 g of nuts
b) 84 g each of cereal and pretzels and 42 g of nuts
c) 200 g each of cereal and pretzels and 100 g of nuts
d) 300 g each of cereal and pretzels and 150 g of nuts
17. a) 90 **b)** 108 **c)** 333
19. about 820 bears
20. 20 and 35
21. b) The ratio of the side to the diagonal is always around 1:1.4.
22. a) 6 cm × 10 cm × 16 cm
b) 24:40:15
c) 632 cm^2
23. 30°, 70°, and 80°

Mid-Chapter Review, p. 63

1. a) $0.\overline{7}$ **b)** $0.\overline{1275}$ **c)** $0.485\,\overline{621}$
2. a) 0.85 **b)** $0.\overline{4}$ **c)** 0.1875 **d)** $0.\overline{90}$

3. If the prime factorization of the denominator of a fraction has only 2s and/or 5s, then the equivalent decimal of the fraction will terminate. Otherwise, it is a repeating decimal.
4. $\frac{17}{25}$, 0.7, 0.72, $\frac{8}{11}$, $0.\overline{75}$
5. a) 34.248 b) 2.6128 c) 0.021 994
6. a) 25.6 b) about 12.757 c) about 12.781
7. \$21.73
8. 16 whole burgers
9. \$117.10/m^2
10. a) 1:11 = 11:121
 b) 5:2:1 = 35:14:7
 c) 1.5:1.25:2.4 = 6:5:9.6
11. 9 kg of nitrogen, 3 kg of phosphorus, and 6 kg of potassium
12. 20 solid, 12 opaque, and 4 transparent beads

2.5 Rates, pp. 66–67

3. a) number of words to minutes: 54 words/min
 b) metres to seconds: about 7.3 m/s
4. a) \$0.45/m b) \$0.13/bottle
10. Chantelle, Carla, Gemsy, and Avril
11. a) Station B b) Store B c) Store B
12. 500 m race
13. 740 g box
14. Argentina 1053.30 pesos, Germany 315.95 euros, India 17 932.78 rupees, Japan 42 530.03 yen, Russia 11 364.70 rubles, South Africa 2588.54 rand, Sweden 2732.32 kronor, United Kingdom 217.21 pounds, United States \$408.86
15. a) 15.9378 km/h b) 2 h 49 min 25 s
16. 1 h 21 min 55.2 s

2.6 Representing Percent, pp. 70–71

4. a) 33% b) 175% c) 1.5%
5. a) \$4.50 b) \$155 c) \$0.25 d) \$82.50
6. a) 450 students b) 9 students
10. 0.3%, 0.72, 77.6%, 1.56, 212%, $4\frac{1}{2}$
15.

Percent	Fraction	Decimal
$187\frac{1}{2}\%$	$1\frac{7}{8}$	1.875
$212\frac{1}{2}\%$	$2\frac{1}{8}$	2.125
$\frac{3}{4}\%$	$\frac{3}{400}$	0.0075

16. a) $66\frac{2}{3}\%$ b) $16\frac{2}{3}\%$

2.7 Solving Percent Problems, pp. 74–75

4. a) 14.4 b) 45% c) 60
5. a) e.g., 20 students
 b) $\frac{60}{100} = \frac{\blacksquare}{30}$
 c) 18 students in the class walk to school.
6. 37.5%
7. a) $\frac{80}{100} = \frac{32}{\blacksquare}$ b) 40 questions
18. a) 12.9%
 b) e.g., How many girls chose the "spending time with friends" option? Answer: 119 girls

2.8 Solving Percent Problems Using Decimals, pp. 77–78

4. discount \$84.99, purchase price \$293.20
6. a) i) PST \$24.00, GST \$21.00
 ii) PST \$88.00, GST \$77.00
 iii) PST \$1.20, GST \$1.05
 iv) PST \$2.60, GST \$2.27
 v) PST \$3.94, GST \$3.45
 vi) PST \$2.02, GST \$1.77
 b) i) \$344.95 ii) \$1264.95 iii) \$17.23 iv) \$37.36 v) \$56.68 vi) \$29.08
7. a) i) discount \$15.00, sale price \$134.95
 ii) discount \$25.00, sale price \$74.99
 iii) discount \$10.65, sale price \$24.84
 iv) discount \$5.95, sale price \$33.74
 v) discount \$14.79, sale price \$14.79
 vi) discount \$7.96, sale price \$31.83
 b) i) \$144.40 ii) \$80.24 iii) \$26.58 iv) \$36.10 v) \$15.83 vi) \$34.06
9. a) interest \$37.50, total amount \$287.50
 b) interest \$87.50, total amount \$587.50
 c) interest \$331.20, total amount \$1531.20
 d) interest \$191.25, total amount \$2741.25
 e) interest \$300.00, total amount \$5300.00
10. second store
11. Plan A
12. \$21.52
13. \$538.00
14. \$708.81
15. \$7511

2.9 Solve Problems by Changing Your Point of View, p. 82

3. a) The sale price is 70% of the regular price.
b) The purchase price is 115% of the sale price.
c) The area can be calculated by subtracting the area of the small rectangle from the large rectangle.
4. \$56.33
5. \$81.81
7. a) 214 cm^2 **b)** 90.0 cm^2
8. 54.4 cm^2
9. 20.52 cm by 30.78 cm

Chapter Self-Test, p. 83

1. a) 0.85, terminate **c)** $0.\overline{67}$, repeat
b) 0.6875, terminate **d)** $0.\overline{285\,714}$, repeat
2. a) 3.726 **b)** 3.9345 **c)** 120.52
3. a) 4.0 **b)** 234.50 **c)** 24.45
4. a) $<$ **b)** $=$
5. a) 28 **b)** 8.1 **c)** 1.7, 21.0
6. a) 37.4% **b)** 126%
7. a) 234 **b)** 22.5
8. a) 15 km/h **b)** 2 h 40 min
9. \$1.37
10. 77.49¢/L
11. about 9.1%
12. 45 cats
13. $5\frac{1}{4}$ cups of mix and $2\frac{1}{4}$ cups of water
14. \$861.59

Chapter Review, p. 85

1. a) 0.44 **b)** $0.8\overline{3}$ **c)** $0.8\overline{6}$
2. $\frac{2}{9}$, 0.25, $0.\overline{25}$, $0.2\overline{5}$, $\frac{13}{25}$
3. a) 177.375 **b)** 16.234
4. Only Celine should buy a monthly pass.
5. a) 4 : 7 : 3 = 16 : 28 : 12
b) 15 : 27 : 6 = 5 : 9 : 2
6. peanuts 400 g, cashews 200 g, almonds 150 g
7. a) 1.5 km/min **b)** \$31.00/kg
8. 2 L bottle
9. a) amount of money and number of hours, \$11.25/h
b) distance travelled in metres and number of seconds, 8 m/s
10. a) 0.23 **b)** 2.45 **c)** 0.007 **d)** 1.2
11. equal
12. a) 80 **b)** 40 **c)** 20.8 **d)** 250 **e)** 20 000
13. 940 students
14. \$7
15. a) \$24.13 **b)** \$44.82 **c)** \$6.72 **d)** \$51.54
16. a) interest \$420, total amount \$2170
b) interest \$135, total amount \$1635

Math in Action: Coach, pp. 87–88

1. a) 32.5 strokes/min
b) 36.2 strokes/min
c) about 30.6 strokes/min
Order from least to greatest: 30.6 strokes/min, 32.5 strokes/min, 36.2 strokes/min
2. a) about 6.0 m/s
b) about 5.1 m/s
c) about 4.7 m/s
3. Unit rates help a coach compare the performance of each team. The coach can tell which team is rowing faster and which team needs to improve its speed.
4. a) about 89.0% **b)** about 88.1%
c) If a team meets the gold standard time, the percent would be 100%. If a team does better than the gold standard time, the percent would be greater than 100%. This means the better team has a higher percent. So the men's team did better.
5. 2440 m; It is necessary to include "at this pace" because the team may not be able to row at the same speed for the entire 8 min. They may slow down.
6. about 7 min 14 s
7. e.g., in 6 min, 208.8 strokes and in 8 min, 278.4 strokes
8. 6:01.96
9. 6:48.89

Chapter 3, p. 89

Getting Started, p. 91

1. a) a census **c)** a sample
b) a sample **d)** a census
2. A matches the data for the listening time for all ages, while B matches the data for the listening time for ages 12 to 17.

NFI

3. a) i) about 8500 **iii)** about 10 700
ii) about 10 800
b) 1997–1998; an increase of about 1300

4. a)

Stem	Leaf
4	6
5	5 5
6	3
7	1 5 9
8	1 2 3 4 5 6 7 8 8 9
9	0 1 3

b) e.g., Most students got a mark in the 80s.

5. **Average Monthly Sunshine in September**

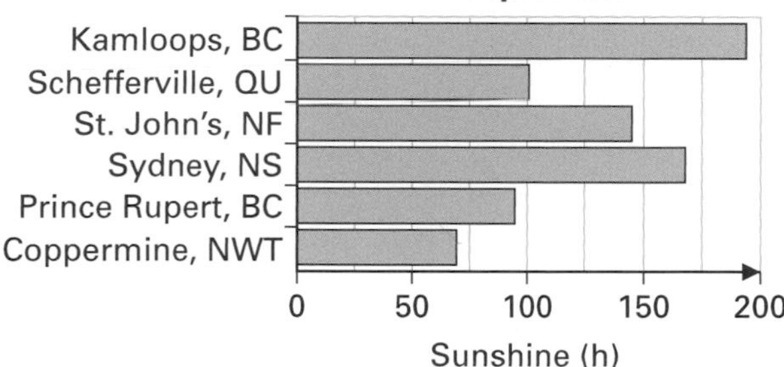

6. mean 23, median 17.5, mode 17

3.1 Organizing and Presenting Data, pp. 93–95

3. a) e.g., line graph **c)** e.g., scatter plot
b) e.g., circle graph **d)** e.g., pictograph

6. a) e.g., **Speed vs. Gasoline Consumption**

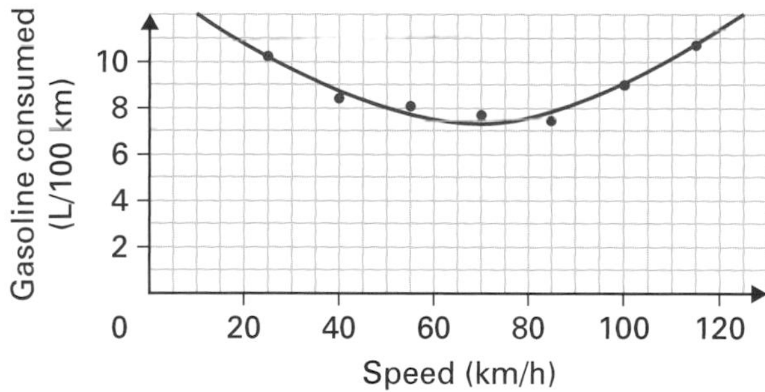

b) e.g., about 85 km/h
c) e.g., about 35 km/h
d) e.g., about 8.5 L

7. a) yes
b) A double-bar graph compares the preference for each snack before and after hearing the guest speaker.

9. A scatter plot would show that there is no relationship between age and wealth.

3.3 Using Electronic Databases, pp. 100-101

3. **Average Number of Hours of Television Viewing per Week**

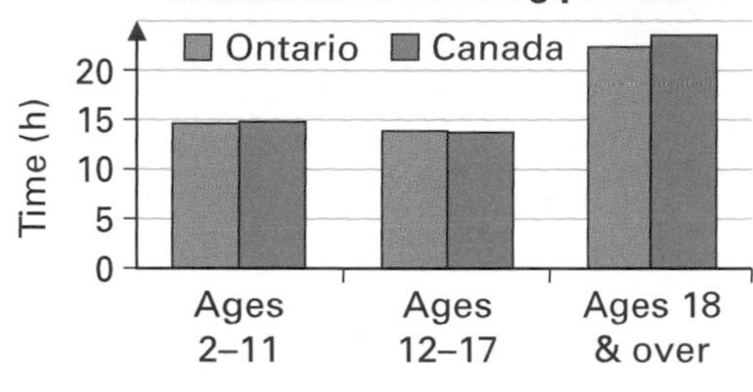

10. a) e.g., The first row of the database can be Country, Area (km^2), Population, Imports to Canada (millions of $), Exports from Canada (millions of $), Continent.
b) e.g., Copy and paste the database to a spreadsheet, then sort the "Continent" column to find all the European countries together. Copy that section and paste it onto another spreadsheet. Sort the "Population" column to find the European country with the largest population.
c) e.g., Copy and paste the database to a spreadsheet, then sort the "Continent" column to find all the Asian countries together. Copy that section and paste it onto another spreadsheet. Make another column by using the "Sum Formula" to calculate the total of exports to Canada and imports from Canada. Lastly, sort the new column to find the Asian country that trades with Canada the most.
d) Spain
e) Canada exports the most to USA and the least to Norway.

Mid-Chapter Review, p. 103

1. a) **Percent of Two Provinces' Adult Population with Various Levels of Schooling**

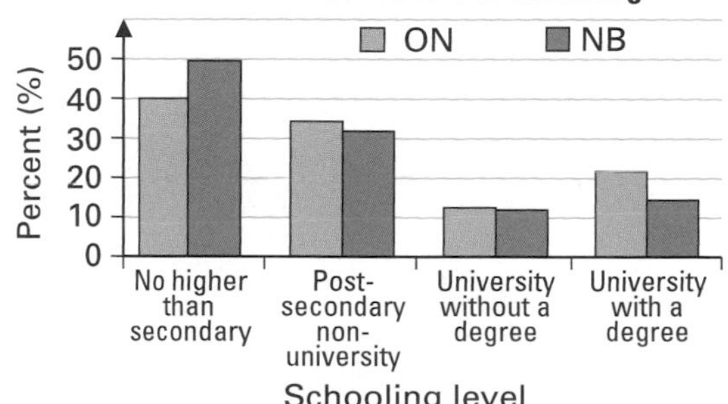

b) 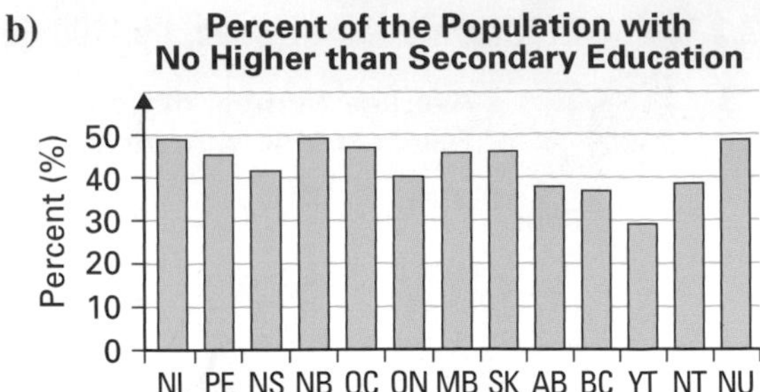

c) Nova Scotia

d) Ontario, British Columbia, and Yukon Territories

e) e.g., New Brunswick and Newfoundland

f) e.g., a comparative bar graph

2. a) e.g., to compare the populations of different provinces

b) e.g., to find a relationship between average temperature and average rainfall per month over the period of a year

3. Magda, because larger samples are generally more representative of the school.

4. b) 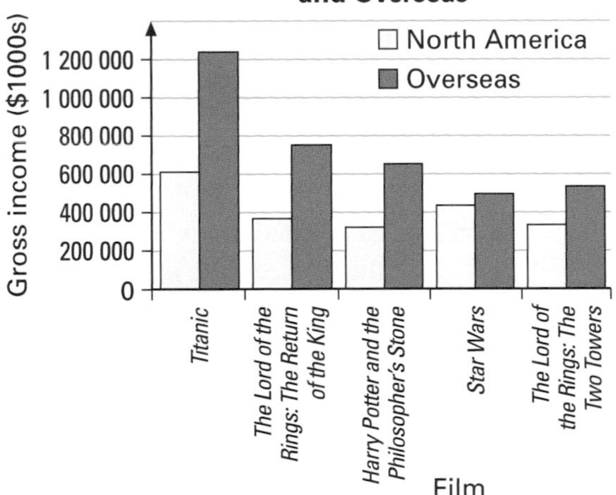

c) *The Lord of the Rings: The Two Towers*

3.4 Histograms, pp. 106–107

3. a) 6; 20 min b) 20–40

4.

Temperature range	Frequency
0–10	5
10–20	4
20–30	4
30–40	6
40–50	5

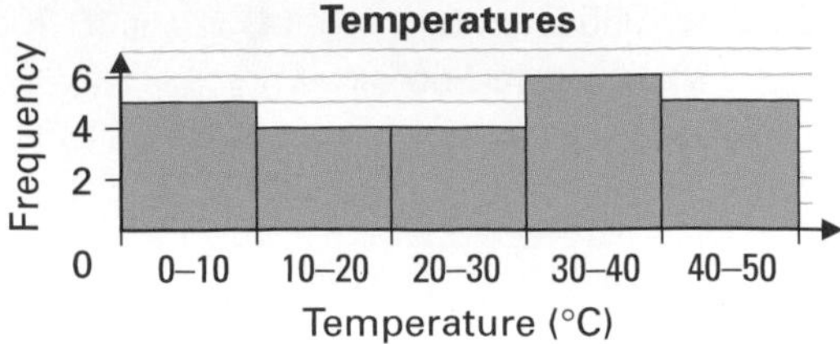

7. c) about 7%

10. e.g.,

Stem	Leaf
0	6 7 7 8 8 8
1	0 0 0 0 1 2 2 7 8
2	1 2 6 6 7 9
3	0 0 0 0 2 3 6 9 9
4	1 1 2 7 8 9
5	0 0 0 0

3.5 Mean, Median, and Mode, p. 110

4. a) mean 18.3, median 18, mode 18

b) mean 18.25, median 18, mode 18

c) mean

5. a) mean 3.8, median 4.5, mode 2.7 and 4.9

b) mean 3.9, median 4.5, mode 2.7 and 4.9; mean

6. 20 167

7. a) 72 b) no c) 97

9. a) mean 6.25, median 6.25

b) mean 6.75, median 6.75

10. a) 75 or 82 or 99 or 102 b) 15

11. b) The lower the average word length is, the easier the material is to read.

3.6 Communicating about Graphs, p. 114

3. e.g., How many meals did you eat or what is the total number of servings of food you had?

5. a) Scandinavia 513, North America 289, the Alps 565, USSR/Unified Team/Russia 275

6. b) e.g., 9.5 billion; I assumed that the current population trends continue.

Chapter Self-Test, p. 115

1. a) 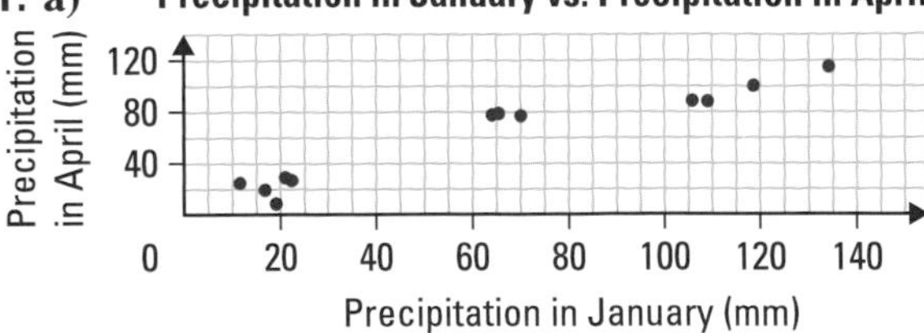

b) A scatter plot is used to determine how closely two sets of data are related.

2. a) 20 000 people, because larger samples are usually more representative of the population.
   b) The sample might be too large. The survey would be expensive and time consuming to conduct.
3. a) The western cities have less precipitation than the eastern cities of Canada. To compare the data from the eastern and western cities, create a comparative bar graph.
   b) No, because there is no data on any cities from British Columbia where some parts of the province are rainforests while other parts are deserts.
4. a)

Height (cm)	Frequency
160–165	2
165–170	5
170–175	6
175–180	7
180–185	6
185–190	4

   b)

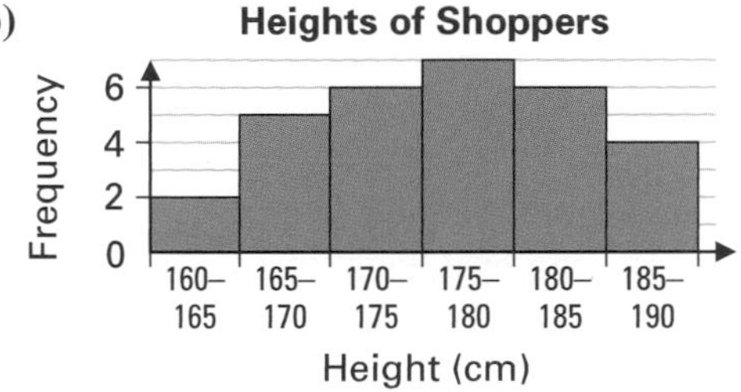

5. a) mean 13.9°C, median 13°C, mode 12°C
   b) mean 13.5°C, median 13°C, mode 12°C; the mean is affected the most because it depends on the number of numbers in the set.

Chapter Review, p. 117

1. a) the higher the life expectancy, the higher the income
   b)

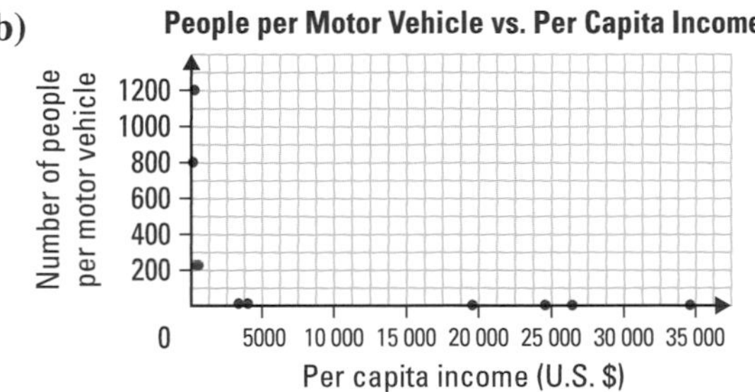

In countries with a higher per capita income, there are fewer people per motor vehicle.

2. A census because it provides results for the entire population.
3. a)

Distance (km)	Frequency
0–10	3
10–20	3
20–30	6
30–40	6
40–50	7
50–60	3
60–70	2

   b)

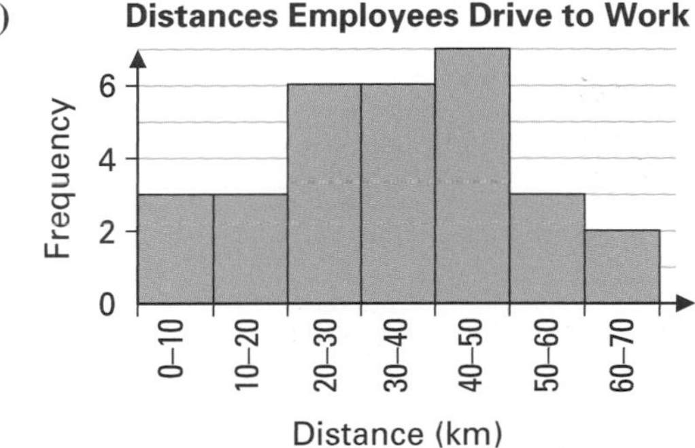

4. a)

Stem	Leaf
15	1
17	0 0 1 4 8 9
18	2 4 5 6 6 6
19	3 4 5 6 7 9
21	9

   b) median 185.5, mode 186
   c) 184.75
   d) mean 184.72, median 185.5, mode 186; the mean is affected the most because it depends on the number of numbers in the set.
5. a) Since 1500 is much larger than any value in the data set, adding it will raise the median to 512.5 and the mean to 583.5.
   b) Since 499 is around the middle of the data, the median will become 499.5 and the mean will become 458.4.
   c) Since 1 is much smaller than the average value of the data set, the median will drop to 497.5 while the mean will become 396.1.
6. a) Grade 7
   b) orange juice, bottled water, and milk

Cumulative Review Chapter 1–3, pp. 119–120

1. B **2.** A **3.** D **4.** A **5.** D
6. A **7.** D **8.** B **9.** B **10.** D

11. a) mean is \$8.62; mean without the highest and lowest hourly pay is \$8.46; e.g., I think the mean without the greatest and least numbers better represents the hourly rates of pay; since the greatest pay of \$10.75 is much higher than the rest of the rates, the mean is greatly affected by it. So, the mean without the greatest and least rates better represents the average hourly rates of pay.

b)

Hourly rates of pay (\$)	Frequency
7.00–7.99	8
8.00–8.99	9
9.00–9.99	7
10.00–10.99	6
11.00–11.99	3
12.00–12.99	3

The lowest rate of pay is \$7.55 and the highest is \$12.95, which gives a range of \$5.40 for the set of data. If multiples of 0.5 are used for the interval labels, there would be 11 intervals. That's too many. If multiples of 1 are used, there would be 6 intervals if starting from \$7.00 and ending at \$12.99. The number of intervals is appropriate, so use multiples of 1.

c) Hourly Rate of Pay

Frequency: 0, 2, 4, 6, 8
Rates of pay (\$/h): 7.00–8.00, 8.00–9.00, 9.00–10.00, 10.00–11.00, 11.00–12.00, 12.00–13.00

The histogram shows that the most common hourly rate of pay is between \$8.00 and \$9.00. But a lot of rates are below \$8.00. Only a few rates are above \$11.00.

d) 15 packages of buttons and 9 packages of bookmarks

Chapter 4, p. 121

Getting Started, p. 123

1. a) 4 **b)** 4 **c)** 22 **d)** 5

2. a)

Figure number	Figure	Number of counters
1		3
2		5
3		7
4		9
5		11

b) You add 2 counters to the middle row of the previous figure to make the new figure.
c) $2n + 1$ **d)** 21

3. a) 15, 18, 21, …; Start at 3 and add 3 each time.
b) 18, 22, 26, …; Start at 2 and add 4 each time.
c) 15, 21, 28, …; Start at 1 and add 2, then add 1 more each time.
d) 25, 36, 49, …; Start at 1 and add the next odd number each time, or the sequence is the squares of numbers, starting at 1 and increasing by 1 each time.

4. a) $n + 4$ **b)** $5n + 2$ **c)** $3n$ **d)** $4n - 1$

5. a) 10.2 **b)** 44 **c)** 79 **d)** 20

6. a) The number of blue tiles stays the same; the number of orange tiles changes.
b) Double the figure number and add 1.
c) $2n + 1$ **d)** 11

7. a)

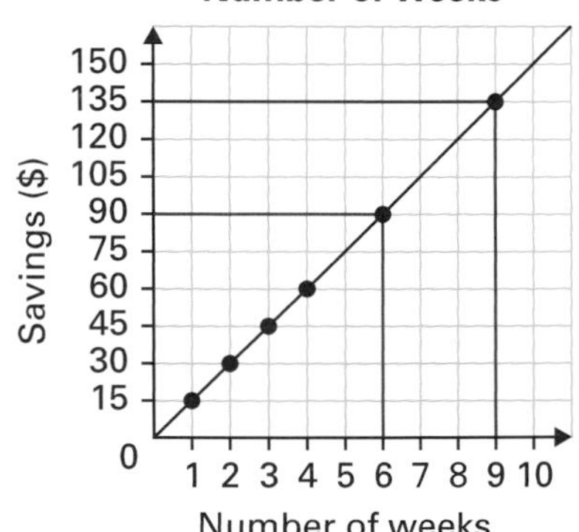

b) \$135 **c)** week 6

4.2 Creating Pattern Rules from Models, pp. 128–129

3. a) The 3 blue tiles in the centre column stay the same. Two red tiles are added each time.

b) $2n + 3$

4. e.g., Start with 2 toothpicks that are vertical and 3 toothpicks that form a triange, then add 3 toothpicks in the form of a triangle to each new figure; $3n + 2$ or $2 + n + n + n$

10. b) 18 blue tiles

13. a) n^2 **c)** $(n + 2)^2$ or $n^2 + 4n + 4$

b) $4n + 4$

4.3 The General Term of a Sequence, pp. 132–133

3. a)

Term number (figure number)	Picture	Term value (number of squares)
1		2
2		4
3		6
4		8
5		10

b) $2n$ **c)** 60

8. c) 11 **d)** 306

9. a) $4n + 1$; 201 **d)** $30n - 20$; 1480

b) $2n + 9$; 109 **e)** $100n + 1$; 5001

c) $5n + 21$; 271

11. a) 31, $4n + 3$ **b)** 35, $2n + 1$

12. a) $-2n + 31$, -69 **b)** $-n + 119$, 69

13. a) $\frac{(n + 2)(n + 3)}{2} + 1$ **b)** 5254

14. a)

Figure number	Number of cubes
1	1
2	3
3	6
4	10
5	15

b) $\frac{n(n + 1)}{2}$ **c)** 55

15. a) 1, 2, 3, 4, 5, 6, … **b)** yes

Mid-Chapter Review, p. 135

1. a) This is like the Fibonacci sequence, but each term is twice the matching term of the Fibonacci sequence.

b) No, because it is odd. All the terms are even.

c) The difference alternates between -4 and 4 for each group of 3 numbers; yes

d) This is similar to the matching relationship for the Fibonacci sequence, but the differences alternate between -1 and 1.

2. a) $3n + 5$

b) The 5 represents the column of five green tiles, and the $3n$ represents the group of columns of three orange tiles.

3. a) e.g.,

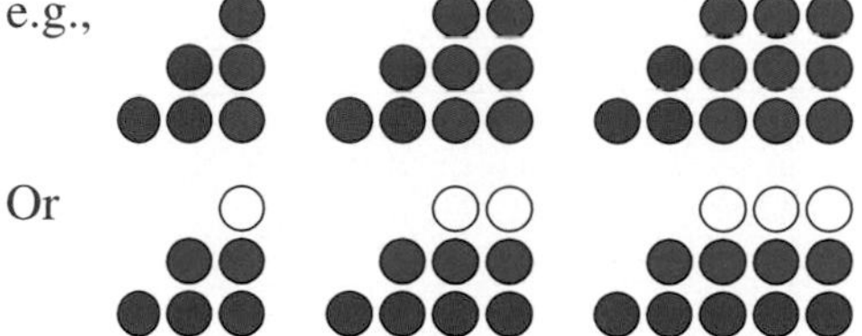

Or

b) e.g., In the first model, the nth term contains $3n + 3$ circles; in the second model, the nth term contains $n + (n + 1) + (n + 2)$ circles.

4. a) $3n + 4$ **b)** $3n + 5$

c) The pattern rules differ by 1.

5. a) $2n + 3$ **b)** 103 **c)** 11

6. a) $6n + 2$, 602 **d)** $n + 8$, 108

b) $3n + 12$, 312 **e)** $16n + 31$, 1631

c) $11n$, 1100

4.4 Solve Problems by Examining Simpler Problems, p. 138

4. 99

5. 41

6. a) Solve the problem using fewer teams.

b) 182

7. 1 h

8. a) 24 **b)** 120 **c)** 3 628 800

9. 10 100 square units

10. a) 4 **b)** 40 **c)** 100

11. 170

4.5 Relating Number Sequences to Graphs, pp. 142–143

3. pattern A: red, pattern B: blue, pattern C: green

4. b) 144

6. b) 70 min **c)** $-200t + 20\,000$

7. b) 3 h

10. A: n^2, B: $n^2 - 1$, C: $n^2 + 1$

11. $n^2 + 2n + 3$

Chapter Self-Test, p. 145

1. a)

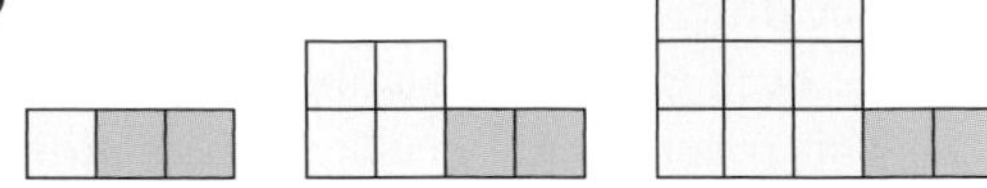

b) The 2 green squares stay the same. The yellow squares increase by a factor of n^2.

c) $n^2 + 2$

2. a)

Term number	Term value	Change
1	7	
2	12	+5
3	17	+5
4	22	+5
5	27	+5
6	32	+5

$5n + 2$

b) 127

3. a) To calculate each term, multiply the term number by 7 and then add 10; $7t + 10$.

b) $7n + 10$ **c)** 549

4. a)

Level	Balls in level	Total number of balls
1	1	1
2	3	4
3	6	10
4	10	20
5	15	35
6	21	56

56 balls

b) 164 more balls **c)** 9 levels

5. 226 pieces

6. b) i) 3 **ii)** 20

7. a) $5n + 4$

b) The figure number is 18.

c) $5(18) + 4 = 94$

Chapter Review, p. 147

1. a) The number of pennies around the centre penny changes; the centre penny stays the same.

b) Multiply the term number by 5, then add 1, to get the term value.

c) $5n + 1$ **d)** 61

2. a)

Term number	Term value	Change
1	5	
2	7	+2
3	9	+2
4	11	+2
5	13	+2

b) $2n + 3$ **c)** 143

3. 153

4. 36

5. a)

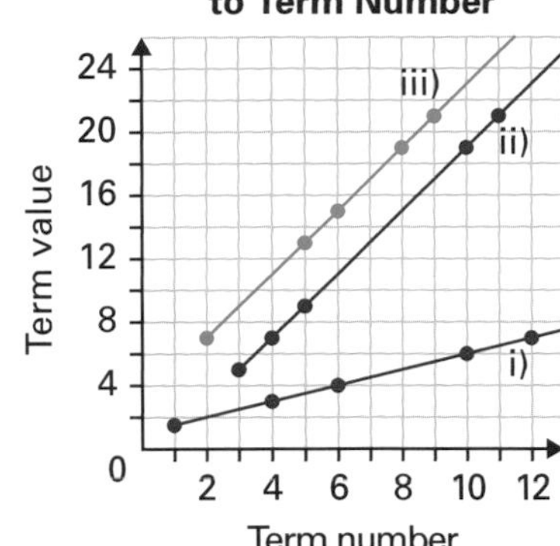

b) i) 7, 1.5 **ii)** 19, 21 **iii)** 19, 21

c) i) $\frac{n}{2} + 1$ **ii)** $2n - 1$ **iii)** $2n + 3$

Chapter 5, p. 149

Getting Started, p. 151

1. a) perimeter **b)** area **c)** perimeter

2. a) 5 cm < 5 m **c)** 1.000 m = 1000 mm

b) 1 m = 100 cm **d)** 13 km > 130 m

3. a) perimeter 72 mm, area 324 mm^2

b) perimeter 20 m, area 16 m^2

c) perimeter 18.8 cm, area 15.0 cm^2

d) perimeter 29.5 cm, area 36.9 cm^2

4. perimeter 23.4 cm, area 29.5 cm^2

5. a) 52.5 m^2 **b)** 38.8 m^2 **c)** 108.8 m^2

6. 3 cm

5.3 Calculating Circumference, pp. 158–159

4. a) 16 cm **b)** 14.8 cm

5. a) 63 cm **b)** 51.5 m

11.

Item	r	d	C
clock	9.0 cm	18.0 cm	56.5 cm
watch	18 mm	36 mm	113 mm
round tea bag	1.9 cm	3.8 cm	11.9 cm
sewer cover	31 cm	62 cm	195 cm
circle protractor	5.9 cm	11.8 cm	37.1 cm
electric fan	101 mm	201 mm	631 mm

14. 94.2 cm
15. 141.3 m
16. 5.3 cm
19. 12.6 cm by 10.0 cm
20. 249.9 m
21. The red arc and the blue circle are the same length.

Mid-Chapter Review, p. 161

2. radius, diameter, circumference
3. e.g., about 9 m
4. **a)** e.g., about 75 cm **c)** e.g., about 60 cm
b) e.g., about 33 m **d)** e.g., about 9 km
5.

Item	Diameter	Radius	Circumference
CD case	12.0 cm	6.0 cm	37.7 cm
coaster	9.0 cm	4.5 cm	28.3 cm
lock	26 mm	13 mm	82 mm
coin	3.8 cm	1.9 cm	11.9 cm

6. **a)** 47 cm **c)** 39.3 cm **e)** 138 cm
b) 188 cm **d)** 53 cm **f)** 63 cm
7. The circumference also doubles.

5.5 Calculating Area, pp. 166–167

4. **a)** 346.2 cm^2 **c)** 531 cm^2
b) 154 cm^2 **d)** 6.2 cm^2
7. **b)** 2.1 cm^2
8. **b)** 17.6 cm^2
9. **b)** 380.0 cm^2
10. **c)** 21.5 m^2
12. **b)** 1.7 cm^2
14. 89.3 cm^2
15. 1766.3 cm^2
16. **a)** 251 015.6 m^2 **d)** $5300.63
b) $313 769.50 **e)** $319 070.13
c) 1927.5 m

5.6 Solve Problems by Working Backward, pp. 170–171

3. **a)** circle of diameter 20.0 cm
b) circle of diameter 20 cm
4. 46
5. 10.0 m
6. **a)** 15 cm, 10 cm, 5 cm
b) 94 cm, 63 cm, 31 cm
c) 392 cm^2, 235 cm^2, 79 cm^2
7. 102 kg
9. **a)** 7.1 m **b)** 22.3 m
11. about 9 m
12. 4.2 cm^2

Chapter Self-Test, p. 173

1.

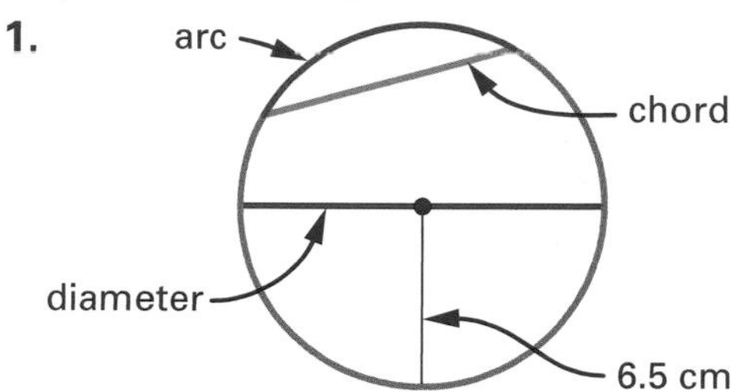

2. **a)** area **c)** circumference
b) area **d)** circumference
3. Divide the diameter by 2.
4. **a)** 15.7 km **c)** 9.4 cm
b) 163 cm **d)** 66 cm
5. **a)** 13 cm^2 **c)** 25.5 cm^2
b) 95 cm^2 **d)** 120.7 cm^2
6. **a)** 225.0 m^2 **b)** 176.6 m^2 **c)** 48.4 m^2
7. 13.9 cm^2
8. 57.1 cm^2
9. **a)** 64.4 m^2 **b)** 15.7 m
10. **a)** circle with radius 6 cm
b) circle with radius 2.7 cm
11. 17.6 m

Chapter Review, p. 175

1. Circle 2 has a radius of 10.0 cm and Circle 1 has a diameter of 10.0 cm.
2. The circumference is just over 3 times as long as the diameter. The ratio is a special number called π (pi).
3. **a)** 16.3 cm **c)** 3.8 km
b) 94 cm **d)** 26.1 cm
4. 157 m

6. a) 1963 km^2 c) 132.7 cm^2
   b) 13 mm^2 d) 95.0 m^2
7. 50.24 m^2
8. 3018 cm^2
9. a) 144.0 m^2 c) 113.2 m^2
   b) 28.3 m^2 d) 30.8 m^2
10. a) circle with radius 5.7 cm
    b) circle with radius 12 cm
    c) circle with radius 5.5 cm

Math in Action: Architect, pp. 177–178

1. e.g., The dome is in the upper portion of the picture, on top of pillars and other supporting structures.
2. a) 75 m b) 452 m^2
3. a) 23 m b) 415 m^2
4. a) e.g., designing a building that is both elegant and practical
   b) e.g., building a perfectly curved wall
5. a) e.g., 15 m by 10 m: perimeter 50 m, area 150 m^2
   b) e.g., Use area formula for circle and work backward to find radius; radius 7 m, diameter 14 m, circumference 44 m
   c) e.g., a circle with diameter 14 m
   d) e.g., circular because it could improve communication

Chapter 6, p. 179

Getting Started, p. 181

1. a) true b) true c) false d) false
2. −26, −7, −5, 0, +7, +13
3. a) +12 b) −6 c) −11 d) +5959
4. a) −5 b) +4
5. +
   =
   =
6. a) −2 c) −11 e) +4
   b) −6 d) +11 f) −10
7. a) counter model:
   + =
   number sentence: (+5) + (−9) = −4
   b) counter model:
   − =
   number sentence: (+3) − (−2) = +5
8. 5 units to the right; 3 units to the left; 5 units to the right; 11 units to the left; 3 units to the left; 10 units to the right
9. a) 0 b) +1

6.2 Relating Integer Subtraction to Addition, pp. 186–187

3. a) −2 0 +5
   b)
   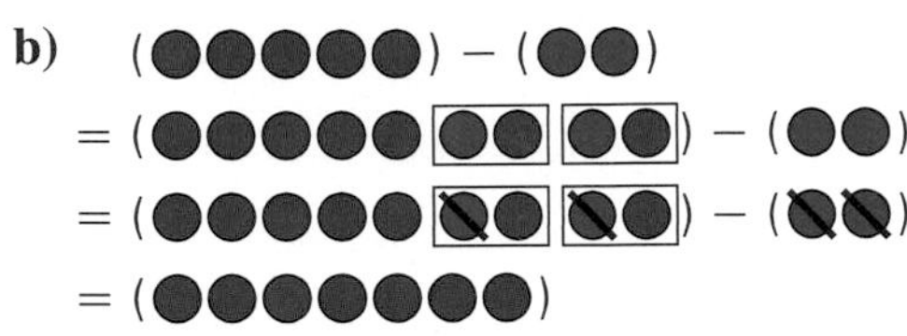
   c) 5 + 2 = 7
4. 10°C
5. 16, 0, −11, −12
19. a) −69 b) 81
20. when the second integer is negative
21. when the second integer is positive

6.4 Multiplying Integers, pp. 192–193

5. a) 6 × 3 = 18 c) (−2) × 9 = (−18)
   b) −5 × (−4) = 20 d) 5 × (−3) = (−15)
6. a) 10 h b) 8 h c) 0 h
16. 105
20. a) 30 b) 120 c) 24
21. a) −20 b) yes
23. The result of any choice will be −6720.

Mid-Chapter Review, p. 196

1. a) −38 b) 79 c) 0 d) 44
   From least to greatest: −38, 0, 44, 79
2. 14°C
3. e.g., 0, 0, and −10; 20, 42, and 12; −6, 0, and −4
4. a) Let a and b be negative integers. The number line shows the sum is less than each integer.

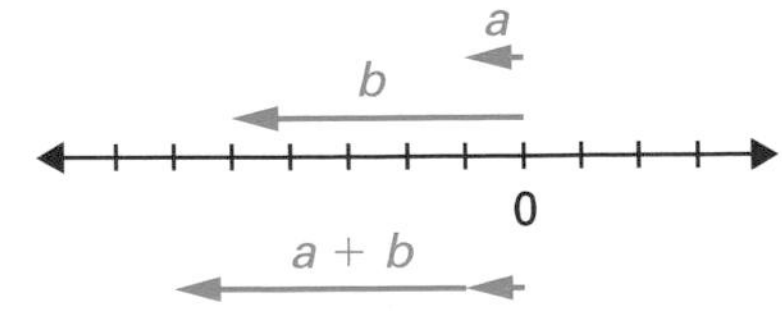

b) e.g., consider $-2 - (-3) = 1$. The difference, 1, is greater than (-2) or (-3).

5. positive

6. yes

7. a) $5 \times (+2) = 10$ **b)** $2 \times (-5) = -10$

8.

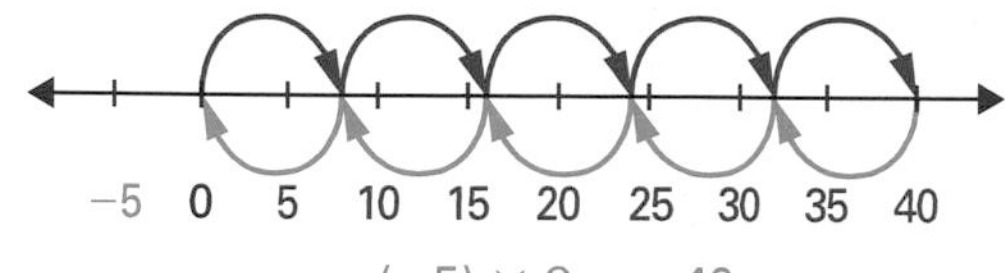

9. a) $5 \times (-6) = -30$ **b)** $(-6) \times 5 = -30$

10. a) 45 **b)** 56 **c)** −88 **d)** 0

11. −$40

12. $3 \times (-8) = -24$; He lost 24 points.

13. no

14. −11

15. a) −1 and 64, −2 and 32, −4 and 16, −8 and 8, −16 and 4, −32 and 2, −64 and 1

b) −1 and 64, −64 and 1

c) −1 and 64

d) The differences come in pairs. −2 and 32 have the same difference as −32 and 2. Each sum is unique.

6.6 Dividing Integers, pp. 201–203

4. a) 9 **b)** 0 **c)** −9 **d)** −8

5. a) B, 2 **b)** C, 2 **c)** D, −2 **d)** A, −2

6. a) negative

b) $[(+4) + (-11) + (-10) + (+15) + (-13)] \div 5 = -3$; −3

17. 1

18. a) −2 dB **b)** 22 dB **c)** 11 dB

19. 40

26. a) yes **b)** yes **c)** yes

27. $\frac{2}{18}$ or $\frac{1}{9}$

28. One integer is negative and the other is positive.

29. −1

6.7 Order of Operations with Integers, pp. 206–207

4. a) −8 **b)** −27 **c)** 22 **d)** 1

6. a) 10 **b)** 35 **c)** −28 **d)** −2 **e)** −39 **f)** 153

7. a) 112 **b)** −51 **c)** −11 **d)** −30 **e)** 60 **f)** 666

9. a) 2 **b)** −1 **c)** −1 **d)** −6 **e)** −1 **f)** −8

11. −440

13. a) 0°C **b)** 100°C **c)** −20°C **d)** −40°C

14. −2°C

15. $130

17. a)

Day	Starting price ($)	Final price ($)	Change in price ($)
Mon.	350	348	−2
Tues.	348	346	−2
Wed.	346	344	−2
Thurs.	344	352	+8
Fri.	352	360	+8

b) $350 **c)** $2

18. a) −4 **b)** −3 **c)** −5

19. a) 13 **b)** −12 **c)** 2 **d)** 1

20. $4 \times 12 - (-5) + (-3) = 50$

6.8 Communicating about Calculations, p. 210

3. a) e.g., multiply by 2, add 31, and subtract 1; add 5, multiply by −4, and subtract 10; multiply by 3, add 42, and subtract 2

b) e.g., add 1, subtract 31, and divide by 2; add 10, divide by −4, and subtract 5; add 2, subtract 42, and divide by 3

4. 3

5. e.g., −2

7. a) −43

8. a) −$12

9. Abby was 2 km west of Lauren's home.

10. e.g., −25, −12, −10, 25

Chapter Self-Test, p. 213

1. a) Atlantic Ocean, 1155 m **b)** Atlantic Ocean

2. a)

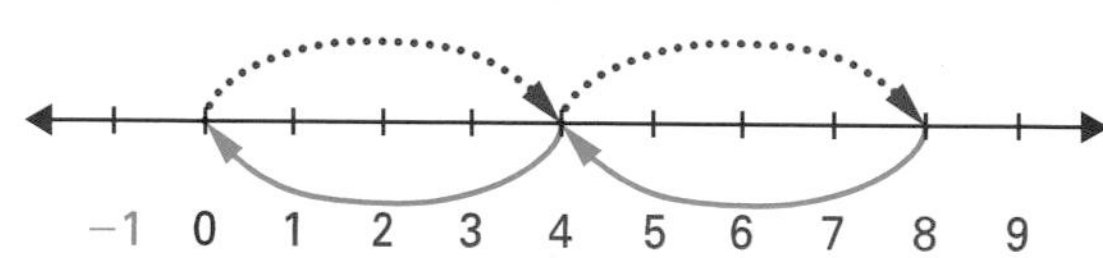

b)

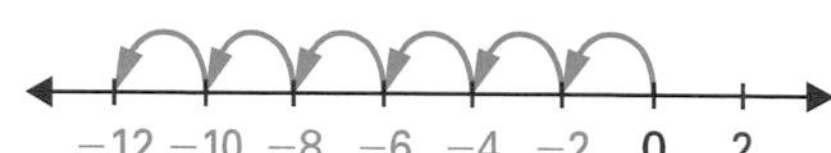

3. a) -3 c) -9 e) -3
b) -13 d) -4 f) -10

4. a) 10 c) -29 e) 30
b) -3 d) 10 f) -9

5. a) -9 b) -12 c) -15 d) -15

6. a) 4 b) -3 c) -56 d) -414

7. a) 60 b) 666 c) -2 d) 33 e) -58

8. lost \$250

9. -12 and 10

10. 39 greater

11. a) subtract before multiplying b) 2

Chapter Review, p. 215

1. 15°C

2. a) e.g., $(-40) + (2) = -38$
b) e.g., $(-36) - (2) = -38$

3. $-83, -97, -61, 64$

4. 530 m

5. -8

6. a) $4 \times (-38)$ d) $-935 \div (-85)$
b) $8 \times (-4)$ e) -3×7
c) $-21 \div 7, 3 \times (-7)$

7. 203

8. a) -36 c) -6 e) -21
b) 0 d) -7 f) 39

9. yes

10. e.g., She could have started at 2.

11. a) $-58 - (-36) + (-15) = -37$
b) $-4 \times (-3) + 28 = 40$
c) $-4 \times (-3 + 28) = -100$

12. a) e.g., -35 c) e.g., 7
b) e.g., -11 d) e.g., 5

13. She is wrong.

Cumulative Review: Chapters 4–6, pp. 217–218

1. B **2.** C **3.** D **4.** A
5. C **6.** A **7.** D **8.** A
9. D **10.** A **11.** D

12. a) 754 m c) 168 m
b) $120 + 2n$ d) 88 623 m^2

13. a) in the 1960s, by one whooping crane
b) 71 whooping cranes
c) about 35 whooping cranes
d) 11 whooping cranes

Chapter 7, p. 219

Getting Started, p. 221

1. $A(-4, 3)$, $B(3, 1)$, $C(2, -3)$, $D(-1, -5)$, $E(0, 1)$

2.

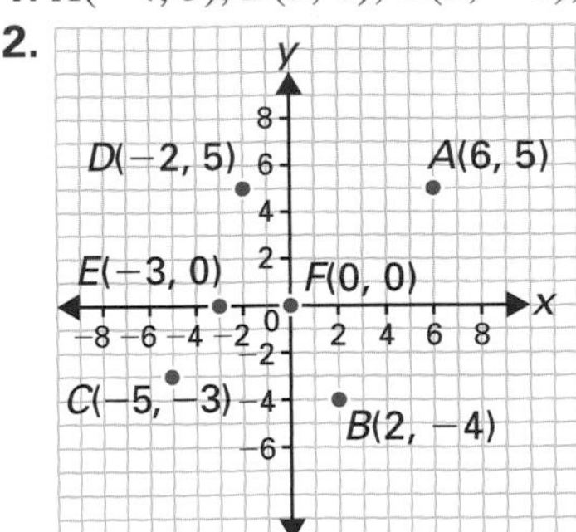

3. a) $(20, -15)$ c) $(15, 32)$
b) $(15, 32)$ d) $(18, -41)$

4. figure *S*

5. figures *B* and *C*

6. figures *W* and *X*

7. a) figure *D* b) figure *B* c) figures *C* and *E*

8. figures *N* and *M*

7.1 Coordinates of Points on a Grid, pp. 224–225

4. $A(-3, 0)$, $B(-1, -3)$, $C(0, 3)$, $D(4, 1)$

5.

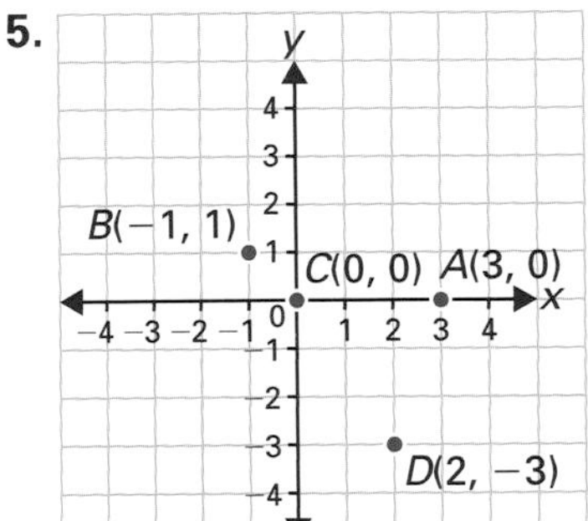

8. a) right triangle d) trapezoid
b) isosceles triangle e) trapezoid
c) rectangle f) rhombus

9. a) e.g., $(-9, 0), (-8, 0), (-7, 0)$
b) e.g., $(-1, -2), (-1, -3), (-1, -4)$
c) e.g., $(-3, 6), (-2, 7), (-1, 8)$
d) e.g., $(-4, 3), (-5, 3), (-6, 3)$

11. e.g., $Q(8, 4)$, $R(8, -1)$, and $S(3, -1)$

12. e.g., $Q(5, 6)$, $R(7, 4)$, and $S(5, 2)$

13. e.g., $K(-2, 7)$, $L(1, 7)$, and $M(0, 4)$

14. e.g., $(1, 3)$ and $(1, -5)$

15. a) Everton is subtracting each of Marisol's numbers, n, from 5.

b)

n	$5 - n$
3	2
2	3
1	4
0	5
−1	6
−2	7
−3	8

c)

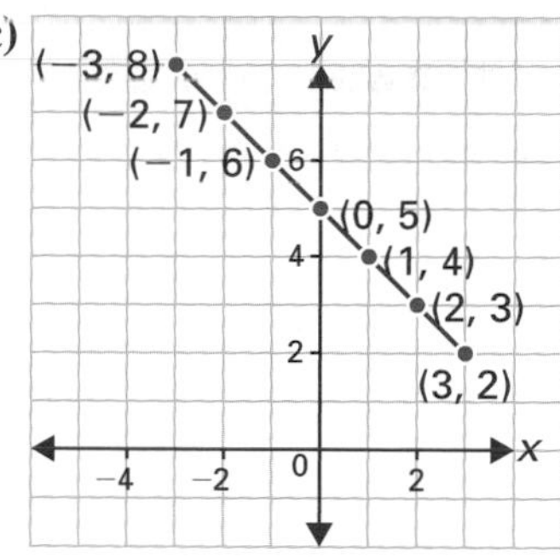

d) The plotted points form a straight line slanting down to the right. The values of n (or x) go down one each time as the values of $5 - n$ (or y) go up one each time.

16. a) 1st or 3rd quadrant **b)** 2nd or 4th quadrant **c)** x axis or y-axis

17. a) 1st or 3rd quadrant **b)** 2nd or 4th quadrant **c)** y-axis, except origin **d)** x-axis

18. a)

n	$3n + 2$	$3n - 2$	$-3n + 2$
−3	−7	−11	11
−2	−4	−8	8
−1	−1	−5	5
0	2	−2	2
1	5	1	−1
2	8	4	−4
3	11	7	−7

c) e.g., straight lines with same length and steepness; different position on Cartesian plane and different direction

7.2 Translations on a Coordinate System, pp. 228–229

4. a) $(-5, 5)$ **b)** $(2, 1)$

5. a)

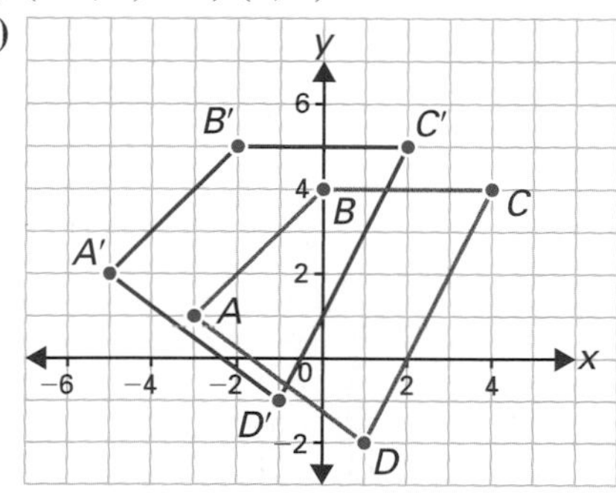

b) $A'(-5, 2)$, $B'(-2, 5)$, $C'(2, 5)$, $D'(-1, -1)$

10. a) $[2, -5]$ **b)** $E(-10, 0)$, $F(0, -2)$

12. $P'(2, 1)$, $Q'(6, 3)$, $R'(4, 6)$

13. c) $[0, -6]$

14. a)

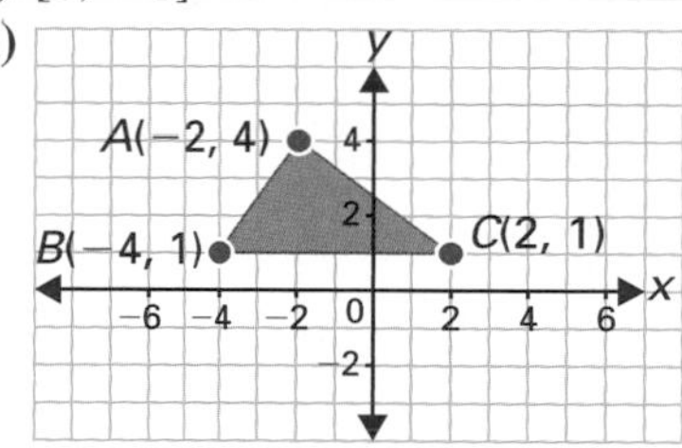

b)

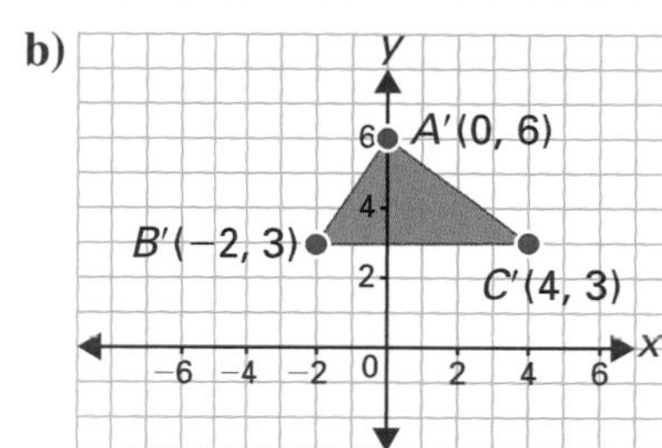

c)

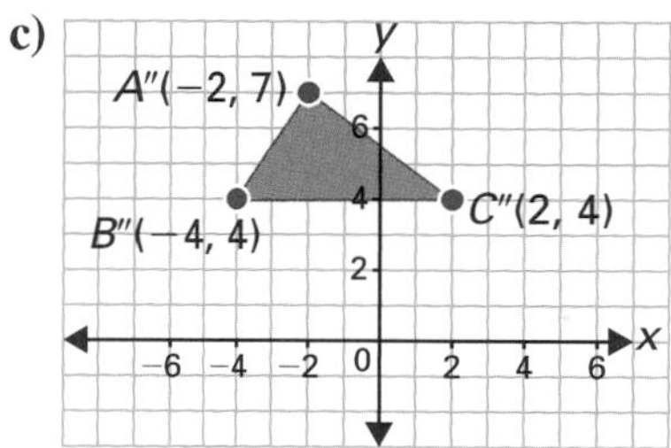

d) $[0, -3]$

e) Add the three translation vectors to get the sum $[0, 0]$, which represents the original position:

$$[2, 2] + [-2, 1] + [x, y] = [0, 0]$$
$$[x, y] = [0, -3]$$

7.3 Reflections and Rotations, pp. 232–233

4. $A'(1, -1)$, $B'(4, -4)$, $C'(7, -1)$, $D'(6, 3)$

5. a) $A'(6, 2)$, $B'(4, 0)$, $C'(2, 5)$
b) $A'(2, -6)$, $B'(0, -4)$, $C'(5, -2)$

6. a) $A'(-2, -5)$, $B'(-5, 1)$, $C'(3, 1)$
b) $A'(5, -2)$, $B'(-1, -5)$, $C'(-1, 3)$
c) $A'(-2, -5)$, $B'(-5, 1)$, $C'(3, 1)$

7. a) $A'(-6, -1)$, $B'(5, 0)$, $C'(-4, 4)$
b) $A'(6, 1)$, $B'(-5, 0)$, $C'(4, -4)$
c) $A'(1, -6)$, $B'(0, 5)$, $C'(-4, -4)$
d) $A'(-1, -6)$, $B'(0, 5)$, $C'(4, -4)$
e) $A'(6, -1)$, $B'(-5, 0)$, $C'(4, 4)$

8. a) $A'(-4, -1)$, $B'(1, -5)$, $C'(4, 3)$, $D'(-2, 3)$
b) $A'(4, 1)$, $B'(-1, 5)$, $C'(-4, -3)$, $D'(2, -3)$
c) $A'(4, -1)$, $B'(-1, -5)$, $C'(-4, 3)$, $D'(2, 3)$
d) $A'(-1, -4)$, $B'(-5, 1)$, $C'(3, 4)$, $D'(3, -2)$

10. Yes, he is right.

13. a) $A'(x, -y)$ **c)** $A'(y, x)$ **e)** $A'(-x, -y)$
b) $A'(-x, y)$ **d)** $A'(y, -x)$ **f)** $A'(-y, x)$

14. The second reflection line is $x = -10$.

Mid-Chapter Review, p. 236

1. a) $A(0, 3)$, $B(-2, 4)$, $C(3, -4)$, $D(4, 0)$
b) B is in the 2nd quadrant; C is in the 4th quadrant

2. parallelogram

3. e.g., $(-14, -5)$, $(2, 3)$, $(10, -1)$

4. a) $A'(-7, -2)$, $B'(-1, 4)$, $C'(3, -3)$, $D'(-5, -5)$
b) $A'(-2, -3)$, $B'(4, 3)$, $C'(8, -4)$, $D'(0, -6)$
c) $A'(-9, -7)$, $B'(-3, -1)$, $C'(1, -8)$, $D'(-7, -10)$

5. a) $[-4, -9]$
b) $A'(-9, -11)$, $B'(-3, -5)$, $C'(1, -12)$, $D'(-7, -14)$

6. $[-3, -4]$

7. $A(4, 3)$, $B(0, 0)$, $C(8, 2)$

8. a) $A'(2, 4)$, $B'(-4, 1)$, $C'(0, -4)$, $D'(3, -1)$
b) $A'(-2, -4)$, $B'(4, -1)$, $C'(0, 4)$, $D'(-3, 1)$
c) $A'(4, -2)$, $B'(1, 4)$, $C'(-4, 0)$, $D'(-1, -3)$
d) $A'(-4, -2)$, $B'(-1, 4)$, $C'(4, 0)$, $D'(1, -3)$
e) $A'(4, 2)$, $B'(1, -4)$, $C'(-4, 0)$, $D'(-1, 3)$

9. a) $A''(-1, -1)$, $B''(1, -1)$, $C''(3, -5)$

10. a rotation of 90° counterclockwise

11. 1st quadrant

7.5 Communicating about Transformations, p. 242

4. When a shape is reflected in the x-axis, the y-coordinate is the opposite of the original; when a shape is reflected in the y-axis, the x-coordinate is the opposite of the original. So after both reflections, both coordinates are the opposite of the originals. That's the same thing that happens after a 180° rotation about the origin.

7. Upper green figure: 90° ccw rotation of the blue pentomino about the bottom left corner of the top left tile
Upper red figure: translate the blue pentomino $[-3, 1]$
Left green figure: 90° cw rotation of the blue pentomino about the bottom left corner of the top left tile, then translate $[-3, 1]$
Lower red figure: translate the blue pentomino $[-4, -2]$
Lower green figure: 90° cw rotation of the blue pentomino about the bottom left corner of the top left tile

8. e.g.,
red figure: translate $[13, -1]$ and then reflect in a horizontal line through $(0, 4)$
orange figure: reflect in a vertical line through $(-5, 0)$ and then translate $[0, -6]$
blue figure: translate $[9, -6]$
light green figure: translate $[11, -2]$
dark green figure: rotate 180° about its top right vertex, then translate $[8, -5]$

Chapter Self-Test, p. 245

1. a) A **b)** B **c)** B **d)** A

2.

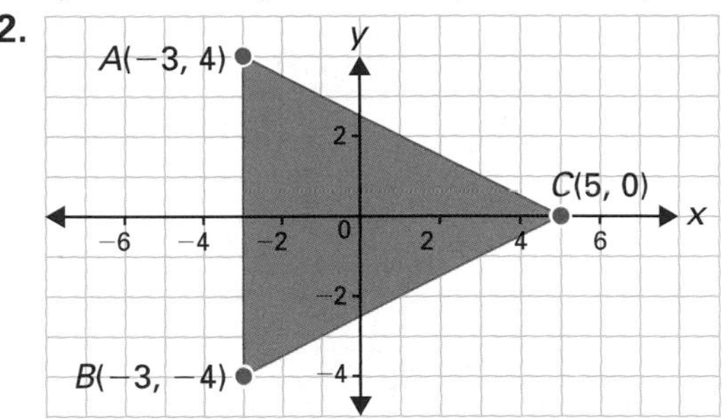

isosceles triangle

3. a) $[6, -7]$ **b)** $[-4, 6]$
c) $A'(-7, 15)$, $B'(-9, 10)$, $C'(-6, 7)$, $D'(-3, 9)$

4. a) $(4, 9)$ **b)** $[-3, 9]$
c) $A'(-1, 6)$, $B'(4, 9)$, $C'(-4, 15)$, $D'(1, 18)$

5. a) $A'(-3, -4)$, $B'(2, 1)$, $C'(7, -1)$
b) $A'(3, 4)$, $B'(-2, -1)$, $C'(-7, 1)$
c) $A'(-4, -3)$, $B'(1, 2)$, $C'(-1, 7)$
d) $A'(3, -4)$, $B'(-2, 1)$, $C'(-7, -1)$

6. a)

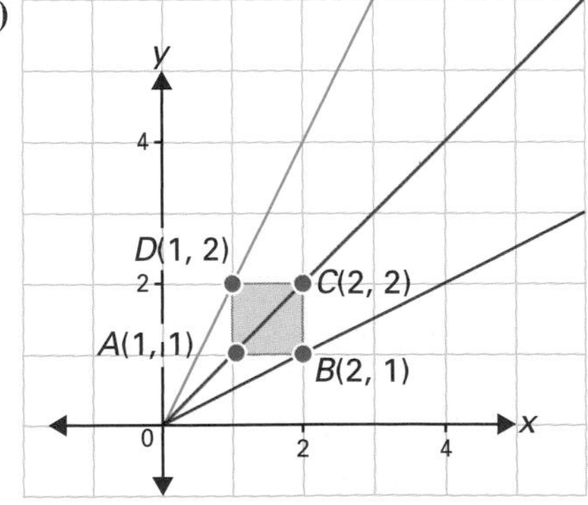

b) $A'(2, 2)$, $B'(4, 2)$, $C'(4, 4)$, $D'(2, 4)$

Chapter Review, p. 247

1. a) $A(-1, 3)$, $B(3, 4)$, $C(-3, -1)$, $D(2, 0)$
   b) A: 2nd quadrant, B: 1st quadrant, C: 3rd quadrant, D: axis between the 1st and 4th quadrants
2. e.g., $P(5, 0)$, $Q(0, 3)$, and $R(-5, 0)$; or, $P(5, 0)$, $Q(0, 7)$, and $R(-5, 0)$
3. a) $A'(0, -1)$, $B'(6, -4)$, $C'(2, -9)$, $D'(-1, -6)$
   b) $A'(-5, 6)$, $B'(1, 3)$, $C'(-3, -2)$, $D'(-6, 1)$
4. a) [3, 1]
   b) $A'(1, 5)$, $B'(7, 2)$, $C'(3, -3)$, $D'(0, 0)$
5. a) $A'(6, -6)$, $F'(-2, -6)$

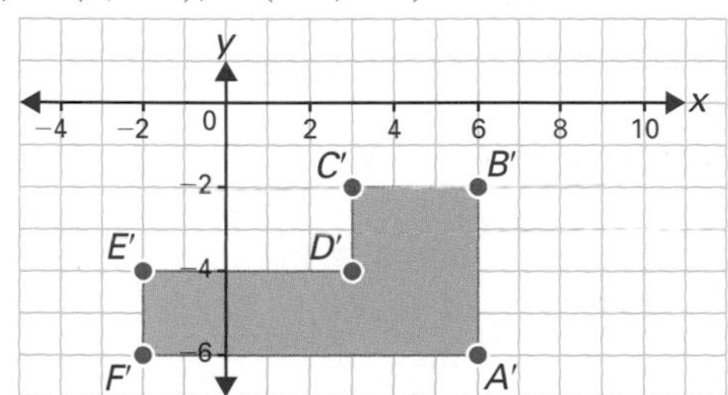

   b) $A'(-6, 6)$, $F'(2, 6)$

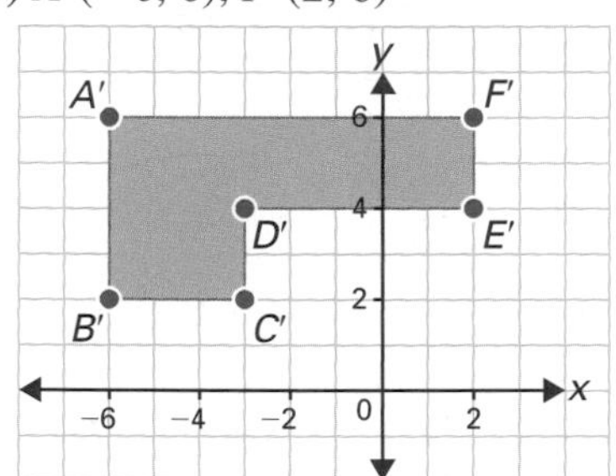

   c) $A'(-6, 6)$, $F'(-6, -2)$

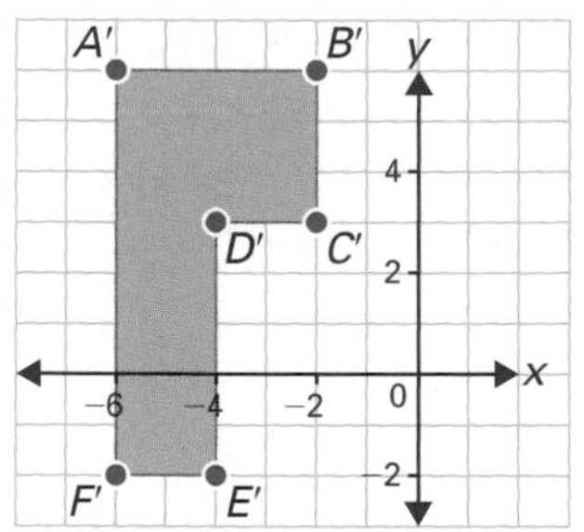

   d) $A'(-6, -6)$, $F'(2, -6)$

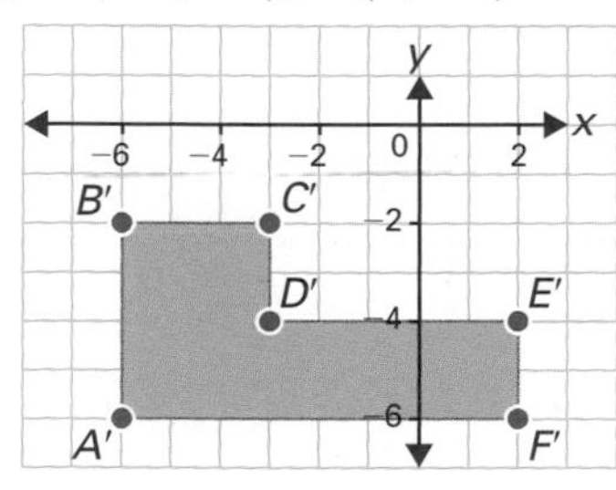

   e) $A'(6, -6)$, $F'(6, 2)$

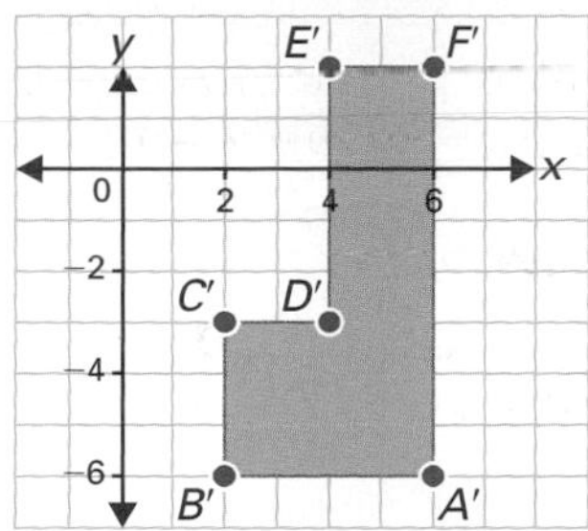

6. b) e.g.,

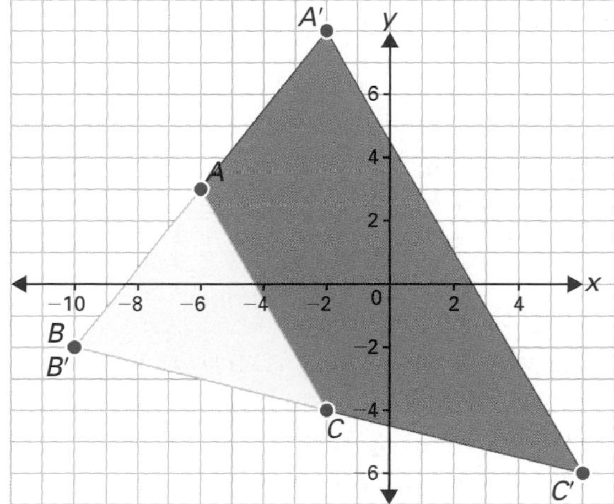

   c) e.g.,

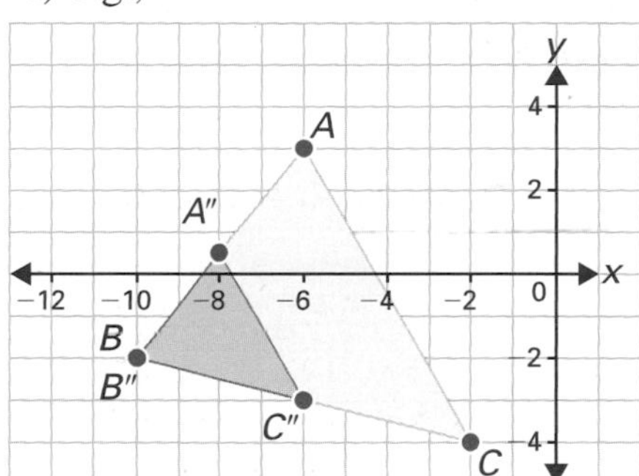

Chapter 8, p. 249

Getting Started, p. 251

1. a) 23	b) 30	c) 32	d) 12
2. a) 12	b) 7	c) 50	d) 2
3. a) $2n + 3$	b) $m + 1$		

4. a)

Figure number	Number of counters
1	3
2	7
3	11
4	15
5	19
6	23

b)

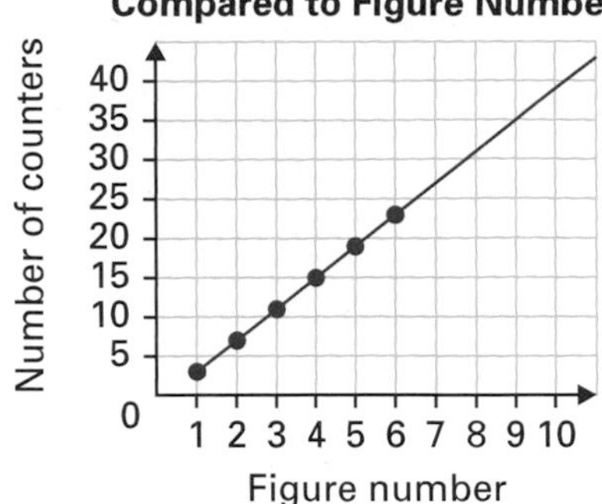

c) 39

5. a) \$9.60 b) 4 kg

6. Figure 12

7. a) $t = 8$ b) $w = 12$ c) $a = 8$ d) $y = 9$

8. a) $m = 19$ b) $s = 2$ c) $w = 4$ d) $y = 5$

9. a) $n = 5$ b) $n = 23$ c) $n = 17$ d) $n = 2$

8.1 Solving Equations by Graphing, pp. 254–255

3. $n = 7$

4. a)

Figure number	Number of tiles
1	3
2	4
3	5

b) $n + 2$ c) $n + 2 = 22$

d)

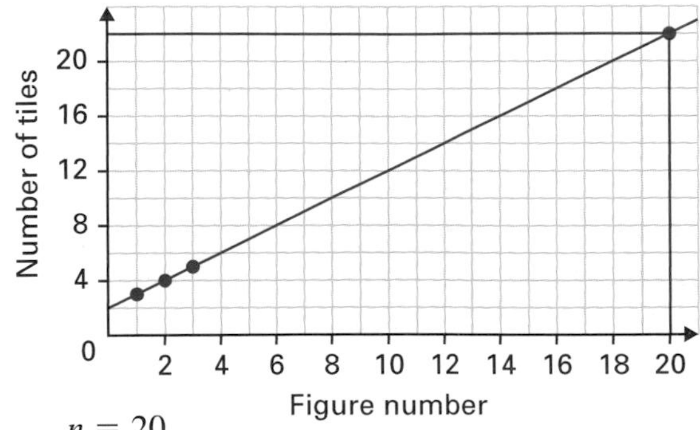

$n = 20$

6. d) after 11 weeks e) after 19 weeks f) \$105

7. a) Figure 32 b) Figure 48

8.

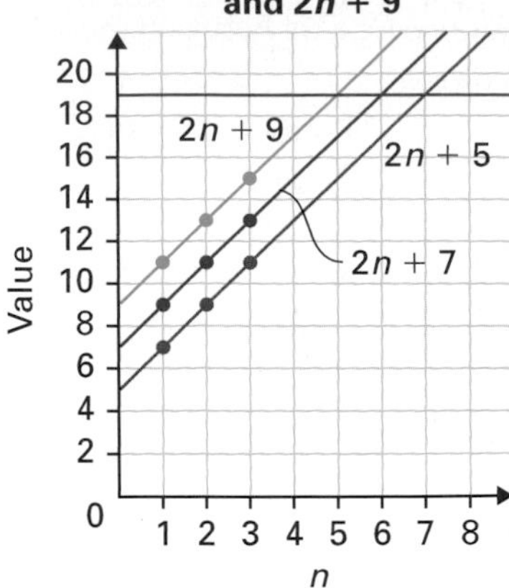

a) $n = 7$ b) $n = 6$ c) $n = 5$

9.

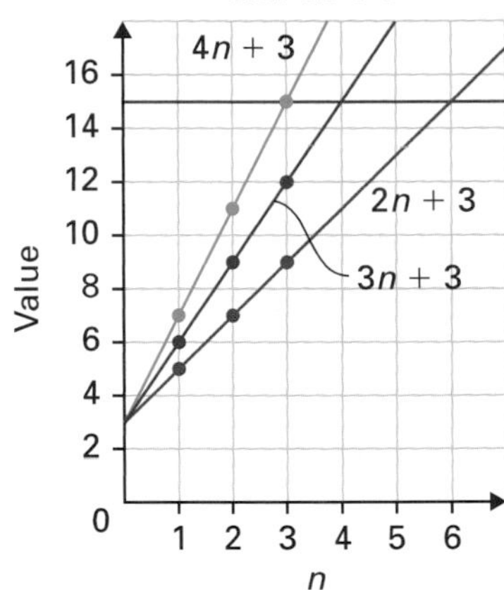

a) $n = 6$ b) $n = 4$ c) $n = 3$

10. a)

Figure number	Area of pond	Number of border tiles
1	1	8
2	4	12
3	9	16
4	16	20

b) Area of pond: $n \times n$
Number of border tiles: $4n + 4$

c)

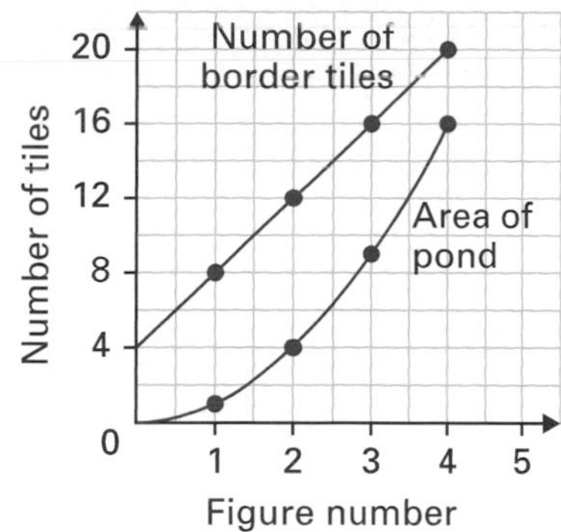

d) The pattern rule for the area of the pond has an n^2, while the pattern rule for the number of border tiles has no exponents. The line representing the area of the pond is curved upward, while the line representing the number of border tiles is straight.

e) $4n + 4 = 56$; Figure 13

f) $n \times n = 121$; Figure 11

8.3 Creating and Evaluating Algebraic Expressions, pp. 259–261

4. a) $1.50m + 1.25j$ **b)** \$95

5. a) 31 **b)** 17.5 **c)** 9.3 **d)** 28 **e)** 4

6. a) 46 **b)** 7 **c)** 31.6 **d)** 15 **e)** -9

7. a) $0.10d + 0.05n + 0.25q$ **b)** \$9.50

8. c) $22t + 18t = 40t$ **d)** 6000 L

9. d) 40.6

10. d) 41

11. b) 1195.5 kg

12. c) 39.2 m, 94.1 m^2

13. b) offer ii)

14. a) $2.45s + 2.85b$ **b)** \$39.55

15. a) $s^2 + t^2$

b) e.g., If $s = 1$ and $t = 1$, then $s^2 + t^2 = 2$.

c) sometimes, e.g., if $s = 3$ and $t = 4$

16. a) $l - 2$ **b)** $l(l - 2)$ **c)** $w(w + 2)$ **d)** 80 cm^2

17. a) $4.25s - 2.50s$, $1.75s$ **b)** \$304.50

Mid-Chapter Review, p. 263

1. a)

Day number	Number of golf carts
1	9
2	15
3	21
4	27

b) $6n + 3$ **c)** $6n + 3 = 51$; day 8

2. a)

Figure number	Number of counters
1	11
2	15
3	19

b) $4n + 7$ **c)** $4n + 7 = 63$ **d)** Figure 14

3. a) $n = 12$ **b)** $n = 14$

4. a) 7.6 **b)** -22 **c)** 8.8 **d)** 5

5. a) $182.73 + 12.50n$ **b)** \$282.73

8.4 Solving Equations I, pp. 266–267

4. a)

b) $15n - 100 = 425$

c) 35 lawns

e) e.g., yes, because my answer from solving the equation matches my answer from the graph

5. a) $n = 6$ **b)** $n = 2.5$ **c)** $n = 3.1$ **d)** $n = 4$

7. a) e.g., $x \doteq 10$ **c)** e.g., $a \doteq 35$ **e)** e.g., $p \doteq 2.5$

b) e.g., $c \doteq 3$ **d)** e.g., $h \doteq 2$ **f)** e.g., $n \doteq 6$

8. a) incorrect; $n = 15$ **d)** correct

b) correct **e)** correct

c) incorrect; $t = 54.9$ **f)** incorrect; $w = 3$

9. a) $b = 4$ **c)** $n = 1.2$ **e)** $t = 4.83$

b) $x = 1$ **d)** $t = 4.25$ **f)** $n = 4$

10. a) $6n = 48$; $n = 8$

b) $2p - 10 = 37$; $p = 23.5$

c) $7w + 2.5 = 58.5$; $w = 8$

11. b) \$39.95

12. d) 31

13. d) 13 cartons

14. 11, 12, and 13

15. Madison earns \$30.75, and Daryl earns \$10.25.

16. Holly scored 59 points, and Julia scored 48 points. The difference is 11 points.

17. a) $m = -6$ **b)** $m = -3$ **c)** $t = -9$

8.5 Solving Equations II, pp. 270–271

5. a) Double the number of counters and double the number of bags on the right side.
b) Subtract 4 counters on the right side.
6. $2n + 3 = 17; n = 7$
7. a) $t = 12$ **b)** $a = 3$ **c)** $b = 3$ **d)** $x = 16$
8. $n = 4$
9. a) $m = 17$ **c)** $n = 1280$ **e)** $w = 110$
b) $a = 12$ **d)** $n = 32.5$ **f)** $n = 24$
10. a) $a = 1.1$ **c)** $n = 11$ **e)** $n = 27.8$
b) $t = 1.3$ **d)** $x = 7.95$ **f)** $n = 65$
11. 6 stones
12. a) $2n + 6 = 66$; 30 stones
b) $3m - 7 = 32$; 13 stones
13. a) $x = 2.4$ **b)** $n = 2.2$ **c)** $x = 27$ **d)** $n = 27.5$
14. $2.95
15. $13.95
16. $4.85
17. 22.5 kg
18. 0.25 kg
19. $x = 10$
20. a) $x = -10$ **c)** $x = 9$ **e)** $n = -2$
b) $n = 5$ **d)** $n = 4$

8.6 Communicating about Equations, p. 276

4. a) e.g., Alec bought 2 boxes of cereal and a carton of milk. The milk cost $1.50. If his total before tax was $5.50, then how much did each box of cereal cost?
b) e.g., $2.00
c) e.g., I created this problem thinking about buying items from a store and letting the cost of one of the items be the variable and the cost of another item be $1.50. The total of the items purchased before tax could be $5.50. I solved my problem by balancing the equation and then I checked my solution to make sure that it was correct.

Chapter Self-Test, p. 277

1. $n = 15$
2. a)

Figure number	Number of counters
1	1
2	5
3	9

b) $4n - 3$ **c)** $4n - 3 = 161$ **d)** $n = 41$
3. a) 115.35 **b)** -37
4. a) $x = 13$ **c)** $m = 14$
b) $n = 6$ **d)** $t = 104.25$
5. a) $n = 7$ **c)** $t = 5.37$ **e)** $p = 3$
b) $x = 18.3$ **d)** $h = 4$ **f)** $n = 4.4$
6. a) $n + 7.1 = 10.3$ **c)** $2m = 49$
b) $6n = 48.6$ **d)** $3p + 2.5 = 83.5$
7. a) $2s = 150.62$; $s = \$75.31$
b) $3h + 7.65 = 27.90$; $h = \$6.75$
8. $39 + 2.5s = 51.5$; 5 pairs of socks

Chapter Review, p. 279

1. a) $n = 8$ **b)** $2n + 4 = 12; n = 4$
2. a)

Figure number	Number of counters
1	13
2	19
3	25

b) $6n + 7$ **c)** Figure 23
3. $59.25
4. a) $b = 5$ **c)** $n = 0.8$ **e)** $t = 4.75$
b) $a = 1.6$ **d)** $x = 36$ **f)** $m = 9.2$
5. a) $n + 3.21 = 16.05; n = 12.84$
b) $3.21n = 16.05; n = 5$
c) $2n - 3.21 = 16.05; n = 9.63$
6. $34c + 351 = 895$; $16.00 per team
7. e.g., Eva noticed a sale at the bookstore: any book for $10.99. If her total without tax was $21.98, how many books did Eva buy? Answer: 2 books
8. e.g., What was the cost of each individual ticket? Answer: $25.50

Math in Action: Entrepreneur, pp. 281–282

1. (1) the months the business was open; (2) the sales in dollars for each month; (3) the amount of money borrowed in dollars each month; (4) the total amount of money in dollars the business received each month; (5) the amount of money in dollars spent on buying equipment each month; (6) the amount of money in dollars needed to pay employees each month; (7) the cost in dollars of renting equipment each month; (8) the amount of money in dollars withdrawn from the business each month; (9) the amount of money in dollars used to pay the loan each month;

(10) the total amount of money in dollars the business paid out each month; (11) the overall change in money for each month; (12) the overall change in money from the beginning of April after each month

2. =B2+B3

3. =B5+B6+B7+B8+B9

4. =B4−B10

5. a) negative

b) the business broke even—no gains, no losses

6. a) for B12: =B11; for C12: =B12+C11

b) for B12: =B11; for C12: =B11+C11

c) e.g., B12: =B11; C12: =B12+C11; D12: =C12+D11; E12: =D12+E11; F12: =E12+F11; G12: =F12+G11; H12: =G12+H11

7. a) Row 4: B4 = 6900, C4 = 6500, D4 = 4200, E4 = 6900, F4 = 7800, G4 = 3800, H4 = 1100
Row 10: B10 = 7140, C10 = 11 815, D10 = 1160, E10 = 2410, F10 = 2630, G10 = 1920, H10 = 6350
Row 11: B11 = −240, C11 = −5315, D11 = 3040, E11 = 4490, F11 = 5170, G11 = 1880, H11 = −5250
Row 12: B12 = −240, C12 = −5555, D12 = −2515, E12 = 1975, F12 = 7145, G12 = 9025, H12 = 3775

b) It is the first month that the business is open, so there are no previous month's to influence the cumulative cash flow.

8. e.g., The cash flow increases and then decreases as it gets warmer and then colder again.

9. e.g., Yes, she should generate enough income to be able to pay back the loan, as well as cover all her expenses, and still make a profit.

Chapter 9, p. 283

Getting Started, p. 285

1. a) e.g., $\frac{6}{16}, \frac{9}{24}$

b) e.g., $\frac{10}{6}, \frac{15}{9}$

c) e.g., $\frac{22}{4}, \frac{33}{6}$

d) e.g., $\frac{18}{24}, \frac{27}{36}$

2. $\frac{3}{8}, \frac{3}{5}, \frac{6}{7}, \frac{12}{5}$

3. $\frac{2}{8} + \frac{3}{8} = \frac{5}{8}$

4. a) $\frac{2}{3} - \frac{1}{6} = \frac{1}{2}$, $\frac{1}{2}$ of the circle represents how much more yellow there is than red.

b) $\frac{3}{4} - \frac{1}{3} = \frac{5}{12}$, $\frac{5}{12}$ of the strips represents how much more yellow there is than red.

5. a) $\frac{3}{5} + \frac{1}{3} = \frac{14}{15}$

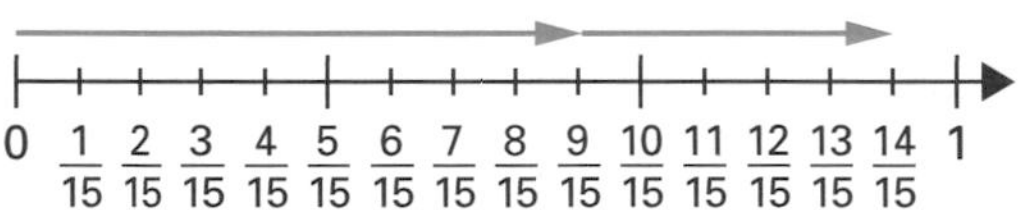

b) $4 \times \frac{2}{5} = \frac{8}{5}$, or $1\frac{3}{5}$

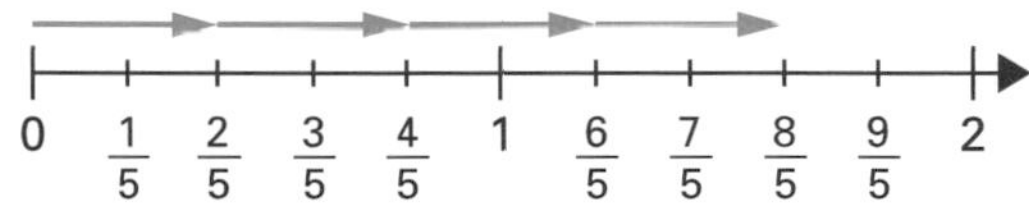

6. a) $\frac{17}{20}$

b) $\frac{3}{20}$

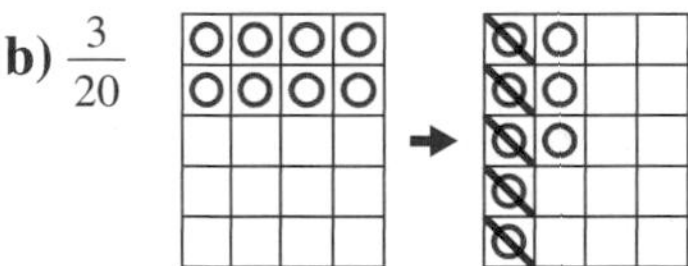

c) $\frac{9}{5}$ or $1\frac{4}{5}$

d) $\frac{18}{10}$ or $1\frac{4}{5}$

7. a) $\frac{9}{10}$ **b)** $\frac{7}{6}$ or $1\frac{1}{6}$ **c)** $\frac{11}{8}$ or $1\frac{3}{8}$

8.

Repeated addition	Multiplication	Result
$\frac{2}{3} + \frac{2}{3} + \frac{2}{3} + \frac{2}{3}$	$4 \times \frac{2}{3}$	$\frac{8}{3}$ or $2\frac{2}{3}$
$\frac{5}{8} + \frac{5}{8} + \frac{5}{8}$	$3 \times \frac{5}{8}$	$\frac{15}{8}$ or $1\frac{7}{8}$

9. a) 16 slices **b)** $1\frac{1}{3}$ pizzas

10. 4 full glasses, and one glass that was $\frac{2}{3}$ full.

9.1 Adding and Subtracting Fractions Less Than 1, pp. 288–289

4. a) $\frac{7}{6}$ or $1\frac{1}{6}$ 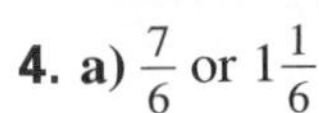 e.g.,

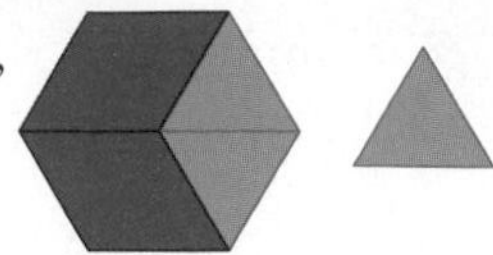

b) $\frac{1}{8}$ e.g.,

1/8	1/8	1/8	1/8	1/8	1/8	1/8	1/8
1/4		1/4		1/4		1/4	

5. a) $\frac{5}{28}$ **b)** $\frac{49}{60}$

6. $\frac{2}{3}$ is greater than $\frac{1}{5}$ by $\frac{7}{15}$.

7. $\frac{1}{2} + \frac{1}{5}$

8. $\frac{3}{14}$

10. a) $\frac{5}{6}$ **b)** $\frac{11}{10}$ or $1\frac{1}{10}$ **c)** $\frac{1}{14}$ **d)** $\frac{5}{4}$ or $1\frac{1}{4}$

12. a) $1\frac{2}{21}$ **b)** $1\frac{6}{35}$ **c)** $1\frac{19}{36}$ **d)** $\frac{5}{12}$ **e)** $\frac{7}{20}$ **f)** $\frac{11}{24}$

15. $\frac{5}{12}$

16. a) $\frac{7}{4}$ or $1\frac{3}{4}$ **b)** $\frac{3}{4}$

17. B

19. $\frac{1}{6} + \frac{4}{5} + \frac{2}{3}$

20. $\frac{41}{75}$

21. $\frac{3}{5}$

9.2 Adding and Subtracting Fractions Greater Than 1, pp. 292–293

4. $4\frac{1}{6}$ cups

5. a) $4\frac{11}{12}$ **b)** $\frac{5}{8}$

6. a) $8\frac{17}{24}$ **b)** $2\frac{11}{30}$

7. a) $6\frac{3}{10}$ **b)** $1\frac{17}{20}$

8. a) $5\frac{1}{5}$ **c)** $\frac{43}{6}$ or $7\frac{1}{6}$ **e)** $7\frac{11}{12}$

b) $8\frac{14}{15}$ **d)** $7\frac{7}{15}$ **f)** $10\frac{1}{30}$

9. a) $1\frac{3}{5}$ **b)** $2\frac{5}{28}$ **c)** $\frac{17}{20}$ **d)** $\frac{41}{10}$ or $4\frac{1}{10}$

10. $\frac{5}{6}$ h

13. b)

18. e.g., $\frac{3}{4}$ and $\frac{3}{8}$

20. $6\frac{9}{20}$ cars

21. a) $12\frac{1}{3}$ small bags **b)** $3\frac{1}{12}$ large bags

22. a) $9\frac{2}{3} - 1\frac{4}{6} + 7\frac{5}{8} = 15\frac{5}{8}$

9.4 Fractions of Fractions, pp. 298–299

4. a) $\frac{2}{7}$ **b)** $\frac{2}{9}$

5. b), c), a)

6. $\frac{1}{4}$ of $\frac{2}{3}$ is $\frac{1}{6}$.

12. a) $\frac{5}{8}$ **b)** $\frac{8}{9}$ **c)** $\frac{1}{10}$

16. a) e.g., $\frac{1}{5}$ is $\frac{1}{2}$ of $\frac{2}{5}$. **c)** e.g., $\frac{5}{12}$ is $\frac{5}{6}$ of $\frac{1}{2}$.

b) e.g., $\frac{2}{8}$ is $\frac{1}{3}$ of $\frac{3}{4}$. **d)** e.g., $\frac{3}{7}$ is $\frac{3}{4}$ of $\frac{4}{7}$.

18. The darkest section is an eighth of the circle.

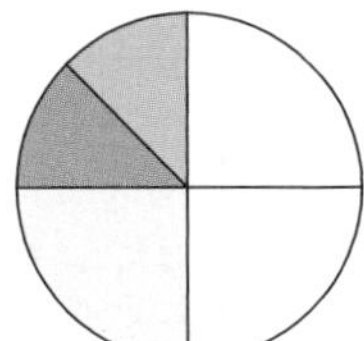

19. a) $\frac{1}{3}$ **b)** $\frac{3}{7}$ **c)** $\frac{3}{8}$ **d)** $\frac{3}{5}$

20. e.g.,

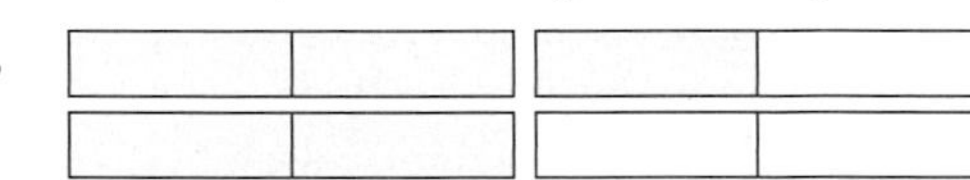

21. a) $\frac{9}{20}$ **b)** 20

22. e.g., It is more accurate and requires fewer calculations to use fractions. It requires many calculations to multiply 0.6 by a repeating decimal and it's relatively easy to think of $\frac{1}{3}$ of $\frac{3}{5}$ as $\frac{1}{5}$.

9.5 Multiplying Fractions, pp. 302–303

4. a) $\frac{4}{9} \times \frac{3}{4}$ **b)** $\frac{3}{7} \times \frac{2}{3}$

5. $\frac{6}{20} = \frac{3}{10}$

6. $\frac{2}{110} = \frac{1}{55}$

8. a) $\frac{3}{16}$ b) $\frac{4}{15}$ c) $\frac{1}{15}$ d) $\frac{1}{4}$

18. a) about $\frac{9}{40}$ b) about 67.5 million

19. a) $\frac{1}{6}$

b) The probability of landing on A is $\frac{1}{2}$ and the probability of landing on red is $\frac{1}{3}$, so the probability of both is $\frac{1}{2} \times \frac{1}{3}$.

20. $a = 7$

21. $\frac{1}{100}$

Mid-Chapter Review, pp. 306–307

1. a) $\frac{5}{6}$ b) $\frac{1}{2}$

2. a) $\frac{19}{12}$ or $1\frac{7}{12}$ b) $\frac{5}{24}$

3. a) less than c) greater than e) less than
b) greater than d) greater than f) greater than

4. a) $\frac{7}{8}$ b) $\frac{11}{30}$ c) $\frac{29}{45}$ d) $\frac{7}{40}$ e) $\frac{4}{63}$ f) $\frac{67}{110}$

5. a) $\frac{2}{3} + \frac{3}{4} = 1\frac{5}{12}$ b) $\frac{5}{20} + \frac{8}{20} = \frac{13}{20}$

6. a) $\frac{13}{12}$ or $1\frac{1}{12}$ c) $\frac{3}{8}$ e) $\frac{25}{18}$ or $1\frac{7}{18}$
b) $\frac{16}{15}$ or $1\frac{1}{15}$ d) $\frac{3}{20}$ f) $\frac{3}{5}$

7. a) e.g., $\frac{1}{5} + \frac{2}{5}, \frac{3}{10} + \frac{3}{10}, \frac{1}{10} + \frac{5}{10}$

b) e.g, $\frac{4}{5} - \frac{1}{5}, \frac{5}{5} - \frac{2}{5}, \frac{6}{5} - \frac{3}{5}$

8. e.g., $\frac{2}{8} + \frac{2}{8} + \frac{3}{8}, \frac{1}{16} + \frac{9}{16} + \frac{1}{4}, \frac{1}{2} + \frac{3}{16} + \frac{3}{16}$,
and $\frac{4}{8} + \frac{1}{4} + \frac{2}{16}$

9. $\frac{5}{12}$ **10.** $\frac{1}{12}$ **11.** $5\frac{1}{4}$ days

12. a) 10 b) 3 c) 5 d) 0 e) 1 f) $2\frac{1}{2}$

13. a) $8\frac{3}{4}$ b) $5\frac{7}{9}$ c) $5\frac{14}{15}$ d) $3\frac{1}{3}$ e) $2\frac{1}{3}$ f) $1\frac{1}{12}$

14. e.g., $2\frac{4}{5} + 3\frac{1}{5} = 6$

15. The model shows how to get from $1\frac{2}{3}$ to 4, so first add $\frac{1}{3}$ to get to 2 and then another 2 to get to 4. Thus, you are adding $\frac{1}{3} + 2$ to find the difference between 4 and $1\frac{2}{3}$.

16. a) $\frac{1}{8} - \frac{1}{16} = \frac{1}{16}, \frac{1}{16} - \frac{1}{32} = \frac{1}{32}, \frac{1}{32} - \frac{1}{64} = \frac{1}{64}$

b) $\frac{1}{512} - \frac{1}{1024} = \frac{1}{1024}$

17. $\frac{2}{3}$ of $\frac{3}{8}$ is $\frac{1}{4}$

$\frac{1}{8}$	$\frac{1}{8}$	$\frac{1}{8}$	$\frac{1}{8}$	$\frac{1}{8}$	$\frac{1}{8}$	$\frac{1}{8}$	$\frac{1}{8}$
$\frac{1}{8}$	$\frac{1}{8}$	$\frac{1}{8}$	$\frac{1}{8}$	$\frac{1}{8}$	$\frac{1}{8}$	$\frac{1}{8}$	$\frac{1}{8}$

18. e.g.,

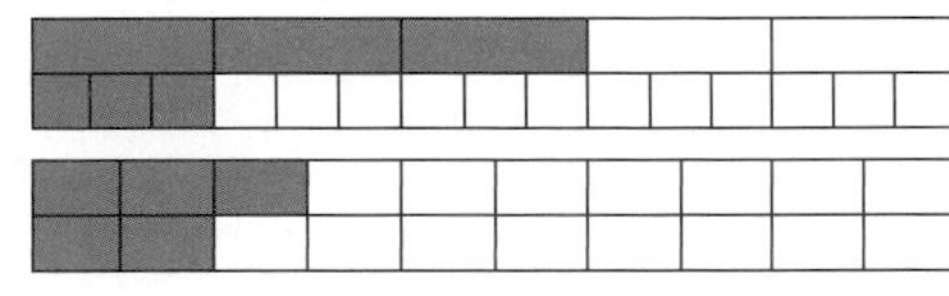

19. a) $\frac{1}{14}$ b) $\frac{3}{4}$ c) $\frac{1}{3}$

20. a) $\frac{1}{18}$ b) $\frac{12}{35}$

21. a) $\frac{3}{6} \times \frac{2}{5} = \frac{6}{30}$ c) $\frac{3}{5} \times \frac{1}{2} = \frac{3}{10}$
b) $\frac{2}{4} \times \frac{6}{7} = \frac{12}{28}$

22. a) $\frac{1}{56}$ b) $\frac{6}{55}$ c) $\frac{5}{8}$ d) $\frac{1}{27}$ e) $\frac{6}{25}$ f) $\frac{81}{100}$

23. yes

24. no

25. a) $\frac{1}{35}$ b) $\frac{1}{12}$ c) $\frac{7}{20}$

26. e.g., Jane's room is $\frac{2}{3}$ as long as Andy's and only $\frac{3}{5}$ as wide. What fraction of the area of Andy's room is Jane's room?

9.6 Multiplying Fractions Greater Than 1, pp. 310–311

4. a) 3 b) 49

5. a) $4\frac{4}{5}$ b) $2\frac{2}{7}$

6. a) $\frac{17}{18}$ b) $15\frac{21}{25}$

7. 1 dozen

8. a) $1\frac{1}{2}$ b) $\frac{15}{16}$ c) $\frac{8}{15}$ d) $2\frac{1}{8}$ e) $1\frac{3}{7}$ f) $\frac{7}{27}$

9. a) 2 b) $1\frac{1}{7}$ c) $6\frac{29}{30}$

10. a) $7\frac{1}{2}$ b) $3\frac{3}{4}$ c) $4\frac{4}{5}$ d) $7\frac{1}{5}$ e) $8\frac{4}{9}$ f) $1\frac{11}{24}$

12. 2 times

14. $2\frac{2}{9}$ the area

15. Mount Columbia is $26\frac{9}{20}$ times as high as the highest point in Prince Edward Island.

16. **a)** $7\frac{41}{50}$ **b)** 7.82 **c)** The answers are the same.

18. $a = \frac{8}{5}$, $b = \frac{5}{4}$, and $c = \frac{7}{3}$

19. e.g., $2\frac{1}{2}$ and $1\frac{1}{4}$

9.7 Dividing Fractions I, pp. 314–315

4. $\frac{2}{3} \div \frac{2}{9}$

5. $\frac{7}{8} \div \frac{1}{4} = 3\frac{1}{2}$

1/8	1/8	1/8	1/8	1/8	1/8	1/8	

1/4	1/4	1/4		

6. **a)** $\frac{5}{6}$ **b)** $3\frac{3}{4}$

7. $6\frac{2}{3}$ times

9. **a)** 15 **b)** $2\frac{1}{10}$ **c)** $6\frac{2}{3}$ **d)** $\frac{18}{25}$

10. $2\frac{1}{2}$ h

11. 13 or 14 times

13. **a)** $\frac{3}{10}$ **b)** $5\frac{5}{7}$ **c)** $\frac{1}{8}$ **d)** 3

14. $7\frac{1}{8}$ times

18. **a)** about 7 sections

19. **a)** $\frac{1}{8}$ is half the size of $\frac{1}{4}$.

b) $\frac{6}{8}$ is twice as long as $\frac{3}{8}$.

20. $\frac{5}{6}$

21. e.g., $\frac{13}{8}$ and $\frac{1}{2}$, or $\frac{13}{5}$ and $\frac{4}{5}$

9.8 Dividing Fractions II, p. 319

5. **a)** $\frac{3}{4}$ **b)** $2\frac{5}{8}$

6. $2\frac{1}{2}$ small cans

9. b) and d)

10. **a)** ii) and iii)

11. **a)** $2\frac{2}{9}$ **b)** $4\frac{1}{6}$ **d)** $2\frac{5}{8}$

13. **a)** $13\frac{1}{3}$ pages/min **b)** 15 pages/min **c)** 8 pages/min

14. $3\frac{3}{4}$ pitchers

15. **a)** $6\frac{2}{3}$ laps **b)** $4\frac{4}{9}$ laps **c)** $3\frac{1}{3}$ laps

18. e.g., $\frac{1}{3}, \frac{2}{3}, \frac{14}{15}$

19. **a)** $\frac{9}{16}$ **b)** $\frac{1}{4}$

20. e.g., $\frac{1}{2}$ and $\frac{1}{2}$, $\frac{1}{6}$ and $\frac{1}{3}$, $\frac{1}{12}$ and $\frac{1}{4}$

9.9 Communicating about Multiplication and Division, p. 322

3. 1.2 is $1\frac{2}{10}$. This is the same as $1\frac{1}{5}$. So, I need 3.55 and another $\frac{1}{5}$ of 3.55. To calculate $\frac{1}{5}$ of 3.55, you can take $\frac{1}{5}$ of each hundredths grid. $\frac{1}{5}$ of the first hundredths grid is 20 hundredths. Similarly, $\frac{1}{5}$ of the second and third grids is also 20 hundredths each. $\frac{1}{5}$ of the last grid is $55 \div 5 = 11$ hundredths. This gives a total of $20 + 20 + 20 + 11 = 71$ hundredths. Express 71 hundredths as a decimal to finish the calculation, that is $3.55 + 0.71 = 4.26$.

4. e.g., $4.25 \times 2.1 = \frac{425}{100} \times \frac{21}{10}$. You get the answer by multiplying 425×21 for the numerator and using 1000 for the denominator.
$42.5 \times 0.21 = \frac{425}{10} \times \frac{21}{100}$. You still have the same numerator of 425×21 and the same denominator of 1000.

12. $\frac{15}{8} \div \frac{5}{4}$ means how many sets of $\frac{5}{4}$ are in $\frac{15}{8}$.
$\frac{15}{8} \div \frac{5}{8}$ means how many sets of $\frac{5}{8}$ are in $\frac{15}{8}$.
Since $\frac{5}{4}$ is exactly twice the size of $\frac{5}{8}$, it will fit in exactly half as many times.

13. No, since 4 is less than 8, $4 \div 8$ will be less than 1. Since 0.4 is greater than 0.08, $0.4 \div 0.08$ will be greater than 1. So, $0.4 \div 0.08$ will be greater than $4 \div 8$, not $\frac{1}{10}$ of it.

9.10 Order of Operations, pp. 325–326

3. **a)** 9 **b)** $\frac{25}{36}$

4. e.g., $\frac{2}{5} \div \frac{1}{4} + \frac{3}{8} = \frac{79}{40}$, or $1\frac{39}{40}$
$\frac{2}{5} \div \frac{3}{8} + \frac{1}{4} = \frac{79}{60}$, or $1\frac{19}{60}$
$\frac{2}{5} + \frac{1}{4} \div \frac{3}{8} = \frac{16}{15}$, or $1\frac{1}{15}$

5. a) e.g., $\frac{1}{2}-\frac{2}{9}\div\frac{4}{5}=\frac{2}{9}, \frac{4}{5}-\frac{2}{9}\div\frac{1}{2}=\frac{16}{45},$
$\frac{4}{5}\div\frac{1}{2}-\frac{2}{9}=1\frac{17}{45}$

b) Yes; e.g., $\left(\frac{4}{5}-\frac{1}{2}\right)\div\frac{2}{9}=\frac{27}{20}$, or $1\frac{7}{20}$

6. a) $\frac{97}{60}$ or $1\frac{37}{60}$ c) $\frac{37}{10}$ or $3\frac{7}{10}$ e) $\frac{19}{24}$

b) $\frac{29}{120}$ d) $\frac{112}{135}$ f) $\frac{25}{36}$

7. A and B

8. a) $\frac{9}{35}$ c) $\frac{25}{2}$ or $12\frac{1}{2}$ e) $\frac{52}{9}$ or $5\frac{7}{9}$

b) $\frac{79}{12}$ or $6\frac{7}{12}$ d) $\frac{103}{140}$ f) $\frac{256}{63}$ or $4\frac{4}{63}$

9. 144

10. $2+\left(\frac{1}{4}+\frac{1}{3}\right)\times\frac{3}{7}-\frac{2}{5}\times\frac{3}{8}\div\left(\frac{1}{10}+\frac{1}{5}\right)$

11. e.g., $a=\frac{35}{36}, b=\frac{1}{36}, c=\frac{5}{6}$ and $a=\frac{48}{49}, b=\frac{1}{49}, c=\frac{6}{7}$

12. A, B, D

13. a) e.g., $a=\frac{1}{2}$ and $b=\frac{1}{3}$ c) e.g., $d=\frac{1}{6}$

b) e.g., $c=\frac{1}{3}$

14. e.g., $\frac{4}{5}+\frac{1}{3}\times\frac{3}{5}$

15. a) 3 b) 2

Chapter Self-Test, p. 327

1. a) $\frac{5}{4}$ or $1\frac{1}{4}$ c) $\frac{14}{15}$ e) $\frac{1}{6}$

b) $\frac{7}{9}$ d) $\frac{3}{10}$ f) $\frac{5}{12}$

2. c), a), b), d)

3. e.g.,

1	1	1
1		

4. a) $5\frac{1}{5}$ b) $6\frac{1}{8}$ c) $5\frac{1}{10}$ d) $1\frac{5}{6}$

5. $\frac{5}{6}$

6. a) $\frac{2}{12}=\frac{1}{6}$ b) $\frac{6}{18}=\frac{1}{3}$ c) $\frac{6}{7}$

7. e.g., Multiplying by $\frac{5}{6}$ means taking $\frac{5}{6}$ of something; that's only part of it, not all of it, so the answer is less than the number you start with.

8. a) $\frac{3}{8}$ b) $\frac{5}{18}$ c) $\frac{1}{14}$ d) $\frac{15}{112}$

9. a) e.g.,

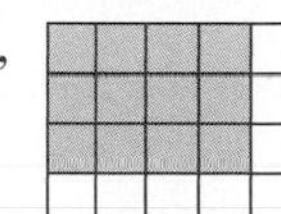

10. e.g., If you have $\frac{3}{4}$ of a can of paint and only need to use $\frac{1}{2}$ of it for a project, what fraction of the can will you use?

11. e.g.,

$$1\frac{2}{3}\times 2\frac{1}{4}=1\times 2\frac{1}{4}+\frac{2}{3}\times 2\frac{1}{4}$$
$$=2\frac{1}{4}+\frac{2}{3}\times\frac{9}{4}$$
$$=\frac{9}{4}+\frac{6}{4}$$
$$=\frac{15}{4}, \text{ or } 3\frac{3}{4}$$

OR

$$1\frac{2}{3}\times 2\frac{1}{4}=\frac{5}{3}\times\frac{9}{4}$$
$$=\frac{45}{12}$$
$$=\frac{15}{4}, \text{ or } 3\frac{3}{4}$$

12. a) $\frac{33}{10}$ or $3\frac{3}{10}$ c) $\frac{49}{20}$ or $2\frac{9}{20}$

b) $\frac{189}{40}$ or $4\frac{29}{40}$ d) $\frac{32}{27}$ or $1\frac{5}{27}$

13. a) e.g.,

$\frac{1}{8}$	$\frac{1}{8}$	$\frac{1}{8}$	$\frac{1}{8}$	$\frac{1}{8}$	$\frac{1}{8}$	$\frac{1}{8}$	$\frac{1}{8}$

$\frac{3}{4}\div\frac{5}{8}=1\frac{1}{5}$

b) $\frac{3}{4}\div\frac{5}{8}=\frac{3}{4}\times\frac{8}{5}$

$=\frac{24}{20}$, or $1\frac{1}{5}$

14. a) 2 b) $\frac{25}{8}$ or $3\frac{1}{8}$ c) $\frac{8}{25}$ d) $\frac{28}{10}$ or $2\frac{4}{5}$

15. e.g., When you multiply $\frac{34}{10}$ by $\frac{41}{10}$, the denominator is hundredths and not thousandths.

16. a) $\frac{9}{16}$ b) $\frac{25}{144}$ c) $\frac{9}{16}$

Chapter Review, pp. 330–331

1. a) $\frac{31}{35}$ b) $\frac{11}{35}$

2. a) $\frac{19}{15}$ or $1\frac{4}{15}$ b) $\frac{1}{15}$ c) $\frac{6}{5}$ or $1\frac{1}{5}$

3. a) $\frac{23}{24}$ **b)** $\frac{19}{12}$ or $1\frac{7}{12}$ **c)** $\frac{19}{35}$ **d)** $\frac{3}{10}$ **e)** $\frac{17}{63}$ **f)** $\frac{5}{24}$

4. $\frac{3}{20}$

5. a) $5\frac{4}{5}$ **b)** $6\frac{3}{10}$ **c)** $5\frac{2}{3}$ **d)** $5\frac{1}{20}$

6. e.g., $a = 8$ and $b = 9$ or $a = 7$ and $b = 8$

7. a) $5\frac{11}{30}$ **b)** $2\frac{1}{6}$ **c)** $6\frac{2}{5}$ **d)** $2\frac{5}{12}$

8. $2\frac{5}{12}$ cups

9. a) $\frac{12}{80}, \frac{12}{160}, \frac{12}{320}$ **b)** $\frac{12}{5120}$

c) The second fraction is half of the first. To get a common denominator, I have to double the first fraction ($2 \times 4 = 8$). I then add the numerator of the second fraction to get $8 + 4 = 12$.

10. a) $\frac{1}{10}$ **b)** $\frac{3}{9} = \frac{1}{3}$ **c)** $\frac{2}{4} = \frac{1}{2}$ **d)** $\frac{4}{12} = \frac{1}{3}$

11. a) $\frac{3}{5}$ **b)** $\frac{1}{2}$ **c)** $\frac{2}{3}$ **d)** $\frac{5}{6}$

12. a) $\frac{1}{4}$ **b)** $\frac{1}{10}$ **c)** $\frac{3}{4}$ **d)** $\frac{3}{5}$

13.

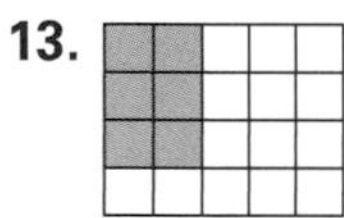

14. A

15. a) $\frac{5}{12}$ **b)** $\frac{1}{4}$

16. a) $\frac{4}{63}$ **b)** $\frac{9}{25}$ **c)** $\frac{8}{27}$ **d)** $\frac{5}{12}$ **e)** $\frac{1}{7}$ **f)** $\frac{6}{35}$

17. $\frac{9}{16}$

18. $\frac{7}{5}$ or $1\frac{2}{5}$

19. a) $\frac{3}{2}$ or $1\frac{1}{2}$ **b)** $\frac{16}{25}$ **c)** $\frac{20}{9}$ or $2\frac{2}{9}$ **d)** $\frac{27}{5}$ or $5\frac{2}{5}$ **e)** $\frac{165}{16}$ or $10\frac{5}{16}$ **f)** $\frac{102}{5}$ or $20\frac{2}{5}$

20. e.g.,

21. Since both sets of numbers have the same denominators, we only need to compare their numerators. So, $\frac{4}{6} \div \frac{3}{6} = \frac{4}{3}$ and $\frac{4}{5} \div \frac{3}{5} = \frac{4}{3}$ as well.

22. a) 5 **b)** $\frac{5}{2}$ or $2\frac{1}{2}$ **c)** $\frac{10}{3}$ or $3\frac{1}{3}$ **d)** $\frac{27}{16}$ or $1\frac{11}{16}$

23. $\frac{9}{2} \div \frac{1}{4}$

24. $\frac{8}{9}$

25. a) e.g., $\frac{5}{6}$ and $\frac{1}{2}$ **b)** e.g., $\frac{8}{3}$ and $\frac{8}{4}$ **c)** e.g., $\frac{5}{6}$ and $\frac{1}{10}$

26. e.g., 4.5 is $4\frac{1}{2}$ and that's $\frac{9}{2}$. $0.5 = \frac{1}{2}$, so I multiply $\frac{9}{2} \times \frac{1}{2} = \frac{9}{4}$. That's $2\frac{1}{4} = 2.25$.

27. A. $\frac{49}{120}$ **B.** $\frac{28}{120}$ **C.** $\frac{25}{120}$; A has the greatest value.

28. $\left(\frac{3}{5} + \frac{1}{4}\right) \div \frac{2}{3} + \frac{1}{3} = \frac{193}{120}$

Cumulative Review, Chapters 7–9, pp. 333–334

1. A **2.** A **3.** D **4.** C **5.** A
6. B **7.** B **8.** D **9.** B

10. a) 3.75 m **b)** 256 m **c)** 4 round trips **d)** \$40 946.10 **e)** $\frac{1}{20}$

f) Reflect in the x-axis and then in the y-axis, or reflect in the y-axis and then in the x-axis.

Chapter 10, p. 335

Getting Started, p. 337

1. a) 8 **b)** 3 **c)** 7 **d)** 3.2 **e)** 4.9 **f)** 1.4

2. A: right, scalene; B: acute, equilateral; C: right, isosceles; D: acute, scalene; E: obtuse, isosceles

3. a) $\angle CAB = \angle CBA$ **b)** $\angle EDF = \angle EFD$

4.

	Pairs of parallel sides	Pairs of perpendicular sides
a)	*a* and *c*, *b* and *d*	*a* and *b*, *b* and *c*, *c* and *d*, *d* and *a*
b)	*h* and *f*, *e* and *g*	none
c)	*i* and *k*	none

5. $\angle 1 = 120°$, $\angle 2 = 60°$

6. a) $\angle D$
b) $\angle B = \angle E$, $\angle C = \angle F$

7. a) e.g.,

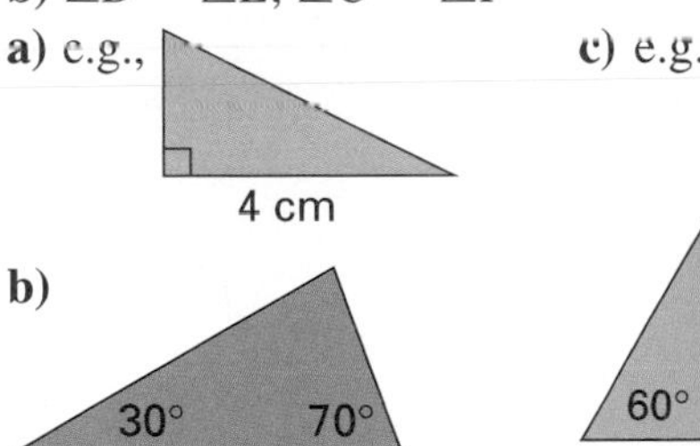

c) e.g.,

40°
60°
5 cm

10.2 Intersecting Lines, Parallel Lines, and Transversals, pp. 342–343

4. 60°
5. a) 50° b) 130°
6. 100°
11. $\angle 1 = 50°$, $\angle 2 = 80°$, $\angle 3 = 50°$
13. a) equal
b) The "C" pattern shows supplementary angles; the "F" pattern shows equal corresponding angles.
14. a) 3 by 1 3 by 3 3 by 4 3 by 5 3 by 2

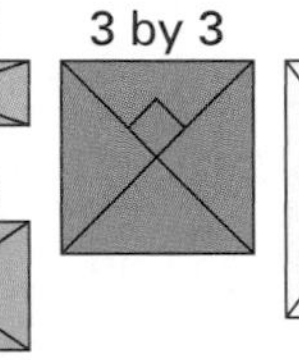

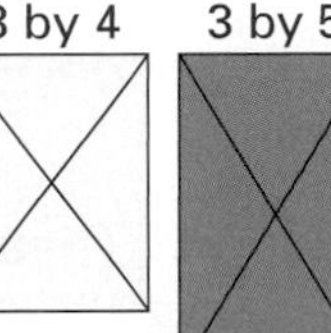

b) The angles created by the diagonals range from acute to right to obtuse (or obtuse to right to acute); the right angles occur in the square.
15. a) The angle opposite the 40° angle is 40° and the other pair of opposite angles are 140°.
b) the angle measures at the intersection point of PQ and the transversal

10.3 Angles in a Triangle, pp. 346–347

3. 65°
4. a) 15°
b) $\angle q = \angle r = 40°$
5. 70°
14. a) $\angle a = 50°$, $\angle b = 60°$, $\angle c = 70°$, $\angle d = 70°$, $\angle e = 60°$, $\angle f = 50°$
16. b) two triangles c) 360°
17. a)

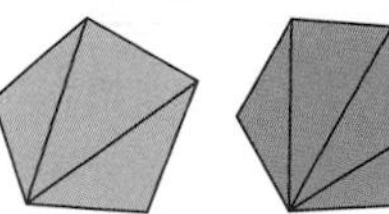

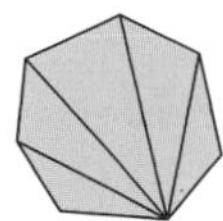

b) pentagon 540°, hexagon 720°, heptagon 900°

18. The length of the rectangle is half the base of the triangle, $\frac{1}{2}b$. The width of the rectangle is half the height of the triangle, $\frac{1}{2}h$. So, the area of the rectangle is $\frac{1}{2}b \times \frac{1}{2}h$, or $\frac{1}{4}bh$. Since the triangle is made up of two of these rectangles, the area of the triangle is $2 \times \frac{1}{4}bh$, or $\frac{1}{2}bh$.

Mid-Chapter Review, p. 351

1. a)

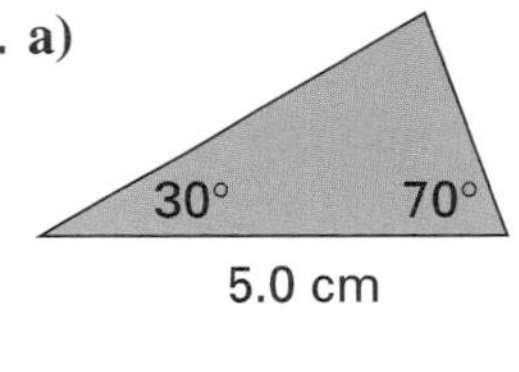

b)

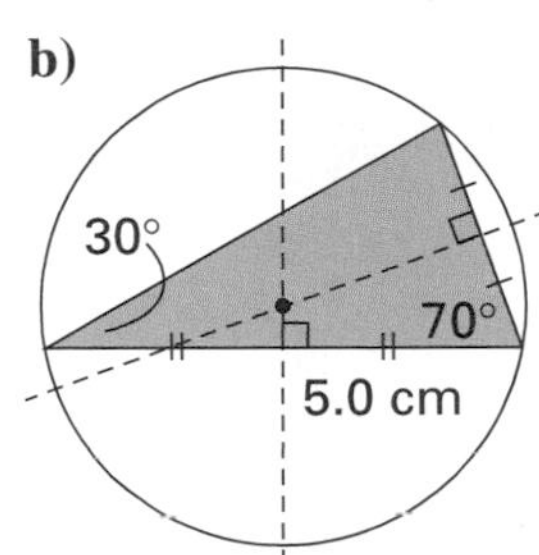

c) 2.5 cm
2. a) $\angle 1 = 105°$, $\angle 2 = 75°$, $\angle 3 = 105°$
3. $\angle 7 = 120°$, $\angle 8 = 60°$
4. 95°; Since the two tracks are parallel, a straight road crossing both will create equal angles.
5. 80°
6. a) The sum of the measures is greater than 180°.
b) e.g., 90°–80°–10°, or 89°–80°–11°, or 90°–79°–11°
7. a) 90°; right scalene triangle
b) 65°; acute isosceles triangle
c) 49°; obtuse scalene triangle
d) 4°; acute isosceles triangle
8. $\angle a = 45°$, $\angle b = 105°$, $\angle c = 30°$
9. a) 360° b) 90°
10. The diagonals intersect at 90° when it is a rhombus.

10.6 Applying the Pythagorean Theorem, pp. 356–357

3. a) 10.0 cm b) 11.6 cm
4. a) 7.8 cm b) 5.7 km c) 4.1 cm d) 5.8 cm
5. a)

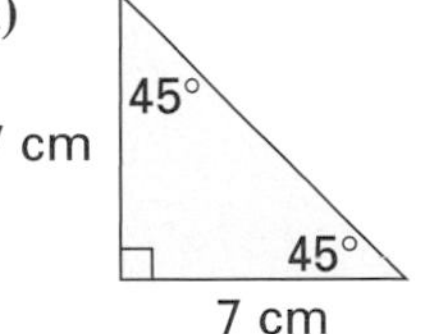

b) no

c) No, because then one of the smaller sides would also be 7 cm.

6. a) C
   b) Since $7^2 + 7^2 = 98$, $\sqrt{100} = 10$, and $\sqrt{81} = 9$, $\sqrt{98}$ must be between 9 and 10.
7. about 16 m
8. 3000 m
9. a) 24 m   b) 23.9 m
10. 15.6 cm^2
11. a) 420 m   b) seconds
12. right triangle; $50^2 = 30^2 + 40^2$
13. 6.9 cm

10.7 Solve Problems Using Logical Reasoning, pp. 360–361

4. C
5. Gregory
6. yes
7. 3 bananas
9. Figure 4, Figure 3, Figure 1, Figure 2

Chapter Self-Test, p. 363

1. Join the points to form 2 chords. Then find the perpendicular bisector of each chord. The intersection of the perpendicular bisectors is the centre of the circle.
2. $\angle a = 138°$, $\angle b = 42°$, $\angle c = 138°$
3. e.g.,
4. a) 8
   b) $\angle 3$ and $\angle 6$, $\angle 16$ and $\angle 9$
   c) 360°
5. $\angle a = 81°$, $\angle b = 25°$, $\angle c = 74°$, $\angle d = 25°$
6. a) 45°
   b) $180° - 98° - 37° = 45°$
   c) obtuse and scalene
7. a)

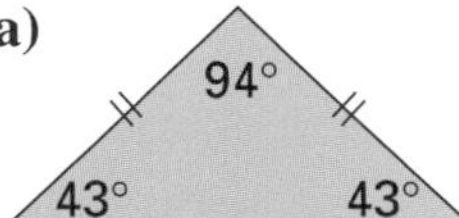

   b) a rhombus and a chevron
   c) 90°
8. a) 5.7 m   b) 12.0 cm
9. 10 cm
10. 2.01 km

Chapter Review, p. 365

1. a) $\angle a$ and $\angle c$, $\angle b$ and $\angle d$
   b) opposite angles
2. $\angle 1 = \angle 3 = \angle 5 = \angle 7 = 82°$,
   $\angle 2 = \angle 4 = \angle 6 = \angle 8 = 98°$
3. $\angle b$, $\angle e$, $\angle p$, and $\angle s$
4. 35°
5. a) yes   b) rectangle
   c) The diagonals will not meet at a right angle.
6. e.g., 3 cm and 4 cm
7. a) 85°   b) 8.1 cm
   c) 15°
   d) 78°

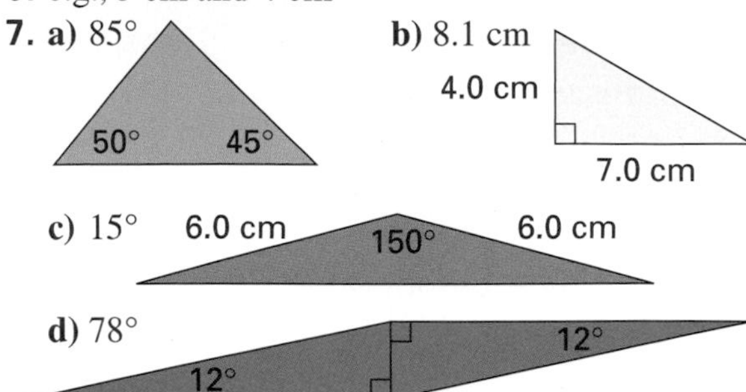

8. a) cyclist A
   b) $a^2 = 5.5^2 + 3.4^2$, $b^2 = 3.4^2 + 5.0^2$
   c) Otherwise you cannot use the Pythagorean theorem

Math in Action: Theatre Technician, pp. 367–368

1. a) 2   b) yes   c) $\angle b = 9°$
2.

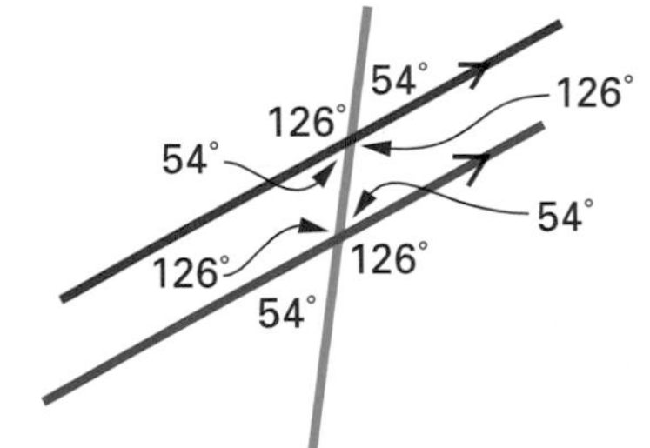

3. Yes, the angles are 76°, 104°, 76°, and 104°, and each of these is within 15° of 90°.
5. 1.45 m
6. a) 40°   b) 70°

Chapter 11, p. 369

Getting Started, p. 371

1. a) litres   c) square centimetres
   b) centimetres   d) cubic centimetres

2. **a)** e.g.,

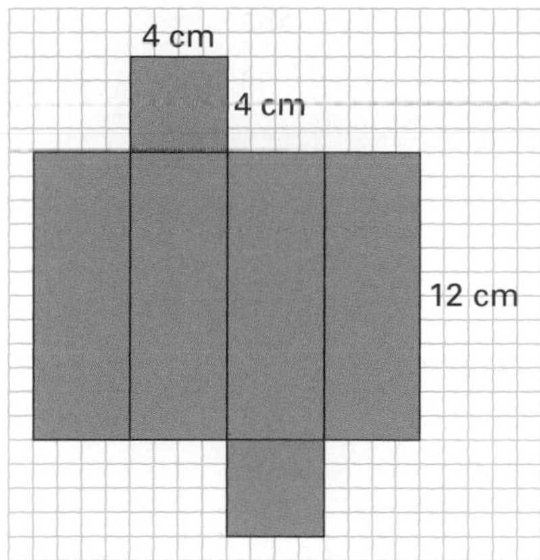

surface area = 224 cm²

b) e.g.,

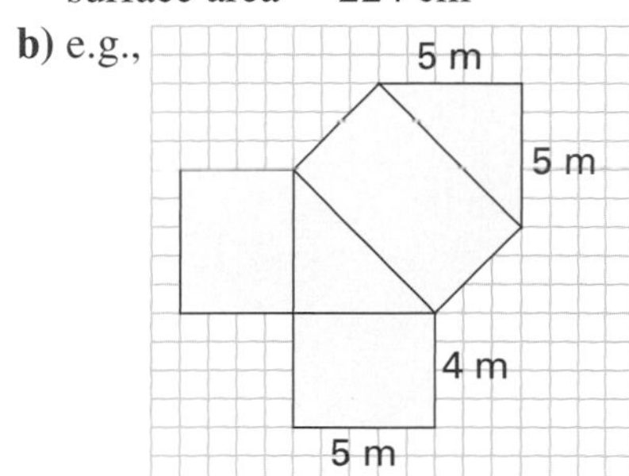

surface area ≐ 93 cm²

3. 306 cm²

4. **a)** area ≐ 50.2 cm², circumference ≐ 25.1 cm
b) area ≐ 15.9 m², circumference ≐ 14.1 m

5. **a)** about 234.4 cm³ **b)** 36 cm³

6. **a)** 234.4 mL **b)** 36 mL

7. **a)** 9 edges, 5 faces, 6 vertices
b) 18 edges, 8 faces, 12 vertices

8. e.g.,

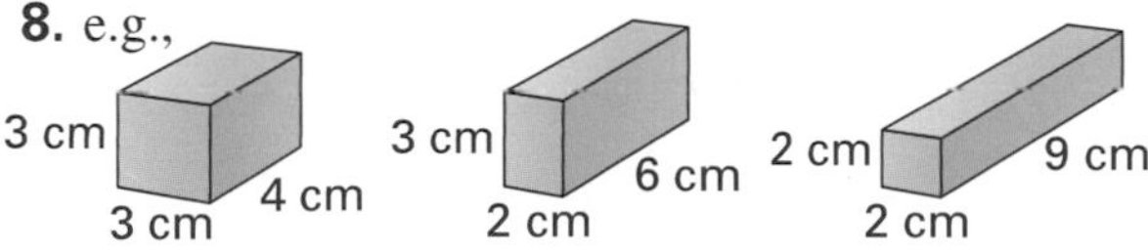

9. **a)** area of trapezoid = 3560.0 cm², area of rectangle = 1683.0 cm²
b) volume of trapezoidal prism = 1 352 800.0 cm³, volume of rectangular prism = 639 540.0 cm³
c) 1 992 340.0 cm³

11.2 Surface Area of a Cylinder, pp. 376–377

4. **a)** about 314 cm² **b)** about 184.3 cm²

5. **a)** about 251 cm² **b)** about 353.3 cm²

6. **a)** about 110.4 cm² **b)** about 93.5 cm² **c)** about 126.3 cm²

7. **a)** about 162.9 m² **b)** about 2491.6 m² **c)** about 201.0 cm²

9. **a)** about 188.9 m² **b)** about $175.00

11. about 27 m²

12. about 603 cm²

13. about 113 cm²

11.3 Volume of a Cylinder, pp. 380–381

4. **a)** e.g., about 300 m³ **b)** e.g., about 300 cm³

5. **a)** about 8204.0 cm³ **b)** about 143.3 cm³

6. **a)** e.g., about 96 cm³ **b)** e.g., about 270 cm³

7. **a)** about 1570.0 cm³ **b)** about 1570.0 mL

8. **a)** about 628 cm³ **b)** about 40.9 m³

9. **a)** about 27.5 m³ **b)** about 27 500 L **c)** 550 min or about 9 h

10. e.g., about 846 cm³

11. about 220 cm³

12.

Radius of base	Diameter of base	Height	Volume
4 cm	8 cm	11 cm	553 cm³
6.0 m	12.0 m	5.0 m	565.2 m³
3.5 cm	7.0 cm	8.0 cm	307.7 cm³
6.0 m	12.0 m	2.0 m	226.1 m³

13. about 10.0 cm

14. about 8.0 cm

15. **a)** about 6051.0 cm **b)** about 5000.8 cm

16. cylinder

17. cylinder with a diameter of 10.0 cm and a height of 7.0 cm

18. **a)** about 4.5 cm **b)** can of mushroom soup

19. Volume would quadruple.

20. e.g., 8.0 cm × 8.0 cm × 15.6 cm for the juice carton and a height of 12.7 cm with a radius of 5.0 cm for the water bottle

11.4 Solve Problems Using Diagrams, p. 384

3. volume ≐ 8.8 m³, surface area ≐ 25.2 m²

4. volume ≐ 11.6 m³, surface area ≐ 39.7 m²

7. **a)**

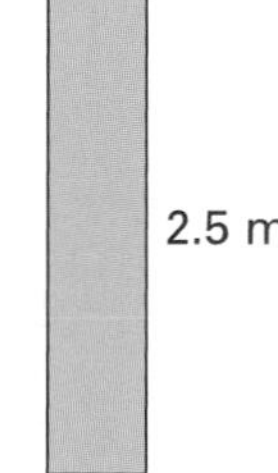

b) about 1.4 m²

9. 200 squares
10. 24
11. about 671 m
12. 3.24 L

Mid-Chapter Review, p. 387

1. a) about 301 cm^2 c) about 1548.0 cm^2
   b) about 1059.8 cm^2 d) about 16 485.0 cm^2
2. about 2.8 m^2
3. e.g., First, measure the height and the diameter of the roll. The surface area of the roll is twice the height multiplied by the circumference, or $SA = 2 \times h \times 2\pi r$.
4. a) about 77 401 mm^2 b) about 678.2 cm^2
5. about 980 cm^2
6. a) about 10 613 cm^3 c) about 6280 cm^3
   b) about 2653.3 cm^3
7. about 22 078 mL
8. about 469.0 m^3
9. about 13.3 L
10. largest container is about 9420 cm^3, middle-sized container is about 6280 cm^3, small container is about 3140 cm^3

11.6 Polyhedron Faces, Edges, and Vertices, pp. 392–393

3. 6
4. $F + V - E = 4 + 4 - 6$
   $= 2$
6.

Number of faces	Number of edges	Number of vertices
6	9	5
6	12	8
6	11	7
20	30	12
16	24	10
8	12	6

12. b) 5 faces c) 9 edges d) 6 vertices
13. b) 6 faces c) 10 edges d) 6 vertices
14. $F + V - E = 8 + 6 - 12$
    $= 2$
15. a) $n + 2$ faces
    b) $3n$ edges
    c) $2n$ vertices
    d) $F + V - E = (n + 2) + (2n) - (3n)$
    $= 2$
16. a) $n + 1$ faces
    b) $2n$ edges
    c) $n + 1$ vertices
    d) $F + V - E = (n + 1) + (n + 1) - (2n)$
    $= 2$

Chapter Self-Test, p. 395

1. For the larger candle:

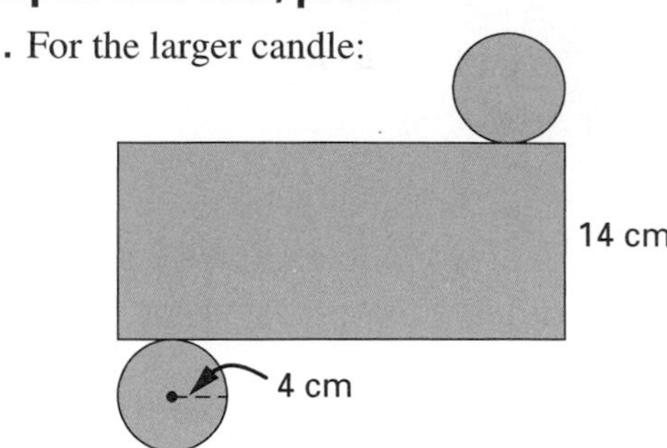

For the smaller candle:

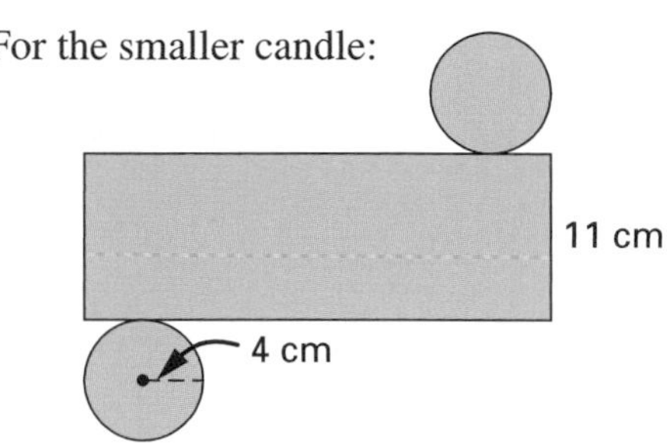

2. *a*, *d*
3. a) surface area $\doteq$ 297 cm^2, volume $\doteq$ 382 cm^3
   b) surface area $\doteq$ 517.5 cm^2, volume $\doteq$ 844.5 cm^3
   c) surface area $\doteq$ 246.6 cm^2, volume $\doteq$ 212.3 cm^3
   d) surface area $\doteq$ 376.8 cm^2, volume $\doteq$ 549.5 cm^3
4. about 138.3 m^3
5. about 785 cm^3
6. Since the angle at each corner of a square is 90°, if more than three squares meet at a vertex, then the total interior angle of the vertex will be greater than or equal to 360°. This means that the shape would either be flat or turned upward, neither of which can make a polyhedron. So, no more than three congruent squares can meet at a vertex to form a Platonic solid because a Platonic solid must be a polyhedron.
7. 90 edges

Chapter Review, p. 397

1. about 196.9 m^2
2. about 212.0 cm^3
3. a) "Crash" b) "Crash"

4. about 96.2 mL
5. e.g., radius 4.9 cm, height 10.0 cm
6. e.g.,

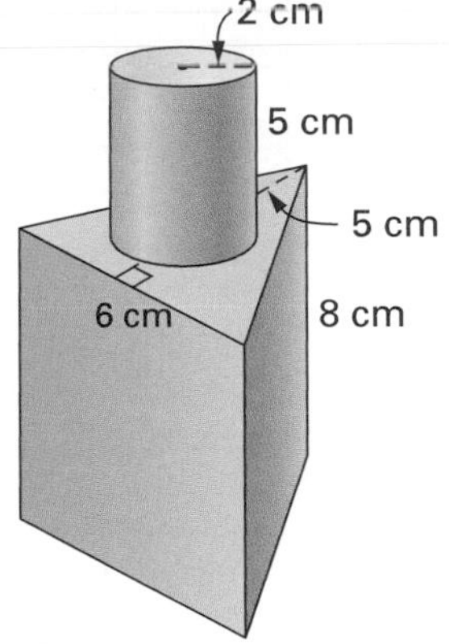

7. Since having six or more equilateral triangles meeting at a vertex would result in an interior angle of 360° or greater, the shape would be flat or turned upward. Since a Platonic solid must be a polyhedron, six or more equilateral triangles cannot meet at a vertex.
9. **a)** 5 faces
   b) e.g.,

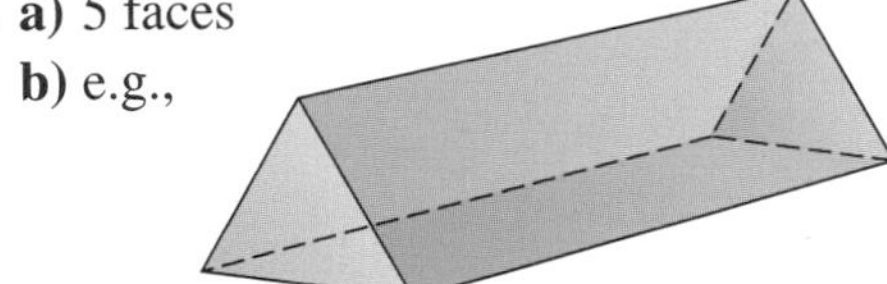

10. 10 edges
11. 6 vertices

Chapter 12, p. 399

Getting Started, p. 401

1. **a)** 3 **b)** trials 6 to 10 and 21 to 25 **c)** increasing **d)** $\frac{1}{6}$
2.

Event	Fraction form of probability	Decimal form of probability	Percent form of probability
4	$\frac{1}{13}$	0.077	7.7%
number card greater than 5	$\frac{5}{13}$	0.385	38.5%
red	$\frac{1}{2}$	0.5	50%

3. a) $\frac{57}{100}$ **b)** $\frac{1}{2}$ **c)** 50
4. a) $\frac{1}{6}$ **b)** $\frac{1}{3}$ **c)** $\frac{1}{3}$
5. 70%
6. **a)** The event will happen for certain.
   b) It is impossible for the event to happen.
7. The bar for 30 to 39 would drop to 14, and the bar for 40 to 49 would increase to 15.

12.2 Theoretical and Experimental Probabilities, pp. 406–407

3. **a)** $\frac{1}{6}$ **b)** $\frac{1}{2}$ **c)** $\frac{1}{3}$
4. **a)** 7, 8, 9, and 10 **b)** $\frac{1}{10}$
5. **a)** $\frac{1}{2}$ **b)** $\frac{1}{5}$ **c)** $\frac{1}{2}$ **d)** $\frac{1}{2}$ **e)** $\frac{3}{5}$ **f)** $\frac{4}{13}$ **g)** $\frac{3}{4}$
7. **a)** P(greater than 8) **b)** P(9)
8. **a)** $\frac{3}{8}$ **b)** 0 **c)** 1
10. **a)** blue $\frac{1}{2}$, red $\frac{1}{3}$, green $\frac{1}{6}$
11. **a) i)** $\frac{1}{10}$ **ii)** $\frac{1}{2}$ **iii)** $\frac{1}{5}$
    b) 250, 37 or 38
12. **b)** box A $\frac{3}{8}$, box B $\frac{2}{5}$, box C $\frac{5}{12}$
    c) Box A
13. e.g., rolling a die and not getting 6
14. No, because each outcome is not equally likely.

12.3 Calculating Probabilities, p. 410

5. **a)** $\frac{1}{2}$ **b)** $\frac{1}{2}$ **c)** $\frac{2}{3}$
7. **b)** $\frac{3}{8}$ **c)** $\frac{1}{2}$ **d)** $\frac{1}{8}$
9. $\frac{1}{8}$
10. **b)** $\frac{7}{8}$ **c)** $\frac{7}{16}$
11. It is more likely that both Anthony and Peter will receive ribbons.
12. **a)** $\frac{1}{9}$
    b) 4 and 1, 1 and 4, 2 and 3, 3 and 2
    c) $\frac{1}{2}$
13. $\frac{7}{18}$

Mid-Chapter Review, p. 413

1. a) $\frac{1}{13}$ **b)** $\frac{1}{6}$ **c)** 0 **d)** $\frac{1}{2}$

2. a) e.g., After 10 trials, I had rolled 3 ones.
b) e.g., After 30 trials, I had rolled 7 ones.
c) As the number of trials increases, the experimental probability gets closer to the theoretical probability.

3. a) $\frac{5}{9}$ **b)** $\frac{1}{9}$ **c)** $\frac{14}{18}$ **d)** $\frac{9}{18}$

4. Jeff, a greater number of trials usually means a more accurate experimental probability.

5. a)

4-sided die	6-sided die	Sum
1	1	2
	2	3
	3	4
	4	5
	5	6
	6	7
2	1	3
	2	4
	3	5
	4	6
	5	7
	6	8
3	1	4
	2	5
	3	6
	4	7
	5	8
	6	9
4	1	5
	2	6
	3	7
	4	8
	5	9
	6	10

b) i) $\frac{1}{24}$ **ii)** $\frac{5}{24}$ **iii)** $\frac{19}{24}$

6. rolling a number that is not a multiple of 3 and not spinning C

7. a)

Pants	Shirt	Jacket
blue	blue	black
		white
		navy blue
	pink	black
		white
		navy blue
	white	black
		white
		navy blue
	green	black
		white
		navy blue
black	blue	black
		white
		navy blue
	pink	black
		white
		navy blue
	white	black
		white
		navy blue
	green	black
		white
		navy blue
brown	blue	black
		white
		navy blue
	pink	black
		white
		navy blue
	white	black
		white
		navy blue
	green	black
		white
		navy blue

b) $\frac{5}{9}$ **c)** $\frac{1}{3}$

12.4 Solve Problems Using Organized Lists, p. 417

3. $\frac{1}{2}$

4. b) 1 coin
c) 25 coins
d) yes, 2 dimes and 5 pennies

5. b) with a free throw, 13 more

6. b) 12 **c)** $\frac{1}{2}$

7. a) $\frac{1}{4}$

b) Omit P: $P(\text{word}) = \frac{1}{24}$; Omit O: $P(\text{word}) = \frac{1}{8}$;

Omit T: $P(\text{word}) = \frac{1}{8}$; Omit S: $P(\text{word}) = \frac{1}{12}$

c) 5

d) Leaving out the E gives you the best chance.

12.5 Using Simulations to Determine Probability, p. 420

3. a) B **b)** D **c)** A **d)** C

6. a) e.g., Represent a male with 1, 2, 3 and a female with 4, 5, 6.

b) e.g., Represent a male with a black card and a female with a red card.

c) e.g., Represent a male with half of the spinner sections and a female with the other half.

d) e.g., Have two different coloured marbles in the bag: one colour represents a male and the other colour represents a female.

Chapter Self-Test, p. 423

1. Experimental probability is the observed probability of an event based on data from an experiment. Theoretical probability is how likely an event is to occur, expressed as a number from 0 (will never happen) to 1 (certain to happen).

2. The experimental probability should get closer to the theoretical probability of $\frac{1}{6}$.

3. a)

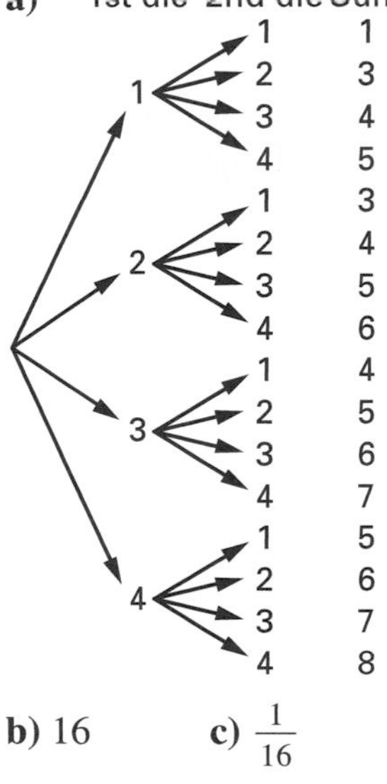

b) 16 **c)** $\frac{1}{16}$

4.

Marie	Dennis	Adele	Sum of ages
15	10	5	30
15	9	6	30
15	8	7	30
14	11	5	30
14	10	6	30
14	9	7	30
13	12	5	30
13	11	6	30
13	10	7	30
13	9	8	30
12	11	7	30
12	10	8	30
11	10	9	30

5. a) 13 **b)** 3

6. a) A **b)** D **c)** C

7. You could simulate this event by creating a 10-section spinner. Label 6 sections green and 4 sections red. The green sections represent a goal, and the red sections represent a miss.

Chapter Review, p. 425

1. a)

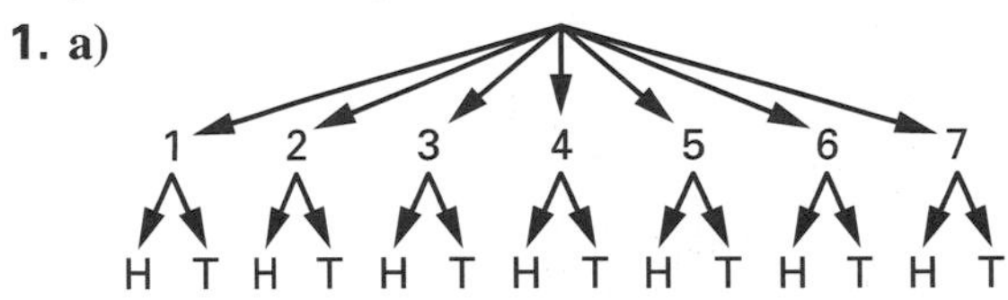

b) i) $\frac{1}{14}$ **ii)** $\frac{2}{7}$ **iii)** $\frac{5}{14}$ **iv)** $\frac{1}{7}$ **v)** $\frac{1}{7}$

2. a) $\frac{1}{10}$ **b)** $\frac{7}{30}$ **c)** $\frac{3}{5}$ **d)** $\frac{1}{15}$

3. a) $\frac{3}{8}$ **b)** $\frac{5}{8}$ **c)** $\frac{1}{4}$ **d)** $\frac{11}{16}$

4. a) Let I represent Asif, S represent Sean, B represent Bill, F represent Francis, and A represent Andrew:
ISB, ISF, ISA, IBS, IBF, IBA, IFS, IFB, IFA, IAF, IAB, IAS, SIB, SIF, SIA, SBI, SBF, SBA, SFI, SFB, SFA, SAI, SAB, SAF, BIS, BIF, BIA, BSI, BSF, BSA, BFI, BFS, BFA, BAI, BAS, BAF, FID, FIB, FIA, FSI, FSB, FSA, FBI, FBS, FBA, FAI, FAS, FAB, AIS, AIB, AIF, ASI, ASB, ASF, ABI, ABS, ABF, AFI, ASI, ASB

b) $\frac{3}{5}$

5. a) 45 pennies **b)** 7

6. a) C **b)** B

Cumulative Review, Chapters 10-12, pp. 427–429

1. D **2.** B **3.** D **4.** C **5.** A **6.** B
7. D **8.** D **9.** C **10.** B **11.** C **12.** C
13. C **14.** A **15.** B **16.** D **17.** C **18.** B

19. a) 106 m
b) height 2.1 m, area 2.5 m^2
c) angle in triangular panel is 60°; angle in hexagonal panel is 120°
d) 0.113 m^3 **e)** $\frac{1}{12}$ **f)** $\frac{1}{4}$

Review of Essential Skills from Grade 7, p. 430

Chapter 1: Number Relationships, pp. 430–431

1. a) 1, 2, 3, 4, 6, 8, 12, 24
b) 1, 5, 7, 35
c) 1, 2, 4, 8, 16, 32, 64
d) 1, 2, 4, 5, 10, 20, 25, 50, 100

2. a) 1, 2, 4, 8; GCF: 8 **b)** 1, 5; GCF: 5

3. 20, 300, 128

4. e.g., 15, 30, 45, 60, and 75

5. a) 6 **b)** 18

6. a) 2, 3, 5, 7, 11, 13 **b)** 4, 6, 8, 9, 10, 12, 14, 15

7. No; e.g., 25 is an odd number, but it is not prime since $5 \times 5 = 25$.

8. a) $2^4 = 16$ **c)** $7^2 = 49$
b) $5^3 = 125$ **d)** $12^3 = 1728$

9. a) 5^2 **b)** 2^3 **c)** 9^2 **d)** 10^3

10. a) $A = 3 \text{ cm} \times 3 \text{ cm} = (3 \text{ cm})^2$
b) $V = 2 \text{ cm} \times 2 \text{ cm} \times 2 \text{ cm} = (2 \text{ cm})^3$

11. 1, 4, 9, 16, 25, 36, 49, 64, 81, 100

12. a) 8 **b)** 11 **c)** 4 **d)** 25

13. Since $\sqrt{144 \text{ cm}^2} = 12$ cm, each side of the square is 12 cm long.

14. a) 19 **b)** 10 **c)** 2

Chapter 2: Proportional Relationships, pp. 432–434

1. a) 0.9 **c)** 0.25 **e)** 0.75 **g)** 0.44
b) 0.5 **d)** 0.6 **f)** 0.65

2. a) $\frac{4}{5}$ **c)** $\frac{1}{4}$ **e)** $\frac{3}{4}$ **g)** $\frac{9}{20}$
b) $\frac{13}{20}$ **d)** $\frac{3}{10}$ **f)** $\frac{11}{25}$

3. a) $\frac{1}{4}, \frac{2}{5}, \frac{1}{2}, \frac{7}{10}, \frac{3}{4}, \frac{22}{25}$
b) 0.03, 0.1, 0.35, 0.7, 0.75, 0.82

4. a) 1.41 **c)** 0.6572
b) 0.1314 **d)** 2.647 92

5. a) 29.12 **c)** 10.4125
b) 6502.56 **d)** 215.625

6. a) 3:7 **b)** 3:10 **c)** 7:10

7. 18:42, 9:21, 3:7, and $\frac{6}{14}$

8. a) 36 **b)** 3 **c)** 7 **d)** 2

9. a) e.g., 2 goals/game and 4 goals/2 games
b) e.g., 2 km/15 min and 8 km/60 min
c) e.g., 12 km/L and 24 km/2 L

10. a) $\frac{\$15.00}{2 \text{ h}} = \frac{\$■}{8 \text{ h}}$; \$60.00
b) $\frac{90 \text{ markers}}{6 \text{ boxes}} = \frac{■ \text{ markers}}{1 \text{ box}}$; 15 markers

11. 25%

12.

Fraction	Ratio	Decimal	Percent
$\frac{1}{4}$	1:4	0.25	25%
$\frac{4}{20}$	4:20	0.2	20%
$\frac{6}{8}$	6:8	0.75	75%

13. a) $\frac{3}{5} = \frac{60}{100} = 60\%$ **b)** $\frac{21}{25} = \frac{84}{100} = 84\%$

14. a) 95% **b)** 20% **c)** 52% **d)** 70%

15. a) 9 **b)** 24 **c)** 80 **d)** 140

Chapter 3: Collecting, Organizing, and Displaying Data, pp. 435–437

1. a) bar graph **c)** \$10 000
b) \$8000 **d)** \$17 000

2. a) line graph **b)** about 55 km **c)** 90 min
d) They travelled in the opposite direction for 5 km.
e) 1.5 km/min

3. a) pictograph **c)** 700 books **e)** 480
b) 100 books **d)** September and October

4. a) e.g., a bar graph

b)

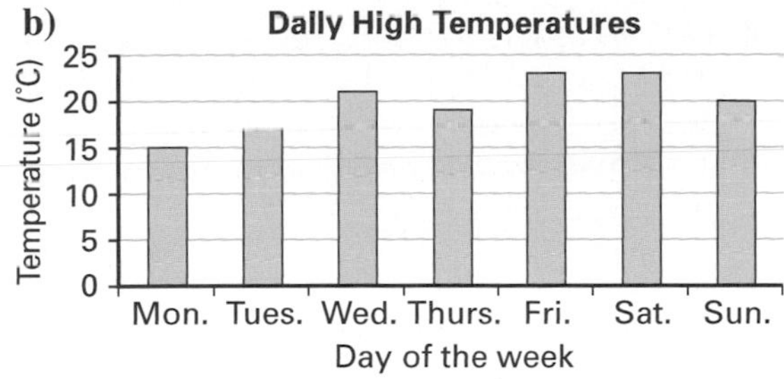

5. a) time spent studying
   b) test score
   c) e.g., generally, the more time spent studying, the higher score on the test
6. a)

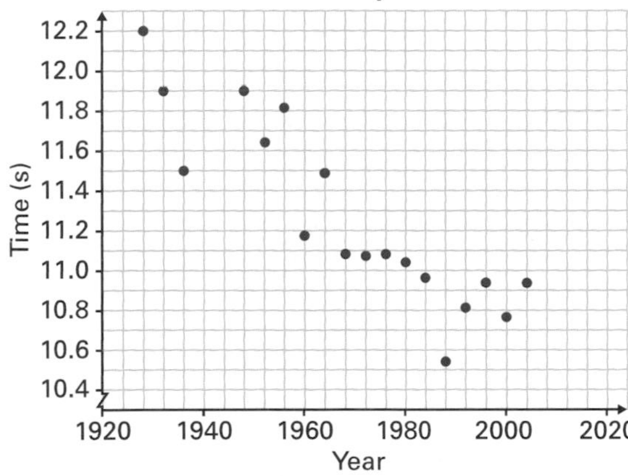

   b) The graph shows the winning time has decreased over the years.
7. a) mean 7.625, median 8.5, mode 9
   b) mean 4.778, median 4, mode: 6
8. a) mean 72.9%, median 74%, mode: 90%
   b) e.g., take a sample of 7 percentages: 58%, 66%, 78%, 82%, 69%, 100%, 72%; mean 75%, median 72%, mode none
9. a) 15 students
   b) lowest score: 35, highest score: 50
   c) 6 students
10. mean 44.07, median 45, mode 50
11. a)

Heights of Arjun's Classmates (cm)	
Stem	Leaf
12	9
13	3 5 8
14	6 6 7
15	2 4 5 6 7 7 8
16	0 2 3 4 6 8
17	0 4

   b) 156.5 cm

Chapter 4: Patterns and Relationships, pp. 438–439

1. a) Start at 3. Add 5 to each term to get the next number in the sequence. The next three terms are 28, 33, and 38.
   b) Start at 2. Multiply each term by 2 to the next number in the sequence. The next three terms are 128, 256, and 512.
   c) Start at 100. Subtract 4 from each term to get the next number in the sequence. The next three terms are 80, 76, and 72.
2. 7, 9, 13, 21, 37
3. a) 2nd hour: $60, 3rd hour: $30, 4th hour: $15
   b) $236.25
4. a) 15, 21, and 28
   b) For whatever term number you want, add all of the numbers less than and equal to that term number together.
   c) 55
5. a)

Term number	Number of squares
1	5
2	8
3	11
4	14
5	17
6	20

   b) Start with 5 and add 3 to each term value to get the next one in the sequence.
6.

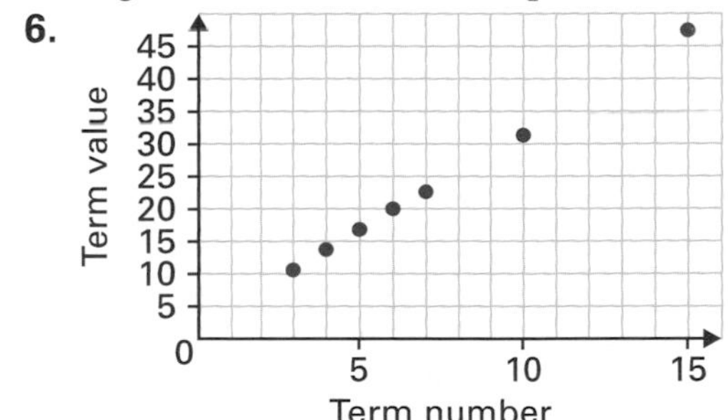

missing term numbers: 6, 7
missing term value: 32

7. a)

Figure number	Number of red triangles	Number of blue triangles
1	0	1
2	1	3
3	4	5
4	9	7

b) **Red Triangles in the Pattern**

Number of red triangles: 0, 1, 2, 3, 4, 5, 6, 7, 8, 9

Term number: 0, 1, 2, 3, 4, 5

c) **Blue Triangles in the Pattern**

Number of blue triangles: 0, 1, 2, 3, 4, 5, 6, 7, 8, 9

Term number: 0, 1, 2, 3, 4, 5

Chapter 5: Measurement of Circles, pp. 440–441

1. a) 520 mm **b)** 680 mm **c)** 710 mm **d)** 73 000 mm

2. a) 7.0 cm **b)** 1050 cm **c)** 600 000 cm **d)** 31 700 cm

3. a) 7000 m **b)** 0.79 m **c)** 0.062 m **d)** 8.72 m

4. a) 0.345 km **b)** 8.000 km **c)** 0.205 km **d)** 0.026 km

5. a) 24 cm **b)** 31.1 cm

6. 26 m of fencing

7. a) 6 square units **b)** 12 square units

8. a) 39 m^2 **b)** 5.25 mm^2

Chapter 6: Integer Operations, pp. 442–444

1. $A = -9$; $B = -6$; $C = -3$; $D = 1$; $E = 4$

2. −8 −5 −3 −2 0 3 7 9

The integers from least to greatest are −8, −5, −3, −2, 0, 3, 7, and 9.

3. a) < **b)** > **c)** < **d)** < **e)** > **f)** >

4. a) $(+5) + (+8) = +13$
b) $(+9) + (-5) = +4$
c) $(-6) + (+9) = +3$
d) $(-3) + (-3) = -6$

5. a) $(-6) + (+10) = +4$
b) $(-3) + (-7) = -10$
c) $(+15) + (-12) = +3$
d) $(-3) + (-8) + (+11) = 0$
e) $(-16) + (+16) = 0$
f) $(-23) + (-37) = -60$
g) $(+25) + (-32) = -7$
h) $(-25) + (-18) + (+41) = -2$

6. a) $(+4) - (-2) = +6$
b) $(-5) - (-1) = -4$
c) $(+4) - (+2) = +2$
d) $(-2) - (+3) = -5$
e) $(-2) - (-3) = +1$

7. a) $(+5) - (-3) = +8$
b) $(-6) - (-4) = -2$
c) $(+7) - (+12) = -5$
d) $(-12) - (+6) = -18$
e) $(-15) - (-15) = 0$
f) $(-26) - (+24) = -50$
g) $(+37) - (+42) = -5$
h) $(-42) - (-12) = -30$

Chapter 7: Transformations, pp. 445–447

1. Shape B

2. 4 units down and 9 units to the right

3.

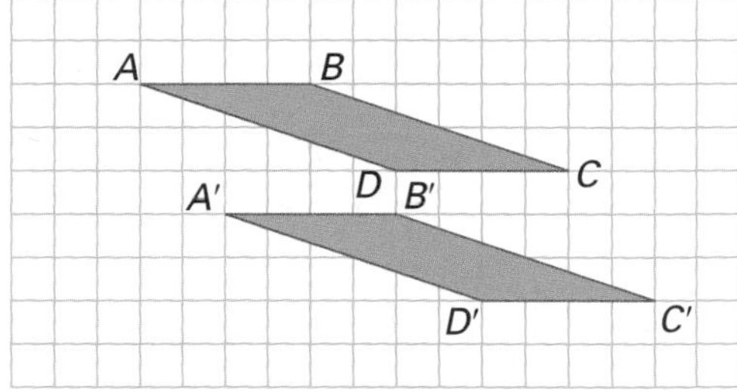

4. Shape B

5. 270° clockwise or 90° counterclockwise

6.

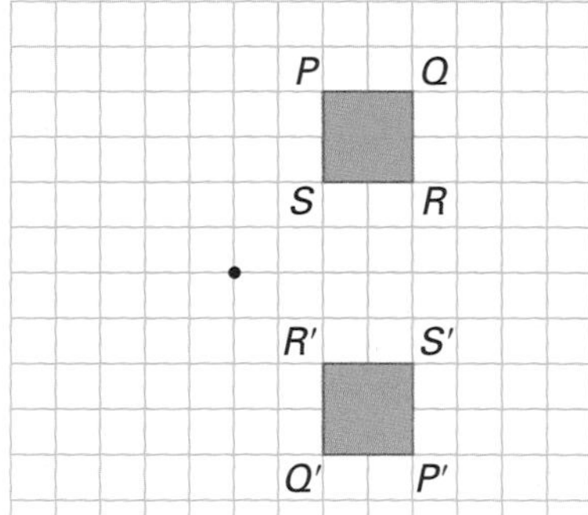

7. Shape B

8.

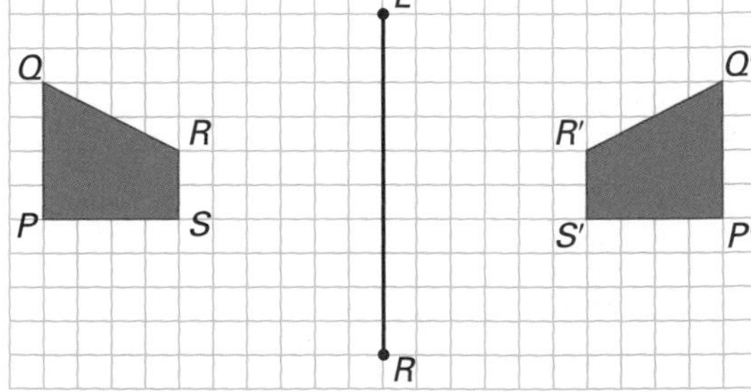

9. a) Shapes B and F, C and D are congruent.
   b) Shapes A, B, C , D, and F are similar since they are all identical in shape.

Chapter 8: Equations and Relationships, pp. 448–449

1. a) The number of red counters always stays the same; the number of black counters changes.
   b) There is always one red counter in the middle, but the number of black counters increases by 2 every time.
   c) $2n + 1$
2. a) The first number is the square of 1; the second number is the square of 2; the third number is the square of 3; the fourth number is the square of 4; and the fifth number is the square of 5, and so on.
   b) n^2
3. ●●●●● ●●●●●●●●● ●●●●●●●●●●●●●
4. a) 48 b) −5 c) 38
5. a) Let h represent the number of hot dogs. The total cost for h hot dogs is $2h$.
   b) The variable l can represent the term number. The length is $6l$.
   c) The variable q can represent the number of quarters and the variable d can represent the number of dimes. The total value is $25q + 10d$.
6. a) $n = 4$ c) $p = 9$ e) $v = 10$
   b) $c = 10$ d) $x = 3$ f) $s = 8$
7. a) $2d + 5 = c$ b) $2d + 5 = 25$ c) $d = 10$
8. a) $c = 70$ c) $c = 14$
   b) $d = 13$ d) $g = 24$
9. a) $b = 6$ cm b) $h = 4$ cm

Chapter 9: Fraction Operations, pp. 450–454

1. a) $\frac{3}{4} + \frac{1}{8} = \frac{7}{8}$ b) $\frac{1}{3} + \frac{1}{4} = \frac{7}{12}$
2. a) 1 c) $1\frac{1}{4}$
   b) $1\frac{2}{8}$ or $1\frac{1}{4}$ d) $1\frac{3}{20}$
3. $\frac{3}{8} + \frac{1}{2} = \frac{3}{8} + \frac{4}{8}$
   $= \frac{7}{8}$, which is less than 1
   Therefore, his tank is not full.
4. a) $\frac{2}{3} - \frac{1}{9} = \frac{5}{9}$ b) $\frac{8}{7} - \frac{1}{2} = \frac{9}{14}$
5. a) $\frac{1}{5}$ b) $\frac{1}{4}$ c) $\frac{1}{4}$ d) $\frac{11}{20}$
6. The pitcher of juice is $\frac{5}{8}$ full.
7. a) $1\frac{3}{4} + 2\frac{2}{4} = 4\frac{1}{4}$ b) $1\frac{2}{8} + 1\frac{3}{8} = 2\frac{5}{8}$
8. a) 7 b) $8\frac{3}{4}$ c) $4\frac{5}{8}$
9. a) $4 - 3\frac{1}{5} = \frac{4}{5}$ b) $5 - 1\frac{1}{3} = 3\frac{2}{3}$
10. a) $4\frac{2}{3}$ b) $2\frac{1}{4}$ c) $3\frac{4}{5}$
11. $1\frac{1}{8}$ of the pizza is left.
12. a) $\frac{3}{4} \times 3 = 2\frac{1}{4}$ b) $\frac{2}{3} \times 6 = 4$
13. a) $1\frac{1}{2}$ b) $4\frac{1}{2}$ c) $1\frac{1}{2}$
14. Akiko has 15 h of music lessons each month.

Chapter 10: Angles and Triangles, pp. 455–457

1. a) 45° b) 90°
2. a) acute b) right
3. a) A, 30°, B, C
   c)

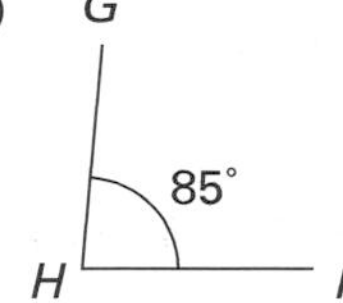

   b)

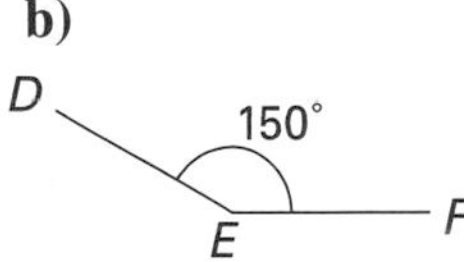

   d)

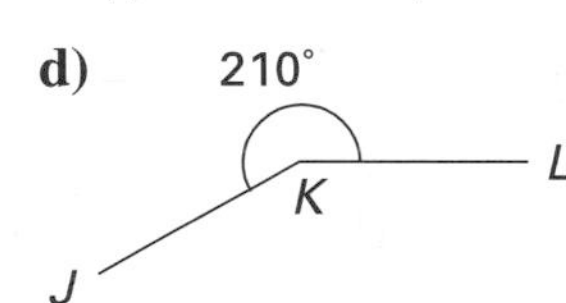

4. a) acute and scalene c) obtuse and scalene
   b) right and isosceles
5. a) rhombus b) trapezoid c) rectangle

Chapter 11: Geometry and Measurement Relationships, pp. 458–459

1. 319.2 cm^2
2. a) 54 cm^2
   b) 12.54 m^2
   c) 5928 cm^2
   d) 432 cm^2
   e) 90.0 cm^2
   f) 1242 cm^2

3. a) 64 cm^3 **c)** 600 m^3 **e)** 864 cm^3
b) 320 cm^3 **d)** 320 cm^3 **f)** 19.152 cm^3

4. a) 2.76 m^3 **b)** 75.0 m^3

Chapter 12: Probability, pp. 460–461

1. a) both coins Heads: $\frac{1}{5}$

one coin Heads and the other Tails: $\frac{1}{2}$

both coins Tails: $\frac{3}{10}$

b) both coins Heads: $\frac{1}{4}$

one coin Heads and the other Tails: $\frac{1}{2}$

both coins Tails: $\frac{1}{4}$

c) one coin Heads and the other Tails

2. a) i) $\frac{1}{10}$ or 0.1 or 10%

ii) $\frac{3}{10}$ or 0.3 or 30%

iii) $\frac{2}{5}$ or 0.4 or 40%

iv) $\frac{0}{10}$ or 0.0 or 0%

b) i) $\frac{1}{20}$ or 0.05 or 5%

ii) $\frac{1}{2}$ or 0.5 or 50%

iii) $\frac{1}{5}$ or 0.2 or 20%

c) i) $\frac{1}{4}$ or 0.25 or 25%

ii) $\frac{1}{4}$ or 0.25 or 25%

iii) $\frac{3}{4}$ or 0.75 or 75%

3. a) $\frac{1}{8}$ **b)** $\frac{3}{8}$ **c)** $\frac{7}{8}$ **d)** $\frac{1}{4}$

4. a)

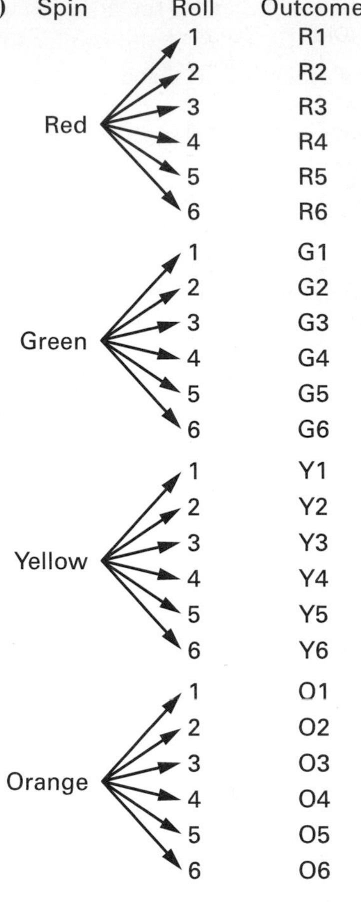

b) i) $\frac{1}{24}$ **ii)** $\frac{1}{8}$ **iii)** $\frac{1}{4}$ **iv)** $\frac{3}{8}$

c) It is not possible to roll a 7.

NEL

5. a) 2, 3, 4, 5, 6, 7, 8, 9, 10, 11, and 12

b)

Die 1	Die 2	Sum
1	1	1 + 1 − 2
	2	1 + 2 − 3
	3	1 + 3 = 4
	4	1 + 4 = 5
	5	1 + 5 = 6
	6	1 + 6 = 7
2	1	2 + 1 = 3
	2	2 + 2 = 4
	3	2 + 3 = 5
	4	2 + 4 = 6
	5	2 + 5 = 7
	6	2 + 6 = 8
3	1	3 + 1 = 4
	2	3 + 2 = 5
	3	3 + 3 = 6
	4	3 + 4 = 7
	5	3 + 5 = 8
	6	3 + 6 = 9
4	1	4 + 1 = 5
	2	4 + 2 = 6
	3	4 + 3 = 7
	4	4 + 4 = 8
	5	4 + 5 = 9
	6	4 + 6 = 10
5	1	5 + 1 = 6
	2	5 + 2 = 7
	3	5 + 3 = 8
	4	5 + 4 = 9
	5	5 + 5 = 10
	6	5 + 6 = 11
6	1	6 + 1 = 7
	2	6 + 2 = 8
	3	6 + 3 = 9
	4	6 + 4 = 10
	5	6 + 5 = 11
	6	6 + 6 = 12

c) $\frac{1}{6}$

Index

NEL

D

E

Credits

This page constitutes an extension of the copyright page. We have made every effort to trace the ownership of all copyrighted material and to secure permission from copyright holders. In the event of any question arising as to the use of any material, we will be pleased to make the necessary corrections in future printings. Thanks are due to the following authors, publishers, and agents for permission to use the material indicated.

Statistics Canada information is used with the permission of Statistics Canada. Users are forbidden to copy this material and/or redisseminate the data, in an original or modified form, for commercial purposes, without the expressed permission of Statistics Canada. Information on the availability of the wide range of data from Statistics Canada can be obtained from Statistics Canada's Regional Offices, its World Wide Web site at http://www.statcan.ca, and its toll-free access number 1-800-263-1136.

Chapter 1 Opener page 1: © Joseph Sohm; Visions of America/CORBIS; page 3: One Mile Up/Fotosearch; page 20: © Nature Picture Library/Alamy; page 25: UPI/Landov; page 30: Marcus Fuehrer/EPA/Landov; page 44: Courtesy of the UNFPA

Chapter 2 Opener page 45: © Stephanie Maze/CORBIS; page 46: © 2005 JupiterImages and its Licensors. All Rights Reserved; page 52: David Leahy/Getty Images; page 59: photolibrary.com pty. ltd./Index Stock; page 61: © Galen Rowell/CORBIS; page 64: CP PHOTO; page 67: LASZLO BALOGH/Reuters /Landov; page 68: Benelux Press/First Light; page 72: Ghislain & Marie David de Lossy/Getty Images; page 74: © Jeff Greenberg/Photo Edit. All rights reserved; page 76: Jostein Hauge/Shutterstock; page 80: © Conrad Zobel/CORBIS; page 82: left, Hugh Threlfall/Alamy; right, JIM YOUNG/Reuters /Landov; page 87: top, Courtesy Alan Morrow; centre, Courtesy of Alan Morrow; page 88: Courtesy Alan Morrow

Chapter 3 Opener page 89: © J. Barry Mittan; page 91: "Radio Listening Time," adapted from the Statistics Canada website http://www.statcan.ca/english/Pgdb/arts17.htm, extracted on July 27, 2004; page 92: CP PHOTO/Peterborough Examiner-Clifford Skarstedt; page 93: Graph based on data from the Canadian Disaster Database Web site; page 94: Table based on data from Euromonitor; page 100: "Average Number of Hours of Television Viewing per Week," adapted from the Statistics Canada website http://www40.statcan.ca/l01/cst01/arts23.htm; page 102: "New housing price index," adapted from the Statistics Canada website http://www40.statcan.ca/l01/cst01/manuf12.htm?sdi=housing%20price%20index; page 103: "Population by highest level of schooling," adapted from the Statistics Canada website http://www40.statcan.ca/l01/cst01/educ43a.htm; "Highest-grossing films," based on data from http://actionadventure.about.com/gi/dynamic/offsite.htm?site=http%3A%2F%2Fwww.the-movie-times.com%2Fthrsdir%2Ftop100world.html; bottom right, © CLOSE MURRAY/CORBIS SYGMA; page 104: www.PerfectPhoto.CA, © Rob vanNostrand; page 110: AP Photo/Keith Srakocic; page 114: top right, table based on data from http://www.infoplease.com/ipsa/A0115207.html; page 115: Table based on data from Environment Canada; page 117: top left, table adapted from HUMAN GEOGRAPHY by DRAPER/FRENCH/CRAIG. © 2000. Reprinted by permission of Nelson, a division of Thomson Learning: www.thomsonrights.com. Fax 800 730-2215; bottom right, © Will & Deni McIntyre/CORBIS; page 118: left, Chris LeBoutillier PIXRGB.com/Shutterstock; centre, RubberBall/Alamy; right, Bernd Weissbrod/EPA/Landov

Chapter 4 Opener page 121: John Lamb/Getty Images; page 123: © Chuck Savage/CORBIS; page 125: © GK Hart/Vikki Hart/Getty Images; page 139: Deutsche Bundesbank, Money Museum; page 140: © Brian Sytnyk/Masterfile www.masterfile.com

Chapter 5 Opener page 149: Dreamcatcher, handcrafted by Gordon Hill, designed by Vanessa Fraser, Cardinal Glass Studio, 2004; page 159: Photodisc Green/Getty Images; page 164: Photodisc Green/Getty Images; page 166: from top, © SuperStock, Inc./SuperStock; Dave Mager/Index Stock; Siede Preis/Getty Images; One Mile Up/Fotosearch; page 168: CORDELIA MOLLOY/SCIENCE PHOTO LIBRARY; page 175: from top, © Kristiina Paul; © Kristiina Paul; Jim Wark/Index Stock; © 2005 JupiterImages and its Licensors. All Rights Reserved; page 177: All images, Douglas J. Cardinal Architect Ltd.; page 178: © COREL

Chapter 6 page 182: left, © 2005 JupiterImages and its Licensors. All Rights Reserved; right, © 2005 JupiterImages and its Licensors. All Rights Reserved; page 184: Frans Lemmens/The Image Bank/Getty Images; page 187: © John and Lisa Merrill/CORBIS; page 197: left, © 2005 JupiterImages and its Licensors. All Rights Reserved; right, © 2005 JupiterImages and its Licensors. All Rights Reserved; page 207: B&C Alexander/First Light; page 217: Coin designs© courtesy of the Royal Canadian Mint; page 218: top, MARCELO DEL POZO/Reuters/Landov; bottom, © Steve Kaufman/CORBIS

Chapter 7 Opener page 219: Michel Jean Paller/Shutterstock; page 220: M.C. Escher's "Symmetry Drawing E08" © 2005 The M.C. Escher Company - Holland. All rights reserved. www.mcescher.com; page 243: © Eyecon Images/Alamy

Chapter 8 page 258: © Michael Newman/Photo Edit; page 260: © Jose Carillo/Photo Edit; page 267: CP PHOTO/Aaron Harris; page 272: Yvette Cardozo/Index Stock; page 281: Courtesy of Kate Hennessy; page 282: top, Courtesy of Kate Hennessy; bottom, Courtesy of Kate Hennessy

Chapter 9 page 286: CP PHOTO/Andrew Vaughan; page 299: © Anna Peisl/Corbis; page 300: © 2005 JupiterImages and its Licensors. All Rights Reserved; page 301: © 2005 JupiterImages and its Licensors. All Rights Reserved; page 311: Morning light on Mount Columbia, Canadian Rockies. Photo by Alan Kane; page 319: © Photodisc Blue/Getty Images; page 334: Kim Langille/Shutterstock

Chapter 10 Opener page 335: Stephen Studd/Getty Images; page 336: © Royalty-Free/CORBIS; page 344: Photo by Geoff Suderman-Gladwell. Courtesy of Graham and Joyce Gladwell; page 347: Ken Straiton/First Light; page 366: Don Farrall/Getty Images; page 367: Courtesy of Patrick Brennan; page 368: Courtesy of Patrick Brennan

Chapter 11 Opener page 369: Courtesy of Kenton Otterbein, Killbear Provincial Park; page 377: centre right, NASA Kennedy Space Center (NASA-KSC), ksc-372c-0617; bottom left, Patsy A. Jacks/Shutterstock; page 380: © Francisco Cruz/SuperStock; page 393: top, © COREL; bottom, Luis Veiga/Getty Images; page 395: top right, Patsy A. Jacks/Shutterstock; bottom right, C Squared Studios/Photodisc/Getty Images; page 397: Photodisc Collection/Getty Images; page 398: © Richard A. Cooke/CORBIS

Chapter 12 Opener page 399: Jim Reed/Photo Researchers, Inc.; page 408: right, www.PerfectPhoto.CA, © Rob vanNostrand; page 417: Photodisc/Getty Images; page 429: top, © Library and Archives Canada. Reproduced with the permission of the Minister of Public Works and Government Services Canada (2005). Source: Library and Archives Canada/Expo 67 (Montreal) collection/Accession 1970-019/Image e-000995982; bottom, © Library and Archives Canada. Reproduced with the permission of the Minister of Public Works and Government Services Canada (2005). Source: Library and Archives Canada/Expo 67 (Montreal) collection/Accession 1970-019/Image e-000990869